ENGLISH PSALMS IN THE MIDDLE AGES, 1300–1450

English Psalms in the Middle Ages, 1300–1450

ANNIE SUTHERLAND

OXFORD
UNIVERSITY PRESS

OXFORD
UNIVERSITY PRESS

Great Clarendon Street, Oxford, OX2 6DP,
United Kingdom

Oxford University Press is a department of the University of Oxford.
It furthers the University's objective of excellence in research, scholarship,
and education by publishing worldwide. Oxford is a registered trade mark of
Oxford University Press in the UK and in certain other countries

First Edition published in 2015

Impression: 1

Published in the United States of America by Oxford University Press
198 Madison Avenue, New York, NY 10016, United States of America

British Library Cataloguing in Publication Data
Data available

Library of Congress Control Number: 2014954691

ISBN 978–0–19–872636–4

Printed and bound by
CPI Group (UK) Ltd, Croydon, CR0 4YY

For Chris, Ruby, and Zebedee, and in grateful memory of
Graham Sutherland, 1939–2014

Acknowledgements

For academic conversation, advice, and encouragement over the years, I would like to thank Helen Barr, Vincent Gillespie, Malcolm Godden, Ralph Hanna, Barbara Harvey, Eddie Jones, David Lawton, Francis Leneghan, Nick Perkins, and Almut Suerbaum. For specific guidance and advice in the writing of this book, I am very grateful to Michael Kuczynski, Nicholas Orme, Elizabeth Solopova, and Jane Toswell. Richard Hitchman provided welcome assistance with the translation of some Latin material and Ayoush Lazikani was meticulous in proofreading and correcting an earlier draft of the book. I would also like to thank the anonymous readers engaged by Oxford University Press for their rigorous and constructive criticism of this work in its various forms. I am also grateful to the Small Grants fund of the British Academy for an award that allowed me, in partnership with Professor Anne Hudson, to have old editions of three Middle English Psalter translations digitized. The John Fell Oxford University Press Research Fund is also to be thanked for awarding me a grant which facilitated the completion of this book. My greatest debt, however, is to Anne Hudson who has, over the years, been my most valued and meticulous academic mentor.

Permissions

Some material in Chapter 2 appeared first as 'Psalms as Polemic: the English Bible Debate', in *Polemic: Language as Violence in Medieval and Early Modern Discourse*, ed. A. Suerbaum and B. Thompson (Aldershot, 2014). I am grateful to Ashgate for permission to reproduce here.

Some material in Chapters 3 and 5 appeared first as 'English Psalms in the Middle Ages', *Bodleian Library Record* 28 (2009). I am grateful to Bodleian Library Publishing for permission to reproduce here.

Some material in Chapter 5 appeared first as 'Performing the Penitential Psalms in the Middle Ages', in *Aspects of the Performative in Medieval Culture*, Trends in Medieval Philology 18, ed. M. Gragnolati and A. Suerbaum (Berlin and New York, 2010), pp. 15–37. I am grateful to De Gruyter for permission to reproduce here.

Contents

List of Illustrations

List of Abbreviations

Add.	Additional (in manuscript references)
BJRL	*Bulletin of the John Rylands Library*
BL	London, British Library
BLJ	*British Library Journal*
BLR	*Bodleian Library Record*
BN	Bibliothèque Nationale
BodlL	Oxford, Bodleian Library
CCCC	Corpus Christi College Cambridge
CUL	Cambridge University Library
EETS	Early English Text Society (1864–); volumes with prefix OS are in the Original Series, those with prefix ES are in the Extra Series; those with prefix SS are in the Supplementary Series
EHR	*English Historical Review*
ELH	*English Literary History*
EUL	Edinburgh University Library
EV	Early Version of the Wycliffite Bible
GUL	Glasgow University Library
IMEP	*Index of Middle English Prose* (Cambridge, 1984–)
IPMEP	*Index of Printed Middle English Prose*, ed. R. E. Lewis, N. F. Blake, and A. S. G. Edwards (New York and London, 1985)
JEBS	*Journal of the Early Book Society*
JEGP	*Journal of English and Germanic Philology*
JMEMS	*Journal of Medieval and Early Modern Studies*
JRH	*Journal of Religious History*
JRL	John Rylands University Library
LALME	*A Linguistic Atlas of Late Mediaeval English*, ed. A. McIntosh, M. L. Samuels, and M. Benskin, 4 vols (Aberdeen, 1986)
LV	Later Version of the Wycliffite Bible
MA	*Medium Aevum*
MED	*Middle English Dictionary*, ed. H. Kurath, S. M. Kuhn et al. (Ann Arbor, 1952–99)
MLN	*Modern Language Notes*
MLR	*Modern Language Review*
MLQ	*Modern Language Quarterly*
MP	*Modern Philology*
MRS	*Medieval and Renaissance Studies*
MS	*Mediaeval Studies*
N&Q	*Notes and Queries*
NML	*New Medieval Literatures*
NM	*Neuphilologische Mitteilungen*
NT	New Testament
OED	*Oxford English Dictionary* (Oxford, 1933; online version updated)
OT	Old Testament

PBA	*Proceedings of the British Academy*
PQ	*Philological Quarterly*
PL	*Patrologia Latina*
RES	*Review of English Studies*
RV	Revised versions of Rolle's *English Psalter* commentary
SE	*Studies in English*
SN	*Studia Neophilologica*
TCC	Cambridge, Trinity College Library
TCD	Dublin, Trinity College Library
TEAMS	Consortium for the Teaching of the Middle Ages
TSE	*Texas Studies in English*
Vulgate	*Biblia sacra iuxta Vulgatem versionem*, ed. R. Weber et al. (4th edn, Stuttgart, 1994)
WB	*The Holy Bible . . . made from the Latin Vulgate by John Wycliffe and his Followers*, ed. J. Forshall and F. Madden, 4 vols (Oxford, 1850, repr. New York, 1982)
YES	*Yearbook of English Studies*

All Vulgate quotations are taken from Weber

All translations of the Vulgate are taken from the Douay-Rheims version

Punctuation in both is modernized when necessary

Unless otherwise stated, all other translations are my own

In all but Chapter 6, manuscript abbreviations have been silently expanded and punctuation added.

Introduction

The pre-eminent position occupied by the psalms in the traditions of Western Christianity is widely known. Their centrality to the Church's rhythms of prayer, both corporate and personal, was—and is—unmatched by that of any other book of the Bible. As texts which were always intended to be sung, some of which 'offer strong evidence of their use as liturgical texts' in their early Hebrew context, they lend themselves readily to incorporation within the performative rituals of the Christian liturgy.[1] It is with these rituals that we begin our consideration of the psalms.

In the medieval Church, psalm recitation was 'the corner-stone' of the daily cycle of intercessions (the Office), an identity which originated in the practices of the early Christians:

> If a few selected psalms sung regularly (even daily) formed a major part of 'lay' public worship in the early Church, the whole collection recited successively provided a basis for meditation for the early solitary monks. In due course monks gathered together in groups, and so the recitation of psalms developed as a shared practice. And from the monks the custom of successive recitation spread throughout the Church in the West.[2]

The liturgy of the Middle Ages was by no means stable in either form or practice; as John Harper points out in his important book *The Forms and Orders of Western Liturgy*, the liturgical practice of the medieval Church was complex and varied.[3] Nonetheless, as he goes on to suggest, the Western liturgy did reach 'a crucial point of synthesis and stability in the tenth century. From this period it is possible to discern a consistency of liturgical observance supported by written sources that stretches to the present day.'[4] We can, therefore, speak meaningfully of the liturgical continuum within which the recitation of the psalms featured in the late Middle Ages. It is, however, worth noting that the Roman Rite (the framework of liturgical observance in the Western Church) divided into two principal Uses: the monastic and the secular. Distinct from each other in details of form and practice,

---

[1] J. Harper, *The Forms and Orders of Western Liturgy from the Tenth to the Eighteenth Century: A Historical Introduction and Guide for Students and Musicians* (Oxford, 1991), p. 67. For the second quotation, see R. Alter (ed.), *The Book of Psalms: A Translation with Commentary* (New York, 2007), p. xvii.
[2] Harper, p. 67.   [3] Harper, p. 13.   [4] Harper, p. 11.

the two are 'most readily contrasted by their differences in the order of the Night Office of Matins'.[5] Yet for all their discontinuities, in terms of psalm recitation there were certain affinities between monastic and secular Uses:

> Matins included Psalm 94 in the introductory section. Lauds had a group of unchanging daily psalms (66, 148–50); Psalm 62, recited daily in the secular *cursus*, was sung on Sunday in the monastic cycle; and Psalm 50, recited every day in the monastic cycle, was included on weekdays in the secular *cursus*. Compline was also unchanging in its use of Psalms 4, 90, and 133, though the secular use also included the first part of Psalm 30. The secular cycle also had a regular daily pattern for the little Hours of Prime, Terce, Sext and None (partly echoed in monastic Use). The numerical sequence is most evident in Matins and Vespers: broadly speaking Psalms 1–108 form the *cursus* at Matins, while Psalms 109–50 occur at Vespers (allowing in each case for the extraction of psalms used at other Hours).[6]

In both Uses,

> [a] group of psalms was sung at the beginning of each of the Hours, and at the beginning of every section (nocturn) of Matins . . . [the selection of which] reflects the two traditions of the early Church . . . the non-monastic use of a regular, well-known selection to suit the time and the day, and sung in an established pattern; and the monastic practice of singing the psalter from beginning to end in numerical order regardless of theme.[7]

Whether one operated within the monastic or the secular tradition, one's daily prayer life would have been heavily inflected by the language and sentiments of the psalms.

Within the liturgy of the medieval Church, the psalms were used in many different ways. As already indicated, they were most frequently sung, although by whom is not always easy to discern: while some were performed by 'the priest and ministers', others were intended for the entire congregation.[8] Neither is it always clear what the 'singing' of the psalms might have entailed in context: as Susan Boynton suggests, '[t]he liturgy included many different forms of musically heightened declamation that correspond to various points on a continuum between song and the spoken word.'[9] In general, however, we know that the psalms were performed antiphonally in both the Mass and the Office, a refrain (antiphon) being sung either at the beginning and end of each individual psalm, or at the beginning and end of each group of psalms. While the psalms themselves remained fairly

---

[5] Harper, p. 14. In secular Use, the rhythms of which inform much of the material discussed in my book, it was the Use of Salisbury (i.e. liturgical observances derived originally from those followed in the cathedral at Salisbury) which was most widespread in the Middle Ages. The Use of Salisbury is also referred to as the Sarum Rite.

[6] Harper, p. 70.

[7] Harper, pp. 69–70. As Harper points out, in the Middle Ages, there was an increasing number of proper psalms (i.e. psalms that change from day to day according to season and feast) which often replaced the ordinary psalms (i.e. those psalms which are constant) at Matins and Vespers.

[8] Harper, p. 69.

[9] S. Boynton, 'Plainsong', in *The Cambridge Companion to Medieval Music*, Cambridge Companions to Music, ed. M. Everist (Cambridge, 2011), pp. 9–25, p. 10.

constant from one week to the next, the antiphons 'changed week by week, season by season, and feast by feast'.[10] The one antiphonal constant, though, is that their texts tend to be 'drawn from the psalms with which they alternated': in liturgical terms, the psalms are statements or queries to which they themselves provide the response.[11] This sense that the psalms can function dialogically also informs the other liturgical uses to which they were put. As Harper points out, '[t]hough in the medieval Office the bulk of the psalmody was sung early in each service, extracts from psalms provided a response to scriptural readings or the texts of dialogues in intercessions' at other moments.[12]

Of course, all public (and much private) liturgical celebration involving the psalms took place in Latin throughout the Middle Ages. Although we do have some evidence suggesting the limited incorporation of vernacular prayers into public ritual, none involves the psalms.[13] Even if the congregation was invited to participate in the antiphonal recitation of the psalms, the non-Latinate majority would not necessarily have had much (if any) understanding of what it was that they were responding to and saying. Harper reads the situation thus:

> The medieval liturgy had little place for the active involvement of the laity. Their role was passive and devotional. Even in modest parish churches the priest was distanced physically from the people at the east end . . . By the fifteenth century there was some response to the presence of the people: in the Salisbury Use vernacular prayers were said towards the end of the procession before the Mass (the Bidding of Bedes), and in some churches there were vernacular prayers at the Offertory. But for the most part the laity were excluded entirely from active participation in both Mass and Office, even in parish churches.[14]

For Eamon Duffy, such geographical and linguistic exclusion is overstated: the screen separating clergy from laity was 'both a barrier and no barrier. It was not a wall but rather a set of windows, a frame for the liturgical drama, solid only to waist-height, pierced by a door wide enough for ministers and choir to pass through and which the laity themselves might penetrate on certain occasions.'[15] And while 'the available models of prayer . . . were all in Latin', much of their content 'would have been familiar even to lay people, and their meaning well

---

[10] Harper, p. 71.

[11] Boynton (2011), p. 11. As she points out, 'greater textual variety characterizes the antiphons for feast days'.

[12] Harper, p. 71.

[13] Richard Pfaff provides some examples of reference to the vernacular in liturgical contexts. The eleventh-century portiforium which almost certainly belonged to Bishop Wulfstan, for example, contains an extensive vernacular prayer for forgiveness as well as 'a bilingual votive office of the Cross in which each Latin petition is followed by its English equivalent', headed *aliae orationes latine et anglice* (p. 129). Pfaff also points out that a number of late-medieval Sarum missals contain one or two rubrics 'specifying certain words to be said *lingua materna*' (p. 419). Finally, he reminds us that for the Bridgettine nuns of Syon, 'an early and high degree of the vernacular' was incorporated in the rubrics of service-books (p. 531). See R. W. Pfaff, *The Liturgy in Medieval England: A History* (Cambridge, 2009). We know, of course, that they had access to Richard Rolle's English translation of the psalms.

[14] Harper, p. 40.

[15] E. Duffy, *The Stripping of the Altars: Traditional Religion in England c. 1400–1580* (New Haven and London, 1992), p. 112.

understood'.[16] Even those Latin rituals (particularly that surrounding the celebration of mass) which remained incomprehensible served a purpose, since their 'very element of mystery gave legitimacy to the sacred character of Latin itself, as higher and holier than the vernacular'.[17]

Duffy's reading of Latin's 'mystery' as 'sacred' certainly recalls the sentiments of some medieval commentators. The anonymous author of the late fourteenth-century *Chastising of God's Children*, for example, refers approvingly to Hildegard of Bingen's efficacious repetition of Vulgate Psalm 69 ('Deus in adiutorium meum intende' [O God come to my assistance]) 'al be it þat she vndirstode nat what she saide or radde'.[18] However, while it was certainly the case that Latin remained dominant in the context of formal liturgy and, on occasion, less formal devotion, the profusion of vernacular psalm translations in England in the fourteenth and fifteenth centuries suggests that the *status quo* was not without its discontents. Nor does it offer unequivocal support for the notion that Latin was invariably seen as mysteriously superior to English as a sacred language. Of course, there is no evidence to indicate that any of the texts with which we deal in the course of this book was intended to supplant the recitation of the Latin psalms in the formal context of the public liturgy. There is, however, abundant evidence that many of them were intended to supplement and comment on such Latinate practices, and even to replace them in private contexts.

In making this claim, I do not seek to propose a reading of late-medieval devotional culture which insists rigidly on a competitive division between Latin liturgy and paraliturgical English devotion.[19] Although elements of this may creep into the narrative that the book outlines, my real interest lies in considering the ways in which vernacular psalm versions, both complete and paraphrased, can be read as relating and responding creatively to liturgical patterns and practices. Borrowing terminology from Bruce Holsinger, I argue that these English translations might 'be seen as in part an *effect* of liturgy' and that 'far from exercising a conservative or regressive grip upon vernacular invention, liturgical cultures functioned as powerful engines of vernacular making'.[20] In making this claim, the present volume also

---

[16] Duffy (1992), pp. 219–20.   [17] Duffy (1992) p. 218.

[18] E. Colledge and J. Bazire, *The Chastising of God's Children and the Treatise of the Perfection of the Sons of God* (Oxford, 1957), chapter 24.

[19] The term 'paraliturgical' (and quasi-liturgical) is used in this book 'to describe Christian observances which are not part of the prescribed liturgy, but which relate to it in structure or intent' (definition that of Harper, Glossary, p. 309). Conventionally, 'liturgy' has been understood to refer to 'all the prescribed services of the Church, as contrasted with private devotion' (E. A. Livingstone, *The Concise Oxford Dictionary of the Christian Church*, revd. 3rd edn (Oxford, 2013), p. 306), while 'devotion' has been taken to denote rather more personal, informal intercessory practice. However, recent years have witnessed some debate regarding such delineated use of the terms 'liturgy' and 'devotion', as scholars have begun to argue that private devotion can allude to and involve devices conventionally associated with the liturgy, and vice versa (for further exploration of this area, see S. Boynton, 'Prayer as Liturgical Performance in Eleventh- and Twelfth-Century Monastic Psalters', *Speculum* 82 (2007), 896–931).

[20] B. Holsinger, 'Liturgy', in *Middle English*, Oxford Twenty-First Century Approaches to Literature, ed. P. Strohm (Oxford, 2007), pp. 295–314, p. 296 and p. 300. In this essay, Holsinger is beginning to explore ideas which are investigated more fully in K. Zieman, *Singing the New Song: Literacy and Liturgy in Late Medieval England*, The Middle Ages Series (Pennsylvania, 2008). In

owes something to the work of Katherine Zieman, whose recent study *Singing the New Song: Literacy and Liturgy in Late Medieval England*, attempts to counter underestimations of the importance of the Latin liturgy in the history of vernacular literature and literacy. For Zieman, and for my own work, it is important that we dispute general perceptions of 'the cultural function of the liturgy [as] one of conservative repetition, not innovation or creation'.[21]

Focusing on this generation of specifically English literature, I do not consider the finer details of Latinate liturgical practice, but bear it constantly in mind as a productive source and companion. I do not, however, focus on the English psalms only as 'liturgical effects' but also consider their status as translations and situate them in the context of translation theory and practice, arguing that there is no sense in isolating them from their contemporary cultural milieu, in which the literary activity of translation played such a central role. While some are close and literal vernacularizations, the work of translators conscious of the imperative for fidelity to the source, others are free and confident paraphrases, whose authors use the psalms as a basis for both exposition and prayer. Like their literary contemporaries, those responsible for the various vernacular renditions clearly conceptualized the role of the translator in different ways and had different aims and audiences in mind. The late-medieval English psalms can, however, be distinguished from many contemporary translations by virtue of the fact that they are vernacularizations of specifically biblical material. They must all therefore also be seen to participate in the sometimes fraught late-medieval discussions of the propriety of the English Bible in particular and of vernacular devotion in general.

Intended for a wide range of readers with varying expectations of their encounter with the book of psalms, these late-medieval English translations were not restricted in use to a 'passive' laity, the only stratum of society unschooled in Latin. As we know, by no means all members of the medieval clergy (particularly those in lower orders) were as proficient in Latin as they might have been. William Langland's Sleuthe, boasting of his liturgical and biblical ignorance, is a fictional case in point:

> I han be preest and person passynge thritty wynter,
> Yet kan I neyther solve ne synge ne seintes lyves rede,
> But I kan fynden in a feld or in a furlang an hare
> Bettre than *Beatus vir* or *Beati omnes*
> Construe clausemel[e] and kenne it to my parisshens.[22]

Many of the translations and paraphrases which I investigate would have been of use to such individuals, not all of whom should be reduced to the level of Sloth's

context, Holsinger is talking about the ways in which 'the liturgy provides an economic, material and even creative foundation of literary production' from the late Middle Ages 'through the first decades of the English Reformation'. My interest in this book is focused on the liturgy as *creative* foundation for vernacular literary production only.

[21] Zieman, p. ix.

[22] A. V. C. Schmidt, *The Vision of Piers Plowman. A Critical Edition of the B-Text based on Trinity College MS.B.15.17*, 2nd edn corrected (London, 2011), Passus V, p. 57/416–20.

drivelling caricature. And that they did function in this way is often suggested, and sometimes confirmed, by manuscript evidence. While the interests of the devout laity were no doubt a significant factor in the popularity of the English psalms, their use was by no means restricted to this group.

Yet for all their variety of uses and audiences, and for all their awareness of their own identity as translations of the Vulgate and as companions to Latinate liturgical practice, the one characteristic uniting the widely differing psalm translations considered in this book is their vernacularity: all provide a resource and means of expression for those who cannot, or choose not to, read the Latin. Among the psalm verses which resonate most insistently and powerfully in medieval devotional culture is 50: 17 ('Domine labia mea aperies et os meum adnuntiabit laudem tuam' [O Lord, thou wilt open my lips and my mouth shall declare thy praise]), its pre-eminence due to the fact that in secular Use, it introduces a dialogue at the beginning of Matins. Beginning with the first half of the verse ('Domine labia mea . . .'), the response is formed from the second ('Et os meum . . .'). The next antiphon is taken from the first verse of the aforementioned Psalm 69 ('Deus in adiutorium meum intende' [O God, come to my assistance]), while the response is the second half of the same verse ('Domine ad adiuvandum me festina' [O Lord, make haste to help me]).[23] Translated into English, Psalm 50: 17 ('Lord, opene thou my lippis and my mouth schal telle thi preysyng') also consistently introduces the Matins of Our Lady (also known as the Little Office of the Virgin) with which late-medieval vernacular primers begin. Central to much of this book's exploration and analysis, these underexplored primers (akin to Books of Hours) provide us with compelling evidence that, in the late Middle Ages, the translated psalms offered an unparalleled opportunity for the opening of a multitude of lips in vernacular praise, prayer, and penance. The repetition of both plea ('Lord, opene thou my lippis') and statement ('and my mouth schal telle thi preysyng') at the beginning of each of these volumes serves as an apt and evocative illustration of the ways in which English psalm translation enabled the liberation of a new voice in the late Middle Ages, at once devotional and literary. The central role that the psalms played in the 'explor[ation] and exten[sion] [of] vernacular literary voice' has recently been highlighted in an important essay by David Lawton, in which he suggests that '[t]he Psalms are the place where Christianity does its most urgent and extensive thinking about voice and persona, both religious and literary'.[24] But where Lawton argues that the vernacular psalms operate most forcefully in the post-Arundelian era, I would suggest that productive psalmic experimentation in English begins a little earlier, in the fourteenth century.

The role that the psalms play in encouraging the liberation of this vernacular voice should not surprise us: the Psalter has long been seen as containing some

---

[23] In monastic Use, 'the order of the opening dialogue was commonly reversed, and Psalm 3 preceded the Invitatory and hymn' (Harper, p. 90). The opening of the lips in praise is not, therefore, as obviously foregrounded as it is in secular Matins.

[24] D. Lawton, 'Voice after Arundel', in V. Gillespie and K. Ghosh, *After Arundel: Religious Writing in Fifteenth-Century England*, Medieval Church Studies 21 (Turnhout, 2011), pp. 133–51, p. 144 and p. 146.

of the Bible's most powerfully personal intercessions. For example, in his *De Usu Psalmorum*, the eighth-century ecclesiastic Alcuin of York characterizes them thus:

> In psalmis invenies tam intimam orationem, si intenta mente perscruteris, quantum non potes per teipsum ullatenus excogitare.[25]

> (In the psalms, if you study them with an attentive mind, you will find prayer so intimate that you would not yourself be able to devise any greater.)

More than this, however, the psalms are texts which foreground 'the voice' as their very theme. They are insistent in drawing attention to themselves as personal utterances and frequently appear caught between anxiety lest God will not hear:

> Hear, O Lord, my prayer: and let my cry come to thee. Turn not away thy face from me. In the day when I am in trouble, incline thy ear to me. In what day soever I shall call upon thee, hear me speedily. (Psalm 101: 2–3)

and certainty that He is able to hear:

> For the Lord hath heard the voice of my weeping. The Lord hath heard my supplication, the Lord hath received my prayer. (Psalm 6: 9–10)

This preoccupation with voice is read by Robert Alter as a preoccupation with language, and his sense of the psalms' fascination with their own vocality is apt in the context of this book:

> One of the most ubiquitous themes in the various genres of Psalms is language itself. There seems to be a development from a formal organising device to the self-conscious investigation of a theme. That is, as befits poems which may often have been recited in a cultic setting, many of the thanksgiving poems begin and end with the declared intention of praising, extolling, thanking God, and many of the supplications begin and end by entreating God to hear the plea, pay heed, and rescue. But the poets very often proceed from these formulas of inception and conclusion to ponder the uses and power of the medium of language they employ. The supplication often quite explicitly raises questions about the efficacy of man's speech to God, the possibility of an answering speech from God to man, the tensions between speech and silence, the different functions of language for crying out in anguish and for exploring the enduring enigmas of man's creaturely condition.[26]

It is the proliferation of specifically vernacular psalmic voices with which we are now going to deal. Confident on occasion, troubled on others, these voices both assert an identity independent of their Latin source and ask to be heard in dialogue with that source. In prose and poetic form, in literal and fluent tones, they demand our attention.

This study of the English psalms is a starting point rather than a conclusion. Raising as many questions as I answer, I aim to alert us to productive lines of future research. In assembling material for the volume, I have chosen to focus only on

---

[25] Alcuin of York, *De Usu Psalmorum, PL* 101: 465D. This phrase is quoted in R. Fulton, 'Praying with Anselm at Admont: A Meditation on Practice', *Speculum* 81 (2006), pp. 700–33, p. 712.
[26] R. Alter and F. Kermode, *The Literary Guide to the Bible* (London, 1987), R. Alter, 'The Psalms', p. 260.

texts whose obvious identity is that of psalm translation or paraphrase. This leaves us with an unexplored body of lyrical and devotional literature inspired by the psalms as well as a mine of information relating to the use and understanding of the Psalter in contemporary vernacular sermons. Such texts must form the subject of a future study. For now, let us turn our attention to the English psalms themselves, and set the scene, in Chapter 1, with an examination of their manuscript dissemination. Chapter 2 steps back from the texts and their material context to consider the English psalms in the light of inherited and contemporary translation theory. In Chapters 3 and 4, we return to the texts themselves and examine the practice of psalm translation in the late Middle Ages. Chapter 5 explores patterns and habits of psalm reading and in Chapter 6, attention turns to questions raised by consideration of the English psalms in their manuscript context. Given the appearance, in the majority of manuscripts, of at least parts of the text of the Latin Psalter, how English, might we ask, were the 'English' psalms?

1

Psalm Dissemination

THE CIRCULATION OF THE PSALMS

We begin by tracing the dissemination of versions of the vernacular psalms in late-medieval England. Shedding light on who owned and read these texts, this chapter establishes the evidential basis on which the rest of the book builds. It does so by consideration of the information supplied by the manuscripts themselves and by examination of testamentary documents.

The limitations of wills and testaments as indexes of the reading population are well attested.[1] It is widely acknowledged that they cannot be relied upon to itemize all the books that might have been owned by the testator, that they tend to advertise the testator's religious volumes rather more forcefully than those of an obviously secular nature, and that they probably privilege Latin over vernacular texts.[2] It must also be acknowledged (from experience if nothing else) that there is often a difference between owning a book and actually reading it, and further, that the activity of 'reading' in a medieval context must have differed in many ways from 'reading' as understood today.[3] Extant wills are also inconsistent in their social coverage; not only do significantly more wills survive from some areas than from others, but while many fourteenth-century wills are of aristocratic origin, it was

---

[1] Strictly speaking, the will was a document in which lands were disposed, whereas testaments dealt with moveable goods. In practice, however, many testators did not distinguish between the two, often leaving a 'last will and testament' (see A. M. Dutton, 'Passing the Book: Testamentary Transmission of Religious Literature to and by Women in the England 1350–1500', in *Women, the Book and the Godly: Selected Proceedings of the St. Hilda's Conference, 1993*, ed. L. Smith and J. H. M. Taylor (Cambridge, 1995), pp. 41–54). Henceforth this chapter will use the term 'will'.

[2] C. M. Meale, '"alle the bokes that I haue of latyn, englisch, and frensch": Laywomen and their Books in Late Medieval England', in *Women and Literature in Britain 1150–1500*, Cambridge Studies in Medieval Literature 17, 2nd edn, ed. C. M. Meale (Cambridge, 1996), pp. 128–58. See especially her comment that '[i]nterpretation of the evidence provided by the will is not . . . straightforward: the nature of the document and the solemnity and formality which characterises it, undoubtedly had some influence on the kinds of books which were specified by a testator, in terms of both their content and their value' (p. 130).

[3] Carol Meale's comments on specifically female 'reading' are applicable to a much broader cross-section of society: '[i]t is quite possible that women who were unable to read or write possessed books . . . In an age when "reading" could be a communal activity, whether in aristocratic circles such as those of Cecily Neville and Margaret Beaufort or in artisan households such as those of the female Lollards in Norwich, the term "reader" may need radical redefinition if we are to understand women's use of books' (Meale, p. 133).

not until the late fifteenth century that 'will-making as an activity . . . percolated down the social scale to include a far wider cross-section of the population'.[4]

Bearing all of these limitations in mind, it is nonetheless the case that surviving wills paint a compelling picture of a population intent upon the psalms; after all, Psalters are among the most commonly bequeathed books of the late Middle Ages, along with primers, Missals, Breviaries, and other liturgical and devotional volumes.[5] The contents of primers will be discussed later, but the term 'Missal' designates a book containing a priest's texts for the celebration of mass, while a Breviary contains all of the psalms, collects, and readings used in the daily services of the church.[6] We can assume Missals and Breviaries to have been Latin texts. The language of the great majority of these Psalters is unspecified and it would be wise to assume most to have been Latin.[7] Nonetheless, consideration of their popularity and of the popularity of the closely related primer is a valuable precursor to more detailed analysis of the circulation of English translations, since it makes us aware of the traditions of psalm ownership and reading from which the vernacular versions grew and to which they responded.

Unsurprisingly, male ownership of Psalters in the Middle Ages is extremely well attested. It would be much harder to find a will or inventory that does not include the book than it is to find one that does, and evidence suggests that ownership was spread fairly evenly between monastic communities, clerics in high orders, and individual members of the laity. There is also considerable evidence of Psalters belonging to parish churches, which comes as no surprise since we know that repeated synodal statutes required such ownership.[8] Possession of Psalters by individual parish clergy is also extremely common and wills tell us that it was by no means unusual for priests to own their own copies of liturgical volumes.[9] Evidence of female interest in the psalms is equally notable and that the earliest recorded bequest to a nunnery (in the 1349 will of William de Thorneye, a London pepperer) contains a Psalter is a useful indicator of the popularity of this book among

---

[4] Dutton, p. 44.

[5] As Susan Cavanaugh has demonstrated, '[a]t least half the books mentioned in medieval wills are liturgical or devotional. Bequests of such books occur regularly enough to show that they were owned by a great many individuals from all levels of society.' S. Cavanaugh, *A Study of Books Privately Owned in England: 1300–1450* (unpublished PhD thesis, University of Pennsylvania, 1980), p. 10.

[6] For explanation of key liturgical terms, the reader is referred to Harper, 'Glossary of Ecclesiastical and Liturgical Terms', pp. 286–319.

[7] Specific references to English Psalters will be examined later in this chapter. It is, however, worth noting that several wills mention French Psalters. In 1392 Sir Robert de Roos left a 'Psalterium de gallico' [French Psalter] to his daughter Eleanor (Cavanaugh, pp. 747–8). The two Psalters glossed in French left by Eleanor Bohun, Duchess of Gloucester, to her daughters in 1399 will be discussed later in this chapter (Cavanaugh, pp. 110–11), alongside the 1401 will of Isabella Percy of York, which includes three Psalters (one 'de gallico' [in French], another 'anglice' [English], and a third described as 'parvum' [small]) (Cavanaugh, p. 648).

[8] See, for example, the 1240 statutes of Walter de Cantilupe, Bishop of Winchester, requiring ownership of the following books: Missal, Breviary (usually listed as Portiphorium rather than Brevarium), Gradual, Antiphoner, Troper, Psalter, Manual, and Ordinal (see N. Morgan, 'Books for the Liturgy and Private Prayer', in *The Cambridge History of the Book in Britain*, vol. 2, 1100–1400, ed. N. Morgan and R. M. Thomson (Cambridge, 2008), chapter 12, pp. 291–316, p. 295).

[9] See Morgan, pp. 291–316.

communities of religious women.[10] As Mary Erler states, Psalters were 'the most characteristic fourteenth-century book bequest' to nunneries, and conceding that extant evidence is patchy at best, Richard Pfaff also points out that 'those books which survive and can be attributable to a specific female house are overwhelmingly psalters (and Horae)'.[11] The wills of many wealthy women also indicate the popularity of Psalters amongst female readers beyond the cloister, several of whom owned more than one copy.[12] The 1356 will of Elizabeth Bohun Countess of Northampton, for example, mentions two Psalters (one of which was left to her daughter Elizabeth and another to 'fr dauid de servington') and that of Eleanor Bohun Duchess of Gloucester (1399) includes four (one left to her son Humphrey, one to her daughter Joan, and two to her daughter Isabel, a nun in the minoresses of Aldgate, London).[13] In her will dated 1400 (proved 1401) Isabella Percy of York bequeathed three Psalters, one to William Flaxton, chaplain, one to Johanna Chetwyn, and another to 'domino Henrico', chaplain of the parish church of All Saints North Street, York.[14] Later in the fifteenth century Elizabeth Fitzhugh Lady of Ravensworth left one 'sauter' to her son Robert and another to her daughter Darcy, and in the 1438 will of Lady Matilda Mauley we find three, of which one was bequeathed to William Darell, one to Richard Plumpton, and another to Robert Cross.[15]

In fact, the remarkable extent of psalm circulation in the Middle Ages can make it difficult to delineate specific groups of readers. The above bequests indicate not only the popularity of the Psalter among women, but also—and equally importantly—its fluid lines of dissemination; all demonstrate that these volumes passed easily between men and women. Those of William de Thorneye and Eleanor Bohun also illustrate the trend for lay bequests to religious establishments (or to individuals within those establishments), while that of Isabella Percy exemplifies circulation between members of the laity and the clergy.[16] Neither was it uncommon for lay bequests to be made directly to ecclesiastical establishments; in 1412, for example, Sir Ivo FitzWaryn left two 'libros vocatos Sawters' [books called

[10] Cavanaugh, pp. 856–7. His bequest was to the Prioress and nuns of S. Elena, London (St Helen's Bishopsgate) and also included a cup to hold the host, a portifory, and a silver-gilt chalice.

[11] M. C. Erler, *Women, Reading and Piety in Late Medieval England*, Cambridge Studies in Medieval Literature 46 (Cambridge, 2002), p. 39, and Pfaff, p. 342. See also D. N. Bell, *What Nuns Read: Books and Libraries in Medieval English Nunneries* (Kalamazoo, 1995).

[12] See A. Blamires, 'The Limits of Bible Study for Medieval Women', in *Women, the Book, and the Godly* ed. Smith and Taylor (Cambridge, 1995), pp. 1–12. See also Meale's comments: 'Many of the finest Psalters and books of hours from the fourteenth century were produced at the instigation of women, and this tradition seems to have continued into the fifteenth century' (Meale, p. 137).

[13] Cavanaugh, pp. 108–11. She also suggests that the Book of Hours and Psalter in Oxford, BodlL Dept. Astor. A.1 was executed for Elizabeth, and later left to Blackfriars, Norwich. We know also that the Psalter in NLS, Advocates 18.6.5 was commissioned by Eleanor de Bohun in the late fourteenth century. Eleanor was married to Thomas of Woodstock, Duke of Gloucester (d. 1397). An inventory of goods seized in his castle at Pleshy after his death includes an impressive collection of books, secular and devotional (see Cavanaugh, pp. 844–51).

[14] Cavanaugh, p. 648.   [15] Cavanaugh, p. 347 and p. 578.

[16] For further lay bequests to female religious, see for example the 1430 (proved 1431) will of William Stowe of Ripon in which he bequeaths 'unum parvum psalterium' [a small Psalter] to the prioress of Nun Monkton, West Yorkshire (Cavanaugh, pp. 828–9).

Psalters] to 'ecclesie cathedral Saresburie' [the cathedral church of Salisbury] and in a rather more modest gesture, the 1419 will of Matilda Constable bequeathed 'unum psalterium' [a Psalter] to the Church of All Saints Halsham, Yorkshire.[17] The complexity of Psalter circulation is perhaps best illustrated by two specific fifteenth-century wills; in his 1450 will, Sir Thomas Cumberworth included a 'gret boke of Dauid sauter'. Having apparently belonged to 'the ffrerys' ('my gret boke . . . as was the ffrerys') before it passed into Thomas' hands, the 'sauter' is then bequeathed by Thomas to 'the parson of Someretby'.[18] Transferred from religious to lay to clerical ownership, the movements of this volume exemplify effectively the broad appeal of the Psalter. Turning to a second will, in 1417 Edmund Thorpe, Knight of Ashwellthorpe, Norfolk, bequeathed two Psalters. Following a common pattern of dissemination, the first was left to Thomas Arteys, chaplain. However, the second ('unum aliud psalterium' [another Psalter]) traces a rather more complex path; bequeathed by Edmund to Robert Bussh, it had belonged to Edmund's wife, Joan (d. 1414), having been left to her by 'magister [master/tutor] Karolus Aleyn'.[19] Passing from male teacher to female (student?), to noble husband, and then to one 'Robert Bussh', the movement of this Psalter bears witness to its multiplicity of readers and, presumably, uses.

In bequeathing more than one Psalter, Edmund Thorpe was by no means unusual, as indicated by the contents of many other wills cited in this chapter. Not only do such wills reveal individual ownership of multiple Psalters, but they also indicate great variety among these volumes; no one Psalter was identical to any other. As with many book bequests in the Middle Ages, it is not uncommon to find them distinguished by appearance, and most simply by the colour of their covering; the Psalter left by the aforementioned Elizabeth Fitzhugh to her son, for example, was 'couered with rede velwet', while that left to her daughter was 'cou'ed in blew'.[20] The two Psalters bequeathed by Ivo FitzWaryn are differentiated in the same way ('unus coopertus . . . cum nigro worsted et alius coopertus cum albo correo' [one covered . . . with black cloth and another covered with white leather]) and the three Psalters in the 1438 will of Lady Matilda Mauley are, respectively, 'coopertum cum blodio velvett' [covered with blue velvet], 'nigrum' [black], and 'rubeum' [red].[21] Neither is it rare to find them apparently identified by size; Agnes Stapilton's much-cited will (1447) refers to 'meum magnum psalterium' [my great Psalter] which she left to her grandson William Plumpton, and the 1450 will of the aforementioned Sir Thomas Cumberworth includes the 'gret boke of Dauid sauter'.[22] That left by Eleanor Bohun to her son

[17] Cavanaugh, pp. 348–9 and p. 206. See also the 1347 will of Margaret de Thorp, wife of Lord William de Thorp, in which she leaves 'psalterium meum' [my Psalter] to 'Sanctae Trinitatis Capellae de Thorp' [de Thorp chapel of the Holy Trinity] (pp. 861–2).

[18] Cavanaugh, pp. 224–5. The possibility that Sir Thomas Cumberworth's 'gret boke' was a copy of Rolle's English translation and commentary will be discussed later in this chapter.

[19] Cavanaugh, p. 863.   [20] Cavanaugh, p. 347.

[21] Cavanaugh, p. 349 and p. 578.

[22] For Stapilton's will, see Cavanaugh, pp. 815–16. Agnes Stapilton, married to Sir Brian Stapilton, had three children (Brian, Joan, and Elizabeth). Elizabeth married Sir William Plumpton (to whom

(a 'psauter bien et richement enlumines oue lez claspes dor enamailes oue cignes blank et les armes de mon seignor et piere enamailes sur lez claspes et autres barres dor sur les tissues en maner des molets') with the accompanying request that it be passed down from heir to heir, is clearly a volume of some worth and proportions.[23]

Other wills refer somewhat cryptically to 'small' Psalters. In 1392 Sir Robert de Roos left, among other books, 'unum parvum psalterium' [a small Psalter] to Thomas his son, and a 'parvum psalterium quod fuit matris ejus' [a small Psalter which was her mother's] to his daughter Katherine.[24] That left to William Flaxton by Isabella Percy was also a 'parvum psalterium', and in 1450 Joan Buckland, widow of Richard Buckland of Edgcott, Northamptonshire, bequeathed 'my litill Sawter' to one Richard Clarell.[25] On such occasions, it is difficult to know whether the 'smallness' refers to physical dimensions, to contents, or to both. It is possible that a 'parvum psalterium' denotes a volume containing an abbreviated selection of psalms such as one finds in the primer, or a text of the psalms unaccompanied by liturgical additions; in all likelihood, such a book would also be physically small when compared with some of the grander volumes already mentioned. Equally, 'small' could be a straightforward reference to physical size, having little to do with contents; as Nigel Morgan points out, even a tiny Psalter volume could contain the complete biblical text.[26]

Despite this opacity, many extant wills do distinguish between Psalters by means of explicit reference to their contents. The description of the heirloom Psalter (presumably Latin) bequeathed to her son by Eleanor Bohun (discussed earlier) differs substantially from that of the French Psalter bequeathed to her daughter Joan. Described as 'un liure oue le psautier primer et autres deuocions oue deux claspes dor enamaillez oue mes armes quele liure iay pluis use oue ma beneison'), this is a well-used 'working' book, albeit an impressive one, apparently containing, in addition to the psalms, a copy of the primer and other devotional pieces.[27] In the nature of its additional contents as well as its language (French), this Psalter resembles one of the two which she also bequeathed to her daughter Isabel, described as a 'liure nouel du psautier glosez de la primer, domine exaudi, tanque a omnis

Agnes left 'unum librum cum orisons' [a book with prayers]) and it was their son, also called William, to whom Agnes left her Psalter. For Sir Thomas Cumberworth, see pp. 224–5. See also, for example, the 1319 will of Margery de Crioll, which refers to 'mon graund sauter' [my large Psalter] (pp. 222–3).

[23] Cavanaugh, pp. 110–11 ['a psalter well and richly illuminated with enamelled clasps of gold as well as white swans and the arms of my lord and enamelled stone on the clasps and other gold strips on the rich cloth in the pattern of stars']. See also the 1368 will of John de Grandisson, Bishop of Exeter, which refers to 'duo Psalteria majora et meliora' [the two bigger and better Psalters] as well as 'pulchrius psalterium meum' [my more beautiful Psalter] (pp. 371–2). See also the 1435 will of Thomas Hebbeden, Dean of Aukland, which refers to 'unum pulcrum psalterium sb'aliter (? *specialiter*) scriptum' [a beautiful Psalter written (? in a particular style)] (p. 404).

[24] Cavanaugh, pp. 747–8.   [25] For Buckland, see Cavanaugh, p. 148.
[26] The specific example to which Morgan alludes is a *c.* 1270–180 Psalter, PML MS. 679 (51 x 37mm) in which the text takes up 400 folios (Morgan, p. 311).

[27] ['a book containing, in addition to the Psalter, a primer and other devotions, with two clasps enamelled with gold as well as my arms, which book I use most frequently, along with my blessing']. The primer and its relationship with the Psalter will be discussed later in this chapter.

spiritus laudet dominum'.[28] Other wills refer frequently to similar content beyond
the psalms; that of Beatrice Milreth, for example, includes 'a book with primer
and psalter in one volume' (1448) and a 1493 will also mentions 'my prymere
with the sawter and oþere praiers'.[29] Some bequests were of Psalters which were
clearly deployed as service books; such is the case with the 1434/5 will of Johannes
Gylby, rector of Knesall, Nottinghamshire, in which 'unum parvum Psalterium
cum Ympnario, et multis devotis orationibus' (the 'parvum' possibly referring to
the Psalter rather than the volume as a whole) was left to his church.[30] The will
of William Phelip, Lord Bardolph (1438, proved in 1441) refers to a 'magnum
psalterium novum cum hymnario et servicio mortuorum' [a great new Psalter with
a hymnal and an Office of the Dead] which was left to his chapel, and that of Sir
Thomas Chaworth, dated 1458, includes a 'Sawter with Placebo and Dirige and
an Hympner in the same', left to his son William.[31]

It should come as no surprise that we find Psalters thus distinguished by additional content. In medieval usage, the term 'Psalter' very rarely designated a volume containing only the psalms. As Nigel Morgan has demonstrated, a medieval
Psalter almost invariably included a Calendar, a Litany, and the Canticles. It could
also be combined with a Hymnal; such are the volumes bequeathed by William
Phelip and Thomas Chaworth.[32] Morgan also notes that in the late twelfth and
thirteenth centuries Psalters sometimes contained the Office of the Virgin and
many also included the Office of the Dead. The fact that the Psalters of Phelip
and Chaworth also contained the Office of the Dead indicates that such combined texts remained in circulation in the fourteenth and fifteenth centuries and

---

[28] ['a new book (containing) a psalter? *glossed/annotated* according to the primer (from) 'Hear, O
Lord, my prayer' as far as 'Let every spirit praise the Lord'], Cavanaugh, pp. 110–11. What Eleanor
means by a 'psautier glosez de la primer' is not entirely clear, but it may be a version of the psalms
marked in some way for liturgical use. 'Domine exaudi' refers to either Psalm 101 or 142 (the fifth and
seventh Penitential Psalms respectively) and 'Omnis spiritus laudet dominum' to Psalm 150: 5. She
also leaves to Isabel a 'psautier veil tanqe a la nocturn de Exultate glosez' [an old Psalter glossed/anno-
tated until the nocturn 'Let (every spirit) praise (the Lord)']. R. S. Wieck, *Time Sanctified: The Book of
Hours in Medieval Art and Life*, 2nd edn (New York, 2001) points out that '[d]uring the course of the
twelfth and thirteenth centuries, the Hours of the Virgin became attached for a time to the Psalter, the
prayerbook commonly used by the laity during these two hundred years, and formed a type of book
called the Psalter-Hours.' But such books were obviously lengthy and cumbersome. It is possible that
Eleanor is referring to such a volume.
[29] Cavanaugh, pp. 585–6. For another composite volume, see the inventory appended to the 1449
will (proved in 1451) of John Clerk, chaplain of the chapel of St Mary Magdalene near York, in which
we find 'unum Psalterium cum Placebo et Dirige, commendac' cum vij Psalmis penitencialibus in
eodem contentis' [a Psalter with *Placebo* and *Dirige* and the Psalms of Commendation with the seven
Penitential Psalms contained in the same]. The additional contents sound very like the contents of the
average primer, minus the Little Office of the Virgin (Cavanaugh, p. 194). For the 1493 will, see E.
Bishop, 'On the Origin of the Primer', in H. Littlehales, *The Prymer or the Lay Folk's Prayer Book*, 2
vols, EETS OS 105 (1895) and OS 109 (1897). Reprinted in E. Bishop, *Liturgica Historica: Papers on
the Liturgy and Religious Life of the Western Church* (Oxford, 1918), pp. 211–37.
[30] ['A small psalter with a hymnal and many devout prayers'], Cavanaugh, p. 361.
[31] Cavanaugh, p. 651 and pp. 181–2. Sir Thomas' Psalter is to be found in his 'closet at the
chapell', accompanied by an 'olde Messe boke with a boke of Placebo and Dirige' and other liturgical volumes. Sir Thomas was the great-great-grandson of Sir Geoffrey Luttrell, for whom the Luttrell
Psalter was made.
[32] Morgan, p. 302.

were, indeed, still being commissioned (Phelip refers to his volume as 'psalterium novum'). Some also added the 'basic prayers to be learned by a child as specified in the 1262/5 episcopal statutes of Winchester', which tallies with what we know of the role of Psalters in elementary education.[33]

While institutional ownership of the Psalter seems to have remained constant throughout the late Middle Ages, several studies of lay literacy have noted that Psalters are mentioned less frequently in wills of the mid- to late fifteenth century than they are in those of the fourteenth and early fifteenth. P. J. P. Goldberg's reading of 2,286 fifteenth-century York wills, for example, finds that while nineteen Psalters were bequeathed in the first half of the century, there were only six such bequests in the second.[34] Noting that Psalters declined in fashion over the period, he states:

> Conversely, primers, works specifically designed for lay use and easily the most numerous of service or devotional books in lay hands, became increasingly popular as the fifteenth century wore on [. . .] It would thus appear that the growing popularity and availability of the primer tended to displace the psalter, and perhaps the missal, for lay use.[35]

Goldberg's findings are broadly paralleled by those of Norman Tanner who, in his study of late-medieval Norwich, also notes a drop in the circulation of the Psalter amongst the laity. For Tanner as well, the decline of the Psalter is matched by a fifteenth-century peak in the popularity of the primer. His examination of 1515 lay wills finds that a total of twelve primers were bequeathed in the years 1440–89, as compared with one in the years 1370–1439 and one in the years 1490–1517.[36]

The apparent decline in Psalter circulation is read by some as indicative of a broader movement away from strictly liturgical devotion, which tended to be performed publicly, to more private, para-liturgical forms of personal devotion.

---

[33] Morgan, p. 308. On the role of the psalms in education, see the work of Nicholas Orme; '[f]or boys and girls alike, schooling began by learning the alphabet—usually the Latin alphabet—written on a board or in a small book. This was followed by reading practice, starting with basic prayers like the Paternoster, Ave Maria and Apostles' Creed in Latin or English and, especially in formal schools for boys, the sight-reading, pronunciation and chanting of Latin texts from the Psalter and antiphonal which were used in church services.' Nicholas Orme 'Schools and School-Books', in *The Cambridge History of the Book in Britain*, vol. 3, 1400–1557, ed. L. Hellinga and J. B. Trapp (Cambridge, 1999), pp. 449–69, p. 451.

[34] P. J. P. Goldberg, 'Lay Book Ownership in Late Medieval York: The Evidence of Wills', *The Library* 16 (1994), 181–9, p. 185.

[35] Goldberg, p. 185. Prior to Goldberg, Jo Ann Hoeppner-Moran's examination of York diocesan wills finds that five primers were bequeathed from 1370–99 as compared with seventy-three in the period 1400–49 and ninety-two from 1450–99. She comments, '[P]rimers, the basic medieval reading text, were bequeathed in growing numbers, reflecting perhaps the growth in reading schools, or possibly the increased popularity of private devotions during Mass.' See *The Growth of English Schooling 1340–1548—Learning, Literacy and Laicization in Pre-Reformation York Diocese* (Guildford, 1985), p. 196.

[36] N. P. Tanner, *The Church in Late Medieval Norwich 1370–1532*, Pontifical Institute of Medieval Studies, Studies and Texts 66 (Toronto, 1984). He unearths a similar peak in clerical bequests. Looking at a total of 289 clergy wills, he finds that six primers were bequeathed between 1440 and 1489 as compared with only one between 1370 and 1439.

Mary Erler, for example, in her investigation of lay bequests to female religious houses, concludes that they demonstrate a shift in the nature of reading, 'notably by the mid-fifteenth century, from liturgical to devotional'.[37] Gone are the 'thoroughly traditional' bequests of Eleanor de Bohun (made in 1399), replaced by the five vernacular works found in the 1448 will of Agnes Stapilton (three in French and two in English).[38] There is certainly some truth in Erler's claim; Psalter bequests do decline and we do witness an increase in the circulation, among both lay and religious, of more obviously devotional literature, some of which is avowedly English. However, to trace such a trajectory is misleading since it suggests a straightforward separation between public and private devotion in the Middle Ages, and a simple movement from the former to the latter.[39] In its oversimplification, it also fails to note that 'the rise of vernacular theology is contemporaneous with the development of Books of Hours and other technologies of Latin prayer'. As Katherine Zieman has recently pointed out, '[e]vidence of book ownership . . . suggests that this burgeoning market [for liturgical texts] catered to the same audience as that of speculative vernacular texts.'[40] Erler's reading further misses the nuances of the de Bohun and Stapilton wills, the ways in which the later recalls as well as revises the earlier. Attention to the remarkable collection of vernacular devotional material in Agnes Stapilton's will tends to overshadow the fact that it also contains two rather more familiar volumes: a 'magnum psalterium' [great Psalter] left to her grandson William Plumpton and a 'primarium cum duobus claspis' [primer with two clasps] left to her granddaughter Agnes Ingelby.[41] Such bequests obviously recall the 'psauter bien et richement enlumines' [well- and richly illuminated Psalter] which Eleanor de Bohun left to her son Humphrey, the combined Psalter/primer which she left to her daughter Joan and which she had reserved for personal use ('quele liure iay pluis use' [which book I used most frequently]), and the 'psautier glosez de la primer' [the Psalter glossed/annotated according to the primer] which she left to her daughter Isabel. Clearly, as close consideration of these wills illustrates, personal and liturgical devotion complemented and enriched each other throughout the Middle Ages, to such an extent that it is often difficult to discern a clear division between the two. Much of the material under consideration in this book, of course, provides us with a clear illustration of this fact.

---

[37] Erler, pp. 41–2.

[38] Erler, p. 40. Stapilton's two obviously English books are *The Prick of Conscience* and *The Chastising of God's Children*. In addition, *Vices and Virtues* may have been an English book, and it is likely that 'librum meum vocatum Bonaventure' [my book called Bonaventure] was a translation of the pseudo-Bonaventuran meditations on the life of Christ. The 'librum cum orisons' [book with prayers] which she left to her son-in-law William Plumpton may well also have been English. She also bequeathed two unidentified French books ('librum de ffrensshe') as well as a 'librum de ffrensshe de vita sanctorum' [a French book of the lives of the saints] (Cavanaugh, pp. 815–16).

[39] As Nigel Morgan has argued, '[a] simplistic division between public liturgy and private devotion is most certainly not characteristic of late medieval religion in which the social and the personal penetrate and overlap.' Morgan, p. 306.

[40] For both quotations, see Zieman, p. 116.

[41] Agnes Ingelby was the daughter of Joan Stapilton and William Ingelby.

THE PRIMER

The difficulty of dividing liturgical from personal devotion makes more sense once we understand that the primer (often associated with private prayer) is based in large part on the Psalter (often associated with public performance, although also used extensively in private contexts). The growing popularity of the former, coupled with the waning lay circulation of the latter, should not therefore be read as heralding an irreversible decline in the popularity of the psalms as individual texts or groups of texts. Rather, it tells us that there was a hunger for a more digestible version of the Psalter, and that in its relatively brief and ordered contents the primer went some way towards satisfying this hunger. Presenting psalms and prayers drawn from liturgical tradition, it 'provided a well-structured series of texts for private devotion' which the traditional, full-scale Psalter lacked.[42] It is no surprise that the psalms should have been regarded as suitable for private devotional use as well as public liturgical performance; as Nigel Morgan points out, the Psalter had, 'since the early Middle Ages, been used for private devotion, both by clergy and lay people'.[43] In fact, the manuscript context and circulation of the psalms demonstrate more effectively than those of any other texts 'that any consistent distinction between liturgy as a category of practices performed only in public and devotion as predominantly private is elusive indeed'.[44]

But what did the late-medieval liturgical primer contain?[45] The simplest answer is that provided by Edmund Bishop in the late nineteenth century. Asserting that primers in general present 'certain practically unvarying elements', he lists the Office of the Blessed Virgin, the Office of the Dead, the Penitential and Gradual Psalms, the Litany, and Commendations.[46] More recently, Bishop's summary has been refined and elaborated upon by Nigel Morgan, who states that the 'average' medieval primer circulating in England contains:

> [T]he short version of the Hours of the Virgin, the Office of the Dead and the Litany. Other votive Offices of the Cross, the Passion, the Holy Spirit and the Trinity were sometimes additional texts. The gradual and penitential psalms are included, although the former are more frequent in early manuscripts and by 1400 they seldom occur in Books of Hours. Various devotions to the Virgin are included such as her joys and sorrows, in various numbers . . . and prayers to God, Christ, the Holy Trinity, the Holy Cross, the Holy Face, the Five Wounds, Mary and the saints.[47]

The short version of the Hours of the Virgin (distinct from the full Office of the Virgin), comprised of a series of devotions to Mary according to the eight liturgical Hours (Matins, Lauds, Prime, Terce, Sext, None, Vespers, and Compline), had the psalms as its backbone.[48] The Office of the Dead ('the fixed texts of the

---

[42] Morgan, p. 309. [43] Morgan, p. 306. [44] Boynton (2007), p. 896.
[45] I distinguish a 'primer' from a '*liturgical* primer' for reasons which will become clear.
[46] Bishop (1897), p. xii.
[47] Morgan, p. 310. See also the summary of the basic contents of 'Horae' in Wieck (2001), pp. 27–8.
[48] This Office is frequently called 'The Little Office of the Virgin' to distinguish it from the full Commemorative Office of the Virgin.

Offices of Vespers, Matins, and Lauds, recited on the day of burial, or as a daily or occasional commemoration of the dead') also relied on antiphonal psalm recitation and, in the case of Matins (or Vigils), on a series of readings from the book of Job.[49] Recitation of the seven Penitential (6, 31, 37, 50, 101, 129, 142) and fifteen Gradual (119–33) psalms was a manageable intercessory activity, and inclusion of the Litany (along with further variable supplementary materials) made for a comprehensive yet compact devotional handbook.[50] As Edmund Bishop put it, '[w]e may feel sure that but one prayer-book [i.e., the primer] was in common use in the Middle Ages'; its appeal is readily comprehensible.[51]

The principal devotions of the medieval primer, as outlined, were drawn from long-standing liturgical tradition. Once again, Bishop's comments are elucidatory:

> [T]he *Prymer* consisted of those devotional accretions to the Divine Office [. . .] invented first by the piety of individuals for the use of monks in their monasteries, which accretions were gradually and voluntarily adopted in the course of two or three centuries by the secular clergy so generally, that by the fourteenth century they had, by virtue of custom, come to be regarded as obligatory, and practically a part of the public daily (or only Lenten) office itself.[52]

It is easy to see why these particular accretions became so popular in later medieval devotion; originating, in many cases, from practices of personal piety, they were readily adapted to the personal/public hybrid of the primer. The Little Office of the Virgin, for example, was often recited aloud in the monastic choir, but on other occasions (or at specific times of the year) it was 'said individually either in or out of choir'. And in some monastic foundations, 'a section of the community was detailed to recite the [Little Office of the Virgin] in a Lady chapel, or else special singers (including boys) were engaged to undertake this task, together with the antiphon sung after Compline'.[53] The popularity of the Office of the Dead in private devotion has already been noted, and the intensely introspective Penitential Psalms, first isolated as a distinct group by Cassiodorus in his sixth-century *Expositio Psalmorum*, have self-explanatory appeal as expressions of individual devotion.[54] The short Gradual psalms (other than Psalm 131, not one has more than nine verses) are also obviously convenient units for meditation, recitation, and memorization.

As with the Psalter, the popularity of the primer is indicated by its frequent inclusion in wills, its earliest appearance probably dateable to Elizabeth Bacon's 1323 bequest of 'a primer that was my sister Margaret's' to her brother Sir John

---

[49] Harper, p. 308. Although there were some minor variations in different Uses, the Vespers (*Placebo*) psalms were 114, 119, 120, 129, 137, and 145. The Matins (*Dirige*) psalms were 94, 5, 6, 7, 22, 24, 26, 39, 40, and 41. Those of Lauds were 50, 64, 62, 148–50, and 129 (as listed in Harper, pp. 105–8).

[50] There is 'some uncertainty' as to why the Gradual psalms are so described (see Harper, p. 300).

[51] Bishop (1897), p. xxxvii.   [52] Bishop (1897), p. xxxvii.   [53] Harper, pp. 133–4.

[54] For a comprehensive exploration of the background to the Seven Penitential Psalms, see M. Driscoll, 'The Seven Penitential Psalms: Their Designation and Usage from the Middle Ages Onwards', *Ecclesia Orans* 17 (2000), 153–201. See also discussion of the origins of the Penitential Psalm grouping in C. Costley King'oo, *Miserere Mei: The Penitential Psalms in Late Medieval and Early Modern England*, Reformations: Medieval and Early Modern (Notre Dame, 2012), pp. 4–5.

de la Ware.[55] It was among the most widely owned books of the late Middle Ages and '[m]any hundreds, perhaps thousands, of instances occur of mediaeval allusions to the *Prymer, Primer* or *Primarium*'.[56] Here, however, we should pause and ask what, in these testamentary contexts, is meant by 'primer', a term 'apparently special to England', since it seems that it does not always denote the liturgical volume whose contents were enumerated earlier. Rather, the term appears to have operated as something of a catch-all in the Middle Ages, used to refer to both liturgical and educational books which often contained supplementary catechetic and devotional material. Nicholas Orme points out that the word means 'first [book]', and may have come into use, as John Hilsey believed in 1539, because a prayer book or book of hours was 'the first book that the tender youth was instructed in'.[57] 'Primer' can, therefore, mean an elementary schoolbook containing the ABC and basic prayers, which need not necessarily be accompanied by liturgical material, although it can also denote a more prominently liturgical volume. Admittedly, the distinction between the two is not always clear-cut (liturgical volumes were often intended for and used in educational contexts), but it does have some valency and it is important that we bear it in mind.

The term 'primer' makes one think of a schoolbook, and the well-known reference to the 'litel child' sitting 'in the scole at his prymer' (ll. 516–17) in Chaucer's *Prioress' Tale* confirms that it was a book used in educational contexts. The work of Orme and others has provided us with ample evidence of this.[58] The fact that it was not unusual for churches and individual clerics to own primers provides further evidence of their use in education; outside the context of formal schooling, elementary learning was supplemented by parish priests and clerks, as well as by chantries and collegiate churches.[59] And, of course, primers also played their role in private family life and education:

> In the great lay households, boys and girls of the nobility were trained for lay careers rather than ecclesiastical ones, with greater emphasis on the vernacular than on Latin.

[55] Cavanaugh, pp. 61–2. In his article 'The Prymer in English', Edwyn Birchenough states that '[t]he word is first found in the Latin form of *primarium* in the will of Matthew of the Exchequer in 1294', but he offers no further information (E. Birchenough, 'The Prymer in English', *The Library* (1937) 18, 177–94, p. 177).

[56] A. Barratt, 'The Prymer and its Influence on Fifteenth-Century English Passion Lyrics', *MA* 44 (1975), 264–79, p. 264, and Bishop (1897), p. xliii. The advent of printing led to a dramatic increase in the number of primers in circulation. Eamon Duffy states that '[o]n the eve of the Reformation there were probably over 50,000 Books of Hours or Primers in circulation among the English laity. No other book commanded anything like such a readership.' Duffy (1992), pp. 8–9.

[57] N. Orme, *Medieval Children* (New Haven and London, 2001), p. 264.

[58] See in particular N. Orme, *English Schools in the Middle Ages* (London, 1973) and his *Medieval Children* (2001). See also the remarks of Alexandra Barratt (1975): '[I]t was not only the devout that came into contact with the prymers and similar books: it is doubtful whether any literate layman could be untouched by their influence, for they were used to teach children to read' (p. 264). The question of primer usage will be discussed in detail in Chapter 4. Zieman opens her 2008 book with consideration of this Chaucerian moment.

[59] Orme (1973), particularly chapter 2 'The Schools of Medieval England'. Although 1323 appears to mark the earliest appearance of a primer in a will, Henry Littlehales located an earlier reference to a primer in a church inventory. Elaborating on his claim that some parish churches possessed primers before the Reformation, he points us to the 1297 inventory of the property of Ardley Church, Essex,

For them, learning the alphabet was probably followed by learning to read prayers from the primer . . . (sometimes in Latin, sometimes in English) containing the basic prayers and simple office (or hours) of the Virgin Mary which the laity used for their private devotions.[60]

As suggested by these comments, in the hands of their users, the primers' educational function must have merged with their devotional purpose to such an extent that it is difficult to draw a firm line between the two.[61] Progress in functional literacy was, inevitably, progress in devotional literacy; as one learned to read, one learned to pray. In fact, the two activities were, ideally, indistinguishable; '[r]edunge is god bone', as the *Ancrene Wisse* author put it in the thirteenth century.[62] That the alphabets (ABCs) which appear on the opening pages of some late-medieval primers often begin with a cross (hence the name 'cross-rows') and end with 'amen' confirms this; as Orme puts it, '[t]he ABC is no longer a mere list of letters; it has become something that you offer to God, just as you do when you pray.'[63] Therefore, when Roger Elmesley, servant to a London waxchandler, bequeathed to 'Robert Sharp goddis-child . . . a prymmer for to serve god with', the 'service' envisaged was not only that of prayer but, more basically, that of acquiring a devotional vocabulary, a language with which to pray.[64]

which includes 'Item vnum primarium cum septem psalmis, et XV., et Placebo et Dirige' [A primer with the seven [penitential] psalms and the fifteen [gradual] and Placebo and Dirige [the Office of the Dead] (Littlehales (1897), p. 2). Orme (2001) also points out that the 'Carthusian priory of Hinton (Som.) owned two books called "primers of children" in 1343', p. 264.

[60] Orme (1999), pp. 455–6. He also states that '[t]here is evidence that children learning to read were made to decipher the Paternoster as their first piece of prose after learning the basic letters' (2001, p. 205).

[61] Hoeppner-Moran highlights the role of the primer in education, pointing out that '[a]fter learning the elementary primer, a reading scholar would move on to learn the psalm *De Profundis*, perhaps then *Dirige and Placebo* . . ., parts of the daily mass, particularly the Matins and Hours of the Virgin, and finally, the entire Psalter' (p. 46). She also points out that although the more complex Books of Hours were commonly used by the laity as a devotional manual during the church service, they could also be used as school-texts. This is illustrated by Bishop Grandisson's 1357 circular, which instructed teachers to parse the Matins and Hours (construere et intelligere faciunt Oracionem Dominicam cum Salutacione Angelica, Symbolum, et Matutinas, ac Horas de Beata Virgine, et dicciones ibi declinare ac respondere de partibus earundem, antequam eosdem ad alios libros transire permittant'). F. C. Hingeston-Randolph, *The Register of John de Grandisson*, 3 vols (London and Exeter, 1894–9), vol. 2, p. 1193 ['They make [them] construe and understand the Sunday Office with the Salutation of the Angels, with the Apostles' Creed, and Matins and the Hours of the Blessed Virgin, and there to decline the phrases and respond to the parts of the same, before they permit them to pass to other books.'].

[62] B. Millett, *Ancrene Wisse—A Corrected Edition of the text in Cambridge, Corpus Christi College MS 402 with Variants from Other Manuscripts*, 2 vols, EETS OS 325 & 326 (Oxford, 2005), vol. 1, 109/1554–5.

[63] Orme (2001), chapter 7 'Learning to Read', p. 249. Orme's comments on the cross with which alphabets began are also worth quoting; '[i]t led the letters like a cross-bearer and the letters marched behind it like a force of crusaders or a parish procession.' (p. 251) For examples of ABCs in English language primers, see Columbia University Library Plimpton 258; Oxford, BodlL Rawlinson C. 209; Manchester, JRL 85; and GUL Hunter 472 (v. 6. 22). These manuscripts contain only catechetic (and some devotional) material. The occurrence of an ABC in GUL Hunter 472 is particularly interesting, as this is a primer which contains liturgical material as well as catechesis. For full discussion of English language primers, see later in this chapter.

[64] For the 1434 will of Roger Elmesley, see Cavanaugh, p. 288. The primer is the only book mentioned in Elmesley's will, which also includes a considerable collection of domestic moveable goods, as

From the context in which they appear, the vast majority of primers mentioned in fourteenth- and fifteenth-century wills seem to have served personal devotional purposes, and are volumes which we might feel more comfortable designating 'Books of Hours'. However, we have drawn too rigid a distinction between the primer as unglamorous schoolbook and the more illustrious Book of Hours (the very notion of which 'conjures up images of richly gilt initials, jeweled covers [and] exquisite miniatures').[65] The fact that this modern distinction between the two is flawed was noted by Bishop over one hundred years ago:

> It is unfortunate that MS. Prymers should, in Libraries, be classed as Books of Hours, or Horae. The MSS. so called, whether they contain the common contents of the *Prymer*, or whether they contain any kind of Hour Office, are as a rule all classed together under that heading, though in most cases they prove to be Prymers[66]

and has been remarked upon more recently by Nicholas Orme. Maintaining that there was a distinction between a 'book of basic prayers' (containing the Pater Noster, Ave, Creed, etc.) and a 'book of hours' (containing 'shorter, simpler versions of the daily church services said by the clergy'), Orme notes that in contemporary practice, 'primer' was used to describe both.[67] The observations of both Littlehales and Orme are borne out by examination of contemporary wills. While, as noted, primers feature frequently in such documents, it is very rare for the term 'Book of Hours' to be used; Susan Cavanaugh's study includes only 'mes heures ou je di mes choses les quelles furent a la Royne descosce' [my hours in which I say my ?things which were ?in the kingdom of Scotland] and 'mon journal en quoi je dy mes heures' [my journal in which I say my hours] bequeathed in the 1376 will of Marie de Seintpol, Countess of Pembroke.[68] Several of the volumes explicitly designated 'primers' are nonetheless of the grandeur that we associate with 'Books of Hours'. The 'primarium magnum cum litteris illuminatis' [large primer with illuminated letters] left to Joanna, wife of William Beckwith, by Sir John Depeden in 1402 is a case in point, as is the 'primarium largum cum ymaginibus intus scriptis ad modum Flandr' [the large primer with images inside written in the style of Flanders] bequeathed by William Revetour, chaplain of York, to his granddaughter Isabel in 1446.[69]

well as some small financial bequests (F. J. Furnivall, *Fifty Earliest English Wills in the Court of Probate, London A.D 1387 1439*, EETS OS 78 (London, 1882)).

[65] Duffy (1992), p. 211.   [66] Bishop (1897), p. xliii.

[67] Orme (2001), p. 264. For examples of English language primers which contain basic prayers in the absence of liturgical material, see later in this chapter.

[68] Cavanaugh, pp. 778–9. For discussion of Marie de Seintpol, see S. L. Field, 'Marie of Saint-Pol and her Books', *EHR* 125 (2010), 255–78. She leaves the 'journal' to Emma of Beauchamp, Abbess of Bruisyard. Noting that the term 'journal' is ambiguous, Field argues that it 'suggests a highly personal volume used in Marie's personal devotions' (p. 262). The 'heures ou je di mes choses' are left to Jeanne of Bourbon, Queen of France and Marie's great-niece. Field suggests that the Queen of Scotland to whom the book belonged formerly is likely to have been Joan (b. 1321), youngest daughter of Edward II and Isabella. Again, he points out that 'the precise meaning of *choses* here is difficult to determine but presumably implies daily prayers' (p. 267).

[69] Cavanaugh, p. 244 and pp. 723–4.

It should also be noted that when wills mention volumes designated 'Matins of the Virgin' (which they do more commonly than 'Books of Hours'), they are very probably referring to primers. Given the centrality to the primer of the Little Office of the Virgin, this alternative designation makes perfect sense. When, for example, Elizabeth Bohun bequeaths 'j librum matutinarum de beata virgine' [a book of the matins of the blessed virgin] to her daughter Elizabeth in 1356, we can be fairly sure that she is describing a primer of sorts, and the same is true of the 1421 will of Lady Elizabeth Trivet (proved in 1433) which leaves 'meum meliorum librum de matutinis Beate Marie et aliis devocionibus' [my best book of the matins of the blessed Mary and other devotions] to Alice Compton.[70] It has been asserted that such volumes were particularly popular among women, and although they do appear with notable frequency in women's wills, in which they are often bequeathed to other women, they were also owned by men, and sat quite comfortably alongside heavyweight liturgical volumes.[71] The book containing 'the Matins of the B.V.M., placebo and dirige, and the visitation of the sick' and 'a book of the matins of the B.V.M' left by Henry Brokeland, Canon of Exeter (1404), are likely to have been primers, as is the 'librum rubeum de matutinis Beate Marie et de aliis devocionibus contentis in eodem' [the red book of the matins of the Blessed Mary and other devotions contained in the same] mentioned in the 1429 will of Simon Northew, Canon of Chichester.[72]

Like Psalters, late-medieval primers varied dramatically in size and in value. Several wills specify large volumes, some of which, as mentioned, are identified as illuminated.[73] A comparable number include small primers, although reduced size in itself need not necessarily indicate lessened value; many ornately illuminated English primers are of diminutive proportions.[74] It was very common for individuals to own more than one copy, with multiple primers appearing to have been particularly popular among women. In 1391, for example, Margaret Courtenay Countess of Devon left 'mes deux primers' [my two primers] to her daughter, the 1392 will of Isabella Duchess of York includes 'mon large primer' [my large primer] as well as 'mez deux petit premers' [my two small primers], and the will

---

[70] Cavanaugh, p. 108 and pp. 887–8. For further evidence of female ownership of such volumes, see the 1402 will of Constance Skelton and the two 'liber matutinarum beate marie' [book[s] of the matins of the blessed Mary] listed among items in the chamber of Isabella, Queen of Edward II (Cavanaugh, p. 789 and p. 459).

[71] Goldberg's investigation of York wills uncovers much evidence of female primer ownership: 'The testamentary evidence . . . suggests that whereas psalters and (somewhat less surprisingly) missals were largely in male ownership, primers were commonly owned by women and regularly bequeathed to women.' Goldberg, p. 185.

[72] Cavanaugh, pp. 141–2 and p. 618. For further evidence of male ownership of such books, see for example the 'parvus liber de Matutinis de Domina, cum vij. P.' [small book of the Matin of [our] Lady, with the 7 [penitential] Psalms], one of the ninety plus books left by Nicholas of Hereford (d. 1392) to Evesham Abbey.

[73] For example, in his 1375 will (proved in 1377) Hugh de Courtenay, Earl of Devon, left 'mon graunt primer' [my great primer] to 'Margrete ma fille' [my daughter] and in her 1378 will Margareta de Eure of Witton Castle bequeathed 'Radulpho de Eur' unum primarium magnum' [a great primer] (Cavanaugh, pp. 212–13 and p. 324).

[74] As an example, Nigel Morgan points us to London, BL Harley 928 (112 x 77 mm) (p. 313).

of Elizabeth Darcy, widow of Philip Lord Darcy (1412) mentions 'duos Primarios' [two primers].[75] Rather more remarkably, in her 1450/1 will, Hawisia Aske of York bequeathed a total of five primers.[76] In such situations, primers, like Psalters and other books, were often distinguished by their colour and covering. So, in her will dated 1415 (proved 1416), Isabella Wyleby, daughter of Sir Hugh de Annesley, left to 'Isabellae, uxori filii mei . . . unum primarium coopertum cum nigro velvet' [Isabel, wife of my son . . . a primer covered with black velvet] and to 'Margaretae filiae meae . . . unum novum primarium coopertum' [Margaret my daughter . . . a new, covered primer], and in his will dated 1450, Sir Thomas Cumberworth left 'my litill rede Primer lynyd with blak bawdekyn'.[77] The will of Matilda Countess of Cambridge, dated 1446, demonstrates again that size was also used as a distinguishing factor; leaving 'meum primarium viride' [my green primer] to her cousin Beatrice Watirton, she also left her 'parvum nigrum primarium' [small black primer] to Katherine FitzWilliam and 'meum magnum primarium optimum' [my great, best primer] to Alesia Countess of Salisbury.[78] As the mention of 'meum magnum primarium *optimum*' illustrates, several wills also distinguish between primers by reference to their value, although it is not always clear whether monetary or devotional value is implied, or, indeed, whether the two can ever be entirely distinguished. For example, in 1415 Michael da la Pole, Earl of Suffolk, left his 'magnum primarium' [great primer] to Katherine his wife until the end of her life 'et volo quod post mortem suam dictus primarius detur heredi meo, et ipse qui erit heres oneretur quod idem primarius remaneat heredi suo et sic de herede in heredem quamdiu Deo placuerit'.[79] Pole's insistence (by no means unusual) that the primer should remain within his family suggests both that it is a volume of some material worth and that it has played a valuable role in the family's devotional life and should continue to do so 'quamdiu Deo placuerit' [as long as it will please God].[80]

---

[75] Cavanaugh, pp. 229–30, pp. 460–1, and p. 213.

[76] Cavanaugh, pp. 56–7. Hawisia was the daughter of William Mowbray, head of an important Yorkshire family. Her first husband was William Selby, first Lord Mayor of York, and after his death she married Roger Aske, head of another influential Yorkshire family. Hawisia left 'unum primarium' to her husband Roger Aske (son and heir of Conan Aske). She left a further three to the children of her nephew John Mowbray ('unum primarium cum uno clasp argento parato et deaurato' [a primer furnished with one silver gilded clasp] to Isabella Mowbray, 'unum aliud primarium' [another primer] to Isabella's sister Margaret, and 'unum aliud primarium luminatum cum duobus claspis argento paratis et deauratis' [another illuminated primer furnished with two gilded silver clasps] to Margaret's sister Hawisia). Her last primer ('unum parvum primarium cum uno clasp argento parato quod quondam fuit patris sui' [a small primer furnished with one silver clasp which once belonged to her father]) was left to Elizabeth Pudsay. Elizabeth's father, to whom Hawisia refers, was probably Sir John Pudsay of Bolton, married to Margaret Eure. The life and associations of an individual woman who bequeathed five primers clearly merit further exploration.

[77] Cavanaugh, p. 934 and pp. 224–5.   [78] Cavanaugh, pp. 575–6.

[79] [And I desire that after her death the said primer is given to my heir and that he who will [then] be heir is given the responsibility [of ensuring] that the same primer passes to his heir and thus from heir to heir as long as it will please God], Cavanaugh, p. 236. He also leaves to his son 'unum parvum primarium' [a small primer] which used to belong to John his brother.

[80] See also the 1449 will of Margaret la Zouch in which she leaves 'my best primer' to her daughter Elizabeth (Cavanaugh, pp. 954–5).

PRIMER OWNERSHIP

It is unsurprising that, as indicated by the earlier discussion, primer ownership should have been so common among the gentry and nobility. What is more surprising is the extent of primer ownership among men and women of the emerging middle classes. In 1426, for example, William Chichele, citizen and grocer of London, drew up a will indicative of a real interest in literacy. As well as bequeathing 'x li. to be bestowed on bokes notable to be layde in the newe librarye at the Gildehall at London', he also left his 'premer' to his daughter Florence and her heirs, his Bible to his son John, and his Psalter to 'lye in the quere at Hiegham for ever'.[81] The 1433 will of Thomas Roos, citizen and mercer of London, included 'primarium meum teintum cum rub' rubric cum le bagge' [my primer dyed with red rubric with the bag] and 'meum paruum primarium cum le bagge' [my small primer with the bag], both of which he left to his son Guy, as well as 'meum librum vocatum stimulum consciencie' [my book called *The Prick of Conscience*] and 'meum librum vocatum piers plowman' [my book called *Piers Plowman*].[82] The fact that Roos' primers are accompanied by 'bagges' suggests that they were valuable volumes in need of protection, and reminds us of the considerable wealth amassed by many members of the middle classes in the late Middle Ages.

It was by no means uncommon for such individuals to own more than one primer, as confirmed by the contents of the 1442 will of John Welles, citizen, grocer, and alderman of London, in which he left 'meum optimum primarium' [my best primer] to Elizabeth Marchall and to Beatrice Knolles 'meum primarium secundum optimum' [my second best primer].[83] Although a degree of value is implied by the designation 'optimum', late-medieval primers were not always very costly. As Eamon Duffy writes, 'even before the dramatic shift in the sociology of book ownership produced by printing, many editions of the primer were produced for a wider and less affluent clientele' and contemporary documents provide us with some evidence of this.[84] The 1376 bankruptcy inventory of the chattels of John Cogsdale, citizen and haberdasher of London, for example, includes 'vnum primarium prec. xij. d' [a primer priced at 13 shillings], and that of William Cost, citizen and grocer of London, includes 'unum librum vocatum prymer' prec' xvj. D' [a book called a primer priced at 16 shillings] and a further 'librum vocatum prymer' prec' iiij. d' [a book called a primer priced at 4 shillings] as well as 'ij libros de Englyssh prec' viij. d' [two books of English prayers priced at 8 shillings].[85] Although medieval prices cannot accurately be equated with modern ones, a book

---

[81] Cavanaugh, p. 188. As Cavanaugh points out, William was the brother of Henry Chichele, Archbishop of Canterbury, and was, as such, rather well connected.

[82] Cavanaugh, p. 749–50. The will was proved in 1434.

[83] Cavanaugh, pp. 915–16. He also leaves 'meum psalterium in Latinis discriptum' [my Psalter written in Latin] to Thomas Knolles, citizen and grocer of London. For further evidence of middle-class ownership of such texts, see the 1437 will (proved in 1439) of John Notyngham, Grocer of Bury St Edmund's, in which he left a missal, a Psalter, a portifer, and a primer (p. 625).

[84] Duffy (1992), p. 211.

[85] Cavanaugh, p. 201 and p. 210. William Cost's inventory was drawn up in 1392. From the contents of the will, Hanna (2005) suggests that Cost might have been (or might have been supplying) 'a practising scribe or stationer' (p. 13).

worth a few shillings is clearly not a deluxe volume, some examples of which were valued at over £60 in the Middle Ages.[86]

We can also learn something of the ways in which primers were used by looking at other books bequeathed alongside them. In a very few wills, such as that of Roger Elmesley, the primer is the only book mentioned, but in the majority of cases those who owned primers also owned other books. The most tantalizing will in this regard is that of Margaret Plays, wife of Sir William Plays, who in 1400 left 'unum librum primarium meum optimum' [my best primer book] to her daughter Elizabeth and 'omnes libros meos' [all my [other] books] to John Ferrour, chaplain.[87] Most commonly, however, primers are found in wills which also contain Psalters and other liturgical and devotional books. On occasion the wording indicates that the primer and Psalter were very different volumes; we are reminded, for example, of the distinction between the grand Psalter left by Eleanor Bohun to her son and heirs, and the 'liure oue le psautier primer . . . quele liure iay pluis use' bequeathed to her daughter. The former is clearly a valuable heirloom suitable for public display, while the latter is a functioning volume used in private devotion. This pattern of Psalter bequests to men and primer bequests to women can be observed in some other wills of the period; in 1449 Margaret la Zouch, for example, left her 'best primer' to her only daughter and her 'fair gret Sawter' to one 'Thomas Nevile of Da(u)rlton', and in 1442 the aforementioned John Welles left two primers to women whilst bequeathing 'meum psalterium in Latinis discriptum' [my Psalter written in Latin] to his son Thomas Knolles, citizen and grocer of London.[88] More often, however, wills which contain Psalters and primers do not appear unduly troubled by the recipient's gender. Elizabeth Bohun, for example, left one Psalter to her daughter and another to 'fr' dauid de Seruington', while the aforementioned Hugh de Courtenay left 'mon graunt primer' [my great primer] to one daughter and 'mon sauter' [my Psalter] to another. The 1427 will of Elizabeth Lady Fitzhugh, discussed earlier in the chapter, includes a particularly impressive collection of Psalters and primers, listed thus:

Als so I wyl yat . . . my son Rob't (have) a sauter coucred with rede velwet and my doghter Mariory a primer cou'ed in Rede and my doghter Darcy a suater cou'ed in blew & my doghter Malde Eure a prim' cou'ed in blew . . . And yong Eliyzabeth ffitzhugh my goddoghter a book cou'ed in grene with praiers y' inne.[89]

---

[86] Cavanaugh, p. 13. She notes that 'Edward III paid £66.13s.6d for a book of romance in the ninth year of his reign, and William de Montacute paid the same amount for a French *Historia scholastica* which was taken from King John in 1356 at the Battle of Poitiers.' Cavanaugh points out (p. 12) that wealthy individuals are also known to have owned inexpensive books. The 1397 inventory of the goods of Thomas of Woodstock, Duke of Gloucester, 'lists numerous manuscripts valued at a few shillings or even pence' (see pp. 844–51). For further discussion of the monetary value of books in the Middle Ages, see H. E. Bell, 'The Price of Books in Medieval England', *The Library* 17 (1936), 312–32.

[87] Cavanaugh, p. 656.

[88] Cavanaugh, pp. 954–5 and pp. 915–16. One primer was left to Beatrice Knolles, sister of his executor Thomas Knolles. In this context, it is also worth remembering that William Chichele left his primer to his daughter and his Psalter to the church.

[89] Cavanaugh, p. 347.

The wording here suggests an equivalence between the volumes. With the possible exception of the 'sauter couered with rede velwet', they appear to be of interchangeable value and suitability as devotional bequests. It seems unlikely that Margery, Darcy, and Maud would have fallen out over who had been left the Psalter and who had got the primers.

Such bequests of multiple Psalters and primers do, however, beg a further question. What, prior to bequeathing them to one's children, did one do with all of these copies? Why did Isabella, Duchess of York, and Matilda, Countess of Cambridge, need three primers, what did Hawisia Aske do with five, and why did Elizabeth Lady Fitzhugh own two Psalters and two primers? Although there was inevitably considerable duplication of contents among these volumes, and although the wording of the Fitzhugh will in particular suggests a degree of equivalence, the broad answer must be that they were felt to be distinct from each other in some way, as indicated by testamentary references to 'best' and 'second best' primers, to large and small copies, to illuminated editions passed from generation to generation, and to volumes 'quo cotidie utor' [which I use every day]. In addition, the variable content of the primer (and the Psalter) and its catechetic and devotional additions may have created situations in which individuals felt that one copy of the primer needed to be supplemented by another.

PRIMERS AND THE VERNACULAR

For the purposes of this book, some of the most interesting primer bequests appear in wills which also include vernacular devotional material. We encountered just such a will in our discussion of Agnes Stapilton, whose 1448 bequests included several English and French books in addition to a primer and Psalter. Perhaps unsurprisingly, given the ubiquity of both texts, the primer is often found in wills which also contain *The Prick of Conscience*. That of Thomas de Roos (1399) includes a primer and a Psalter alongside other books including a 'librum Stimuli Conscienciae' [a book of *The Prick of Conscience*] and that of Robert Cupper, Burgess of Great Yarmouth, Norfolk (1434) mentions 'my Psalter', 'my best Primer', and a 'certain book called Stimulus consciencie' [*The Prick of Conscience*].[90] Bequests made by William Revetour, Chaplain of York (1448), include 'Stimulus Conscientiae in Anglia' [*The Prick of Conscience* in English] as well as a primer, a Psalter, and various other biblical and liturgical volumes, and London merchant Thomas Roos (no relation of Thomas de Roos), whose two primers 'cum le bagge' have already been mentioned, also bequeathed 'librum vocatum stimulum constiencie' [a book called *The Prick of Conscience*] and 'meum librum vocatum piers plowman' [my book called *Piers Plowman*] in 1433.[91] In the 1438 will of Eleanor Roos (sister of Thomas de Roos) we find a 'primarium de Sancto Spiritu' [primer/hours of the Holy Spirit] keeping company with the first book of Hilton's *Scale of Perfection* ('unum librum

---

[90] Cavanaugh, p. 748 and pp. 225–6.   [91] Cavanaugh, pp. 723–4 and pp. 749–50.

Anglicum vocatum librum primum Magistri Walteri' [an English book called the first book of Master Walter]) and the 1451 will of Mercy Ormesby includes two primers, a missal and 'vnum librum Anglie vocatum, the Chastesing of goddes children' [an English book called *The Chastising of God's Children*], a volume which also appears alongside the primer in Agnes Stapilton's will.[92] Such combinations of primers, Psalters, and English religious writings support the hypothesis, put forward earlier in this chapter, that liturgical and quasi-liturgical activity persisted within an increasingly vernacular devotional climate and that the latter developed and built upon rather than eroded the former.

The complementary relationship between liturgical tradition and vernacular devotion can be seen most clearly in those late-medieval volumes in which conventionally Latin texts have been translated into English. Pre-eminent among such volumes are those containing vernacular versions of the psalms, and here primers are of particular note. The assumption underlying the foregoing discussion has been that primers were Latin, and in the vast majority of cases, this is likely to have been true. That surviving primers are overwhelmingly Latin provides ample testament to this fact. However, vernacular primers were produced in England in the late Middle Ages, and some seventeen are now extant.[93] In addition to their liturgical contents, most of these primers also contain variable amounts of catechetic material of the type that proliferated in the aftermath of Archbishop Pecham's 1281 Syllabus and the subsequent provincial constitutions of John Thoresby, Archbishop of York (1357).[94] None of these vernacular primers has been dated earlier than the end of the fourteenth century, or later than the end of the fifteenth.[95] While some of

[92] Cavanaugh, p. 749 and pp. 629–30. The short Hours of the Holy Spirit find a place in several primers of the period.

[93] For a list of English language primers which include English translations of the psalms, see Appendix I.

[94] For discussion of manuscripts containing such catechetic material, see V. Gillespie, 'Vernacular Books of Religion', in *Book Production and Publishing in Britain 1375–1475*, ed. J. Griffiths and D. Pearsall (Cambridge, 1989), chapter 13, pp. 317–44. (Gillespie does not discuss vernacular primers, however.) For a list of English language primers which include vernacular catechetic additions, see Appendix II. Also extant are some English language primers which include basic Christian prayers and catechesis (sometimes alongside other devotional material) but exclude psalm translation. Such, for example, are [1] Columbia, University Library Plimpton 258. For a facsimile reproduction of most of the manuscript, see G. A. Plimpton, *The Education of Chaucer: Illustrated from the Schoolbooks in Use in his Time* (London, 1935) and for discussion, see P. Acker, 'A Schoolchild's Primer (Plimpton MS 258)', in *Medieval Literature for Children*, ed. D. T. Kline (New York and London, 2003), chapter 9, pp. 143–54; [2] Oxford, BodlL Rawlinson C.209. Of this manuscript, Gillespie (1989) writes: 'The book is written in one hand and the separate items are unified by a standard apparatus, forming a collection of the sort that might well have been professionally produced for casual sale' (p. 318); [3] Manchester, JRL English 85 (contents described in *IMEP* II, pp. 14–24); [4] London, BL Add. 60577 ('The Winchester Anthology') which contains a sequence of independent texts on the syllabus, preceded by a cross and an alphabet. See E. Wilson (with an account of the music by Iain Fenlon), *The Winchester Anthology: A Facsimile of British Library Additional 60577* (Cambridge, 1981). For a somewhat problematic attempt to classify such manuals into five groups, see C. A. Martin, 'Middle English Manuals of Religious Instruction', in *So Meny People Longages and Tonges: Philological Essays in Scots and Medieval English presented to Angus McIntosh*, ed. M. Benskin and M. L. Samuels (Edinburgh, 1981), pp. 283–98.

[95] The number of primers in English has tended to be underestimated. Nigel Morgan, for example, states that '[i]f the constituent texts of the Books of Hours are considered in their Anglo-Norman

them are decorated with very fine borders and illuminations, in the context of Latin liturgical volumes they could not be described as grand. It is perhaps unsurprising that it is very difficult to find explicit reference to them in wills.[96] The oft-quoted 1479 bequest of 'my litill englissh booke like a prymer' to one 'Joane ffitzlowes' is ambiguous, indicating that any English copy of the primer was an approximation of the real thing, the default language of which was Latin.[97] Evidence confirms that this was generally the case, but a clearer and earlier reference to an English primer does survive, in the will of Henry, Lord Scrope. Executed in 1415 for his apparent involvement in a plot against Henry V, Lord Scrope was clearly a devout and literate individual, as indicated by his lengthy will which includes several volumes in Latin, English, and French, almost exclusively of a religious nature. Among these is 'unum primerium cum matutinis beatae Mariae Virginis in Anglicis' [a primer with the matins of the blessed Virgin Mary in English] which he left to one Sybil Beauchamp 'pro remembrancia' [for remembrance].[98] Scrope's specification that the volume is 'in Anglicis' [in English] indicates that the language of this primer was the exception rather than the rule, but its appearance is significant. The 1415 date tallies with the aforementioned dating of English primer manuscripts, and the fact that it was owned by a member of the aristocracy provides evidence that these sometimes humble volumes could keep illustrious company; as demonstrated by the aforementioned case of Thomas of Woodstock, ownership of inexpensive books by the wealthy was not uncommon.[99]

  With the obvious exceptions of Edmund Bishop and Henry Littlehales, scholars have paid little attention to these volumes.[100] Such interest in vernacularity as there has been has tended to focus on those Latin primers which contain

translation, only two manuscripts are extant of the Hours of the Virgin, two of the Hours of the Cross, one of the Office of the Dead, and one of the Penitential Psalms. There are two surviving texts of the Hours of the Virgin in Welsh, and just a few more of the Middle English Primer, whereas the Latin version seems to have been overwhelmingly the most popular version of the text.' Morgan, pp. 314–15. Eamon Duffy is closer to the mark when he states that '[f]ewer than a dozen and a half pre-Reformation primers in English survive' (1992), p. 213.

[96] See Littlehales (1891), vol. 2: 'The prymer in English differs from the Latin version in the fact that it has no illuminations and little ornament of any kind beyond an occasional border or fine capital, from which we may perhaps infer that the latter, being ornamental, and in Latin, would amongst the richer classes take the place of the prymer in English' (p. x).

[97] Bishop (1897), p. xlii. By this date, the 'litill englissh booke' may well have been a printed edition.

[98] Cavanaugh, pp. 773–7. Some of Henry, Lord Scrope's volumes are service books, but there are also two books 'de meditationibus' [of meditations], an Apocalypse 'in Latinis & Gallicis' [in Latin and French], 'i pulchrum librum de matutinis & aliis orationibus' [a beautiful book with Matins and other prayers], two of Rolle's Latin works, two Psalters, and 'unum librum in Anglicis, qui vocatur Stimulus conscientiae' [a book in English which is called *The Prick of Conscience*], among several other bequests.

[99] However, the fact that the primer was bequeathed to serve a memorial purpose ('pro remembrancia') implies that it might not have been an unimpressive volume.

[100] M. Deanesly, *The Lollard Bible and other Medieval Biblical Versions* (Cambridge, 1920) makes some reference to English primers. More recently, they have been discussed by Barratt (1975) and alluded to by Alcuin Blamires (see 'The Limits of Bible Study for Medieval Women', in Smith and Taylor (1995), pp. 1–12).

additional English (and French) prayers, of which, as Nigel Morgan points out, there are many:

> [P]rayers and devotional texts not found in the Breviary occur very frequently in Anglo-Norman and Middle English, and these vernacular prayers are often found as additional texts in Latin Psalters and Books of Hours, or as independent prayer collections in books, rolls or as additions on flyleaves or blank spaces in manuscripts of various texts.[101]

However, volumes in which the constituent texts of the primer were translated into English appear to have enjoyed some popularity (the extant manuscripts are well used), although we have little information about who actually read them.[102] Only one (Oxford, BodlL Douce 246), inscribed on fol. 8ᵛ 'Deyd Agnes Orges my wyff Hausaber in Harflu(r?) in the 3ere of our Lord miiijᶜᶜᶜᶜxlvj', contains an obvious contemporary indication of ownership.[103] That English primers have gone under the radar is not surprising, and given that they were composed in a climate of anxiety regarding the role of the vernacular in devotion, it has been suggested that this was quite deliberate. In somewhat cursory analyses, several historians have argued that the circulation of English primers may have been curtailed by 'panic over Lollardy' and that many more than currently survive could have been written.[104]

---

[101] Morgan, pp. 314–15. Eamon Duffy (1992) also states that '[t]hough the basic texts of the primers remained in Latin until after the break with Rome, the demand for vernacular material was evident in the evolution of the early sixteenth-century primers, as more and more English material was added' (p. 80). The work of Charity Scott-Stokes is also relevant here. Focusing on women's Books of Hours, she states that '[i]nasmuch as the vernacular languages were used, Anglo-Norman French was the more frequently used vernacular language up to the late fourteenth or early fifteenth century; then it gradually ceded to English.' For the 'most active trilingual combination of Latin and the vernacular languages', she points us to the *De Mohun Hours* (Boston Public Library 124), the *DuBois Hours* (New York, Pierpont Morgan Library, M. 700), the *Taymouth Hours* (BL Yates Thompson 13), and the *Percy Hours* (BL Harley 1260). 'The tendency in such cases is for the Anglo-Norman items to be part of the original compilation, and for the English texts to be later additions' (C. Scott-Stokes, *Women's Books of Hours in Medieval England: Selected Texts Translated from Latin, Anglo-Norman French and Middle English with Introduction and Interpretive Essay* (Woodbridge, 2006), pp. 21–2). Scott-Stokes does point out that, unusually, English occurs in part of the Little Office of the Virgin in Oxford, BodlL Liturg 104 (*c.* 1340). Here, the vernacular prayers do not involve psalm translation.

[102] As Littlehales (1891) points out, '[f]ew entries of names, dates, family events, or other occurrences, have been inserted by the owners in the flyleaves, calendar, or elsewhere, in the Prymers' (vol. 2, p. xv).

[103] The dust-jacket illustration is taken from BodlL Douce 246, f. 11r and shows the beginning of Matins. In the Middle Ages, Harfleur was the principal sea port of north-western France, over which the English and the French fought for possession. At the time of Agnes' death, the town was in English possession. That the Douce inscription points towards use, if not ownership, by a woman is not surprising. It is likely that English primers were particularly popular among women. As Nicholas Orme points out, '[t]he study of Latin by girls was rare until about 1500, when an increasing perception of its value to the laity caused the daughters of Henry VII to be taught the language, a practice which spread to other aristocratic girls during the sixteenth century' (Orme (1999), p. 451).

[104] The phrase is Duffy's: 'In the fourteenth and early fifteenth centuries English versions of the primer had circulated, but the panic over Lollardy had made them suspect. Fewer than a dozen-and-a-half pre-Reformation primers in English survive, none of them dating from after the mid fifteenth century. The mere possession of one might be grounds for suspicions of heterodoxy in the early sixteenth century' (1992, p. 213). For similar reasoning, see Hoeppner-Moran, p. 44, where she also suggests that the small number of extant manuscripts might also be due to 'the ephemeral nature of such slight texts'. Margaret Deanesly also suggested that English primers were associated with Lollardy

Later evidence adduced by F. J. Furnivall would seem to support this; pointing us to a list of thirty 'suspect bokes, bothe in Englissh and in Laten' proscribed in 1531, he indicates that it includes both '[t]he Prymer in Englissh' and '[t]he Psalter in Englissh'.[105]

The fact that some rely quite closely on the Later Version of the Wycliffite Bible for their rendition of the psalms while others differ somewhat, suggests that they were being produced in more than one place, by individuals with access to (or preference for) different versions of the Psalter.[106] There is, however, a degree of uniformity in their presentation of liturgical material—all include some Latin. In most cases, this takes the form of red ink cues (or *incipits*) to individual clauses or verses in prayers and psalms, which are followed by full English translations. Such cues presumably functioned as prompts for users, alerting them to the correlation between the English that they were reading and the Latin with which they would have been at least aurally familiar. The cues are so abbreviated that these primers cannot have been intended to teach Latin as well as foster devotion (as Rolle suggests that his Psalter is), although the resourced and resourceful reader could of course locate the cue in a Latin primer or Psalter, in which the given text could then be read in its entirety.[107] However, in two English primer manuscripts (Oxford, University College 179 and Glasgow, Hunter 512), the languages are weighted equally; both provide Latin clauses or verses in full, followed by the English equivalent.[108] In such cases, it is clear that the book could

and that some copies might have been destroyed by burning. 'Between 1424 and 1430 more than one hundred persons were arraigned for Lollardy in the diocese of Norwich. In 1429 John Baker was convicted of having a book of the pater noster and other prayers in English, which looks as if English primers had fallen under general suspicion, as being English and therefore Lollard' (Deanesly, p. 357). In a number of the vernacular primer manuscripts, the catechetic additions have been identified as Wycliffite.

[105] F. J. Furnivall, *Political, Religious and Love Poems* EETS OS 15 (London, 1866), pp. 62–3. He takes the list from London, Lambeth Palace Library 306 (f. 65). The proscribed volumes were obviously printed and we are told that they were 'opynly, by the autorite of my lorde of london vnder his Autentycal seale, by the doctor that that day prechide, prohibite, and straytely commaunded of no maner of man to be vsed, bought, nor solde, nor to be red, vnder payne of suspencioun, and a greter payne, as more large apperyth in forsayde autoryte.'

[106] The detail and implications of this apparent use of the Wycliffite translation will be discussed in Chapter 3. Only one primer manuscript (CUL Dd. 11. 82) has been mapped in *LALME* (I: 66); the language is localized to Bedfordshire, and the scribe is assigned LP 81060. Raymo suggests that '[a] majority of the manuscripts localise in the southwest Midlands; others show a more northerly or easterly provenance' (Volume 7, XX *MWME*, p. 2367). In an unpublished Cambridge MLitt thesis, J. M. Harris-Matthews agrees, suggesting that most can probably be located in 'a triangular area bordered to the West by Worcester, to the East by Warwick and to the South East by Banbury'. However, she locates Cambridge, Emmanuel College 246 'further east than the others, perhaps in Huntingdonshire', and suggests that London, BL Add. 17010 and 17011 'appear to have been produced further to the North East, perhaps nearer to South Leicestershire' (pp. 100–1). One primer (Oxford, University College 179) 'bears no relation in its translation' to the others. It is written in a mid fifteenth-century cursive hand and 'may have originated in a Staffordshire provenance' (J. M. Harris-Matthews, *Lay Devotions in Late Medieval English Manuscripts*, MLitt thesis, University of Cambridge, 1980, p. 101).

[107] A case in point is the English primer in Oxford, BodlL, Ashmole 1288 (1) in which the red Latin incipits to prayers and psalms are minimal.

[108] Hunter 512, f. 37r (the beginning of Matins) is reproduced as Figure 1.1, including Psalm 50: 17 and 69: 2. The Latin is underlined and given in full clause by clause (with standard abbreviations),

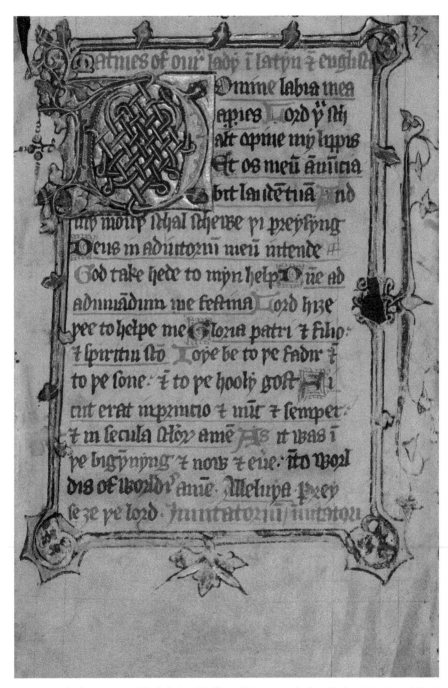

Fig. 1.1. The beginning of the bilingual Office of Matins, including Psalms 50: 17 and 69: 2

University of Glasgow MS Hunterian 512, f. 37r. Reproduced by kind permission of the University of Glasgow, Special Collections

serve a dual purpose, encouraging both devotional and linguistic development by means of fully comparative reading. These primers not only provided their readers with material for ordered, quasi-liturgical vernacular prayer but also with the opportunity to expand their Latin vocabulary. The way in which these bilingual primers manage to 'face both ways' is fascinating and can be read as an attempt to negotiate a pathway through a shifting terrain in which the laity were looking to develop their own vernacular devotional literacy whilst maintaining their dependence upon (and even developing their understanding of) the traditional Latinity of the church. Neither should it be forgotten that, as discussed earlier, these primers were in production and circulation at a time when the role of the vernacular in devotion (specifically in the translation of biblical material) was hotly contested. A prayer book equally reliant on Latin and English was, therefore, not only practically useful but also culturally sensitive.

The fact that English primers generated discussion in their own day is indicated by comments in *The Chastising of God's Children*. An anonymous compilation of recent and patristic material focusing on the subject of spiritual temptation, *The Chastising* was probably composed by a Carthusian monk in the late fourteenth century.[109] Apparently intended for a specific 'religious sister', it nonetheless reached a wide audience as suggested by its appearance in the aforementioned wills of Mercy Ormesby and Agnes Stapilton, in both of which it is accompanied by a primer (language unspecified) as well as other devotional volumes. Preoccupied with exploring the challenges of living the Christian life, the *Chastising* author is particularly concerned to recommend a suitable devotional routine for his addressee(s) and towards the end of the treatise, he offers the following advice:

> Þanne it is nedeful, as ferforþ as I feele and as I haue lierned, þat we do oure besynesse to preie ententifli in tyme of oure seruise, þat is to seie in tyme whan we seie oures of þe niȝt and þe day, and in þe tyme þat we seien masse or heere, to whiche we bien bounded to seie or to heere aftir þe ordynaunce of holi chirche, and in þe maner as it was ordeyned of oure hooli fadirs. I seie in þe maner as it was ordeyned, for sum now in þese daies vsen to sei on ynglisshe her sautir and matyns of oure ladye, and þe seuen psalmes and þe letanye. Many men repreuen it to haue þe matyns or þe sautir or þe gospels or þe bible in englisshe, bicause þei mowe not be translated into vulgare, word bi worde as it stondiþ, wiþoute grete circumlocucion, aftir þe feelynge of þe first writers, þe whiche translated þat into latyn bi techynge of þe holi goost. Naþeles, I wil

and is followed by the English in full, not underlined. Throughout Hunter 512, liturgical material is given in both Latin and English ('Matines of oure Ladye in latyn and englisch') while the basic prayers and catechesis are given in English only. In University College 179, the basic prayers and the liturgical material are written in alternate Latin and English throughout.

[109] *The Chastising of God's Children* was edited in the mid twentieth century (see E. Colledge and J. Bazire, *The Chastising of God's Children and The Treatise of Perfection of the Sons of God* (Oxford, 1957)). For discussion of the text, see M. Cré, 'We are united with God (and God with us?): Adapting Ruusbroec in *The Treatise of Perfection of the Sons of God* and *The Chastising of God's Children*', in *The Medieval Mystical Tradition in England—Exeter Symposium VII*, ed. E. A. Jones (Cambridge, 2004), pp. 21–36. See also A. Sutherland, '*The Chastising of God's Children*—A Neglected Text', in *Text and Controversy from Wyclif to Bale—Essays in Honour of Anne Hudson*, ed. H. Barr and A. Hutchison (Turnhout, 2005), pp. 353–86.

nat repreue suche translacion, ne I repreue nat to haue hem on englisshe, ne to rede on hem where þei mowen stire ȝou more to deuocion and to þe loue of god; but uttirli to usen hem in englisshe and leue þe latin, I holde it nat commendable, and namly in hem þat bien bounden to seien her sautir or her matyns of oure lady, for if a mannes confessour ȝiueþ hym in penaunce to seie his sautir wiþoute ony oþer wordis, and he gooþ forþ and seiþ it in englisshe and nat in latyn as it was ordeyned, þis man, I wene, dooþ nat his penaunce.[110]

In guidance equally relevant to a religious audience and to devout lay readers, the author reveals himself to be anxious about the role of the vernacular in devotion. His anxiety is not that translation renders widely accessible material which should remain the preserve of the learned, a charge which often featured in anti-Wycliffite rhetoric. Rather, he registers the opinion of those who say that to translate 'þe matyns or þe sautir or þe gospels or þe bible' is problematic since English—and English translators—are simply not up to the job ('þei mowe not be translated into vulgare, word bi worde as it stondiþ, wiþoute grete circumlocucion, aftir þe feelynge of þe first writers, þe whiche translated þat into latyn bi techynge of þe holi goost'). Although he claims to 'nat repreue suche translacion', neither does he advocate a complete abandonment of the Latin, retaining a respect for the efficacy of the latter in the context of liturgical devotion ('uttirli to usen hem in englisshe and leue þe latin, I holde it nat commendable . . . for if a mannes confessour ȝiueþ hym in penaunce to seie his sautir wiþoute ony oþer wordis, and he gooþ forþ and seiþ it in englisshe and nat in latyn as it was ordeyned, þis man, I wene, dooþ nat his penaunce').[111]

Aware of controversy surrounding the translation of 'þe gospels' and 'þe bible' into English, the *Chastising* author is nonetheless particularly concerned with vernacular versions of the 'sautir and matyns of oure ladye, and þe seuen psalmes and þe letanye', repeating the first two of these towards the end of the passage quoted. 'Matyns', the 'seuen psalmes', and the 'letanye' are clearly allusions to texts contained within the 'standard' late-medieval primer, which, as we have seen, was sometimes accompanied by a complete Psalter. It is about vernacular versions of this volume, used by 'sum now in þese daies', that he is talking. While he offers qualified approval for the use of these translations by some, he remains more sceptical about their appropriateness for 'hem þat bien bounden to seien

[110] Bazire and Colledge, chapter 27, 220/27–221/22. Italics mine.
[111] Writing about Books of Hours in which the liturgical material is in Latin, while additional prayers are in the vernacular, Nigel Morgan states, '[o]ne could conclude from this that the Latin texts used in the public liturgy had particular authority in that language, whereas para-liturgical texts were considered more permissible in the vernacular' (Morgan, pp. 314–15). One imagines that the *Chastising* author would concur with the first part of this statement, although he does allow room for manoeuvre. In this context, the primer apparently written by John Lacy, recluse at Newcastle (Oxford, St John's College 94), is fascinating. The Hours and further liturgical material common to primers are provided in Latin while Lacy's additional catechetic and devotional texts are in English. On f. 101v, an inscription reads '[p]reyeth for þe saul of frere jon lacy anchor and reclused in þe new castel vpon tynde þe wiche þat wrooth þis book and limned hit to his awne vse and aftur to othur in exitynge hem to deuocion and preyers to god and þerfor for þe blessing and loue of god and oure lady and of seint michael and of him þat made þis book þat neuer man ne woman lete departe þe engeliche from þe latyn for diuers causes þat ben good and lawful to my felynge' (*IMEP* VIII, pp. 87–9).

her sautir or her matyns of oure lady', presumably the professed religious, as well as those living lives of regulated piety in the world. In general, the complete abandonment of Latin in favour of English is not advisable ('uttirli to usen hem in englisshe and leue þe latin, I holde it nat commendable'). Preserving the text of the Latin Psalter in partial incipit or in full quotation, English language primers must have done much to facilitate such an apparently problematic mode of liturgical reading.[112]

VERSE PARAPHRASES

Of course, these primers were by no means the only late-medieval texts to contain English translations of the psalms central to the liturgy—and neither were they the earliest. They have been privileged in this chapter since the widespread circulation of primers in general is so well attested, but English translations of individual psalms and, slightly later, groups of psalms can be found in many other manuscripts. These translations distinguish themselves from those found in the primer by virtue of the obvious fact that they are almost all verse. They also differ insofar as they are not set specifically in the context of the liturgy, although some appear in manuscripts which also contain liturgical material. They do not seem to have been intended explicitly for use as part of a quasi-formal daily devotional routine, although they may well have been used in such a way. Yet these translations are obviously similar to those of the primer in that they render accessible to a lay (or at least non-Latinate) audience psalms central to the liturgy.[113] Like the psalms of the vernacular primer they are often found in manuscripts which also contain basic prayers and catechesis in English; in fact, the company that they keep has much to tell us about the ways in which they were read.

The earliest extant example of a freestanding Middle English paraphrase of an individual psalm is that which appears in the Auchinleck Manuscript. Dateable to the 1330s, NLS Advocates 19.2.1 provides us with our first instance of 'lay and commercial' book production in England.[114] It is particularly significant in that it offers 'a rare snapshot of the kind of English literary [specifically poetic] texts

---

[112] This is a passage also discussed by Zieman (pp. 123–4), who concludes: 'Ultimately [the liturgical speech act] comes to be defined by exteriority—a gap between speaker and speech that can be measured temporally (services are not the immediate exclamations of the devout soul but externally regulated services) and linguistically (services must be performed in Latin rather than in English). The writer disdains the possibility of "sautir and matyns of oure ladi" in English but does not object to their use under all circumstances. His interest, rather, lies in assigning the use of English to the realm of private devotion.' As indicated in my Introduction, Zieman does not consider manuals such as the Middle English primers, which both complicate and substantiate what she has to say.

[113] In their manuscript contexts, several of the verse paraphrases include the Latin in more or less abbreviated form. They thus facilitate the same sort of quasi-liturgical reading as that encouraged by the primer.

[114] Ralph Hanna downplays the extent to which Auchinleck anticipates 'forms of fifteenth-century book-production in which shared scribal work enables production economies' (see R. Hanna, 'Reconsidering the Auchinleck Manuscript', in *New Directions in later Medieval Manuscript Studies—Essays from the 1998 Harvard Conference*, ed. D. Pearsall (Woodbridge, 2000), pp. 91–102, p. 93).

which were in circulation in the period before Chaucer'. [115] Most famous for its collection of verse romances, it contains a wealth of further material including two poems dealing in basic Christian doctrine, both of which are unique to (or at least found in unique versions in) this manuscript.[116] The first of these, a treatment of catechetic essentials, is a 308-line homily in rhyming couplets, setting out the Seven Deadly Sins, the Ten Commandments, the Paternoster, the Creed, and the Hail Mary, followed by an account of the Passion (ff. 70ra–72ra). Its full title in the manuscript is missing, since the top of the folio has been cut away, leaving only the word 'sinnes'.[117] However, given the foregrounding of the Seven Deadly Sins at the beginning of the poem, it seems likely that they formed at least part of the title. It is followed immediately by a second poem in rhyming couplets dealing with doctrinal basics. Entitled *þe paternoster undo on englissch* (ff. 72ra–?72rb or?72va stub), the text runs to 136 lines and ends imperfectly, but is, as it stands, a vernacular meditative response to the Latin prayer, clause-by-clause quotation of which it includes in its rhyme scheme.[118] Although this second Paternoster paraphrase is unrelated to the briefer version in *On the Seven Deadly Sins*, the similar tone and outlook of the two poems must have been recognized by the manuscript's compiler(s) and readers. Copied by the same scribe (scribe three, who also copies the next four poems) and sharing a folio at the beginning of booklet three, the goal of both is the English verse transmission of 'þe bileue'.

Advocates 19.2.1 contains several other religious poems which are broadly distinguished from the Paternoster and the Deadly Sins by virtue of their narrative rather than expository emphasis.[119] However, towards the end of the manuscript as it is now bound (booklet eight, ff. 280rb–280vb) is a unique devotional text which has some affinities with the two earlier poems. Prefaced by the title 'Dauid þe Kyng', it is a vernacular response in rhyming couplets to Psalm 50, the fourth of the seven Penitential Psalms.[120] Using each verse of the psalm as a starting point, the poem moves between paraphrase of, and response to, David's prayer. Its treatment of the sinner's agonized penitence is almost entirely generalizing (David's tormented 'I' becomes an undifferentiated 'we'), leading some to call the poem

[115] D. Burnley and A. Wiggins, *The Auchinleck Manuscript*, National Library of Scotland (5 July 2003). Accessed 14 October 2010. Version 1.1 <http://digital.nls.uk/auchinleck/> <http://digital.nls.uk/auchinleck/editorial/importance.html>.

[116] In addition to further religious verse, other genres represented in the Auchinleck manuscript include hagiography, comedy, moral verse, satire, and chronicle.

[117] Red-ink titles are appended to most of the texts in the manuscript, apparently after copying and decoration were complete: 'They appear to have been an afterthought, squeezed into any available space' (Burnley and Wiggins, <http://digital.nls.uk/auchinleck/editorial/physical.html#titles>). For the printed facsimile of the manuscript, see D. Pearsall and I. C. Cunningham, *The Auchinleck Manuscript—National Library of Scotland Advocates MS. 19.2.1* (London, 1977).

[118] The surviving lines of Auchinleck's *Paternoster* correspond to lines 269–1330 in the Vernon text.

[119] Excluding hagiographies, the narrative religious poems include the fragmentary *Life of Adam and Eve*, *The Harrowing of Hell*, *The Clerk who would see the Virgin*, *The Life of St. Mary Magdalene*, *The Nativity and early Life of Mary*, and *The Assumption of the Blessed Virgin*.

[120] Only the top two-thirds of this title are visible, the bottom concealed by patching of the hole made by the miniature hunters who cut out the illustration (presumably an enthroned David) at the head of the paraphrase. The same fate has befallen the majority of Auchinleck's miniatures.

'unsophisticated', a 'distortion[] of the Latin text'.[121] But this is to miss the point, for the significance of *Dauid þe Kyng* lies not in its reductiveness but in its vernacularity. It does not pretend to translate verbatim, but it does offer its audience an opportunity to engage, in the vernacular, with the resonances of a Vulgate text central to the liturgical life of the late Middle Ages, with the 'psalme most hauntid in halykirke'.[122] In providing this opportunity, *Dauid þe Kyng* has obvious affinities with the two earlier poems which similarly provide vernacular access to liturgical cornerstones. In particular, it is notably akin to Auchinleck's *Paternoster* in its modelling of a simple response to a core text of Christian doctrine; both poems advertise their reliance on the Latin by reproducing it in the manuscript, each verse followed by its English elaboration.[123]

Of course, one should not make too much of the connection between these particular poems. The manuscript contains other poems in similar short couplets, and *Dauid* appears much later and is the work of a different scribe; there is no indication that they were linked by the compiler or by readers. Preceded by *The Sayings of St. Bernard* (with which it shares f. 280r) and followed by *Sir Tristrem* (which begins on a new folio in booklet nine), *Dauid* is one of the texts that Hanna and others have designated a 'filler'.[124] Nonetheless, its inclusion in the Auchinleck manuscript alongside romance, chronicle, comedy, and satire, as well as other devotional pieces, highlights its fourteenth-century acceptability as matter for lay reading, listening, and devout meditating. And although it differs from the later primers in that it paraphrases psalm material in verse rather than translating it in prose, it also anticipates them in its maintenance of an overt reliance on the liturgically important Latin. Further, its position in Auchinleck suggests that in the early fourteenth century it was already playing its part in the programme of basic catechesis that would later form part of so many vernacular primers.

For the second extant freestanding paraphrase of Psalm 50, we must look to London, BL Add. 31042 (the London Thornton manuscript), which contains an

---

[121] J. J. Thompson, 'Literary Associations of an Anonymous Middle English Paraphrase of Vulgate Psalm L', *MA* 57 (1988), 38–55, pp. 42–3.

[122] H. R. Bramley, *The Psalter or Psalms of David and certain canticles with a translation and exposition in English by Richard Rolle of Hampole* (Oxford, 1884), p. 183. (All quotations from Rolle's uninterpolated *English Psalter* are taken from Bramley's edition.)

[123] Palaeographically speaking, *Dauid þe Kyng* makes more of the Latin than the *Paternoster*. Although its Latin verses are abbreviations ending in '&c', their importance is emphasized by the red ink in which they are written. The *Paternoster*'s Latin, by contrast, is in the same brown ink as the English text, although it is highlighted by enlarged blue initials decorated with red penwork. In literary terms, the two poems also treat the Latin differently; the poet of *Paternoster* attempts to integrate the Latin within the rhyming couplets of the English poem (although he does not always manage it) while *Dauid þe Kyng* excludes its abbreviated Latin verses from the vernacular rhyme scheme.

[124] The Psalm 50 paraphrase appears in booklet 8, although Hanna cautions against reading too much into the order of the manuscript as it survives: 'The extant manuscript is numbered to 334 folios and includes forty-four text items. But what remains, large as it is, is only wreckage: there's evidence for more than eighty lost leaves and fifteen to twenty additional texts. There's consensus that the book was not produced as a piece, but in twelve definable booklets, independent units, many of them substantial. Thus, there is no necessary connection between the bound order of the book we have—this was imposed on the booklets at the end of the procedure—and the various stages of its production' (Hanna (2000), pp. 91–102, p. 92).

incomplete verse rendition.[125] Like Auchinleck, London Thornton is an important collection of Middle English verse, although we know rather more of its origins. Composed in the mid fifteenth century by Robert Thornton of East Newton in North Yorkshire (who also produced Lincoln Cathedral 91, famous for its collection of romances), the London Thornton manuscript seems to have been intended for domestic use and remained within the Thornton family for many generations.[126] Perhaps best known for its unique preservation of the fragmentary *Wynnere and Wastoure*, it also contains a substantial amount of devotional verse including material from *Cursor Mundi*, two accounts of the Passion, and (most notably) four lyrical 'songs' ('a louely song of wysdome'; 'a song how þat mercy passeth rightwisnes'; 'a song how mercy comes before þe iugement doo mercy bifore thy iugement'; and 'a songe how þᵗ mercy passeth alle thynge').[127] It is indicative of late-medieval reading tastes that poetic paraphrases of Psalm 50 find a place in the broad literary collections of both Auchinleck and Thornton (even if only as 'filler' in both), and like Auchinleck, the Thornton paraphrase preserves the abbreviated Latin at the head of each stanza, facilitating liturgical reference in the manner of the primers with which it was roughly contemporary. Beyond this, however, the two vernacular poems generated by the biblical text differ in almost every respect. Where the earlier tends towards communal generalization, the later models a more personal response to the psalm and involves closer paraphrase of the Vulgate which segues into an introspective first-person expansion.

Most obviously, the Thornton poem differs from the Auchinleck version by virtue of its poetic skill. In purely literary terms, it is much more accomplished than Auchinleck's *Dauid* and has literary as well as devotional appeal. Where the earlier relies on a scheme of simple rhyming couplets, the later is arranged in twelve-line alliterating stanzas rhyming ababababcdcd, in which the eighth and ninth lines

---

[125] The paraphrase appears on ff. 102r–v. Thompson refers to its 'consistent and economical presentation in the manuscript' and states that, along with *The Quatrefoil of Love* and the *Prayer to the Guardian Angel*, it shows 'every sign of having been added to Thornton's collection as "filler[]" '. He reads it as an example of 'Thornton's evident desire always to present material in the most legible format possible' being 'compromised by the limited amount of available blank space' (J. J. Thompson, *Robert Thornton and the London Thornton Manuscript—British Library MS Additional 31042* (Cambridge, 1987), p. 39).

[126] Thompson points out that although there are 'general thematic similarities' between some of the Middle English material in the two Thornton manuscripts, 'there is no duplication of items . . . Seen as a whole, therefore, this two-volume collection, on occasions made up of shared stocks of watermarked paper, would seem to represent the sustained efforts of a fifteenth-century Yorkshire gentleman to organise a mass of the reading material available for his use into some kind of "shape" ' (Thompson (1987), p. 1). It is worth noting, as does Thompson, that the Lincoln manuscript contains a copy of Psalm 50 in Latin (f. 258r–v).

[127] For a full list of contents, see Thompson (1987), pp. 10–118. The four devotional 'songs' appear later in the manuscript ('a louely song of wysdome' (120r–122rb) in alternately rhyming eight-line stanzas; 'A Song How þat mercy Passeth Rightwisnes' (122va–123ra) in eight-line stanzas with a refrain; 'A song How mercy comes before þe iugement Doo mercy Bifore thy iugement' (123ra–vb) in twelve-line stanzas with a refrain; 'A Songe how þᵗ mercy passeth alle thynge' in twelve-line stanzas with a refrain). In the manuscript as it survives, Psalm 50 is followed immediately by an incomplete copy of Lydgate's *Virtues of the Mass* which includes a vernacular version of Psalm 42. Given the complexities of foliation, it would be unwise to read this juxtaposition as deliberate.

are linked by concatenation. Each Vulgate verse is allotted a stanza, the first eight lines of which paraphrase the Latin, while the final quatrain emphasizes personal application and culminates in the direct appeal 'God/Ihesu þou haue mercy on me'.[128] In fact, in its literary sophistication, the Thornton version differs not only from Auchinleck but from all other surviving Middle English psalm paraphrases. Attempts to find connections between Thornton's paraphrase and other Middle English Psalm translations have been unconvincing, not least because the language and structure of the Thornton poem is so closely dictated by its particular rhyming and alliterative demands. Much more productive, however, have been readings of the text which position it within a contemporary tradition of overtly literary verse of a doctrinal and devotional nature; as John J. Thompson has pointed out, '[t]his poem invites comparison with other Middle English didactic works which also draw attention to their own artifice and employ similar stylistic features such as heavy alliteration, concatenation, the use of a refrain and informal quatrain division within the twelve-line stanza.'[129] Most famous among alliterative poems in the twelve-line stanza is of course *Pearl*, although there is no evidence to suggest that the Thornton paraphrase or any other devotional poem was directly influenced by the dream vision. Rather, as Thompson argues, 'it seems likely that these writers were responding variously to a prevailing literary trend that can be linked quite closely not only to a vogue for imitation of the French ballade stanza, but also to the growth in the demand for suitable reading-material in the period'.[130]

Most notably, the Thornton paraphrase has stylistic features in common with the sequence of refrain poems extant in the Vernon and Simeon manuscripts, with which the Thornton manuscript shares 'A song how þat mercy passeth alle thynge'.[131] The paraphrase also resonates with the tradition of devotional and catechetic versification that we witness in Cambridge, Magdalene College Pepys 1548 and Cambridge, CUL Ff. 2. 38, with both of which Thornton shares 'A louely song of wysdome'.[132] And although the Thornton paraphrase is unique, the manuscript also shares two 'songs' ('A song how þat mercy passeth rightwisnes' and 'A song how mercy comes bifore þe jugement') with a sequence in London, Lambeth Palace Library 853, the second of which also appears in London, BL Add. 39574 (the Wheatley manuscript).[133] Building on the fourteenth-century taste for versified doctrine, which we witnessed in Auchinleck, these poems are indicative of

---

[128] For an edition of the Thornton paraphrase, see J. J. Thomson, 'Literary Associations of an Anonymous Middle English Paraphrase of Vulgate Psalm L', *MA* 57 (1988), 38–55 (edition on pp. 52–5). See also S. Greer Fein, '*Haue Mercy* of Me (Psalm 51): An Unedited Alliterative Poem from the London Thornton Manuscript', *MP* 86 (1989), 223–41 (edition on pp. 236–41).

[129] Thompson (1988), p. 44.   [130] Thompson (1988), p. 44.

[131] In both Vernon and Simeon, 'A song how þat mercy passeth alle thynge' is the first in the sequence.

[132] As will be discussed, both Pepys 1548 and Ff. 2. 38 also contain the variant ('B') version of Thomas Brampton's *Penitential Psalms*. Some similar texts teaching basic Christian doctrine are also extant in London, BL Harley 1706 and Harley 2339 (both of which contain prose as well as verse).

[133] M. Day (ed.), *The Wheatley Manuscript*, EETS OS 155 (1921). London, BL Harley 1704 also contains a copy of 'A song how mercy comes bifore þe jugement' as well as a copy of Brampton's *Penitential Psalms*.

a considerable audience for such easily memorable vernacular material, and in their self-conscious artistry and exploitation of contemporary literary trends they plough a quite different furrow from that ploughed by the primer. Yet in their devotional and catechetic emphasis, the manuscripts which contain these texts echo the late-medieval primer's dual focus on prayer and catechesis.

As earlier discussion has indicated, one of the key features of late-medieval primers is their presentation of liturgical material alongside catechesis. The manuscripts mentioned earlier do not present anything as formal as the liturgy, but they do contain vernacular (generally verse) paraphrases of liturgical material. The Wheatley manuscript contains Richard Maidstone's metrical paraphrase of the Penitential Psalms followed immediately by a prose version of *Lessons from the Dirige*, and both Cambridge, Magdalene College Pepys 1548 and CUL Ff. 2.38 contain copies of Brampton's paraphrase of the same seven psalms. The two Cambridge manuscripts also contain copies of a mid fifteenth-century verse paraphrase of the nine lessons that form part of the Office of the Dead (the 'Dirige'), known as *Pety Job*. As discussed earlier in this chapter, the Office of the Dead is, like the Penitential Psalms, a regular component of the primer, both Latin and vernacular. Sharing with Thornton and others the popular twelve-line stanza, this version of *Pety Job* also concludes each stanza with a repeated refrain ('parce mihi domine' [spare me, Lord]).[134] It also has in common with Thornton (and Auchinleck) the fact that it models a vernacular response to Vulgate material which is of great liturgical significance in both monastic and secular traditions. Broadly and expansively replicating many of the more codified contents of the vernacular primer, these manuscripts exhibit a sustained interest in rendering available to a wide audience, in the vernacular, some of the key components of the liturgical day. The obvious difference from the primer is that these texts couple liturgical material with penitential and catechetic commentary in verse; they do the devotional 'work' which the rather more spartan primer leaves to its audience.

This trend for the English versification of key liturgical texts coupled with devotional gloss can be seen on a larger scale in the widespread circulation of two versions of the Seven Penitential Psalms, both of which were mentioned in the previous paragraph. The first is attributed to Richard Maidstone (d. 1396), a Carmelite friar and fierce opponent of John Wyclif, and the second (early fifteenth century) to the Franciscan friar Thomas Brampton.[135] Both create from the Penitential Psalms one

---

[134] The twelve-line stanza version of *Pety Job* survives in five manuscripts: Oxford, BodlL Douce 322; Cambridge, TCC R.3.21; London, BL Harley 1706; Cambridge, CUL Ff.2.38; and Cambridge, Magdalene College Pepys 1584 (the Pepys and CUL manuscripts also contain Thomas Brampton's paraphrase of the Seven Penitential Psalms). The twelve-line stanza *Pety Job* lacks Thornton's concatenation and its rhyme scheme is the slightly more demanding ababababbcbc. For the most recent edition of *Pety Job*, see S. Greer Fein (ed.), *Moral Love Songs and Laments* (Kalamazoo, 1998). There is also an eight-line stanza version extant in Oxford, BodL Digby 102, which also contains Maidstone's metrical paraphrase.

[135] For biographical material on Richard Maidstone, see V. Edden (ed.), *Richard Maidstone's Penitential Psalms* (Heidelberg, 1990). She points out (p. 10) that several works have been attributed to Maidstone. Although relatively few survive, 'there does not seem to be any reason to doubt his authorship of the *Penitential Psalms*; his name appears in two of the surviving twenty-seven manuscripts and

long poem of eight-line stanzas (although their rhyme schemes differ) and in both, each stanza paraphrases and comments on an individual verse. In fact, such are the formal similarities between the two versions that it seems quite possible Brampton knew of Maidstone's version when he was composing his own.[136]

Richard Maidstone's paraphrase was very popular, appearing in whole or in part in twenty-seven manuscripts.[137] Further evidence of its popularity is provided by the fact that the text preserved in these manuscripts varies widely, 'no doubt due to much memorisation and consequent oral-auditory transmission', as well as to 'individual devotional taste'.[138] Maidstone's modern editor, Valerie Edden, divides the manuscripts into three variational groups (α, β and γ, of which β is the earliest) and states that '[t]hese groups cannot be accounted for as genetic groups deriving ultimately from a common exemplar, though it is possible to establish some familial relationships between particular manuscripts.'[139] It is in Psalm 50, which survives (in version β) in isolation from the rest of Maidstone's poem in a total of six manuscripts, that the text proves most variable.[140] The popularity of vernacular versions of this psalm has already been indicated by discussion of their inclusion in Auchinleck and Thornton and it is in keeping with this trend that Maidstone's Psalm 50 paraphrase seems to have taken on a devotional life of its own.

---

the treatise is also recognised as his by Bale'. By contrast, very little is known about Brampton; 'except as author of the metrical version of the *Seven Penitential Psalms*, the name of Thomas Brampton does not appear anywhere in the many available accounts of literature and literary figures of the Middle Ages', and although his treatise survives in six manuscripts, only two name him as author'. J. R. Kreuzer, 'Thomas Brampton's Metrical Paraphrase of the Seven Penitential Psalms', *Traditio* 7 (1949), 359–403, p. 365.

[136] Maidstone reads ababbab and Brampton ababbcbc. Lynn Staley, 'The Penitential Psalms: Conversion and the Limits of Lordship', *JMEMS* 37 (Spring 2007), pp. 221–69, also speculates that Brampton might have read Maidstone's version (p. 224).

[137] For a complete list of the manuscripts, see Edden (1990). For a list of those manuscripts which preserve Maidstone's text in full, see Appendix III at the back of this book. For discussion of the possibility that Maidstone's translation is indebted to the Late Version of the Wycliffite Bible, we must wait until later in the book.

[138] For the first quotation, see A. I. Doyle, *A Study of the Origins and Circulation of Theological Writings in the Fourteenth, Fifteenth and Early Sixteenth Centuries with Special Consideration of the Part of the Clergy therein*, 2 vols (unpublished PhD thesis, Cambridge, 1953), vol. 2, p. 147. For the second, see Day (1921), p. xiii.

[139] Edden, pp. 20–1. Positing β as the earliest group 'leaves open the question as to whether the other large variational groups present Maidstone's revisions or those of an intelligent scribe or compiler'. Edden also suggests (p. 39) that '[t]he γ revisions are not likely to be authorial and present a text inferior to β, both on the grounds that some of the revisions do violence to the rhyme scheme and also because the common ancestor of γ contained a corrupt text of β . . . The case that β is preferable to α is more contentious . . . [It is a case of] of literary judgement rather than firm fact, but it is further supported by the difficulty of establishing the text of α or finding a good α manuscript, since there is considerably more variation among α manuscripts than β ones.' Her observation that among the γ revisions are some changes to the translation, making it more accurate, will be considered in Chapter 4.

[140] Edinburgh, NLS Advocates 19.3.1 (first half of 15thC); London, BL Add.10036 (early 15thC); CUL Dd. 1. 1 (early 15thC); Oxford, BodlL Eng. poet. a. 1 (late 14thC); Oxford, BodlL Rawlinson C. 891 (first quarter of 15thC) (in part); Oxford, BodlL Douce 141 (early 15thC). In addition, CUL Dd. xii. 39 has one stanza of Maidstone's Psalm 50 on its endleaf. As Doyle points out, on f. 75v, this manuscript has the inscription 'Thes ys master thornes bok clothworker of London' (xvi in.) (Doyle (1953), vol. 2, p. 33).

The manuscripts in which this psalm appears in isolation from the rest of the paraphrase are all relatively early (the earliest being Vernon, assembled in Maidstone's lifetime), clearly indicating, as Edden states, that Psalm 50 was 'chosen as an anthology piece' in the initial stages of the poem's circulation. [141] In each, Psalm 50 plays its part in a more or less developed sequence of devotional and catechetic material (often in verse) of the type commented on in relation to Thornton and Auchinleck. In the early fifteenth-century London, BL Add. 10036, it takes its place in a sequence of poems including the Pater Noster, the Ave, the Seven Deadly Sins, the Ten Commandments, and the Seven Works of Mercy. [142] 'A very small book', Additional 10036 appears to have been intended for use as a personal manual and it is easy to see how Maidstone's paraphrase could function effectively in such a context. [143] In the early fifteenth-century NLS Advocates 19.3.1, a much larger-scale miscellany of secular as well as devotional material, it is fitting that Psalm 50 should appear in a booklet comprised of religious verse. [144] Like the psalm paraphrase, almost all of these poems are in eight-line stanzas, two of them also occurring in the aforementioned Vernon/Simeon sequence. That their focus is more penitential than catechetic, more exploratory than expository, indicates the adaptability of Maidstone's psalm as well as the fluidity of the categories 'catechesis' and 'devotion'. Participating in both catechetic ('God make in me my herte clene, / þi ri3tful goost in me þou newe, / Fro *synnes seuen* þou make hit shene') and meditative ('þi self was offered a childe [ful] 3yng, / And afturwarde on rode tre / Whenne of þi hert blood can sprynge; / þerfore my herte I offer to þe') discourses, the poem reminds us of the ease with which the doctrinal could become devotional and vice versa. Vincent Gillespie is right to say that it is 'a long way from catechesis to contemplation', but the journey from catechesis to devotion is less arduous. Vernacular versions of the psalms, and the company that they keep, demonstrate this more effectively than any other late-medieval text. [145]

Maidstone's Psalm 50 appears again alongside conventional texts of basic catechesis in Douce 141, which also contains the monumental *Prick of Conscience*, similarly accompanying Maidstone's Psalm 50 in Rawlinson C. 891. [146] Once

---

[141] Edden, p. 36. She suggests that there is a possibility that Psalm 50 was written first, though offers no further substantiation of this.

[142] The manuscript also contains a fragment of *Titus and Vespasian* and a poem on the Assumption of Our Lady.

[143] Doyle (1953), vol. 2, p. 32.

[144] As Philippa Hardman points out, the Edinburgh manuscript is made up of a series of nine booklets, possibly composed together. She suggests that booklet six, containing Maidstone's paraphrase, forms a self-contained 'anthology' of religious verse. See P. Hardman, 'A Mediaeval "Library" In Parvo', *MA* 47 (1978), 262–73 for a full list of contents. The two poems that it shares with Vernon and Simeon are 'Merci God and graunt merci' and 'Deo Gracias'.

[145] V. Gillespie, 'Anonymous Devotional Writings', in *A Companion to Middle English Prose*, ed. A. S. G. Edwards (Cambridge, 2004), chapter 9, pp. 127–49, p. 129.

[146] For an edition of the poem in Douce 141, see J. R. Kreuzer, 'Richard Maidstone's Version of the Fifty-First Psalm', *MLN* 66 (1951), 224–31. For descriptions of all manuscripts containing *Prick*, see R. E. Lewis and A. McIntosh, *A Descriptive Guide to the Manuscripts of the Prick of Conscience* (Oxford, 1982). Oxford, BodlL Rawlinson C. 891 also contains brief annals of England from creation to 1377. Although the Rawlinson manuscript now preserves only part of Psalm 50 (f. 127v), it may originally have contained more. The five leaves following have been cut out.

more, the paraphrase is dwarfed by the company that it keeps in Cambridge, CUL Dd. 1.1, where it is found with texts including *The Northern Homily Cycle* and the vast anonymous compilation *Memoriale Credencium* (which, despite its Latin title, was composed for 'lewed men that konne not understonde latyne ne frens-she').[147] This manuscript also contains the vernacular psalm commentaries *Qui Habitat* and *Bonum Est*, attributed to Walter Hilton, which are also found in Part IV of the Vernon manuscript in the company of other Hilton and Rolle material. An incomplete rendition of Maidstone's Psalm 50 is also found in Vernon (Part II, ff. 113v–114ra) and is given the title 'miserere mei deus secundum magnam misericordiam tuam in engleis and laten' [Have mercy on me God according to your great mercy in English and Latin] in the list of contents.[148] As was the case with the Auchinleck and Thornton paraphrases, Vernon's version reproduces the Vulgate text with standard abbreviations, alongside a two-line decorated initial which introduces each stanza. In Vernon, Maidstone's poem is preceded by *La Estoire del Evangelie* and other devotional pieces and followed by a series of prayers, the majority of which are penitential; '[a]fter general addresses to Jesus or the Virgin, the prayers become more specifically addressed to sins of omission, such as not fulfilling the ten commandments or not accomplishing the works of mercy.'[149] Its position at the head of such a sequence affirms, once again, Psalm 50's central-ity to the devotional catechesis of the late Middle Ages. And that the sequence is followed (f. 116r–v) by English translations of the liturgical hymns *Horae de Cruce* and *Veni Creator* reminds us of the psalm's role in collections of private, primer-related piety. In the case of both hymns, part of the Latin text is provided, followed by the English verse translation.[150] As noted in the discussion of primers, such a

[147] *Memoriale Credencium* (c. 1400, extant in full in four manuscripts) distinguishes itself from the *Prick of Conscience* and most other manuals of instruction for the laity by virtue of its ambi-tion. '[R]ather than seek straightforward and basic instructional materials directed toward private devotion, [the anonymous author] founded his work upon some extremely sophisticated texts, Latin works written for clerical, rather than lay, instruction'. R. Hanna, 'The Text of *Memoriale Credencium*', *Neophilogus* 67 (1983), 284–92, p. 284. *IMEP* XIX dates Dd. 1. 1 to s.xv[1] and points out that on f. 206v there is a reference to a London merchant, Antonie Mericke (s. xvi) and that on f. 218v we find 'To hir very frind John Hunt merchaunt of London (s. xvi). On f. 225v, the scribe signs himself twice as 'Staundone, R'. Of this manuscript, Doyle comments: 'A tall narrow volume of paper and vellum, written (xv in/med) by R. Staundone . . . Many of the items are of mendicant origin or adaptation . . . and some have peculiar texts in common with the Vernon and Simeon manuscripts, so that they must go back to a common source, an important volume (xiv med/ex.). The elaborate Latin rubrics of Dd may also be derived from that or an intervening volume with other additions. The combination of clerical learning and popular matter suggests the friars, but there is nothing indicating the precise context of this manuscript' (Doyle (1953), vol. 2, p. 60).

[148] Doyle states that there was also '(now lost) a complete copy of Maidstone's Psalms' in Vernon (Doyle (1953), vol. 2, p. 147). Certainly, the list of contents refers to 'þe seuene psalmes' (f. 1v), but it is not clear that these were those of Maidstone.

[149] N. F. Blake, 'Vernon Manuscript: Contents and Organisation', in *Studies in the Vernon Manuscript*, ed. Pearsall (Cambridge, 1990), pp. 45–59, p. 51.

[150] After another devotional poem, these two liturgical paraphrases are followed in by the *Psalterium Beatae Mariae*, a Latin poem by Albertus Magnus, and then by a similar poem based on a Latin text attributed to Thomas Aquinas. The *Psalterium Beatae Mariae* is divided into stanzas prefaced by the Latin *incipits* to the psalms, but the poem bears no relation to the Psalter.

practice facilitates a mode of reading which allows one to keep track of the formal liturgy while meditating on its implications in the vernacular.

This is also the practice in manuscripts containing Maidstone's Penitential Psalms in full.[151] Of course, his vernacular rendition of the biblical material is too loose for there to be any real possibility of non-Latinate readers using the English to parse the unfamiliar language, as, for example, the Hunter 472 and University College 179 primers may well have been used. Yet the presence of the (often abbreviated) Latin text clearly grounds the vernacular in the authority of the Vulgate and, as indicated, is sufficiently close to the wording of the original to facilitate unmediated rumination on liturgically familiar material. The placing of Maidstone's psalms immediately prior to a prose version of *Lessons from the Dirige* in the Wheatley manuscript reminds us that they were at home in the company of 'Englished', primer-related liturgy. The same is indicated by their position immediately following the aforementioned eight-line stanza version of *The Lessons of the Dirige* in Oxford, BodlL Digby 102 and by their inclusion alongside Richard Rolle's commentary on the *Benedicite* and *Quicunque Vult* in Oxford, BodlL Laud Misc 174.[152] Uniquely, they also find their place alongside a Latin primer contained in New York, Pierpont Morgan Library M.99. A liturgical volume, written and illuminated at St Peter's Abbey, Gloucester (*c.* 1405–1415), the manuscript contains the Hours of the Virgin, of the Passion, and of the Lamentation of the Virgin. These are followed by a copy of Maidstone's poem (ff. 92r–132r) before the manuscript reverts to a litany and additional material in Latin.[153]

The poem's appearance in a Latin liturgical volume is, however, exceptional. In all other cases, Maidstone's psalms sit comfortably alongside quasi-liturgical and more broadly devotional material, generally in the vernacular but sometimes in Latin.[154] Given their Christocentric emphasis, they fit easily with Passion meditation such as that found in the Wheatley manuscript, and they circulated particularly frequently

---

[151] For a list of manuscripts containing Maidstone's Penitential Psalms in their entirety, see Appendix III. There are several others that lack between one and four stanzas and a few with more substantial *lacunae*. There are only three manuscripts in which the text of the psalms is entirely fragmentary: Oxford, BodlL Eng. poet E. 17 (some fragments of the psalms bound into a volume containing a selection of fragments from different periods); CUL Dd.12.39 (contains only stanza 21, on a final flyleaf); TCD 156 (lines 9–273 only).

[152] For Wheatley, see Day (1921). For Digby, see H. Barr, *The Digby Poems—A New Edition of the Lyrics*, Exeter Medieval Texts and Studies (Exeter, 2009). As Barr points out, Digby's paraphrase 'bears very close resemblance to the Middle English version of the liturgy' (p. 304). In Digby, Maidstone's poem is presented as prose. Note also the inclusion of Maidstone's psalms in Oxford, BodlL Digby 18, which also includes a (Latin) kalendar and litany, and in Aberystwyth, National Library of Wales Porkington 20 and London, BL Harley 3810 Part I. Both of these manuscripts also contain the English liturgical text *Trentalle Sancti Gregorii* which specifically recommends the recitation of the Penitential Psalms as well as the *Placebo* and *Dirige*: 'He moste say with good deuocioun, / Ouer Euen þe commendacyoun, / Placebo & dyryge also, / The sowle to brynge out of woo: / And also þe salmis seuenne / For to brynge þe sowle to heuen' (see F. J. Furnivall, *Political, Religious and Love Poems*, EETS OS 15 (1866), pp. 114–22, p. 121).

[153] For a full description of the manuscript, see *Corsair—The Online Catalog of the Pierpont Morgan Library* <http://corsair.themorgan.org/>.

[154] It is worth noting that some of the manuscripts containing Maidstone's psalms also contain non-devotional material. Such, for example, is Oxford, Bodleian Library Ashmole 61. In addition,

with the writings of Rolle, to whom they are attributed in Oxford, BodlL Digby 18, which also contains his *Form of Living* and *Emendatio Vitae* (in its English translation).[155] They also circulate alongside Rolle's *Emendatio Vitae* in the original Latin in two further manuscripts: Windsor, St George's Chapel E.1.1 and Oxford, BodlL Rawlinson A.389.[156]

The Rawlinson manuscript is of particular note for several reasons. Used as the base text in Valerie Edden's edition of the psalms, it preserves an ascription to 'Frere Richard Maydenstoon, In Mary ordre of þe Carme þat bachliere is in dyvinite', and is a compilation of Latin and vernacular material, the majority of which is devotional.[157] Probably copied in Lichfield, Edden comments that '[t]he peculiar and important Latin texts it contains . . . suggest that it may have been compiled . . . for and by the interest of clerks in a position to acquire them—as more than a few of the cathedral clergy were.'[158] In fact, the two names mentioned in the manuscript ('liber M Thomas Rynold' and 'liber M Iohannis Reedhill') have been identified by Ker as belonging to two fifteenth-century holders of the same prebend in Lichfield Cathedral.[159] Further manuscripts containing Maidstone's poem seem likely to have had clerical associations; the aforementioned Windsor miscellany, for example, contains the inscription 'Robert bewych . . . Ao. Xxij hcij. vijti', a name which Doyle tentatively linked with a Robert Bexwyke, incumbent of E. Lambrook, Somerset, 1502–10.[160] And Edden has suggested that London, BL Royal 17. C. xvii, a large devotional compilation which also contains John Mirk's *Instructions for Parish Priests* as well as part of *The Prick of Conscience*, may have been 'a priest's handbook'.[161] In addition to the Royal manuscript and to the

London, BL Harley 3810 (Part 1) contains the psalms and other devotional poetry along with (for example) *Sir Orfeo*, astronomical material and medical recipes, as well as the aforementioned *Trentalle Sancti Gregori*.

[155] Of Digby 18, Doyle writes '[a] well written small book; the kalendar and litany not exceptional, but emphasise rather more Benedictine English saints than usual' (Doyle (1953), vol. 2, p. 88). Maidstone's psalms (ff. 38r–64v) follow the *Emendatio Vitae* and precede the Latin litany.

[156] The fifteenth-century Windsor Chapel manuscript also contains, among other devotional material, the commandments in verse, Latin and vernacular poetry, a prose Life of Our Lady, and a series of meditations on the Passion (see J. N. Dalton, *The Manuscripts of St George's Chapel, Windsor Castle* (Windsor, 1957)).

[157] For description of the manuscript, see Edden (1990), pp. 12–14. See also R. Hanna, *The English Manuscripts of Richard Rolle—A Descriptive Catalogue*, Exeter Medieval Texts and Studies (Exeter, 2010), pp. 171–4.

[158] Doyle (1953), vol. 2, p. 146.

[159] N. R. Ker, 'Patrick Young's Catalogue of the Manuscripts of Lichfield Cathedral', *MRS* 2 (1950), 151–68 (166–7).

[160] Doyle (1953), vol. 2, p. 35. He also points out that a 'Robert Bewyk was to be buried in St Clement-without-the-bars, London, 1513'. Doyle also speculates on the clerical associations of the aforementioned Oxford, BodlL Laud Misc 174. Noting the inscriptions 'Iste liber pertenit ad me Sir Rychard Kechyn' (a Richard Kechen on Croydon died in 1515) and, in the same hand (xvi in.) 'Richard clark off huckyn' (f. 91), 'Item unto Welliam Ryepyle of barwyck', he comments '[i]t was, it seems, a priest, not the testator mentioned who had this volume' (vol. 2, p. 34).

[161] Edden (1990), p. 15. The suggestion that Royal 17 C. xvii was a priest's handbook originates in Lewis and McIntosh (1982); dating the manuscript to s. xv. in., they state that 'from the contents, the manuscript would appear to be a priest's handbook, and because it contains a unique copy of *The Legend of the Blood of Hayles*, it may have connections with Hailes Abbey in Gloucestershire' (pp. 153–4). The manuscript contains almost all of Book Four of the *Prick* (ff. 117–24).

two manuscripts in which Psalm 50 circulates with *The Prick of Conscience*, three further *Prick* manuscripts also contain the full version of Maidstone's poem.[162] We know that the *Prick* was popular among the secular clergy. And even when clerical associations for manuscripts cannot be proved, it is useful to remember that the company the poem tends to keep is avowedly 'pro-ecclesiastical' and 'pro-sacerdotal'.[163] For clerics and for their lay parishioners, the paraphrase provided a template for orthodox meditation on biblical material. Implicitly bolstering the authority of the Church, it also facilitated independent quasi-liturgical activity of the sort so popular among the laity of the late Middle Ages.

As demonstrated by the existence of catechetic additions in vernacular primers and by the variety of devotion and catechesis contained in so many late-medieval anthologies and miscellanies, quasi-liturgical texts in English very rarely circulated in isolation from supplementary material. By and large, the dissemination of Maidstone's paraphrase conforms to this pattern and, in its manuscript contexts, it tends to gain force from the presence of its devotional companions. However, in two small manuscripts (both early fifteenth century) the poem has survived alone and it is clear that one of these (Oxford, BodlL Douce 232) circulated as an independent booklet from early in its history, if not from its creation. Preserving the complete paraphrase in a neat Anglicana with the Latin in a more formal script, Douce's dimensions are diminutive (155 x 120 mm), making it a portable aid to personal devotion, and that it was used as such is suggested by the heavy marking on its first and last folios.[164] London, BL Add. 11306, the second extant manuscript to contain the psalms alone, is more unusual in that although it has now been cut into pages, it originally consisted of a roll written on both sides.[165] While this is the only manuscript to preserve Maidstone's poem in such a form, prayer rolls do find mention in wills of the period, and a number are still extant, mostly dating from the late fifteenth century.[166] It seems likely that such prayer rolls were intended for

---

[162] Maidstone's psalms are the first item in Philadelphia, University of Pennsylvania Library, English 1, before *The Prick of Conscience* (Lewis and McIntosh date this manuscript to *c.* 1400 (p. 123)). Aberystwyth, National Library of Wales, Porkington 20 has already been mentioned as, in addition to Maidstone's poem and the *Prick*, it contains the English liturgical text *Trentalle Sancti Gregori*. Manchester, JRL English 50 (s. xiv ex.) contains the *Prick* and some fragments in a later hand. TCD 156 also contains the *Prick* in addition to a fragment of Maidstone's poem (T. K. Abbott, *Catalogue of the Manuscripts in the Library of Trinity College Dublin* (Dublin and London, 1900)).

[163] Edden (1990), p. 12. This is a point also made by Helen Barr in her edition of the Digby 102 lyrics. Containing an incomplete C text of *Piers Plowman*, twenty-four lyrics, Maidstone's paraphrase, and *The Debate between the Body and Soul*, the codex has a 'fiercely penitential focus' and is 'demonstrably orthodox'.

[164] Douce 232's presentation of the text is economical. There is no decoration and although the Latin (in full, with standard abbreviations of individual words) is in a more formal script than the English, it is in the same brown ink. As is the case with most manuscripts of Maidstone's poem, there is no space between the individual psalms, facilitating a continuous reading experience.

[165] It is impossible to determine the date at which the roll was cut into pages.

[166] The 1448 will of Beatrice Milreth, as already discussed, includes 'a roll of the passion of our Lord Jesus Christ' and a roll of fifteen 'Gaudes beate Marie' (Cavanaugh, pp. 585–6). And the 1450 will of Sir Thomas Cumberworth contains a 'roll of prayers', bequeathed to 'the reclus of the grese fote' (Cavanaugh, pp. 224–5). The devotional text which survives most frequently in roll form is the *Arma Christi* (a versified description of the instruments used in the torture of Christ) and although Rossell Hope Robbins suggested that such rolls, which tend to be illustrated, were intended for

46   *English Psalms in the Middle Ages, 1300–1450*

use as easily transportable devotional tools, placing Additional 11306's copy of the poem on a level with that found in Douce 232.[167]

Thomas Brampton's slightly later paraphrase of the Penitential Psalms also survives alone in one fifteenth-century manuscript, London, BL Sloane 1853.[168] Like Maidstone's poem, however, it appears more frequently in the company of other texts and varies considerably between manuscripts. Sloane contains what Kreuzer has called the 'normal' (A) version (also found in London, BL Harley 1704 and Cambridge, Magdalene College Pepys 2030), while the remaining manuscripts contain the 'variant' (B) version (TCC R.3.20; Cambridge, Magdalene College Pepys 1584, and CUL Ff. 2.38).[169] In three manuscripts, Brampton's poem is accompanied by devotional material similar to that found in the majority of volumes containing Maidstone's paraphrase. In Cambridge, Magdalene College Pepys 2030, it is the first text, followed by a prose fragment from a preface to the Fifteen Oes of St Bridget and an imperfect version of Peter Idley's *Instructions to his Son*.[170] As discussed, it also finds a place in CUL Ff. 2.38. Between 'þe mirror of vices & of vertues' and 'a salutacion of oure lady', Brampton's poem shares the eight-line stanza with many of its companions, including the aforementioned 'Louely song

congregational use, to be displayed in churches, Pamela Robinson has pointed out that 'the extant rolls are not nearly large enough for their pictures to be seen at a distance' (see R. H. Robbins, 'The 'Arma Christi' Rolls', *MLR* 34 (1939), 415–21, and P. Robinson, 'The Format of Books: Books, Booklets and Rolls', in *Cambridge History of the Book in Britain*, vol. 2, ed. Morgan and Thomson (2008), chapter 3, pp. 41–54, p. 44).

[167] That both of these manuscripts belong to Edden's a family might suggest that the poem did not circulate as a discrete entity at an early point in its history.

[168] For an edition of the Sloane Brampton, see W. H. Black, *A Paraphrase of the Seven Penitential Psalms in English Verse*, Percy Society 7 (London, 1842). Black's comments on the nature of Middle English devotional verse are worth quoting: 'The religious poetry of the Middle Ages consists, for the most part, of dull versification, ennobled with few of the lofty sentiments that pure Christianity inspires, and enlivened with few flights of imagination, except those derived from a wild and dreary superstition. That of our own language is therefore chiefly valuable for its philological data, and as constituting a part of our national literature' (p. v).

[169] For a reproduction of Sloane 1853, f. 14v (the end of Brampton's Psalm 37 and the beginning of Psalm 50), see Figure 1.2. See Kreuzer (1949). Kreuzer's edition is of the B text, and is a collation of Pepys 1584 and CUL Ff.2.38. Kreuzer is indebted to Carleton Browne for his A and B versions. He states that although Carleton Brown's two versions 'unquestionably stem from the same original', '[t]he variant version differs from the normal version in about 130 lines scattered throughout the poem.' In some places, only a few words are changed, and in others, entire stanzas are altered; it has been suggested that while A is an anti-Lollard text, B's alterations are decidedly pro-Lollard' (p. 359). While the various versions of Maidstone's poem are probably attributable to the vicissitudes of memory as well as devotional preference, the purposes behind the alterations to Brampton are rather different and will be discussed in Chapter 3. For a list of Brampton manuscripts, see Appendix III.

[170] For *Instructions*, see C. D'Evelyn, *Peter Idley's Instructions to his Son* (Oxford, 1935). Pepys 2030 is a paper manuscript written in one hand; '[a]ll of the texts are imperfect, and the physical evidence conflicts with the textual at various points. There are no catchwords or quire and leaf signatures visible. The present sewing suggests that there are, perhaps, ten gatherings . . . but these seem unlikely to reflect the original construction of the volume.' R. Mckitterick and R. Beadle, *Catalogue of the Pepys Library at Magdalene College Cambridge*, vol. 5, Manuscripts. Part I: Medieval (Cambridge, 1992), p. 47. Brampton's poem lacks the first six stanzas, and most of the seventh, as well as stanzas 121–4. Mckitterick and Beadle point out that on fol. 101v there is a merchant's mark displayed on a shield incorporated into an initial and also found elsewhere in the manuscript. 'It appears to be identical with [a merchant's mark] found "on a stone in the wall of an old house on the East side of the Duke's Palace Yard" in Norwich.'

Now flefchly frendys haue y none.
Lord to the my foule y take.
Y hope and trufte in the alone.
Shat thou wylt me neuer forfake.
Thou mayft left my forwe aflake.
Departe not lord awey fro me.
So thi mercy my mone y make.
Ne reminifcaris dñe.
A wende in adiutozium meum?
dñne deus falutis mee.

Howz y in flefch be fyke and fede.
Of my foule god lord take hede.
Yn the only is hope and hele.
Thou art myn helpe at euery nede.
yn mercy thou wylt no man forbede.
Wyl the body and foule departyd be.
panne is to late to feye fynge oz rede.
Ne reminifcaris dñe.

Iferere mei deus? fecundum
magnã miferrcozdiam tuam.
Crye lord y calle and crye.
Thi mercy is wyd in euery place.

Fig. 1.2. The end of Thomas Brampton's Psalm 37 and the beginning of his Psalm 50
London, British Library MS Sloane 1853, f. 14v. Reproduced by kind permission of the British Library. © The British Library Board

of wysdome' also found in Vernon, Simeon, the London Thornton manuscript, and Pepys 1584.[171] Its associations with these texts are both devotional and literary.

In the fifteenth-century paper manuscript Pepys 1584, the twin 'at least in part' of the CUL manuscript, 'containing a number of the same texts in the same order', the poem is given the heading and running title 'The seale of mercy'. [172] Last in the sequence of three eight-line stanza poems with which the manuscript begins, it is followed immediately by a copy of the twelve-line stanza *Pety Job* also found in CUL Ff. 2.38.[173] Here, again, Brampton's poem plays its part in a manuscript whose structure and versified contents approximate the structure and prose contents of the vernacular primer. Just as the primer begins with liturgical matter which it tends to follow with catechetic material, so Pepys begins in devotion and quasi-liturgy before turning its attention to versified catechesis.[174] The deliberate nature of this structure is emphasized by f. 1r's list of contents and incipit, '[t]his litill boke is compilid of full notabill expl. and so folowyng euery matir oon aftir anodir.'[175] What we have in Pepys is, arguably, a deliberate attempt to replicate the form and function of elements of the primer, and the suitability of Brampton's poem for such an enterprise is obvious. Marked at the conclusion of each stanza by the refrain 'ne reminiscaris domine' [Lord, do not remember . . .] borrowed from the antiphon which concludes the recitation of the Seven Penitential Psalms in both Sarum and York Uses, the paraphrase advertises its indebtedness to the liturgical traditions that it both replicates and supplements.

However, despite the poem's clear links with primer-related devotion, its manuscript presentation actually suggests a degree of movement from the trend of linking vernacular paraphrase to quotation of the liturgical/biblical Latin which we saw in volumes containing Maidstone's text. In comparison with the latter, it is

---

[171] For the manuscript facsimile, see F. McSparron and P. R. Robinson, *Cambridge University Library MS Ff.2.38* (London, 1979). Ff. 22–27 of the manuscript are missing, meaning that Brampton's poem (ff. 28r–31v) begins abruptly at l.451 of the edition as printed by Kreuzer. Other eight-line stanza poems in the manuscript include 'The Complaint of God', 'Markys of Medytacyouns', and 'Twelve Profits of Anger' as well as the aforementioned 'mirror of vices & of vertues'.

[172] Mckitterick and Beadle point out that some of the texts found in Pepys 1584 and CUL Ff. 2.38 are also found grouped together in London, BL Harley 1706 and London, BL Harley 2339 (p. xxv). Pepys 1584's explicit to Brampton's poem gives it the alternative title '[or] the vij salmes'. 'Pety Joob' is the heading and running title given to the poem, but in the incipit it is referred to as 'the ix lessons of dyrige that is clepid pety Jobe'.

[173] In an unpublished PhD thesis, 'The Middle English *Pety Job*: A Critical Edition with a Study of its Place in Late Medieval Religious Tradition' (University of Texas, 1979), K. A. Crawford points to similarities in metrical form, style, and treatment between *Pety Job* and Brampton's metrical paraphrase. She suggests that, at the least, they may be products of the same school of poetry.

[174] For a full list of Pepys 1584's contents, see Mckitterick and Beadle, p. 23. Its catechetic contents are fairly standard (The Ten Commandments; The Seven Works of Mercy; The Five Bodily Wits; The Five Ghostly Wits; The Seven Deadly Sins; The Seven Virtues, etc). The last (imperfect) text in the manuscript, 'Thes ben þe iiij doweris', is prose.

[175] Mckitterick and Beadle note that there is 'one practised and current secretary hand' throughout the manuscript (p. 23). The link between the contents of CUL Ff. 2.38 and, by extension, of Pepys 1584 were noted by the editors of the former's facsimile edition some years ago, who pointed out that they 'imply not only a poet but also an audience familiar with the contents of the Primer' and provide 'further evidence for the association of the Primer with the development of lay piety in the fifteenth century, an association which has not yet been fully assessed'. McSparron and Robinson, p. ix.

noteworthy that in CUL Ff. 2.38 and Pepys 1584 Brampton's poem is not accompanied by any reproduction of the Vulgate psalms. In the versions found in both manuscripts, the only appearance that Latin makes is in the aforementioned 'ne reminiscaris' refrain, which is not distinguished from the rest of the text by means of script, colour, or size. The effect of such treatment is, obviously, that readers are not reminded repeatedly of the status of Brampton's poem as a paraphrase of biblical material. The title '[t]he seale of mercy' given as an alternative to 'the vij salmes' in Pepys 1584 suggests further that an attempt is being made to assert a literary identity for the poem independent of its psalmic indebtedness.

The claim made by devotional poetry to participate in a coherent school of accomplished vernacular poetry which need not always advertise its indebtedness to biblical *auctoritas* has already been witnessed in discussion of the traditions of versification found in Thornton, Vernon, Simeon, and others. But it is perhaps at its most obvious in the case of Thomas Brampton's paraphrase which, on two notable occasions, is found in manuscripts that also contain Chaucerian material. In London, BL Harley 1704 (which contains the 'A' version), the poem features alongside not only *The Abbey of the Holy Ghost, The Charter of the Abbey of the Holy Ghost*, and *The Three Kings of Cologne* (among others), but also a copy of Chaucer's *Prioress' Tale*.[176] And in TCC R.3.20 (which contains the 'B' version) it stands at the head of a volume containing a substantial collection of Chaucer and Lydgate.[177] It is particularly interesting that the Chaucer represented in this anthology is not quite the Chaucer whom the Retractions would want us to remember and who would be an obvious companion to Brampton in his devotional preoccupations. Rather, it is the Chaucer responsible for *Troilus and Criseyde, Anelida and Arcite*, and *The Complaint of Venus* (among others), and the Chaucer who curses his scribe for playing fast and loose with his literary reputation. In prefacing an anthology including such material with Brampton's poem, the compiler of the manuscript is staking a claim for his psalms to be considered alongside it. Brampton's paraphrase

---

[176] For studies of the circulation of some of these texts, see J. Boffey, ' "Many grete myraclys . . . in divers contreys of the eest": The Reading and Circulation of the Middle English Prose *Three Kings of Cologne*', in *Medieval Women: Texts and Contexts in Late Medieval Britain: Essays for Felicity Riddy*, ed. J. Wogan-Browne et al. (Turnhout, 2000), pp. 35–47, and J. Boffey, '*The Charter of the Abbey of the Holy Ghost* and its Role in Manuscript Anthologies', *YES* 33 (2003), 120–30. Only stanzas 62–116 of Brampton's poem survive in this manuscript.

[177] A note at the beginning of this manuscript attributes the poem to one 'Frater Thomas Brampton sacrae Theologiae Doctor fr. Minorum pauperculus confessor de . . .' and continues in a later hand 'whoose name was Fratae Thomas bramptone sacre Theologiae doctor fratrum minorum pauperculus confessor de latino in Anglicum. Anno domini m.cccc.xiiij ad dei honorem et incrementum devocionis.' ['Brother Thomas Brampton, consectrated Doctor of Theology, Friars Minor, humble confessor from Latin into English. In the year of our Lord m.cccc.xiiij to the honour of God and increase of devotion']. Linne Mooney states that the manuscript was written by John Shirley and that it was probably originally joined with Sion College M. Arc. L. 40. 2/E. 44 in a single volume and possibly also with BL Harley 78, ff. 80–3 (L. Mooney, *Manuscripts in the Library of Trinity College, Cambridge (IMEP* XI), p. 22). See also Seth Lerer 'British Library MS Harley 78 and the Manuscripts of John Shirley', *N&Q* (1990), 400–3, in which he alludes to the 'growing scholarly consensus' that Sion College Arc.L.40.2/E.44 and the Cambridge manuscript originally formed part of the same compilation (p. 400).

is obviously being read by a literary audience to whom Chaucerian sophistication appealed.

COMPLETE PSALTERS

Moving from the richly suggestive evidence of use and readership supplied by verse paraphrases of the psalms, we turn finally to the complete English Psalters and begin with the earliest of the extant translations, the so-called *Surtees* or *Metrical Psalter*, which is, coincidentally, entirely in verse (rhyming couplets with some quatrains). Edited twice in the nineteenth century but attracting little attention since, the *Metrical Psalter* distinguishes itself from the other complete Middle English translations not only by its identity as verse but also by its very limited circulation.[178] Dated variously to the second half of the thirteenth century and the beginning of the fourteenth, it survives in six manuscripts.[179] Defined as a 'truly local text' by Ralph Hanna, it appears to originate from 'a coherent small portion of the West Riding [of Yorkshire]' and not to have disseminated far beyond this area.[180]

In keeping with Hanna's reading, the *Linguistic Atlas of Late Mediaeval English* maps Bodley 425 (LP 601) to the West Riding, an area to which it also maps three further manuscripts containing the *Metrical Psalter*; Harley 1770 (LP 191), Vespasian D. vii (LP 364), and Egerton 614 (LP 603).[181] In their EETS edition of the late fourteenth-century alliterative poem *The Siege of Jerusalem*, Ralph Hanna and David Lawton provide us with some useful further information regarding these manuscripts.[182] Examining the dialect of *The Siege*, they isolate eight linguistic features which, they argue, 'could represent a geographically specific authorial dialect—a small area in the West Riding of Yorkshire, a neighbourhood centred around Barnoldswick and Earby'.[183] Going on to suggest that this 'linguistic community most closely resembles the forms provided by six of LALME's linguistic profiles', they point out that four of these profiles are those of the *Metrical Psalter* manuscripts already listed.[184] The scribal dialect of Cambridge Corpus Christi 278 (LP 589) is not entered on LALME's maps, but is also located to the West

---

[178] For these two editions, see J. Stevenson, *Anglo-Saxon and Early English Psalter*, Publications of the Surtees Society, vols 16 and 19 (London, 1843–7), and C. Horstmann (ed.), with a new preface by A. C. Bartlett, *Yorkshire Writers: Richard Rolle of Hampole, an English Father of the Church and his Followers* (Woodbridge, 1999), vol. 2, pp. 129–273. Neither editor was aware of Corpus Christi 278, nor of the two Bodley manuscripts containing the *Metrical Psalter*.

[179] For a list of *Metrical Psalter* manuscripts, see Appendix IV.

[180] R. Hanna, 'Yorkshire Writers', *PBA* 121 (Oxford, 2003), pp. 91–109, p. 101, footnote 23.

[181] A. McIntosh, M. L. Samuels, and M. Benskin, *A Linguistic Atlas of Late Mediaeval English*, 4 vols (Aberdeen, 1986). The abbreviation 'LP' refers to the linguistic profile assigned to the scribal dialect of individual manuscripts.

[182] R. Hanna and D. Lawton, *The Siege of Jerusalem*, EETS OS 320 (Oxford, 2003).

[183] Hanna and Lawton, p. xxix.

[184] Hanna and Lawton, pp. xxix–xxx. The other two manuscripts are London, BL Egerton 927, which contains an adaptation of Grosseteste's *Château D'Amour* ascribed to a Salley monk, and London, BL Cotton Vespasian A. iii, which contains *Cursor Mundi*.

Riding of Yorkshire. And while Bodley 921 is the only manuscript of the *Metrical Psalter* that is not assigned a linguistic profile nor mapped in LALME, preliminary investigations would suggest that it too originated and circulated in a distinctly northern context.

What, then, might explain the *Metrical Psalter*'s limited dissemination? After all, this chapter has provided us with decisive evidence of the popularity of English versions of the psalms and we might legitimately expect the earliest complete translation to have garnered favourable attention. Answers to that question can only ever be partial and provisional, but it seems possible that, as Hanna suggests, its circulation was 'truncated by the success of Rolle's more scholarly and explanatory prose Psalter', another complete translation with a northern provenance.[185] There is also a sense in which the *Metrical Psalter* was the author of its own demise; featuring dialect terms of distinctively and (to the outsider) obscurely northern origin, it may have limited its own possible readership. Added to this is the dubious attribute of monotony: a literal rendition of the entire book of psalms in couplets (some quatrains) which rely for their rhyme on a succession of repeated, monosyllabic tags, it is not always a stimulating read. Lacking both the expansive commentary which makes Rolle's equally literal translation more palatable, and the concision which characterizes individual psalm paraphrases, it is relatively easy to see why the *Metrical Psalter* might have fallen by the wayside in the devotional marketplace of the late Middle Ages. Nonetheless, that it survives in a total of six manuscripts is worthy of comment, indicating that it was by no means insignificant as a 'local' text.[186]

Codices containing the *Metrical Psalter* are, in general, frustratingly opaque on the question of ownership. Only one, Harley 1770, can be located decisively to a monastic centre: marked 'Liber Monasterii de Kirkham' [Book of the Monastery of Kirkham], we know it to have belonged to the house of Augustinian Canons. Cambridge, Corpus Christi 278 also has a monastic shelfmark which, while it appears in Norwich books, is fairly universal and not, therefore, 'especially definitive for localisation'.[187] That these two manuscripts (the first certainly, the second probably) were at some point in monastic hands might, however, tell us something about ways in which the *Metrical Psalter* was read and used. In addition to the English verse translation, both preserve an Anglo-Norman (Prose) Psalter and Harley 1770 also contains a complete Latin (Gallican) text.[188] The details of these Psalters and their *mis-en-page* will be discussed in Chapter 6, but it is worth noting here that these bi- and tri-lingual manuscripts recall, in admittedly humble fashion, the parallel Hebrew and Greek Psalters of the thirteenth century used by

[185] Hanna (2003), p. 101, footnote 23.
[186] By way of contrast, the so-called *Prose Psalter*, the second of the complete English psalm translations, is extant in only four copies, but has attracted much more scholarly notice.
[187] Private communication with Ralph Hanna, to whom I am grateful for this information.
[188] The Anglo-Norman Psalter in both has been identified by Dean and Boulton as the so-called Oxford Psalter, a twelfth-century prose rendition of the Gallican Psalter, made in England (see R. J. Dean and M. B. M. Boulton, *Anglo-Norman Literature: A Guide to Texts and Manuscripts* (London, 1999), no. 445, pp. 239–41).

English scholars for purposes of comparative study.[189] As Ian Doyle notes, such volumes 'have always been means of advanced study by persons proficient in each language'.[190] The *Metrical Psalter* may well have functioned in the (theoretically at least) learned environs of monasticism as a vernacular experiment in the mirroring of the Vulgate, of interest for reasons of comparison as well as in and of itself. That it was not, however, a text of notable distinction or value (either devotional or financial) is perhaps indicated by the fact that neither Harley 1770 nor any of the other extant codices are elaborately illuminated or ornamented. Although it was by no means carelessly copied, manuscript presentation of the *Metrical Psalter* would suggest that it was regarded as a functional rather than decorative text.

In two manuscripts, the *Metrical Psalter* appears in isolation. One of these, Cotton Vespasian D.vii, is of a size which would suggest that it was intended for personal use. The other, Egerton 614, is more substantial, but may have functioned in a similar way. Although neither contains full Vulgate Psalters, in common with all manuscripts of the *Metrical Psalter*, Vespasian and Egerton preserve Latin incipits to individual psalms (and, sometimes, to individual verses), indicating that they were probably used, or meant to be used, by readers keen to follow the rhythms of the psalms in their liturgical context. Bodley 921, which contains the *Metrical Psalter* in its entirety (fols. 1r–99v) as well as (fol. 101v) a fourteenth-century French form of the *Prognosticon Milonis Toletani de coniunctione facta anno Domini 1357*, also lends itself to use in such a setting.[191] Of eminently portable dimensions, containing Vulgate cues, it is again an entirely functional volume.

Although we know nothing of the provenance of Bodley 425 (beyond its LP which assigns it to the West Riding of Yorkshire), its contents additional to the *Metrical Psalter* also indicate an interest in the psalms in their liturgical context, and in the verse vernacularization of liturgical material more generally. Beginning imperfectly at Psalm 16: 3, the *Metrical Psalter* introduces the volume but is interrupted at f. 66v by a sequence of versified, vernacular liturgical material (the five Gospel Capitula, the Athanasian Creed, the *Veni Creator*, and the *Ave Maris Stella*). At f. 72v, the *Metrical Psalter* resumes and is followed by a sequence of five Anglo-Norman poems (punctuated by the unexplained repetition of some of the versified liturgy).[192] Bodley 425's preoccupation with verse is not surprising, particularly given its Yorkshire context: as Ralph Hanna and others have pointed out, verse paraphrase and instruction are among the 'prevailing norms of canonical literary production' in the north of medieval England, characterizing not only the *Metrical Psalter* (and the further contents of Bodley 425), but also devotional texts including *Cursor Mundi*, *The Prick of Conscience*, and the *Northern Homily Cycle*.[193] This being the case, the manuscript's English contents are of little help in identifying a specific intended audience.

---

[189] For discussion, see B. Smalley, *The Study of the Bible in the Middle Ages*, 3rd edn (Oxford, 1983).
[190] Doyle (1953), p. 102.
[191] *Summary Catalogue of Western Manuscripts*, vol. 2, p. 569.
[192] For a full list of contents, see A. Sutherland, 'English Psalms in the Middle Ages', *BLR* 28 (2008), 75–92.
[193] Hanna (2003), p. 101.

Its Anglo-Norman elements (in the same hand as the English material), however, may assist us in our conjectures as to readership. Linked thematically as texts of a moral and advisory nature, the poems (all of which are identified by Dean and Boulton) begin with Nicholas de Bozon's *Le Char d'Orgueil*, a late thirteenth-century allegorical treatise in quatrains which is, broadly speaking, an exhortation to virtue and a guide to confession, although it also has some material in the middle satirizing the vanity of women.[194] They continue with the *Proverbes de Bon Enseignement*, generally rhyming in couplets, and widely accepted as the work of de Bozon.[195] The third and fourth poems are both preoccupied with the theme of courtesy, one addressed to an unidentified Edward, and the other beginning 'Bon enfant doit a son leuer / corps e alme a Dieu comande' ('A good child must, on his lips / commend body and soul to God').[196] And the final text is also an Anglo-Norman poem in couplets, listed by Dean and Boulton as a thirteenth-century treatise on morals, manners, and conduct for boys and young men.[197] What this selection suggests is a compiler and/or scribe consciously aiming his material at a male audience. It is not impossible that Bodley 425, like Harley 1770 and Corpus Christi 278, was intended to function in a monastic milieu. Unlike these manuscripts, however, it may have been meant for an audience of limited experience and expertise. Its advisory Anglo-Norman material would have been of general relevance to the novice monk while its versified English material, consistently keyed by incipits into the Latin sources from which it derives, could well have assisted in the comprehension of liturgical basics.

While we can, then, suggest a monastic provenance for at least some of the manuscripts containing the *Metrical Psalter*, we find ourselves in somewhat different territory when investigating the circulation of the slightly later *Prose Psalter* (sometimes referred to as the *Midland Prose Psalter*), not to be confused with Richard Rolle's *English Psalter*.[198] Extant in four manuscripts, the *Prose Psalter* is a translation of a glossed Anglo-Norman text which is, itself, a translation of a glossed version of the Gallican Psalter.[199] The precise source remains unidentified and it has generally been assumed that there is no extant copy of any such text in England. However, as I will demonstrate in subsequent chapters, the *Prose* text is a translation of a glossed version of the Anglo-Norman 'Oxford Psalter', a later copy of which is preserved in London, BL Add. 44949 (the 'Tywardreath Psalter'). The fact that none of the surviving manuscripts of the *Prose* translation preserves the

---

[194] Dean and Boulton, no. 687, pp. 373–4.   [195] Dean and Boulton, no. 252, pp. 140–1.

[196] Dean and Boulton, nos. 232 and 233, pp. 131–2.

[197] Dean and Boulton, no. 231, pp. 130–1. This text, surviving in a total of eleven manuscripts, is incomplete in Bodley 425. It is also transcribed in a different (probably later) hand.

[198] Until 2012, the only edition of the *Prose Psalter* was K. Bülbring, *The Earliest Complete English Prose Psalter*, EETS 97 (Oxford, 1891). Bülbring was aware of only two manuscripts of the Psalter (London, BL Add. 17376 and TCD 69), and the limitations of his edition will become apparent in the course of this book. In 2012, as this volume was undergoing a process of revision, a further edition was published: R. R. Black and R. St-Jacques, *The Middle English Glossed Prose Psalter edited from Cambridge, Magdalene College, MS Pepys 2498*, Middle English Texts 45, 2 vols (Heidelberg, 2012). While Bülbring's edition will be used as the basis for quotation in this book, reference to Black and St-Jacques' edition will also be made.

[199] For a list of manuscripts containing the *Prose Psalter*, see Appendix IV.

Anglo-Norman source is an oddity which will also be addressed later in the book, as will their presentation of the glossed Latin. The text's dissemination has little in common with that of the *Metrical Psalter*. Not only do we have clear evidence of its circulation outside monastic settings, but it also identifies itself, in manuscript context, as a resolutely London text, far from the northern provenance of the former. The two may, however, be closer in terms of composition date than has been generally assumed. Although the mid fourteenth century has been conventionally proposed for the *Prose Psalter*, with characteristic precision Ralph Hanna has adduced evidence which suggests that the text was probably composed 'at the latest, early in the fourteenth century'.[200] Such a date would also position the *Prose Psalter* earlier than Rolle's English translation, probably written in the late 1340s.

In only one manuscript, Princeton, University Library Scheide deposit 143, does the *Prose Psalter* survive in isolation. In each of the other three witnesses, it is accompanied by a substantial body of vernacular material. Dublin, Trinity College 69, for example, opens with the *Prose Psalter* and follows it with the prose Apocalypse, 'a tale of charite' (the sixtieth sermon of the London sermon cycle, the *Mirror*, translated from an Anglo-Norman source) and 'an early copy of a widespread instructional text involving biblical exposition, as well as a tract on the 10 Commandments. It also contains a Latin description of Jerusalem and a copy of *The Prick of Conscience*.'[201] Some of its contents are mirrored by those of the late fourteenth-century Cambridge, Magdalene College Pepys 2498 which contains, in addition to the *Prose Psalter*, the prose Apocalypse, the full text of the *Mirror* (also translated from Robert de Gretham's Anglo-Norman *Miroir*), and a commentary on the Ten Commandments. This manuscript also houses a Gospel Harmony (with which it begins), a heavily interpolated copy of *Ancrene Riwle* (identified as 'þis good book Recluse'), the prose *Complaint of Our Lady*, and a copy of the popular Gospel of Nichodemus, as well as some additional prayers.[202] In the last, but possibly earliest (mid fourteenth-century), of the manuscripts containing the *Prose Psalter* (London, BL Add. 17376, Part 1) it follows 'Latin materials suitable for use by a parish priest.'[203]

As Hanna has amply demonstrated, the text was firmly embedded in London literary culture of the early fourteenth century. In '[d]efining the corpus of London texts', he singles out ten manuscripts whose contents are written in Samuels' 'Type II' London English.[204] Two of these contain copies of the *Prose Psalter*: Additional 17376, which he dates palaeographically to *c.* 1330–70, and Pepys 2498, dated to

[200] R. Hanna, *London Literature, 1300–1380*, Cambridge Studies in Medieval Literature 57 (Cambridge, 2005), p. 21. He bases his supposition on evidence supplied by the copy of the *Prose Psalter* in London, BL Add. 17376. In this manuscript, Psalm 13: 6's 'sub labiis eorum quorum os maledictione' appears as 'of whiche þe mouþe ys ful of þaryynge'. As Hanna suggests, 'the translator's rendition . . . is not, as written, Middle English . . . the anomalous "þaryynge" must represent the appropriate "waryynge"'. The scribe appears to have mistranscribed the exemplar's archaic letter *wynn*. On this, he comments: 'The demise of this grapheme is a roughly datable feature. In some contexts, this old runic form was becoming passé by the 1270s, and I should not put the latest example I have noticed, in a book copied near King's Lynn, after 1320.' In Pepys 2498, we read 'wari3inge' (Black and St-Jacques, p. 9. In TCD 69, we find 'cursyng' (Black and St-Jacques, p. 108).
[201] Hanna (2005), p. 17.
[202] For the full description, see McKitterick and Beadle, pp. 86–8.
[203] Hanna (2005), p. 8.   [204] Hanna (2005), pp. 4–7.

c. 1365–75.[205] The evidence offered by the two other copies of the *Prose Psalter* (in Trinity 69 and Scheide deposit 143, both of which Hanna offers as examples of the 'dispersed transmission' of the text) also implies 'an unusually concerted access to London texts', even if they are not written in London language. Further linking the four codices is the fact that the majority of Trinity 69's contents mirror those of Pepys in reverse ('although the two books have certainly been derived from different exemplars').[206] And Scheide deposit 143, which contains only the *Prose Psalter*, has been 'copied by the same Sussex scribe who copied Trinity College MS 69'.[207]

Isolating Pepys 2498 as particularly significant, Hanna argues that:

> These [London] manuscripts do not simply share, as Samuels argues, a distinctive local language, but an extensive group of texts as well. Particularly central in this regard is Pepys 2498, devoted entirely to a lengthy sequence of prose texts. In addition to their prose form, unusual at this date, these share a variety of other features: all provide reasonably direct access to biblical texts, all encourage a relatively learned textual consumption through their inclusion of explanatory commentaries, and all have been translated from Anglo-Norman sources.[208]

He goes on:

> So far as manuscript survivals allow one to tell, Pepys 2498 represents the most extensive project of English vernacular book-production undertaken before the close of the fourteenth century.[209]

United with contemporary London codices and with other *Prose Psalter* manuscripts, Pepys' contents indicate an interest not only in prose texts, translation from Anglo-Norman, and biblical translation but also in specifically English doctrine and devotion. In formal terms at least, we are a long way from the exclusively poetic contents of Bodley 425 (although the latter shares with the London manuscripts an interest in Anglo-Norman material, albeit of a different genre). In fact, we are closer to the manuscript contexts of Brampton's and Maidstone's paraphrases which, as we know, indicate that these translations were also being read in conjunction with specifically English doctrine, devotion, and instruction.

To whom, then, would the *Prose Psalter* and its companions have appealed? Evidence supplied by two of the manuscripts would suggest a readership among the emerging mercantile classes of the late Middle Ages, the type of audience among which primers also appear to have circulated. Trinity 69, for example, was owned at an early stage by one 'John Hyde', a name which, Hanna comments, 'may imply a London provenance for the book . . . although equally, Hyde might be a Winchester surname'.[210] And Doyle suggested that Additional 17376 might have

---

[205] Hanna (2005) points out that the front nine leaves (all Latin) of Add.17376 are now preserved separately as Bodleian Library, Lat. Th. e. 32. He also suggests that '[t]he style of one colophon (fol. 198rv in part II, not in London language but the same hand), outlining indulgences which "are granted by Archbishop Simon" . . . may permit a narrower placement, *c.* 1330–48' (p. 6).

[206] Hanna (2005), p. 17.

[207] Hanna (2005), p. 18. He goes on to speculate thus: 'In this context, it is difficult to be certain that the Trinity/Scheide scribe was not a London workman . . . His Sussex language may simply represent the early training of a person then immigrant to London, *c.* 1400.'

[208] Hanna (2005), p. 7.   [209] Hanna (2005), p. 153.   [210] Hanna (2005), p. 18.

circulated in a similar context; he read, under ultraviolet light, the name 'William Pelka civis London'.[211] It is also highly likely that Pepys 2498 was intended for a London audience; Hanna suggests that it 'could well be seen as the anti-romantic response to a[nother London] book like Auchinleck' and argues that '[s]o imposing a volume seems explicable only as a lectionary or as a stationery reference volume, for group use in a household or chapel'.[212] The evidence of an extant 1349 will also indicates that the text may well have circulated in London: following Doyle, Hanna suggests that the 'psalter written in Latin and English' willed by the London vintner Robert Felstede, to John de Foxton, clerk of another prominent London vintner, Henry la Vanneve, may well have been the *Prose Psalter*.[213] It is also possible that the 'j. veil' sauter glosez d'engleis pris xx. d' [an ancient Psalter glossed in English, price 20 shillings] listed in the inventory of the goods of Thomas of Woodstock was a copy of the *Prose* text.[214]

Clearly, the *Prose Psalter* originated and circulated in a context entirely different from that of the earlier *Metrical Psalter*: available evidence points towards its popularity among a devout lay audience with a voracious appetite for biblical learning and doctrinal instruction in the vernacular. By contrast, although we have no evidence that the *Metrical Psalter* was not used by lay readers, the indications that we have suggest only a monastic provenance. The two are not entirely distinct, however, as indicated by the fact that both have some relation with the thirteenth-century Anglo-Norman Oxford Psalter. While the *Metrical* text is accompanied by this translation in two extant manuscripts, the *Prose Psalter* is itself a translation of a late, glossed version of the Oxford Psalter. Written at different times, with different priorities and used by different audiences, the two Psalters nonetheless share an association with this Anglo-Norman translation, very popular among devout readers in the English Middle Ages. The fact that the *Prose Psalter*, by contrast, does not appear to have gained much momentum in terms of circulation beyond its immediate southerly context is not entirely surprising. As proceeding chapters will demonstrate, its translation is uneven and it is possible that its inclusion of glosses alienated readers looking for an English equivalent to the Vulgate. Although Rolle's translation is, it might be argued, equally problematic (for entirely different reasons), its literality serves a purpose and is, in any case, clarified by the glossing commentary with which it is accompanied. The *Prose Psalter* must have suffered by comparison.

It is to Rolle's *English Psalter* that we now turn.[215] Distinguishing itself from all other complete Middle English psalm translations by virtue of the fact that it

---

[211] Hanna (2005), p. 6 comments that he can no longer see this inscription.

[212] Hanna (2005), p. 153.

[213] Cavanaugh, p. 336. He also wills a book called 'le Byble' to John de Heurle. As Hanna indicates, 1349 is too early to imagine that a copy of Rolle's Psalter might have been circulating in London.

[214] Cavanaugh, pp. 844–51.

[215] Thus far, Rolle's Psalter has been edited only once, by H. R. Bramley. Anne Hudson's edition of the Wycliffite interpolated Rolle commentary is published by EETS (A. Hudson, *Two Revisions of Rolle's English Psalter Commentary and the related Canticles*, 3 vols, EETS OS 340, 341, 343 (2012–14). Kevin Gustafson and Jill C. Havens are planning a new edition of the uninterpolated text. For a list of manuscripts containing Rolle's uninterpolated *English Psalter* see Appendix IV.

contains an extensive commentary as well as a closely literal rendition of the Latin, Rolle's Psalter reached a remarkably extensive and diverse audience, extending far beyond the northern context of its composition, and was by far the most widely read of all the complete Middle English psalm translations. For extensive evidence of the text's provenance, circulation and manuscript companions, the reader is referred to Ralph Hanna's 2010 descriptive catalogue of the English manuscripts of Richard Rolle. To duplicate Hanna's observations would not be valuable, and I do not intend to do so. It is, however, important to isolate salient features of manner and extent of the text's presentation and dissemination.

Rolle's Psalter, in more or less complete form, survives in a total of nineteen manuscripts and, as is well known, (a) Wycliffite interpolated version(s) also circulated in several further codices. With notable exceptions, which will be discussed in some detail later in the book, manuscripts containing Rolle's *English Psalter* tend to be substantial in size; they are not, generally, books which would have functioned comfortably in the context of private devotion. Presenting the text clearly and often professionally, the majority of volumes are eminently readable.[216] While most include enlarged and/or decorated initials at liturgically important moments in the Psalter, sometimes accompanied by marginal illumination, most are not, however, luxurious volumes. The obvious exception to this rule is the imposing and elaborate Oxford, BodlL Bodley 953, produced for Thomas IV, Lord Berkeley. Unusual among *English Psalter* manuscripts, it contains several figural illuminations, the majority of which include King David.[217] Cambridge, Corpus Christi College 387 is also notable for its finely executed champs, again including representations of David.[218] Cambridge, MA Harvard University Library Richardson 36, containing an interpolated copy of Rolle's Psalter (Hudson's RV1), also has, at the beginning of Psalm 1, 'an eleven-line historiated initial (David enthroned) with vinet' in addition to further elaborate champs marking each of the seven Nocturns.[219] In such manuscripts Rolle's vernacular translation and commentary is accorded the illustrative reverence that we tend to associate with copies of the Vulgate Psalter.[220] However, the high value accorded to Rolle's *English Psalter* by contemporary readers is suggested not only by such aesthetic elaborations but also, rather differently, by the existence of fairly extensive marginal annotations and corrections in a number of manuscripts.[221] For many readers, it would appear that what the text said

[216] There are, of course, some exceptions to this rule. Hanna describes London, BL Arundel 158, for example, as a 'pretty rough and ready job' (2010), pp. 84–5, no. 44.
[217] Hanna (2010), pp. 145–6. See also R. Hanna, 'Sir Thomas Berkeley and his Patronage', *Speculum* 64 (1989), 878–916.
[218] Hanna (2010), pp. 5–6, no. 2.
[219] Hanna (2010), p. 44, no. 23. Richardson 36 is unusual among Rolle Psalter manuscripts insofar as it contains only the prologue, translation, and commentary and is not accompanied by any liturgical Canticles or additional catechesis.
[220] See also the interpolated copy (breaking off at Psalm 88) in London, Lambeth Palace Library 34, which is, as Anne Hudson states, 'a splendid and expensive production'.
[221] Eton, Eton College Library 10 (s. xv²/⁴): the Psalter is accompanied by 'a fair number of marginal corrections with signes de renvoi' (p. 63); Oxford, University College 56 (s. xv¹) has a 'fair number of marginal later hand notes, quarrels, clarifications' (p. 182); *olim* South Queensferry (West Lothian), Dalmeny House, the Earl of Rosebery (s. xv. in and xv²/⁴); '[T]he text has been assiduously

was as important as how the text looked; content was as, if not more, important than form. This is confirmed by the fact that, in several manuscripts, while the Psalter and commentary are complete, the decorative system accompanying them is not. Word takes precedence over image in the context of Richard Rolle's *English Psalter*.[222]

It is very rare to find Rolle's *English Psalter* (including prologue, commentary, and translation) circulating in isolation; in almost all extant manuscripts it is accompanied by other material which is, on occasion, extensive.[223] Most consistently, the Psalter is followed by a selection of canticles ('other biblical psalm-like utterances').[224] Mirroring the conventions of Latin liturgical Psalters, manuscripts containing such material suggest that in the late Middle Ages, Rolle's Psalter was read in awareness of, if not active conjunction with, the liturgical context in which the psalms featured so dominantly. Although relatively little in Rolle's commentary indicates that he was, in its composition, concerned with linking exegesis to liturgical role, manuscript context (as well as decoration) implies scribes/compilers and readers were keen to do so. On occasion, we also find Rolle's *English Psalter* in the company of catechetic material, which, from its contents, suggests clerical use. The uninterpolated copy in London, BL Harley 1806, for example, is followed by not only the Canticles and Magnificat but also a text of *De informacione simplicium sacerdotum*, the instructional programme from John Pecham's 1291 Lambeth Canons.[225] Additionally, Oxford, BodlL Hatton 12 contains, as well as the prologue, Psalter, Canticles, and Magnificat, a substantial body of catechetic and devotional material. According to Hanna's catalogue, this includes tracts on the Ten Commandments and Creed and verses containing material from the Pecham syllabus.[226] And the uninterpolated copy in *olim* South Queensferry (West Lothian), Dalmeny House, the Earl of Rosebery is followed, after the Canticles

corrected by later hands' (p. 200); Worcester, Cathedral Library, f. 158 (s. xv ½): corrections in relatively informal anglicana, s. xv med (p. 215) (all page references to Hanna (2010)).

[222] Cambridge, Sidney Sussex College 89 (s. xiv/xv): the manuscript is only partially finished; in addition to many blanks for initials, the final 2 leaves in 11 of the quires are either completely undecorated or, on two occasions . . . followed by undecorated leaves' (p. 13); London, BL Royal 18 D. i (s. xv in.): Hanna (2010) records 'an unfilled eight-line space for an initial at the opening of the prologue, a ten-line one at the opening of Ps. 1, and six- or seven-line examples, some with spaces for headings, at the Nocturns (p. 106); London, BL Add 74953 (s. xv in.) (a continuation of London, BL Royal 18 D. i): Hanna records 'unfilled blanks with guide letters, five and seven lines respectively, at the heads of the nocturns (fols 50rb, 123va)' [in scribe 3's unfinished stint] (p. 108); Oxford, BodlL, Bodley 467 (s. xv²ᐟ⁴, perhaps a little later): 'unfinished'; Oxford, University College 74 (s. xv in.): A fragment of interpolated (RV1) Psalter 'only partially finished. Headings in red. But although the scribe provided running titles, his five- and seven-line spaces for decorated initials . . . to precede the Latin, and paraphs have not been filled' (p. 186).

[223] As indicated, in Cambridge, MA Harvard University Library, Richardson 36, the Psalter and prologue are unaccompanied by any additional material. Unusually, in Aberdeen, University Library 243, the Psalter is not prefaced by a copy of Rolle's prologue. It is accompanied by the Old Testament Canticles and Magnificat, the additional Canticles, and the Lessons of Dirige.

[224] Hanna (2010), p. xxxii.

[225] Hanna (2010), pp. 100–1, no. 50. The prologue is missing but was, presumably, originally present: the *English Psalter* begins late in 1: 1 'after an excised first leaf'.

[226] For a full list of contents, see Hanna (2010), pp. 158–9, no. 86.

and Magnificat, by an instructional tract and a copy of The Twelve Degrees of Meekness.[227] The survival of Rolle's *English Psalter* with such companions indicates that it was a text interpreted and used in pastoral as well as liturgical contexts: it was understood to provide moral and spiritual guidance in addition to functioning as a vernacular prompt aiding readers in following the rhythms of Latinate devotion. That these dual roles are by no means incompatible with the contexts of the commentary will become clear later in the book.

It is in keeping with the *English Psalter*'s liturgical functionality that the earliest evidence of ownership we have suggests a religious readership, both female and male. As Doyle suggests, the first copies that we have are roughly dateable to the end of the fourteenth century and 'may be judged from their execution and early markings to have been of monastic provenance'.[228] As is well known, the unique metrical preface in Oxford, BodlL Laud Misc 286 tells us that the book was, at some point, in the possession of the nuns of Hampole, and Robert Est, priest of York, in his will of 1474, bequeaths the nuns of Hampole 'psalterium glosatum de propria scriptura Beati Ricardi heremitae' [a Psalter glossed with the individual composition of Blessed Richard the hermit].[229] The author of *The Mirror of Our Lady* also implies that a copy/copies were in the early possession of the Bridgettine nuns of Syon. We know as well that copies of the English text were in the ownership of male monastic communities. For example, Henry of Kirkstede, in the *Catalogus de Libris Autenticis et Apocrifis*, probably referring to a book in the library of Bury St Edmunds (Suff., OSB), lists among works of Rolle 'super Psalterium duntaxat [l. dupliciter?] Latine et Anglice' [on the Psalter?*twice*, in Latin and in English].[230] And the aforementioned splendidly illuminated Cambridge, Corpus Christi College 387 (s. xv med.) is inscribed, in the lower margin of f. 2 (similarly fol. 82v): 'Iste liber Constat Dompno Iohanni Colman Abbati Monasterij de Lesnes' (on the second occasion adding 'in Comitatu Kanc", i.e. Westwood (OSA, Kent), near Woolwich.[231] An inscription in Oxford, BodL Bodley 467 (s. xv²/³) also indicates a monastic provenance ('Iste est liber domini Hugonis Eyton, supprioris monasterij Sancti Albani Anglorum prothomartiris').[232]

Evidence adduced earlier in this chapter suggests that, from a relatively early date, Rolle's *English Psalter* was also circulating among lay readers. We know, additionally, that Sir Thomas Berkeley owned a remarkably elaborate copy (the aforementioned Bodley 953) and it is also possible that Henry, Lord Scrope of Masham possessed one. He bequeathed to his brother John 'unum psalterium novum

---

[227] Hanna (2010), pp. 200–2, no. 109. As he points out, the Psalter begins imperfectly at 7: 18 and is, therefore, missing the prologue.

[228] Doyle (1953), p. 108. He points out that it is from the beginning of the fifteenth century that 'the evidence of dissemination precipitates'. Bequests suggest that 'the eminent members of the secular clergy and laity who had copies must have obtained them about the turn of the century, and that it had about then just reached several parts of England'. He also supposes that it may have spread to south and west through monastic channels 'or with the increasing secular and lay interest.'

[229] Hanna (2010), pp. xxxv and xxxvii.   [230] Hanna (2010), pp. xxxvi–xxxvii.

[231] Hanna (2010), pp. 5–6. As Hanna points out, 'Sum Willelmi Eden' also appears on fol. 113 (lower margin, s. xv/xvi).

[232] Hanna (2010), pp. 138–9.

glossatum, elumpnatum, cum armis meis et uxoris meae' [a newly glossed psalter, illuminated, with my arms and those of my wife] and while he does not specify Rolle, date and location make it most likely to have been his. It should be remembered, though, that Scrope may refer to Rolle's Latin text: as Hanna points out, the inventory of his goods includes 'a good deal of Latin Rolle'.[233] Turning, finally, to the aforementioned likelihood of clerical ownership of Rolle's *English Psalter*, while a lack of specificity as to language makes the evidence difficult to read, it is possible that two extant wills indicate possession in such a context. In 1449, for example, Thomas Loxley, chaplain of St Martin Orgar, London, bequeathed a fellow chaplain 'unum psalterium per hampol glosatum' [a Psalter glossed by Hampole]. And in 1446 Thomas Beelby, 'persona' of the church of York, bequeathed Mr William Duffield 'domino meo', 'j. Psalterium de tractatu Ricardi Hampole' [a Psalter with the commentary of Richard Rolle]; as Hanna points out, the volume appears subsequently in the 1453 inventory of Duffield's goods.[234] As discussed, it also seems likely that London, BL Harley 1806 and Oxford, BodlL Hatton 12 were at some point in clerical hands. And that the same applies to the aforementioned *olim* South Queensferry is suggested by Hanna, who observes that 'Latin *distinctiones* of a sort conventional for preachers [are] added in lower margins, fols 150–163 *passim*, imply[ing] early use as a clerical practitioner's book'.[235]

As already indicated, surviving manuscript evidence tells us that Rolle's commentary was, at a relatively early stage, appropriated and interpolated by Wycliffite revisers: clearly, the Lollards were well aware of the Yorkshire hermit's psalmic activity and redeployed it to their own ends. What is, however, particularly interesting about their revisions is the fact that, with few exceptions, they feature in the commentary alone: by and large, the Wycliffites leave Rolle's vernacularization untouched. It would appear that, for them, Rolle is more interesting as a commentator on the psalms than he is as a translator. The fact that it was the hermit's status as psalm reader which appealed to a (loosely defined) heterodox audience is indicated by the occasions on which we find Rolle's impassioned and expository prologue accompanied not by his own translation but by that associated with the Wycliffites (LV). In the remarkable San Marino Huntington Library 501, for example, the hermit's prologue features as the last in a sequence of four prologues to the psalms, and is followed by the Wycliffite LV Psalter. London, BL Add. 10046 also contains Rolle's prologue, following it with excerpts from the General Prologue to the Wycliffite Bible as well as the LV psalms and canticles. It also appears in Worcester Cathedral Library F. 172, accompanied by the LV Psalter and other material, and in London, BL Add. 31044, followed by the LV psalms, canticles, and sapiential books. And we find it finally in Dublin, Trinity College 75 where it is accompanied by two other prologues to the psalms (both by Jerome and often

[233] Hanna (2010), p. xxxvi.

[234] Hanna (2010), p. xxxvi. Duffield was a canon of York and a former fellow of Merton College, Oxford.

[235] Hanna (2010), pp. 200–2. He also observes that the name 'Elizabeth' [the surname cut away with the lower margin] appears on f. 177 (s. xv/xvi).

prefaced to the Wycliffite Psalter) but no Psalter, either Wycliffite or Rollean. The preference of some compilers/readers for the Wycliffite LV translation over that of Rolle is not surprising: the former is much more fluent and comprehensible. It is, nonetheless, testament to Rolle's extraordinary influence as psalm commentator that these compilers/readers insisted on the presence of his prologue.[236]

Discussion of manuscripts in which Rollean and Wycliffite material circulate in conjunction leads us, finally, to consideration of the Wycliffite psalms in both the Early and Later Versions. Of extant manuscripts containing the complete Wycliffite Bible, twenty contain the Psalter.[237] But of these, only four (TCD 66; Oxford, BodlL Douce 369; Oxford, Christ Church 145; Oxford, Corpus Christi College 4 and Wolfenbuttel, Herzog-August-Bibl., Guelf. Aug. A. 2) include the EV psalms: all others are LV Bibles. Fifteen further manuscripts include the psalms in complete or partial Old Testaments.[238] Of these, only two contain the EV psalms (Cambridge, CUL Add. 6681 and Oxford, BodlL Bodley 959) and one (Cambridge, CUL Ee 1.10) contains a revised copy of parts of the EV Old Testament, including extracts from the psalms. In two further manuscripts, LV psalms appear with New Testament material only; in Cambridge, St John's College E.18 the psalms of the passion are accompanied by an LV John and the Articles of the Faith and in Worcester Cathedral Library F. 172, Psalms 1–83 appear alongside LV Acts and a selection of devotional prose.[239] Noteworthy among Wycliffite Psalters for containing the complete Latin and English texts (matched only in London, BL Harley 1896), Worcester F. 172 will be discussed later in this book. Twice the LV psalms also appear in the context of selections of both Old and New Testament material; in Oxford, BodlL Bodley 771 where they feature in a complete EV Old Testament accompanied by extracts from the Epistles and Acts and in Oxford, BodlL Laud Misc 182. In the latter, Psalms 1, 2, 4, 5, 6, 36, 50, 70, and 98 are included in a selection of complete LV chapters (Old and New Testaments) and selected verses from other psalms are quoted again later in the codex.[240] In New Haven, Yale University, Beineke Library 360, LV Psalms 2: 9–150 are accompanied by a primer (as previously footnoted) and in Dublin, Trinity College Library 70 the same psalms appear, accompanied by basic catechetic material. To this group should be added the Middle English primers discussed earlier in the chapter: almost all manuscripts containing the primers include translations of the psalms related in some way to the Wycliffite versions.

Finally, although there are no extant copies of the EV Psalter alone, the LV psalms are found in isolation (other than the Canticles and, on occasion, a litany and/

---

[236] It should also be pointed out that small extracts from Rolle's Psalter have been noted in further manuscripts. See Oxford, BodlL Laud Misc 210, which contains a fragment of his commentary on Psalm 18: 15. See also Beineke 360, which has an excerpt from his commentary on Psalms 6: 1 and 37: 1. See also London, BL Harley 3913 which contains two excerpts from the interpolated commentary (Hudson's RV1) on Psalms 30: 31 and 18: 15.

[237] For a list of manuscripts containing the complete Wycliffite Bible including the Psalter, see Appendix IV.

[238] For a list of these manuscripts, see Appendix IV.   [239] See Appendix IV.

[240] See Appendix IV. For a full description of Laud Misc 182, see Ogilvie-Thomson, *IMEP* XVI, pp. 24–5.

or lectionary and/or some prefatory material) in seven manuscripts. London, BL Add. 10047 contains a copy of Psalms 1–73 and Add. 35284 has Psalms 45–150, as well as the Canticles and a Litany. In Oxford, New College 320 and London, BL Harley 1896 we find the psalms accompanied by the Canticles; as mentioned earlier, the latter is, like Worcester F. 172, notable for its inclusion of the complete Latin and English for each verse. Dublin, Trinity College Library 72 contains a lectionary, the LV prologue to the psalms, the psalms and the Canticles, and the aforementioned London, BL Add. 10046 has part of chapter 12 of the prologue to the Wycliffite Bible, the psalms and Canticles as well as the Quicunque Vult, with Rolle's commentary. Finally, Oxford, BodlL Bodley 554, which will be discussed later in the book, contains a heavily glossed copy of the psalms, in addition to the Canticles.[241] We should also note the psalms have been removed from Oxford, St John's College 7, an otherwise complete LV New Testament, 'presumably for ease of use'.[242]

The Wycliffite psalms (particularly those of LV) appear, then, to have enjoyed significant popularity, both as independent texts and when accompanied by additional biblical material. Like Rolle's Psalter, they also circulated with basic catechetic doctrine and, on two occasions, in codices whose contents also reveal an anthologizing interest in psalm-based material. Most strikingly, in the aforementioned San Marino, Huntington Library HM 501, the LV psalms are accompanied by no less than four prologues to the Psalter (including Rolle's, introduced as 'þe fourþe prolog on þe salmes of þe sauter þat Richard Hampol made') as well as an apparently unique unpublished abbreviated Psalter consisting of a selection of LV psalms 'chosen to exhibit God as a just king demanding righteous behaviour from his people' and a copy of the so-called 'St Jerome Abbreviated Psalter' in English. In addition to this psalmic material, the manuscript contains further biblical texts (Wycliffite LV Old Testament as well as 'þe gospel of Ascensioun Day') as well as catechetic information and instruction and some liturgical matter including a Litany and the Old and New Testament canticles.[243] And in Beineke 360 the LV psalms are accompanied not only by a full liturgical primer and two brief extracts from Rolle's commentary but also by a further copy of St Jerome's Abbreviated Psalter in English, mirroring that in Huntington 501.

Many of the volumes which contain the LV psalms accompanied by liturgical material and catechesis are of small dimensions, and, as will be discussed later in the book, those which omit the catechesis are even smaller. It is, however, unlikely that their size is due to fears surrounding censorship; they appear to have circulated quite freely. Neither do they give the impression of being volumes designed to be

---

[241] See Appendix IV. A reproduction of Bodley 554, f. 21r appears as Figure 1.3.

[242] M. Dove, *The First English Bible: the Text and Context of the Wycliffite Versions*, Cambridge Studies in Medieval Literature 66 (Cambridge, 2007), p. 63.

[243] For a full list of contents, see Hanna, *IMEP* I, pp. 25–30. As he points out, the abbreviated Psalter consists of quotations taken from Psalms 77: 1–2; 48: 2–3; 18: 6–12; 1 complete; 2: 10–13; 81: 3–4; 4: 5–6; 10: 5–8; 9: 10–13; 32: 1–9; 33: 6–23; 92 complete; 63: 11; 65: 2; 68: 33–37; 71: 11–14; 91: 13–15; 14 complete; 23 complete; 13: 2–3 (ending imperfectly with a folio lost), 88: 43–53 (beginning imperfectly), 89 complete; 91: 1–8; 93: 1–9.

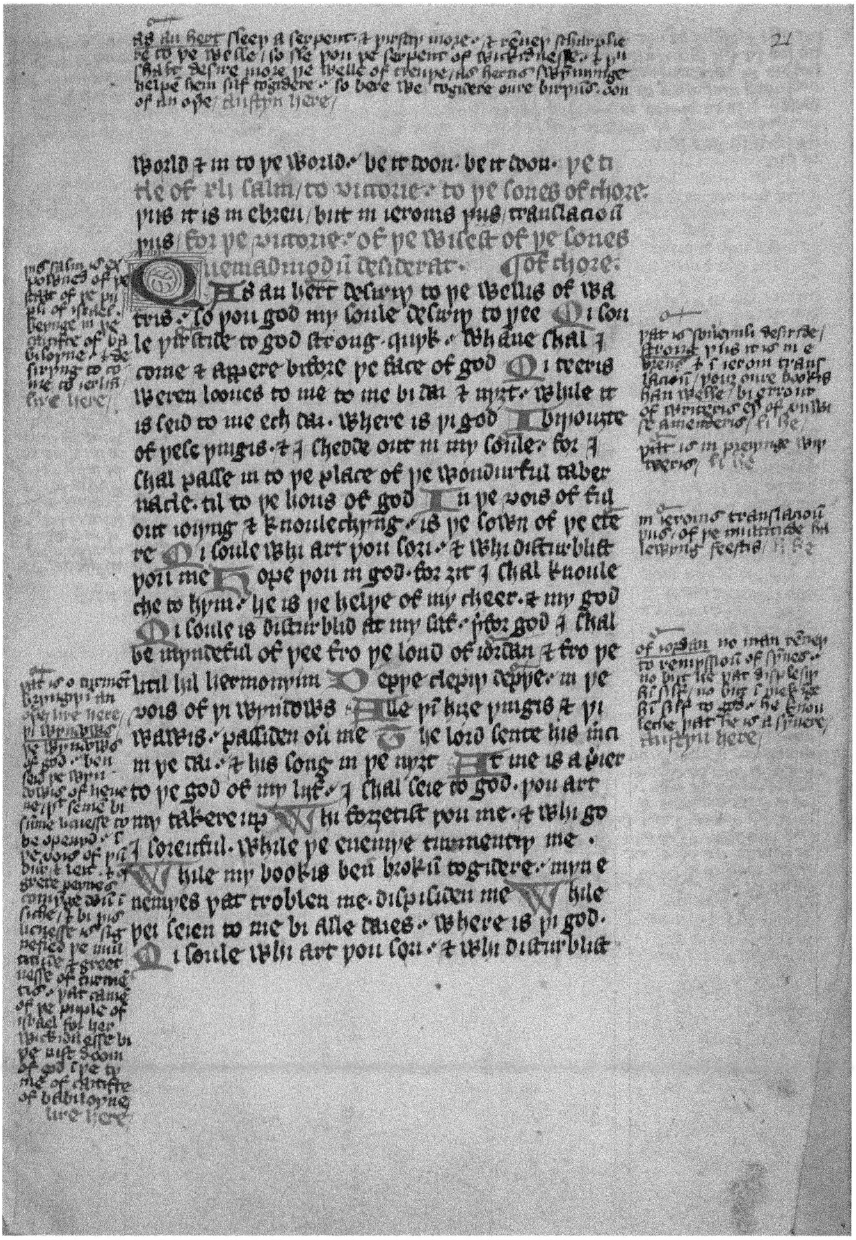

Fig. 1.3. Psalm 41 in the glossed Wycliffite Psalter (LV).
Bodleian Library MS Bodley 554, f. 21r

hidden away; they are, by and large, very careful and professional productions, and many are delicately illuminated. These are obviously manuscripts designed for personal, devotional use and, in this, they distinguish themselves from the majority of complete Wycliffite Bibles which tend to be large, lectern volumes apparently intended for corporate deployment of some sort. What, however, links the smaller psalm-based volumes with their larger complete counterparts is the interest that both display in the Bible as it operates in liturgical contexts. As Dove has pointed out, at least eighty-nine of the *c.* 250 complete Wycliffite Bibles that survive 'include a lectionary, complete or partial', enabling readers to discover and locate the lections which 'were going to be read at mass on any particular day'.[244] While the lectionary covers only the New Testament gospels and epistles, 'individual psalms can [also] be readily located in Wycliffite Bibles' by means of the Vulgate incipits which more or less invariably introduce them. As Dove suggests, 'in most manuscripts of the Wycliffite Psalms, alternating blue and red one-line capitals mark the opening of each verse of each psalm, so that the psalm could be read antiphonally where appropriate, or a listener could keep track of the text of a psalm read or sung antiphonally'.[245] Far from dislocating their users from the practices of the church community or from its acceptable teachings (as indicated by the inclusion, in many manuscripts, of uncontentious catechesis), these were volumes which could well have been used to complement entirely orthodox devotional activity. Despite the early fifteenth-century Arundelian legislation under whose shadow they were apparently intended to fall, the Wycliffite psalms thrived and are testament to the evocative power of these biblical texts in the context of late-medieval England.

[244] Dove (2007), p. 61.   [245] Dove (2007), p. 63.

2

Theorizing Translation

As the previous chapter has demonstrated, the psalms were translated in many different ways by many different people over the 150 years covered by this book. The vernacular Psalter survives in prose and in verse, in complete and abbreviated form, and in literal and paraphrasing renditions. All were written in different circumstances, intended for different audiences and read in manifold ways. Yet all have in common the fact that they are indebted, ultimately, to the Vulgate Psalter and that they 'turn' a Latin source into an English translation.[1] As translations, those responsible for them must have had an opinion, whether consciously articulated or not, of what the labour of vernacularization involved and of the nature of the relationship between original and 'copy'. In the translation of a biblical text from apparently authoritative Latin to a widely used vernacular, questions of linguistic status and propriety must also have arisen. What does one *do* to the Word of God when one turns its habitation from a high-status language to one of arguably less lofty associations?

In order to be meaningful, any discussion of late-medieval psalm translations must situate these texts in the context of such questions and issues, considering inherited attitudes to the processes of translation and the responsibilities of the translator. Equally, it must position the vernacular psalms in the broader contemporary milieu of late fourteenth-century interest in translation as a literary activity. Given the 'close relation between religious and secular writing in the period', it makes no sense to view the activity of biblical translation in isolation from contemporary practices of translation from classical and continental sources.[2] It is only when such theoretical questions associated with translation have been considered that we can proceed to an informed investigation of the practice of English psalm vernacularization.

---

[1] The precise identity of the Latin Psalter(s) lying behind the English translations will be discussed in the next chapter.

[2] For the quotation, see N. Watson, 'Censorship and Cultural Change in late Medieval England: Vernacular Theology, the Oxford Translation Debate and Arundel's Constitutions of 1409', *Speculum* 70 (1995) 822–64, 823–4.

MODELS OF TRANSLATION

As the work of Rita Copeland has demonstrated, the chief model of translation which the Middle Ages inherited from the Roman era was one of 'differentiation from the source text', even of 'contestation and displacement'.[3] In the context of medieval hermeneutics, '[t]ranslation, like exegetical commentary, does not simply "serve" its "master" texts: it also rewrites and supplants them.' She goes on:

> Like commentary, translation tends to represent itself as a "service" to an authoritative source; but also like commentary, translation actually displaces the originary force of its models.[4]

For Copeland, this tendency is traceable back to a specifically Roman understanding of translation as a rhetorical activity, the object of which is dissimilarity with the source. A translation does not attempt to forge imitative identity with its exemplar, but aims for a sort of 'inventive difference':

> The aim of translation is to reinvent the source, so that, as in rhetorical theory, attention is focused on the active production of a new text endowed with its own affective powers and suited to the particular historical circumstances of its reception. Thus in translation, the force of rhetorical invention should produce difference with the source.[5]

In the case of the Romans, 'the aim of inventive difference in the replicative project of translation . . . emerges from a disturbing political agenda in which forcibly substituting Rome for Greece is a condition of acknowledging the foundational status of Greek eloquence for *Latinitas*'.[6]

Copeland's model rests on her assertion of there being a difference, in Roman understanding, between 'translation as a form of commentary and translation as a form of imitation'.[7] At the most basic level, imitation involves the copying of an original while commentary involves the explanation or decoding of an original. As already indicated, for the Romans, the translator has most in common with the commentator. His task is to create the new from the old, and is 'comparable to the act of inventing one's own argument out of available topics'.[8] The most famous (and aggressive) proponent of this model of translation was Cicero; as Copeland comments, '[t]hroughout Cicero's scattered remarks on translation, the question of active differentiation from the original text is theorized in the much more aggressive terms of contestation and displacement.'[9] His most notorious formulation of this model is found in the late treatise *De optimo genere oratorum* when he is discussing his translation of the speeches of Demosthenes and Aeschines:

> And I did not translate them as an interpreter, but as an orator, keeping the same ideas and the forms, or as one might say, the "figures" of thought, but in language which

---

[3] R. Copeland, *Rhetoric, Hermeneutics and Translation in the Middle Ages: Academic Traditions and Vernacular Texts*, Cambridge Studies in Medieval Literature 11 (Cambridge, 1991), p. 33.
[4] Copeland (1991), pp. 3–4. [5] Copeland (1991), p. 30.
[6] Copeland (1991), p. 31. [7] Copeland (1991), p. 10.
[8] Copeland (1991), p. 30. [9] Copeland (1991), p. 33.

conforms to our usage. And in so doing, I did not hold it necessary to render word for word [*non verbum pro verbo necesse habui reddere*], but I preserved the general style and force of the language. For I did not think I ought to count them out to the reader like coins, but to pay them by weight, as it were. The result of my labor will be that our Romans will know what to demand from those who claim to be Atticists and to what rule of speech, as it were, they are to be held.[10]

Two particular features of this Ciceronian proclamation are of significance to us in the context of this chapter. First is the phrase 'non verbum pro verbo' (not word for word), frequently cited in responses to classical translation theory and practice. And second is the implication of opposition, even competition, between 'their' (the Greeks') language and ours (the Romans'). The 'fortunes' of both precepts in later patristic tradition are of real importance to Western medieval conceptualizations of the process of translation and the responsibilities of the translator, as we will see.[11]

To deal first with 'non verbum pro verbo', if interpreted as a straightforward endorsement of non-literal translation, the phrase suggests that the preservation of source's meaning should be the translator's priority. As glossed by Jerome (that most prolific of biblical translators), it theoretically relegates language to a position of inferior importance in the activity of translation; a text's true significance lies not *in* but *behind* its words. Here Copeland is worth quoting *in extenso*:

As early Christian semiology accords human language a secondary, although necessary, role in relation to the primacy and stability of divine signification, so patristic translation theory is concerned mainly with recuperating a truthful meaning beyond the accidents of human linguistic multiplicity . . . The problem of difference, of linguistic and literary heterogeneity, is of course a central theme in patristic theory; but whereas Roman theory seeks to erase difference (even as it recognizes it) by foreclosing the originary claims of the source and substituting Latin for Greek, patristic criticism seeks more to resolve difference by pointing towards a communality of source and target in terms of the immanence of meaning.[12]

As a rhetorician, Cicero's priorities lay with the crafting of an accomplished 'new' product as the outcome of any act of translation. His injunction to 'translate "non verbum pro verbo," but rather preserving the force and figures of the language and the general *sententiae* represents a principle of conservation directed, not to the service of the source text, but to the benefit of the target language'. In its original Ciceronian context, '[t]his injunction against literalism is not framed in a context that favors meaning above language or that directs attention to the preservation of the signified, despite the way that this precept was later interpreted within the patristic tradition of translation theory.'[13] Jerome, as theologian rather than rhetorician, might be argued to have misappropriated Ciceronian terminology, since his

[10] Copeland (1991), p. 33.
[11] See R. Copeland, 'The fortunes of "non verbum pro verbum": or why Jerome is not a Ciceronian', in *The Medieval Translator. The Theory and Practice of Translation in the Middle Ages*, ed. R. Ellis (Cambridge, 1989), pp. 15–35.
[12] Copeland (1991), p. 43.   [13] Copeland (1991), pp. 33–4.

theory of translation suggests 'a priority of the claims of meaning over and apart from language as the vehicle of intention' although in his practice he was a little more flexible.[14] Jerome's recognition of the necessity of non-literal translation is expressed most clearly in the preface to his translation of Eusebius' Chronicle:

> A meaning may be conveyed by a single word: but in my vocabulary I have no comparable word; and when I try to accommodate the full sense, I take a long detour around a short course . . . If I translate word for word it sounds silly; if by necessity I change some aspect of word order or diction, I will seem inadequate to the task of translator . . . The point of all this is that it should not seem strange to you if our translation offends, if its hesitant speech is uneven with consonants and its vowels open with hiatus . . . Learned men will have sweated over this work.[15]

Influenced by neo-Platonic theory, the trends of patristic thought favoured the notion that behind the accident of the text there lies an extra-linguistic, transcendental signified which it is the task of the translator to recuperate and preserve. This somewhat utilitarian view of the process of translation, in which language itself is relegated to a position of secondary importance, was by no means shared by the consummate rhetorician Cicero, but the misappropriation of his terminology was perpetuated into the later Middle Ages.

Turning to the second of Cicero's propositions (that the translator is a merchant transferring ideas from one nation's currency to another's and trying to make a profit in the process), Copeland argues that this was more or less silenced in patristic reception of Roman thought. The theorizing of translation as contestation, if not displacement, of the original, has little place in a tradition devoted to the interpretation and translation of biblical and theological texts. Most specifically, how—or why—could a translation of a biblical text claim to be of more authority than its divinely inspired original? Nor is there any nationalistic or overtly political agenda informing such translations, as there is very clearly in the Roman model of 'translatio studii et imperii' (the translation of knowledge and power). What Copeland illuminates most clearly in the course of her work is that, while borrowing extensively from Roman terminology, patristic tradition does not in any sense represent an unproblematic continuation of classical models.

MEDIEVAL THEORIES OF TRANSLATION

It was largely through the transmission of such patristic tradition that Roman translation theory became known in the medieval West.[16] Particularly influential

---

[14] Copeland (1991), p. 50.

[15] Quoted in Copeland (1991), p. 47. See *Liber de Optimo Genere Interpretandi (Epistula 57)*, ed. G. J. M. Bartelink (Leiden, 1980), pp. 43–63.

[16] As Copeland points out, Roman theories were also transmitted via the 'rhetorical compendia of late antiquity'. However, the patristic route was the most common. Copeland (1991), p. 41.

was the aforementioned Hieronymian justification of non-literal translation. His recognition of the difficulty and, on occasion, undesirability, of verbatim translation finds its way into chapter 15 of the Prologue to the Wycliffite Bible, which relies both explicitly and implicitly on Jerome's model. In his most notable (though unsignposted) recollection of Jerome, the English author tells us that the 'best' mode of translation is not strictly verbatim:

> Firste it is to knowe þat þe best translating is, out of Latyn into Englisch, to translate aftir þe sentense and not oneli aftir þe wordis, so þat þe sentence be as opene or opener in English as in Latyn, and go not fer fro þe lettre. And if þe lettre mai not be sued in þe translatyng let þe sentence euere be hool and open, for þe wordis owen to serue to þe entent and sentence, and ellis þe wordis ben superflu or false.[17]

But while, as we have seen, Jerome did recognize the need for non-literal translation in certain circumstances, he made something of an exception in the case of specifically biblical translation. In fact, in the scriptural situation, he actually advocated the strictest literalism 'so as not to violate the sacred mystery immanent in the very words of scripture'. For Jerome, 'the very order of the words in the Bible is a mystery, and the meaning of scripture is not to be falsified by the linguistic liberties of a translator'.[18] In contrast with the general tenor of the prologue's chapter 15, the Hieronymian ideal of biblical translation is one of close fidelity to the language—and even the syntax—of the source. It is, in fact, a model which Boethius adapted to his project of philosophical translations. As Copeland points out, in Boethian thought:

> It is in the very language of the text that the translator is to find its uncorrupted truth; and any departure from the linguistic directive of the source represents a departure from its substantive directive. Thus to compensate for the inevitable loss of meaning in translation, the margin of difference must be as small as possible.[19]

Predicated on a neo-Platonic understanding of meaning as ideally residing outside the problematic realm of language, in such theories of biblical and philosophical translation, the words themselves are actually heavily freighted with significance. The meaning ('sentence') of a text cannot be divorced from the language ('lettre') in which it is communicated. Such a sacramental, incarnational view of words themselves necessitates a mode of translation which, problematically, allows for very little difference between the source and target languages.

At moments throughout his literary career, Chaucer poses as a translator working to uphold such ideal. Presenting himself as meekly reliant on the authority of his source, he articulates an ostensibly straightforward theory of translation as

---

[17] M. Dove, *The Earliest Advocates of the English Bible—The Texts of the Medieval Debate*, Exeter Medieval Texts and Studies (Exeter, 2010), p. 81/2812–17. All quotations from the Prologue to the Wycliffite Bible are taken from Dove's edition. That the Wycliffites, in a sophisticated hermeneutical manoeuvre, were able to classify 'non verbum pro verbo' translation as a form of literal translation will be discussed later in the book.

[18] Copeland (1991), p. 51 and p. 53.   [19] Copeland (1991), p. 53.

the substitution of one language for another. This, for example, is how he introduces his rendition of the *Canticus Troili* in Book I of *Troilus and Criseyde*:

> And of his song naught only the sentence,
> As writ myn auctour called Lollius,
> But pleinly, save oure tonges difference,
> I dar wel seyn, in al, that Troilus
> Seyde in his song, loo, every word right thus
> As I shal seyn; and whoso list it here,
> Loo, next this vers he may it fynden here.[20] (I, 393–9)

He will not, he says, simply reproduce the 'sentence' of his source, but will replicate 'every word right thus', the 'every word' referring, appropriately, to the terminology of both original and translation. Nothing will be changed in the course of vernacularization.[21] But quite apart from the fact that he is invoking a fictional source, Chaucer's casual dismissal of 'oure tonges difference' as an impediment to 'plein' translation is obviously tongue in cheek. He is, of course, eminently aware of both the pitfalls and the potential inherent in the reality of linguistic difference. And, in common with Cicero et al., he is also alert to the nature of translation as an inventive activity. Roger Ellis' analysis of his manoeuvres is most effective and apt:

> Characteristically, Chaucer presents himself as humbly dependent upon an authoritative original which he is proposing to make more widely available, under correction from the learned, to readers who would otherwise have no access to it. He thus appears to conform to the religious model of translation associated with Sts Jerome and Augustine, one which, in Eagleton's phrase, makes a fetish of the original text . . . But in a number of places he is significantly more radical in his theorisings, and makes common cause, while nowhere acknowledging them, with the . . . Roman authors for whom translation from Greek into Latin was a matter of national pride and self-aggrandizement.[22]

In their *Medieval Literary Theory and Criticism*, Minnis and Scott point out that, in medieval Latin, the word *translatio* (translation) was often taken to be synonymous with *expositio* (interpretation).[23] This Latinate blurring of the boundaries between imitation and invention, inherited from Roman thought, carries through into practices of vernacular translation, where:

> [i]f . . . taken seriously, it provides a justification for understanding vernacular translations not simply as attempts to transfer meaning unchanged from one language to

---

[20] L. D. Benson, *The Riverside Chaucer*, 3rd edn (Oxford, 2008). All Chaucer quotations are taken from *The Riverside*.

[21] For a further instance of Chaucer posing as an unskilled literal translator, see the prologue to *The Second Nun's Tale*: 'This yet preye I yow that reden that I write, / Foryeve me that I do no diligence / ilke storie subtilly to endite, / For bothe have I the wordes and sentence / Of hym that at the seintes reverence / The storie wroot, and folwen hire legende / And pray yow that ye wole my werk amende' (78–84).

[22] R. Ellis, 'Translation', in *A Companion* to Chaucer Blackwell Companions to Literature and Culture, ed. P. Brown (Oxford, 2000), pp. 446–7.

[23] A. J. Minnis and A. B. Scott, *Medieval Literary Theory and Criticism, c. 1100 – c. 1375: The Commentary Tradition*, rev. edn (Oxford, 1991), p. 374.

another but as *readings* of source texts, part of whose purpose may indeed lie in their difference from those texts.[24]

For all his posturing as literal copyist, Chaucer is in no doubt as to the affinities between the activities of translation and commentary. His remarks on his own narration of Troilus and Criseyde's romance offer a compelling indication of this:

> But sooth is, though I kan nat tellen al,
> As kan myn auctour, of his excellence,
> Yet have I seyd, and God toforn, and shal
> In every thyng, al holly his sentence;
> And if that ich, at Loves reverence,
> Have any word in eched for the beste,
> Doth therwithal right as youreselven leste. (III, 1324–30)

Claiming inadequacy to the task of translation, he nonetheless admits, with disarming nonchalance, to having 'in eched' words 'for the beste', the activity of 'eching' involving both addition and improvement. In fact, identifying Chaucer's *Legend of Good Women* and Gower's *Confessio Amantis* as examples of what she calls 'secondary translation', Copeland argues that both authors 'redefine the terms of vernacular translation itself: they use the techniques of exegetical translation to produce, not a supplement to the original, but a vernacular substitute for that original'.[25] Viewed from such a perspective, translation is anything but the straightforward substitution of one language with another, which Chaucer pretends that it is in the previously quoted stanza from book 1 of *Troilus*. It is, in line with the Ciceronian model, a fully fledged appropriation of the source, if not a displacement of its authority.

Copeland's reading of the medieval situation is compelling and she is certainly right in her central claim that:

> [t]he essential paradox of the enterprise of translation as replication through difference, through displacement, substitution, and cultural or canonical appropriation, . . . gain[s] new importance in the Middle Ages.[26]

In this context, one of Chaucer's particularly effective manoeuvres is his querying of the notion that the Latin language is endowed with a uniquely resonant authority. For Chaucer, as for other of his contemporaries, Latin is simply a vernacular tongue, of no greater or lesser weight than any other vernacular. It has no special status as a mythical point of origin. As is well known, such reasoning is articulated with particular clarity in Chaucer's preface to his *Treatise on the Astrolabe*, where he positions 'Englissh', 'Grek', 'Arabien', 'Ebrew', and 'Latyn' on a par in their capacity to communicate scientific fact:

> But natheles suffise to the these trewe conclusions in Englissh as wel as sufficith to these noble clerkes Grekes these same conclusions in Grek; and to Arabiens in Arabik,

---

[24] J. Wogan-Browne et al., *The Idea of the Vernacular: An Anthology of Middle English Literary Theory 1280–1520*, Exeter Medieval Texts and Studies (Exeter, 1999), p. 317.
[25] Copeland (1991), p. 179.   [26] Copeland (1991), p. 36.

and to Jewes in Ebrew, and to Latyn folk in Latyn; whiche Latyn folk had hem first
out of othere diverse langages, and writen hem in her owne tunge, that is to seyn, in
Latyn. And God woot that in alle these langages and in many moo han these conclusions ben suffisantly lerned and taught, and yit by diverse reules; right as diverse pathes
leden diverse folk the righte way to Rome.[27] (28–40)

It is, then, tempting to read Chaucer as inheritor and proponent of the classical
model of translation as contestation. Latin has no special claim to authority and
English translations (and translators) have the right to be considered on an at least
equal footing. In fact, if we read Chaucer's reference, in *The House of Fame*, to
'Englyssh Gaufride' (l. 1470) as an allusion to himself, we have clear grounds for
arguing that he was specifically and deliberately endorsing just such an equality
of authority. In his literary preoccupations, he is one of those 'besy for to bere up
Troye', alongside:

> [. . .] the gret Omer;
> And with him Dares and Tytus
> Before, and eke he Lollius,
> And Guydo eke de Columpnis. (1466–9)

In such a hermeneutic, the vernacular *auctor* accrues to himself the status traditionally associated with Latinity.[28]

However, Copeland's above-quoted association of Chaucer with an apparently
aggressive model of translation as substitution may require some nuancing. He
does not, it seems, attempt to displace the authority of his sources with his vernacular renditions so much as to question the notion that any version of any text
in any language (including Latin) has any definitive claim to authority. To borrow from Roger Ellis' previously cited characterization of Chaucer, he certainly
makes common cause with 'Roman authors for whom translation from Greek
into Latin was a matter of national pride and self-aggrandizement', but nowhere
does he suggest the wholesale displacement of source by translation. 'Englissh
Gaufride' is positioned alongside 'Omer', 'Dares', 'Tytus', and 'Guido' (the mention of Lollius is, presumably, for comic effect) but he does not threaten to topple
them. This modification of Copeland's reading of Chaucer alerts us to the wider
limitations inherent in her competitive model of translation. As Wogan-Browne
et al. point out (and as Copeland herself recognizes), her *Rhetoric, Hermeneutics
and Translation* is 'restricted to texts produced as self-conscious contributions to
high literary culture' and 'the competitiveness inherent in *translatio studii* . . .
focuses the discussions that arise from the model on a narrow range of issues to

---

[27] For a similar recognition of the equivalent status of Latin and other vernaculars, see John
Trevisa's *Dialogue between the Lord and the Clerk on Translation*: '*DOMINUS*: . . . Aristotils bokes and
other bokes also of logik and of philosophy were translatid out of Grue into Latyn. [Also holy writ was
translated out of Ebru into Grue and out of Grue into Latyn], and than out [of] Latyn into Frensshe,
than what hath Englisshe trespassed that hit myght not be translated into Englisshe?' (Wogan-Browne
et al. (1999), p. 133/95–100).
[28] The possibility that 'Englyssh Gaufride' might be identifiable with Chaucer rather than, as conventionally assumed, Geoffrey of Monmouth, was suggested by Helen Cooper. See 'The Four Last
Things in Dante and Chaucer: Ugolino in the House of Rumour', in *NML* 3, ed. D. Lawton, W.
Scase, and R. Copeland (Oxford, 1999), pp. 39–66.

do with language and *prestige*.[29] But 'however much it mattered', status was not invariably the only issue at stake in the activity of translation into Middle English. Late-medieval vernacular writers were, in fact, concerned with a range of other issues, 'having to do not simply with authority but with reading and audience, instruction, pleasure and truth in history and fiction, and theories of meaning'. And this often resulted in a mode of translation which was 'neither derivative nor competitive but pragmatic'.[30] Latin and English were by no means always antagonistically opposed in late-medieval vernacular culture. In a rather different context, Katherine Zieman's *Singing the New Song—Literacy and Liturgy in Late Medieval England* also productively queries a narrative which presents the vernacular, associated with 'an aspiring laity', as 'competing with, and even subverting, Latin as the firmly installed language of privilege'.[31] For Zieman, in late-medieval England, the vernacular is often 'a counterpoint to, not a replacement for, Latin'.[32]

Nonetheless, the continued coexistence of the two languages in contemporary culture, combined with the proliferation of translations from Latin into English, did have the effect of tying 'the theory and practice of vernacular writing permanently to the question of its status in relation to Latin'. In an evocative characterization of the manoeuvres involved in such a situation, Wogan-Browne states that '[i]n annexing Latin's cultural authority, vernacular literatures demonstrate their ability to do anything Latin can do, while marking their difference from Latin; asserting the prestige of Latin texts and *auctores*, they also seek to assimilate that prestige, in an endless shuttling between gestures of deference and gestures of displacement.'[33] This 'shuttling' back and forth is aptly illustrated by *Troilus and Criseyde*'s closing envoy, in which Chaucer asserts ownership of a vernacular work of literary merit while simultaneously bowing to the authority of antecedent texts:

> Go, litel bok, go, litel myn tragedye . . .
> But litel book, no makynyg thow n'envie,
> But subgit be to alle poesye;
> And kis the steppes where as thow seest pace
> Virgile, Ovide, Omer, Lucan, and Stace. (V, 1786–92)

Such a reading of the relative status of the two languages could scarcely be of more relevance to the issues of biblical translation to be explored in this book.

BIBLICAL TRANSLATION AND THE TRANSLATION DEBATE

The inapplicability of the model of displacement to any project of biblical translation has already been noted in this chapter. Middle English scriptural translators

---

[29] Wogan-Browne et al. (1999), p. 321. [30] Wogan-Browne et al. (1999), p. 322.
[31] Zieman, p. ix.
[32] Zieman, p. 151. She is here talking specifically about the role that both Latin and English play in the writings of Chaucer and Langland.
[33] Wogan-Browne et al. (1999), pp. 321–2.

serve, rather than contest, the authority of their divinely inspired source. They tend to vernacularize literally and unidiomatically, and to favour a mode of translation which is basically imitative rather than commentative. [34] Their approach is, according to Copeland, utilitarian and 'counter-rhetorical'. She comments:

> This medieval tradition derives its assumptions from Jerome's precepts about translation of non-scriptural texts, and takes a utilitarian view of translation, seeing it as a form of transparent access to a stable and transmissible set of ideas. [35]

Such a model could certainly explain the resolutely literal translation which we find throughout the *Metrical Psalter*. The earliest of the complete Middle English versions, this rendition has the dubious honour of being an extremely faithful translation in verse, meaning that it relies on somewhat repetitive tag rhymes which are really the only 'fillers' in an otherwise very close vernacularization. As will be discussed, it seems possible that the Metrical translator was indebted to Old English traditions of interlinear glossing, although nothing like this is ever reproduced in the text's manuscript layout. Copeland's 'counter-rhetorical' model is also applicable to Richard Rolle's complete English translation of the psalms, comments on the impenetrability of which are common. As with the *Metrical Psalter*, its close literalism can make it almost impossible to decipher without recourse to the Latin original (or to the more idiomatic translation often embedded in the commentary section) and it too seems to hark back to traditions of Old English glossing. [36]

As is well known, towards the end of the prologue to his *English Psalter*, Rolle provides a somewhat awkward justification of the method and nature of his translation:

> In this werke I seke na straunge ynglis, bot lyghtest and comonest and swilk that is mast lyke til the latyn, swa that thai that knawes noght latyn by the ynglis may com til mony latyn wordis. In the translacioun I folow the lettere als mykyll as I may. And thare I fynd na propire ynglis, I folow the wit of the worde, swa that thai that sall red it thaim thare noght dred errynge. (pp. 4–5) [37]

The claim that '[i]n the translacioun I folow the lettere als mykyll as I may' is unproblematic; Rolle has produced a literal rendition of the psalms. But exhibiting a defensiveness not unusual in his writing, Rolle also seems to pre-empt (or respond to?) criticism by claiming that 'straunge ynglis' has not been his intention. What, however, is 'straunge ynglis' as distinct from 'lyghtest and comonest'? And how do we square his claim to a 'comon[]' vernacular with his apparent admission that he has coined new terms ('thare I fynd na propire ynglis, I folow

---

[34] At a very early stage in *Rhetoric, Hermeneutics and Translation*, Copeland states that '[t]he important question of biblical translation lies outside the scope of this study.' Somewhat later, she also points out that '[b]ecause the patristic position is articulated largely with reference to translation of the Bible and of theological texts, the question of displacement, so much a motive in Roman theory, is naturally ruled out here as an ideal.' Copeland (1991), p. 5 and p. 43.

[35] Copeland (1991), p. 226.

[36] For discussion of Alford's (1995) claim that Rolle is directly indebted to such traditions, see Chapter 3. The pressing question of how these and other *English Psalters* were actually *used* will be addressed later in the book.

[37] All quotations from Rolle's uninterpolated *English Psalter* are taken from Bramley (1884).

the wit of the worde')? His professed goal is that the Psalter should be used as a 'prompt' of sorts, the vernacular translation leading the non-Latinate to a knowledge of the Latin ('thai that knawes noght latyn by the ynglis may com til mony latyn wordis'); we know from the previous chapter that this was common educational practice in the Middle Ages.[38] But he is perfectly aware that the non-idiomatic constructions which this leads him to produce might appear 'straunge' (as in recondite or obscure) to readers, as could the regular vernacular coinages (calques) which he uses in mirroring individual elements of Latin words and which, while they might be 'mast lyke til the latyn', are not necessarily either 'lyght[]' or 'comon[]'.[39]

The unease in this passage of the prologue should not be read, however, as suggesting a lack of sophistication in the planning and execution of Rolle's *English Psalter* (after all, we know him to have been an accomplished Latinist). On the contrary, his explicit reflections on the difficulties of the process of translation arguably demonstrate an erudite attempt to move towards a theory of biblical vernacularization as fundamentally sacramental: so as to preserve the 'substance' of God's Word, the 'accident' of language should be as little changed as possible. Rolle is following in a well-developed, ultimately Hieronymian, tradition of biblical translation. But how, in practice, is such a model of translation to be realized? While the prologue cannot answer this question fully, it does outline some of Rolle's basic principles; first, that he will not permit himself simply to transliterate a Latin word and second, that where possible he will provide 'native equivalents for both elements of compound Latin words, so that the whole translated word exactly duplicates its Latin original'.[40] His goal is not to produce a vernacularization of literary merit but to open the 'garthen closed, wel enseled, paradyse ful of all appils' (p. 3) of the Latin original to the non-Latinate reader. Like the later narrator of Chaucer's *Troilus and Criseyde* (though without the irony) he minimizes the significance of 'oure tonges difference'. In the Rollean hermeneutic, translation is a basically replicative rather than creative activity.

However, it is worth noting that deference for the Vulgate is not the only reason why Rolle translates in the way that he does. For as Ellis has pointed out, and as Wogan-Browne et al. have reiterated, the medieval translator cannot be

---

[38] As Roger Ellis has put it, 'Rolle's translation is not a substitute for the original, which, in any case, he copies out in full, but a means of familiarising the reader with the Latin: almost an interlinear gloss.' R. Ellis, 'The Choices of the Translator in the Late Middle English Period', in *The Medieval Mystical Tradition in England—Papers read at Dartington Hall, July 1982*, ed. M. Glasscoe (Exeter, 1982), p. 29. The claim that Rolle 'copies out [the original] in full' must be queried; although this may have been Rolle's own practice, relatively few extant manuscripts reproduce the Latin in full, as discussed in Chapter 1. See also Nicholas Watson: '[i]t even seems possible that the structure of the English Psalter—the way in which it persists in focussing the reader on Latin verses she may only partially understand—is the product of an undeclared assumption on Rolle's part that canor itself is ideally a Latin experience.' See N. Watson, *Richard Rolle and the Invention of Authority*, Cambridge Studies in Medieval Literature 13 (Cambridge, 1991), pp. 247–8.

[39] For the definition of 'straunge' see *MED* 2(d).

[40] Ellis (1982), p. 29. He goes on to claim that 'if this view is correct, Rolle is here arguing for the translation of abstract and compound words in ways that will not be heard of again until the sixteenth century' (pp. 29–30).

characterized simply as either deferent or defiant. On the contrary, (s)he must have had in mind many 'competing demands' while engaged in the labour of translation:

> Like the author of an original work and the scribe who makes a copy of it, the translator realises his work only in relation to the competing demands of four elements whose collaboration vitally informs it: the demands of his original, his audience, himself, and the tradition within which he is working.[41]

The manner of Rolle's translation not only respects the authority of the original and follows in established tradition, but it also (theoretically at least) serves the needs of an audience wanting, for perhaps none other than practical reasons, to follow the cadences of the Latin Psalter. The monumental demands with which this strategy in fact burdens the reader, as well as the challenges of executing it whilst using a manuscript which contains only vestiges of the Latin, are matters for a later chapter.

The notion of deference to an authoritative original is also (though for different reasons) insufficient to explain the close literalism which characterizes the slightly later Wycliffite EV, in particular the section beginning with the psalms and ending at Baruch 3: 20.[42] In many respects akin to the translation strategy behind Rolle's Psalter, that underpinning the EV of the Wycliffite Bible is one of literal fidelity to the Gallican text, complicated at points by dispute as to the precise wording of the 'true' source. For obvious reasons, it is tempting to view the EV translation as the less accomplished precursor to the more idiomatic LV but on reflection it seems much more likely that its literalism was quite deliberate, not to say idealistic, an important step on the journey towards an English text as—or more—'trew' than that of the Latin original.[43] Commenting on the word-order of EV, Conrad Lindberg suggests that 'the very first turning of the text was a slavish imitation of the Latin, later Englished' and that it began life as a word-for-word interlinear rendition of the Vulgate.[44] Such a supposition is interesting, and although Dove suggests that 'the surviving manuscripts provide no evidence' of such a rendition, the existence of significant variants between extant EV manuscripts could be read as indicating that what we call EV was not in fact the first translation of the Wycliffite Bible but that it was preceded by earlier vernacularizations. Dove does agree, however, that the literalism of EV is deliberate rather than naïve:

> Fully aware of the dissimilarities between Latin and English, the Wycliffite translators must have been highly conscious of the difficulty of producing a literal translation.[45]

---

[41] Ellis (1982), p. 18.

[42] Of EV, Dove comments that the translation from the psalms to Baruch is 'even closer to the Latin than the translation of Genesis to Job'. As she suggests, this may be an indication that 'different parts of the Bible were apportioned to different translators' (2007), p. 139. As has also been pointed out, composite Latin verbs are more precisely rendered in this part of the Bible than elsewhere (see H. Tanabe, 'On Some English Readings in the Vocabulary of the Wycliffite Bible', in *Philologia Anglica: Essays presented to Professor Yoshio Terasawa on the Occasion of his Sixtieth Birthday*, ed. K. Oshitari et al. (Tokyo, 1988)).

[43] Dove (2010), p. 81/2845–6.

[44] C. Lindberg, 'The Alpha and Omega of the Middle English Bible', in *Text and Controversy from Wyclif to Bale—Essays in Honour of Anne Hudson*, Medieval Church Studies 4, ed. H. Barr and A. M. Hutchison (Turnhout, 2005), pp. 191–200, p. 195.

[45] Dove (2007), p. 137. As she states, 'there is no evidence for any earlier stage of the translation than that preserved in the Earlier Version' (p. 138).

Like Rolle, then, the Wycliffites deliberately chose to translate literally. Beyond this, however, the similarities cease: the rationale informing the two translations is quite different. Unlike Rolle's rendition, the Wycliffites' does not seem to have been intended as a crib for those trying to grasp the basics of the Latin language. What, then, was its purpose? Dove suggests that it was provisional from the outset and was not meant to be circulated:

> I argue that the Earlier Version was never intended to be copied as a translation in its own right, but that the translators producing the Later Version lost control of what happened to the Earlier Version in the early 1380s. The Wycliffites who arranged to have the Bible copied in the Earlier Version almost certainly knew that the stylistic and textual work on the translation were still in progress, but they chose to go ahead without waiting for the Later Version to be completed.[46]

But while this is a fascinating conjecture, it would be impossible to prove.[47] Yet, if extant manuscripts of the Wycliffite Bible teach us anything, it is that we cannot always divide the two 'versions' from each other to this extent.[48] For all the idealism lying behind the Wycliffite EV, it and LV bled into each other from a relatively early stage. There is, however, a discernible difference between the imperative driving EV and that driving many of the revisions behind LV, and this is as true—if not truer—of the psalms as it is of any other biblical book.

Whatever their precise purpose, the Wycliffite EV psalms also differ from Rolle's insofar as their literalism is driven by a very particular concern to produce a 'correct', authoritative vernacular text of the Bible. They want, as already pointed out, to create an English text as—or more—'trew' than that of the Latin original. Integral to their realization of this desire is their refusal to regard the Latin language as any more inherently authoritative than any other language. According to chapter 15 of the Prologue to the Wycliffite Bible (a text to which we have referred and will return), Latin is simply another vernacular, no different in status from English:

> And Austin and many mo Latyns expowneden þe Bible for many partis into Latyn, to Latyn men among which þei weren, and Latyn was a comyne langage to her puple aboute Rome and biȝende and on þis half, as Englich is comyn langage to oure puple (83/2914–18)

---

[46] Dove (2007), p. 3. This differs from received wisdom, which would have LV, once complete, superseding EV, already in circulation (see *The Holy Bible, containing the Old and New Testaments, with the Apocryphal Books, in the Earliest English Versions made from the Latin Vulgate by John Wycliffe and his Followers*, ed. J. Forshall and F. Madden, 4 vols (Oxford, 1850), vol. 1, p. xxxii). Dove comments further that 'Forshall and Madden . . . impl[y] that Wyclif and the translators expected the Earlier Version to be copied for the use of English readers until the revised version became available . . . [but] . . . it seems much more likely that they expected that their English Bible would begin to be copied and circulated only when the translation had been corrected and revised.'

[47] It is conceivable that EV was intended originally for a readership of learned individuals with a critical interest in the processes of translation and in the capacity of the vernacular to reproduce the sonorities of biblical Latin. Again, however, this is a conjecture impossible to substantiate.

[48] See, for example, A. Hudson, *The Premature Reformation—Wycliffite Texts and Lollard History* (Oxford, 1988), chapter 5 'Lollard Biblical Scholarship'; Dove (2007), chapter 6 'The Text'.

This being the case, the Vulgate's authority does not derive from the language in which it is written; it too is nothing more or less than a translation:

> Ierom, þat was a Latyn man of birþe, translatide þe Bible boþe out of Ebreu and out of Greek into Latyn (83/2912–14)[49]

Viewed in this light, the Wycliffite psalms might be said to contest, rather than defer to, the authority of their immediate source. While, as Copeland points out and as we have already reiterated, a challenge to the authority of God's Word *per se* is obviously irrelevant to any model of biblical translation, contestation of the authority of the language in which that Word happens to be expressed is not. And as has been widely recognized, in their querying of uncritical deference for Latin, the Wycliffites and Chaucer share common ground. There is much to be gained from viewing the two in conjunction.

The Wycliffite Bible and attitudes towards it should be set not only in the context of Chaucerian and wider 'secular' theorizings of translation but also in that of broad late-medieval controversies surrounding the translation of the scriptures and the use of the vernacular in devotion and pastoral instruction. The role of English in piety and the propriety of English biblical versions had been a frequent topic of discussion from the Anglo-Saxon period onwards, and prompted by the production and dissemination of the Wycliffite Bible, debate on the matter reached something of a peak in the late fourteenth century.[50] As is well known, the 1407 Constitutions of Archbishop Arundel 'inhibited' the circulation of biblical translations produced during and since Wyclif's time.[51] The impact of these Constitutions (promulgated in 1409) has been much debated.[52] For the purposes of our discussion, though, what is most striking about them is their deployment of the name 'Wyclif'. It indicates not only the 'arch-heresiac's' centrality to the fraught consciousness of the late-medieval Church but also the pivotal role which the ecclesiastical establishment perceived him to have played in the Bible translation project. Certainly the scriptures were vernacularized by 'men sympathetic to Wyclif' and it is more than likely that he had a direct and influential hand in the enterprise at its outset.[53] But the mention of his name, whilst polemically powerful, is not entirely helpful, contributing to the misapprehension that advocacy of

---

[49] See the similar arguments rehearsed in John Trevisa's *Dialogue Between a Lord and a Clerk*, prefacing his English translation of Ranulph Higden's *Polychronicon* (1380s): 'holy wryt was translated out of Hebrew ynto Gru and out of Gru into Latyn, and þanne out of Latyn ynto Frensch. Þanne what haþ Englysch trespased þat hyt my3t no3t be translated into Englysch?' (for an edition of Trevisa's *Dialogue*, see J. A. Burrow and T. Turville-Petre, *A Book of Middle English*, 3rd edn (Oxford, 2005). For this quotation see p. 220/115–18).

[50] On the dating of the Wycliffite Bible, Dove (2007) writes 'I think it likely that the project was in the planning stage at the beginning of the 1370s . . . and that work on the translation started before the middle of the decade' (p. 80). She suggests (2010) that the LV was completed *c.* 1390 (p. xix).

[51] See Dove (2010), p. xix where she also points out that this legislation remained in place until 1529.

[52] See, in particular, N. Watson, 'Censorship and Cultural Change in late Medieval England: Vernacular Theology, the Oxford Translation Debate and Arundel's Constitutions of 1409', *Speculum* 70 (1995), 822–64. See also the essays collected in Gillespie and Ghosh, *After Arundel*.

[53] Dove (2010), p. xix.

the English Bible was the sole preserve of the heterodox.[54] In fact, by no means all supporters of biblical vernacularization were Wycliffite.[55] Several English tracts, circulating in the very early fifteenth century, strongly endorse the availability of 'God's law in the people's language' and not all of these can be identified as Wycliffite.[56]

In the context of our discussion, one of the most remarkable aspects of these vernacular tracts is their rebuttal of any notion that English is an inherently 'lesser' language than Latin. As for Chaucer and the Wycliffites, so for the authors of these tracts, Latin is simply one vernacular among many. The so-called *First seiþ Bois*, for example, drawing on the orthodox Richard Ullerston's 1401 Latin defence of vernacular translation, points out that the Vulgate itself is a translation:

> Also seuenti docturis withouten mo byfore þe incarnacioun translatiden þe Bibile into Greek ou3t of Ebrew, and aftur þe ascencioun many translatiden al þe Byble, summe into Greek and summe into Latyne, but seint Ierom translatide it out of Ebrew into Latine, wos translacioun we vsen most (145/63–6)

The author goes on to present 'Latyn' as equivalent to 'Englyssche or . . . Frensche or . . . Duchyssche oþer . . . eny oþer langage after þat þe peple haþ vnderstondyng' (162/54–9). This sense of equivalence is also articulated at the very beginning of the so-called Cambridge Tract VII:

> Siþen þat þe trouþe of God stondiþ not in oo langage moo þan in anoþer, but whoso lyueþ best and techiþ best plesiþ moost God, of what langage þat euere it be, þerfore þe lawe of God written and tau3t in Englisch may edifie þe commen pepel as it doiþ clerkis in Latyn (118/1–4)

and is recalled at the outset of *Pater Noster II*:

> And syþþe þe treuþe of God stondeþ nou3t in one langage more þan in anoþer, bot whoeuere lyueþ best [and]techeþ best pleseþ most God of what langage euer he be, þerfore þis prayere declared in Englysche may edifye þe lewede peple as it doþ clerkes in Latyn' (160/3–6).

The 'treuþe of God' is extra-linguistic; it does not reside in the material words in which it is expressed. Drawing on neo-Platonic theories of meaning, Copeland

---

[54] For an interesting discussion of this issue, see Fiona Somerset's 'Professionalising Translation at the Turn of the Fifteenth Century', in F. Somerset and N. Watson (eds), *The Vulgar Tongue—Medieval and Postmedieval Vernacularity* (Pennsylvania, 2003), pp. 145–57.

[55] The most famous orthodox proponent of biblical translation is Richard Ullerston. On this matter, see A. Hudson, 'The Debate on Bible Translation, Oxford 1401', *EHR* 90 (1975), 1–18.

[56] Dove (2010), p. xix. Dove's volume is a very useful edition of these tracts. She includes texts whose associations with the Wycliffite movement are clear (the Prologue to the Wycliffite Bible, the Prologue to Isaiah and the Prophets, and the Prologues and Epilogue to the Glossed Gospels). But the heterodox associations of many of the other tracts that she edits are much less clear. As Dove also points out, not all of the texts that she edits contain arguments in favour of a complete English Bible in written form; some suggest simply that the gospel should be preached to all people (e.g. Cambridge Tracts III and IV). (All quotations from the vernacular tracts are taken from Dove (2010).)

is right to claim that the proponents of biblical translation are in many senses counter-rhetorical. Yet in the context of Wycliffite thought and in the specific case of the Wycliffite practice in LV, liberation from the imperative of strict fidelity to the syntax and terminology of the immediate source leads to a practice of translation which, if not fully rhetorical in the Ciceronian mode, is at least more supple than verbatim. It is able to accommodate a perception of translation as commentary rather than as straightforward imitation.

As is well known, and as has been pointed out, it is in chapter 15 of the prologue to their Bible that the Wycliffites articulate the beginnings of an ambitious and unprecedented theory of translation into English. The prologue's oft-noted discussion of the differences between inflected and uninflected languages and the difficulties of translating bears witness to a concern with readability. It is generally accepted to be commenting on the specific circumstances of LV's composition and there is no denying that LV is a more accessible text than EV.[57] But it seems unlikely that it states anything that the translators were not aware of when working on EV, when readability was not necessarily the goal, nor need we assume that it was written post-EV and pre-LV.[58] Although it endorses an apparently freer mode of translation than that of EV, in which attention is paid to the differences between inflected and uninflected languages, and although its application gives rise to the more 'user-friendly' LV, it is unlikely that the author would have intended it to be read as condoning a style of translation in which readability takes precedence over fidelity to the source. Translation as commentary is as faithful an activity as translation as imitation. In the context of Wycliffite thought, it is a liberation of divine 'entent', of biblical 'sentense'. The key term here is 'fidelity': to what exactly is the translator expected to be faithful? The author suggests that there is a difference between fidelity to the 'sentense' and to the 'wordis', and privileges the former over the latter:

> [t]he best translating is, out of Latyn into Englisch, to translate aftir þe sentense and not oneli aftir þe wordis, so þat þe sentence be as opin or openere in English as in Latyn[.]

before reminding us that the translator should 'go not fer fro þe lettre'.[59] But in (admittedly inconsistent) Wycliffite thought, fidelity to the 'sentense' does not necessarily result in a less literal translation than does fidelity to the 'lettre'. It produces a version of the Bible as 'literal' as a verbatim vernacularization if the mind of the translator is in a condition of charity and if, by the 'literal', we mean 'that sense

---

[57] In any consideration of the General Prologue to the Wycliffite Bible, it is worth bearing in mind Anne Hudson's caution: 'Important as the General Prologue is for the modern critic, because of its limited dissemination it cannot be regarded as a text that is likely to have been widely influential at the time.' (Hudson (1988), p. 238.)

[58] As Anne Hudson points out, from the fact that none of the copies of the Prologue is attached to unrevised EV texts of the Bible, it is clear that it was written after the process of revising had begun. However, this need not mean that it was written after EV was completed and before LV was begun; as she says of a different moment in the prologue, 'the natural reading of the passage is that it relates to the whole process from the very beginning down to the revised LV' (1988), p. 243.

[59] Dove (2010), p. 81/2812–18.

intended by God in all its "spiritual" fullness'. As Kantik Ghosh has demonstrated, in his own writing Wyclif vacillates between this 'revolutionary concept' of the literal and a second, more traditional understanding of it 'as the surface or historical sense which is the basis for deeper, "mediately elicited" significances'.[60] Something of this equivocation finds its way into the General Prologue's discussion of translation, which veers between viewing 'sentense' and 'lettre' as distinct from, and integral to, each other. Although the author complains that previous translators and interpreters of the psalms have 'taken litil heede to þe lettre but al to þe gostli vndurstonding', it seems that for him the most 'literal' (in the 'revolutionary' sense of the word) mode of translation is that which operates on the basis that the letter and the spirit are mutually informing, if not, ideally, identical.[61]

It is logic such as this which lies behind the more idiomatic and readable LV Bible and which might also be argued to inform the glossing translation found in the mid fourteenth-century *Prose Psalter* as well as the affective style of vernacularization which informs the many abbreviated and paraphrased psalm versions of the late Middle Ages. These are not aggressively Ciceronian texts, but in their recognition that accurate translation can legitimately depart from verbatim reproduction of the source, they have affinities with contemporary notions of literary vernacularization as an 'in eching' of the original. And in their oft-expressed awareness of the provisionality of any language, including Latin, as a vehicle of truth, the late-medieval proponents of biblical translation share common ground with that most eloquent of theorists, Chaucer.

THE CASE OF THE PSALMS

The psalms occupy a particular place in the tradition of Middle English biblical translation. Circulating in various versions prior to the emergence of Wycliffite controversy, they appear to have escaped the worst effects of Arundel's censorship (although the effect that Arundel's censorship actually had more broadly is perpetually under discussion). In fact, Rolle's *English Psalter* is cited approvingly more than once in tracts related to the translation debate. In his aforementioned 1401 *determinacio* in favour of an English Bible, the orthodox Richard Ullerston makes no less than three references to Rolle. First he adds him to his impressive list of precedents for biblical translation, referring to 'Ricard[us] . . . heremita . . . qui totum psalterium transtulit in uulgare' [Richard the hermit who translated the entire Psalter into English].[62] Slightly later he quotes 'Richardus hampole' on

---

[60] K. Ghosh, *The Wycliffite Heresy—Authority and the Interpretation of Texts*, Cambridge Studies in Medieval Literature 45 (Cambridge, 2002), p. 37.

[61] Dove (2010), 58/2015–16. As has been remarked frequently, there is arguably a tension between this insistence on the 'letter' and the Wycliffite foregrounding of the Pauline tenet 'þe lettre sleeþ but þe spirit, þat is, gostli vndurstonding, quykeneþ' (2 Corinthians 3: 6; chapter 12 of the Prologue in Dove (2010), 63/2196–7).

[62] The unedited *determinacio* is in Vienna, Österreichische Nationalbibl. 4133, ff. 195ra–207vb. I am grateful to Anne Hudson for the loan of her transliteration of the text (f. 198va).

Psalm 118: 43 ('And take not thou the word of truth utterly out of my mouth') in support of the gospel in English:

> Ne aufferas de ore meo uerbum ueritatis vsque quamque ubi sic scribit. Nonnulli sunt qui pro deo uolunt sustinere uerbum falsitatis sciencioribus et melioribus credere nolentes similes amicis Iob quia cum deum defferendere intebantur, offendunt tales inquit si occidantur quamuis miracula faciant sunt tamen ut uulgus dicit fetentes martyres. Hec Ricardus.[63]

The fact that this excoriating exegesis originates in Rolle's Latin Psalter rather than in his English rendition is an interesting anomaly in a *determinacio* so fulsome in its praise of Rolle as translator, but given Ullerston's academic credentials (he was a fellow of Queen's College, Oxford from 1391), it is not entirely surprising.[64] The third and last of his approving references to Rolle comes in the conclusion to the treatise, where he cites the hermit as definitive precedent for the 'lawfulness' of biblical translation:

> Sicut licuit Ricardo heremite trium linguarum principalium periciam non habenti transferre psalterium in uulgare, ita licet alijs parem ydoneitatem habentibus & eodem spiritu dei ductis.[65]

Two of these references to Rolle surface again in *First seiþ Bois*. Another early fifteenth-century tract in favour of the English Bible, the majority of *Bois* is a 'translation or paraphrase' of Ullerston's *determinacio*.[66] The translator expands on Ullerston's first citation of Rolle; the 'totum psalterium' vernacularized by the hermit becomes, in the English tract, the 'Sauter wiþ a glose of longe process, and lessouns of Dirige and many oþer tretis, by wiche many Engliche men han ben gretli

---

[63] Ullerston, f. 199ra. [*Take not thou the word of truth utterly from my mouth* where thus he writes. There are some who for God wish to sustain a word of falseness, unwilling to trust more knowledgeable and better men, like the friends of Job because when they contemplated defending God, they offend. Such men, he says, if they were slain, even if they did miracles, they are, as the common people say, stinking martyrs. This is what Richard says.]

[64] At the same point (Psalm 118: 43) the uninterpolated English gloss (in Bramley's edition) reads '[m]any ere rad and dare noght ay say the soth. forthi he prayes til god. that he be nan of thaim. bot that god suffire noght sothfastnes be reft fra him. for life na for ded. for in thi domys. that is, in pynys, thorgh whilke thou chastis, I ouyrhopid. that is, that punyssynge refes me noght hope, bot ekis it ouyre that it was bifore' (p. 416). The gloss in RV is all but identical to that in the uninterpolated text. However, the commentary in Rolle's Latin Psalter reads: 'Nota quod dicit verbum veritatis quia nonnulli pro deo volunt sustinere verbum falsitatis, alijs credere nolentes quamuis melius literalis: hi sensu proprio sunt indurati, et non possunt vinci, sed fugiendi tales. Si occidantur, quamvis miracula faciant, tamen, vt vulgus dicit, sunt foetentes martyres [quia in iudicijs tuis] id est, in flagellis iustorum [super speraui] quod non sunt condignae passiones huius temporis ad futuram gloriam.' Quotation taken from the unpublished PhD thesis of M. L. Porter, *Richard Rolle's Latin Commentary on the Psalms to which is prefaced a Study of Rolle's Life and Works* (Cornell University, 1929). [Note that he says the word of truth because some for God wish to sustain a word of falseness, unwilling to trust others though better lettered: these men are in the proper sense hardened, and cannot be defeated, but such men are to be fled from. If they were killed, even though they did miracles, yet, as the common people says, they are stinking martyrs [because in your judgments] that is, in the whips of just men [I have hoped above] because the passions of this time are not worthy for future glory.]

[65] Ullerston, f. 207v. [Just as Richard the hermit was permitted to translate the psalms into the vernacular, not having knowledge of the three main languages, so others are permitted who have an equal suitability and are led by the same spirit of God.]

[66] Dove (2010), p. xlix.

edified' (p. 146/112–13). But *Bois* retains the second citation (of Rolle on Psalm 118: 43) without alteration, thus providing an English translation of a passage of commentary which is actually derived from Rolle's Latin:

> Þer he seiþ þus: 'þer ben not fewe but many þat wolen sustene a word of falsenes for God, not willing to beleue to konynge and better þan þei ben. Þei ben liche to þe frendes of Iob, þat wiles þei enforsiden hem to defende God þei offendeden greuosly in hym. And þou3 suche ben slayne and don myracles, þei neuerþeles ben stynkyng martirs'. (147/121–6)

Presumably the author was working from a copy of Ullerston's text without independently verifying his quotations. But whatever the reason, the fact remains that the English psalms, and Rolle's *English Psalter* in particular, played a vital role in the polemical writing of those who advocated a vernacular Bible in the late Middle Ages.

Part of the reason for the psalms' centrality to the Bible translation debate lies simply in the fact that the Psalter was generally thought of as the central book of the Bible, a more complete compendium of morality and devotion than any other. Its very particular centrality lay in its versatility: as this volume demonstrates, it was regarded as both a handbook to basic Christian morality and a guidebook for the spiritual sophisticated. In addition, it was—and is—as indicated at the outset of this book, uniquely preoccupied with the role played by the human voice in interactions with the divine. This voice, according to the Psalmist, can be devotional but it can also be polemical and deployed to polemical ends.

It is in the aforementioned early fifteenth-century vernacular tracts endorsing texts of vernacular devotion that the psalms can be seen to function in their most overtly polemical mode. Psalm quotation and exegesis form the backbone of arguments in favour of specifically vernacular spirituality. That which survives in a unique copy in the common-profit book of John Colop and which begins '[t]he holi prophete Dauid seiþ' is, for obvious reasons, particularly noteworthy.[67] Arguing against the monopoly on biblical interpretation held by immoral 'clerkis' and for the availability of the scriptures in a language comprehensible to the many, at its outset *The Holi Prophete Dauid Seiþ* makes dramatic use of a catena of psalm quotations:

> The holi prophete Dauid seiþ, in þe persone of a iust man, 'Lord, how swete ben þi spechis to my chekis', þat is, to myn vndirstondyng and loue, and þe prophete answeriþ and seiþ 'þo ben swettere þan hony to my mowþ'. Eft þe same prophete seiþ, in þe persone of a iust man, 'Lord, I was glad of þine spechis as he þat fyndiþ many spoilis eiþir praies'. Eft þe same prophete seiþ 'þe domes of þe Lord ben trewe and iustified in hemsilf; þo ben more desiderable þan gold and precious stones and swettere þan hony and honeycomb; forwhi þi servant kepiþ þo and moche reward is to kepe hem'. (p. 150/1–8)[68]

---

[67] See Vincent Gillespie's invaluable essay on the common-profit books (Gillespie (1989)). See also W. Scase, 'Reginald Pecock, John Carpenter and John Colop's "Common-Profit" Books: Aspects of Book Ownership and Circulation in Fifteenth-Century London', *MA* 61 (1992), 261–74.

[68] Dove (2010). The psalm quotations are taken from the Wycliffite LV. Notable in this context is Psalm 118: 130. *HPD*'s translation reads 'Þe declaryng of þyne wordis 3yueþ goostli li3t, and 3yueþ

Quoting from Psalm 118: 103 (How sweet are thy words to my palate! more than honey to my mouth), 118: 162 (I will rejoice at thy words, as one that hath found great spoil) and 18: 10–12 (The fear of the Lord is holy, enduring for ever and ever: the judgments of the Lord are true, justified in themselves. More to be desired than gold and many precious stones: and sweeter than honey and the honeycomb. For thy servant keepeth them, and in keeping them there is a great reward), this opening sequence focuses on God's 'spechis', his 'lawe', his 'comaundement', and his 'word'. It goes on to include Psalm 118: 165 (Much peace have they that love thy law, and to them there is no stumbling block), 1: 1 (Blessed is the man who hath not walked in the counsel of the ungodly, nor stood in the way of sinners, nor sat in the chair of pestilence), 118: 105 (Thy word is a lamp to my feet, and a light to my paths), 18: 9 (The justices of the Lord are right, rejoicing hearts: the commandment of the Lord is lightsome, enlightening the eyes), and 118: 130 (The declaration of thy words giveth light: and giveth understanding to little ones). The opening catena then concludes:

> For þise auttorites and siche oþere, sum men of good wille redin besili þe text of holi writ for to kunne it and kepe it in here lyuynge, and teche it to oþere men bi hooli ensample, and for þe staat þat þei stondyn ynne and for þis werk, þei han þe blissyng of God. (p. 150/23–6)[69]

The so-called Cambridge Tract I also deploys the psalms to polemical purpose, highlighting flaws in the logic of those who would prohibit the circulation of the vernacular scriptures:

> Men of holy chirche euery day preien to God not only for hemself but principaly for þe pepel, seynge on þis manere: '*da michi intel[le]ctum et scrutabor legem tuam et custo-diam illam in toto corde me [118: 34]. Da michi intell[e]ctum ut s[c]iam testamonia tua [118: 125]; da michi intell[e]ctum ut vivam [118: 144].*' Lord, seiþ he, 3eue me vnder-stondynge and I schal ransake vp þi lawe and kepe it wiþ al my hert; 3y[f] me vnder-stondynge and I schal kunne þi witnes and þi comaundementis, and so leue wiþouten eende. And siþen þei preien so bisili þat cristyne peple schulde vnderstonde Goddis lawe wu[n]der I haue whi þei ben so looþe to teche Englyshe pepel Goddis lawe in Englische tunge. For wiþouten Englische tunge þe lewed Englische pepel mowen not knowe Goddis lawe. And me merueleþ moche why þei ben so besi to let folke for to vnderstonde Goddis lawe and holy writ. (p. 100/397–408)

If 'men of holy chirche' preach the Word of God, and draw attention to the value of that Word, in a language incomprehensible to the majority of their audience,

---

vndirstondyng to meke men' (p. 150/21–2), echoing the LV translation '[d]eclaring of thi wordis li3tneth; and 3eueth vnderstonding to meke men'. It is the 'meke men' (a translation of the Latin 'parvulis') which is of interest here; by contrast, EV has 'litel childer' and Rolle 'smale'. In its glossing translation, LV is obviously following in well-worn exegetical tradition; in his commentary, Rolle also glosses 'parvulis' as 'meke saules'.

[69] Dove suggests that *The Holi Prophete Dauid* might be by the person responsible for the Prologue to the Wycliffite Bible (Dove (2010), pp. 89–102). For a compelling reading of Lollard psalm usage, see M. P. Kuczynski, 'An Unpublished Lollard Psalm *Catena* in Huntington Library MS 501', *JEBS* 13 (2010), 95–138.

they are occupied in futile, hypocritical activity. They are, in fact, no better than the 'stynkyng martirs' alluded to by the author of *First Seiþ Bois*. By contrast, chapter 15 of the General Prologue to the Wycliffite Bible relies, at its outset, on the authority of the vernacular psalms to bolster its argument that 'þe gospel shal be prechid in al þe world':

> [. . .] Crist seiþ þat þe gospel shal be prechid in al þe world, and Dauiþ seiþ of þe postlis and her prechyng 'þe sown of hem 3ede out into ech lond and þe wordis of hem 3eden out into þe endis of þe world' [18: 5], and eft Dauiþ seiþ 'þe Lord shal telle in þe scripturis of pupils, and of þese princes þat weren in it' [86: 6], þat is, in hooli chirche, and as Ierom seiþ on þat vers 'hooli writ is þe scripture of puplis for it is maad þat alle puplis shulden knowe it'. (p. 80/2777–83)

This foregrounding of the voice of David in polemic advocating an English Bible (or at least some vernacular version of the basics of the faith) should come as no surprise. Voiced by one who meditates on God's law, who receives instruction from God, who speaks to him from the depths of despair and from the heights of joy, and who tells others of his glories, the psalms urgently dramatize the necessity of access to the divine unmediated by any barrier of language.[70] And of all the psalms, it is in 118 (used with the greatest frequency by advocates of the vernacular) that this urgency is most extensively articulated. Given the powerful voice in which this psalm speaks of hunger for God's word ('[m]y soul hath fainted after thy salvation and in thy word I have very much hoped') and of thirst for his commandments ('I opened my mouth and panted because I longed for thy commandments'), its appeal to those arguing for the availability of the scriptures in a comprehensible vernacular is clear.[71]

---

[70] In referring to the psalms as voiced by 'one' I am reading them as they were so often read in the Middle Ages, i.e. as the personal utterance of David.

[71] Psalm 118: 81; 131.

3

The Practice of Translation
Complete Psalters

Whether overtly articulated or not, a range of theoretical positions underpins the English versions of the psalms produced in the late Middle Ages. Preoccupied, as they are, by the importance of maintaining a clear and direct line of communication between God and man, it is not surprising that they feature so forcefully in polemic advocating the translation of the scriptures. It is the task of this chapter and the next to investigate these vernacular psalm versions as manifesting various conceptions of the role of the translator and of his/her translation(s) in practice. It is entirely possible to locate the activity of psalm translation firmly within the wider contemporary context of interest in the status of the vernacular as a language of literary and devotional resonance. This will entail a comparative consideration of the many contemporary English versions, covering complete Psalters in this chapter and paraphrased renditions in the next.

A CHAIN OF TRANSLATION?

In an article published in 1957, Henry Hargreaves spoke of English psalm translations of the later Middle Ages as forming a 'chain'.[1] The article focuses exclusively on the Middle English psalms; it is not Hargreaves' goal to consider the ways in which these texts might be responding to theorizations of translation, nor does he consider them in the context of broader late-medieval interest in the practice of vernacularization. The implication of his 'chain' metaphor is quite specific: the many surviving Middle English psalm versions are linked, deriving from and contributing to each other. It suggests that not only do they share a 'genetic' relationship with the Vulgate Psalter but that, independently of their shared source, they also interact consciously and creatively with each other as translations. Hargreaves' article investigates what he perceives to be one particular link in this 'chain', that between the northern *Metrical Psalter* and Rolle's translation, but several others have been suggested. The 'chain' of translation has also been argued to extend

---

[1] H. Hargreaves, 'The Vocabulary of the Surtees Psalter', *MLQ* 17 (1956), 326–39, p. 326.

beyond the boundaries of the late Middle Ages; continuities with Anglo-Saxon traditions of Psalter glossing have been discerned and it has been argued that the Wycliffite Bible in particular exerted an influence on the 1611 Authorized Version.[2] However, the focus of this chapter and the next is on the Middle English versions, complete and paraphrased, and their possible relationships with each other.[3] Written in the awareness of long-standing and significant scholarship on the Wycliffite translation project and of emerging work on the Rolle text, they do not attempt a detailed analysis of these central Psalters, spending a little more time on the lesser-known versions and paraphrases.[4] Their real contribution to the burgeoning field of late-medieval devotional studies lies in their consideration of continuities and discontinuities. Recalibrating a question posed by Muir in 1935, these two chapters ask, '[w]as there established in the Middle Ages an English tradition for translating the Psalms?'[5]

The revisiting of Muir's question, focusing it on a geographically diverse activity of translation over a space of 150 years, raises methodological issues. Extant psalm translations, both complete and partial, literal and paraphrasing, were composed by different people, for different audiences, at different times, and in different parts of England. They all occupy distinctive positions in the devotional marketplace of the late Middle Ages; some were disseminated very widely, while the circulation of others appears truncated. Any attempt to trace a straightforward line of descent from one to another, if that is what we mean by the words 'chain' and 'tradition', would be flawed. If, however, we understand the terms to imply a nexus of connections in which texts have the freedom to respond to each other critically as well as imitatively, they can be deployed more effectively. In this late-medieval psalmic nexus, differences and discontinuities are found to be as striking as similarities and continuities, and where relationships can be discerned, they are not always those that we might expect.

---

[2] Chapter 15 of the prologue to the Wycliffite Bible cites the Anglo-Saxon examples of Bede and Alfred in bolstering their case for a contemporary English Bible. Note particularly 'kyng Alurede, þat foundide Oxenforde, translatide in his laste daies þe bigynnyng of þe Sauter into Saxoyn, and wolde more if he hadde lyued lengere'. (Dove (2010), 84/2935–9.)

[3] Some consideration of continuities with Old English glossing traditions nonetheless plays a part in this chapter's analysis of the *Metrical Psalter*. For discussion of early modern psalm translation, the reader is referred to (for example) R. Zim, *English Metrical Psalms: Poetry as Praise and Prayer 1535–1601* (Cambridge, 1987), and H. Hamlin, *Psalm Culture and Early Modern English Literature* (Cambridge, 2004).

[4] The most significant work on the Wycliffite translation project is, of course, that of Anne Hudson. More recently, the work of Mary Dove has been illuminating. Although Rolle's *English Psalter* has not been edited since 1888, Anne Hudson's EETS edition of the revised version of the text will do much to further our knowledge and to facilitate future scholarship. The first (containing Hudson's Introduction, Rolle's Prologue, and Psalms 1–34) and second (containing Psalms 35–115) volumes were published by EETS in 2012 (see A. Hudson, *Two Revisions of Rolle's English Psalter Commentary and the Related Canticles* EETS OS 340 and 341 (Oxford, 2012)). The final volume, containing the rest of the Psalter and Canticles, was published in 2014 (EETS OS 343). I am grateful to Anne Hudson for providing me with access to the proofs of Psalms 35–150.

[5] L. Muir, 'The Influence of the Rolle and Wycliffite Psalters upon the Psalter of the Authorised Version', *MLR* 30 (1935), 302–10, p. 302. While Muir's interest is in a tradition extending into the sixteenth and seventeenth centuries, this chapter focuses his question on the thirteenth to fifteenth centuries.

THE SOURCE TEXT AND THE DIFFICULTY
OF PSALM TRANSLATION

For any investigation of these texts and the possible relationships between them to be meaningful, it must be prefaced by consideration of the source to which they were all indebted, the Vulgate 'blueprint' which ultimately lies behind all Middle English psalm translations, diverse as they are. The notion of a Vulgate 'blueprint' might suggest that a single, authoritative text underpins all vernacular renditions of the Psalter. The situation is, however, rather more complex than this since, as is well known, the Latin Psalter survives in four versions. The earliest is the Vetus Latina (Old Latin), translated from the Greek Septuagint, and is followed by the Romanum, also translated from the Septuagint and traditionally associated with Jerome. The third is the Gallicanum, another translation from the Septuagint by Jerome (commonly found in Vulgates), and the last is the Hebraicum, Jerome's final version, which draws on the original Hebrew.[6] In the Middle English period covered by this book, the Psalter that circulated most widely was the Gallican and it is primarily on this version that the three complete English translations of the psalms rely.[7] Yet even here the situation is slightly muddled, making it difficult to talk in terms of discrete 'versions' as sources. Rolle, for example, uses the Gallican with some Old Latin readings as does the *Metrical Psalter*, and the Wycliffite EV and LV Psalters appear on occasion to translate source texts which differ in minor details.[8]

A telling example of the confusion that this intermingling of 'versions' can cause is found in Richard Rolle's vernacular dealings with Psalm 37: 8. In the Old Latin the verse reads 'quia lumbi mei repleti sunt *ignominia* et non est sanitas in carne mea' [for my loins are filled with *ignominy* and there is no health in my flesh] and in the Gallican 'quoniam lumbi mei impleti sunt illusionibus et non est sanitas in carne mea' [for my loins are filled with *illusions*; and there is no health in my flesh]. Although Bramley's edition of Rolle's *English Psalter* prints the Gallican text, the hermit's translation is actually of the Old Latin:

> ffor my lendis ful ere fild of *hethyngis [ignominia]:* and hele is not in my fleysse. (p. 139)[9]

To complicate matters further, Rolle's commentary remarks on the Gallican text while preserving the Old Latin translation:

> My lendes, that is my fleysse, is fild of hethyngis of the deuel. for I syn not anly for my frelte, bot alswa of the fende, that tourmentis my body and trauails my saule in *vayn ymagynaciouns* [illusionibus]: and swa makis he me his hethynge. (p. 139)

---

[6] For an accessible summary of the Latin versions of the Psalter available in the Middle Ages, see C. Sisam and K. Sisam, *The Salisbury Psalter*, EETS OS 242 (Oxford, 1959), pp. 98–104.

[7] For a discussion of the role played by choice in Middle English translations, see Ellis (1982).

[8] For discussion of Rolle's source text, see H. E. A. Allen, *English Writings of Richard Rolle, Hermit of Hampole* (Oxford, 1931), p. 7.

[9] As in previous chapters, all quotations from Rolle's uninterpolated *English Psalter* are taken from Bramley (1884).

The Revised Version of Rolle's Psalter seems to note the problem; it does not replace the Old Latin with the Gallican but does delete the commentary's reference to 'illusionibus', suggesting that the reviser(s) was paying careful and critical attention to the coherence of the relationship between translation and gloss. The earlier *Metrical Psalter* also appears to translate the Old Latin (for mi lendes filled with bismers are, / And hele in mi flesche es na mare') as does the later Wycliffite LV (for my leendis ben fillid with scornyngis). The Wycliffite EV, however, translates the Gallican (for my leendis ben fulfild with deceytis), as does the *Prose Psalter* (for myn baches ben fulfild of illusiouns).[10] The difference is relatively minor, but it does alert us to the variability of the Latin Psalter in the Middle Ages.

The difficulty of locating a stable text of the Psalter is commented on in chapter 15 of the Prologue to the Wycliffite Bible:

> þe Sauter . . . of alle <oure> bookis discordiþ m<oost fro Ebrew, for þe chirche rediþ noȝt þe Sauter bi þe laste translacioun of Ierom, out of Ebreu into Latyn, but anoþere translacioun of oþere men þat hadden myche lasse kunnyng and lasse hoolynesse þan Ierom hadde.[11]

As indicated by this remark, supplemented by another in chapter 11 ('[n]o book in þe elde testament is hardere to vndurstondyng [than the Psalter] to vs Latyns for oure lettre discordiþ myche fro þe Ebreu'), for the Wycliffites the very particular difficulty of understanding and translating the Psalter lies in the fact that it was composed originally in Hebrew, which differs profoundly from Latin.[12] Returning to a point discussed extensively in Chapter 2, they were, like Chaucer and other contemporaries, overtly critical of any simplistic understanding of Latin as a mythical point of origin. According to the above quotation from chapter 15 of the prologue, Jerome's 'laste translacioun' (the Hebraicum) is the only version to engage with this difficulty, yet is regrettably not in common use. While there is no reason to doubt this observation of contemporary practice, the comment is slightly disingenuous since the Wycliffite Psalter itself is not a translation of Jerome's Hebraicum, but of his earlier Gallican version, translated from the Greek, with some variant readings (including, in LV, the 'ignominia' discussed earlier). Remarks in chapter 15 of the prologue suggest that the translators accessed the Hebrew scriptures by means of the writings of earlier commentators:

> And where þe Ebreu, *bi witnesse of Ierom and of Lire and oþere expositours*, discordiþ fro oure Latyn bookis, I haue set in þe margyn bi þe maner of a glose what þe Ebreu haþ, and hou it is vnderstonden in sum place[.][13]

---

[10] For discussion of other occasions on which the Wycliffite EV and LV appear to be translating from different Latin texts of the psalms, see later in this chapter.

[11] Dove (2010), 82/2856–60. For discussion of this point, see Hudson (1988), p. 244. In his *Dialogue*, Trevisa also notes the existence of various translations of the psalms ('Jerom translatede þryes þe Sauter'). He is not, however, commenting on the particular difficulty of psalm translation but on the challenges of translation in general ('Clerkes knoweþ wel ynow þat no synful man doþ so wel þat he ne myȝte do betre, noþer makeþ so good a translacyon þat he ne myȝte make a betre.' Burrow and Turville-Petre, 221/137–41).

[12] Dove (2010), p. 58/2014–15.   [13] Dove (2010), p. 82/2853–5. Italics mine.

and although EV Bibles include the letters of the Hebrew alphabet in Psalm 118, Proverbs 31 and Lamentations, they do so in imitation of Latin Bibles.[14] The prologue states that these marginal glosses on 'what þe Ebru haþ' are most necessary in the case of the Psalter 'because of the great disparities between the text of the Gallican Psalter and the text of the Hebrew Psalter', but as Dove points out, 'there is only a smattering of glosses of this kind in two or three manuscripts'.[15] The most intensively glossed Psalter is that in Bodley 554 (B_554), *c.* 1400. Preserving a text of the LV psalms only, Bodley 554 couches its comments on readings from the Hebrew Psalter 'in the context of very extensive glossing from Lyra, Augustine, and other authorities' as the earlier-quoted remarks in the prologue would lead us to expect.[16] The other two LV manuscripts containing glosses related to those in Bodley 554 are Oxford, BodlL Fairfax 2 (K), and London, Lambeth Palace Library 1033 (V).[17] But in all three, as Dove points out, the glosses relating to the Hebrew Psalter are 'as much concerned with moral and spiritual as with literal interpretation of Psalms'.[18]

Nonetheless, the Wycliffites stand out amongst their fourteenth-century contemporaries in their concern to establish an authoritative biblical text on which to base their vernacular translation; as is stated in their General Prologue, they sought 'to gedere manie elde biblis, and oþere doctours and comyn glosis, and to make o Latyn Bible sumdeel trewe'.[19] As indicated by the comments quoted, it was well recognized that this was a particularly challenging enterprise in the case of the Psalter. By contrast, the reliability of the source text is not an issue on which Rolle reflects explicitly. Remarks in his prologue indicate that he recognizes the Psalter to be the most challenging and comprehensive of biblical books:

> [I]n [this boke] is perfeccioun of dyuyne pagyne. for it contenys all that other bokes draghes langly. that is, the lare of the ald testament. & of the new. (p. 4)

But on only one occasion, in commenting on Psalm 17: 12 ('And he made darkness his covert, his pavilion round about him, dark waters in the clouds of the air'), does he reflect explicitly on the particular difficulties of translating the Bible:

> Her may we see that nan sould be swa hardy to translate or expound haly writ. bot if he felid the haly gast in him. that is makere of haly writ. for soen sall he erre that is noght led with him.[20] (p. 61)

---

[14] Dove (2007), p. 141. Of LV Bibles, only Hereford Cathedral O.VII.I includes the Hebrew letters in Psalm 118.

[15] Dove (2007), p. 160.

[16] Dove (2007), p. 161. Michael Kuczynski is currently completing work on an edition of B_554 entitled *A Glossed Lollard Psalter: MS Bodley 554*. Dove states that 'Bodley 554 may incorporate some or all of the translators' marginal glosses on the Hebrew Psalter, but its text is probably not very close to the glossed Psalms the writer describes in the prologue'. She does not elaborate on this conclusion.

[17] MS Fairfax 2 (described in Dove (2007), pp. 257–9) contains a complete Wycliffite Bible and lectionary in LV. On fol. 385r is the following note: 'þe 3eer of þe lord m.cccc & viiij þis boke was endid', with the fourth 'c' erased. Dove comments that it 'shares many title-glosses and textual glosses (written within the text) in Psalms with B_554V, and has some unique glosses in Ps.; the title-glosses are added later, and sometimes related to the wrong psalm'. Lambeth 1033 contains 2 Chronicles—Baruch in LV and is dateable to *c.* 1410–20 (Dove (2007), p. 293).

[18] Dove (2007), p. 161.   [19] Dove (2010), p. 80/2803–5.

[20] In chapter 15 of the prologue to the Wycliffite Bible we find a similar comment: 'Þerfor a translator haþ greet nede to . . . lyue a cleene liyf and be ful deuoit in preieris and haue not his wit occupied

In his prologue, he is in fact as aware of the perils in store for those who read the translated Psalter as he is for those who have translated it:

> And thare I fynd na propire ynglis I folow the wit of the worde, swa that thai that sall red it thaim thare noght dred errynge. (p. 5)

As discussed in the previous chapter, in attempting to produce English that is 'mast lyke til the latyn', Rolle tries, in a sense, to translate without actually translating.

However, in 'Englishing' the psalms, translators did not invariably rely directly on the Latin of the Gallican version (with variant readings). In two notable instances, we find translators apparently working from French or Anglo-Norman renderings of the Gallican Psalter.[21] The first of these is the *Prose Psalter*, extant in four manuscripts in each of which the English follows, verse by verse, a lightly glossed Latin text which it appears to translate (including glosses) with reasonable accuracy.[22] Despite manuscript appearances, however, what the English translates is not the glossed Gallican but an Anglo-Norman translation of that glossed Gallican.[23] Critical studies of the *Prose Psalter* (of which there have been few) have not always registered its indebtedness to this intermediary despite the fact that its existence was posited by Anna Paues as early as 1902.[24] The only published attempt to identify the source has been that of Ole Reuter (1938), supplemented by Raymond C. St-Jacques (1989), both of whom suggest that a fifteenth-century copy of the lost French source behind the *Prose Psalter* can be found in Bibliothèque nationale de France 6260.[25] Dean and Boulton, however, inadvertently alert us to the

---

aboute worldli þingis, þat þe Hooli Spirit, auctour of wisdom and kunnyng and treuþe, dresse hym in his werk and suffer him not for to erre' (Dove (2010), p. 84/2956–61). The ultimate source of both is, of course, Jerome.

[21] I use the term 'Anglo-Norman' (the same language is also known as 'Insular French' or the 'French of England') to refer to the variety of French spoken and written in post-1066 England until the fourteenth or fifteenth century. In spelling and pronunciation there are some differences from continental French, though the lines are not always easy to draw. Since it seems clear that at least one version of the Psalter which ultimately lies behind the *Prose Psalter* was copied and circulated in England (BL Add 44949), I refer to the prose text's background as Anglo-Norman. Since less is known about the possible source of Eleanor Hull's commentary on the Penitential Psalms, I refer to it as either French or Anglo-Norman.

[22] The fact that the translation varies somewhat between manuscripts will be discussed in Chapter 4. In failing to include the glossed Latin text in his EETS edition of the *Prose Psalter*, Bülbring obscures the interesting work that this Psalter does. In their 2012 edition of the *Prose Psalter*, Black and St-Jacques use Pepys 2498 as their base text, with variants from the other three English manuscripts. In Part 2, they provide the glossed Latin Psalter verses from Pepys 2498 as well as the full Anglo-Norman text from BN 6260. Throughout this chapter, and elsewhere in the book, quotations from the *Prose Psalter* are taken from Bülbring (1891). Comparative reference is made to Black and St-Jacques (2012).

[23] That biblical translations were made from French is not surprising; as Anna Paues pointed out in 1902, the English translator may well have found it 'an easier and more congenial task to turn a familiar French text of the psalms into English than the more difficult Latin psalter' (A. C. Paues, *A Fourteenth-Century English Biblical Version* (Cambridge, 1902), p. lx). The introductory material in this 1902 volume ('printed for private circulation in May 1902 as a thesis for the degree of Phil. Dr. at the university of Upsala') differs from that in Paues' 1904 edition, which does not contain the above comment).

[24] See, for example, S. Dodson, 'The Glosses in "The Earliest Complete English Prose Psalter"', *SE* 12 (1932), 5–26.

[25] R. C. St-Jacques, 'The *Middle English Glossed Prose Psalter* and its French Source', in *Medieval Translators and their Craft* Studies in Medieval Culture 25, ed. J. Beer (Kalamazoo, 1989), pp. 135–54.

existence of an earlier, Anglo-Norman copy of this source closer to home. Listed in their *Anglo-Norman Literature—A Guide to Texts and Manuscripts,* we find the late fourteenth-century Tywardreath Psalter (London, BL Add. 44949), a glossed version of the widely disseminated Oxford Psalter (which Dean and Boulton identify as circulating twice in the same manuscript as the *Metrical Psalter*).[26] The glosses contained in this manuscript have close affinities, and are in fact often identical, with those in BN 6260.[27] It is primarily to the Anglo-Norman Psalter preserved in the English manuscript that I will make comparative reference in this chapter.[28]

Distinct from the *Prose Psalter* by virtue of its later date, its emphasis on the Seven Penitential Psalms alone, and its status as expansive commentary rather than straightforward translation, Eleanor Hull's Seven Psalms nonetheless shares with the earlier text its status as translation from the French (Anglo-Norman?).[29] According to a note recorded in the hand of Richard Fox at the end of the commentary in its sole extant manuscript, 'Dame Alyanore Hulle Transelated [the vij Psalmus] out of Frensche in to Englesche', a claim which is repeated in the same hand at the end of the next text ('Alyanore Hulle drowe out of Frensche alle this before wreten in this lytylle Booke').[30] Although, as with the *Prose Psalter,* the precise source from which Hull was working has not been identified, there is no compelling reason to doubt the accuracy of Fox's remarks. As Barratt states, 'he was an educated lay administrator of St Albans with pronounced literary and theological interests [so] his evidence must be treated with respect, if not regarded as conclusive', and it is highly likely that the French source is the sort of text that Hull might have come across in the monastic library at St Albans.[31] It is of course

St-Jacques' article is, however, a somewhat unsatisfactory abbreviation of a much more substantial paper by Ole Reuter: 'A Study of the French Words in the *Earliest Complete English Prose Psalter*', *Societas Scientiarum Fennica—Commentationes Humanarum Litterarum* 9 (1938), 1–60.

[26] Dean and Bolton, no. 445, pp. 239–41. Several Anglo-Norman Psalters circulated in England from the twelfth century onwards; in addition to the Oxford Psalter (a complete prose translation made *c.* 1115), 'three, possibly four, other distinct translations of the Gallican Psalter' had been made in England prior to 1170 (see G. Rector, 'An Illustrious Vernacular: The Psalter *en romanz* in Twelfth-Century England', in *Language and Culture in Medieval Britain—The French of England c.1100–c.1500*, ed. J. Wogan-Browne et al. (Woodbridge, 2009), pp. 198–206, p. 201.

[27] BN 6260 contains only the Anglo-Norman Psalter, without any trace of the Latin Psalter on which it draws. BL 44949, however, contains the glossed Latin as well as the Anglo-Norman translation, making it more immediately useful as a comparator with the English manuscripts.

[28] In their 2012 edition of the *Prose Psalter,* Black and St-Jacques make no reference to the Tywardreath Psalter.

[29] Although, strictly speaking, discussion of Eleanor Hull's commentary belongs in the next chapter, which deals with paraphrased and abbreviated Psalters, it is considered here, as a response to a French/Anglo-Norman source, in the company of the *Prose Psalter.*

[30] For discussion of these attributions, see A. Barratt, 'Dame Eleanor Hull: A Fifteenth-Century Translator', in Ellis (1989), pp. 87–101. For discussion of Fox's identity, see p. 92.

[31] Barratt (1989), p. 92. For discussion of Hull's possible source see Barratt (1989), pp. 98–101, refined somewhat in the introduction to her edition of the Psalter commentary. A. Barratt, *The Seven Psalms: A Commentary on the Penitential Psalms, translated by Eleanor Hull,* EETS OS 307 (Oxford, 1995), p. xiii: 'the French text from which *The Seven Psalms* was translated has proved impossible to locate, although a number of treatises similar to the putative original are extant'. See also p. 100: 'I suspect that Eleanor found *her* original in the St Albans monastery library rather than acquired it through her contacts at the English court or in France.' As Barratt suggests, the likelihood of a French

possible that the source is a trope, invented by the scribe or by Hull herself so as to create the impression of an appropriate distance between the female locutor and her scriptural material.[32] But this seems to be an unnecessarily suspicious reading of Eleanor Hull, buying into a tendency to underestimate the skills and education of women in the late Middle Ages. And if Hull were going to invent a source text, why did she not invent a Latin one? After all, as Barratt points out, 'claims of a French source . . . would add no particular lustre to a biblical commentary, a genre for which French was no more the 'prestige dialect' than English'.[33]

These translations are of particular interest because they preserve suggestions that French/Anglo-Norman interactions with the Bible could differ somewhat from English. The elegance with which Eleanor Hull's translated commentary manages to combine attention to the grammar and 'lettre' of the Latin original with a remarkably fluent vernacularization of the psalms is unmatched elsewhere in Middle English devotional writing. And while the tone of the *Prose Psalter* is somewhat stilted, it too provides a more idiomatic translation than that of its contemporary Rolle or its successor, the Wycliffite EV Psalter. That the Anglo-Norman (and therefore the English) is a translation of a glossed Psalter might also be read as suggesting a differently nuanced attitude to the text of the Bible. Although, as later discussion will indicate, the glosses are uncontentious and can, for the most part, be matched in traditions of psalm exegesis, their inclusion in the body of the text and its translation is striking. Rolle's Psalter is rigorous in its division of text from glossing commentary and Wycliffite theory at least insists on the importance of preserving the unglossed 'naked' text of scripture.[34] The fact that the Anglo-Norman Psalter, its Latin source, and all manuscripts containing its English translation should include the gloss in the main body of the text is striking, and contributes to a sense that in the late Middle Ages, biblical translation into French/Anglo-Norman was less fraught with anxiety than was translation into English.

THE *METRICAL PSALTER*

Turning from questions of sources and origins, and taking a step back from the highly charged atmosphere of the later fourteenth century, we begin our exploration of the practice of Middle English psalm translation by looking at the earliest of the complete versions—the northern *Metrical Psalter*, dateable to the very early

source is compounded by the fact that 'there is a Gallic tinge to [Hull's] vocabulary and orthography' (1989), p. 94.

[32] Note the similar arguments put forward by Lynn Staley in reference to Margery Kempe. See L. Staley, *Margery Kempe's Dissenting Fictions* (Pennsylvania, 1994).

[33] Barratt (1989), p. 93.

[34] In the introduction to her edition of the Wycliffite RV of Rolle's *English Psalter*, Anne Hudson points out that manuscripts containing the interpolated text tend to be more rigorous in their division of text, translation, and commentary than those containing the uninterpolated. See Hudson, vol. 1 (2012), p. xxix. That Wycliffite *practice* somewhat problematizes this distinction will be discussed later.

fourteenth century.[35] As indicated in Chapter 2, the anonymous translator of this text follows in a tradition of closely literal psalm vernacularization. At no point, however, does he reflect explicitly on his practice of translation: none of the extant manuscripts preserves a prologue, like that of Rolle, or the Wycliffite chapter 15, in which a theoretical model is outlined. Nonetheless, the text is a consistently verbatim rendition of the Latin, and it is the *Metrical Psalter*'s remarkable literality, combined with its metricality (to which we will return), which makes his text unique among complete Middle English psalm translations. The translator goes to great lengths in his attempts to preserve the word order of the Gallican text and, anticipating the later Rolle and Wycliffite EV Psalters, makes extensive use of calques in an effort to mirror the morphology of his Latin original. Examples of both techniques can be found throughout the Psalter, but taking an illustrative instance from the second of the Penitential Psalms, Psalm 37: 6 ('putruerunt et corruptae sunt cicatrices meae a facie insipientiae meae' [my sores are putrefied and corrupted because of my foolishness]) becomes:

> Stanke and roten mine erres ere ma,
> Fra face of mine vnwisdome swa. (p. 169)[36]

In preserving the verb–subject syntax of the Latin, the translator has made little concession to the differences between an inflected and uninflected language. Even Rolle's characteristically close rendition, in admitting the clarifying third-person plural pronoun as well as the direct object, sounds idiomatic by comparison:

> Thai rotid and thai ere brokyn, myn erres: fra the face of myn vnwit. (p. 138)

Reversing the verb–subject order of the Latin, the translation in the Wycliffite EV ('[m]yne woundis stunken, and ben roten; fro the face of myn vnwisdam' (p. 774)) is also more accessible.[37] They are all alike, however, in their rendition of the Latin

---

[35] Although Stevenson's 1843–4 Surtees Society edition is the earliest, this chapter uses that by Horstmann since it has Vespasian D.vii as its base text, but contains variant readings from the Egerton and Harley manuscripts. (See Horstmann with a new preface by Anne Clark Bartlett (1999).) When I refer to the *Metrical Psalter* I am referring to the text as contained in Vespasian and as appears in Horstmann (1999), although footnotes point out interesting and important variants from the other five manuscripts.

[36] The word-order is the same in Egerton although the rhyme is different ('Stanke & wemmed min eires are þai / Fra face of mine wisdom *(sic)* ai.') In Harley, the word-order has become more idiomatic ('Mine erres stanc and þai ram / Fra face of mine unwisdam'). CCCC 278 reads 'Stanke an vemmed are mine eres rom / Of þe face of mine unwisdom' (f. 22v). Bodley 425 has 'min ille eres stanc and broken þar þai / fro face of mine unwisdam ai' and Bodley 921 'mine ille eres stanc and broke are þai / ffro face of mine unwisdome ai.'

[37] A similar observation could be made of Psalm 101: 4 ('quia defecerunt sicut fumus dies mei et ossa mea sicut gremium aruerunt' [For my days are vanished like smoke: and my bones are grown dry like fuel for the fire]) which, in the *Metrical Psalter*, reads: 'For waned als reke mi daies swa, / And mi banes as krawkan dried þa' (p. 233). By contrast, Rolle reverses the Gallican's verb–object word-order in the first clause, although he retains the Latinate syntax of the second ('Ffor my dayes failyd as reke: and my banys as kraghan dryid' (p. 352)). Syntactically, EV is very similar ('For my daȝis han failed as smoke; and my bones as croote han dried'). A similar pattern can also be observed, for example, in the *Metrical* translation of Psalm 101: 16 ('et timebunt gentes nomen Domini et omnes reges terrae gloriam tuam' [And the Gentiles shall fear thy name, O Lord, and all the kings of the earth thy glory]), which reads 'And drede sal genge, lauerd, þi name þat is, / And alle kinges of erthe þi blis' (p. 233).

prefix 'in-' as 'vn-' ('insipientia' is 'vnwisdome' in the *Metrical* and EV, 'vnwit' in Rolle).[38] The same calquing technique can also be seen, for example, in the metrical translation of Psalm 85: 11 ('Deduc me Domine in via tua et *ingrediar* in veritate tua. Laetetur cor meum ut timeat nomen tuum' [Conduct me, O Lord, in thy way, and I will walk in thy truth. Let my heart rejoice that it may fear thy name]):

> Lede me, lauerd, in þi wai þat esse,
> And I sal *inga* in þi sothnesse;
> Euer faine mote mi herte,
> Swa þate ite drede þi name in querte. (p. 219)

It is also found in Rolle's version ('Lede me lord in thi way, that I *inga* in thi sothfastnes: fayn be my hert that it drede thi name' (p. 312)). Both translations are also close renditions of the Latin. At this point EV does not use the calque ('Leed mee thenes, Lord, in thi weie, and I shal *gon in* thi treuthe; glad myn herte, that it drede thi name'), although it is similarly faithful to the Latin word-order. In fact, 'inga' is not a form of the verb that EV ever uses, preferring the simple verb with following preposition, 'go in' or, less commonly, 'entire', a translation which, on occasion, Rolle prefers to 'inga'.[39] It is, however, used consistently in the *Metrical Psalter*, which is remarkably creative in its attempts to mirror individual elements of Latin words.[40]

In the examples cited, it is notable that the only departures from close reproduction of Vulgate word-order and terminology occur when the translator needs to create a rhyme. Apparently anxious to remove nothing from the Latin original, on such occasions the translator tends to 'pad' the text with additional words.[41] In the vast majority of cases, this 'padding' does nothing to alter the meaning, and little to alter the emphasis, of the original. Psalm 37: 6's 'ma'/'swa' is a good example;

Rolle, however, reads 'And genge sall drede thi name, and all kyngis of erth thi ioy' (p. 354) (cf. EV 'And Jentilis shul dreden thi name, Lord; and alle kingis of erthe thi glorie').

[38] All quotations from the *Wycliffite Bible* in this chapter and throughout the book are taken from Forshall and Madden.

[39] Although the rhyme is different in Egerton ('ai'/'dai'), in Egerton, Harley, and CCCC 278, 'inga/ingo' remains as a translation of 'introibo'. Bodley 425 reads 'lede me louerd in wai þine / And þi soghnes is sal go ine / ffaine mot mi hert with in me / so þat hit drede þe name of þe' and Bodley 921 'lede me louerd in wai þine / and in þi sothnes i sal go inne / faine mote mi hert with in me / so þat hit drede þe name of þe'.

[40] A good example can be seen in the translation of Psalm 143: 3 ('Domine quid est homo quia *innotuisti* ei aut filius hominis quia reputas eum' [Lord, what is man, that thou art made known to him? Or the son of man, that thou makest account of him?]). The *Metrical Psalter* very precisely reproduces the elements of 'innotuisti' as 'inknew'. Rolle, by contrast, uses 'made knawyn', as does EV. However, the translator (or scribes) evidently had trouble with the translation of 'in'; at the same point, CCCC 278 has '*ne*kneu him', Egerton '*ne* knewe hym', and Bodley 425 '*ne*knewist him'. Additionally, in Psalm 78: 10, the *Metrical* translator erroneously translates (or the scribe erroneously copies) '*in*notescat' [made known] as '*vn*knawen' (Rolle has 'be knawn' while the EV has '*ful* knawen', the 'ful' functioning as a translation of 'in'). This error appears in all manuscripts.

[41] I am grateful to Ralph Hanna for pointing out the similarity between the *Metrical Psalter*'s 'padding' technique and that of *The Destruction of Troy* where second half-lines are customarily 'fillers' (for discussion, see D. A. Lawton, '*The Destruction of Troy* as translation from Latin Prose: Aspects of Form and Style', *SN* 52 (1980), 259–70). This is, he suggests, 'provocative' since despite *The Destruction of Troy*'s later date, it was composed in Whalley, just over the Lancashire border from the extreme west of Yorkshire, where LALME locates the *Metrical Psalter* manuscripts that it maps.

although neither adverb originates in the Vulgate, neither affects significantly our interpretation of the verse. In fact, 'swa' is one of the most frequently used tags in the *Metrical Psalter*, rhyming with a succession of easy monosyllables ('þa', 'ma', 'are', 'wa', '(in)ga', 'twa', 'fra', etc.). And by and large, the *Psalter*'s padding is of this sort; formulaic, inevitably repetitive, and often reliant on the recycling of limited groups of conjunctions, verbs, adverbs, adjectives, and pronouns (e.g. 'soþli '/'forþi'/'witerli'/' . . . I'; 'al'/'wiþ-al'; 'þai'/'ai'/'dai'/'wai'/'awai'; 'me'/'be'/'he'/'se'; 'nou'/'þou'; 'mine'/'þine'; 'þus'/'us'; 'isse'/'hisse'/'blisse'/'þisse', etc.).[42] Less frequently, it relies on formulaic phrases to facilitate rhyme; 'þe wilde and tame' makes a somewhat random appearance in the rendition of Psalm 117: 25–6 ('O Domine salvum me fac, o Domine bene prosperare. Benedictus qui venturus in nomine Domini' [O Lord, save me, O Lord, give good success. Blessed be he that cometh in the name of the Lord]):

> A lauerd, saufe make þou me;
> A lauerd, in querte to be.
> Blissed be, þe wilde and tame,
> Whilke þat comes in lauerdes name. (p. 251)[43]

And rather less unexpectedly, 'dai and night' and 'night and daie' are used, respectively, once (103: 18) and twice (26: 11; 105: 48), to facilitate rhyme. While such formulae are not sanctioned by the original, the crucial point is that they take nothing from it, whilst adding little of significance to it. In fact, it is difficult to see what role these formulaic rhymes play, beyond their probable function as aids to memorization.

On other occasions, though, the impact of the padding is stronger. This is often the case when the translator uses nouns as rhymes; unlike the conjunctions, pronouns, and many of the verbs, adverbs, and adjectives that he uses and which clarify or intensify that which is already in the text, the nouns introduce a concrete or, more usually, abstract element which is not found in the original. Such is the case with Psalm 85: 11's rhyme on 'herte'/'querte', quoted above and repeated below:

> Euer faine mote mi herte,
> Swa þate ite drede þi name in querte. (p. 219)

While 'herte' is obviously a translation of 'cor', 'querte' (whose meanings include 'spiritual well-being') is an addition and softens the impact of the fear of which the

---

[42] On some fortunate occasions, the translation fulfils the dual demands of literality and rhyme without resorting to tags. See, for example, Psalm 50: 17 ('*labia mea* aperies et Domine os meum adnuntiabit *laudem tuam*' [O Lord, thou wilt open my lips: and my mouth shall declare thy praise]), which reads 'Lauerd, þou salte open *lippes mine* / And mi mouth sal schewe *lof þine*' (p. 183). The translator retains the noun–possessive pronoun order of the Vulgate while also rhyming (at the same moment, Rolle reads 'Lord thou sall oppyn my lippis, and my mouth sall shew thi louynge' (p. 187) and EV 'Lord, my lippis thou shalt opene; and my mouth shal beforn telle thi preising'). In fact, one suspects that the demands of rhyme contributed more to the translator's decision than did the imperative to remain close to the Vulgate; after all, 'Lord, þou shalt opene . . .' is an idiomatic rearrangement.

[43] 'þe wilde and tame' also appears as padding in Egerton, Harley, and CCCC 278. It does not appear in Bodley 425 ('Blissed be als so þe same / whilk þat comes in godes name') or 921 ('Blissed be als so þe same / whilk þat comes in loudes name').

Vulgate speaks.[44] My heart will not simply 'drede þi name' as in Rolle and the EV's verbatim rendition, but it will 'drede þi name *in querte*'.[45] Some adverbs operate in a similar way; a case in point is 'inwardeli' which is used as a rhyme six times and which, on each occasion, 'pads' the Vulgate original. Inevitably given its meaning (internally, intensely), its repeated use emphasizes the intimate nature of the relationship between psalmist/speaker and God, and it is deployed for the most part in the evocation of personal prayer:

> Life ofe lauerd asked I,
> Þat sal I seke *inwardeli*:
> Þat [i] wone hous ofe lauerd ine
> Alle þe daies ofe life mine (Psalm 26: 4) (p. 157) [46]

Of course, it could be that the translator is simply looking for a rhyme with 'I' and 'inwardli' is as suitable as any; he could have used 'sothli', 'forþi', or 'witterli' just as easily, as he does elsewhere. But he does not, and neither does he ever use the contrary rhyme 'outewardli' (openly, publicly), although it would serve the same metrical purpose. He seems focused on the personal and the individual, and, with that in mind, it is interesting that Vespasian D.vii, the one manuscript which contains all six 'inwardeli' rhymes, stands out among the *Metrical* manuscripts as obviously intended for personal, private use.[47]

Such instances of arguably thoughtful rhyme have, however, been overlooked in assessments of the aesthetic qualities of the *Metrical Psalter*. Henry Hargreaves, for example, states that 'the literary value of the translation is slight' and that 'the translator is content to turn the Latin of the Vulgate word for word into English'. He concludes:

> [T]he result is sometimes incomprehensible without the help of the original, and always unnatural and stilted; nor is it improved by his reliance upon a continual succession of rhyming tags—there are, indeed, many psalms in which every rhyme depends on their use.[48]

---

[44] 'Querte' (n) can also be used to refer to general or physical well-being as well as to a sense of ease or peace (see *MED*).

[45] 'Querte' is used as a rhyme twenty-three times in the *Metrical Psalter*. On twenty-two occasions, it rhymes with 'herte' and once (Psalm 88: 27) with 'erte'. It appears only once in a non-rhyming position when in Psalm 117: 25 it translates the Vulgate's 'bene prosperare' [give good success] (quoted above). It does not appear as frequently in other manuscripts, which all rhyme differently at this point; see Egerton (In þi sothnes, faine mot hert mine / So þat it drede ai name þine), Harley (Faine sal mi hert þe same / Swa þat it ai drede þi name'), and CCCC 278, f. 53r ('Faine mot mi hert niht and dai / So þat it drede þi name ai'). At the same moment the two Bodley manuscripts rhyme on 'me'/'þe', although they use a 'hert'/'quert' rhyme in the next couplet.

[46] See also its use in Psalm 4: 2; 28: 2; 70: 14; 133: 2. The only occasion on which it jars is when it is used in Psalm 47: 10 ('We onfanged, god, þi merci / In mid of þi kirke inwardeli' (see p. 179)). The conjunction of 'we' and 'inwardli', while potentially plausible, is awkward in its collision of the communal and the private, though it perhaps indicates the fluid boundary between public liturgical celebration and personal devotional practice.

[47] Egerton and Harley have different rhymes in Psalm 4: 2 and 26: 7. Harley's is different in 70: 14, and Egerton's in 47: 10, 28: 2, and 133: 2. Neither Bodley 425 nor 921 has the 'inwardli' rhyme in Psalm 26: 7. It does, however, appear at Psalm 47: 10 and 70: 14.

[48] H. Hargreaves, 'The Vocabulary of the Surtees Psalter', *MLQ* 17 (1956), 326–39, p. 326.

Certainly, as our discussion has demonstrated, most of the endless tags are pain-ful, and equally certainly, the sense of the translation is often difficult to grasp. But to say that 'the translator is content to turn the Latin of the Vulgate word for word into English' is misleading, suggesting that little effort was expended in the production of the Psalter. On the contrary, the labour must have been intense, and the challenges of producing a vernacularization both rhyming *and* literal cannot be overestimated. Hargreaves' comment suggests further that the reason for the literality is that the translator was unambitious, 'content' to produce a virtually unreadable text. Certainly, as Everett pointed out, he was not an accomplished Latinist (his knowledge of Latin was 'clearly inferior to Rolle's') and it is possible that a stilted, verbatim reproduction was all that he could manage.[49] However, neither Hargreaves nor Everett takes account of the very real probability that the translator was deliberately following in a tradition of verbatim, quasi-sacramental, psalm translation. Combining this with the translator's faithful labouring over the rhyme, what we have in the *Metrical Psalter* is, arguably, a remarkably ambitious text. While, as pointed out previously, we have no evidence that the translator worked with the theoretical underpinnings of Rolle, who states that his translation is literal so as to facilitate its use as a crib, or of the translators of the Wycliffite Bible, who were concerned to produce as authoritative and accurate a vernacular text as possible, it may well have been that he intended his *English Psalter* to be used in conjunction with its Latin source. In such a situation, close reproduction of word-order and careful mirroring of terminology would be advantageous. And as is suggested by its manuscript context, the *Metrical Psalter* was indeed used in just such a way.

Literary considerations aside, however, one must agree with Hargreaves' asser-tion that 'the vocabulary of the text is of considerable interest'.[50] In his discussion of this matter, Hargreaves isolates three areas of particular significance, some of which are more important than others. For example, he cites as one 'the inven-tion by the translator of new words, formed from existing English elements, to translate Latin words for which he knew no native equivalent'.[51] Among such new formations he lists existing words with added suffixes and prefixes, and comments that 'sometimes it would appear that the author is able to form a new word by translating literally the various elements of any compound word'.[52] But as this chapter illustrates, such calquing is a feature of Middle English biblical transla-tion and, Ralph Hanna argues, of late-medieval vernacularization in general.[53]

---

[49] D. Everett, 'The Middle English Prose Psalter of Richard Rolle of Hampole, II', *MLR* 17 (1922), 337–50, p. 344 [1922b]. As Everett points out, where a Latin word is capable of more than one trans-lation, he sometimes chooses the wrong one, and he frequently mistranslates verb forms. He is not unusual in this, but his mistranslations are generally different from those of Rolle, whom she describes as 'the greater scholar' (p. 350). This article is one in a series of three published by Dorothy Everett; see also *MLR* 17 (1922), 217–27 [1922a] and *MLR* 18 (1923), 381–93.

[50] Hargreaves (1956), p. 326.   [51] Hargreaves (1956), p. 327.

[52] Hargreaves (1956), pp. 335–8, p. 337.

[53] See R. Hanna, 'The Difficulty of Ricardian Prose Translation: the Case of the Lollards', *MLQ* 51 (1990), 319–40. Hargreaves' argument is also based on a lack of evidence of local usage, as will be discussed.

Although the metrical translator may be particularly assiduous in this area, his predilection is by no means unusual. Hargreaves' second feature of interest ('the tendency to use native words other than those found in the Old English Psalters to render Latin words which all other Middle English Psalters translate by Romance words—apparently a deliberate avoidance of Romance words') is also problematic, but it is an area to which I will return.[54] For now, our focus is on what Hargreaves, and Everett before him, identifies as the Psalter's 'resemblances to the Old English glossed psalters'.[55]

Hargreaves argues that the *Metrical Psalter* draws directly on Old English glosses, while Everett suggests that the debt is likely to be to a 'partially modernised' text, 'an early Middle English (Northern) interlinear gloss'.[56] Both of these theories are problematic; while it is not impossible that a translator working in the mid to late thirteenth century could read and understand Old English, it should not be assumed. And we have no extant 'partially modernised' Old English Psalters with which to corroborate Everett's suggestion. The extraordinary twelfth-century Eadwine Psalter (Cambridge, Trinity College R.17.1), in which an interlinear Old English gloss accompanies a Roman Psalter, is probably the latest of the thirteen Anglo-Saxon examples and is often described as 'a Middle English corruption of an Old English gloss'.[57] But its 'orthographical and phonological peculiarities' make it unreliable as a comparator with the *Metrical* text and it is, in addition, a Psalter of southern origin while the *Metrical* is northern. In fact, in looking for evidence of an association between Old English glosses and the early Middle English metrical translation, we repeatedly face the same problem; apart from the earliest Old English Psalter, Vespasian A. i, which is Mercian, the origins of all the others are widely regarded as southern.[58] It is noteworthy, then, that despite these limitations, close analysis of the vocabulary of the *Metrical Psalter* still reveals it to have affinities with extant traditions of Old English glossing, although not always those

---

[54] Hargreaves (1956), p. 327. Everett (1922b) cites evidence from the following *Old English Psalters*: Vespasian, Stowe, Eadwine, and Cambridge. To these Hargreaves adds Regius. I have the advantage of *The Complete Corpus of Old English*, providing me with access to an increased amount of material. See also P. Pulsiano, *Old English Glossed Psalters—Psalms 1–50*, Toronto Old English Series 11 (Toronto, 2001) in which he states '[s]ome forty psalters and fragments of psalters survive from Anglo-Saxon England. Of these, eleven contain interlinear glossing in Old English, one is partially glossed, two contain scattered glosses, two are binding straps from the same manuscript and one contains King Alfred's prose translation of psalms 1–50 and a poetic translation of psalms 51–100.' The thirteen more or less complete Old English glossed Psalters are: Vespasian, Junius, Cambridge, Regius, Eadwine, Stowe/Spelman, Vitellius, Tiberius, Lambeth, Arundel, Salisbury, Bosworth, and Blickling/Morgan. Of these, seven gloss the Romanum text and six the Gallican (Eadwine is a triple Psalter in Latin, Anglo-Norman, and Old English. The Old English glosses the Romanum, the Anglo-Norman the Hebraic, and the Latin glosses the Gallican).

[55] Hargreaves (1956), p. 327. See also Dorothy Everett's 3 *MLR* articles. In the second of these, she discusses possible relationships between Rolle, the *Metrical Psalter*, and earlier English psalm glosses.

[56] Everett (1922b), p. 347, p. 350. Both Everett and Hargreaves are inspired by Horstmann's similar assertion.

[57] P. P. O'Neill, 'The English Version', in *The Eadwine Psalter—Text, Image and Monastic Culture in Twelfth-Century Canterbury*, ed. M. Gibson, T. A. Heslop, and R. W. Pfaff (London and Philadelphia, 1992), chapter 6, p. 123.

[58] I am grateful to Malcolm Godden for his advice on this point.

asserted by Everett and Hargreaves.[59] And it is the cumulative effect of these affinities which is most striking.

Reading the *Metrical Psalter* in the light of evidence provided by Old English Psalters, perhaps the most arresting links are those involving compound words. For example, in translating Psalm 89: 9 ('quoniam omnes dies nostri defecerunt in ira tua defecimus anni nostri sicut aranea meditabantur' [for all our days are spent; and in thy wrath we have fainted away. Our years shall be considered as a spider]), the metrical text reads:

> Oure yheres til vs ere ai,
>   Als spinnandweb thoght þai;
>   Daies ofe oure yheres in þa
>   Sexti yhere and ten als-swa (p. 224)

What is striking here is the word 'spinnandweb' (aranea), unattested elsewhere in Middle English and used only once in the *Metrical Psalter* (in Psalm 38: 12, 'irain' translates 'aranea'). It is possible that this is related to the Old English kenning 'gangewæfre/wæfregange' meaning 'weaver as he goes', which is used in the Vespasian (gongeweafran), Vitellius (gangewefram), Cambridge (gangewæfre), Junius (gongewefran), and Arundel (gangenwefram) Psalters and elsewhere.[60] While neither of the pairs of elements is synonymous, both the Old and the Middle English use a compound word to describe the spider in terms of its actions. And the use of the compound in Vespasian D.vii is not wholly idiosyncratic; although the Egerton and Harley manuscripts of the *Metrical Psalter* have 'irain' in place of 'spinnandweb', it is echoed in Corpus Christi:

> Oure yheres als spinnan web þoht are here (f. 56r)

while the two Bodley manuscripts have 'wanranweb'. The metrical translations of Psalm 86: 1 ('Fundamenta eius in montibus sanctis' [the foundations thereof are in the holy mountains]):

> Groundewalles his in hali hilles;
> Lauerd he loues, als his wille es,
> Yhates of Syon, wele mare
> Ouer alle teldes þat Iacobes ware. (p. 219)

and 136: 7 ('memor esto Domine filiorum Edom diem Hierusalem qui dicunt exinanite usque ad fundamentum in ea' [remember, O Lord, the children of Edom in the day of Jerusalem, who say: Rase it, rase it, even to the foundation thereof]):

> Mine, lauerd, ofe Edom sones, þat tem,
> In daie ofe Ierusalem,
> Þat saies: "lesses, lesses yhite,
> Vnto þe grondstaþelnes in ite!" (p. 264)

---

[59] An exhaustive analysis of these affinities would fill a book, and may deserve to do so. For now, we must content ourselves with selected highlights.

[60] Other translations in the Old English Psalters include 'attercoppan', 'ryngan', 'ceosol', and 'ætterloppan'. See Pulsiano, *Old English Glossed Psalters—Psalms 1–50*, Toronto Old English Series 11 (Toronto, 2001), p. 526.

are similarly noteworthy. In the first, 'fundamenta' becomes 'groundewalles' and in the second, 'fundamentum' becomes 'grondestaþelnes'.[61] As with 'spinnandweb', these compounds appear to be unattested elsewhere in Middle English, but certainly hark back to Old English usage. 'Grundwealles' features as a translation of 'fundamenta' in the Cambridge, Arundel, and Lambeth Psalters, and in the last of these, 'fundamentum' is translated as both 'grundweal' and 'staðolfæstnunga'.[62] Other Old English Psalters tend to use the more familiar 'staðolas' to translate 'fundamenta', a translation which also appears on occasion in the three texts already named. Clearly, 'grundwealles' was by no means universal in the glossing tradition, but it did feature and seems, by some means, to have found its way into the Middle English *Metrical Psalter*.[63]

Although not a compound, the *Metrical Psalter*'s use of 'ferinkli' as a translation of 'subito' [suddenly] (63: 6; 72: 19) is also striking in the context of Old English connections. Everett, in fact, lists it among her 'remarkable' instances of similarity, suggesting that it echoes 'færinga' in the Vespasian and Cambridge Psalters (to this pair should be added Arundel and Junius).[64] As with 'spinnandweb', its appearance in Vespasian D.vii is not idiosyncratic; it is also used in the Egerton and Harley manuscripts of the *Metrical Psalter* (the Bodley manuscripts have 'feringli') but is unattested beyond these witnesses. Yet as with the 'groundewalles', the metrical translator's choice is arguably eclectic; the majority of Old English Psalters render 'subito' by the rather more common 'sona'.[65]

Whatever the nature of the links between the *Metrical Psalter* and its extant Old English antecedents, it is clear that they are neither direct nor unproblematic.[66] The Latin 'facies' [face], for example, is always rendered 'anleth' (Psalm 26: 14; 37: 4; 43: 25) in the Vespasian metrical version.[67] Used very rarely in Middle English (the *MED* lists its occurrence in the *Metrical Psalter* as its latest), 'anleth' derives from Old English 'andwlita'. But while 'andwlita' appears throughout Old English psalm glosses, it is almost invariably used as a translation of 'vultus' which, in the *Metrical Psalter*, is always translated 'face' or 'likam'.[68] Where 'facies' appears in the Latin (both Roman and Gallican), it tends, in the Old English tradition, to

---

[61] In the two Bodley manuscripts, we read 'groun staþeling' rather than 'grondstaþelnes'.

[62] Unlike 'gangewæfre/wæfregange', both of these words are attested outside the Old English Psalters. As Pulsiano only lived to publish the first (Psalms 1–50) of his projected four-volume *Old English Glossed Psalters*, I have relied on evidence supplied by *The Complete Corpus of Old English* for variant translations in later psalms.

[63] The Egerton and Corpus Christi manuscripts have 'groundewalles' but Harley reads 'groundes of him', as do the two Bodley manuscripts.

[64] Everett (1922b), pp. 348–9. Everett cites only Psalm 63: 4. In Psalm 72: 19, Cambridge has 'ferlice', which is used twice in Lambeth.

[65] Tiberius, Vitellius, Regius, Stowe, and Salisbury all agree in using 'sona' on both occasions.

[66] As Everett (1922b) states, '(t)he author of the *Metrical Psalter* did not use as source any copy of the O.E. Glosses known to us' (pp. 349–50).

[67] The other *Metrical* manuscripts are not as consistent as Vespasian; their translations vary between 'face' and 'licham'.

[68] 'Anleth' is not a word discussed by either Everett or Hargreaves. As Everett suggests, 'lickam' appears to be one of the *Metrical Psalter*'s mistranslations. It is not a translation that any of the other manuscripts corrects. 'Ansene' meaning 'face' does appear in a handful of twelfth-century texts, but does not seem to feature any later than this.

be translated 'ansien'. 'Onfanged' as a translation of 'suscepit' [took up, received] is noteworthy for similar reasons; its appearance throughout the *Metrical Psalter* mirrors its consistent use in the Old English glossing tradition, yet again there is a curiosity. In the metrical text, 'onfanged' is also used to translate 'concepit' [conceived] (Psalm 7: 15 and 50: 7), but this does not tally unproblematically with Old English usage.[69] Anglo-Saxon Psalters are fairly equally divided in their translation of 7: 15; while some use variations on 'geecnað', others use variations on 'onfeng' (Regius has 'he onfeng' as do Eadwine, Stowe, and Tiberius. Salisbury has 'he feng').[70] But none of the extant Old English Psalters uses a term close to 'onfeng' in translating 50: 7's 'concepit'; as Pulsiano points out, it is generally translated 'geecnad' (with dialectal variations). While Salisbury uses 'afeng', all of the others use 'cende'.[71]

It should also be added that striking as some of the echoes of Old English practice undeniably are, not all of those adduced by Everett and Hargreaves are as convincing or straightforward as they propose. A case in point is Hargreaves' citation of 'weued' (translating the Latin 'altare' [altar]) which obviously recalls the Old English 'weofod' and which, he suggests, is used in deliberate preference to the Latinate 'auter'.[72] But in making this claim, Hargreaves does not take account of the fact that 'auter' is also used in the Old English glossing tradition, appearing, for example, in Tiberius, Vitellius, and Regius.[73] There is, in other words, no guarantee that the *Metrical Psalter*'s consistent use of 'weued' ('auter' never appears) is directly inspired by the practice of Anglo-Saxon Psalters. Or, to take another example, Hargreaves cites the *Metrical Psalter*'s use of 'steuen', obviously derived from Old English 'stefn', to translate 'vox' [voice] as evidence of the later text's links with earlier glosses.[74] If viewed in comparison with the vocabulary of its closest temporal and geographical contemporary, the use of 'steuen' is noteworthy; Richard Rolle's *English Psalter* is consistent in its use of 'voice'. But 'steuen' is not in itself an unusual term, appearing in a wide variety of texts throughout the Middle Ages. While its use in the *Metrical Psalter* in conjunction with so many other words of Old English origin is evocative, it cannot easily be deployed in building a case for direct indebtedness. In fact, if there is a link between the language of the *Metrical Psalter* and that of the Old English glossing tradition, it seems most likely that it was the result of something rather more general than direct indebtedness. Perhaps the translator had access to, or had at some point encountered, a Gallican

---

[69] The MED lists the *Metrical Psalter* as the only Middle English text to use 'onfongen' to mean 'to conceive a child'. That in this context it might have been unfamiliar to the scribe of Vespasian D. vii is suggested by his use of the otherwise unattested 'onfogh' to translate 'concepit' in the second half of 50: 6 (Egerton and Harley both opt for 'onfong'). That the scribe of Bodley 921 might have struggled as well is suggested by his use of 'shunfonged' in Psalm 7: 15 ('onfonge' is used in 50: 7).

[70] Pulsiano, p. 63.   [71] Again, this is not picked up on by Everett or Hargreaves.

[72] Hargreaves (1956), p. 330. 'Weued' appears in Psalm 25: 6; 42: 4; 50: 21; 83: 4; and 117: 27. It is a translation used consistently in all six manuscripts.

[73] It is odd that Hargreaves does not note this, given that Regius is one of the Old English Psalters which he uses and given that he notes (p. 331) that 'auter' is a word of 'long standing' in the language, used for example by Aelfric.

[74] Hargreaves (1956), p. 331.

Psalter with Old English glosses, and recalled its terminology as he was working. Assuming (as we probably should) the anonymous translator to have had religious affiliations, such a volume may well have been accessible to him in a well-stocked monastic library.

To give them their due, both Everett and Hargreaves do recognize that to prove a link between the *Metrical Psalter* and Old English glossing traditions would be difficult; as well as the remarkable continuities, there are some undeniable dissimilarities.[75] Yet Hargreaves in particular continues to insist that even when the Middle English translation is not obviously inspired by earlier glosses, its language is still archaic, 'quite untypical of its age'.[76] And it is true that its vocabulary often appears somewhat quaint in comparison with more widely circulated texts of the same period. Its use of 'swykedome' (from Old English 'swicdom') to translate 'dolus' [deceit] (9: 28; 31: 2; 34: 20; 35: 4; 49: 19; 54: 12; 72: 18) is a case in point. At the same moments, Rolle invariably uses 'treson', and according to the MED, which lists its latest occurrence as *c*. 1330, 'swykedome' is an uncommon term. Yet its use in the *Metrical* text does not obviously derive from extant Old English Psalters, which are entirely consistent in their use of 'facn' as a translation of 'dolus'.[77] The use of 'methful' to translate 'soporatus' [taken rest] (Psalm 3: 6) where Rolle uses 'soked' is striking for similar reasons.[78] It certainly derives from Old English 'mæþful', but this is not a term used at the same moment in the surviving Old English glosses, which use variously 'slæpingan', 'ic swodrode', 'ic swefnode', and 'geswefod'. Yet the fact that 'methful' is a term also used in a further handful of Early Middle English texts should caution us against agreeing too readily with Hargreaves' reading of the Psalter's language as 'quite untypical'.[79] Elements of its vocabulary may strike as unfamiliar even a seasoned reader of Middle English, but our knowledge of the spoken and written language of the early Middle Ages (particularly that of the north) is too patchy for us to dismiss as archaic that which may have been common usage. If there is a 'chain' of psalm translation running through the Middle Ages, its tantalizing links with Anglo-Saxon traditions of glossing appear rather less secure and direct than Hargreaves supposed.

RICHARD ROLLE'S *ENGLISH PSALTER*

It may be, however, that a 'chain' of translation is easier to discern once we leave the Anglo-Saxon Psalters behind and locate ourselves more securely in the biblical literature of the later Middle Ages. Although references in the previous section to

[75] As Everett points out, '[t]here are several archaic or curious words used in the *Metrical Psalter* which do not correspond to anything' in extant Old English Psalter glosses (1922b), p. 350.

[76] Hargreaves (1956), p. 338.

[77] At 9: 28 Harley has 'sorgh' and CCCC 'sorh' rather than 'swikedome', and at 35: 4 both have 'swikelic'. Other than this, the manuscripts agree in their use of 'swikedome'. At 9: 28 and 35: 4 Bodley 921 has 'swicdom'.

[78] In Egerton, 'methful' is written 'methuf', which might suggest that it is a word unfamiliar to the scribe. Bodley 921 has 'sober'.

[79] MED lists 'methful' as occurring in *Vices and Virtues*, *Sawles Warde*, and *Ancrene Wisse*.

Richard Rolle's *English Psalter* have highlighted differences between the *Metrical* text and that of the Yorkshire hermit, the two translations actually share many similarities throughout. The existence of apparent continuities between these two Psalters has, as indicated at the beginning of this chapter, been observed by Hargreaves, and some striking instances are presented below.[80]

Rolle	Metrical
Psalm 4: 4 ('et scitote quoniam mirificavit Dominus sanctum suum Dominus exaudiet me cum clamavero ad eum' [Know ye also that the Lord hath made his holy one wonderful. The Lord will hear me when I shall cry unto him])	Psalm 4: 4
And wites for lord selkouthid has his haligh: Lord sall here me when I haf cried til him.	And wites þat lauerd his haligh selkouþede *he* / When I to him crie, lauerd sal here me.
Psalm 17: 9 ('ascendit fumus in ira eius et ignis a facie eius exarsit carbones succensi sunt ab eo' [There went up a smoke in his wrath and a fire flamed from his face; coals were kindled by it])	Psalm 17: 9
Reke stegh in the ire of him, and ire brent of his face: coles ere kyndild of him.	Upstegh reke in his ire, / And ofe face ofe him brent þe fire; / koles *þat ware dounfalland* / kindled ere ofe him *glouand*.
Psalm 58: 7 ('convertentur ad vesperam et famem patientur ut canes et circuibunt civitatem' [They shall return at evening, and shall suffer hunger like dogs: and shall go round about the city)]	Psalm 58: 7
Turnyd be thai at euen, and hungire suffire thai as hundes: and thai sall vmga the cite.	Þai be torned at euen, and hunger thole *þa* / als hundes, and cite þai sal vmga.
Psalm 105: 5 ('ad videndum in bonitate electorum tuorum ad laetandum in laetitia gentis tuae et lauderis cum hereditate tua' [That we may see the good of thy chosen, that we may rejoice in the joy of thy nation, that thou mayst be praised with thy inheritance])	Psalm 105: 5
ffor to see in the goednes of thi chosen, forto be glade in gladnes of thi genge: that thou be louyd with thin heritage.	In godenes of þi chosen to se / to faine in faines of þi genge *þat be;* / þat þou be loued *nighte and dai* / with þine heritage *in ai*.

In his recent catalogue of the English manuscripts of Richard Rolle, Ralph Hanna refers to the possibility of Rolle's indebtedness to the *Metrical Psalter* as a 'recurrent minor topic in past discussions'.[81] He cites the work of Everett and Hargreaves, who maintain two different schools of thought whilst both asserting that there is a link between the texts. Everett suggests that the connection

---

[80] The *Metrical Psalter*'s additional words inserted for the sake of rhyme have been italicized.

[81] Hanna (2010), p. xxxv, note 29. As Everett (1922b) points out, the *Metrical Psalter* was included by C. Horstman in the second volume of his edition of the works of Richard Rolle, with the remark that 'a tradition ascribes this Psalter to R. Rolle'.

is indirect, that the partially modernized Northern Old English gloss which she supposes to have influenced the metrical translator was also read, somewhat later, by Rolle ('[t]he facts seem to indicate that the same source was used in both').[82] Hargreaves, however, revises her tentative conclusion, arguing that the 'remarkable similarities between [the metrical text] and Rolle's own *Psalter* may well be due to a direct reliance of the later writer on the earlier and not, as [Everett] was led to suggest, to the use of a common source'.[83] As with Everett's and Hargreaves' arguments discussed in the previous section of this chapter, there are problems with both of these readings. To deal first with Everett's, it is worth asking why, in the fourteenth century, Rolle would have been interested in using a 'partially modernised' Old English gloss (for the existence of which we have no evidence)?[84] Furthermore, can we assume that he would have been able to read such a text? After all, as little as fifty years later, the author of *First Seiþ Bois* comments that the Anglo-Saxon gospels 'ben 3[i]t in many places of so oolde Englische þat vnneþe can any man rede hem'.[85] And to turn to Hargreaves' suggestion, if Rolle's *Psalter* does borrow directly from the metrical text, why does he never reproduce any of the latter's distinctive tag rhymes? As Everett points out:

> Supposing that Rolle were reading the *Metrical Psalter* verse by verse, or were repeating what he remembered of it to himself, it would have seemed inevitable that he should have introduced some of the tags which that version contains. Yet there is no instance of this in the whole of his Psalter; he does not even incorporate the little word 'swa', which occurs so often in the Metrical version for the sake of the rhyme.[86]

The total absence from Rolle's text of any trace of the *Metrical Psalter*'s insistent rhymes seems to provide conclusive proof that any link between the two is not direct.

Yet the affinities of both lexis and syntax cited by Everett and Hargreaves are sufficiently striking to require some examination, in recognition of the possibility, apparently unconsidered by either earlier scholar, that many of them can be explained in ways that do not involve any indebtedness of one to the other, direct or not. It is, for example, highly likely that their frequent use of similarly non-idiomatic constructions is due to the fact that they are following in an established tradition of literal psalm translation. It could also be explained by the fact that both translators are aiming to produce the same sort of text, namely an English Psalter that can be used (in very different ways) alongside the Latin. As noted previously, in such circumstances a closely literal translation, reproducing the syntax and mirroring the morphology of the original, is eminently desirable. In conjunction with this, we must take into account the fact that both of the Psalters are originally northern texts and that it is therefore inevitable that on occasion they will share a

---

[82] Everett (1922b), p. 338.   [83] Hargreaves (1956), p. 339.

[84] According to Pulsiano's 2001 datings, the latest of the more or less complete Old English glossed Psalters are Eadwine (which he dates to *c.* 1155–60) and Arundel, which he locates in the second half of the eleventh century. Everett supposes her hypothetical gloss to have been interlinear: 'the hypothesis of an early Middle English (Northern) interlinear gloss on the Vulgate would, I think, solve the problem of the connexion between the two versions' (1922b), p. 347.

[85] Dove (2010), p. 145/80–4. This point is borrowed from Ullerston's *Determinacio* (f. 198va).

[86] Everett (1922b), pp. 346–7.

distinctive northern vocabulary.[87] Of course, arguments positing a shared 'north-ern' vocabulary are hampered by the fact that there are no remains of northern English dateable to earlier than the late thirteenth or early fourteenth centuries; it is therefore 'extremely difficult to have the same sense of historical usage' as one has with other Middle English dialects.[88] Bearing this limitation in mind, it does seem, however, that their shared northern origins might account for a significant proportion of the lexical agreements between the Psalters. The verb 'romien' [to roar/lament], for example, which appears in both of these texts but in neither the Wycliffite versions nor the *Prose Psalter* (21: 14, 37: 9, and 103: 21), must simply reflect local usage; although the MED suggests it extends to the Midlands, it does not tend to appear further south. And a similar argument can be made regarding the translation, in both, of 'fumus' [smoke] as 'reke' (a word to which we will return), 'fletus' [weeping] as 'gret/gretinge', and 'camus' [a horse's bridle/bit] as 'kevil'; all appear to have had particular currency in northern England.[89] A strik-ing example is 'lopird', used to translate 'coagulatus/coagulatum' [curdled] in both Rolle and the metrical text (Psalm 67: 16; 118: 70). Everett cites this as one of her 'rare' and 'unusual' words, the appearance of which in both texts points definitively to a connection between the two.[90] However, as Ralph Hanna suggests, it may well have been common in local usage; it is 'a living technical term, if you live in an area committed to pastoral agriculture and thus making cheese from byproducts of your fleeces'.[91] He makes a similar point about the formulation 'gif . . . samen', used by both Rolle and the metrical text to translate 'ne simul trahas' [draw [me] not away together] (Psalm 27: 3). While Everett pinpoints this as unusual, Hanna suggests that it is simply local usage.

However, Rolle's Psalter distinguishes itself from the earlier *Metrical* text by vir-tue of its explicit claim to be phrased in an English that is 'lyghtest and comonest and . . . mast lyke til the latyn'. In practice, the realization of this aim actually leads to many similarities with the *Metrical Psalter*: in terms of 'likeness' to Latin on a syntactical level, Rolle's unidiomatic mirroring of Latin syntax, already discussed, is on occasion actually less extreme than that of the metrical text. And in terms of the *English Psalter*'s lexical Latinity, Rolle's consistent calques, echoing though not exactly reproducing those of the earlier translation, have also been mentioned. More literal than the later Wycliffite EV, his translation regularly reproduces individual

[87] Everett (1922b) expresses doubt as to the *Metrical Psalter*'s northern origins (p. 338). Given its limited circulation in a small area of north Yorkshire, to argue for a non-northern origin would seem counter-intuitive.

[88] I am grateful to Ralph Hanna for this observation. The work of William Rothwell has done much to suggest that the spread of Anglo-Norman was somewhat sporadic in the northern parts of England. See, for example, W. Rothwell, 'The Role of French in Thirteenth-Century England' *BJRL* 58 (1976), 445–66. This obviously causes one to revise Hargreaves' point (1956) '. . . the translator evidently had a decided preference for native words over Romance words . . . this preference was so strong that he was prepared to extend the meaning of a native word rather than borrow from French or Latin' (p. 334).

[89] For 'reke', see Psalm 17: 9; 36: 20; 67: 3; 101: 4. For 'gret/gretinge', see 6: 9; 29: 6; 101: 10. For 'kevil', see 31: 12.

[90] Everett (1922b), p. 342.   [91] Personal communication.

elements of Latin words: 'ante-' regularly becomes 'bifore-', 'circum-' becomes 'vm-', 'cum-' is often '–togeder', 'ex-' is often '–out', 'in-' becomes '–in', 'super-' becomes '–aboue' or '–ouere', and 'trans-' is sometimes '-ouer'.[92] Etymologically speaking, however, Rolle's vocabulary is undoubtedly more Latinate than that of his predecessor: where the earlier text uses 'anleth' to translate 'facies', Rolle has 'face', where the earlier has 'hine' (servus), Rolle has 'servant', and where the earlier has 'steuen' (vox), Rolle has 'voice'. And such moments can be multiplied; 'vani-tates' [foolishnesses], translated 'fantoms' in the metrical text, is 'vanytes' in Rolle and 'aedificantur' [built], translated 'bigged' in the metrical text, is 'edified' in Rolle.[93] Of course, such differences in vocabulary are due in large part to the wider influence of romance languages on Middle English; they do not suggest that Rolle is always deliberately mirroring Latin terms. In fact, such divergence from the *Metrical Psalter* actually tells us more about the vocabulary of the earlier text than it does about Rolle, whose language is more familiar than that of his predecessor at least in part because it is later.

Nonetheless, that Rolle's vocabulary is sometimes distinctively northern and, therefore, difficult to understand, is suggested by the fact that manuscripts copied and circulated further south tend to gloss if not replace particular terms. In an article published in 1990, Sara Nevanlinna makes some interesting observations on the uninterpolated Rolle Psalter found in London, BL Arundel 158. Although a number of her comments on the manuscript must be treated with caution, her dis-cussion of the explanatory glosses which often accompany northern dialectal or Old Norse words is worth noting.[94] She points out that 'reke' is glossed 'Þat is smoke', 'genge' is glossed 'Þat is folk' or 'companie', and 'lered' is glossed 'Þat is yta3t'.[95] Such glossing in Middle English translations is not unusual, as we will see when we look at the Wycliffite psalms.[96] It is, however, particularly striking in the context of Rolle's Psalter, suggesting that scribes who copied the text retained a degree of respect for the hermit's original: they do not replace his translation but offer occa-sional clarifying alternatives. Interestingly, they appear to accord his version the same sort of respect which he, and other literal translators, accorded the biblical text. Glossing is acceptable, but silently altering the terminology of the source is not.

---

[92] For a comprehensive discussion of Rolle's calques, the reader is referred to the introduction to Hudson, vol. 1 (2012).

[93] For 'vanitates' see Psalm 4: 3; 30: 7; 38: 6; 39: 5; 61: 10; 118: 37. For 'aedificantur', see 50: 20; 77: 69; 88: 3.

[94] S. Nevanlinna, 'Glosses in three Late Middle English Texts: Lexical Variation' in *Historical Linguistics and Philology*, Trends in Linguistics—Studies and Monographs 46, ed. J. Fisiak (Berlin and New York, 1990), pp. 273–89. Nevanlinna states that in Arundel 158 the dialect 'has been sys-tematically translated into the language of the South-East Midlands . . . with some Southern features' (p. 274). Hanna (2010), however, points out that the manuscript is the work of three scribes and that they 'vary in usage and sporadically retain Northern archetypal features', and that '[a]ll show diverse and individual forms generally placeable in north Gloucs. (perhaps south Worcs. or extreme west Oxon.)' (p. 85).

[95] Nevanlinna, p. 277.

[96] Roger Ellis (1982), p. 27 comments on the 'well-established and well-noted' prevalence of such glosses in Middle English translations, pointing out that they tend to exist either as simple doublets ('and', 'or', 'of') or as more extensive additions ('that is', 'as if').

The situation with manuscripts of the Wycliffite interpolated Rolle Psalter is slightly different. While, as the work of Anne Hudson demonstrates, many of the scribes seem conscious of the need to clarify northern terms, they do so by silently replacing the original term more frequently than they do by glossing. So, in several manuscripts 'reke' becomes 'smoke', and in all but one, 'genge' becomes 'folk'.[97] 'Lered' seems to have presented less of a challenge; it sometimes becomes 'lerned' or (less frequently) 'tau3t' but the straightforward original often remains. Other distinctively northern terms, however, did present some scribes of the Wycliffite revisions with difficulties. A case in point is the aforementioned 'lopird' (coagulatus [curdled]): in several manuscripts it becomes 'croddid' or 'cruddid' (a much more widespread rendering of 'coagulatus'), and in one we are given the alternatives 'loprid or cruddid' but it seems to have defeated another scribe who renders it 'leprid'.[98] Most scribes, however, simply replace dialectically unfamiliar words with more familiar alternatives; the 'kevil' which features as a translation of 'camus' (a horse's bridle/bit) in both the *Metrical* and Rolle Psalters, for example, is absent from all but two of the RV manuscripts, replaced with 'bernakle'.[99] It is not only dialectically unfamiliar words that are glossed or replaced; some scribes of the Wycliffite RV also substitute Rolle's calques with more accessible alternatives or clarifying circumlocutions. Such practice is in keeping with the fact that they tend, in some manuscripts, to make the impenetrable word-order of Rolle's original rather more idiomatic.[100] So the hermit's 'vmgang' for 'circuitu' [circumference] becomes on occasion 'aboutegoyng', 'goynge aboute', or 'cumpas'. And 'vmgyue' for 'circumdabit' [surrounded/passed around] becomes 'aboute 3eue' (Oxford, University College 74), 'gone aboute (Cambridge MA, Harvard University, Houghton Library Richardson 36), 'cumpasse aboute' (Oxford, BodlL. Bodley 877 and Dublin, Trinity College Library 71) and 'enverone' (Oxford, BodL. Tanner 16 and London, BL Royal 18.D.i + Add. 74953).[101] While the scribes of the Wycliffite RV make remarkably few changes to Rolle's translation (as Anne Hudson remarks, they 'retain Rolle's translation of the biblical text, neither substituting the rendering from the Wycliffite Bible nor providing one of their own'), those which they do make are generally uncontentious, undertaken for reasons of clarity and comprehensibility.[102]

---

[97] According to Anne Hudson's textual notes in her edition of RV, only one manuscript presents us with a glossing alternative to 'reek': see 101: 4 'reek or smeche' in Dublin, Trinity College 71. 'Folk' is used in all manuscripts other than Lincoln Cathedral, Chapter Library 92, which retains it in the gloss.

[98] For 'loprid or cruddid', see Cambridge, MA, Harvard University, Houghton Library Richardson 36.

[99] Oxford, BodlL Tanner 16 has the misreading 'bemakle' and only London, BL Royal 18.D.i + Add. 74953 retains 'keuyl'.

[100] As Hudson's introduction to RV illustrates, although the revisers generally retain Rolle's non-idiomatic translation, they sometimes move towards a more fluent vernacularization. See Hudson, vol. 1 (2012), pp. xc–cix.

[101] As Nevanlinna points out, such words are also often glossed in MS Arundel 158 (pp. 275–7).

[102] Hudson (1988), p. 259. She also points out that 'the layout in the manuscripts, distinguishing Latin text, translated biblical material, and commentary, and so creating a visual hierarchy, regularises that of manuscripts containing Rolle's original text'.

THE WYCLIFFITE PSALMS

Rolle's *English Psalter* was obviously known well and in some detail by many of those involved in the Wycliffite movement. It is tempting to speculate that the latter's translation of the book of psalms was influenced by the former, forming another link in the putative 'chain' of translation.[103] In fact, Mary Dove suggests that on at least one occasion, this may well have been the case. Highlighting Psalm 103: 17 ('erodii domus dux est eorum' [the highest of them is the house of the heron/stork]), she points out that 'erodius', which means 'heron/stork', is mistranslated as 'falcon' by Rolle and 'gerfauken' in both EV and LV.[104] While this is a tantalizing observation, it would be unwise to set about building an argument on such flimsy foundations; the appearance of 'faucons' at the same point in the *Prose Psalter* might suggest that it was simply common usage.[105] Further, preoccupied as they were with the assembling of reliable Latin originals from which to construct their authoritative English Bible, it is arguably unlikely the Wycliffite translators and revisers would have been interested in basing their work on any antecedent vernacularizations. Such a text would not have served their purposes, unless it was functioning simply as a comparator rather than a source or 'standard'.[106]

This is not to say, however, that the Wycliffite EV and LV Psalters have nothing in common with Rolle's work. While the latter's translation makes even fewer concessions to idiomatic word-order than the EV Psalter, and while they differ somewhat in their mirroring of the individual elements of Latin words, the two share an identity as close renditions of their Vulgate original.[107] Even in LV, in which the conventions of verbatim translation have been relaxed, it is 'unquestionable' that 'the Wycliffite translators intended to give English readers access to the naked, literal text of scripture', although by 'literal' we mean here the ' "true literal sense", encompassing all the figurative senses intended by the writer

---

[103] On this subject, Michael Kuczynski is currently investigating glosses to the Psalter in the EV Wycliffite Bible, Longleat House, Marquis of Bath 3, which he believes may be derived from Rolle (see Hanna (2010), pp. xxi–xxii, note 5).

[104] Dove (2007), pp. 174–5. She points out that a marginal note in CCCC 147, probably in the hand of Blyth, who annotated the Prologue in this Bible, accuses Wyclif of being ignorant of Latin here, insofar as he mistranslates 'erodius' as 'gefauken'. Bramley's edition of Rolle actually has 'gerfawkyn' and this is retained in RV manuscripts.

[105] The *Metrical Psalter* has 'wilde haukes' at the same moment.

[106] In the aforementioned 1990 article, Sara Nevanlinna suggests that the mildly glossed Rolle translation in Arundel 158 is the work of someone 'familiar with the Wycliffite Bible, because over 40% of the glosses registered in A, involving twenty-four different word-stems, occur there in the same context' (pp. 284–5). Such a conclusion is probably unwarranted; both the Wycliffite Bible translators and the glossator of Arundel simply share words that are in common currency.

[107] Although Rolle's *Psalter* and the Wycliffite psalms share the use of calques, they sometimes differ in their rendition of individual elements of words. In EV 'invocare' [call upon, invoke] is normally translated 'inwardli clepen' from Genesis to Ezekiel (from Daniel to the Apocalypse the normal translation is 'ynclepen'). And 'exaudire' [hear clearly] is normally translated '(ful) out heren' from Genesis to Job and Ezekiel onwards. (In the first verse of the fourth psalm, LV retains 'inwardli clepede' but deletes 'fulout' (except for Bodley 277, which restores the EV reading). Dove (2007), p. 139). Rolle does not use 'inwardli' and '(ful) out' in the same way.

and all the Christological significations the Holy Spirit has inscribed within the text'.[108] This does not mean, however, that they forewent glosses entirely; as Dove points out, '[w]hatever the translators may have anticipated in advance, in practice they discovered that there is no hard and fast line between literal translation and supplementary explanation.'[109] Translation and commentary are, as the Romans knew well, only two sides of the same coin. For Rolle, by contrast, the clear and consistent division between verbatim vernacularization and interpretative commentary obviates the need for anxiety on this score. In manuscripts of the Wycliffite Bible, supplementary clarification tends to take one of two forms; not only do we often find 'explanatory glosses' ('. . . *þat is* . . .') of the sort that we see in non-northern and revised manuscripts of Rolle's Psalter, but we also frequently come across 'variant translations' ('. . . *eiþer/or* . . .').[110] Both types of gloss appear in EV and LV and, as we will see, are of real importance in the Psalter.[111] An example of the latter can be found in LV Psalm 118: 70, in which 'coagulatum' [curdled], rendered 'lopird' in Rolle and the *Metrical Psalter*, is translated 'cruddid' as it also is in some manuscripts of the Wycliffite revised Rolle Psalter. In London, Lambeth Palace 25 and 1033 (U and V) and Oxford, BodlL Bodley 554 (B_554), however, 'cruddid' is further clarified by the variant translation 'ether maad hard', perhaps indicating a concern with comprehensibility.[112] The vast majority of such glosses in the Psalter seem similarly focused on clarification; Psalm 73: 22 ('God, rise vp, deme thou thi cause; be thou myndeful of thin *vpbreidyngis*, of tho that ben al dai of the vnwise man') becomes 'schenschipis ether vpbreidyngis' in several manuscripts, and Psalm 96: 3 ('[f]ier schal go bifore him; and schal *enflawme* hise enemyes in cumpas') often becomes 'enflawme ether sette a fier'.[113]

---

[108] Dove (2007), p. 152 and p. 159. In referring to the 'true literal sense', Dove acknowledges Karlfried Froehlich.

[109] Dove (2007), p. 153. For Rolle this problem is solved by the fact that he can untie the knots of his translation in his paraphrasing commentary. It is irresolvable for the translator of the *Metrical Psalter*.

[110] Dove (2007), p. 154. She distinguishes between these two types of gloss, commenting that Lindberg calls the latter 'synonymous variants'.

[111] In EV, supplementary explanation becomes much more common after Baruch 3: 20, 'one of several pieces of evidence suggesting a hiatus in the translation at or near that point, followed by a reconsideration of translation practice' (Dove (2007), p. 154). With regard to variant translations, the same pattern can be observed in EV, and they are common throughout the text of LV.

[112] After the gloss, U adds 'Austin here' (see Dove (2007), p. 219). The other occurrence of 'coagulatus' in the Psalter (67: 16) is not glossed in any EV or LV manuscript. However, that comprehensibility might have been an issue is suggested further by Oxford, BodlL Douce 369 (Part 1) (EV), which omits 'cruddid' entirely from its translation of 118: 70, reading simply 'as mylc the herte of hem'. Admittedly, though, this could be a straightforward case of scribal error.

[113] In B_554, 'eþ set a fier' and 'eþir upbreidyngis' are underlined in black in the main body of the text (f. 52v and f. 39v). For similarly minded glosses see Psalm 129: 3 'Lord, if thou kepist wickidnessis; Lord, who schal *susteyne*?' which becomes 'susteyne ether abide' in several manuscripts, including Bodley 277 (see C. Lindberg, *King Henry's Bible. Bodley 277—The Revised Version of the Wyclif Bible*, 4 vols (Stockholm, 1999), vol. 2, p. 526). Bodley 277 provides this alternative to 'susteyne' on several occasions. In B_554, 'eþer abide' is underlined finely in black in the margin (f. 72r). See also the glossing of Psalm 111: 10's 'faile' as 'ether wexe rotun' in several manuscripts including Bodley 277 (see Lindberg (1999), vol. 2, p. 518).

However, clarifications can blur into interpretations, particularly on occasions when the concrete is glossed by the abstract. In such circumstances, the Wycliffites are often influenced by Nicholas of Lyre, as will become clear. Such is the case, for example, with the glossing of Psalm 106: 29 ('And he ordeynede the tempest therof in to a soft wynde; and the wawis therof weren stille').[114] In several manuscripts, 'softe wynde' is glossed 'ether pesiblete'. While there is nothing inherently contentious in this small-scale allegorization, it could not be classed as a 'synonymous variant' (the term used by Lindberg to describe what Dove calls 'variant translations') in the same way as the glosses already discussed. It is presumably such material that Dove has in mind when she states that there is 'a very fine line between a gloss that helps the reader to understand the literal sense of the biblical text and a gloss that interprets the literal sense of the biblical text', and that the Wycliffite translators 'sometimes overstep the mark'.[115] Yet for these very scholars, the offering of such alternatives could be justified by the rationale, outlined in chapter 15 of the General Prologue, that as long as the words used in translation 'serue to þe entent and sentence', they are neither 'superflu or false'.[116] They are, in fact, a key aspect of any understanding of translation as an interpretation, if not a rhetorical reinvention, of a source text. However, given the Wycliffites' concern for the transmission of 'true', unadulterated scriptures, it is not surprising that they should betray some anxiety regarding the translation of 'wordis equyuoke . . . þat han many significaciouns vndur o lettre' and that might require the provision of an alternative or explanation. As stated at the close of chapter 15 of the prologue to the Bible:

> [A] translator haþ greet nede to studie wel þe sentence boþe bifore and aftir, and loke þat sich equyuoke wordis acorde wel wiþ þe sentence, and he haþ greet nede to lyue a cleene liyf and be ful deuout in preieris and haue not his wit occupied aboute worldli þingis, þat þe Hooli Spirit, auctour of wisdom and kunnyng and treuþe, dresse hym in his werk and suffre him not for to erre.[117]

It is only then that the translator's negotiation of ambiguous words (by means of explanation, alternative, or simply translation choice) will prove reliable.

As this quotation demonstrates, our reading of the Wycliffite Bible as vernacularization can—and should—be informed by the prologue's reflections on the process of translation. Given the existence of the Bible in both earlier and later versions, we also have the luxury of being able to trace a changing practice of

---

[114] Unless otherwise specified, all quotations from the Wycliffite EV and LV are taken from Forshall and Madden. As it is imagined that most readers will access this text in its electronic format, page numbers have not been supplied. See <http://quod.lib.umich.edu/c/cme/browse.html>.

[115] Dove (2007), p. 159.   [116] Dove (2010), p. 81/2816–17.

[117] Dove (2010), p. 84/2946–61. The examples that the author adduces ('sharp' and 'swift'; '3onge trees' and 'avoutrie') are from Romans 3: 15 and Wisdom 4: 3, and it is worth noting that in both cases, and in both EV and LV, Wycliffite translation practice tallies with Wycliffite translation theory. On neither occasion are alternatives ('*eiþer/or*') or explanations ('*þat is*') offered; equivocation is resolved before translation takes place. Forshall and Madden do, however, point out that in BL Cotton Claudius E. II (LV) Wisdom 4: 3's 'avoutrie' is glossed 'þat is, alle wicked men, that ben the fendis sones bi goostli auoutrie. Lire here.' Although the initial equivocation has been resolved, supplementary explanation is felt to be necessary.

translation from one to the other. Their respective manuscript traditions further distinguish the two versions; as Anne Hudson has observed, there is a significant degree of 'divergence between manuscripts of EV', much more 'than Forshall and Madden allowed for'. Manuscripts of LV, by contrast, contain a text which 'seems stylistically homogeneous, and amazingly stable'.[118] Contributing to this sense of consistency is the fact that dialectal differences between LV manuscripts are much slighter; the language of almost all is broadly identifiable as Midland.[119] Bearing these broad distinctions in mind, we must nonetheless exercise caution when categorically distinguishing the Earlier Version from the Later and attempting to trace a straightforward line of descent from one to the other, as previously suggested. Although the labels are by no means redundant (there are certainly discernible differences between the translations, more pronounced in the Old Testament than they are in the New), it seems that EV as defined by Forshall and Madden was always already on the verge of becoming something else.[120] A salutary reminder of this is provided by Oxford, BodlL Bodley 959 (*c.* 1380–90) which contains a copy of Genesis to Baruch 3: 20 in EV. Described by Forshall and Madden as 'the original copy of the translator', the work of Fristedt has demonstrated that Bodley 959 actually already exhibits some idioms characteristic of LV.[121] And Hudson has suggested further that the extensive corrections found in Bodley 959, 'even if they are not authoritative', probably illustrate the ways in which EV was modified in the direction of LV: 'interlinearly, and marginally, written evidently before the bifolia were even sewn into quires . . . and by a number of hands, some overlapping with each other and many at work only over a relatively short span'.[122]

A number of Bodley 959's most significant corrections appear in the Psalter. The most striking and well-known example occurs in the translation of Psalm 91: 11 and 15 ('et exaltabitur sicut unicornis cornu meum et senectus mea in *misericordia uberi* . . . adhuc multiplicabuntur in *senecta uberi*' [But my horn shall be exalted like that of the unicorn: and my old age in *plentiful mercy* . . . They shall still

---

[118] Hudson (1988), p. 239 and p. 246. These observations are echoed by Dove (2007), who agrees that '[a]part from marginal glosses . . . the manuscripts of the Later Version generally present a more uniform text than the manuscripts of the Earlier Version' (p. 148). As Hudson also points out, there are some inconsistencies in the vocabulary of the LV which suggest that the text may originally have been divided between different translators and that the Old Testament may have been assigned to one group of translators, and the New Testament to another. And as already touched upon, there are also indications that there was a change of translators in the latter part of the Old Testament, somewhere between Baruch and Amos.

[119] Dove comments that '[w]hile this desire for dialectal homogeneity on the part of at least one of the translators is not quite the same as awareness of an emerging standard, we can see how the concern that the Bible in English should be as "opin" as possible might, during the life of the translation project, have evolved into a shared awareness that the dialect of the Central and South-East Midlands was the most widely comprehensible kind of English' (2007), p. 148.

[120] As Anne Hudson points out, 'the processes of modification needed to produce the idiomatic LV out of the stilted Latinisms of the EV were long and complex, and . . . stages in it are to some extent reflected in extant manuscripts that [Forshall and Madden] broadly categorised as "EV"' (1988), p. 239.

[121] Forshall and Madden (1850), vol. 1, p. xvii. For the reference to Fristedt, see Hudson (1988), p. 239, note 64. Hudson comments that Bodley 959 presents a text which 'may already have been modified somewhat in the direction of fluency'.

[122] Hudson (1988), p. 239. 'There are corrections/revisions throughout (typically three or four per page), some in scribal hand(s) but many more in another hand' (Dove (2007), p. 257).

increase in a *fruitful old age*]). In the translation of both verses 'uberi' is misread as a noun rather than an adjective, resulting in the nonsensical 'mercy of the tete' and 'age of the tete', in preference to the correct 'plentiful mercy' and 'plentiful/fruitful age'.[123] But on both occasions in Bodley 959, the erroneous translations have been crossed out and replaced with 'plenteuous mercy' and 'plenteuous age' respectively, which is how they appear in manuscripts containing the LV Psalter. This is a clear-cut example of an erroneous interpretation being corrected; the fault was the translator's and the misreading does not point to there being anything amiss in the original from which the translator(s) was working. On innumerable other occasions, however, alterations and/or explanatory glosses which appear in the LV psalms but are not to be found in most manuscripts containing EV do suggest that the Latin source has been re-examined or that a different version of that source has been consulted. In their work of revision, the Wycliffite scholars were not simply re-assessing the EV translation but were re-examining the Gallican source(s). To return to Hargreaves' increasingly problematic metaphor, there was no straightforward 'chain' leading from EV to LV; the production of LV involved a return to the source material as well as the implementation of a different style of translation.

In a chapter concerned with the practice of psalm translation in the late Middle Ages, it is worth pausing for a moment over the character of the LV Psalter's differences from EV. In this context, it is particularly important to note the increasing role played by glossing in the later translation. If—as seems to be the case—it is more productive to think in terms of a vibrant late-medieval psalmic nexus than of an ancestral chain of psalmic descent, it is interesting to note the broad affinities between Wycliffite glossing and Rollean preoccupations. In an important article published in 1955 (the year before the article in which he alluded to a chain of Middle English psalm translation) Henry Hargreaves draws attention to several of the occasions on which the Wycliffite revisers of EV appear to be working from a source differing in some detail from that used by the original translators, and he points out that in the places where LV alters EV, all LV manuscripts normally have the revisions in common.[124] The observation is an important one, but it is unfortunate that Hargreaves phrases it in terms of 'correction', suggesting that on many occasions the revisers are deliberately rectifying errors or inferior readings 'characteristic of late-medieval latin bibles'.[125] As Anne Hudson points out, this is an anachronistic approach; '[n]o medieval scholar had access to the range of

---

[123] The earlier translator of the *Metrical Psalter*, who, as already noted, is not a remarkable Latinist, avoids this error. At the same moments, he has 'merci ofe fulhed' and 'felefold in elde'.

[124] H. Hargreaves, 'The Latin Text of Purvey's Psalter', *MA* 24 (1995), 73–90. Dove (2007) provides us with one exception to this general rule: the erroneous reading of Psalm 41: 3, preserved in several LV manuscripts.

[125] He continues thus: 'It is well known that [the LV translator(s)] followed the earlier translation closely, making changes that imparted a more naturally English air to the style and avoiding the sometimes painful literalisms of [the EV translator(s)], but otherwise depending considerably on his work. It must therefore be assumed that he worked with a copy of the earlier translation in front of him, and all divergences from it on his part must be deliberate . . . corrections' (p. 80). Note that Hargreaves also suggests that there are many places where the Latin reading that is the basis of EV is 'more correct than that which is the basis of LV' (p. 76).

copies now known, let alone to the modern assessment of the value of each.'[126] In addition to their increased fluency and readability, the LV psalms do differ in some textual details from those of EV, but while it is clear that the revisers had access to a different version(s) of the Latin Psalter, it is not clear that the alterations would always have been felt to be 'improvements' on a deficient first attempt.

What Hargreaves is right to point out, however, is that many of the revisions which find their way into the LV psalms appear to derive from the Postilla of Nicholas of Lyre, although this should not surprise us given the aforementioned Wycliffite fondness for this glossator.[127] It seems clear that Lyre played a part in the expanded notion of the literal sense of scripture lying behind the apparently freer LV. As Kantik Ghosh puts it, what emerges from his work, alongside that of Aquinas and Richard Fitzralph, is 'a redefinition of the "literal" which does not substantially alter but instead "repackages" inherited exegetical norms. The older distinction between the "literal" and the "spiritual" is recast as a distinction between two aspects of the "literal".'[128] The apparent liberties which this allows one to take with the text of the scriptures are then, in reality, no such thing. Most often cited as an example of Lyran influence on the LV Psalter is Psalm 44: 3.[129] Reading 'speciosus forma prae filiis hominum, diffusa est gratia in labiis tuis. Propterea benedixit te Deus in aeternum' [Thou art beautiful above the sons of men, grace is poured abroad in thy lips. Therefore hath God blessed thee for ever] in the Gallican, it is translated verbatim in EV:

> Fair in forme befor the sonus of men, grace is held out in thi lippis; therfor blesside thee God in to with oute ende.

In LV not only has the translation been recast more idiomatically, but it has also been addressed directly to Christ:

> Crist, thou art fairer in schap than the sones of men; grace is spred abroad in thi lippis; therfor God blessid thee withouten ende.[130]

---

[126] Hudson (2012), vol. 1, p. lxxxvi. [127] Hargreaves (1955), p. 81.

[128] Ghosh (2002), p. 14.

[129] Hargreaves (1955) cites many further convincing instances of Lyran influences on LV psalms. For example, Psalm 8: 5's 'filius hominis' is translated as 'the son of man' in EV, but 'the sone of a virgyn' in LV, a reading which is also found in Lyra ('aut filius hominis i. filius virginis' [or son of man, that is, son of a virgin]) (p. 81). As Hargreaves points out, this suggestion is also made by Bede (Rolle, the *Metrical*, and the *Prose Psalters* all translate 'son of man/man's son'. Bodley 959's EV psalms make no reference to the gloss). See also Psalm 15: 5 'Dominus pars hereditatis meae et calicis mei' [The Lord is the portion of my inheritance and of my cup], translated '[t]he Lord the part of myn eritage, and of my chalis' in EV, but '[t]he Lord is part of myn eritage, and of my passion' in LV. Bodley 959 preserves 'chalis'. Rolle has 'Lord is part of myn heritage. and of my chalice' (p. 53), and the *Metrical Psalter* 'Lauerd dele ofe mine heritage isse / And ofe mi drinke, with mikel blisse'(p. 146). The *Prose Psalter*, however, is closer to the LV in its glossing of 'calicis' as 'ioie' ('Our Lord is part of myn heritage and of mye ioie' (p. 15)). Finally, see Psalm 41: 8 'abissus ad abissum invocat in voce cataractarum tuarum' [Deep calleth on deep, at the noise of thy flood-gates], translated '[t]he depnesse depnesse inwardli clepeth; in the vois of thi gooteris' in EV, but '[d]epthe clepith depthe; in the vois of thi wyndows' in LV. This is a reading very obviously inspired by by Lyre ('cataractae dei dicuntur fenestrae caeli' [the windows of heaven are called the floodgates of God]). Bodley 959 has 'gooteris'. Rolle translates 'catharactarum' as 'gutters', but the *Prose* version is the entirely glossing '[h]elle blameþ þe fendes for þy deþ of þe croice' (p. 51). The *Metrical Psalter* has the somewhat impenetrable '[d]epnes depnes inkalles hegh, / In steuen of þi takenes slegh' (p. 174).

[130] Although the EV psalms of Bodley 959 contain some readings and corrections characteristic of LV, they have no 'Crist' at this moment. See C. Lindberg, *MS Bodley 959: Genesis to Baruch 3: 20*

The sanction for this addition lies with Lyre; his gloss, included in most manuscripts of LV, states 'þis salm is seid of Crist and of hooli chirche modir and virgin, for Poul in [Hebr. 1: 8–9] aleggiþ þis salme seid of Crist to þe lettre [*ad litteram*]'.[131] It is, however, a reading common in Middle English psalm literature. Rolle reads the entire psalm as concerned with Christ ('[t]his psalme spekis of the weddynge of crist and his spouse') and like the Wycliffite LV, the *Prose Psalter* names Christ in its translation ('Fair artou, Christ, in fourme to-fore mennes sones; grace is shadde in þy lippes; for-þy blisced God þe wyþ -outen ende.')

A small group of LV manuscripts provides us with an insight into the sustained process of glossing undergone by the Wycliffite psalms.[132] The first of these, London, Lambeth Palace Library 1033 (V) (*c.* 1410–20), contains 2 Chronicles 2: 7—Baruch and has glosses in the psalms and some unique glosses in Job.[133] The second (Oxford, BodlL Fairfax 2 (K)) is a complete Bible and lectionary, and has many glosses including several in the psalms, some of which are unique.[134] The third (Oxford, BodlL Bodley 554 (B_554) *c.* 1400) is particularly noteworthy. Containing only the psalms and the canticles, it is very heavily glossed throughout, generally attributing its glosses to Lyre. Although the presentation of the glosses in each of these manuscripts differs somewhat (in K they are written within the text, and in V and B_554 they are marginal) and although the glosses differ in length and detail (those in B_554 are extensive, whereas those in K, and to a slightly lesser extent in V, are very brief), they are clearly related to each other. It is possible to divide the glosses according to their focus; while some emphasize points of doctrine and some are allegorizing, a significant number insist on a moral reading of the psalms. Still others point to the psalms' Christocentric nature and some seem to gesture towards a polemical reading. Taken as a whole, they indicate a confident approach to the scriptural text and the responsibilities of the translator. The Psalter's sacrosanct nature is never in doubt, but in the right hands its translation can be legitimately accompanied by clarification and explanation.

A doctrinal emphasis is visible, for example, in the glossing of Psalm 1: 5 ('Therfor wickid men risen not aȝen in doom; nethir synneres in the councel of

---

in the Earlier Version of the Wycliffite Bible Stockholm Studies in English 6, 8, 10, 13, 20, 29, 81, 87 (8 vols) (Stockholm, 1959–97), vol. 4, p. 191.

[131] See Dove (2007), p. 159. As background, see Aquinas on the literal sense: in our reading of the Bible 'even rhetorical figures—metaphor, fictive similitude, and parable or rhetorical allegory—as linguistic phenomena, are assimilated to the literal sense' (R. Copeland, 'Rhetoric and the Politics of the Literal Sense in Medieval Literary Theory: Aquinas, Wyclif and the Lollards', in *Interpretation: Medieval and Modern*, ed. P. Boitani and A. Torti (Cambridge, 1993), pp. 1–23, p. 8).

[132] The majority of LV manuscripts include glosses at the beginning of many of the psalms, in effect mini-prologues, as far as Psalm 72 (and a few include such glosses for later psalms). According to Dove, the manuscripts which include glosses for the later psalms are Oxford, BodlL Fairfax 2; Oxford, New College 66; CUL Dd. I. 27; CCCC Parker Library 147; London, Lambeth Palace Library 25; and London, Lambeth Palace Library 1033.

[133] Dove (2007), p. 293, no. 50.

[134] Dove (2007), pp. 257–9. On f.385r 'þe ȝeer of þe lord m.cccc & viij þis boke was endid' with the fourth 'c' erased.

iust men'). After 'doom', K adds 'that is, to ther saluacion, but more to ther dampnacion' and V the almost identical 'that is, to han saluacioun, but to dampnacioun more'. Bodley 554 makes it clear that Lyre is behind this gloss, commenting
in marginal red 'Þat is to her saluacioun but more to dampnacioun of bodi and
soule *Lire here*' (f. 1r). At the corresponding moment, Rolle has 'fforthi wicked rise
noght in dome: ne synful in counsaile of rightwis', but his commentary makes the
same point as the Wycliffite gloss:

> If we speke of the last day of dome. wickid sall noght rise in dome for to deme, bot for
> to be demed & dampned. (p. 8)[135]

More frequent are those glosses which present the psalms as articulating and reflecting on matters of morality, particularly as they apply to the penitent individual.
For example, the 'thorn' of Psalm 31: 4 ('For bi dai and ny3t thin hond was maad
greuouse on me; Y am turned in my wretchednesse, while the thorn is set in') is, in
B_554, marginally glossed thus:

> Þat is of contricioun *is set yn*. For at Þe word of nathan Þe profete he was contrite and
> knoulechide his synne (f. 14v)

An abbreviated version of this gloss ('. . . the thorn, that is, of contricion . . .')
also appears in K and it is again worth noting that a similar reading is enjoined
by Rolle, who glosses the thorn as 'compunccioun' (p. 112).[136] The penitential
reformation of the individual is again emphasized in the Wycliffite gloss on Psalm
50: 19 ('A sacrifice to God is a spirit troblid; God, thou schalt not dispise a contrit
herte and maad meke'). In Bodley 554, the marginal comment on 'spirit troblid'
reads 'þat is sori for synne *lire* here' (f. 26r) and this is duplicated in K and V,
without the attribution to Lyre. Rolle's gloss here is similar in emphasis but rather
more sacramentally precise; the 'contrit hert' is, specifically, the 'hert contrite
in penaunce and mekid in shrift' (p. 187).[137] It is perhaps unsurprising that the
Wycliffite gloss should make no reference to 'shrift', given the movement's troubled relationship with the practice of auricular confession. K, V, and B_554 also
share a gloss on Psalm 54: 20–1 ('For chaungyng is not to hem, and thei dredden
not God; he holdith forth his hoond in 3elding. Thei defouliden his testament');
in all three, the 'chaungyng' is specified to be 'fro synne to penauns'.[138] That this
specification is not paralleled by Rolle should not distract us from the fact that
affinities with many of the Wycliffite moral glosses can be found in his *English*

[135] The same verse in the *Prose Psalter* reads 'For- þi ne schal nou₃t þe wicked arise in iugement, ne
þe sinniers in þe conseyl of þe ry₃tful.' (p. 1)
[136] At the same moment, the *Prose Psalter* reads 'For þyn honde ys greued vp me day and ny₃t; ich
am turned in my chaitifte, þer-whiles þat vices ben ficched in me.' (p. 35) The 'thorn' has disappeared
from this glossing translation, replaced by 'vices'.
[137] The *Prose Psalter* makes no reference to individual sorrow for sin or penance, but addresses God
as though he were a feudal lord ('þan shal tou take sacrifice of ry₃t, seruice, and honours; hij shul þan
setten godenesses to-fore þy throne' (p. 62)).
[138] Psalm 50 is heavily glossed throughout in Bodley 554; on this verse it reads 'þat is fro synne to
penaunce *lire here* (f. 28r).

Psalter.[139] These glosses in K, V, and B_554 are entirely conventional in the readings that they propose.[140] And what is interesting about them is the way in which they marry the psalms with basic penitential doctrine, making them applicable to the devotional life of the reader. The translated psalms can speak directly to the circumstances of the contrite Christian.

It is not only these three manuscripts which contain glosses emphasizing the moral application of the psalms. Oxford, BodlL Bodley 277 (I) (*c.* 1425–35), a complete, stylistically revised LV Bible, also preserves a substantial body of glosses throughout.[141] As Dove points out, some of its Psalter glosses are shared with K, V, and B_554, but others are apparently unique. A case in point is its glossing of Psalm 6: 7's bed ('I traueilide in my weilyng, Y schal waische my bed bi eche ny3t') with 'or conscience'.[142] While this reading is not found in any other LV manuscript, it appears in Rolle ('I sall waysch my bed, that is his consciens' (p. 23)) who derives it from the Lombard ('vel lectum vocat conscientiam' [alternatively, he calls the bed conscience] *PL* 191: 0107B), reminding us that it is nothing other than conventional.[143] This rendering figurative (conscience) of the literal (bed), perhaps more properly described as the rendering 'truly literal' of the literal, is also seen in other manuscript glosses on the psalms. In K, for example, Psalm 25: 8 ('Lord, Y haue loued the fairnesse of thin hows') is glossed 'hous, that is, cristen mannes soule'.[144] And in several manuscripts the 'foot' of Psalm 25: 12 ('Mi foot stood in ri3tfulnesse; Lord, Y schal blesse thee in chirchis') is read as 'affection' or 'affecciouns'. Again, both of these glosses find echoes in the earlier Rolle Psalter: the hermit glosses foot as 'luf' (25: 12) and is lyrically expansive in his reading of God's house as the self (25: 8):

> That is, i luffid to make my self a feyre howse to the: not suffrand any filthe be thar in.
> that shuld mys pay the. Mony lokes how fowle thei my3t make thaim to the deuel: &
> i lufid the sted of the wonnyng of thi ioy. that is, i lufid to make me asted in the whilk

---

[139] Although the *Prose Psalter* does not refer to penance, its translation does emphasize a movement from sin: 'For chaunge nis nou3t to hem of her iuel lif, and hij ne drad nou3t God; he putt forþe his vengeaunce in-to 3eldyng' (p. 65).

[140] See also the 'mouth' of Psalm 48: 14. In K and V it is glossed 'that is, bosting of lustful lijf' and in B_554 'for þei auaunten hem of sich lustful liyf' (f. 24v). Rolle's commentary reads the verse similarly: '[t]his way, that is, this life of tha, for it ledis thaim til hell, is slawndire til thaim. that is, stangynge and sorow and cheson of thaire dampnacioun' (p. 177). The *Prose Psalter* has 'þys her way his sclaunder to hem; and efter hij shul plesen uiciouseliche in her mouþe' (p. 58).

[141] For a brief description of the manuscript, see Dove (2007), pp. 253–5. The manuscript has been edited by Conrad Lindberg (1999). He describes it as 'a final product of the makers of the Wycliffite versions of the Bible. Based on the Later Version, with traces of the Early Version, it constitutes a revised form of this Bible . . . [t]his royal bible manuscript unites features of all the previous stages into an authoritative whole worthy of the originator' (p. 2). While admitting the significance and idiosyncracy of several of I's revisions, Dove disagrees with Lindberg's reading of it as a 'final' version (Dove (2007), pp. 150–2).

[142] Lindberg (1999), vol. 2, p. 456.

[143] B_554 does not have a gloss on 'bed' but provides this marginal gloss on 'woodnesse': 'Þat is for sorewe of herte wherefor in ebru & in ieroms translacioun it is of bittirnesse li he' (f. 2v) and the fuller gloss on the whole psalm points out that 'Þis salm mai be expowned of ech synere repentynge verily'. The *Prose Psalter* which, as will be seen, frequently renders figurative that which is literal, stays close to the text at this point: 'Ich trauayled in my sorowynges; ich shal wasshe my bed [by] uch ny3t.' (p. 5)

[144] Although the psalm is glossed extensively in B_554, this particular gloss is absent.

thou wold ioyfully wonne, so that i my3t sumwhat fele & take of thi ioy: the fairhed of
his howse is gode werkis. the sted of the wonnyng of his ioy is the priuete of oure hert,
where is the setyll of holy thowgthis, in the whilk wonnes his ioy. (p. 94) [145]

However, taking the reader on a ruminative journey centred on the image of the
self as 'feyre howse', here Rolle's Psalter highlights one of its fundamental differences from the Wycliffite versions. While the hermit is able, in his often expansive
commentary, to model an affective response to the psalms for his audience, the
Wycliffite Psalter does not have this space.[146]

The Wycliffite glosses on the Psalter also reflect convention in their insistence
on its Christocentric nature. For example, Psalm 12: 6's '[m]yn herte schal fulli
haue ioie in thin *helthe*' becomes, in I, 'helthe 3iuere, Crist' recalling the link made
in Rolle's commentary ('& my hert sall ioy in thi hele. that is in ihesu') (p. 47).[147]
And Psalm 39: 3's '[a]nd he ordeynede my feet on a *stoon*' is glossed 'that is, Crist'
in K, V and B_554, a gloss which also appears in Rolle ('on the stane, that is on
Crist').[148] The 'studyes' [studia] of Psalm 9: 12 are glossed 'that is, the gospel' in
K, and 'þat is þe lawe of þe gospel which he tau3te studiousli bi word & dede: lire
here' in B_554.[149] That in Rolle's commentary they are the 'comaundmentis'
rather than the gospel perhaps reflects the particular importance of the latter in
Wycliffite thought. There are of course other moments when Rolle's commentary
and the Wycliffite glosses differ in emphasis. Psalm 84: 14 ('Ri3tfulnesse schal go
bifore him; and schal sette hise steppis in the weie') provides a striking example.
In both K and V, 'ri3tfulnesse' is glossed 'that is, Johan Baptist', an interpretation
expounded more fully in B_554's 'þat is ioon baptist shal go bifor crist & shal sette
steppis in þe weie of penaunce for he lyuyde in penaunce & tau3te it'. In Rolle's

---

[145] The Lombard offers two alternative readings of Psalm 25: 8's house: it is the self ('id est dilexi
me facere decoram domum tibi' [it is my delight to make honourable your house]) or the church
('Vel ita: Domus Dei Ecclesia est' [or thus: the House of God is the Church) (*PL* 191: 0264D). Psalm
25: 12's foot is glossed 'id est dilectio mea et affectio' [which is my delight and affection] (*PL* 191:
0266B).

[146] In the Wycliffite revision of Rolle's comment on verse 8, the emphasis falls less on the internal
disposition of the intercessor than it does on the obligation for all men (particularly 'fals' clergy) to be
cleansed of sin: 'þe feirehede of þin hous is a clene soule, oute of þe whiche springeþ louyng wordes
and gode werkes, and not riche peyntyng of stockes and of stones, þe whiche price shulde kepe needy
men and wymmen of gode wille fro grutchyng' (Hudson (2012), vol. 1, p. 304/134–8).

[147] See Lindberg (1999), vol 2, p. 459. 'Helþe' is turned to 'helþe 3iuer' elsewhere in this manuscript (see, for example, Psalm 11: 7). Rather than drawing attention to its Christological application,
the Lyran gloss to this psalm in B_554 emphasizes its historical circumstances (f. 5r). Rolle takes
his interpretation from the Lombard: '*Exsultabit*, vel exsultavit cor meum. [Aug., Gl. int.] Quasi
dicat: Speravi in misericordia: unde *exsultabit cor meum in salutari tuo*, id est in Jesu' [My heart will
rejoice or has rejoiced. As though he says: O hoped in mercy: whence *my heart will rejoice in your
salvation*, that is in Jesus] (*PL* 191: 0162B). A Christocentric reading is not found at this moment in
the *Prose Psalter*.

[148] Rolle's reading is borrowed from the Lombard ('*supra petram*, id est Christum' [on the rock,
that is Christ] *PL* 191: 0400A). B_554's Psalm 39 also has an overarching Christocentric gloss: 'þis
salm is expowned of crist in Xᶜ to ebreis in person of Crist himself & in person of his bodi hooli
chirche (lire here)' (f. 19v). Again, the *Prose Psalter* differs at this point, the 'stoon' disappearing altogether from its translation ('And he stablist my fete in stedfastnes, and dresced my goynges', p. 48).

[149] At this point, the *Prose Psalter* reads '[s]ingeþ to our Lord, þat woneþ in heuen; sheweþ his
studyynges amonge men' (p. 9).

commentary, the John the Baptist link is not made and, as is typical of his Psalter, the verse is applied to the internal disposition of the penitent:

[r]ightwisnes of penaunce for oure syn. sall ga bifor him in vs. that is, it sall ren his cumynge in til vs (p. 311)[150]

Yet they are not so far apart; both Rolle and B_554 emphasize a penitential reading of the psalm even if they do so in different ways.

One area in which the Wycliffite glosses do differ from Rolle in emphasis, however, is in their occasional confrontation of social ills in a manner which chimes with preoccupations often (though not exclusively) associated with their movement.[151] For example, the 'cumpas' of Psalm 58: 7 ('[t]hei schulen be turned at euentid, and thei as doggis schulen suffre hungir; and thei schulen cumpas the citee') is glossed, 'that is, go a begging' in K, and that of 58: 15 as 'gon a beggid' in V. Both recall the fuller gloss in B_554 which reads 'in sekinge liyflode *bi beggynge*' (f. 30r) and which claims the authority of Lyre ('*lire here*'). Yet Rolle's glosses indicate entirely different interpretations at this point: that on verse 7 reads '[a]t euen, departand fra thaim the het of couaitis. sum of thaim sall be turnyd, and thai sall hafe hungire to turne other men, as hundis berkand agayn thaire enmys, mayntenand rightwisnes: and thai sall vmga the cite. that is. thai sall warenyss halykirke with lare and vertus' (p. 208). And that on verse 15 claims that '[t]his prophecy is of the iewes, that sal be turned til crist at even, that is, in the end of the worlde, & hunger rightewisnes' (p. 209).[152] A similar instance is provided by K and V's explanatory gloss on Psalm 72: 8 ('[t]hei thou3ten and spaken weiwardnesse; thei spaken *wickidnesse*') as 'blasfemye/blasfemyng a3ens God', again recalling the fuller gloss in B_554 ('þat is blasfemye a3ens god *lire here*' (f. 37v)).[153] Rolle's commentary, by contrast, makes no reference to blasphemy, reading the verse as referring more generally to those who speak 'proudly and apartely' and 'againste the trowthe of haly kirke' (p. 258). A final example can be seen in the interpretation of Psalm 96: 7 ('Alle that worschipen sculptilis be schent, and thei that han glorie in her symelacris'). In B_554, 'sculptilis' is glossed 'þat is idols maad wiþ hondis *lire here*' (f. 52v), a gloss echoed in K, ('[t]hat is, idols maad with hondis. *Austyn here*').[154] This very specific reference to the worship of material idols is, however,

---

[150] The overarching Lyran gloss on this psalm in B_554 focuses on the fact that it is sung 'for þe turnynge a3en of iewis fro þe caitiste of babiloyne' (f. 46r). Such historical circumstances tend not to interest Rolle in the same way.

[151] This is not to say that Rolle does not use his commentary to critical ends, but simply that his criticisms do not tend to coincide with those expressed in the Wycliffite Psalter glosses. For a reading of Rolle's Psalter as sometimes contentious, see K. Gustafson, 'Richard Rolle's English Psalter and the Making of a Lollard Text', *Viator* 33 (2002), 294–309.

[152] Both of Rolle's glosses are inspired by the Lombard. See *PL* 191: 0544C '*circuibunt civitatem, id est munient Ecclesiam contra haereticas impugnationes*' [*shall go round the city*, that is, will safeguard the church against heretical attacks], and 0548A 'Tertia pars, ubi affirmatur salus Judaeorum, et utroque pariete collecto grates aguntur. Quasi dicat: Comprehendantur in superbia sua' [The third part, where the salvation of the Jews is affirmed, and on both sides of the narrow wall. As though he says: may they be grasped in their pride].

[153] In B_554, the translation reads 'þei spaken wickidnesse *and lii3*'.

[154] In I, the 'sculptilis' become 'grauen thingis or ymagis' (Lindberg (1999), vol. 2, p. 507).

entirely absent from Rolle's commentary on this verse, which interprets 'mawme-try' much more broadly:

> Auerice is seruyce of mawmetry. and ilke man makis that his mawmet that he mast lufis. as sum has syluyre his mawmet. sum fayre hors. sum town or kastell. sum vanyte of atyre. Mawmetry is when any man gifis the luf til any creature that aghe to be gifen til god. (p. 345)

Wycliffite confidence in deploying the psalms to pointedly critical, if not polemical, ends is emphasized in chapter 10 of the General Prologue, in which the suggestion that 'doumb prelatis moun ri3tfuli be clepid symylacris or idols' is substantiated by two citations from the Psalter:

> Þei þat maken sich prelatis ben liyk hem, whiche makeris shulen be dampned wiþ sich prelatis, bi þat word of Dauiþ 'þei þat maken þo ben maad liyk þo' . . . symylacris of clei ben fleischli prelatis, of which God seiþ, in þe Sauter, 'I shal do hem awei as þe clei of stretis'.[155]

The writer's further condemnation of corrupt 'lordis and prelatis' is also confirmed by appeal to the psalms:

> And God seiþ in þe Sauter of sich tirauntis 'þei deuouren my puple as þe mete of breed'.[156]

It is worth noting that this anti-clerical reading is anticipated in Rolle's Psalter, where he who 'gredely etis' is likened to one who 'wynnes til the offices of haly kirke for to take riches and honour of men, noght for hele of mannys saule, na for the louynge of god. bot for to ete godis folke as mete of brede' (p. 49). Such a similarity serves as a timely reminder that for all their differences, the hermit and the Wycliffites can and do share significant common ground in their interactions with the psalms.[157]

THE MIDLAND *PROSE PSALTER*

Beginning with the *Metrical Psalter*, this chapter has considered the practice of trans-lation in four of the five complete *English Psalters* of the late Middle Ages. While

---

[155] Dove (2010), p. 49/1675–7, 1680–1. LV Psalm 113: 16 ('Thei that maken tho ben maad lijk tho') and 134: 18 ('Thei that maken tho, be maad lijk tho') are the source of the first (it is interest-ing that I alone contains a gloss on Psalm 113: 8, indicating the same reading as that of the General Prologue: 'þo' is glossed 'symulacris'). LV Psalm 17: 43 is the source of the second ('Y schal do hem awei, as the cley of stretis'). Rolle does not use these verses to polemical ends.

[156] Dove (2010), p. 53/1810–11. See LV Psalm 13: 4: '[w]hether alle men that worchen wickid-nesse schulen not knowe; that deuowren my puple, as mete of breed'.

[157] Rolle's reading is once again related to that of the Lombard: '*Qui devorant plebem meam, seducendo, vel occidendo sicut escam panis*, id est ut sit eis satietas, de deceptione Christianorum. [Aug.] Vel, devorant plebem, ut faciunt illi qui in ministerio suo utuntur ad capienda commoda ab hominibus, non ad salutem hominum, vel ad gloriam Dei. Et hoc sicut escam panis, id est quotidie sicut panis est quotidianus cibus, ita et illi quotidiana rapina simplices Christianos absorbent' [*They who devour my people*, will lead astray or will kill, *as if they were eating the meat of bread*, that is until they are satiated of deception of Christians. Or, they devour people, as those who use their ministry to seize the advantage from men, not to the salvation of men, nor to the glorification of God. And this is like the meat of bread, it is daily as bread is daily food, and in the same way they devour simple Christians with daily robbery] (*PL* 191: 0165C-D).

the notion of a straightforward line of descent from the *Metrical Psalter* through Rolle and to the two Wycliffite versions has been queried, it is clear that in all four translations strict fidelity to the letter of the Bible is prioritized. The fact that this 'strict fidelity' can incorporate a degree of glossing is also apparent throughout the English 'tradition', most obviously in the Wycliffite LV. However, it was not only the Wycliffites who incorporated glossing within the practice of translation. In this final section of the chapter we turn to the fourteenth-century *Prose Psalter*, possibly written before Rolle's translation and certainly before the Wycliffite versions, as evidence of a rather different manner of glossing. Its distinctiveness is twofold; first, the translator reproduces glosses already found in his Anglo-Norman source rather than inserting them himself, and second, he often uses them to emphasize a rather different reading of the psalms. Borrowing from his source, he appears to understand the role of the translator in a manner distinct from, though not entirely dissimilar to, Rolle and the Wycliffites. In his mind, translation is quite legitimately an act of rhetorical invention (or at least a reproduction of that act, performed already in the glossed Anglo-Norman), and in his hands, the Psalter becomes a somewhat altered text. Like Chaucer's disingenuous narrator in *Troilus and Criseyde*, the translator of the *Prose Psalter* has 'in eched' several words 'for the best'. Such 'in echings' endorse, rather than supersede, the terminology of the original; there is no element of competition in the Prose text's model of translation.

It will have been noted in the preceding discussion that while Rolle and the Wycliffite glosses often, although not invariably, agree in their reading of the psalms, the *Prose Psalter* seems to concur with them less often. In fact, of all the instances listed, it shares the same interpretation at only one moment, namely Psalm 44: 3, which all three take to be a description of Christ. In the vast majority of cases, such lack of agreement can be explained by the fact that the *Prose Psalter*'s translations are not invariably glossing. It does not, for example, gloss 6: 5, 9: 12, 12: 16, 25: 8 and 12, 58: 7 and 15, or 84: 14, all of which have been discussed. On such occasions, it is not that the *Prose* text reads the psalms differently but that it does not 'read' them at all; the translation is unsupplemented by gloss.[158] However, at the moments when it does amalgamate gloss and translation, its reading can differ from that of the other two Psalters. Such is the case with Psalm 39: 3 ('And he heard my prayers, and brought me out of the pit of misery and the mire of dregs. And he set my feet upon a rock, and directed my steps'); while Rolle and the Wycliffite glosses read this verse's 'rock' as 'Christ', the *Prose* text loses the rock altogether, replacing it with the abstract noun 'stedfastnes' (p. 48).[159] This silent replacement of original with gloss is a particular feature of the Anglo-Norman and English translations; BN 6260 reads 'Et il estably mes piez en establete' and BL 44949 'Et il establist mes piez sur establete' (f. 99r).[160] Yet BL 44949's Latin, like that of BL 17376, retains both original and gloss, distinguishing them from each other by underlining the latter.[161]

---

[158] That the translation is itself a reading should go without saying.

[159] The English translation in Pepys 2498 also silently erodes the biblical rock (Black and St-Jacques (2012), p. 26).

[160] For BN 6260, see Black and St-Jacques, p. 93.

[161] BL Add. 17376's Latin reads 'et statuit super petram *id est stabilitatem*' [and set upon a rock, *that is stability*] (f. 35v), as does that of BL Add. 44949 (f. 99r).

A similar pattern can be observed in its reading of Psalm 31: 4's 'thorn' ('For day and night thy hand was heavy upon me. I am turned in my anguish, whilst the thorn is fastened'). While Rolle and the Wycliffite glosses interpret it as 'compunccioun' and 'contricion' respectively, the *Prose Psalter* deletes it, replacing the singular 'spina' [thorn] with the plural 'vices' that are 'ficchid to me' (p. 35).[162] This reproduces the Anglo-Norman 'vice est en moi fiche', witnessed in both BN 6260 and BL Add. 44949.[163] Yet although this *Prose* gloss differs from that in the other two complete *Middle English Psalters*, it is not without authoritative precedent: the Lombard glosses 'spina' similarly as 'peccatum' [sins] (*PL*, 191: 0319D)).[164] Neither is it unrelated to the contrition/compunction glosses, since it is the piercing with sin that prompts such penitential states.

On both of the occasions discussed, the glossing English of the *Prose Psalter* appears to be a translation of the glossed Anglo-Norman original, best represented by the aforementioned fourteenth-century Tywardreath Psalter preserved in London, BL Add. 44949.[165] The fact that this is the case is masked by the manuscript context of the text: none of the four extant English witnesses preserves the Anglo-Norman. Their preservation of the glossed Latin which lies behind the French does, however, allow us a second-hand insight into the text's interaction with its primary sources, enabling us to see that Psalm 39: 3's 'stedfastnes' and Psalm 31: 4's 'thorn' do not originate in the English text but are derived ultimately from the Latin. On other occasions, though, the preservation of the Latin is misleading: as analysis of the Tywardreath Psalter suggests, there are occasions on which versions of the Anglo-Norman psalms which lie behind the *Prose* translation contain glosses which do not derive from the Latin. When the *Prose Psalter* introduces glosses that do not feature in the Latin text which accompanies it in the manuscript, it is likely that they are borrowed directly from their Anglo-Norman source. There is no definitive answer to the question of why the English manuscripts do not preserve the Anglo-Norman as well as the Latin: it may have been for reasons for space and time but it could equally be explained by anxiety as to the

---

[162] BL Add.17376 (f. 26r). The Latin Psalter in this manuscript does not contain the gloss at this point. It does, however, appear as an underlined alternative to 'spina' in the Latin text preserved in Pepys 2498: 'dum configitur spina *id est vicium*' (Black and St-Jacques, p. 12). Both Princeton Scheide 143 and TCD 69 retain the two alternatives in their English translation: 'þe þorne[s] or vices' (Black and St-Jacques, p. 114).

[163] For BN 6260, see Black and St-Jacques, p. 86. In BL Add. 44949, see f. 8r.

[164] Hull follows this tradition: 'Ye schul vndyrstond that holy wryt callyth "þornys" the greuous synnys that man doth' and goes on to link the thorn more specifically with the conscience ('And þer-for spake Dauid of þys þorne wher-with hys consyence had be prykkyd'). Barratt (1995), p. 33/328–44.

[165] Occasionally, there seem to be misunderstandings of the Latin. So, the second half of Psalm 78: 1, which reads 'polluerunt templum sanctum tuum posuerunt ierusalem in pomorum custodiam' [they have defiled thy holy temple: they have made Jerusalem as a place to keep fruit], in the Gallican is translated 'and hij filden þyn holy temple, and sett Ierusalem in þe kepeing of a maner of folk þat was cleped Pomos' (p. 98) in the *Prose*. 'Pomorum' become 'apples' in all other Middle English translations of this psalm, following from Augustine and the Lombard: the *Prose Psalter* is the only one that struggles. This appears to a reproduction of an error in the Anglo-Norman; see BN 6260 'de gens appelez Pommes' (Black and St-Jacques, p. 121) and BL Add. 44949 'de gentes apellez pommes' (f. 165r).

credibility of the translation. To suggest a direct line of descent from the Gallican perhaps gives the *Prose Psalter* more authority than it would have were it to admit to an Anglo-Norman intermediary.

Although the Anglo-Norman glossed Psalter is absent from all four manuscripts of the English text, the work of Ole Reuter has demonstrated convincingly that the English translation is indebted to such a source. Leaving aside the glosses for a moment, its indebtedness is often revealed in use of Anglo-Norman loan-words. To take an example from Psalm 31: 4, already discussed, in the *Prose Psalter* the verse in its entirety reads:

> For þyn honde ys greued vp me day and ny3t; ich am turned in my chaitifte, þer-whiles þat vices ben ficched in me. (p. 35)

It is the term 'chaitiste' which is of interest here, differing from the Rollean and Wycliffite 'wrichidnes'. Its ultimate source is of course the Vulgate 'erumpna' [anguish], but it appears to actually translate the French 'chetiveté', meaning 'wretchedness'.[166] Looking again at Psalm 39: 3, similar observations can be made. In the *Prose Psalter* the verse reads '[a]nd he stablist my fete in stedfastnes, and dresced my goynges' (p. 48) and it is the translation of 'statuit' [set (my feet)] as 'stablist' which is noteworthy (in Rolle we have 'sett abouen' and in the Wycliffite LV 'ordeynede'). Although the romance verb 'stablishen' is by no means unusual in Middle English, it seems fairly clear that the translator is here working from the Anglo-Norman 'establir', which appears in BN 6260 and in Add. 44949 at this point.[167] The *Prose* text's indebtedness to an Anglo-Norman source is suggested further not only by its translation of individual words, but of fuller phrases. A case in point is its repetition of 'our(e) lord', a literal translation of 'Nostre Seigneur' for 'all cases of 'dominus', whether or not 'noster' accompanies it in the Latin'; at the same moments Rolle and the Wycliffite versions tend to use '(the) lord'.[168] Its comparative independence of the word-order of the Latin can also be attributed to its reliance on its Anglo-Norman source. As Reuter points out, '[e]ven in case[s] where the Latin order of words would be perfectly natural in English, the French [is often] followed', leading to 'quite a modern impression'.[169] The *Prose Psalter*'s more consistently idiomatic word-ordering distinguishes it further from Rolle, the EV, and even, to an extent, LV.

---

[166] Reuter, p. 21. 'Chetiveté' appears in BN 6260 and in BL Add. 44949 (f. 82r) at this point. The version of the *Prose Psalter* in Pepys 2498 also has 'cheitifte', but in TCD 69 and Princeton Scheide 143, we find 'myschefe' (Black and St-Jacques, p. 20 and p. 114). According to the MED, the *Prose Psalter*'s 'chaitiste' represents the earliest occurrence of the word in Middle English.

[167] Reuter, p. 38. He points out that the version of the *Prose Psalter* in TCD 69 does not use 'stablish'. In fact, it uses 'sette', as does Princeton Scheide 143 (Black and St-Jacques, p. 117). Pepys 2498 has 'stabled' (Black and St-Jacques, p. 26).

[168] St-Jacques, p. 143.

[169] Reuter, p. 11. He goes on to comment that '[i]t compares favourably with Rolle's Psalter, which follows the Vulgate closely, and is exceedingly stiff and unidiomatic', although he does concede, rightly, that an unidiomatic translation was actually what Rolle intended. Reuter provides several striking examples of occasions on which the English translation follows the French (represented by BN 6260). He does, however, point out that sometimes the translator appears to follow the Latin rather than the French.

Putting the readability of the Psalter to one side, the most striking results of the translator's indebtedness to the Anglo-Norman are seen in the glosses that he reproduces in his English text. In Pepys 2498, the glosses are ascribed thus:

> Of þe Sautere on Englisch here is þe gynnynge,
> Wiþ þe Latyn bifore & Gregories expounynge (f. 132)

an ascription which obviously bears some relation to that appearing in Bibliothèque nationale 6260:

> Ci commence l'istoire de la Bible, que l'on list en saincte esglise chascun an, translatée de grec en latin et de latin en françois par saint Gregoire, de la vie des sains patriarchez et prophectes qui estoient ou monde avant que Dieu naisquist. [170] [This begins the story of the Bible, which one reads in Holy Church each year, translated from Greek into Latin and from Latin into French by Saint Gregory, from the life of the holy patriarchs and prophets who were in the world before the Lord was born]

The identity of this supposed Gregory has eluded scholars.[171] For us, however, his identity is not as important as the nature of the glosses for which he is responsible, which indicate a perception of the Psalter as directly applicable to the devotional interiority of the individual Christian reader. In itself this is not surprising; we have already seen something similar in the interpretative work of Rolle and the Wycliffites. Two aspects of the *Prose Psalter*'s glosses do, however, mark them out as distinctive. First, as already suggested, they do not always 'read' the psalms' applicability to the individual reader in a manner which chimes with Rollean or Wycliffite preoccupations. Second, by their inclusion in the text of the translated Psalter rather than in the margins or between the lines, the glosses arguably rewrite (albeit minimally) the Gallican Psalter or at least turn it from what it was into something else. This is compounded in the English manuscripts by the fact that there is nothing in the vernacularization's presentation which alerts one to the presence of these glosses. While they are almost always underlined in red in the Latin, the English translation leaves them unsignposted. For the reader focused on the vernacular alone, they are visually indistinguishable from the biblical text that they replace and, on occasion, supplement. But what exactly is it that these glosses turn the Psalter into and how effective are they in doing so?

The most characteristic feature of these glosses, whatever their source, is their replacement of the concrete with the abstract. Time and again they insist on moral and spiritual readings of the psalms. The Psalter's abundant 'waters', for example, are often deleted: such is the case with Psalm 31: 6 ('verumtamen in diluvio aquarum multarum, ad eum non adproximabunt' [And yet in a flood of many waters, they shall not come nigh unto him]). In Rolle we read '[n]oght forthi in flowynge of many watirs til him thai sall noght neghe' (p. 112) and in LV '[n]etheles in the greet flood of many watris; tho schulen not neiȝe to thee', but in the *Prose Psalter* we find 'for-soþe hij ne shal nouȝt come nere hym in þe gaderyng of mani synnes'

---

[170] See Reuter, p. 4. This reference to Gregory does not appear in the Tywardreath Psalter.

[171] Reuter, p. 4: 'None of the existing commentaries on the Psalms by different St. Gregories which I have searched bear any resemblance to our glosses.'

(p. 35).[172] The translation is confidently idiomatic in comparison with Rolle and LV, and also differs from them in its replacement of the waters with 'þe gaderyng of mani synnes'. Its idiomatic nature stems from its immediate Anglo-Norman source, but in its glossing translation it is indebted, ultimately, to the glossed Latin. We see the same tendency at work in Psalm 22: 4 ('virga tua et baculus tuus ipsa me consolatur sunt') [Thy rod and thy staff, they have comforted me]). The 'virga' (rod) and 'baculus' (staff) have vanished from the *Prose* translation and instead we read 'þy discipline and þyn amendyng conforted me' (p. 26). In all four of the English manuscripts, this follows the glossed Latin which (in Add. 17376, f. 23r) reads '[u]irga *id est disciplina* tua & baculus *id est correctio* tuus ipsa mea consolata sunt' [your rod *that is, discipline* and your staff, *that is correction*, they are my consolation].[173] Potent examples of the effect of such insistent moral glossing can be multiplied throughout the text of the *Prose Psalter*. Taking two instances from the evocative and widely translated Psalm 50, verse 9's powerful plea 'asparges me hysopo et mundabor' [thou shalt sprinkle me with hyssop, and I shall be cleansed] rendered literally as 'ysope' by Rolle and the Wycliffite translations, becomes 'Þou sprengest me, Lord, wyþ þy mercy' (p. 61).[174] And verse 10's haunting image of the 'ossa humiliata' [the bones that have been humbled] which will rejoice, again rendered literally in the Rolle and Wycliffite versions, becomes 'þe mylde dedes of my hert shul gladen' (p. 61).[175] As readings of Psalm 50, there is nothing inherently surprising in these glosses.[176] It is the way in which, in the English translation, they

---

[172] In BL Add. 17376, this gloss appears in the Latin (f. 26v). It is also found in BL Add. 44949 ('diluuio *id est congregacione* aquarum *id est uiciorum*' [flood, *that is congregation* of waters, *that is, of sins*]. Black and St-Jacques (p. 12) record an almost identical gloss in Pepys 2498's Latin: 'in diluuio *id est congregacione* aquarum *id est peccatorum*'. The Anglo-Norman in BL Add. 44949 reads 'congregacion de mult3 uices' [congregation of the most vices] (f. 82v) and in BN 6260 'la congregacion de moult de pechiez' (Black and St-Jacques, p. 86).

[173] BL Add. 44949 reads (f. 69v) 'Virga tua & baculus tuus id est disciplina et correctio ipsa me consolata sunt' [Your rod and your staff, that is, your discipline and correction, they are my consolation]. The translation reads 'Ta discipline & ta correctio . . .' [your discipline and your correction . . .], as does that in BN 6260 (Black and St-Jacques, p. 80).

[174] This is another occasion on which the interpretation is clearly not derived from the Latin which, in BL Add. 17376 (f. 46r) and Pepys 2498 (Black and St-Jacques, p. 20), is unglossed at this moment. The gloss does, however, appear in the Latin text in BL Add. 44949 (f. 116v), where it is underlined in red. The Anglo-Norman in both BN 6260 (Black and St-Jacques, p. 100) and BL Add. 44949 reads simply 'de ta mercy', without any referene to hyssop.

[175] In Pepys 2498, we read 'þe workes of myne hert mylde', and in both Dublin Trinity College 69 and Princeton Scheide 143 we find 'meke dedes' (Black and St-Jacques (2012), p. 33 and p. 120). The Latin in BL Add. 17376 is glossed at this point (f. 46r) and Black and St-Jacques point out that the Latin in Pepys 2498 is also glossed here. In BL Add. 44949 (f.116v) the Latin reads 'ossa *id est facta cordi mei* humiliata' and the Anglo-Norman 'les faitz de mon quoer humbles esioierount'. See also BN 6260 (Black and St-Jacques, p. 100). The Psalter's aversion to bones does not persist throughout the translation. See, for example, Psalm 6: 3; 21: 15; 21: 18; 30: 11; 31: 2; 33: 21; 52: 6; 101: 4; 140: 7. However, Psalm 34: 10's 'omnia ossa mea' [all my bones] becomes 'al myn wittes' (p. 40) in all four manuscripts. And Psalm 41: 11's 'confriguntur ossa mea' [my bones are broken] becomes 'my3tes ben frusced' (p. 51) (Pepys 2498 has 'my mi3ttes ben tobroken' (Black and St-Jacques, p. 27). TCD 69 and Princeton Scheide 143 both have 'bones or my3tes' and 'broke or proschid'. For a further example of vividness erased, see Psalm 87: 13's evocative 'terra oblivionis' [the land of forgetfulness]. Translated 'land of forgettyng' (p. 317) by Rolle, in all four manuscripts of the *Prose Psalter* it becomes 'helle' (p. 107).

[176] For a good example of a conventional reading of the Psalms, see Psalm 50: 16's 'libera me de sanguinibus' [Deliver me from blood]. Translated literally by Rolle and the Wycliffites, it becomes

replace the words of the original which is so striking. Further examples can be gleaned from Psalm 90. In the original unglossed Gallican, verses 12 and 13 read:

> [i]n manibus portabunt te ne forte offendas ad lapidem pedem tuum super aspidem et basiliscum ambulabis et conculcabis leonem et draconem.

> [In their hands they shall bear thee up lest thou dash thy foot against a stone. Thou shalt walk upon the asp and the basilisk and thou shalt trample under foot the lion and the dragon]

In the *Prose Psalter*, this becomes:

> Hij shul bere þe in hondes, þat tou ne hirt nou3t perauenture þy gost wyþ vices. þou shalt gon vp queintis and godenes, and þou shalt de-foule þe fende and helle. (p. 113)[177]

The singular 'lapis' [stone] has become the plural 'vices' while the insertion of 'þy gost' has affirmed that this is an emphatically spiritual reading. The venomous, concrete 'aspis' and 'basilisc' have been replaced by the mild, abstract 'queintis and godenes' and the 'leo' and 'draco' by 'þe fende and helle'.

   Putting aside the 'queintis and godenes', to which we will return, there is nothing 'wrong' with any of these glosses when viewed in light of exegetical tradition. The association of psalmic waters with sin, for example, is commonplace. Rolle glosses Psalm 31: 6 thus:

> Tha that ere in flowynge of many waters. that is, tha that flowis in lust of fleysse and delites of this warld and in sere errours of couaitis. thai sall noght neghe til god as thai wene. (p. 112)[178]

and Eleanor Hull reads 'aquarum multarum' [a flood of many waters] as 'þe trybulacyons of þys world and þe dyuers aduersyteys wher-inne þe man fallyth by his synnes'.[179] Similarly, the association of the 'lapis' (Psalm 90: 12) with sin is logical in this context and not without parallel: Rolle makes a similar link in his commentary, referring more specifically to 'the hard stane of presumpcioun or

'deliuer me of sinnes' in all four manuscripts of the *Prose Psalter*. Such a reading, however, is found in Rolle's commentary, '[t]hat is, delyuer me of fleysly synnes' (p. 187), and in a gloss included in the previously discussed Wycliffite LV manuscript Bodley 277 ('delyuere thou me fro bloodis or synnes'). The Latin in BL Add. 44949 reads 'libera me de sanguinib3 *id est de pecis*' while the Anglo-Norman has only 'de peche3' (f. 117r).

[177] All of these glosses also appear in the Latin in BL Add. 17376, although they are not all underlined (ff. 87r–v), and in BL Add. 44949 (f. 185r) where they are all underlined. In Pepys 2498, we find: 'þai schullen beren þe in hondes þat þou ne schalt no3t hirten, þerauenture, þi gost wiþ vices. Þou schalt gon vpe queyntise in godenesse, and þou schalt defoule þe deuel in helle' (Black and St-Jacques, p. 59). Princeton Scheide 143 again retains both text and gloss in its English translation: 'perauentur þou hurt no3t þi gost or þi fote with vice atte stone' (Black and St-Jacques (2012), p. 135).

[178] Rolle is following the Lombard (who is following Augustine) in associating the waters with sins of the flesh (*Verumtamen.* [Alcuin.] 'Quasi dicat: Licet sanctus oret, licet tempus opportunum sit, [Aug.] verumtamen illi qui sunt *in diluvio aquarum multarum*, id est defluentes in carnalibus concupiscentiis' (*PL* 191: 0321C)) [*And yet.* As though he says: Let the holy pray, let it be an appropriate time. And yet those who are *in a flood of many waters*, that is flooded by carnal desires].

[179] Barratt (1995), p. 42/658–60.

desperacioun' (p. 332).[180] It also makes perfect sense to read 'leo & draco' as 'þe fende and helle'. Augustine and the Lombard read both as aspects of the devil, as does Hilton in his commentary on Psalm 90, while Rolle glosses them as internal vices rather than external entities; the lion is 'all cruelte till his neghbure' and the dragon is 'gilry and priue malice, that bloundiss with the heuyd & smytes with the tayle' (p. 333).[181] The interpretation of 'aspis' [asp/snake] as 'queintis' ('wisdom', from the French 'cointise') and of 'basilisc' as 'godenes' is, however, surprising. For obvious reasons, the psalmic 'aspis' is more often associated with temptation and sin: such is the logic demonstrated by Augustine and the Lombard, for example. It is a reading adopted by Hilton and, in keeping with his focus on personal morality in the exegesis of this psalm, Rolle glosses thus:

> the snake [aspis] is ill eggynge that hurtis men priuely ar thai wit, and with delyte and assentynge till syn bryngis forth the basilysk. that is, grete syn in dede, that with the syght slas all the vertus of the saule: with stynkand smell of ill ensaumpill slas men that cumes nere: and with ill ande. that is, with venymous worde slas the herers. (p. 333)[182]

The *Prose* text's wording, however, indicates that lying behind it is a completely different reading of the verse. The asp and basilisk are not perilous temptations to be avoided as one creeps over them, but spiritual virtues upon which to stand as one progresses towards the vanquishing of the devil and hell. The interpretation may be counter-intuitive, an apparent contortion of the text, but it reads nothing untoward into the words of the psalms.

For understandable reasons, Ole Reuter was unimpressed by the impact that such repeated spiritual and moral glossing had on the Psalter and dismissed the translator/commentator responsible as 'not a very advanced spirit'. '[M]ostly', he says, his glosses are 'very dull and mechanical, substituting a prosaic expression for the beautiful and forceful phrases of the Vulgate'.[183] But this is perhaps to miss the point. Interpretations that Reuter classes as 'dull . . . mechanical [and] prosaic' are likely, in the mind of the translator, to have been justifiable as faithful reproductions of the 'true' literal meaning of the Psalter. So, for example, when David speaks of the threat of 'many waters', the divinely inspired translator legitimately reads reference to 'synnes'. To the devout translator, God's 'rod' and 'staff' are obviously his 'discipline' and 'correction', and the hard 'stone' over which one can stumble is clearly the human vice which we must avoid. Eliding translation and commentary into one activity, the *Prose Psalter* and its glossed sources have reproduced not what the psalmist *said* but what he *meant*. The text's legitimacy rests on our acceptance of the translator's implicit claim to have accessed divine authorial 'entent'.

[180] Rolle may have been inspired by the Lombard, who glosses the stone as the unyielding law of the Old Testament prior to the advent of the Holy Spirit 'in plenitudine amoris' (*PL* 191: 0853B). In this gloss, the Lombard is inspired by Augustine. In *Qui Habitat*, Hilton's reading is quite different: 'þe ston', he says, 'is vre lord' and 'haþ non harm. ffor whon þou, þorw blyndnes of þiself, offendest god in vn-ordeyned loue to eni creature, he is neuer þe wors' (B. Wallner, *An Exposition of Qui Habitat and Bonum Est in English* Lund Studies in English 23 (Lund, 1954), p. 39/1–9).

[181] Wallner, pp. 40–3.

[182] For Augustine, see *PL* 37: 1168 and for the Lombard see *PL* 191: 0853C-D.

[183] Reuter, p. 4.

However, it could be argued that the translator is unpredictable in the execution of his role and that, in particular, he does not gloss consistently. The aforementioned asp, for example, is not invariably read as 'queintis'. In Psalm 57: 5 and 139: 4, for example, it is unglossed.[184] The translation of Psalm 13: 3 offers us two alternative literal renditions:

> Her gorge is an open biriel, hij deden trecherouusliche wiþ her tunges; venim of aspides, id est nedders, is vnder her lippes. (p. 13)[185]

Neither is stone always glossed by 'vices' nor waters by 'synnes'.[186] Such vacillation leads to an inconsistency of tone which, for all the *Prose Psalter*'s readability when compared with Rolle et al., can make it seem oddly indigestible. At such moments, the text appears poised precariously between manifesting two conceptualizations of the role of the translator. On the one hand, the translator has a duty to record the words of the Psalmist as *written*, but on the other (as previously pointed out), his loyalty is to the words as *meant*. In his translation, we seem to glimpse a text in a state of arrested metamorphosis. It attempts to be both a faithful rendering of the language of the Psalter and a conversion of that book into a specifically Christian compendium of spiritual and moral guidance, independent of the circumstances of its original composition. This can be illustrated aptly by the prose text's engagement with the Latin 'vnicornis' [unicorn]. While the mythical creature remains in the translations of Psalm 28: 6, 77: 69 and 91: 11, it is deleted from Psalm 21: 22, which turns from the evocative '[s]alva me ex ore leonis et a cornibus unicornium humilitatem meam' [save me from the lion's mouth and my lowness from the horns of the unicorns] to the exegetically acceptable '[s]auue me fram þe mouþe of helle and my mekenes fram iuels of pride' (p. 24).[187] Before we are too hard on the *Prose Psalter* for this apparent irregularity, however, we would do well to bear in mind the Wycliffite caution, outlined in chapter 12 of the General Prologue to the Bible:

> Also þe same word or þe same þing in scripture is takun sumtyme in good and sumtyme in yuele, as a lioun signefieþ sumtyme Crist and in anoþere place it signefieþ þe deuel . . . And whanne not o þing alone but tweyne or moo ben feelid or vndurstonden

[184] It is also unglossed in BN 6260 and in BL Add. 44949.
[185] This is not a variant translation found in the Latin in BL Add. 17376 (f. 9v). In the English, the alternative *'id est nedders'* [that is, snakes] is underlined in red. Neither is it found in the Latin in BL Add. 44949 (ff. 53r–v), where the Anglo-Norman reads 'venym de serpen3' [venom of serpents]. In the English translation in Pepys 2498, the alternative is not offered and we read simply 'venym of serpentes' (Black and St-Jacques (2012), p. 9).
[186] For unglossed occurrences of 'water(s)' see, for example, Psalm 17: 16; 22: 2; 78: 3; 105: 11. For unglossed 'stone(s)' see 18: 11; 20: 4; 117: 22. The absence (from all four manuscript copies) of a gloss in this last verse ('þe stone which þe biggand reproued, and it is made oȝain þe heued of þe corner') is a little surprising: 'Christ' would be the obvious substitution, but it is not glossed in the Latin of any of the English manuscripts, nor in BL Add. 44949 or BN 6260. In Psalm 101: 15, 'lapides' [stone] is glossed by 'fastnes' (Pepys 2498 reads 'stedfastnesses' (Black and St-Jacques, p. 64)).
[187] These glosses appear, as additions to the Gallican, in the Latin in BL. Add. 17376, Pepys 2498, and BL. Add. 44949. The Anglo-Norman in BL Add. 44949 and BN 6260 silently erases original with gloss.

bi þe same wordis of scripture . . . þat is no perele if it mai be preued bi oþere places of hooli writ þat ech of þo þingis acordiþ wiþ treuþe.[188]

According to such logic, what appears to be an act of random and unsanctioned interpretation can actually be justified hermeneutically.[189]

Whatever its inconsistencies, however, it is undeniable that the overwhelming focus of the *Prose* text is on the psalms as interior psychodrama. It is in keeping with this focus that the Psalter sometimes erases the geographical specifics of the Vulgate, replacing them with abstract nouns or eschatological landscapes. This is particularly the case in its dealings with 'Sion', which disappears altogether from the rendition of Psalm 19: 3 ('mittat tibi auxilium de sancto et de Sion tueatur te' [may he send thee help from the sanctuary and defend thee out of Sion]):

Sende he to þe helpe of þe holy gost, and defende he þe fram iuel. (p. 22)[190]

Once again, such a reading seems counter-intuitive and has no obvious basis in exegetical tradition: Rolle, for example, drawing on the Lombard, equates 'Syon' with 'heghe contemplacioun'.[191] On several other occasions, however, 'Sion' is more conventionally replaced with 'heuen' (see, for example, Psalm 2: 6; 13: 7; 50: 20; 73: 2; 83: 8) and at one notable moment (Psalm 134: 21 'benedictus Dominus ex Sion qui habitat in Hierusalem' [Blessed be the Lord out of Sion, who dwelleth in Jerusalem]) it holds its own in a translation which assigns the signification of heaven to Jerusalem:

Blisced be our Lord of þe folk of Syon þat woneþ in heuen. (p. 164)[192]

In further keeping with this interior, spiritual emphasis is the *Prose Psalter*'s frequent erasure of direct references to physical warfare. So 'sagitta', which is rendered literally as 'arwes/arues/arwis/arowis' in most Middle English psalm translations, become 'a-sautes' (Psalm 37: 3), 'manaces' (44: 6), 'sharp' (56: 5), 'þe turmentes of

---

[188] Dove (2010), p. 65/2237–45. The author refers us to 'Austin in þe þridde book of *Cristen Teching*' as the source of 'al þis and myche more' (*De Doctrina Christiana* III, xxv).

[189] Although 'leo' never signifies Christ in the *Prose Psalter*, it is not consistently presented. On several occasions, the 'leo' of the Gallican remains in the English version (Psalm 7: 3; 9: 30; 16: 12; 21: 14; 103: 21). On other occasions, however, it is glossed. In Psalm 21: 22 the 'ore leonis' [mouth of the lion] is 'mouþe of helle' (p. 24); in 34: 17 'leonibus' [lions] becomes 'fendes' (p. 40); in 56: 5 'de medio catulorum leonum' [from the midst of the young lions] becomes 'sharpnes of tourmentes of fendes' (p. 67) and in 57: 7, 'molas leonum confringet Dominus' [the Lord shall break the grinders of the lions] is 'þe uttemast iuels of þe wicked' (p. 68).

[190] The Latin in BL Add. 17376 (f. 16r) reads 'de sancto & de syon *id est malo* tueatur te' [from the sanctuary and from Sion, *that is*, defend thee *from evil*]. The Latin in BL Add. 44949 contains both of the *Prose Psalter*'s glosses (f. 64r) 'de sancto *spiritu* et de syon *id est malo* tueatur te [from the sanctuary *of the spirit* and from Sion, *that is*, defend thee *from evil*]' while the Anglo-Norman silently replaces original with gloss.

[191] In this reading, Rolle draws on the Lombard (*PL* 191: 0216C) who is inspired by Augustine.

[192] This gloss is found in the Latin in BL Add. 17376 (126r) and in BL Add. 44949 (f. 246r). Cf. Rolle's commentary on this verse: 'Now of syon. that is, of vs, is god blissid. for als long as we life in luf & hope we are in syon. when this life is endid. we shal be with him. thar he wonnys, in ierusalem. of heuen. where we shal se him in endles pees' (p. 456). 'Sion' is by no means invariably glossed in the *Prose Psalter*; see for example Psalm 47: 3, 12, 13; 52: 7; 68: 36; 96: 8; 125: 1.

þe wicked' (63: 8), and 'wreches' (76: 18).[193] Perhaps most striking is the alteration made to Psalm 90: 6, in which '[a] *sagitta volante* in die, a negotio perambulante in tenebris, ab incursu et daemonio meridiano' [of the arrow that flieth in the day, of the business that walketh about in the dark: of invasion, or of the noonday devil] becomes '[o]f *temptacioun waxand* in daie, fram nede goand in derkenes, fram þe curs of þe fende bry₃t shynyng' (p. 113).[194] The glossing of the arrow as temptation is not without precedent; it is an interpretation to which Augustine alludes, and the Lombard refers to it in the context of 'levi tentatione' [light temptation].[195] Following in this tradition, Rolle reads the arrow as 'ese and welth, that thirlis the hertis of many men. and makis thaim to luf mare the iolifte of this warlde. than the kyngdom of heuen' (p. 331) and Hilton glosses it more specifically as 'þe secunde temptacion . . . þat is veyn-glorie, stured in þin herte of þi gode dedes'.[196] In verse 7 of the same psalm, 'temptacioun' appears again; this time, however, it does not gloss a Latin term, but instead supplements a perceived lack in that Latin. So, the Vulgate's 'cadent a latere tuo mille, et decem milia a dextris tuis, ad te autem non adpropinquabit' [a thousand shall fall at thy side, and ten thousand at thy right hand but it shall not come nigh thee], translated closely by Rolle:

> ffall sall fra thi syde a thousand: and fra thi right syde ten thousand. bot til the he sall noght neghe. (p. 331)

is rendered thus in the *Prose*:

> A þousand *temptaciouns* shul fallen fram þi syde, and ten þousandes fram þy ry₃thalf; *þe deuel* for-soþe ne shal no₃t comen to þe. (p. 113)[197] (italics mine)

The association of this verse with 'temptaciouns' (and 'þe deuel') is not out of place in exegetical terms. Although it does not appear to derive from Augustine, who reads the fallen thousands as those who have lived lives of sin, it has some currency in later English exegesis. Hilton, for example, reads the verse as referring directly to 'mony þousend' temptations, and in Rolle's gloss, although the fallen thousands are not the temptations themselves, they are those who have been overcome by these temptations:

> A thousand. that is, many of tha that forsoke all, & semyd perfyt. to deme with the, sall fall fra thi syde. that is. thai sall be ouercomen in temptaciouns thorgh quayntys of the fende. and ten thowsand sall fall fra thi right syde. (pp. 331–2)[198]

---

[193] In Pepys 2498, Psalm 76: 18's 'sagitta' become 'vengeaunces' (Black and St-Jacques, p. 49). The *Prose Psalter* does not gloss 'sagitta' on all occasions. See, for example, Psalm 119: 4 and 126: 4.

[194] Rolle, Hilton, and the Wycliffite translations all preserve 'arrow'. The *Prose Psalter*'s gloss on arrow is also found in the Latin in BL Add. 17376 ('sagitta *id est temptacione* volante *id est emergente*' [from the flying arrow, *that is the approaching temptation*] (f. 87r)). BL Add. 44949 also has these glosses in the Latin (f. 184v).

[195] *PL* 191: 0850C.   [196] Wallner (1954), p. 17/5–6.

[197] Both of these glosses are found at this point in BL Add. 17376 (f. 87). The second ('id est diabolus' [that is, the devil]) is not underlined. Both also appear (and are underlined) in BL Add. 44949 (f. 184v).

[198] Wallner (1954), pp. 24–5.

Once more, the *Prose Psalter*'s reading is not, in itself, unusual. It is its inclusion of this reading within its vernacularization, its elision of the activities of translation and commentary, which marks it out among its specifically biblical English contemporaries.[199]

Sometimes, in fact, the glossing commentary threatens to overwhelm the original. To take Psalm 67: 14 as an example, in the unglossed Gallican we read 'si dormiatis inter medios cleros, pinnae columbae deargentatae et posteriora dorsi eius in pallore auri' ('[i]f you sleep among the midst of lots, you shall be as the wings of a dove covered with silver, and the hinder parts of her back with the paleness of gold'). In the *Prose Psalter*, however, the glossed Latin and the English version respectively read:

Si dormiatis *id est vivatis* inter medios cleros *id est inter leges ueteris testamenti & noui,* penne columbe deargentate *id est fine facta:* & posteriora dorsi eius in pallore auri *id est sed leges posterioris testamenti & noue sunt in pallore auri pro voluntate dei'.* [If you sleep, *that is, live,* in the midst of lots, *that is between the laws of the Old Testament and the New,* you shall be as wings of a dove covered with silver, *that is, made at the end:* and the hinder parts of her back with the paleness of gold, *that is, the laws of the later testament and of the new are in the paleness of gold for the will of God*]

ȝyf þat ȝe liuen bitwix þe lawes of þe olde testament and þe new, þe wil of þe [olde is] seluered, þat his to saie fainteliche made; bot þe lawe of þe last testament, þat hys þe nywe, ben in palenes of gold, þat hys to saye, ben att þe wyl of God. (p. 78)[200]

On such occasions, the commentary can be said to have almost entirely subsumed the original. It would, however, be inappropriate to read this as an aggressive manoeuvre on the part of the translator. Far from silencing the voice of the psalmist, the gloss can be read as generous in allowing the Old Testament prophet David to pronounce confidently on the 'gold' illumination provided by the New Testament.

---

[199] It is also worth noting that in the *Prose Psalter*, hunters sometimes become 'fendes', as in the translation of 90: 3 ('Quoniam ipse liberabit me de laqueo venantium et a verbo aspero' [For he hath delivered me from the snare of the hunters: and from the sharp word]) (in Rolle's translation and in the two Wycliffite versions they are still hunters). Again, the Psalter is following in exegetical tradition here; on the same verse, Rolle comments 'he delyuerd me of the snare of huntand. that is, of fleyssly delytis and lusty thoghtis. the whilke deuels lays as snares to take men' (pp. 330–1). The Psalter is not consistent in glossing 'venator' [hunter] however: the translation of 123: 7 ('anima nostra sicut passer erepta est de laqueo venantium' [Our soul hath been delivered as a sparrow out of the snare of the hunters]) preserves a literal rendition of the 'venator': '[o]ur soule is defended as þe sparowe fram þe gnare of þe fouler' (p. 158).

[200] With minor variations, these glosses also appear in BL Add. 44949 (f. 138r) and in BN 6260 (Black and St-Jacques, p. 110). Rolle's commentary also reads the 'cleros' as the Old and New Testaments, an interpretation which is sanctioned by Augustine (after lengthy consideration) and alluded to by the Lombard (*PL* 191 0621A). There, however, the similarities cease. While the *Prose* text reads 'sleep' as 'life' and the differently toned feathers of the dove as indicating the differences between the Old and New Testaments, Rolle reads the sleep as that of contemplation and the 'fethirs of doufe' as illustrating the 'shynand' vertues of a 'clene saule': 'If ȝe slepe, that is, if ȝe rist in contemplacioun, fra dyn of vices, amange myddis clergis. that is, in the lare and the auctorite of twa testaments. that ȝe last til ȝoure ded, in despite of this warld, and in perfite ȝernynge of heuen. than ȝe sall hafe fethirs of doufe, that is, the vertus of a clene saule. and the hyndire of hire bake. that is, the luf of ȝour saule, whare the rotis of vertus ere festid, sall be shynand in wisdome & discrecion' (p. 233). The glossed translation in Pepys 2498 differs in some minor details (Black and St-Jacques, p. 41).

In this context, also distinguishing the Psalter from its contemporaries is the manner in which its translation includes glosses that erode references to culturally specific Old Testament practice, often replacing them with more generalized statements. So, for example, Psalm 50: 21's discussion of fleshly sacrifice ('tunc acceptabis sacrificium iustitiae oblationes et holocausta. Tunc imponent super altare tuum vitulos' [then shalt thou accept the sacrifice of justice, oblations and whole burnt offerings. Then shall they lay calves upon thy altar]) is erased by a decisively spiritual reading:

> þan shal tou take sacrifice of ry3t, seruice, and honours; hij shul þan setten godenesses to-fore þy throne. (p. 62)[201]

Although, as is generally the case, this reading is exegetically conventional, it is noteworthy for its wholesale nature. It goes much further for instance than Rolle who, even in his commentary, maintains the metaphor of fleshly sacrifice:

> Than, in the tother warld, when the walles ere edified, thou sall accept, that is, it sall be acceptabile til the. the sacrifice of rightwisnes, that is, of louynge that is rightwis: obles and offrandis. that is, that thai be all brennand in godis fire. and in charite: and ded be destroyde in victory. than sall aungels sett on thin autere in heuen kalfis, that is, innocentes withouten 3oke of synn. (pp. 187–8)

In a related manner, the *Prose Psalter* is also prone to removing references to the psalms as song; in 42: 4, 'cithara' [lyre] becomes 'þe in-mast of myn hert', in 32: 2 it features as 'vertu3' and in 80: 3 as 'ioie'.[202] The notion that the 'psalterium' [stringed instrument] too is an instrument that can be played is also threatened in the *Prose* text's glossing translation. For example, in all four manuscripts of the *Prose Psalter*, Psalm 91: 4's 'in decacordo psalterio, cum cantico in cithara' [upon an instrument of ten strings, upon the psaltery: with a canticle upon the harp], is replaced with the 'x. comaundement3, wyþ songe and harpe' (p. 36).[203] And in Psalm 32: 2, the psaltery is again 'þe techynges of þe.x. comaundement3'.[204] In itself, this is well-worn exegesis: Rolle, for example, comments similarly on Psalm 91: 4 '[a]swhasay, 3e sall tell godis mercy and his sothfastnes in kepynge of ten comaundments. with sange of swete louynge in the harpe of slaghtire of fleyssly

---

[201] All of these glosses appear, underlined, in BL Add. 17376 (f. 46v) and in BL Add. 44949 (f. 117v) at this point. For other erasures of 'vitulum', see Psalm 28: 6 and Psalm 21: 13. In the latter, the vivid imagery ('circumdederunt me vituli multi, tauri pingues obsederunt me' [Many calves have surrounded me, fat bulls have besieged me]) is lost entirely ('For many fendes han en-cumpassed me, þe counseil of wicked vmseged me') (p. 24). He does, however, maintain Psalm 49: 9's reference to 'vitulos' and 'gregibus' (Y ne shal nou3t taken chalues of þyn hous, ne kiddes of þyn flokkes) (p. 60) and renders 68: 32's 'vitulum' as '3onge chalf' (p. 82). See also 105: 19 and 20.

[202] Again, these glosses are derived from the Latin via the Anglo-Norman. See, for example, the Latin Psalm 42: 4 in BL Add. 44949, ff. 104r-v (in cythara *id est interio cordis*'), rendered 'en le deufune de mon quoer' in the Anglo-Norman. 'Cithara/harp' does, however, remain in the following: Psalm 56: 9; 70: 22; 91: 4; 97: 5; 107: 3; 146: 7; 150: 3.

[203] That the psaltery should be glossed in a verse which does not gloss the accompanying harp is typical of the Psalter's inconsistency, which may of course originate in the Anglo-Norman original.

[204] Again, Rolle makes the same link. The psaltery does, however, remain in the translation of Psalm 48: 5; 56: 9; 80: 3; 107: 3; 149: 3; 150: 3.

vicys' (p. 334).[205] Its occurrence here reminds us of the central role played by the psalms in basic Christian catechesis of the late Middle Ages.

Yet the *Prose* text's glossing interjections insist on the Psalter's specifically Christian relevance even more persistently than do any other complete Middle English translations. Its references to Christ are particularly pointed in their fore-grounding of his sacrificial death.[206] Although two of them (Psalms 44: 3 and 88: 39) can be attested elsewhere in Middle English translations, the *Prose Psalter* hints at its distinctive background in its glossing of Psalm 71: 7's 'luna' [moon] as Christ:

> Ry3tfulnes and waxing of pees shal arisen, to þat þe soule of Crist be don oway fram hys body. (p. 85)[207]

The most striking insertion of his name, however, occurs in the translation of Psalm 123: 7 ('laqueus contritus est et nos liberati sumus' [the snare is broken and we are delivered]) which reads:

> þe trappe of þe fend is to-broke wyþ þe deþ of Crist, & we ben deliuered fro damp-nacioun. (p. 158)[208]

In keeping with this emphasis on Christ's redemptive death, the cross is mentioned once ('Helle blameþ þe fendes for þy deþ of þe croice' (p. 51)) in the heavily glossed translation of Psalm 41: 8 ('abyssus ad abyssum invocat, in voce catharac-tarum tuarum' [deep calleth on deep, at the noise of thy flood-gates]). In fact, this is one of the most radically substitutive glosses in the *Prose Psalter* insofar as the translation makes no direct lexical reference to the original. The Latin in BL Add. 44949 makes the substitutions apparent:

> Abyssus *id est infernus* abyssum *id est diabolu* inuocat *id est uituperat* in uoce *id est pro morte* catharacturu tuar *id est crucis tue* [deep *that is, hell* calls on *that is, curses* deep *that is, the devil* at the voice *that is, for the death* of your flood-gates *that is, of your cross*]

while its Anglo-Norman performs the same process of erasure ('Enfern blame le deable per ta mort de la croi3' [hell blames the devil for your death of the cross]) as the Middle English.[209]

---

[205] Rolle is here inspired by the Lombard: 'In hoc psalterio psallit qui spiritu vivificato, per obser-vantiam decalogi, cum hilaritate bene agit' [In this stringed instrument plays he who is brought to life by the spirit, through the observance of the Ten Commandments, performed well and with cheerful-ness] (*PL* 191: 0857A-B). The gloss in *Bonum Est* is rather more specific, commenting 'charite is song, & chastite is þe harpe'. See Wallner, p. 58/6.

[206] The *Metrical Psalter* actually names Christ significantly more than does the *Prose Psalter*; it does not, however, provide any interpretative glosses. Rolle mentions Christ in his translation of Psalm 19: 7; in the equivalent position, the *Prose Psalter* inserts 'hys preste anoint wyþ creme' (p. 22).

[207] The Latin in BL Add. 17376 has the gloss at this point (f. 65v) as does that in Pepys 2498 (Black and St-Jacques (2012), p. 8) and BL Add. 44949 (f. 148r). Psalm 44: 3 has already been dis-cussed. On 88: 39, see Rolle ('[t]hou sothly put agayn thou despisyd: thou delayd thi crist' (p. 325)) and the *Metrical Psalter* ('Þou awaipute and þou forsegh, / Forbare þi criste þat es slegh' (p. 223)).

[208] The same glosses are found (without 'damnacioun') in Add. 44949 (f. 247v). The same verse is translated '[s]nare is brokyn and we ere delyuyrd' (p. 442) by Rolle. His commentary, extremely brief at this point, makes no reference to Christ.

[209] See BL Add. 44949 (f. 103r). Rolle's substantial gloss at this point makes no reference to Christ or the cross. It is characteristic of the *Prose Psalter*'s somewhat erratic glossing technique that

'Helle' is referenced several times in the *Prose Psalter* and on one occasion its Harrowing seems to be evoked: translating (at two removes) Psalm 23: 7's 'adtollite portas principes vestras' [lift up your gates, O ye princes], the *Prose* text in all four manuscripts reads '[o]peneþ 3our 3ates, 3e princes *of helle*' (p. 26).[210] Even more strikingly, purgatory makes an appearance in the translation of the glossed Psalm 41: 5 ('quoniam transibo in locum tabernaculi *id est purgatorij* admirabilis *id est pleni penis*, vsque ad domum dei *id est celum*' [for I shall go over into the place of the wonderful, *that is full of punishment*, tabernacle, *that is, purgatory*, even to the house of God, *that is Heaven*]), which reads:

> For hy shal passen in-to þe stede of purgatorij ful of pines, ri3t vn-to heuen. (p. 51)[211]

There is an undeniable sense here of the verse having been exegetically contorted. Rolle's commentary on the same verse makes rather more logical sense, reading the 'tabernaculi admirabilis' as 'halykirke', although agreeing with the *Prose* text on the glossing of the 'domum dei' ('for on this manere I sall passe thorght halykirke. thare is wondirful lufers, incomand with thoght in til godis howse in heuen, takyn with na 3ernynge of this world' (p. 138)).[212]

Having some features in common with Wycliffite and Rollean glosses, while also differing from them on several occasions, the *Prose Psalter* is in some senses the 'outsider' among Middle English translations of the complete book of psalms. This is due, in large part, to its reliance on a different source, a 'ready-glossed' Anglo-Norman Psalter that is itself related to a glossed Gallican text. As this chapter has demonstrated, this results in an English text that goes further than any other contemporary or antecedent complete Psalter in appearing to recognize—and demonstrate—the close affinity between translation and commentary as re-creative

---

this 'Christian' rendition of the Old Testament follows a verse which is not glossed at all. Psalm 41: 7 (ad me ipsum anima mea conturbata est, propterea memor ero tui de terra Iordanis et Hermoniim a monte modico [My soul is troubled within myself: therefore will I remember thee from the land of Jordan and Hermoniim, from the little hill]) is rendered 'myn soule is trubled vn-to my seluen; for- þy, Lord, y shal be þenchand on þe, God, of þe tur[n]ing of folk of þe londe of Jordan and of þe folk of þe littel hille of Hermon' (p. 51). Yet as Rolle's commentary on this verse attests, the exegetical erasure of the specific locations of Jordan and Hermon was eminently possible.

[210] This addition is not found in either Latin or Anglo-Norman in BL Add. 44949, f. 70v. It is, however, in BN 6260's Anglo-Norman 'vous princes d'enferr' (Black and St-Jacques, p. 81). In an interesting divergence, Rolle reads this verse, first and foremost, as a command to the interior self ('[s]en that nane may stand in godis hill. bot that ere swilk as I haf sayd. for thi 3e men that suld be princes of vices and haf the victory of ill stiryngis. takup, that is, doe away fra 3oure saule, 3oure 3ates of couaitis and of warldis dred: that ere 3ates of ded, the whilke the deuel sett in 3ow for his entre: and agayn tha 3atis ye endles 3ates. that is, entre of endles life, as forsakynge of the warld and perfit turnynge til god. 3e ere heghid. that is, 3e suld be heghid in hertis of men: for swa sall inga til 3oure saules the kynge of ioy; crist, in whaim we ioy withouten pride' (pp. 86–7)).

[211] All of these glosses also appear in BL Add. 44949, f. 102v and in BN 6260's Anglo-Norman (Black and St-Jacques, p. 94). As noted previously, TCD 69 and Princeton Scheide 143 tread a line between gloss and translation in their English rendition, reading 'purgatorie ful of paynes into þe hond (Trinity 'hous') of god þat is into heuen' (Black and St-Jacques, p. 117). Pepys 2498 makes no reference to purgatory in Latin or English.

[212] Rolle is inspired by the Lombard here (see *PL* 191: 0417B-D). Purgatory is also mentioned once in Rolle's commentary, on Psalm 37: 1, where he expresses the hope that he will not be one of those 'purged in the fire of purgatory' (p. 138).

activities. But if we insist too stridently on the *Prose Psalter*'s distinctiveness, we run the risk of over-emphasizing the continuities between the other four English Psalters. As this chapter has demonstrated, while they all share genetic characteristics as literal renditions of an unglossed Gallican, more direct relationships are not necessarily provable. Further, the *Metrical Psalter* and the Wycliffite LV in particular also recognize (albeit in very different ways) the inherent creativity of the act of translation; the former in its crafting of a rhyming text from the prose Gallican and the latter in its idiomatic relaxing of Latinate constructions, combined with its intermittent glossing insertions.

It also seems important that we recognize the affinities between the *Prose* text's understanding of the Psalter's nature and function, and what we know of broader contemporary understandings. As indicated in this chapter, the glossing translation insists on the psalms' applicability to the devotional interiority of the penitent reader; the Wycliffite and Rollean Psalters do the same (as, arguably, does the *Metrical Psalter* in Cotton Vespasian D.vii). Equally, it asks us to consider the words of the Old Testament Psalmist from an enlightened New Testament perspective; once again, this is common practice.[213] Replacing allusions to the psalms as song with allusions to the psalms as embodiments of basic catechetic doctrine (specifically the Ten Commandments), the *Prose Psalter* also reveals its affinities with broad trends of psalm interpretation. However, where it (and its source) differs is in what we might call its 'functional' approach to the Psalter. While Rolle, for example, retains the original's 'harp' references in his translation, providing the 'ten comaundments' interpretation only in his commentary, the glossing *Prose* vernacularization silences all reference to the psalms' musicality: the harp on which the Psalmist played is not *like* the Ten Commandments, it *is* the Ten Commandments. The text's emphasis falls squarely, though somewhat inconsistently, on the Psalter as Christian catechesis rather than as Old Testament song. In its emphasis on catechesis, the *Prose Psalter* is in tune with broad traditions of English psalm exegesis, and it is perhaps surprising that it does not seem to have circulated widely beyond its immediate London milieu. Endless speculation on a negative would be fruitless, but it may be that audiences were alienated by its sometimes clumsy blurring of the boundaries between translation and exegesis, although of course the idea of such merging is by no means unusual. It is also likely that it suffered at the hands of the very popular Rolle Psalter, a significantly more cumbersome text that contains, nonetheless, a more direct translation of the psalms. Both of these complete Psalters, however, find themselves increasingly supplemented in the late fourteenth and early fifteenth centuries by more easily digestible paraphrased and abbreviated versions of the psalms. It is to such versions that we now turn.

---

[213] The fact that Rolle's Psalter does this work in its commentary section rather than in its verbatim translation will be discussed in Chapter 5.

4

The Practice of Translation
Abbreviated and Paraphrased Psalters

The previous chapter began with reflection on Henry Hargreaves' metaphor of a 'chain' of English psalm translation and concluded that although there are tantalizing links between the five extant complete Psalters, straightforward connections between any one version and another are unprovable and, in the case of the *Prose* translation, unlikely. It is impossible to demonstrate conclusively that the practice of any single English psalm translator directly influenced, or was directly influenced by, any other. All that we can say with certainty is that each was working in a late-medieval environment in which the nature, status, and function of translation was hotly debated and—in many circles—highly valued. However, to borrow one of Chapter 3's phrases, it is somewhat easier to talk in terms of a 'nexus of connections' when exploring relationships between the many contemporary abbreviated and paraphrased versions of the psalms, as well as between them and the complete translations.

It is on practices of abbreviation and paraphrase that this chapter will focus, in the context of a broader consideration of continuities and discontinuities in the 'tradition' of English psalm vernacularization. As literary activities, abbreviation and paraphrase obviously occupy common ground insofar as neither is wedded to the exact reproduction of an original. An abbreviating version obviously omits elements of its source while a paraphrasing rendition is free to both omit and expand. As we know well, however, in their medieval context, both abbreviation and paraphrase are legitimate aspects of translation. Lying behind both activities is an assumption, whether conscious or not, that the work of translation is inventive: it is the responsibility of the translator to shape a new text rather than reproduce an old. This is particularly, although not invariably, the case with those paraphrases that make poetry out of the Gallican prose; in a manner that recalls while varying the complete *Metrical* translation, they craft a consciously literary response to the psalms. One of the key differences from the *Metrical* text, however, is that rather than 'adding' rhymes to a more or less literal rendition of the Psalter, the paraphrases more obviously interact with their Gallican source, interweaving personal, often affective, commentary with direct translation. In mapping the psalms on to a devotional agenda, the paraphrased versions have something in common with the *Prose Psalter* and, of course, with Rolle's commentary. But while the *Prose* translator's approach (derived from his source) is largely functional, glossing/replacing individual Latin words or phrases with individual English words/phrases, those responsible for the verse paraphrases more frequently and obviously delight in the language of the Psalmist and ask us to delight in their own ruminative elaborations on that language. The fact that these two priorities sometimes appear to be in competition with each other, in line with an aggressive model of translation familiar to us from Chapter 2, will be discussed later.

We begin, however, not with these verse amplifications of selected psalms but with the Prose translations which appear in the Middle English primers and which are abbreviations insofar as they are selected for their liturgical functionality and do not constitute a complete Psalter. As we will see, they appear to participate in the broadly defined vogue for the literal translation of the original Latin, outlined in the previous chapter. In reality, though, they draw on an antecedent Middle English translation of the Psalter rather than (or as well as) on the Vulgate itself. Specifically, they are indebted to some form of the Wycliffite translations. Here, at last, we have a clear case of one Middle English psalm translation having a direct impact on another and it is all the more interesting for its unexpectedness, indicating the circulation of 'heterodox' material in apparently 'orthodox' contexts.

THE PRIMER PSALMS

It is, therefore, to the Wycliffite psalms that we return at the beginning of this chapter. Unlike the *Prose* translation, that of the Wycliffites circulated very widely. As stated in Chapter 1, it was by far the most frequently copied book of their Old Testament, surviving in some forty-eight manuscripts. Twenty appear in complete Bibles (of these only four are EV) and there are fifteen in incomplete or partial Old Testaments (of these only two are EV and one 'revised' EV). LV psalms appear twice with New Testament material only, and on two further occasions they appear with abbreviated selections from both the Old and New Testaments. In two additional manuscripts, they are accompanied by extensive English catechetic and quasi-liturgical material. Finally, there are seven manuscripts which contain the psalms alone, accompanied the canticles on six occasions, once by a litany, once by a lectionary as well as the LV Psalter prologue, and on one further occasion, by an extract from chapter 12 of the Wycliffite General Prologue in addition to the *Quicunque Vult*. All seven of these manuscripts are LV.

However, in addition to these forty-eight manuscripts, we also have eight English language primers (of the seventeen extant) whose psalm translations are all but identical to those of LV. Yet although the appearance of the Wycliffite psalms in Middle English primers was discussed briefly by the tireless Henry Hargreaves and also featured in an unpublished Cambridge MLitt thesis by J.

M. Harris-Matthews, it has otherwise remained largely unexplored.[1] In his note on '[t]he Middle English Primers and the Wycliffite Bible', confining himself to discussion of the three published primers (London, BL Add. 17010 (Maskell); Cambridge, St John's College G.24 and CUL Dd.11.82 (both Littlehales)), Hargreaves states that:

> [W]hat is probably the most important fact of the first and third of these primers seems to have escaped the notice of the original editors and of nearly everyone who has worked on them since their publication . . . [namely] the close connexion in which the translation of the Biblical passages they contain stands to the later version of the Wycliffite Bible.[2]

He goes on to suggest that the second primer (St John's G.24) contains 'an independent translation'. Expanding on Hargreaves' observations, and basing her work on a survey of sixteen English primer manuscripts, Harris-Matthews suggests that they 'can be divided into two groups, with one exception—University College, Oxford 179'.[3] Like Hargreaves, she argues that London, BL Add. 17010 and CUL Dd.11.82 are 'very close' to the Wycliffite LV (they form part of her 'second group'). However, rather than suggesting that Cambridge, St John's College G.2 and others in her first group contain 'an independent translation', she claims that their psalm renditions are 'similar, but not identical, to those of Rolle' and later suggests that they might also depend on a Psalter akin to 'the English versions of St Jerome's'.[4]

I follow Hargreaves and Harris-Matthews in dividing the Middle English primers into two main categories. Where I differ from both, however, is in suggesting that for their psalm translations, the primers in both categories are almost all in some way indebted to the Wycliffite Bible. None of them is, as Hargreaves suggested, entirely independent and neither is there any obvious justification for claiming, as did Harris-Matthews, a substantial link with Rolle's translation. The suggestion of a link with the English version of St Jerome's Abbreviated Psalter is more interesting, and is a point to which we will return. For now it is simply worth noting that since this abridgement of selected psalms survives in only six manuscripts and varies quite considerably between these, it would be unwise to use it as the only basis for comparison.[5] Basing my conclusions on an analysis

---

[1] H. Hargreaves, 'The Middle English Primers and the Wycliffite Bible', *MLR* 51 (1956), 215–17 (it appears in the 'Miscellaneous Notes' section of the journal). For the unpublished thesis, see Harris-Matthews (1980). More recently, Dr Kathleen Kennedy (Pennsylvania State University (Penn State, Brandywine Campus)) has been working on the Middle English primers.

[2] Hargreaves (1956), p. 215. He refers to 'the twelve English versions of the medieval service book known as the Primer or the Book of Hours', but as he does not provide manuscript sigla it is impossible to know the copies of which he was unaware.

[3] Harris-Matthews, p. 43.   [4] Harris-Matthews, p. 43 and p. 98.

[5] The English version of the *Abbreviated Psalter of St. Jerome* survives in the following manuscripts (although it differs in completeness in each): (1) Oxford, BodlL Hatton 111 (as Dove (2007) points out, this manuscript contains an EV Lectionary, Gospels, and James-Apocalypse, as well as the Office of Compline in English and a *capitula*-list for Matt.I-Luke 20 (p. 300)); (2) Oxford, BodlL Bodley 416 (a substantial volume which also contains *Book to a Mother*); (3) Yale University Library, Beinecke 360 (this LV Psalter manuscript, which also contains a primer, was discussed in Chapter 1); (4) GUL

of the language of the Seven Penitential Psalms, I suggest that the first group of primers (here designated Group A) contains translations which are virtually identical to the Wycliffite LV.[6] Although there are some minor differences, they are 'not usually much greater than the discrepancies to be expected between any two manuscripts of a Middle English work liable to the numerous emendations and errors that copying by hand is likely to introduce'.[7] The translations found in the second group (here designated 'B') are more difficult to categorize, but they show undeniable evidence of the influence of the Wycliffite Bible.[8] Sharing obvious features of language and syntax with the EV psalms (and very occasionally sharing readings with Rolle's *English Psalter*) they also often move in the direction of the more idiomatic LV Psalter. I list the manuscripts in their respective categories below, before providing illustrative psalm translations and analysis.

Wycliffite LV Primers (Group A)

Cambridge, CUL Dd. 11. 82
London, BL Add. 17010
London, BL Add. 17011
London, BL Add. 36683
Oxford, BodlL Ashmole 1288 (1)[9]
Oxford, BodlL Rawlinson C. 699
Oxford, Queen's College 324
Yale, University Library Beineke 360[10]

Hunter 496 (V.7.23); (5) San Marino, Huntington Library, HM 501 (this psalm-based anthology, containing parts of the Wycliffite LV Old Testament, was discussed in Chapter 1); (6) Oxford, University College 179 (also containing a primer). As is clear from this list, in four cases the English abbreviated Psalter appears with Wycliffite biblical material. Its links with the Wycliffite translations will be discussed later in the chapter.

[6] Obviously, a collation involving all of the material (biblical, liturgical, devotional, and catechetic) in all eighteen manuscripts is ultimately desirable. Harris-Matthews attempts something approximating this in her 1980 thesis and her preliminary findings suggest that a full analysis, when undertaken, will reveal some complex results. It should be noted that my labelling of the categories as 'A' and 'B' differs from Harris-Matthews' system of identification.

[7] Hargreaves (1956), p. 216. As he also notes, there are also 'a smaller number of readings where the divergence between one or other of the primers and the LV is more marked'. These tend to appear in the non-psalmic material (the sixth and ninth lessons in the Office of the Dead, the *Magnificat*, and the *Benedictus*) (pp. 216–17).

[8] In terms of all their psalm translations (not just the Seven Penitential), Harris-Matthews divides this group of manuscripts into two sub-categories: (i) Add.17010 and Add. 17011; (ii) CUL Dd.11.82; Rawlinson C.699; Add. 36683; Queens 324; Ashmole 1288 (pp. 91–2). She suggests that the (ii) manuscripts follow LV closely throughout while (i) contain some minor variations.

[9] For a reproduction of Ashmole 1288, f. 9r (the beginning of Matins) see Figure 4.1.

[10] The primer material is found between f. 152 and f. 176v. Only the cues to the psalms (in English) are provided, presumably because the user could be expected to locate the entire psalm in the LV Psalter which precedes the primer. This is also the suggestion made by Hanna (2010), pp. 122–3 ('all Psalm references reduced to incipits keyed to the preceding text').

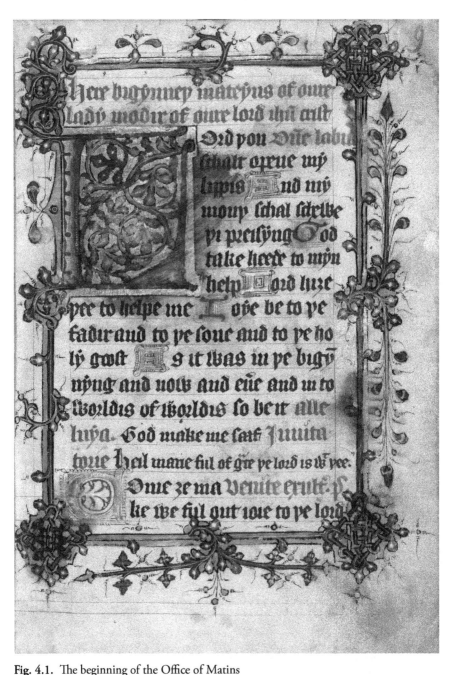

Fig. 4.1. The beginning of the Office of Matins

Bodleian Library MS Ashmole 1288, f. 9r. Reproduced by kind permission of the Bodleian Libraries, the University of Oxford

EV/LV? Primers (Group B)

Cambridge, Emmanuel College 246
Cambridge, St. John's College G. 24
GUL Hunter 472 (v. 6. 22)
GUL Hunter 512 (v. 8. 15)
London, BL Add. 27592[11]
Oxford, BodlL Bodley 85
Oxford, BodlL Douce 246[12]
Oxford, BodlL Douce 275

Uncertain

Oxford, University College 179[13]

SAMPLE ONE

Psalm 6: 2–4 Domine ne in furore tuo arguas me neque in ira tua corripias me. Miserere mei Domine quoniam infirmus sum. Sana me Domine quoniam conturbata sunt ossa mea et anima mea turbata est valde; et tu Domine usquequo? (O Lord, rebuke me not in thy indignation, nor chastise me in thy wrath. Have mercy on me, O Lord, for I am weak. Heal me, O Lord, for my bones are troubled. And my soul is troubled exceedingly; but thou, O Lord, how long?)

Wycliffite EV

Lord, in thi wodnesse vndernyme thou nott me; ne in thi wrathe chastice thou me. Haue mercy of me, Lord, for I am syk; hele me, Lord, for disturbid ben alle my bonys. And my soule is disturbid gretly; but thou, Lord, hou longe?

---

[11] Harris-Matthews suggests that Emmanuel 246 and Add. 27592 are in the same hand (p. 91).

[12] In terms of all their psalm translations (not just the Seven Penitential), Harris-Matthews divides this group of seven manuscripts into three further sub-categories which differ from each other in relatively minor details: (i) St. Johns G.24, Bodley 85 and Hunter 512; (ii) Douce 246 and 275; (iii) Emmanuel 246, Add. 27592 and Hunter 472 (pp. 86–91). Harris-Matthews (p. 89) points out that in the Office of the Dead, the psalm translations in Hunter 512 shift suddenly to Group A (i.e. they have more obvious affinities with LV). She also suggests (pp. 90–1) that the portions of Psalm 118 that survive in the London University Fragment correspond to that found in the Group B primers.

[13] The primer in this manuscript is quite distinct from that in others in terms of its translation and its presentation. Issues of presentation and purpose will be discussed in the next chapter, but here our focus is on its translation. For purposes of comparison, its translation of Psalm 6: 1–3 is as follows: 'Lord yn þi wodenes repreue not me ne yn þi wreþ sle not me. Lord haue mercy on me for y am syke. Hele me lord for my bones be togeder strublid. And my soule ys strubled ful moch. But þou lorde forsoþe'. See also Psalm 31: 1–2 'þey be blessed whace wikkidnesses be for3iffen and whace synnes be hid. þat man ys blissed to wam oure lord put no syn ne in whace spirit ys no trecchry'. (As I have not been able to locate Marquis of Bute, HMC MS 3: 206 as yet, it has not been assigned to a group.)

Wycliffite LV

Lord, repreue thou not me in thi stronge veniaunce, neiþer chastice thou me in thin ire. Lord, haue thou merci on me, for Y am sijk; Lord, make thou me hool, for alle my boonys ben troblid. And my soule is troblid greetli; but thou, Lord, hou long?[14]

GROUP A READINGS

Ashmole 1288

Lord repreue þou not me in þi strong veniance neiþer chastice þu me in þi ire. Lord haue þou merci on me for i am syk. Lord make þu me hool for alle my boones ben troblid. And my soule is troublid gretly. But þou lord how longe.

Rawlinson C.699

This folio is missing from the manuscript, presumably removed because it marked the beginning of the Seven Penitential Psalms and therefore contained some fine borders and illumination.

CUL Dd. 11. 82

Lord, repreue þou not [me] in þi stronge veniaunce; neþer chastise þou me in þin ire! Lord, haue merci on me, for y am sijk! lord, make þou me hool, for alle my bones ben trublid. And my soule is trublid gretli; but þou, lord, hou longe?[15]

BL 17010

Lord repreue thou not me in thi strong vengaunce: neithir chastise thou me in thin ire. Lord, haue thou merci on me, for I am siik: lord, make thou me hool, for alle my bonys ben troublid. And my soule is troublid greetli: but thou lord how longe.

GROUP B READINGS

Douce 275

Lord in thi woodnesse underneme no3t me ne in þi wraþ blame not me. Haue mercy on me Lord for i am syke. Hele me Lord for alle my bones ben troubled. And my soule is troubled gretlyche. But þou lord how long.

Bodley 85

Lord in thi woodnesse undermin nou3t me ne in thi wrathe blame me nou3t. Haue merci on me lord for y am seek. Heel me lord for al mi bonis ben troubled and my soule is troubled gretliche. Bote thou lord hou longe.

---

[14] The revised LV Psalter in Bodley 277 adds 'tariest' at the end of this verse. This is not an addition found in any of the extant primers.

[15] Littlehales (1895), p. 37.

Douce 246

Lord in þy wodenesse undernym noȝte me ne in þy wraþe blame noȝte me. Haue mercy of me god for i am syke. Hele me lord for al my bones ben troubled. And my soule is troubled gretliche. Bot þou lorde how long.

St John's College, G24

Lord in þy woodnesse undermine nouȝt me, ne in thi wraþthe blame nat me. Haue mercy of me lord for y am syyk, hele me lord for alle my bones been trowbled. And my soule is trowbled gretlyche. Bote thow lord how loonge.[16]

SAMPLE TWO

Psalm 31: 1–2 Beati quorum remissae sunt iniquitates et quorum tecta sunt peccata. Beatus vir cui non inputabit Dominus peccatum nec est in spiritu eius dolus (Blessed are they whose iniquities are forgiven, and whose sins are covered. Blessed is the man to whom the Lord hath not imputed sin, and in whose spirit there is no guile.)

Wycliffite EV Psalm

Blissid of whom ben forȝiue the wickidnessis; and of whom couered ben the synnes. Blessid the man, to whom witide not the Lord synne; and ther is not in the spirit of hym trecherie.

Wycliffite LV Psalm

Blessid ben thei, whose wickidnessis ben forȝouen; and whose synnes ben hilid. Blessid is the man, to whom the Lord arrettide not synne; nethir gile is in his spirit.

GROUP A READINGS

Ashmole 1288

Blessid ben þei whos wickidnessis ben forȝouen and whos synes ben hilid. Blessid is þe man to whom þe lord arettide not synne neiþer gile is in his spirit.

Dd. 11. 82

Blessid ben þe, whose wickidnessis ben forȝouun, & whos synnes ben hilid. Blessid is þe man to whom þe lord arettid not synne; neþer gile is in his spirit.

---

[16] See the diplomatic edition in Littlehales (1891), p. 52. I have expanded the contractions and modernized the punctuations.

Rawlinson C. 699

Blessid ben þei whos wickidnessis ben for3ouen & whos synnes ben hilild. Blessid is þe man to whom þe lord arettide not synne, neiþer gile is in his spirit.

BL 17010

Blessid ben thei whose wickidnessis ben for3ouun: and whos synnes ben hilid. Blissid is the man to whom the lord arettide not synne neither gile is in his spirit.

GROUP B READINGS

Douce 275

Blessed be þei whos wickednesses ben for3euen & whos synnes ben heled. Blessed be þat man to whom the lord rehetede no3t synne ne tresoun is not in his gost.

Bodley 85

Blessed ben thei whos wikednes ben for3iue and whos sinnis ben heled. Blessed be that man to whom oure lord retteþ no sinne ne treson is not in is gost.

Douce 246

Blessed be þey whas wickednesse ben for3eue and whas synnes ben heled. Blessed be þat man to wham the lord rettede no3te synne, ne tresone is no3te in his goost.

St John's G.24

Blessed be they whas wikkidnesses been for3yue and whaas synnes been heeled. Blessed be that man to wham oure lord rettede nou3t synne, ne treson is nou3t in his goost.

SAMPLE THREE

Psalm 50: 3 Miserere mei Deus secundum magnam misericordiam tuam et secundum multitudinem miserationum tuarum dele iniquitatem meam (Have mercy on me, O God, according to thy great mercy and according to the multitude of thy tender mercies blot out my iniquity)

Wycliffite EV Psalm

Haue mercy of me, God; after thi grete mercy. And after the multitude of thi grete mercy doingus; do awey my wickidnesse. More ouer wash me fro wickenesse myn; and fro my synne clense me. For my wickidnesse I knowe; and my synne a3en me is euermor.[17]

---

[17] In Bodley 959, 'wickenesse myn' is the more idiomatic 'my wickedness' (p. 194).

Wycliffite LV Psalm

God, haue thou merci on me; bi thi greet merci. And bi the mychilnesse of thi merciful doyngis; do thou awei my wickidnesse. More waische thou me fro my wickidnesse; and clense thou me fro my synne. For Y knouleche my wickid\nesse; and my synne is euere a3ens me.[18]

GROUP A READINGS

Ashmole 1288

Lord haue þou merci on me þoru þi greet merci. And bi þe mochilnesse of þi merciful doynges do þou awei my wickidnesse. Moore waische þou me fro wickidnesse & clense þou me fro my synne. For I knowleche my wickidnesse and my synne is euer a3ens me.

Rawlinson C. 699

God haue þou mercy on me aftir þi greet mercy. And bi þe mychelnesse of þi merciful doyngis do þou awei my wickidnesse. More ouer waische þou me fro my wickidnesse & clense þou me fro my synne. For I knowleche my wickidnesse: & my synne is euer a3ens me.

CUL Dd.11.82

God, haue merci on me! bi þi greet merci, and bi þe mychelnesse of þi merciful doyngis, do þou awey my wickidnes! More, waische þou me fro my wickidnesse, and clense me fro my synne! For y knouleche my wickidnes; & my synne is euere a3enes me.

BL 17010

God, haue merci on me: aftir thi grete merci. And bi the mochilnesse of thy merciful doyngis: do thou awey my wickidnesse. More waishe thou me fro my wickidnesse: and clense thou me fro my synne. For I knowleche my wickidnesse: and my synne is euere a3ens me.

GROUP B READINGS

Douce 275

Haue mercy of me god after thi grete mercy. And after þi mechelnesse of þi mercyes do awei my wickednesse. Wasche me more of my wickednesse & of my synne clense þou me. For I knowe my wickednesse and my synne is euer a3ens me.

---

[18] In Bodley 277, 'more waische' is 'more ouer waische' (p. 481).

Bodley 85

Haue merci of me god after thi mechel merci. And after the mekenes of thin mercies do a wey myn wykenes. Wasche me more of my wyckednes and of my sinnes clense thou me. For y knowe my wyckednes and my synne is euer aȝenis me.

Douce 246

Haue merci of me god after þy gret mercy. And after þe mechelnesse of þy mercyes do aweye my wickednesse. Wasche me more of my wyckednesse & of my synne clense me. For I know my wickednesse and my synne is euer aȝens me.

St John's G.24

Haue mercy of me god: after thy grete mercy. And after the mechelnesse of thi mercyes. do a wey my wickidnesse. Waysch me more of my wickednesse: and of my synne clense me. For y knowe my wickednesse: and my synne is euere aȝens me.

BL Additional 27952

Haue merci of me god: after Þi grete mercy. And after the Þe mechelnesse of Þi mercies do awei my wickednesse. Wasche me more of my wickednesse and of my synne clens me. For I knowe my wickednesse and my synne is euer aȝens me

SAMPLE FOUR

Psalm 129 De profundis clamavi ad te Domine. Domine exaudi vocem meam, fiant aures tuae intendentes in vocem deprecationis meae. Si iniquitates observabis Domine Domine quis sustinebit? Quia apud te propitiatio est propter legem tuam sustinui te Domine. Sustinuit anima mea in verbum eius speravit anima mea in Domino a custodia matutina usque ad noctem speret Israhel in Domino. Quia apud Dominum misericordia et copiosa apud eum redemptio et ipse redimet Israhel ex omnibus iniquitatibus eius. (Out of the depths I have cried to thee, O Lord. Lord, hear my voice, let thy ears be attentive to the voice of my supplication. If thou, O Lord, wilt mark iniquities, Lord, who shall stand it? For with thee there is merciful forgiveness and by reason of thy law, I have waited for thee, O Lord. My soul hath relied on his word, my soul hath hoped in the Lord. From the morning watch even until night, let Israel hope in the Lord. Because with the Lord there is mercy and with him plentiful redemption and he shall redeem Israel from all his iniquities)

Wycliffite EV

Fro depthis I criede to thee, Lord; Lord, full out here thou my vois. Be maad thin eris vnderstondende; in to the vois of my lowe preȝing. If wickidnessis thou shalt al aboute

kepe, Lord; Lord, who shal sustene. For anent thee is mercy doyng; and for thi lawe I sustenede thee, Lord. My soule sustenede in the woord of hym; my soule hopide in the Lord. Fro the morutyd warde vnto the ny3t; hope Irael in the Lord. For anent the Lord mercy; and plenteous anentis hym a3een biyng. And he shal a3een bie Irael; fro alle the wickid\nessis of hym.[19]

Wycliffite LV

Lord, Y criede to thee fro depthes; Lord, here thou mi vois. Thin eeris be maad ententif; in to the vois of my biseching. Lord, if thou kepist wickidnessis; Lord, who schal susteyne [several manuscripts have 'susteyne ether abide']? For merci is at thee; and, Lord, for thi lawe Y abood thee. Mi soule susteynede in his word; my soule hopide in the Lord. Fro the morewtid keping til to ni3t; Israel hope in the Lord. For whi merci is at the Lord; and plenteous redempcioun is at hym. And he schal a3en bie Israel; fro alle the wickidnessis therof.[20]

GROUP A READINGS
Ashmole 1288

Lord i criede to þee fro deppis. Lord wel here þou my vois [this is all there is of this psalm here. The remainder is taken from fol. 52v–53r, the end of Compline]. Þin eeris ben maad ententif into þe vois of my bisechinge. Lord if þou kepist wickidnessis lord who schal susteyne. For merci is at þee and lord for þi lawe I abood þe. My soule susteynede in his word, my soule hopide in þe lord. Fro þe morewetid keping til to ni3t Israel hope in the lord. For whi merci is at þe lord, and plenteuous redempcion is at hym. And he schal a3enbie israel fro al þe wickidnessis þerof.

Rawlinson C. 699

Lord I criede to þee fro depþis. Lord heere þou my vois. Þin eeris be maad ententif in to þe vois of my biseching. Lord if þou kepist wickidnessis lord who schal susteyne. For mercy is at þee & lord for þi lawe I abood þee. My soule susteynyde in his word, my soule hopide in þe lord. Fro þe morewetide keping til in to þe ny3t, israel hope in þe lord. Forwhi mercy is at þe lord and plenteuous redempcioun is at him. And he shcal a3enbie israel fro alle þe wickidnessis þeroff.

CUL Dd.11.82

Lord, y criede to þee fro depþis; lord, here þou my vois! Thyne eeris ve maad ententif in-to þe vois of my biseching! Lord, if þou kepist wickidnessis; lord, who schal susteyne? For merci is at þee; &, lord, for þi lawe y abode þee. Mi soule suseynede

[19] In Bodley 959, 'vnderstondende' is 'vnderstondynge'.
[20] None of the primers offers the alternative 'ether abide'.

in his word; my soule hopide in þe lord. Fro þe morwetid keping til to þe ni3t, Israel, hope in þe lord! For whi, merci is at þe lord; & plenteuouse redempcioun is at him. And he schal a3enbie Israel fro alle þe wickidnessis þerof.

BL 17010

Lord, I cried to thee fro depthis: lord, wel here thou my vois. Thin eeris be maad ententif: in to the vois of my bisechyng. Lord, if thou kepist wickidnessis: lord, who shal susteyne. For merci is at thee: and lord for thi lawe I abood thee. My soule susteyned in his word: my soul hopide on the lord. Fro the morwetide kepinge til to ny3t: israel hope in the lord. For whi, merci is at the lord: and plenteuous redempcioun is at him. And he shal a3enbie israel: fro alle the wickidessis thereof.

GROUP B READINGS
Douce 275

From depnesse I criede to þee lord. Lord here my vois. Be þin eres maad takynge entente to þe voice of my preiere. Lord 3if þu take kepe to wickednessis lord who schal susteyne. For at þe is mercy & for þi lawe I susteynede þe lord. Mi soule susteynede in his word, my soule hopede in oure lord. Fro þe morwe kepinge til þe ni3t hopede israel in oure lord. For at þe lord is mercy & plenteuous a3en biynge is at him. And he schal bie israel of alle his wickednesses.

Bodley 85

Missing. The text moves directly from Psalm 50 to 'domine exaudi' and does so on a single folio (56v)—i.e. it cannot be accounted for by a missing folio.

Douce 246

From depnesse i cried to þe Lord. Lord þou here my voyce. [this is all there is of this psalm here. The rest is taken from the lesson immediately prior to the Penitential Psalms] Be þyne eris made takynge entent to þe voice of my preyere. Lord 3ife thou take kepe to wickednesses lord who schal susteyne. For atte þe is mercy and for þy lawe I susteyned þe lord. My soule susteyned in his word, my soule hoped in oure lord. Fro þe morrow kepynge til þe ny3te hope israel on oure lord. For atte oure lord is mercy and plenteuouse a3en byinge is atte hym. And he schal bye israel of alle his wickednesses.

St John's G.24

From deepnesses y cryede to thee lord: lord here my voys. Be thyn eeres maad takynge entente: to the uoys of my preyere. Lord 3if thou take kepe to wicked-nesses: lord ho schal susteyne. For at thee is mercy: and for thi lawe y susteynede thee lord My sowle susteynede in his word my sowle hopede in oure lord. Fro the morwe kepynge tyl the ny3t: hope isrl on owre lord. For at oure lord is mercy and plentevous a3eynbyinge is at hym. And he schal bye israel of alle his wickednesses.

BL Additional 27952

From depnesse I criede to Þe lord. Lord here my vois. Be thin eres made takynge entente to Þe vois of my preiere. Lord 3if Þou take kepe to wickednesses lord ho schal sustei. For at Þe is mercy and for Þi lawe i susteinede Þe lorde. Mi soule susteyned on his word, my soule hopede in oure lord. Fro the morwe kepinge til the ny3t hope Israel on oure lord. For at oure lord is mercy and plentifous a3enbiynge is at him. And he schal bye Israel of alle his wickednesses.

Looking first at the Group A primers, it is immediately apparent that they are all more or less identical with the LV text printed by Forshall and Madden. In fact, their consistency is quite remarkable. Returning to some of LV's revised Psalter verses, discussed in the previous chapter, it is also worth noting that the Group A primers include their apparently Lyran readings, distinguishing them from those in the EV Psalter. So, while Psalm 8: 5's 'filius hominis' is translated 'the son of man' in EV, LV and the Group A primers have 'the sone of a virgyn', a reading which is derived from Lyra ('aut filius hominis i. filius virginis' [or son of man, that is, son of a virgin]). And while Psalm 41: 8 is translated '[t]he depnesse depnesse inwardli clepeth; in the vois of thi gooteris' in EV, in LV and the Group A primers we find '[d]epthe clepith depthe; in the vois of thi wyndows'. This is, again, a reading obviously inspired by by Lyre ('cataractae dei dicuntur fenestrae caeli' ['the floodgates of God' is called 'the windows of heaven']).[21] It is entirely indisputable that the producers of these primers were working from the Wycliffite LV.[22]

The situation with the Group B primers is more difficult to read. Taking Psalm 6: 2–4 as the first instance, in all of the manuscript samples given, the first verse is identical to EV with the exception of 'blame', which replaces 'chastice'. The similarities persist into the second verse, with 'hele me' rather than LV's 'make me hool'. But after this, the lexical ('troubled' in place of 'disturbid') and syntactical (the idiomatic 'al my bones ben troubled' rather than 'disturbid ben alle my bonys') affinities are with the LV. In the case of Psalm 31: 1–2, the first verse is identical with LV (although Bodley 85 and Douce 246 have the singular 'wikednes/wickidnesse') and the first clause of the second also follows LV's more idiomatic rendition of the Vulgate's 'cui non inputabit Dominus peccatum', using 'retten' rather than

---

[21] At corresponding moments, Group B primers preserve the EV readings.

[22] Among this group, the psalm translations in Rawlinson C.699 are particularly interesting. As indicated, at Psalm 50: 3, it preserves EV's 'more ouer'. On other occasions, it distinguishes itself from other Group A primers by including glosses (underlined in red in the text) which also appear in several LV manuscripts. So, Psalm 131: 6 (f. 50r) reads 'Lo we herde þat arke of testament in effrata *þat is in sylo*' (Cf. CUL Dd.11.82's reading 'Lo! we herden þat ark of testament in effrata'). See also Psalm 114: 1 at the beginning of the Office of the Dead, which reads 'I louyde *þe lord*' in Rawlinson C.699. CUL Dd.11.82 also adds 'þe lord', but Rawlinson's underlining indicates an awareness of it as glossing addition.

LV's 'aretten'. Its final 'ne treson is not in his gost' differs lexically from both EV and LV, although it has idiomatic similarities with the latter. It does, however, echo precisely Rolle's translation of the same verse ('na treson is in his gaste'). Moving to Psalm 50: 3, like EV, the Group B primers delay the vocative 'God' until the end of the first clause and translate the Vulgate's 'secundum' with 'aftir' rather than LV's 'bi'. However, they differ from both Wycliffite versions in their use of 'mercies' (Rolle has 'mercyyngis'), and although their 'my wickednesse' is more idiomatic than EV's 'wickenesse myn', their literal translation of 'a peccato meo munda me' with 'of my synne clense me' echoes the syntax of EV. And although their idiomatic translation of '[q]uoniam iniquitatem meam ego cognosco: & peccatum meum contra me est semper' recalls that of LV, their use of 'knowe' rather than 'knowleche' echoes EV (Rolle also has 'knaw'). Looking finally at Psalm 129, the last of my samples, the B primers again recall EV in delaying the vocative 'Lord' to the end of the first clause, although they differ from both EV and LV in translating 'profundis' as 'depnesse(s)' rather than 'depthes' (Rolle has 'groundis'). Their 'be thyn eeres maad takynge entente' appears to amalgamate aspects of EV ('be maad thin eeris vnderstondende') and LV ('thin eeris be maad ententif').[23] Unlike EV, they move the vocative 'Lord' to the beginning of verse 3, avoiding the awkward collision of 'Lord. Lord'. The syntax of the next phrase ('for at thee is mercy and for thi lawe y susteynede thee lord') echoes that of EV, although 'my soule susteynede in his word' replaces EV's 'woord of hym'. The B primers' 'morwe kepynge' is closer to LV's 'morewtid keping' than EV's 'morutyd warde' (Rolle has 'kepyng of morne'), although they go on, like EV, to delay the vocative 'Israel'. Their 'plentevous aȝeynbyinge' is, like LV, an idiomatic improvement on EV's difficult 'plenteous anentis hym aȝeen biyng' but it shares EV's 'aȝeynbyinge', not adopting LV's 'redempcioun' like the A primers.[24]

What, then, is the relationship between the Group B primers and the Early and Later Wycliffite translations, both of which they undoubtedly echo? What are we to make of the way in which they apparently combine elements of both at the same time as introducing some readings of their own? The most obvious answer would be to suggest that they draw on some sort of 'intermediate' version/versions of the Wycliffite Psalter in which EV's literalism has been at least partially replaced with more idiomatic translations characteristic of LV. However, before proceeding with this line of thought, it is worth pausing to recognize its problems, the most obvious of which is the paucity of manuscript witnesses to such a version/versions

---

[23] At the same moment Rolle has 'thin eeren be made beholdand'.

[24] MS Douce 246 is particularly interesting. A neat contemporary hand occasionally makes alterations to the text, introducing readings characteristic of EV. So, for example, on f. 44v Psalm 31: 3 reads 'whils i crie', but there is a small red ∧ under the 'whils' and in the margin we find 'schulde' ('schuld' is found in Douce 275 at this moment). This replicates the EV reading. LV has 'whiles y criede' and this is found in other Group B primers. See also Psalm 31: 10 (f. 45) where there is an erasure: 'many scourges ~~ben~~ of synful men'. LV reads '[m]any betyngis ben of the synnere' while EV has '[m]anye scourgis of the synnere'. Douce 275 does not have 'ben' at this point but other Group B primers do. Harris-Matthews notes the existence of corrections in Douce 246 (although she does not provide examples) and suggests that they have been made to correspond with the variations found in Douce 275 (p. 90).

of the psalms. In an article published in 1970, Conrad Lindberg cited seventeen Wycliffite Bible manuscripts which contained what he called an *E*LV text ('partly in EV, partly in LV'), implying that they included 'intermediate' readings of the type mentioned earlier. His labelling was, however, somewhat misleading, since he did not clarify whether *E*LV denoted manuscripts which contain some EV biblical material and some LV, or whether it referred to copies which amalgamate readings from both (more often than not, it denoted the former). He went on, in his extensive later work, to clarify and expand his thoughts, listing EV manuscripts 'according to the degree of later revision', but his *E*LV labelling has remained in use, being cited, for example, by Mary Dove in *The First English Bible*.

Re-categorizing six of Lindberg's 1970 *E*LV manuscripts as straightforward LV, Mary Dove's index of Wycliffite Bible manuscripts affords us some help in decoding his initial analyses, although she too is unclear on occasion.[25] She adopts, for example, his ambiguous *E*LV labelling in indexing TCD 75 without providing any further details.[26] Dove does, however, clarify the term when applied to other manuscripts: she points us to two labelled *E*LV by Lindberg (London, Lambeth Palace Library 25 and Manchester, JRL 89) and explains that they contain both EV and LV biblical books. She also points us to a third (Manchester, John Rylands Library English 84) in which Acts 7: 31–10: 6 are EV while the rest of the book is LV, and to a final two (Oxford, New College 66 and Oxford, BodlL Bodley 183) in which LV biblical translations are accompanied by some EV prologues.

More interesting for our purposes is the fact that a further four of the manuscripts which Lindberg labelled *E*LV contain, according to both Lindberg and Dove, 'revised EV' readings rather than a combination of discrete EV and LV materials. New York, Columbia University Plimpton Additional 03, a complete Wycliffite New Testament, has Matthew and Mark in a 'slightly revised' EV while San Marino, Huntington Library HM 134, another complete New Testament, has Matthew 4: 20–13: 33 in revised EV. Cambridge, Sidney Sussex College 99 contains a complete New Testament in a 'slightly revised' EV and London, BL Add. 11858 has Mark, Luke, and part of Matthew in a revised EV 'clearly influenced by LV', while the rest of the New Testament is LV.[27] The existence of such manuscripts is intriguing, and the evidence that they supply could be read in a number of ways. It is possible that they represent an intermediate stage in the Wycliffite translation project and that in their revisions we can discern traces of a gradual movement from the difficult EV to the more accessible LV. As Hudson pointed out, 'the existence of "intermediate" stages [of the Wycliffite Bible] is coming to be recognised',

---

[25] C. Lindberg, 'The Manuscripts and Versions of the Wycliffite Bible—A Preliminary Survey', *SN* 42 (1970), 333–47. Although Dove's index (in her 2007 book) does not refer to Lindberg's labels, her categorization of the following as LV differs from that of Lindberg: London, BL Cotton Claudius E.11; Oxford, BodlL Bodley 277 (which contains, as we know, a revised LV Psalter); Oxford, BodlL Fairfax 2; Oxford, BodlL Rawlinson C.259; Cambridge, CUL Dd.1.27; Cambridge, Jesus College 30.

[26] In *SSE* 7, Lindberg clarifies his earlier description and states that the EV text in TCD 75 shows a considerable degree of revision (for a brief description of manuscript, see Dove (2007), pp. 242–3).

[27] On the claim for 'clear' LV influence here, see Lindberg (1959–97), vol. 7, p. 24. Citing Lindberg, Dove also indexes New Haven, Yale University Beinecke Library 125 (Matthew 3: 4–1 Timothy 1: 15) as containing some revised EV readings.

and as Dove has also suggested, '[t]extual revision . . . seems to have been an ongoing process throughout the Wycliffite Bible project.'[28] Lindberg, for example, lists several manuscripts which contain portions of revised EV New Testament material, and as Hudson has pointed out, an intermediate version of this sort seems to have been used by the compilers of the Wycliffite Glossed Gospels ('[a]ll the commentaries make use of a form of the EV gospel translation, somewhat modified but not yet transformed into the established LV version').[29] These revisions may well have been entirely independent of LV, of which it is conceivable that the revisers were unaware.[30] However, an alternative (or additional) possibility is suggested by Lindberg when, in commenting on BL Add. 11858, he states that the revisions have been 'clearly influenced by LV'. It appears, then, that there may have been occasions on which the revisers of EV worked with an awareness of LV, readings from which they incorporated into their reworked translations. Just because LV was in circulation, this did not mean that it was always preferred to EV.

This is, I suggest, the situation with the psalm translations in the Group B primers. Departing from or idiomatically improving on EV, they sometimes do so in a manner distinct from LV, but they also frequently share striking readings with the latter. The most satisfactory explanation for this is that the B primers are all ultimately indebted to an EV Psalter which contains LV-inspired revisions (i.e. not strictly speaking an intermediate version, since it demonstrates an awareness of LV). It may, however, have been noticed that among the revised EV manuscripts cited previously, there are no copies of the psalms; almost all contain New Testament material only.[31] Finding oneself suggesting a hypothesis in the absence of any specific supporting evidence is awkward, but the unease is alleviated somewhat by a reading of Cambridge, CUL Ee.1.10. Containing a condensed selection of material from 2 Chronicles–2 Maccabees in addition to EV prologues, CUL Ee.1.10 was originally in two volumes and probably preserved an abridgement of the entire Wycliffite Old Testament.[32] As it stands, it contains several extracts from the Psalter (followed by the *Te Deum, Benedictus, Magnificat, Nunc Dimittis,* and *Athanasian Creed*) including some almost complete psalms, some represented by long excerpts, and some by a single verse. In the first volume of their Wycliffite Bible edition, Forshall and Madden describe its text as 'made from the earlier version', the language of which has been 'very slightly altered, chiefly by a different collocation of words, the insertion of an article or pronoun and occasionally of a verbal gloss'.[33] In more recent references to the manuscript, it has been described more decisively as containing a 'revised version' of EV.[34] However, the

---

[28] Hudson (1988), p. 246; Dove (2007), p. 142.   [29] Hudson (1988), p. 250.

[30] Dove (2007), p. 180 suggests that 'at least some parts of the production of the Later Version and some parts of the revision of the New Testament were carried out independently'.

[31] As we know, the EV Psalter in Bodley 959 contains revisions. They do not, however, appear to be related to the revisions that we find in the Group B primers.

[32] For a brief description, see Dove (2007), pp. 239–41. For a fuller description see *IMEP* XIX, pp. 85–6.

[33] Forshall and Madden, vol. 1, p. liv.

[34] Dove (2007), p. 284. Lindberg also refers to its 'revised' text (C. Lindberg, *The Middle English Bible—The Book of Judges* (Oslo, 1989), p. 69), although he did not include it in his 1970 list of *ELV*

most detailed analysis of CUL Ee.1.10, in particular its text of the psalms, remains that of Henry Hargreaves who suggested that the alterations to which Forshall and Madden referred 'were by no means slight; on the contrary, they were so numerous and consistent that they obviously represented a thorough working over of the earlier version'.[35] To Hargreaves, the revisions indicated that the manuscript preserves extracts from an 'intermediate version' of the Wycliffite Bible, which may or may not have influenced LV.

Without necessarily subscribing to Hargreaves' hypothesis that CUL Ee.1.10 contains excerpts from an 'intermediate version' of the Wycliffite Bible (a more convincing suggestion is that it contains a 'blend' of EV and LV readings such as that which Lindberg discerns in BL Add. 11858), its revisions of the psalms are striking insofar as they generate a text which has affinities with that found in the Group B primers.[36] For example, the Ee.1.10 psalms, like those of the Group B primers, sometimes move vocative nouns to the beginning of clauses, revising EV's tendency to leave them in the position which they occupy in the Vulgate. We witnessed this in the case of Group B's Psalm 129 and see it again in the Ee.1.10 and Group B translations of Psalm 131: 1 ('Memento Domine David' [O Lord, remember David]), in both of which 'domine' has been moved forward (Ee.1.10 reads 'Lord, haue minde . . .' and Group B (represented by St John's G.24) 'Lord, by thenk the . . .').[37] The revisions that they make to the syntax of Psalm 50: 17 ('Domine labia mea aperies et os meum adnuntiabit laudem tuam' [O Lord, thou wilt open my lips: and my mouth shall declare thy praise]) also have affinities; both create an idiomatic sentence by making the initial verb precede the subject. So, Ee.1.10 has 'Lord, opene thou my lippis and my mouth shal tell thi preisyng' and St John's G.24 'Lord þou schalt opene my lyppes and my mouþ schal shewe thi preisynge'. Both read more smoothly than EV's 'Lord, my lippis thou shalt opene; and my mouth shal before telle thi preising', although Ee.1.10 is closer than St John's G.24 to LV's 'Lord opene thou my lippis; and my mouth schal telle thi preysyng'.[38] Equally, both Ee.1.10 and the Group B primers are happy, in the interests of idiomatic translation, to make initial subject precede verb when necessary. So, Psalm 31: 1 ('beati quorum remissae sunt iniquitates et quorum tecta

manuscripts. Dove suggests that '[t]he editors and scribes of those Wycliffite Bible manuscripts that contain selected books, chapters and verses of the Bible rather than a continuous biblical text, may well have been hoping to evade the [Arundelian] legislation by concealing the fact that the extracts derived from a complete (and therefore Wycliffite) Bible'. She also points out that Fristedt makes this case in relation to CUL Ee.1.10 (p. 52).

[35] H. Hargreaves, 'An Intermediate Version of the Wycliffite Old Testament', *SN* 28 (1956), 130–47, p. 133.

[36] For the suggestion that CUL Ee.1.10 contains a 'blend' of EV and LV readings, see Dove (2007), p. 240.

[37] Ee.1.10's reading is closer to LV ('Lord, haue thou minde . . .') than is St John's G.24's. Nonetheless, they are both driven by the same imperative. In general, Ee.1.10 is more consistent than the Group B primers in altering the position of the vocative.

[38] However, it is worth noting that, like the Group B primers, the LV psalms in Oxford, BodlL Fairfax 2 (K) read 'lord þou schalt opene my lippis'.

sunt peccata' [Blessed are they whose iniquities are forgiven, and whose sins are covered]) reads identically in both:

> Blessed be they whas wikkidnessis been for3yfe and whaas synnes ben heeled.

This smooth translation mirrors that of LV ('Blessid ben thei, whose wickidnessis ben for3ouun and whose synnes ben hilid') and is in stark contrast with EV's literal 'Blissid of whom ben for3iue the wickidnessis and of whom couered ben the synnes'.[39]

They also both replicate other conventions underlying the LV translation. As Hargreaves points out, in chapter 15 of the General Prologue to the Wycliffite Bible, we are told that it is legitimate for the Vulgate's 'autem' to be rendered in different ways:

> Also, whanne oo word is onys set in a resoun it mai be set forþ as ofte as it is vnder-stonden, or as ofte as resoun and nede asken. And þis word *autem* or *vero* mai stonde for 'forsoþe' or for 'but', and þus I vse comynly, and sumtyme it mai stonde for 'and', as eld grammarians seyn.[40]

Where EV tends to translate 'autem' with 'forsoþe', LV shows greater variety and often moves the term to the beginning of the clause or sentence.[41] A similarly increased flexibility is at work in both Ee.1.10 and Group B. For example, Psalm 125: 6 ('euntes ibant et flebant portantes semina sua venientes autem venient in exultatione portantes manipulos suos' [Going they went and wept, casting their seeds. But coming they shall come with joyfulness, carrying their sheaves]) is translated thus in EV:

> Goende thei 3iden and wepten; sendende ther sedis. Comende forsothe thei shul come; berende with ful out io3ing ther handfullis.

but in LV:

> They goynge 3eden, and wepten; sendynge her seedis. But thei comynge schulen come with ful out ioiynge; berynge her handfullis.

The latter reading has precise and obvious affinities with that in St John's G.24 (the word-order of which is replicated in CUL Ee.1.10):

> Goynge thei 3ede and wepte: sendynge here seedes. Bote comynge they schulle come with gladnesse, berynge here schefes.[42]

Like LV, in the interests of idiomatic translation, they also both frequently supply words absent from the Latin (and from EV). Such is the case, for example, in their

---

[39] For other examples of subject re-placement in both Ee.1.10 and Group B, see Psalms 125: 2 and 130: 1 in both. Neither makes the change in Psalm 50: 4; the word-order of 'a peccato meo munda me' [cleanse me from my sin] is reproduced in both ('of my synne clense me'). This is closer to EV ('fro my synne clense me') than LV ('clense thou me fro my synne').

[40] Dove (2010), pp. 81/2835–8.

[41] For Hargreaves' discussion of this point, see (1956), p. 139.

[42] Rolle has 'Gangand thai ₃ede and grett, sendand thaire sede. Bot cumand thai sall cum with gladnes: berand thaire repis.'

quoted renditions of Psalm 31: 1–2 to both of which the verb 'be(n)' is supplied after 'blessed'. Of course, the text of the psalms found in CUL Ee.1.10 is by no means identical to that in the Group B primers; often it is closer to LV than the latter, although there are some occasions on which Group B's readings align more closely with LV.[43] Nonetheless, the general tenor of the revisions is the same: both have recognizable affinities with EV but move decisively in the direction of greater idiomacy.[44]

The circulation of Wycliffite psalms in the English language primers might seem initially surprising. It is not as easily explicable as, for example, the use of the Wycliffite translation (lightly revised EV) in the Glossed Gospels or in the polemical literature discussing the availability of scriptural material in the vernacular (LV). But it substantiates the observation, made at the beginning of Chapter 3, that where relationships between Middle English psalm translations can be discerned, they are not always those which one might expect. Further, it offers compelling evidence that the EV psalms were the subject of revision in much the same way as parts of the New Testament and is, therefore, richly suggestive. Indicating that the Wycliffite Bible was quarried for its translations as early as the closing decades of the fourteenth century, the primers could also be said to provide intriguing evidence of the swift dissemination of this apparently 'heretical' biblical version in entirely orthodox contexts.[45] And the fact that the translation should have been put to use in the context of the primer is entirely in keeping with the facilitation, in many Wycliffite manuscripts, of the liturgical deployment of the Bible as a whole. As Dove points out, 'at least eighty-nine' contain calendars and lectionaries 'indicating which epistles and gospels are read at mass throughout the year' and the text of the Old Testament mass-lections is added to New Testament in some twenty-five of these.[46] Further, as Christopher de Hamel has demonstrated, the presentation of the Wycliffite psalms also resembles that of liturgical Psalters, and in most manuscripts, 'alternating red and blue one-line capitals mark the opening

---

[43] For a striking example of Group B's closeness to LV, see Psalm 119: 1. EV reads 'To þe lord whan I was trublid I criede' and LV 'Whanne y was set in tribulacioun y criede to þe lord'. Ee 1.10 has 'whanne y was trobled y criede to þe lord', but Group B (represented by Cambridge, St John's College G.24) has 'whanne y was in tribulation y cryede to oure Lord' (Rolle has 'Till lord when I was in anguys I cryid: & he herd me').

[44] I would tentatively suggest that such a revised EV/LV text might also be behind some of the versions of the *St Jerome's Abbreviated Psalter*. Harris-Matthews argues that the links between the Hatton 111 version and the Group B primers are particularly compelling. Cf. Psalm 50: 12 in St John's G.24 'Make a clene herte in me god: and make newe a ri3tful gooste in my guttes' and in Hatton 111 'Make a clene herte in me god & a ri3tful gost mak newe in my guttes' (cf. EV 'A clene herte forme in me, God; and a ri3t spirit inwardli newe thou in my bowelis' and LV 'God, make thou a clene herte in me; and make thou newe a ri3tful spirit in my entrailis'). And cf. 50: 13 in St John's G.24 'Cast nat me fro þi face and þi ri3tful gost bere nat fro me' and in Hatton 111 'Cast me not fro þi face þin holy gost bere nat fro me' (cf. EV 'Ne throwe thou me aferr fro thi face; and thin holy spirit ne do thou awei fro me' and LV 'Caste thou me not awei fro thi face; and take thou not awei fro me thin hooli spirit').

[45] For recent discussion of an instance of the Wycliffite Bible circulating in an orthodox context, see A. Hudson, 'The Carthusians and a Wycliffite Bible', in *Ecclesia-Cultura-Potestas: A Festschrift for Urszula Borkowska OSU*, ed. P. Kras et al. (Kraków, 2006), pp. 731–42. There is nothing inherently 'Wycliffite' in the primers' enabling of the English recitation of the basic liturgical hours; as suggested in Chapter 1, this was long-established practice in educational contexts.

[46] Dove (2007), pp. 58 and 61.

of each verse of each psalm, so that the psalm could be read antiphonally where appropriate, or a listener could keep track of the text of a psalm read or sung antiphonally'.[47] The Latin *incipits* generally used to identify individual psalms in the Middle Ages (and which appear in the English language primers) are also included in most manuscripts containing the Wycliffite psalms, further facilitating liturgical cross-referencing should it be necessary.[48]

However, in addition to the liturgical texts previously discussed, eleven of the extant English language primers contain further catechetic material. BL Add. 27592 has, at its conclusion, short treatises on the Ten Commandments, the Seven Deadly Sins, the Five Senses, the Five Works of Mercy, the Seven Gifts of the Holy Spirit, the Seven Words from the Cross, and the Sixteen Properties of Charity. It follows these with a series of biblical quotations and a copy of Walter Hilton's *Of Angels' Song*.[49] BodlL Ashmole 1288(1) contains a copy of the *Confession of St. Brendan*, a version of which is also found among the extensive catechetic contents of BodlL Rawlinson C. 699.[50] BodlL Bodley 85 ends with a new quire (in the same hand as the liturgical material) containing treatises on the Ten Commandments, the Seven Deadly Sins, the Five Bodily Senses, the Five Spiritual Senses, the Seven Special Virtues, the Seven Works of Mercy, the Seven Gifts of the Holy Spirit, as well as quotations from St Paul and Leviticus (the manuscript is incomplete). BodlL Douce 246 concludes with a prayer to St Catherine, a commentary on the Ten Commandments, *Diliges Dominum*, and some very basic diagrams outlining the Five Senses, the Seven Deadly Sins, the Seven Gifts of the Holy Spirit et al.[51] Oxford, Queen's College 324 has a copy of Edmund of Abingdon's *Speculum Ecclesie*, and Oxford, University College 179 has, among its additional contents, a vernacular prayer about the recitation of the psalms, prayers to be said before eating meals, and a copy of the Abbreviated Psalter of Jerome in alternate Latin and English.[52] Cambridge, Emmanuel College 246 has treatises on the Ten Commandments, the Five Senses et al, as well as a discussion of the Sixteen Properties of Charity.[53] The same subjects are covered (with some exceptions) in Glasgow, Hunter 512 and 472, the last of which also has a series of prayers to be said before eating meals.[54] Yale, University Library Beineke 360 contains, in addition to the primer, a complete *English Psalter* (Wycliffite LV) as well as a copy of the abbreviated Psalter of Jerome in English.

It would be tempting to look for evidence of Wycliffite-related heterodoxy among these additional contents: we would then have something of a context in

---

[47] C. de Hamel, *The Book: A History of the Bible* (London, 2001), pp. 182–3, and Dove (2007), p. 63. As Dove points out, there is never any 'rule' for locating the proper psalms in Wycliffite Bibles.

[48] Unusually, in Oxford, BodlL Laud Misc 182 (which contains selected chapters and verses from the Wycliffite LV including the psalms), the psalms are identified by number rather than *incipit*.

[49] For a fuller description, see the online British Library Catalogue.

[50] For a full description of Ashmole 1288, see *IMEP* IX (Eldredge).

[51] For a full description, see *IMEP* IV (Braswell), pp. 46–50.

[52] For further details, see *IMEP* VIII (Ogilvie-Thomson), pp. 81–3 and pp. 121–4.

[53] For further details, see M. R. James, *The Western Manuscripts of Emmanuel College: A Descriptive Catalogue* (Cambridge, 1904).

[54] On both, see J. Young (continued and completed by P. Henderson Aitken), *A Catalogue of the Manuscripts in the Library of the Hunterian Museum in the University of Glasgow* (Glasgow, 1908).

which to place the primers' reliance on the Wycliffite translation. Such evidence is not, however, easily forthcoming; in the vast majority of primers there is little to suggest anything other than orthodox intentions on the part of their compilers. As already pointed out, the liturgical material in Ashmole 1288, for example, is followed by a copy of *The Confession of St. Brendan*, an uncontroversial prayer encouraging simple self-examination:

> Heere eendiþ þe commendaciouns and here bigynneþ a cristen mannes confessioun to his lord god, which behouiþ deuoutly be seid wiþ herte and mouþ and distinctifly wiþ remorse of his conscience, whoso kan and haþ oportunyte of tyme to do it and seie it.[55]

And this is a prayer which is also found in Rawlinson C.699, where it is prefaced thus:

> Here bigynneþ a confession which is also a preier þat seint Brandon made & it is ri3t nedeful to a cristen mane to seie & worche þeraftir in his lyuyng.[56]

Further, although the commentary on the Ten Commandments found in Douce 246 was categorized by Jolliffe 'a 'compressed' (B) version of the Wycliffite (?) Commentary', it has nothing very controversial to say and although *Diliges Dominum* does keep heterodox company in some manuscripts, there is no suggestion of heterodoxy among its companions in Douce.[57] And most notably, the Bodley 85 primer is accompanied by orthodox catechesis as well as biblical material warning readers against the dangers of pursuing heterodoxy:

> We warne 3ou breþren in þe name of our lord ihesu crist þat 3e wiþdrawe 3ou fro euery broþer goyng inordynatly and not after þe ordynaunce þat þei haue take of us. Ffor 3e wyten wel in what maner it nediþ to folowe us'. . .'I haue wonder seiþ seynt poule þat 3e þus soone han left hym þat clepid 3ou in to þe grace of crist . . . 3if ony man teche 3ou eny gospel wiþouten þat 3e han taken of us cursyd be hee.[58]

Perhaps the closest that we come to inflammatory material is in the additions to BL Add. 27592. Its treatise on 'þe x commandments & þe vii dedly synnes & þe v wittis outward & inward wiþ vij werkes of mercy bodely & gostly & þe vij 3iftes of þe holigost' has much to say about idolatry ('god wol no3t þus be worshiped in dede ymages bote in queke men' f. 42v) and about 'vicious prestes' who 'ben unable to be cleped herdes of mennes soules for holy writ clippeþ wicked prestes

---

[55] See f. 112r. *The Confession of St. Brendan* is 311 in the *IPMEP*, although the Ashmole version is not listed. Eldredge's summary of the contents of Ashmole 1288 does not mention *The Confession* (*IMEP* IX).

[56] See f. 162r. The Rawlinson primer also contains some additional devotional prayers and five tracts from *Pore Caitif*.

[57] Perhaps the most provocative statement in the commentary on the Commandments appears on f. 103v: 'The last maundement is brokyn of many men by many weyes as many coueyten vnlefully to gete goode of þeire breþren as doon þes stark beggers þat spolen þe nei3ebores by gabbynge.' But there is nothing inherently Wycliffite about this; although the Lollards were concerned by begging, so were many (orthodox) others, William Langland being an obvious case in point.

[58] The quotations are from 2 Thessalonians 3: 6-7 and Galatians 1: 6-10. They do not seem to be indebted to the Wycliffite translations.

blinde leiers marchauntes and wolfes of rauen in schepes clothinge' (ff. 43r–v).[59]
It comments also on 'flatringe idel & my3ty freres' (48r) and on the impossibility
of buying salvation ('Þou3 a man 3ife alle his good to pardons & to pilgrimages
& to prest or freres it doþ nou3t aweie his synne' f. 49v). Yet although these comments are overtly anti-clerical, anti-fraternal, and anti-ecclesiastical, they contain
no opinions that would define them as specifically or exclusively Lollard. And it
is most telling that anti-sacramental polemic is entirely absent; its author has no
problem with the sacraments but with the senseless multiplication ('bastard braun-
ches and idel dranes') of those who administer them ('for aresonable noumbre ta3t
in godes lawe sufficiaunt to do þe sacramentes & preche only godes law in word &
dede were inowe to þe cherche' (f. 48v)). The use of the Wycliffite Bible translation
in the English language primers does not, then, appear to have been prompted
by, or played a part in, any heterodox agenda. It serves, rather, to point us to the
early circulation of these psalms in the arena of broadly orthodox devotion, an
arena which sets attention to the 'lettre' of the Bible (the text of the psalms) in the
context of the moral reformation of self and society.

PARAPHRASED PSALMS—AUCHINLECK,
THORNTON, AND LYDGATE

Designed for use in the (quasi-)liturgical context of devotional prayer, the primer
psalms need to remain close to their Latin source. If, as will be speculated in the
final chapter of this book, they are intended to assist readers who want to follow,
or at least remain alert to, the ordered recitation of the Vulgate psalms, a degree
of precision in the translation needs to be maintained. For such an audience, verbatim vernacularization has its own merit. This is not, however, true of many of
the paraphrased and abbreviated verse renditions of the psalms (often, but not
always, the Seven Penitential) which circulated in the late Middle Ages. As noted
at the beginning of this chapter, in their recognition of the act of translation as
a creative reinvention of the source, and of paraphrase as a legitimate articulation of Davidic 'entent', the authors of these texts shift attention away from the
'lettre' of the original. However, in their manuscript context these paraphrases
frequently encourage us to move in the opposite direction (the 'endless shuttling'
back and forth between the two languages that this entails will be discussed in
Chapter 6).[60] Although they do not facilitate cross-referencing with the Latin as
overtly as the primer psalms, they nonetheless maintain an active and visible relationship with their Gallican source by generally including it (or at least parts of it)

---

[59] In his checklist, Jolliffe lists Add. 27592's material on the Seven Deadly Sins (ff. 45v–46v) as
occurring in seven further manuscripts. See Jolliffe (1974), pp. 83–4 (F21(b)). As identified earlier,
two of these (Cambridge, Emmanuel College 246 and GUL, Hunter 472) also contain English language primers. He also identifies its material on the 16 Conditions of Charity (ff. 52v–54r) as occurring in five further manuscripts (p. 86 (G4(f)), two of which are again the Emmanuel and Glasgow
manuscripts.

[60] The phrase 'endless shuttling' is taken from Wogan-Browne et al. (1999), p. 322.

on the page, often either in—or underlined in—red ink. Of course, not all of these psalm-based poems can be crudely characterized as sharing the same perception of themselves as renditions of the Vulgate. As pointed out earlier in this book and as illustrated throughout this chapter, they vary widely in their nature as paraphrases. Nonetheless, all grounding themselves in the same source text, they can be considered legitimately as a group and distinguished from the primer versions. Although every act of translation is an inter*acti*on with its source, a paraphrase's dynamic and responsive relationship with the Psalter is always foregrounded in a way that the more obviously reproductive practice of verbatim translation cannot emulate.

We begin with the earliest of the extant free-standing paraphrases of Psalm 50, Auchinleck's 'Dauid þe Kyng'. As demonstrated in Chapter 1, 'Dauid þe Kyng' shares with the primer psalms its manuscript association with basic catechetic material, and it is easy to see its appeal in this context. Beyond this, however, the similarities cease. Although the poet's interactions with the Vulgate vary throughout, from the outset it is clear that verbatim translation is not the goal. The poet incorporates within his paraphrase a response to the text which insists on the psalm's communal applicability:

> *Miserere mei deus &c*
> *[Have mercy on me, O God, according to thy great mercy]*
> Lord God, to þe we calle,
> Þat þou haue merci on ous alle,
> & for þi michel mekenisse
> Þat we mot comen to þi blisse.[61] (1–4)

In fact, in the extant portion of the poem, it is only in stanza 4 that closer translation coincides with recognition of the prayer's intense, first-person introspection:

> *Quoniam iniquitatem meam &c*
> *[For I know my iniquity, and my sin is always before me]*
> Lord, mi wickednisse y knowe wel,
> Fram ende to ende eueridel,
> & euer is mi sinne oʒaines me;
> Lord, on me haue pite.[62] (15–18)

Among modern critics, the poem has been criticized for its apparently unsophisticated engagement with Psalm 50 and with the complexity of the Psalmist's pronouncements. The original psalm, for example, is punctuated by penitential

---

[61] All quotations are taken from the digital transcript of the Auchinleck manuscript <http://digital.nls.uk/auchinleck/>.

[62] This is a point also made by John Thompson (1988), p. 50, footnote 34. I do not follow Thompson in labelling this pluralization of speakers a 'distortion' of the biblical text (p. 43): it seems to me to be a legitimate response to a psalm which has always been understood to articulate the grief of others beyond David. I do, however, agree that the insistent use of 'we' 'will not easily support the notion that this verse-text was specifically intended for private reading and meditation. In common with several other Auchinleck items which offer elementary religious instruction, and where the impressions of oral-didactic address are even more obvious, this particular version of Psalm l was probably written to encourage a fairly simple piety among an audience that probably included small groups of listeners as well as readers' (p. 43).

unease, seen most clearly in the fact that although the speaker asserts God's cleansing power in verse 9 ('asperges me hysopo et mundabor lavabis me et super nivem dealbabor' [thou shalt sprinkle me with hyssop, and I shall be cleansed, thou shalt wash me, and I shall be made whiter than snow]), by verse 11 he has returned to a pained awareness of his sins ('averte faciem tuam a peccatis meis et omnes iniquitates meas dele' [turn away thy face from my sins, and blot out all my iniquities]). In the hands of this Middle English poet, however, the Psalmist's torment is easily resolved by simple couplets, generally rhyming on words of one or two syllables; most notably, his 'greting' (55) is cancelled prematurely by the prospect of 'holy gost comforting' (56).[63] Following the original (verse 17), the poet prays that God will 'vndo' his 'lippes', but his simple proclamations ('wiþ praiers ichil honour þe / þi godhed & ek þi dignete' (71–2)) have not been read as bearing witness to a liberated vernacular able to articulate the intensity of penitential suffering and release.

Certainly, for a poetic adaptation of a biblical text, the piece has few literary pretensions. Despite its departure from the 'lettre' of its Vulgate original, it does not generate a distinctive tone of its own. Other than passing evocations of a noble court (Jesus is 'hei3e justise' (82) and God a 'debonoure' and 'mi3tful heuen-king' (83–4)), it is a markedly unadorned devotional response to the psalm. In fact, as a paraphrase it erodes much of the Psalmist's most striking language. Verse 4's evocative plea for purgation ('amplius lava me [domine] ab iniquitate mea' [wash me yet more from my iniquity]) becomes:

> An[d] kepe ous alle fram dedli sinne,
> Þat non of ous no dye þerinne; (9–10)

And verse 16's powerful 'libera me de sanguinibus' [deliver me from blood] is turned into:

> Lord Iesu, heuen-king,
> Ous alle schilde fram wicked fonding. (65–6)

To interpret this as a failing on the poet's part is, however, to misunderstand his own perception of his role in producing a vernacular version of Psalm 50. Unlike some of the later paraphrases, which revel in the language and imagery of the original, the Auchinleck translator appears to be constructing a consciously 'limited' response to the psalm. Perhaps somewhat surprisingly for someone making poetry out of the Psalter, he is not very interested in the precise, evocative terminology of the original. In fact, 'Dauid þe Kyng' does not fulfil either of the criteria referred to at the beginning of this chapter as characteristic of many psalm paraphrases. It does not 'delight' in the language of the Psalmist, nor does it craft a technically accomplished commentary on that language. Rather, the poet's goal appears to be the distillation of the psalm's penitential essence into a piece of easily memorable rhyming vernacular devotion accessible to a wide audience. And it is in the keying

---

[63] That this all-too-easy resolution is a risk in many Middle English conventionally Christocentric readings of the psalms will be discussed further in Chapter 5.

of psalmic preoccupations into the common spiritual praxis of its Christian readers that 'Dauid þe Kyng' can be said to participate in the wider trends of English psalm translation in the late Middle Ages.

No vernacular analogue or source has been identified for the Auchinleck paraphrase. Equally, the Psalm 50 paraphrase in the London Thornton manuscript has no known equivalent, nor is there is anything to suggest that the poet knew of the Auchinleck version. However, as indicated in Chapter 1, the Thornton poem does participate in a contemporary 'school' of accomplished devotional verse. That the poem has apparent literary affiliations should alert us to the fact that its author is as interested in the nature of his paraphrase as English verse as he is in its status as English translation. The poet's consciousness of his poem's identity as an accomplished English rendition of a Latin original is most apparent in his systematic use of concatenation, linking lines 8 and 9 of each stanza (ay/ay; highte/highte; moghte/moghte/mare & lesse/lesse & mare; clene/clene; clere/clere; wythdrawe/ withdraw; mende/mende; wynne/wyn; wroghte/wroghte). In thus repeatedly recollecting and varying his own terminology, the poet offers compelling evidence of his interest in the paraphrase as literary artefact. And yet, as we will see, the poem registers no sense of conflict between its own accomplishment and its status as paraphrasing translation of a biblical text. In implicitly debunking the notion that there is a conflict between the two identities, the poet follows in the confident translating tradition of Chaucer et al.

However, it is not only in its nature as a notably accomplished poetic artefact that Thornton differs from Auchinleck but also in the fact that its translations of the Vulgate are markedly more precise. In fact, these two aspects of the paraphrase seem to be related to each other: taking heed of the 'lettre' of the Vulgate, the poet also pays attention to the 'lettre' and style of his own response. To take an obvious example, in the first stanza, verse 3 is translated fairly closely:

> God, þou haue mercy of me,
> After thi mercy mekill of mayne. (1–2)[64]

This translation introduces a twelve-line alliterating and rhyming (abababcdcd) stanza which impresses upon us the urgency of the Psalmist's petition by the three-fold repetition of the translated 'God þou haue mercy on me':

> God þou haue mercy on me,
> And purge my plyghte with penance playne;
> God þou haue mercy on me,
> Þat sakles for my syn was slayne;
> God þou haue mercy on me,
> Þat wrange es gane þou gete agayne.[65] (3–8)

before a final restatement in the last line of the stanza:

> God þou haue mercy on me (12)

---

[64] All quotations are taken from John Thompson's edition in his previously cited 1988 article.
[65] Uniquely, the first stanza actually rhymes abababcaca.

In the midst of a Christocentric elaboration which draws attention to the redemption ('Þat sakles for my syn was slayne'), the Psalmist's own voice still resounds. His Old Testament plea for mercy repeatedly breaks through the New Testament assurances interwoven in the verse commentary. And this is an effect which echoes throughout the poem as whole; after the first, each of the subsequent ten complete stanzas ends with the repeated 'Ihesu/God þou haue mercy on me'. This close attention to the words of the Psalmist facilitates (if not forces) the poet's focus on the prayer's intensely personal nature. The translation of the first part of verse 5 is a case in point:

> Full wele I knawe my self certayne,
> Þe wykkede werkes þat y hafe wroghte (37–8)

In the first two lines, the three-fold repetition of the first-person singular pronouns 'I/y' and 'my' amplifies the Vulgate's own two-fold emphasis ('[q]uoniam iniquitatem *meam ego* cognosco' [for I know my iniquity]), but in a particularly striking instance of mirroring, Thornton's 'I knawe my self' recalls the collision of 'meam' and 'ego' in the original: personal culpability could not be more plain. And it is a clarity which persists throughout the rest of the stanza in which the translation of the remainder of the verse and the responsive commentary are skilfully interwoven and alliteratively linked:

> And how sere synnes my saule has slayne,
> Þerfore to saluyng hafe I soughte;
> My synnes are euer me agayne,
> But thraly euer I thynke in thoghte,
> Þat þi mercy es mare of mayne,
> Þan any syn þat man do moghte. (39–44)

Vernacularizing the Vulgate's 'peccatum meum contra me est semper' [my sin is always before me], the ever-present sins of the speaker ('[m]y synnes are euer me agayne') are set in the reassuring context of the 'saluyng' of the 'slayne' soul. But any platitudinous resolution of the penitent's situation is avoided by the poetically and theologically resonant plea 'Ihesu þou haue mercy on me' repeated at the end of the stanza. Making use of this refrain and combining it with alliteration, concatenation, and a popular twelve-line stanza, Thornton's biblical poet draws attention to his own 'à la mode' craftsmanship. It is, however, a measure of his skill and restraint that he does not do so at the expense of the psalm to which he is responding: although this vernacular poet's 'lippes' are emphatically 'opene', he speaks with, rather than over, the Psalmist. Its model of paraphrase is in no sense combative. Situating his psalmic adaptation in the context of self-consciously literary activity, the Thornton poet reminds us that late-medieval biblical vernacularization must be understood in the broader milieu of contemporary debate surrounding the cultural status and function of translation, both religious and secular.

Another poet who forcefully reminds us of this is John Lydgate, whose psalm renditions become all the more interesting when one considers them in the context of contemporary outworkings of the classical model of translation as contestation of the original. As indicated in Chapter 1, the prolific Bury monk was responsible for four verse elaborations on the psalms: an exposition of *Judica Me Deus* (Psalm 42), incorporated in *The Virtues of the Mass*, paraphrases of Psalms 53 (*Deus in Nomine*) and 102 (*Benedic Anima Mea*), and an exposition of *De Profundis* (Psalm 129). Lydgate's paraphrases, as the proceeding discussion will demonstrate, vary widely in character and emphasis, and their artistry is of a more ostentatious nature than that of the Thornton poem. Nonetheless, the two poets have in common an awareness of the potential for the Vulgate psalms to be transformed into vernacular verse of some power and distinction. However, where the Thornton poet interweaves his voice with the Psalmist's, retaining a degree of exemplary anonymity (compounded, of course, by the fact that we do not know who wrote the poem), Lydgate more insistently draws attention to his own presence within his paraphrases. This is emphasized in particular by the *faux*-modest insertion of his own name into the opening lines of *Judica Me Deus* [Judge me, O God], to be discussed later. The effect of this is by no means always detrimental: Lydgate's psalms are frequently compelling and always powerful. It would, of course, be absurd to suggest that his paraphrases work to usurp the precedence of their biblical source; as Copeland points out, and as was suggested in Chapter 2 of this book, displacement of the original is not a motive in the arena of scriptural translation. Nonetheless, there is a sense in which his English poems are not simply 'serving' their source but are also playing a role as 'new text[s] endowed with [their] own affective powers and suited to the particular historical circumstances of [their] reception'.[66]

Lydgate's Psalm 102 (*Benedic anima mea domino* [Bless the lord O my soul]), in twenty-two stanzas rhyming ababbcbc, provides some pertinent illustrations of his paraphrasing technique. His rendition of verse 1 ('Benedic anima mea Domino et omnia quae intra me sunt nomini sancto eius' [Bless the Lord, O my soul and let all that is within me bless his holy name]) is characteristic of the poem as a whole in its 'padded' paraphrase of the Vulgate supplemented by more general reflection:

> O my soule, gyf laude vn-to þe lord,
> Blesse him and preyse, and forget him nought.
> Alle myn entraylles booþe in deed and word,
> And al þat euer is in myn Inward thought,
> Gyf thank to hym þat þee so deere haþe bought
> Of kyndenes he was no thing to blame,
> Late serche þyn hert with al þat may be thought,
> And ofre al vp vn-to his hooly name. (p. 1/1–8)[67]

Insisting, as does the original, on an intensity of personal emotion, Lydgate follows established tradition by interweaving specifically Christian sentiment ('Gyf thank to hym þat þee so deere haþe bought') with the Psalmist's voice. In this, he is entirely conventional. Nonetheless, the specificity of 'myn entraylles' (responding to the Gallican's 'omnia quae intra me sunt') indicates a particular affective

---

[66] Copeland (1991), p. 30.
[67] All quotations from Lydgate are taken from H. MacCracken (ed.), *The Minor Poems of John Lydgate*, EETS ES 107, vol. 1 (London, 1911 for 1910).

engagement with the text of the psalm: Lydgate appears to have taken the verse and ruminated on it prior to producing his own rendition. 'Entraylles' (in this context meaning 'the inner self' but with overtones of 'the internal organs') is unmatched in the English psalmic tradition. The response to verse 2 ('Benedic anima mea Domino et noli oblivisci omnes retributiones eius' [Bless the Lord, O my soul, and never forget all he hath done for thee]), rhyming insistently on Latinate polysyllables, is more stylistically adorned:

> And þou my soule, yit blesse him efft ageyne,
> Haue euer in mynde his consolacyons,
> Be not forgetful, but be truwe and pleyne,
> Ay to remembre his retribuciouns.
> To him haue ay þy contemplacyouns,
> Sith he þee bought with his precyous blood,
> Be not vnkynde, but in þyne orysouns
> Thenk for þy saake he starff vpon þe rood. (pp. 1/9–2/16)

Here the paraphrase is limited to lines 1–4, while lines 5–8 again extrapolate in an entirely conventional Christocentric manner. Once more, the translation is 'padded', but while it makes no attempt at verbatim translation of the original, its use of 'retribuciouns' recalls the lexis of the Gallican in a way that the *Prose Psalter*, Rolle, and the Wycliffite translations do not (all four use 'ȝeldyngis' for 'retribuciones'). In his aureate approximation of romance language, Lydgate keeps his source in play. The Latinate 'consolacyons' and 'contemplacyouns', punctuated by these divine 'retribuciouns' and echoed by the closing 'orysouns', suggest that the poem is aiming to facilitate advanced spiritual activity ('contemplacyouns' is particularly evocative in this context). Yet it is doing nothing more—nor less—than encouraging a basic Passion-based piety, embodied by the monosyllabic 'blood' and 'rood' which puncture the ostentation of the polysyllabic rhymes.

Lydgate's poetic commentaries do not always move in the direction of Christocentric devotion, however. On some notable occasions, they remain obviously inspired by the language of the Psalter and elaborate elegantly on its imagery. Such elaborations are typified by his response to Psalm 102: 5 ('qui replet in bonis desiderium tuum renovabitur ut aquilae iuventus tua' [who satisfieth thy desire with good things: thy youth shall be renewed like the eagle's]) which reads:

> He accomplissheþe in goodness þy desyres,
> He is in loue so stedfast and so trewe.
> Þyne hert enamoureþe with his goostly fyres,
> And lyke an Egle þy youþe shal renuwe
> Elyche fresshe of face and eek of huwe,
> Cladde with a mantel of Inmortalyte,
> With-oute appalling, of aage elyke nuwe,
> With Citeseyns of þyne hevenly Cite. (p. 2/33–40)

Building evocatively on the psalm's perpetually youthful 'aquile', he evokes an impressively regal, if curiously stultified, 'egle' whose heart is enamoured with 'goostly fyres'. Both embodying and encouraging an affective response to the text of the psalm, he focuses, and asks us to focus, on its own imagery as elaborated in his own verse. Source and paraphrase appear to be working in perfect harmony; there is no rivalry between the two. At other times, however, returning to the competitive model of translation referenced at the beginning of this section, it might be argued that the aureate style of Lydgate's verse threatens to overwhelm entirely the mood of the biblical original. His response to Psalm 129: 6 ('a custodia matutina usque ad noctem speret Israhel in Domino' [from the morning watch even until night, let Israel hope in the Lord]) offers a striking example of this:

> Fro custodye of the morwe gray
> Toward Aurora with hir pale lyght,
> Whan Lucyfer at droukyng of the daye
> Bryngeth Kalendis to glade with our sight,
> From phebus vprist to sprede his bemys bright,
> Fresshest ffygure off Consolacyoun,
> Hoope of Israell tendure tyl yt be nyght,
> Grownd take of Crystys glad resureccyoun.[68] (p. 82/121–8)

Propelling us into the arena of classical allusion ('Aurora', 'Kalendis', 'phebus'), the tone of the stanza jars with the rest of the paraphrase. A comparison with Rolle ('ffro kepyng of morne til the ny3t: israel hope in lord') and the Wycliffite LV ('fro the morewtid keping til to ni3t; Israel hope in the Lord') reminds us of how far we have travelled from the biblical text. We are in the environs of romance ('morwe gray', 'pale light', 'bemys bright') rather than the landscape of devotion, and the invocation of 'Crystys glad resureccyoun' in the closing line, completing a polysyllabic C-rhyme in marked contrast to the consistently monosyllabic A and B rhymes, is in danger of sounding like an afterthought. However, viewed from the perspective of translation as rhetorical invention, the goal of which is the production of 'difference with the source', the stanza is an unqualified success: out of the 'olde feldes' of the scriptures there has emerged an entirely new poem.[69]

---

[68] Cf. Maidstone's response to the same verse. He translates fairly closely and offers an entirely conventional spiritual gloss: 'From morwentide vnto þe ny3te / Lat Israel in God truste & trowen; Israel bitokeneþ euery wi3te / þat God shal seen & gostly knowen; / To knowen God is mannes ri3te, / þat wole his wittes wel bistowen; / þerfore I hope, as he haþ hi3te, / þat heuen blis is mannes owen.' Edden (1990), p. 99/817–24. Brampton's response to the same verse removes almost all traces of the biblical text: 'I tryste fully thou wylte me kepe / From all myschefe day and nyght / Whethur euyr y wake or slepe / Wyth me ys euyr an aungell bright / Thogh he appere not to my syght / Full tendurly he kepeth me / He stereþ myn herte wt all hys might / To *nereminiscaris domine*' (Kreuzer, 1949), p. 399.

[69] The allusion is, of course, to Chaucer's *Parliament of Fowls* ('For out of olde feldes, as men seyth, / Cometh al this newe corn from yer to yere' (385/22–3). That Lydgate was keen to re-anchor this 'classical' elaboration on the words of the Psalmist in the world of Christian exegesis is suggested by the fact that he devotes (uniquely) two stanzas to 129: 6. In the second of these, he 're-glosses' his own classical gloss: 'This is to seyne as Cryst Iesu a-roos / On Esterne morwe by record of scripture, / The stoon vp leff, though it afforn was cloos / Whos glorious rysyng doth our feith assure . . .' (p. 82/129–32). For another 'classicisation' of the psalms, see Lydgate's response to 102: 12 ('Quantum distat ortus ab occidente longe fecit a nobis iniquitates nostras' [As far as the east is from the west, so far hath he removed our iniquities from us]): 'Als fer in seoþe as þe cleer oryent / Is in distaunce whane Phebus shyneþe bright / Frome þe west party of þoccydent, / Right so þe lord which is moost of might / Haþe sette oure synnes asyde out of his sight' (p. 4/89–96).

Lydgate is under no illusions as to the nature of his paraphrases; he shapes them to be creative responses to, rather than direct reproductions of, his source. As he suggests in his paraphrasing response to Psalm 129: 2 ('Domine exaudi vocem meam fiant aures tuae intendentes in vocem deprecationis meae' [Lord, hear my voice. Let thy ears be attentive to the voice of my supplication]), preceded by a twelve-stanza introduction which, oddly, does not contain a paraphrase of verse 1, his interest is in the 'sentence' of the verse:

> Lat oure prayer been this in sentence
> On-to that lord which ys moost of myght,
> O cryst Ihesu, yiff benyngne audyence
> To our requeste of mercy more than riht;
> On us synnerys cast doun thy gracious sight,
> That our prayer thyn erys may atteyne,
> Thylke sowlys that brenne day and nyght
> In purgatorye to relesse ther payne. (p. 81/89–96)

It is only in the ornamental lines 3–4 ('yiff benyngne audience / To our requeste') and in the more straightforward line 6 ('That our prayer thyn erys may atteyne') that attention is paid to the Psalmist's 'lettre', and even here the insistent first-person singular ('meam/meae') has been supplanted by the communal 'our/us'.[70] Only once, in *Judica Me Deus*, does Lydgate refer to himself as 'translating' the psalms— on this occasion, Psalm 42:

> I am ful set to do my dylygence,
> After my sympylnesse, this lytyll Psalme to translate,
> With humble support of your pacience,
> Where as I fayle, the defaute ys [in] Lydegate.[71] (p. 91/85–8)

Yet the fact that verbatim translation is not his primary concern is witnessed throughout the proceeding seven-stanza paraphrase.

His verse-response to Psalm 53 is, however, something of an exception. Whereas in his other three psalm-based poems he has tended to intermingle translation with gloss and paraphrase in the manner of a commentator who does not remain subservient to his authoritative text, in *Deus in Nomine* he is more careful to separate translation from gloss. The former occupies the first two (on one occasion, three) lines of each stanza and is then expanded upon in the final five lines. So, for example, verse 3 ('Deus in nomine tuo salvum me fac et in virtute tua iudica me' [save me, O God, by thy name, and judge me in thy strength]) reads:

> God, in thy name make me safe and sounde;
> And in thi vertu me deme & Iustifie,
> And as my leche serch vnto the grounde
> That in my soule ys seke, and rectifie:
> To haue medicine afore thi dome y crye,

---

[70] This insistence on the 'sentence' recalls an earlier comment in the introduction to the poem: 'Another charge was vpon me leyd / Among psalmys to fynde a cleer sentence' (p. 78/9–10).

[71] A rubric to *Benedic Anima Mea Domino* in TCC R.3.20 reads 'Takeþe goode hede, sirs and dames, howe Lydegate daun Iohan þe Munk of Bury, moeued of deuocyioun, haþe *translated* þe salme Benedic anima mea domine.' Italics mine.

> Wherfore of endeles mercy ax y grace
> That y desposed be vch day to dye,
> And so to mende, whyll y haue tyme & space. (p. 10/1–8)

With the exceptions of 'sounde' and 'iustifie', both of which are necessary for rhyme, lines 1–2's translation is all but identical to Rolle's ('God in thi name make me safe and in thi vertu deme me' (p. 192)) and to the two Wycliffite versions (EV 'God, in thi name mac me saaf; and in thi vertue deme me'; LV 'God, in thi name make thou me saaf and in thi vertu deme thou me'). Such affinities persist throughout the poem: verse 4 ('Deus exaudi orationem meam auribus percipe verba oris mei' [O God, hear my prayer: give ear to the words of my mouth]), for example, is translated:

> God graciously here thou my prayere,
> The wordes of my mouth with ere perceyue. (p. 10/9–10)

This obviously recalls Rolle's 'God here my prayere: with eren persayfe the wordis of my mouth' (p. 192)) and the almost identical Wycliffite LV 'God, here thou my pre-ier; with eeris perseyue thou the wordis of my mouth'.[72] However, where Rolle tends towards the literal reproduction of the Vulgate's word-order, Lydgate often allows himself more idiomatic flexibility, although his word-order is to an extent subject to the different limitations of rhyme. This is witnessed most effectively in his transla-tion of verse 9 ('quoniam ex omni tribulatione eripuisti me et super inimicos meos despexit oculus meus' [for thou hast delivered me out of all trouble: and my eye hath looked down upon my enemies]). Where Rolle's rendition of the second clause ('ffor of all tribulacioun thou toke me out and abouen my faes despised my eghe' (p. 193)) is incomprehensible without recourse to the Latin, refusing to disambiguate the rela-tionship between subject and object, matters are clarified in Lydgate's version:

> For fro all trouble thou hast deluyered me,
> And on enmyes myn eye hath had despite. (p. 12/49–56)

Obviously, Lydgate's fifteenth-century verse translation of Psalm 53 is not identi-cal to Rolle's fourteenth-century *Prose* rendition, but the affinities between them are such that it is tempting to speculate that the later poet is working, consciously or not, under the influence of the earlier mystic. It is, however, worth noting that Lydgate's devotional response to the psalm, articulated in lines 3–8 of each stanza, has few similarities with Rolle's more thoroughgoing commentary. If there is a Rollean influence at work in this poem, it is limited to translation and does not extend to the specifics of interpretation.

PARAPHRASED PSALMS—MAIDSTONE AND BRAMPTON

We turn now from verse paraphrases of individual psalms to verse paraphrases of all seven of the Penitential Psalms; as illustrated by Chapter 1's investigations, these

---

[72] The second clause of the EV translation ('with eris perceyue the woordis of my mouth') is identical. The first is the rather more laboured 'God, ful out here thou myn orisoun'.

were the most widely circulating psalms of the English Middle Ages. Bearing in mind their centrality to devotional practice, their translation into easily memorable rhyming form makes perfect sense. As we know, two complete verse renditions of the Penitential Psalms survive, attributed respectively to Richard Maidstone (late fourteenth century) and Thomas Brampton (early fifteenth century). Neither is credited with anything approaching the literary output or reputation of John Lydgate; in fact, as we will observe in the next chapter, we know of Brampton's existence only because manuscripts credit him with authorship of the text. Nonetheless, both create long poems from the seven psalms, each using consistent eight-line stanzas (Maidstone uses an abababab rhyme throughout and Brampton the slightly more demanding ababbcbc). In common with the two Psalm 50 paraphrases and with Lydgate's more artistically ambitious elaborations, they use each stanza to translate (with varying degrees of literality) and meditate upon each individual verse. Where they differ from the other paraphrases is in their linking together of seven psalms in a continuous and substantial work of devotional verse.[73] It would be misleading, however, to imply that the two mirror each other in all respects. Recognizing, of course, the blurred boundary between translation and commentary in a medieval context, I will focus on their distinctive styles of vernacularization in this chapter and, in the next, discuss differences between their exegetical responses to the psalms.

Throughout most of his poem, Maidstone is careful to divide translation from devotional commentary: the former occupies the earlier part of the stanza, most frequently two lines, though sometimes three or even four, while the latter takes up the remainder.[74] And not only does he keep translation distinct from commentary, but he is also evidently interested in producing an accurate vernacularization. His version of Psalm 6: 7 ('laboravi in gemitu meo lavabo per singulas noctes lectum meum in lacrimis meis stratum meum rigabo' [I have laboured in my groanings, every night I will wash my bed, I will water my couch with my tears]) is a case in point; careful to reproduce correctly the shifting tenses of the original ('laboravi' [I have laboured] is past and 'rigabo' [I will wash] future), he writes:

> I *haue trauailed* in my waylynge,
> My bed *shal I wasshe* euery ny3t,
> And wiþ þe teres of my wepynge
> My bedstre watter, as hit is ri3t.[75] (p. 50/49–50) (italics mine)

---

[73] As we know from Chapter 1, Maidstone's Psalm 50 circulated independently of the rest of the paraphrase in six manuscripts.

[74] All quotations from Maidstone's *Penitential Psalms* are taken from V. Edden (ed.), *Richard Maidstone's Penitential Psalms*, Middle English Texts 22 (Heidelberg, 1990).

[75] Maidstone does not always get the tenses right, however. See, for example, his version of Psalm 37: 9 ('adflictus sum et humiliatus sum nimis rugiebam a gemitu cordis mei' [I am afflicted and humbled exceedingly: I roared with the groaning of my heart]), which reads: 'I was afli3te and made ful meke, / I rored for weylyng of my herte' (p. 63/257–8). He translates the present tense (adflictus sum) as past (was afli3te): this is not a mistake that we see in any of the complete *English Psalters*. Brampton's version of the same is again much looser and, somewhat oddly, turns the Psalmist's anguished roar to silence: 'Sikenes makith me lowe and meke / I am tornyd in wo and payne / þoughe þou woldist my sorowe eke / I had no matir me to pleyne' (p. 380).

His careful accuracy contrasts with Brampton's more consciously affective engagement with the biblical text and his privileging of this over the claims of verbatim translation:

> My travell *is* bothe nyght and day
> To wepe and waile for my syn
> With bitter terys *I schall a say*
> To wasche þe bed þat y ly In.[76]

This is not to say that Maidstone's verse translations are always characterized by literal accuracy. Sometimes, particularly in later psalms, he relaxes the distinction between vernacularization and responsive paraphrase. The stanza focusing on Psalm 101: 7 ('similis factus sum pelicano solitudinis, factus sum sicut nycticorax in domicilio' [I am become like to a pelican of the wilderness, I am like a night raven in the house]) is a case in point. Here, translation (italicized) weaves itself around and between Christocentric expansion:

> *I was made like þe pellican*
> *In wildernes* þat himself sleeþ;
> So redily to þe rode I ran
> For mannes soule to suffer deeþ.
> *& as þe ny3t-crowe in hir hous* can
> Bi ny3te see to holte and heeþ,
> So sauered I to saue man,
> Blessed was þat ilke breeþ. (p. 85/593–600)

The saviour who eagerly races to 'þe rode' embeds himself as speaker of the biblical verse; he is its true, authoritative origin.

In general, however, of all the extant Middle English verse psalm paraphrases, Maidstone's (accompanied by Lydgate's *Deus in Nomine*) is the most accurate in its translation. If a reader had wanted to use the English psalms in conjunction with the Vulgate, in an intercessory routine modelled on liturgical devotions, Maidstone's would have been the text to use. As indicated in Chapter 1, it often circulated in the company of vernacular primer-related material and even, on one occasion, in a Latin Book of Hours (New York, Pierpont Morgan Library M.99). It has been suggested that Maidstone's generally careful vernacularization might be indebted to Rolle's, and if we were to look for an English source, the widely circulating Rolle would be the most obvious contender. However, beyond their shared interest in the techniques of close translation, there is little evidence of a direct link.[77] An example is provided by their rendition of Psalm 6: 2 ('Domine ne in furore tuo arguas me neque in ira tua corripias me' [O Lord, rebuke me not in thy indignation, nor chastise me in thy wrath]). In Rolle we have:

> Lord in thi wodnes argu me noght; na in thi ire amend me. (p. 21)

---

[76] All quotations from Brampton's *Penitential Psalms* are taken from J. R. Kreuzer (ed.), 'Thomas Brampton's Metrical Paraphrase', *Traditio* 7 (1949–51), 359–403.

[77] The relation between Maidstone's commentary and that of Rolle will be discussed in the next chapter.

His non-idiomatic word-order is echoed by Maidstone:

> Lord in þin angur vptake me nou3te
> And in þi wrethe blame þou not me. (p. 47/9–10)

The minimal rearrangement of the Vulgate ('Domine in tuo furore arguas me ne neque in tua ira corripias me') is all but identical in both; Maidstone simply adds 'þou not' in the second line. Their lexical choices ('angur/vptake/wrethe/blame') are, however, quite different. In fact, Maidstone's second line recalls exactly the wording of the Group B primers, alerting us to the fact that if his translation has any obvious parallels, they are to be found in the Wycliffite psalms.[78] The apparent familiarity of the impeccably orthodox Carmelite friar with the Wycliffite Bible could provide us with further evidence of the latter's early circulation in non-heterodox contexts. Yet what is most interesting about Maidstone's Wycliffite echoes is the fact that they recall both EV and LV, leading us to suppose that he might, at some point, have had access to an 'intermediate' or 'blended' Psalter version similar to the type already discussed in reference to the primers. His use of '[m]y bedstre' for Psalm 6: 7's 'stratum meum' [my couch], for example, reproduces LV; Rolle, EV and the Group B primers have 'bedding'.[79] And his translation of verse 8's 'turbatus' [troubled] as 'disturblid' again echoes LV; while EV has the obviously related 'disturbid', Rolle has 'druuyd', and the Group B primers 'trowbled'. Moving to Psalm 31, Maidstone's translation of verse 2 ('beatus vir cui non imputabit Dominus peccatum nec est in spiritu eius dolus' [Blessed is the man to whom the Lord hath not imputed sin, and in whose spirit there is no guile]) reads:

> þat man is blessed to whom God retteþ
> No synne, ne haþ in goost ny gyle. (p. 53/97–8)

The wording of the first clause recalls that of LV ('Blessid is the man to whom the lord arrettide not synne'), but while that of the second echoes LV for 'gile', it recalls the Group B primers (and Rolle) for 'goost'. Verse 3 of the same psalm ('quoniam tacui inveteraverunt ossa mea dum clamarem tota die' [Because I was silent my bones grew old, whilst I cried out all the day long]) is translated thus by Maidstone:

> For I was stille, þerfore my boones
> Eldede whil I shulde crye alday. (p. 53/105–6)

and here it is notable that his 'schulde crye' recalls EV's distinctive usage ('[f]or I heeld my pes; inwardli eldeden my bones, whil I shulde crie al dai'): Rolle and LV, by contrast, both have the simple past tense, as do the Group B primers. His translation of verse 10's 'multa flagella' (many [are the] scourges) as '[m]ony one is þe sore betynge' (p. 58/185), however, recalls LV's 'betyngis' (EV and the Group B primers have 'scourgis' and Rolle 'swyngiyngs'. Brampton has '[t]he scourge of god is scharp and kene' (p. 377)).

---

[78] This is a point also made by Valerie Edden.
[79] The *MED* does not contain a listing for 'bedstre' and the *Middle English Compendium* locates it only in the Wycliffite Bible.

Turning to Psalm 37, his translation of verse 8's 'quoniam lumbi mei impleti sunt *illusionibus*' [for my loins are filled with illusions] is noteworthy. Reading '[f]or *fairy* haþ fulfilled my reynes' (p. 62/249), it recalls, though does not reproduce, EV's 'For my leendis ben fulfild with *deceytis*': both suggest untruth and delusion.[80] LV, however, uses 'scornynges', which also appears in the Group B primers. 'Scornynges' is, of course, a translation of the Old Latin 'inlusionibus' [deceits, mockings], suggesting that at this point the LV revisers were working from a source text which differed in this detail (we may recall that Rolle's source text also appears to have read 'inlusionibus' which he translates as 'hethyngis'). But like that of EV, Maidstone's text preserves the Gallican reading. Its status as a problematic translation is, however, emphasized by the fact that in three manuscripts of the paraphrase, it has been replaced with a translation closer to the Old Latin 'inlusionibus', and, therefore, to LV's reading: in one we find 'stornyng', in a second 'flattery', and in a third 'hurtynges'.[81] In the majority, though, the Old Latin/EV 'fairy' is retained. Further affinities with EV can also be seen later in the poem: Maidstone's translation of 50: 4's 'amplius' ('amplius lava me ab iniquitate mea, & a peccato meo munda me' [wash me yet more from my iniquity, and cleanse me from my sin]), for example, reproduces EV's 'moreouer'; LV and the Group B primers use 'more'. And his rendition of 101: 27's 'opertorium' [vesture] as 'couerlite' recalls EV's 'couertour', replaced by 'hiling' in LV and the Group B primers.[82] Clearly, if Maidstone did at some point have access to an intermediate/blended Wycliffite Psalter, it had more affinities with EV than did that which lies behind the Group B Primers. Having said that, however, in the remainder of Maidstone's poem there are some notable occasions on which it differs from both EV and LV. Psalm 129: 4's 'propter legem tuam sustinui te Domine' (and by reason of thy law, I have waited for thee, O Lord), for example, is translated 'I haue [þe] suffrede, lord, for þi lawe' (p. 98/802) and 'sustinuit anima mea in uerbo eius' (my soul hath relied on his word) becomes '[m]y soule haþ suffred in his word' (p. 99/809). The translation of 'sustinui/sustinuit' as 'suffrede/suffred' obviously differs from both LV's reading ('for thi lawe Y abood thee. Mi soule susteynede in his word') and that of EV ('for thi lawe I sustenede thee, Lord. My soule sustenede in the woord of hym'): Maidstone's wording here appears to be his own. But what is interesting is that all three of Edden's γ manuscripts use 'susteined/systeyne', reverting to a translation of verse 4 more akin to that of EV.

It could, however, legitimately be objected that 'susteined' is simply the obvious translation of 'sustinuit': there is no reason to assume that Maidstone's reviser(s) are

---

[80] This is also the suggestion in Brampton's paraphrase of the verse: 'My sprite and my flesch in fere / The fend is besy *to be gile*' (italics mine). The version of Maidstone's poem in Windsor, St George's Chapel Ee.1.1 and Oxford, BodlL Digby 18 and Laud Misc 174 (Edden's group γ) actually reads 'diceites'.

[81] For mss, see Philadelphia, Pennsylvania English 1; London, BL Royal 17 C.xvii; and London, BL Add. 11306. The implications of revisions which imply a re-reading of the source text will be discussed in Chapter 5.

[82] At the same moment, Brampton has 'cloþes'. In London, BL Add.11306, Maidstone's poem has 'couerture ty3te'.

here working under the influence of the Wycliffite EV. Such a basic observation is important in alerting us to the dangers of indiscriminately locating Wycliffite resonances throughout his poem, although it does seem obvious that there are some. For all Maidstone's apparent familiarity with both EV and LV, any comparative reading of all three reveals that for much of the time his translation differs from both. Aesthetically, his paraphrase has more obvious affinities with the psalm-based poetry already discussed; it is a creative elaboration on its source text, a rhetorical reinvention (to borrow Copelandian terminology) of the Psalter. Maidstone is not, though, preoccupied with his own artistry; his rhyme-scheme is undemanding and much of his imagery and language formulaic: 'þe world, þe fend, þe flesshe', for example, are 'mankynde enemyes þre' against which the speaker must strive (p. 52/85–6), and it is 'feiþ and hope & charite' (p. 96/766) which will aid him in his struggle.[83] Relying on alliterative blueprints, the speaker also tells us that:

[]*foule wiþ feþer ny fische wiþ fynne*
Is noon vnstidfaste but I. (p. 49/35–6) Italics mine

and that:

> []he þat *liþ in lustes longe*
> And doþ no bettur þan *beest or bride*,
> He may be siker of *stormes stronge*,
> Þere wrecches beþ ful woo bitidde. (p. 52/93–6) Italics mine

Maidstone very clearly positions his poem in the mainstream of popular devotional and catechetic literature, in the process making psalmic paraphrase accessible to a wide and varied audience.

On occasion, it might be said that Maidstone is overwhelmed by the possibilities of image-based vocabulary which a verse elaboration on the psalms offers him. For example, in his response to Psalm 129: 4–5 ('sustinuit anima mea in verbum eius, speravit anima mea in Domino' [my soul hath relied on his word: my soul hath hoped in the Lord]) he suggests that he has been made lame by sin:

> For synne is sharpe [as] knyf or sword,
> Hit makeþ hem lame þat lyuen in [luste]

then continues in an entirely different vein, imagining himself as rusting rather than limping:

> þerfore Ihesu, my louely lorde,
> þer I am roten, rubbe of þe ruste,

He then diverts to a nautical setting, for which he is presumably inspired by the conventional exegetical reading of this psalm as spoken by the prophet Jonah:

> Or I be brou3te wiþinne shippes bord
> To sayle into þe dale of duste.[84] (p. 99/811–16)

---

[83] For further reference to the conventional three enemies of man, see p. 65/291–2.

[84] Rolle's rather abbreviated commentary on Psalm 129 makes no reference to any of the images which inform Maidstone's reading. Neither does his reading have affinities with Brampton's at this point.

But while this shifting between differently imagined affective elaborations on the verse might seem confusing, it offers devout readers a variety of positions in which to visualize their penitent selves before God. At such moments, Maidstone is providing rich ruminative fodder for his attentive audience. For this audience, the poem has the potential to encourage a disciplined affective engagement with the resonances of the Psalmist's words. In a translation striking in its simple expression of hope, for example, Psalm 31: 10 ('sperantem autem in Domino misericordia circumdabit' [but mercy shall encompass him that hopeth in the Lord]) becomes:

> But he þat is in God trustyng
> Shal mercy clippe [on] euery syde. (p. 58/187–8)

The vivid image of a mercy which 'clippe[s] on euery syde' contrasts favourably with the more laboured translations of Rolle ('bot hopand in lord mercy sall vmgif') and EV ('the hopere forsothe in the Lord, mercy shal enuyroune'). It is phrased idiomatically in a manner which recalls LV ('but merci schal cumpasse hym that hopith in the Lord'), but the use of 'clippe' (embrace) for 'circumdabit' gives the translation a very particular air of intimacy. And it is not only the translation which has the power to resonate evocatively: Maidstone's versified glosses can also have a forceful impact. The desperation of the penitent speaker, for example, is communicated effectively by his response to Psalm 37: 6 ('putruerunt et corruptae sunt cicatrices meae, a facie insipientiae meae' [my sores are putrified and corrupted, because of my foolishness]). Beginning with an apparent reference to drowning:

> For siþen I firste in synne sanke,
> To late I gan for mercy crye.

Maidstone then returns to the verse's own focus on rotting wounds, invoking the New Testament exemplum of Lazarus, tied to the drowning sinner by means of rhyme and alliteration ('sanke/stanke'):

> But Crist þat quykedest him þat stanke,
> Þe broþer of Martha & of Marye,
> So brynge me fro þis breery banke
> To bene in blis aboue þe skye. (p. 61/235–40)

This figuring of the wounded penitent as the shrouded, decomposing Lazarus is an affectively bold move, and reminds us forcefully of the poem's devotional power.[85]

---

[85] Maidstone's invocation of Lazarus makes for a more vivid devotional response to the verse than that of Brampton: 'My soule is cumbred wt sorowe and syn / Lord haue pite on my grevance / My woundis be Rotyn and festirith wt in / Because of onwise gouernaunce / Who so will ascape this carefull chaunce / Whan all our life demyd schall be / He must by fore make purviance / Of * * * *Ne reminiscaris et cetera*.' Rolle's commentary, focusing on the distinction between assent to sin and performing of sin, is inspired by the Lombard ('Myn erres, that is, the wondis of my synnes, hale thurgh penaunce, rotid whils I eft assentid til syn. and thai ere brokyn when I synned eft in dede: and all this is fra the face of myn vnwit: that is, fore my foly, that I wild not halde me in the grace that god had gifen me. on this maner myn alde synnes rotis til my self, and ere brokyn and stynkis til other men' (p. 138)). Cf. *PL* 191: 0383A. Neither the Lombard nor Augustine nor Cassiodorus (*PL* 70: 0274A-B) makes any reference to Lazarus at this point.

In her perceptive article on the Penitential Psalms, Lynn Staley calls Maidstone's poem 'a quietly dazzling paraphrase that testifies to his sensitivity to both voice and theme'; this Lazarus moment is certainly one of its most 'dazzling'.[86]

In the same article, Staley suggests that Thomas Brampton may have known of Maidstone's text and had it in mind when composing his own penitential paraphrase.[87] This is certainly a very real possibility, but while there are obvious affinities between the two (i.e. they both create rhyming devotional monologues from the Penitential Psalms using eight-line stanzas, each based on an individual verse) and while they occasionally share an idiosyncratic translation, they differ throughout in both emphasis and style.[88] Most notably, as we have seen, Brampton elides interpretative commentary with biblical translation more consistently than his forebear. His priority is not verbatim reproduction of the Psalmist's 'lettre' but divinely inspired imaginative insight into the Psalmist's 'entent' (although, of course, these two priorities are not necessarily at odds with each other).[89] Even more than Maidstone's, Brampton's poem is, therefore, a reinvention of its biblical source, a powerful display of both devotion and rhetoric. It is in keeping with Brampton's particular awareness of the literary status of his paraphrase that it should have circulated in some obviously literary manuscript compilations, as we saw in Chapter 1, and his elaborate fictionalizing prologue, a key component of the poem's self-awareness, will be discussed in Chapter 5. For now our focus is on the impact that his consciousness of the poem as literature has on his presentation of text/translation and gloss/commentary. Engaging his speaker and readers in a strained narrative from the beginning of the paraphrase, Brampton varies the Gallican's verbs and tenses. A striking instance can be found in his translation of Psalm 6: 2 ('Domine ne in furore tuo arguas me neque in ira tua corripias me' [O Lord, rebuke me not in thy indignation, nor chastise me in thy wrath]), the first verse of the first Penitential Psalm. Where the Latin uses the present tense 'arguas' (rebuke) and 'corripias' (chastise), which Maidstone translates precisely as present tense 'vptake' and 'blame', Brampton has:

> Lord wilt þu not me schame ner schend
> When þu schalt be in thy fersenes
> To dredefull dome whan I schall wend
> Hold not thy wrathe on my frelenes. (p. 371)

[86] Staley (2007), p. 230.   [87] This was also pointed out in Chapter 1.

[88] See, for example, their rendering of Psalm 129: 1's 'de profundis' (out of the depths). Maidstone has '[f]ro dales depe' (p. 97/777), Brampton 'from þys depe dale' (p. 398). No other contemporary translation refers to 'dale(s)'.

[89] There are occasions on which Maidstone's closer translation of the psalms resounds more evocatively than Brampton's expansive response. A case in point is the former's rendition of Psalm 129: 3 ('si iniquitates observabis Domine Domine quis sustinebit' [if thou, O Lord, wilt mark iniquities, Lord, who shall stand it]). Where Maidstone's vernacularization reproduces the urgency of the original ('If þou rewarde al wickednesse, / Lord, lord, who shal hit susteyne?' (p. 98/793–4)), in Brampton's version the intensity is somewhat diluted by a shift in emphasis to the verse's communal applicability: 'If thou woldyst venge þe anoon / Whan we haue synned and no þyng spare / Oure lyfe in erthe schulde sone be gone' (p. 398).

Making it clear that he understands the Vulgate's present tense to have future meaning (the conventional exegesis of this verse is that it refers to the coming Judgement), we read '*wilt* þu not me schame' and 'þu *schalt* be'. Positioning his speaker in a state of anxious anticipation ('[t]o dredful dome whan *I schall* wend'), Brampton manages to evoke a degree of tension from the poem's outset. We are poised at the brink of a drama from which we will not be released until the end of paraphrase, when the speaker anticipates his escape into heavenly security:

> Alle the fendys ferse and felle
> That wole my soule schame and schende
> They schulle be dampned to peynes of helle
> Whan y wt god to blysse schalle wende. (p. 403)

Accompanying this expansive and dramatic style of vernacularization is Brampton's aforementioned embedding of translation and gloss within each other. His response to Psalm 6: 3 models this tendency: while the Vulgate reads 'miserere mei Domine quoniam infirmus sum. Sana me Domine quoniam conturbata sunt ossa mea' (have mercy on me, O Lord, for I am weak. Heal me, O Lord, for my bones are troubled), in Brampton's version we find:

> *Sith þu woldist no man wer lost*
> Haue mercy on me for I am sike
> Hele me for my bonys bene brest.[90] (p. 372)

Setting the Psalmist's despair in the comforting context of God's love ('sithen þu woldist no man wer lost'), Brampton's words and those of the biblical text are mutually informing. The fifteenth-century poet is reassured by hearing the Psalmist speak of God's mercy, and the Psalmist, in turn, has his plea for this same mercy framed by the later speaker's Christian reassurance. Such interaction between the two is, as noted earlier in this chapter, a key feature of evocative paraphrase. On other occasions, Brampton takes this tendency further, often subsuming the voice of the biblical text within the voice of the contemporary speaker. For example, in responding to Psalm 31: 2 ('beatus vir cui non inputabit Dominus peccatum nec est in spiritu eius dolus' [blessed is the man to whom the Lord hath not imputed sin, and in whose spirit there is no guile]), the focus on the hypothetical 'beatus vir' is supplanted by a rendition of the verse which identifies the subject with the penitentially reformed speaker himself:

> *If god þt made all thyng of nought*
> Of no syn me schall apeche
> *In dede done or hert þought*
> Nothir gile ne falsnes *in my speche*
> *Than if it be as clerkis teche*
> *Of endless blis I doute not me*
> *This worde schall saue my soule fro wreche.*[91] (p. 374)

---

[90] The italics are mine and indicate Brampton's own framing of the biblical text. At the same point, Maidstone's translation reads: 'Mercy, Lord, for I am seke; / Hele me, forbrused beþ alle my bones, / My flesshe is freel . . .' (p. 48/17–19).

[91] Again, the italics are mine and indicate the elaborations on the translation, which is in plain text. Cf. Maidstone 'Þat man is blessed to whom God retteþ / No synne, ne haþ in goost ny gyle' (p. 53/47–8).

Instead of speaking *about* a third-person 'vir', the psalm is spoken *by* Brampton's reader, who is presented as having internalized fully the biblical voice. This is not, however, a misappropriation of the scriptural text; it is a legitimate form of personal commentary, indicating an exegetical outliving of psalmic precepts. At times, following in the traditions of academic commentary discussed in Chapter 2, such exegesis threatens to consume the biblical text on which it relies. The response to Psalm 6: 9 ('discedite a me omnes qui operamini iniquitatem quoniam exaudivit Dominus vocem fletus mei' [depart from me, all ye workers of iniquity, for the Lord hath heard the voice of my weeping]) is a case in point. In the face of Brampton's anguished awareness of the coming Judgement, the biblical speaker struggles to get a word in edgeways:

> *Whan þu schalt deme bothe great and smale,*
> *That day nedis we most abide*
> *From Iosophat þt dredfull vale*
> *Ther is no man þat may hym hide*
> *Than set me lord on thy Right side*
> And wicked wrecchis depart from me
> *Ther is no socour a gayn that tide*
> *But ne reminiscaris etc* [92] (p. 373)

Throughout this entire stanza, it is only in line 6 ('[a]nd wicked wrecchis depart from me') that direct reference is made to the biblical text ('discedite a me omnes qui operamini iniquitatem'). Comparison with Maidstone at this point reminds us of the markedly different character of the two poems:

> 3e þat done wronge, goþ fro me alle,
> For God my wepyng voice haþ herd. (p. 51/65–6)

The above translation of the Latin 'exaudivit Dominus vocem fletus mei' ('God my wepyng voice haþ herd') also alerts us to an irony in Brampton's version. Where the speaker of the Vulgate text (and Maidstone's translation) insists on the fact that his voice has been heard by God, in Brampton's response this original voice appears to have been almost entirely silenced. But it is unlikely that Brampton or his readers would have regarded this as a problem; the speaker's elaborations on the Psalmist's words are an integral aspect of Davidic meaning in this poem.

Direct translation is not Brampton's intention and in its place he here evokes an atmospheric eschatological landscape (the 'dredfull vale' of 'Iosophat') in which the exposed sinner awaits the impending Doom. The fact that he does so alerts us to a particular feature of his paraphrase; namely its recurrent focus on judgement at the expense of mercy. For all his positioning of Psalm 6: 2 within the reassuring context of God's love and for all his concluding emphasis on the anticipated journey of his soul to 'blysse', throughout the poem Brampton's speaker is haunted by the possibility of a lack of mercy, of a God who does not hear. Nowhere is this seen more clearly than in his response to Psalm 6: 9–10. Where verse 9 refers to a

---

[92] Brampton's habit of concluding each stanza with Latin 'ne reminiscaris domine' will be discussed in the next chapter.

God who 'exaudivit' the penitent's prayer, and verse 10 to one who not only 'exaudivit' but also 'suscepit' our intercessions, Brampton expresses no such assurance.[93] His response to verse 9 has already been quoted, and that to verse 10 ('[e]xaudivit Dominus deprecationem meam, Dominus orationem meam suscepit' [the Lord hath heard my supplication, the Lord hath received my prayer]) reads:

> Whan gode and euyl thair mede schall take
> As they be worthy wo and wele
> Let me not than be for sake
> Sith I haue left my synnys fele
> Suffir no fende me ther appele
> Sore wepyng I pray to þe
> This charite of mercy to me assele
> Wt * * * *Ne re et cetera* (pp. 373–4)

While he refers to himself as praying whilst 'sore wepyng', there is none of the Psalmist's certainty that God has heard his cries and we are a long way from Maidstone's confidence at this same point:

> Oure lord haþ herkened my prayere
> And receyued myn orisoun,
> For alle þe bedes þat we sayen here
> To him þei beþ [ful] swete of soun. (p. 51/73–6)

Balanced between the 'fende' who 'appele(s)' and the mercy which 'assele(s)', the fate of Brampton's speaker is undecided.[94] In this context, it is interesting that he in effect deletes God's reassuring voice from Psalm 31: 8 ('intellectum tibi dabo et instruam te in via hac qua gradieris. Firmabo super te oculos meos' [I will give thee understanding, and I will instruct thee in this way in which thou shalt go. I will fix my eyes upon thee]). Maidstone translates the verse directly:

> Vndirstondynge I shal þe sende,
> And I shal teche þe þerwiþalle,
> And in þe waye þat þou shal wende,
> On þe myn eჳen sette I shalle.

and glosses as though it were the word of God:

> "I am þi God, haue me in mynde,
> I made þe fre, þere þou were þralle,
> Þat þe no dedly synne shende,
> Lete witte & wisdam be þi walle" (p. 57/161–8)

---

[93] In Maidstone's version, all three verbs are translated: 'herd', 'herkened', 'receyued'.

[94] For another striking example of Brampton's focus on God's judgement rather than mercy, see his response to Psalm 31: 10 ('multa flagella peccatoris, sperantem autem in Domino misericordia circumdabit' [many are the scourges of the sinner, but mercy shall encompass him that hopeth in the Lord]). Where Maidstone's translation reads: 'Mony one is þe sore betynge / þat to þe sinful shal bityde; / But he þat is in God trustyng / shal mercy clippe [on] euery syde', Brampton's response focuses on only the first half of the verse: 'The scourge of god is scharp and kene / Whan syn among men is Ryve / Full oft he betith þem be dene / To drawe þem from þair cursid lyve / He sparith nothir man ner wife / Nor noan astate of no degre / Ther may no thyng stynt yor stryfe / But * * *.'

In Brampton's version, however, God does not speak, and it is left to the speaker to request that which the psalm actually offers:

> Graunte me grace wisedome and witt
> Thy lawe to lere and vndirstond
> That I neuer forlet ageynst it
> Wher euer I be in any lond
> Bynd me wt that blissid bond
> And if I brek it behold and se
> Howe I take þis worde in hond
> * * * *Ne re et cetera* (p. 377)

There is no suggestion that this request will not be granted, but that it needs to be made at all ('graunt me grace wisdome and witt') is striking when viewed in light of the Vulgate's apparent emphasis on God's own offer ('I will give thee understanding'), indicating once again that the lines of communication between Brampton's speaker and the God whom he attempts to both address and hear are perpetually clogged by the mire of sin.

It is in the conjunction of Brampton's confident awareness of the literary and formal qualities of his poem (it is classed, variously, as a 'preyer', a 'mornenyng', a 'bylle', and a 'songe') with his speaker's oft-expressed anxiety as to its devotional efficacy that we can locate this penitential paraphrase's very particular power. Following the Psalmist (50: 17), Brampton's speaker asserts that in paraphrasing the psalms, his mouth has been opened in praise:

> My mouthe schall preyse þe day and ny3t
> My lyppys to þe schullen open wyde (p. 338)

and certainly the poem presents us with a forceful response to the Pentitential Psalms. Yet the most evocative moments of Brampton's text are not those in which the speaker reflects on his tongue's release from imprisonment but those in which he ponders his own speechlessness and isolation. The self-consciously eloquent uncertainty that this generates is encapsulated in his response to Psalm 101: 6–7 ('a voce gemitus mei adhesit os meum carni meae. Similis factus sum pelicano solitudinis, factus sum sicut nycticorax in domicilio' [Through the voice of my groaning, my bone hath cleaved to my flesh. I am become like to a pelican of the wilderness, I am like a night raven in the house]). While the paraphrase of verse 6 emphasizes his verbal inadequacy:

> For sorowe my lyppys cleuen to gydre
> My mouthe hath no myght to speke.[95] (p. 391)

---

[95] Brampton's paraphrase is founded on a mistranslation of the Latin 'os' meaning 'bone' as 'os' meaning 'mouth'. Maidstone translates correctly: 'Fro þe voyce of my weyling / Vnto my flesshe my boon con shrink' (p. 84/585–6) as do *Prose*, Rolle, EV, and LV. In fact, of all extant Middle English psalm translations, it is only in the *Metrical* that we find the same error: 'Fra steuen of mi sighingnesse / Kliued mi mouth to mi flessche.'

his response to verse 7, involving an extraordinary, exegetically unprecedented image of himself as solitary, night-dwelling bat, provides ample testimony to his powers of poetic imagination:

> To dredefull dethe y am dyght
> As a pelycan in wyldyrnesse
> And as a back þat fleyth be nyght
> I am wyth drawe from all goodnesse. (p. 391)

In Brampton's hands, a vernacular response to the literature of the psalms becomes, in itself, a literary accomplishment. In this, his particular affinities are with Lydgate, and it is easy to see why his poem would have circulated in the company of Chaucerian and Lydgatean material.

PSALM COMMENTARIES—HILTON AND HULL

As we have seen demonstrated in this chapter, the elusive 'chain' of translation which Hargreaves attempted to locate in the context of complete *Middle English Psalters* is more readily discernible in the context of paraphrased and abbreviated versions. In the demonstrable link that the primer psalms have with the Wycliffite versions, in the likely connection that Maidstone has with Wycliffite material and in the possible relationship that Brampton has with Maidstone, these translations participate in a creative nexus of relationships. In their nature as verse renditions of the psalms (with the exception of the primer psalms), the paraphrases also all share a particularly literary understanding of translation as an act of creative invention, a crafting of the new from the old. Key to this is their shared understanding of translation and commentary as closely related activities; it is the task of the translator to interpret as he proceeds.

However, it is not only in the context of verse that translation and commentary can work effectively together. In this closing section, we return to late Middle English prose, looking at three texts which explicitly set out both to translate and to interpret selected psalms; the commentaries on Psalms 90 and 91 conventionally attributed to Walter Hilton, and Eleanor Hull's commentary on the Seven Penitential Psalms. Their status as prose rather than poetry affects the ways in which we read these texts; they appear more formal than their verse counterparts. They are vernacular approximations of academic discourse rather than—or as well as—aids to (quasi-) liturgical activity. In fact, in terms of technique, the Hiltonian commentaries have more in common with Rolle's complete English translation and commentary than they do with any of the verse paraphrases. While both accompany translation with expansive gloss, both are equally rigorous in separating the two from each other. Structurally, they both proceed verse by verse, following close vernacularization with commentary. The one exception is in Hilton's response to verse 1 ('Qui habitat in adiutorio Altissimi in protectione Dei caeli commorabitur' [He that dwelleth in the aid of the most High shall abide under the protection of the God of Jacob]), where the translation is delayed briefly by the insertion of a framing introduction, pointing out that '[a]lle men þat wol liuen in þis world cristenliche, schal suffre persecucions, as þe Apostel seiþ' and that 'þe prophete, at þe inspiracion of þe holi gost' wrote the psalm to warn us of 'þe temptacions þat fallen in þis lyf'.[96]

More precise recollections of Rolle are also to be found in *Qui Habitat*'s translations themselves. Its rendition of the verse 1 ('[he that dwelleth in the aid of the most High shall abide under the protection of the God of Jacob]), for example:

He þat woneþ in help of þe hi3est: in hully[n]g of god of heuene he schal dwelle. (p. 2)

is virtually identical in syntax and lexis to that of Rolle:

He that wonys in helpe of the heghest; in hillynge of god of heuen he sall dwell. (p. 330)

The same is true of verse 16 ('in longitudine dierum replebo eum et ostendam illi salutare meum' [I will fill him with length of days and I will shew him my salvation]), which Hilton translates:

In lengþe of dayes i schal fulfille him: & I schal schewen to him myn hele. (p. 48)

recalling Rolle's equally precise reproduction of the Vulgate word-order ('[i]n lenght of dayes i sall fill him: and i sall shew til him my hele').

On other occasions, however, Hilton appears to echo Rolle's terminology while allowing himself an idiomatic turn of phrase more characteristic of the Wycliffite LV.[97] His translation of verse 12's 'ne forte offendas ad lapidem pedem tuum' (lest thou dash thy foot against a stone) as 'leest happilich þou hurte þi fote at a ston' (p. 38), for example, rearranges the Latinate word-order retained in Rolle's 'leswhen thou hurt til stane thi fote' and in EV's 'lest parauenture thou offende at the ston thi foot', and is virtually identical to LV's 'leste perauenture thou hirte thi foot at a stoon'. At other times, his word-choices recall those of the Wycliffite Psalter rather than Rolle; verse 2's 'refugium meum' (my refuge), for example, becomes 'my refuit' (p. 3), in common with EV, LV, and the *Prose Psalter*, all of which differ from Rolle who uses 'fleynge'. And in verse 8, he shares a reading with EV; both translate 'peccatorum' as 'sins' (p. 25), where Rolle, Prose, and LV have 'synful/syn3ers/synneris'. Yet it is generally the case that echoes of the translation habits of both Wycliffite Psalters and Rolle persist throughout Hilton's commentary: his rendition of verse 4 ('in scapulis suis obumbrabit te et sub pinnis eius sperabis' [he will overshadow thee with his shoulders and under his wings thou shalt trust]), for example, reads:

His soþfastnes schal vnbigo þe with a scheld: and þou schalt not dreden for þe nihtes drede. (p. 13)

[96] All quotations from *Qui Habitat* and *Bonum Est* are taken from B. Wallner (ed.), *An Exposition of Qui Habitat and Bonum Est in English*, Lund Studies in English 23 (Lund, 1954). For this quotation, see p. 1.

[97] If we follow Wallner in dating *Qui Habitat* to relatively early in Hilton's career, before his post-1375 entry into the Augustinian house at Thurgarton, it is possible that he was aware of LV when writing it. See Wallner, p. xl.

The word-order is much more idiomatic than that of the hermit, who translates:

> With shelde sall vmgif the his sothfastnes: and thou sall noght drede of the drede of nyght. (p. 331)

The 'vnbigo' calque, however, echoes Rolle's 'vmgif' (EV has 'enuyroune' while the *Prose* and LV have 'compass/cumpasse') and in his use of calques throughout the commentary, Hilton recalls the widespread English habits of close translation discussed earlier in the book. Verse 6's 'incursu' [invasion], for example, becomes 'in-rennynge' (p.17), which is also used in EV (Rolle uses the similarly constructed 'inras' while LV has 'asailing') and verse 15's 'eripiam' (I will deliver (him)) becomes 'out take' (p. 46), which is also used by Rolle (EV has 'taken . . . out' while LV has 'delyuere').

Accompanying *Qui Habitat* in all but one of the manuscripts in which it appears, *Bonum Est* (on Psalm 91) has often been attributed to Hilton, but as indicated previously, the case for his authorship of this commentary is not as strong as that for *Qui Habitat*. Structurally, *Bonum Est* follows the pattern modelled by *Qui Habitat*: translated in sequence, each verse is kept distinct from the commentary which follows. However, when compared with *Qui Habitat*'s translations, those in *Bonum Est* are more strikingly idiomatic from the outset. Psalm 91: 2 ('Bonum est confiteri Domino et psallere nomini tuo Altissime' [It is good to give praise to the Lord and to sing to thy name, O most High]), for example, becomes:

> Hit is good to schriuen to ure lord: and singen to þi name, þou allerhi3est. (p. 51)

which is identical in word-order to LV's '[i]t is good to knouleche to the Lord; and to synge to thi name, thou hi3este'. Rolle, EV, and the *Prose Psalter*, by contrast, all retain the Latinate 'goed/good/gode (it) is'. And we see the same tendency at work in the translation of verse 7's 'vir insipiens' (the senseless man): Rolle and the *Prose Psalter* reproduce the Latinate word-order ('man vnwys'), but in *Bonum Est* and both Wycliffite versions, it becomes 'vnwise mon/man' (p. 65). On other occasions, however, the vernacularizations do adhere rigidly to the Latin: verse 9 ('tu autem Altissimus in aeternum Domine' [but thou, O Lord, art most high for evermore]), for example, is reproduced without the verb ('lord, þou hi3est with-outen ende' (p. 72)) exactly as it is in Rolle and the EV. LV, by contrast, adds the clarifying verb 'Lord, art the hi3est, withouten ende', as does the *Prose Psalter*. And the verbatim rendition of verse 12 ('et despexit oculus meus inimicis meis, et insurgentibus in me malignantibus audiet auris mea' [my eye also hath looked down upon my enemies and my ear shall hear of the downfall of the malignant that rise up against me]) as:

> Myn e3e haþ dispised myn enemys: & of in-rysyng in me, uuel willende, myn ere schal heren (p. 80)

recalls that of Rolle ('And my eghe despisyd my enmys & of rysand in me illwiland here sall myn ere' (p. 335)).

To suggest that either commentary is directly or consciously indebted to either Rolle or the Wycliffite Psalters would, however, be unproductive. While both have affinities with all three of these complete Psalters (and, sometimes, with the *Prose* text), they are not consistent or striking enough to use in building a case for deliberate imitation. The use of calques in both, for example, bears witness to a previously discussed trend in late Middle English translation, and while their varyingly maintained literalism certainly recalls that of EV and Rolle, the similarities seem most likely to be coincidental. We are a long way from the obvious links with the Wycliffite translations that we can discern in the primer psalms and (probably) in Maidstone's penitential paraphrase. In the case of *Qui Habitat* and *Bonum Est*, the largely commonplace similarities reveal nothing other than that the goal of all three texts is direct and faithful reproduction of the language and syntax of the biblical text. This is not to say, however, that the Hiltonian treatises share nothing of the verse paraphrases' awareness of translation as invention. In accompanying biblical vernacularization with glossing interpretations, they too create a 'new' text, albeit one which appears to insist more rigidly on commentary's role as 'servant' to its authoritative original. The biblical source seems to be rather more obviously ring-fenced in the tradition of English Prose commentary than it does in that of English verse paraphrase.

However, turning from the specifically English tradition, it is worth noting that Eleanor Hull's Prose commentary on the Seven Penitential Psalms (translated from French/Anglo-Norman) does not 'ring-fence' the biblical original in quite the same way, but is more comfortable eliding the distinction between translation and commentary.[98] In this, Hull might be thought to have something in common with the inventive technique of the verse paraphrasers. But where Auchinleck, Thornton, Maidstone, Brampton et al. tend to absorb (in very different ways and to very different extents) psalm translation within their rhyming commentary, on occasion dissolving the biblical 'letter' in a richly affective gloss, Hull manages to combine attention to literality and affectivity in a quite remarkable way. Notably focused on the literal meaning of the Bible and paying close and learned attention to its wording, she is also quite content to allow vernacularization and commentary to intermingle. Assured in her own—and her audience's—grasp of the 'lettre' of the original, she is quite free to relax the boundaries between the two.

Hull's intermingling of translation and interpretation will be discussed more fully in the next chapter, but it is her attention to the letter of the biblical text that merits comment here, since its manner is entirely unmatched in other Middle English responses to the psalms. It does not lead to verbatim translations such as we find in Rolle and the Wycliffite EV, but plays its part in a remarkably supple and learned piece of prose, as comfortable remarking on grammatical details as it is exploring the Psalter's strongly affective impact. A striking example of this aspect of Hull's writing can be found in the commentary on Psalm 6: 7 ('Laboravi in

---

[98] Further, although its progress through the seven psalms is broadly linear, Hull's commentary does not follow Rolle and Hilton in focusing on each verse (translation and commentary) in turn. Where the latter both reveal Lombardian influence in their clear-cut division of one verse from the next, Hull's commentary (despite its recollections of the Lombard, to be discussed in the next chapter) is more Augustinian in its movement between verses, sometimes jumping ahead of itself, only to return at a later moment.

gemitu meo, lavabo per singulas noctes lectum meum; in lacrimis meis stratum meum rigabo' [I have laboured in my groanings, every night I will wash my bed; I will water my couch with my tears]). Beginning with a series of ruminative moral glosses on the words (which she vernacularizes expansively and in passing), Hull nonetheless makes some precise grammatical observations:

> [T]her-for he seythe: *Lavabo per singulas noctes*, and þen aftyr: *Lacrimis meis stratum meum rigabo*. He seyth, 'I haue traueylyd in my waylyngys,' that ys time passyd, and þen aftyr he seythe: *Lavabo et rigabo*, that ys tyme to come, as ther he wold sey, 'That I haue traueylyd in my sorowis and in my weylyng, hit sofficyt not oonly for he þat verreyly repentith hym schold euer weyle and sorow for hys synnys, þer-of I haue afore thys tyme; ȝet must I now and euer whilys I lyue labour and traueyle in verrey repentance.' And ther-for he seyth, 'Y schal wassche my bedde, that ys my fowle surte . . .'[99]

She then states '[n]ow lete ous contenu the lettre' before recollecting the significa-tion of 'stratus meus' and, after some hesitation ('But þe rigabo is not yet disclosyd. God opyn hit to ous yf hit lyke hym'), defining that of 'rigabo'. There is nothing remarkable in her noting the difference of tense between 'laboravi' on the one hand and 'lavabo/rigabo' on the other; as we have seen already, Maidstone's translation registers the distinction, as do those of Rolle and the Wycliffite versions. What is unusual, however, is the way in which the commentary foregrounds the detailed attention that it pays to the biblical 'lettre' (Rolle's gloss, by contrast, makes no reference to the possible significance of the tenses) and uses it to both model and facilitate confident and informed meditation on the psalms.

Hull's response to Psalm 31: 4 ('quoniam die ac nocte gravata est super me manus tua. Conversus sum in aerumna mea dum configitur mihi spina' [for day and night thy hand was heavy upon me. I am turned in my anguish, whilst the thorn is fastened]) provides us with another good illustration of her techniques. Beginning by quoting the Vulgate verse in full, she introduces it with her charac-teristic '[a]nd þer-for seythe the lettre aftyr'. But the expansive commentary, which is again characteristic of the whole in its divergence to discussion of other biblical passages, delays for some fifty lines (in Barratt's edition) her translation of the verse which is, in any case, partial and glossing:

> Quoniam die ac nocte etc. 'Ye schul vndyrstond,' so as he seythe, 'for that your hand ys made heuy ouyr me, that ys, your resonable punyschyng þat han take me for my synnys, and that nyht and day, that ys bothe body and soule.' (pp. 32–3)

This merging of translation and commentary is replicated by the format of the one manuscript in which the text survives, for although it distinguishes Latin text from English translation by means of slightly enlarged script for the former (and one psalm from another by means of large blue capitals with red penwork), it does not differentiate vernacularization from surrounding or interweaving gloss. Neither, incidentally, does it do anything to assist the reader in tracing his/her path

---

[99] All quotations from Hull's Penitential Psalms are taken from A. Barratt (ed.), *The Seven Psalms: A Commentary on the Penitential Psalms, translated by Eleanor Hull* EETS OS 307 (Oxford, 1995). This quotation is from p. 17.

from biblical text to much later translation. Both commentary and manuscript leave much to the discretion of the audience. The manner in which Hull's treatise (and, presumably, its source) caters for users of some learning and sophistication is emphasized by its dealings with the second part of Psalm 31: 4. Picking up on the reading of 'nyht and day' as 'body and soule', it proceeds:

> And for þys doble greuance *conuersus sum in erumpna mea dum configitur spina*. Þis is to sey þat y am conuertyd in-to my wrecchydnes and retorned in-to the knowleche of my grete wykkydnes, for my consyence schewyt me that I am in captyuyte ferre from the fre loue of God in-to þe greuous iugement of hys wretthe. And þer-for y am verryly a caytyfe when my consyence remordyth me and that nec in-merito, *dum configitur spina*.

Vernacularizing 'conversus sum in aerumna' as 'conuertyd in-to my wrecchydnes', it leaves the Vulgate's last four words ('dum configitur mihi spina') untranslated, but continues immediately with:

> Ye schul vndyrstond that holy wryt callyth 'þornys' the greuous synnys that man doth. (pp. 33–4)

By not explicitly equating the 'þornys' with the Latin 'spina', Hull suggests that the reader should be capable of doing some of the work of translation on his/her own. She does go on, some lines later, to imagine these words voiced by David ('and þer-for he seythe: *Conuersus sum in erumpna mea* etc., as þer-of he seyd, 'Lord God mercy, for y fele my sowle persyd with a venimous þorne that ys þe dedly synne in my flessche') but again, this is in no sense a verbatim translation, nor is it intended to be. Hers is a commentary which refuses to spoon-feed its readers, inviting them instead to embark on a ruminative, expansive journey through the biblical text, in which attention to the 'lettre' liberates rather than limits.

In combining a close focus on the 'lettre' of the Penitential Psalms with a highly developed awareness of their affective impact, Hull's translated commentary marks itself out as distinctive among English paraphrased psalm translations and commentaries. In fact, it alerts us to continuities in the vernacular tradition of partial paraphrase and commentary outlined in this chapter. While generalizations are inimical, it would seem fair to say that the English abbreviations and paraphrases—particularly verse—privilege affective engagement with the psalms over encouraging an awareness of their grammatical complexities. This is not to suggest that the paraphrases are unlearned; on the contrary, they deal knowingly and fluently with their biblical source text. They are, however, aware of the audience that they are trying to reach and skilfully position the English psalms in the context of Christian catechesis and devotion. The reality that an affective (and moral) engagement with the Psalter and its implications is as demanding as an engagement with its grammatical niceties will be illustrated amply in the next chapter.

5

Reading the English Psalms

THE LITERARY PSALMS

In Chapters 2, 3, and 4 of this book, the focus fell squarely on issues of translation and the relationship that Middle English psalm translators had with the sacred text that they were vernacularizing. The Bible's status as a product of divine inspiration—and the implications that this had in terms of translation principles and practice—featured prominently in our discussions. In the remaining two chapters, attention will turn to questions of reading: what do we know of how the English psalms were read and of the interpretative frameworks that were applied to them? Of course, the subject of reading is one on which preceding chapters have inevitably touched, since any translation is also a reading of its source. In this chapter, however, I examine not only how translators responded to the Latin original, but also how readers of the Middle English translations were invited to respond and, in some cases, actually responded, to the vernacularized scriptures. I deal, in other words, in questions of biblical exegesis in the English tradition. Keeping in mind the contemporary, uncontested understanding of the scriptures as ultimately authored by God alone, I nonetheless focus on late-medieval recognition of the Bible as a compendium of literary texts with human *auctors*, among which the Psalter is of preeminence. In foregrounding the literary qualities of the Psalter, this chapter recalls the book's earlier insistence that the English psalms should be positioned firmly in their broad cultural context of rich vernacular creativity. In its early stages, the chapter's specific task is to ask whether translators and readers in the Middle Ages had a sense of the psalms as literary texts, written by (a) particular individual(s) at a particular time in a particular place.[1] In its latter part, it will build on these foundations to consider specific instances of Middle English readings and re-readings of the psalms.

Thanks to the important work done by Alistair Minnis, scholars are alert to the ways in which much medieval exegesis laid emphasis on the literary nature of biblical texts alongside their literal meaning. As he points out, 'the study of

---

[1] For discussion of patristic and medieval attitudes towards the composite authorship of the psalms, see A. J. Minnis, *Medieval Theory of Authorship—Scholastic Literary Attitudes in the later Middle Ages*, 2nd edn (Aldershot, 1988), pp. 43–58 and pp. 90–4. See also Minnis and Scott.

the bible occasioned much of the most sophisticated literary theory of the later Middle Ages', often in the context of academic prologues to *auctores*.² The twelfth-century scholastic exegete, Peter Lombard, played an important role here, appealing 'to the art of rhetoric' and providing his commentary on the psalms with 'an elaborate *accessus*', including discussion of the Psalter's authorship, its intention, the significance of the number of psalms it contains, as well as its *materia* and *modus tractandi*.³ Following logically from this developing focus on the literary and the literal was, as Minnis suggests, an increased emphasis on the role played by human *auctores* in the composition of the scriptures, inspired by God as *auctor* of all. Preeminent among these *auctores* was, of course, David, supposed author of many, if not all, of the psalms.⁴ But how did such emphases manifest themselves in Middle English psalm translations, commentaries, and paraphrases? The person of David, figured variously as king, prophet, sinner, and proto-Christ, certainly featured prominently in the devotional imagination of the Middle Ages. In vernacular contexts he is foregrounded through insistent appeals to the authority of his name, life, and words. As 'prophete', 'Goddes derlyng', and simply 'David', he is invoked throughout the corpus of Middle English devotional writing. In Langland's *Piers Plowman* his is the most frequently cited biblical name and voice, and both Chaucer and Gower also have reason to appeal to David's unparalleled authority.⁵ His visual presence in the form of miniatures in Latin Psalters and Books of Hours is well documented, but he also makes occasional appearances in the specific context of English psalm versions.⁶ We might remember, for example, the Auchinleck manuscript's rhyming response to Psalm 50, prefaced by the title 'Dauid þe Kyng' and probably originally accompanied by a miniature depicting the enthroned king. Equally, we might recall Oxford, BodlL. Bodley 953's copy of Rolle's *English Psalter*, which boasts four miniatures depicting David, or the Wycliffite interpolated copy in Harvard University Library, Richardson 36 which has, at the opening of Psalm 1, an eleven-line historiated initial of David enthroned.⁷ We might also

---

² Minnis, chapter 1. For quotation, see p. 36.

³ M. L. Colish, '*Psalterium Scholasticorum*: Peter Lombard and the Emergence of Scholastic Psalm Exegesis', *Speculum* 67 (1992), 531–48, pp. 539–40.

⁴ Peter Lombard follows dominant tradition (Ambrose, Augustine, Cassiodorus) in asserting that David was author of all the psalms (Jerome registered such a viewpoint but also 'affirmed his belief in the multiple authorship of the Psalter.' Minnis, p. 43). For a summary of views on David's authorship of the psalms, see Minnis, pp. 103–12. Michael Kuczynski has also written extensively on David and his problematic exemplarity, and I do not wish to repeat that which he has said so well. See M. P. Kuczynski, *Prophetic Song: The Psalms as Moral Discourse in Late Medieval England* (Philadelphia, 1995), especially chapters 1, 2, and 3.

⁵ While this may seem a cursory summary, it would take another book to explore adequately the citation of David's name and voice in contemporary literature.

⁶ As Wieck points out, in fifteenth-century European Books of Hours the Penitential Psalms were traditionally headed by a miniature depicting David at prayer. The fact that in the thirteenth and fourteenth centuries (and in some areas the first half of the fifteenth) the traditional image is 'Christ as Judge at the end of the world or as the King of Heaven' will be discussed later (see chapter 7, p. 89).

⁷ For a brief description of the Bodley manuscript see Hanna (2010), pp. 145–6 (no. 79). The David miniatures preface Psalms 1, 26, 38, and 68. Hanna also suggests that the miniature prefacing Psalm 109 depicts either David or God. On the Harvard manuscript, see p. 44 (no. 23). As Hanna's comments suggest, it is decorated handsomely throughout: '[a]t the opening of the prologue,

be reminded of the EV Wycliffite Bible now in Wolfenbüttel, Guelf.A.2 Aug.2 in which a miniature of David with his harp appears at the start of the Psalter.[8]

Inspired by Nicholas of Lyre, Wycliffite exegesis also foregrounds David as a historical individual and is, for this reason, particularly notable in the context of Middle English psalmic literature, whose interest in David is more often based on a non-historicized reading of him as a typological prefiguring of Christ and the Christian penitent.[9] Quoting extensively from the *Postilla Litteralis* of Lyre, the contents of the General Prologue to the Wycliffite Bible indicate an awareness of the historical circumstances of Old Testament narrative. Of particular relevance to this study is chapter four, which offers us 'highlights' of David's life and career as narrated in I and II Kings. Although it does not allude specifically to David as composer of the psalms, it references his musical skill ('[f]or reuerence and deuocioun Dauiþ made grete mynstrelsie and mekid himsilf bifor þe arke [of God]').[10] It also recalls 'a greet song of Dauiþ which he spak to God whanne he hadde delyueride him fro þe hond of alle his enemyes'.[11] Finally, it references his post-adulterous repentance before Nathan, widely associated with the composition of Psalm 50:

> þanne God sente Nathan þe profete to repreue Dauiþ of þis synne, and he took mekeli his repreuyng, and knoulechide þat he synnede aȝenus God, and God forȝaf þe synne.[12]

Although the author makes no direct mention of Psalm 50 at this point, his wording of David's reported confession (he 'knoulechide þat he synnede aȝenus God') recalls the Wycliffite LV translation of 50: 5 ('Y knouleche my wickidnesse'): it is clear that he has the psalm in mind. The titles that preface individual psalms in many manuscripts of the LV Wycliffite Bible (most notably B_554) would also have served to remind audiences of their human authorship and the historical circumstances of their composition.[13]

a four-line violet champ with gold leaf and a demivinet. At the opening of Ps. I, an eleven-line historiated initial (David enthroned) with vinet (including the intercolumnar space). Seven- to nine-line champs with demivinets like that of the prologue at the openings of the Nocturns.' This historiated initial from Richardson 36 is reproduced in colour on the dust-jacket of Hudson (2012). A historiated initial 'B' containing the enthroned David playing his harp also appears in London, BL Harley 1896, an LV Psalter which also contains the complete text in Latin.

[8] For reference to figural decorations in the Wolfenbüttel manuscript, see Hudson (2006), p. 734. De Hamel (2001) has a plate on p. 174.

[9] Lyran influence on Wycliffite interpretation of the Psalter was also discussed in Chapter 3. As Minnis points out, although Lyre viewed David as the principal *auctor* of the psalms, he was 'concerned to give each contributor to the Psalter his due and, where authorities differed concerning the names of the *auctores*, he recorded the differing opinions, lest a name be lost' (p. 92). In their overwhelming, though not exclusive, interest in David as type, English psalm glosses share the moral and Christological emphasis of Peter Lombard's *Commentarium in Psalmos*.

[10] Dove (2010), p. 17/503–4. See 2 Samuel 6: 5: 'But David and all Israel played before the Lord on all manner of instruments made of wood, on harps and lutes and timbrels and cornets and cymbals.'

[11] Dove (2010), p. 19/567–8.

[12] Dove (2010), p. 17/514–17. In keeping with Lyre's emphasis, chapter 4 of the prologue also emphasises David's nature as a 'noble kyng' (17/501).

[13] On these titles, see Dove (2007), p. 156, where she points out that '[t]he majority of Later Version manuscripts include glosses at the beginning of many of the psalms, in effect mini-prologues, as far as Psalm 72 (and a few include such glosses for later psalms).' B_554 includes such glosses on all the psalms.

On a much smaller scale, this emphasis on the historical circumstances of the Psalter's composition is recalled by Lydgate who refers, in his accomplished paraphrase of Psalm 42 (*Judica Me Deus*), to the fact that 'Lira doth recorde' that it is here that the Israelites mourn their captivity in Babylon:

> This same Psalme set in the sawtyer
> For a memoriall of the captyuyte,
> Howe Ierusalem stod in gret daungyer
> At Babyloun, that froward fel cyte.[14] (p. 90/61–4)

Lydgate's acute awareness of Psalm 42's relevance to his contemporary Christian audience is affirmed by his recommendation, in the lines immediately preceding those quoted above, that it should be spoken by penitent individuals prior to participation in the Mass:

> Sey furst thys Psalme, with looke erect to heuyn,
> Iudica me deus, of hool hert entyer,
> Theyr conscience purge from the synnes seuyn
> Or they presume to go to the Awtyr. (p. 89/57–90/60)

It is a measure of his accomplished versatility as both biblical exegete and poet that Lydgate manages to combine, in a single stanza, awareness of the psalm's devotional applicability with an understanding of its historical context.

Lydgate's interest in the psalms as texts with an *auctor* and a historical point of origin is matched by his awareness that they are texts to which the tools of literary criticism can be applied. This is illustrated most pertinently in the lengthy verse preamble to his translation of Psalm 129. Fictionalizing the process of the poem's construction, he tells us that he has been charged with finding out:

> Why De Profundis specyally ys seyd
> For crystyn sowlys, with devout reuerence,
> Of fervent loue, and benyvolence,
> Seid as folk passe by ther sepulturys (p. 78/(11–14))

Invoking a conventional modesty topos, he goes on to inform us that although he has no aptitude for the task ('[t]hough yt so be I haue noon Elloquence / In hooly wryt' (p. 78/15–16)) he will nonetheless attempt to 'dresse' his 'stile' '[o]nto thys psalme' (p. 78/21–2). Most notably, in language rich in its associations with Chaucerian notions of literature as containing both 'sentence' and 'solaas', both 'kernel' and husk', he then promises that he will:

> With ffygurys, wych I schall Expresse,
> Voyde the chaff, & gadryn out the corn. (p. 78/23–4)

This notion that the psalms, like fables, contain 'chaff' as well as 'corn' is also recalled in *Judica Me*'s opening instruction to '[t]ake of thys Psalme the moralyte' (p. 90/73). But what can Lydgate mean? How can a psalm's 'moralyte'

---

[14] As in previous chapters, all quotations from Lydgare are taken from H. MacCracken (ed.), *The Minor Poems of John Lydgate*, EETS ES 107, vol. 1 (London, 1911 for 1910).

be distinguished from any other aspect of it? And wherein lies psalmic 'chaff'? Lydgate's remarks leave us in an exegetical conundrum reminiscent of the confusion in which Chaucer's Nun's Priest, refusing to guide our interpretation, leaves us at the end of his tale:

> Taketh the fruyt, and lat the chaf be stille. (VII, 3443)

But where Chaucer playfully encourages us to question our own reading of the text, the same cannot be said of Lydgate: his literary positioning of the psalms does not stretch to encompass an interrogation of their value.

In his reading of Lydgate's paraphrases, Kuczynski suggests that *Judica Me*'s injunction is 'pushy', implying that 'if the poet were not enjoining his reader to avoid it, he might take up the chaff of the psalm text (whatever this might be), to the neglect of the fruit'.[15] It seems to me, however, that in both *Judica Me* and *De Profundis* (which are, as pointed out in the previous chapter, deliberately paraphrasing rather than literal in their evocation of the Psalmist's words), Lydgate makes it perfectly clear that, for his and his readers' purposes at this point, the texts' 'moralyte'/'corn' is to be found in the Psalmist's 'entent' rather than in a literal translation of his original. In the context of medieval translation theory, both are equally valid ways of accessing the 'true' meaning of the Psalmist's words. The fact that this is the case is foregrounded at the beginning of *De Profundis* when, as discussed in the previous chapter, Lydgate states openly that the goal of the paraphrase is to find the 'sentence' (which in this context denotes the 'meaning') of the psalm, not to produce a verbatim translation. But while the logical reading of the *Judica Me* 'chaff/corn' statement is, then, that the 'chaff' is the 'letter' of the psalm and the 'corn' is the 'sentence', this cannot be quite what Lydgate means. No biblical exegete, however confidently paraphrasing he/she was, would dismiss the literal meaning of scripture as little more than waste product in comparison with its figurative significance. Further, as we have seen, Lydgate is fascinated by the literal meaning and historical situatedness of the Psalmist's words: after all, he invokes the authority of Lyre, champion of the *littera*, at the very beginning of *Judica Me Deus*. For Lydgate, as for most readers of the psalms in the Middle Ages, the literal is the necessary basis of the figurative and, as discussed in Chapter 2, can be itself an aspect of figurative meaning. By using the trope of the corn and the chaff, Lydgate is making an important point about the relative value of biblical 'fygure(s)' (p. 90/70) and 'letters' in his paraphrasing poem, but there is also a sense in which he is deploying literary-critical terminology for rhetorical effect. There can be no such thing as psalmic 'chaff'.

Putting the powerful yet puzzling Lydgate to one side for a moment, other than the Wycliffite glosses, the only Middle English psalm commentary to display a sustained interest in David as *auctor* and in the historical circumstances of the Psalter's composition is Eleanor Hull's on the Seven Penitential Psalms. She refers, for example, to the fact that Psalm 6 was 'en-joyned to the Jues in

---

[15] Kuczynski (1995), p. 140.

penance', an observation of 'historical' practice that is not found in the Lombard, apparently the Anglo-Norman/French original's most immediate source.[16] In a similarly historically minded observation on Psalm 50's language of sacrifice, the commentary offers a detailed description of 'þe sacryfyce that þe kyngys made in þer paske', involving the boiling in fire and rubbing between the hands of 'þe tender erys of corne', going on to outline the sacrifices also made in 'pentecost' and 'þe cenofegia'.[17] Turning to the Psalmist himself, the name of David and remarks on his rhetorical activity as one who speaks, prays, and cries out to God, resound throughout the commentary. She reads Psalm 31: 3 ('quoniam tacui inveteraverunt ossa mea dum clamarem tota die' [because I was silent my bones grew old whilst I cried out all the day long]), for example, as an utterance of David 'the verrey repentant for hymselfe and for vs' (p. 30/192–3). Although there is nothing unusual in this *per se*, the Lombard provides no precedent for the manner in which she proceeds to elaborate very specifically on the verse's relevance to David's own circumstances, presenting her own commentary as a confession voiced by the penitent Psalmist:

> 'Feyre Lord,' seyd Dauid, 'to moche I held my pesse with herte and mouthe, and to lytel I callyd the to helpe when the lusty yen of my dezyre and of my fowle flesschly syht be-held the spouse of a-noþer and I fynyd neuer to crye with the foule wyl of myn herte and [multyplyyng] wordys tyl I was fal in-to the derke nyht of a-voutrye.'[18] (p. 30/202–6)

Less surprisingly, Hull is also meticulous in situating Psalm 50 in its historical context, delineating precisely and in great detail the sequence of events leading to David's confession before Nathan.[19]

Hand in hand with Hull's awareness of the psalms as texts with a historical context and an *auctor* is her close reading of the psalms as literary texts, mentioned in the preceding chapter. In fact, her commentary begins in an adept and schematic application of literary critical terms to the Psalter. She outlines first the significance and function of psalm titles:

> *Domine, ne in furore tuo arguas me: neque in ira tua corripias me.*
> *Titulus in finem psalmi Dauid pro octaua.* 'This tytle is seyd, in the ende of the psalme of Dauid for the viij.' Ye schal vndyrstond and know what tytyl menyth. Tytyl is as moche to sey as a keye forto opyn the vndyrstondyng of the lettre of the salme and the spyrytuelle sygnifyance. For ryght as me openyth the dore of the house wher-in me

---

[16] As Barratt's (1995) notes suggest, the commentary is apparently indebted to numerous antecedent sources, including Augustine, Cassiodorus, Gregory, and (pseudo) Jerome. All of these authoritative sources are named in the commentary itself.

[17] Of the first ritual, Barratt (1995), p. 246 states that '[t]his practice is not mentioned in the account of the Passover rituals given in Lev. 23: 9–14 and the commentator must derive his account of it from the Latin Josephus . . . of which 200 manuscripts survive.' As in the previous chapter, all quotations from Eleanor Hull's *Penitential Psalms* are taken from A. Barratt (ed.), *The Seven Psalms: A Commentary on the Penitential Psalms*, translated by Eleanor Hull EETS OS 307 (Oxford, 1995).

[18] The lengthy confession actually continues until line 217. Neither does Augustine read the verse as making specific reference to David's sin of adultery.

[19] See Barratt (1995), pp. 100/16–102/100.

wold entre, ryght so hit be-houyth by couenable exposicions of the tytyl for-to entre
in-to the vnderstondyng of the salme of whyche the tytyl gothe be-fore.[20] (p. 3/4–12)

Then, citing Peter Lombard, she offers a definition of the term 'psalm':

And now hit ys syttyng that ye know what psalme ys to mene. Spalme, as the scripture
seythe, ys hymne: *Himnus est laus dei cum cantico. Canticum est exultacio mentis habita
de eternis in uocem prorumpens.* 'Hymnus,' he seythe, 'ys preysyng of God with songe;
the songe that the man syngyth ys a swete ioye of the corage that only delytyth hym
in euerlastyng ioye.[21] (p. 3/13–18)

Her audience is left in no doubt as to the literary status of the psalms and, in the
discussion of 'tytyl[s]', they are given specific interpretative guidance. In fact, references to the significance of 'tytyl[s]' and to the nature of 'psalme[s]' as 'hymne[s]'
recur throughout Hull's prose, most notably at the beginning of the commentary
on Psalms 37, 50, 129, and 142. Clearly, it is important to Hull's purposes that we
bear in mind the formal characteristics of the Penitential Psalms as we read them.
Equally, she is interested in the Psalmist's style, commenting, for example, on the
three-fold repetition of the plea for God's ear in Psalm 101: 2–3 ('*Hear, O Lord, my
prayer: and let my cry come to thee.* Turn not away thy face from me: in the day when
I am in trouble, *incline thy ear to me.* In what day soever I shall call upon thee, *hear
me speedily*' [italics mine]) that:

Here ys a figure that ys callyd [*epimone*], that is *crebra repeticio sentencie*, that ys ofte
repetyng. (p. 141/71–142/73)

Inspired by the Lombard ('Et est hic figura epimone, per tres versus, id est crebra rep-
etitio sententiae' [And this is the figure *epimone*, through three verses, that is frequent
repetition of sentences] (0906D–0907A)), the commentary's stylistic preoccupation
is particularly noteworthy in its Middle English context. For although, as we know,
Rolle is heavily indebted to the Lombard, this is not a comment which he reproduces. He is, by contrast, interested in the moral application of the text at this point:

*DOMINE exaudi oracionem meam: & clamor meus ad te veniat. Lord here my prayere;
and my cry cum til the.* That is, the cloude of synnys let noght the affecte of myn
askynge. *Non auertas faciem tuam a me: in quacumque die tribulor inclina ad me aurem
tuam. Turne noght away thi face fra me: in what day that I am in anguys held til me thin
ere.* That is, the lyght of thi mercy shyne ay on me, that my fas ouercum me noght, that
angirs me & tempis me. *In quacunque die inuocauero te: velociter exaudi me. In what
day that I hafe inkald the: swiftly thou here me.* That is, in what hete of persecucioun
I kall the in til me. swiftly thou here me: for I aske noght erth bot heuen. (p. 352)[22]

The fact that the majority of these moral glosses actually derive from the Lombard
(*PL* 191 0906C–0907D) reminds us of the careful selectivity of Rolle's approach

---

[20] As Barratt points out, for this description of the title, the commentary is indebted to (Pseudo-)
Jerome, *PL* 26: O824A.

[21] See *PL* 191: 58A.

[22] As in previous chapters, all quotations from Rolle's uninterpolated *English Psalter* are taken from
H. R. Bramley (ed.), *The Psalter or Psalms of David and certain canticles with a translation and exposition
in English by Richard Rolle of Hampole* (Oxford, 1884).

to his principal source. And it is a mark of Hull's accomplishment as exegete that she, like the Lombard, is as alert to moral readings of the Psalter as she is to its literary qualities. She, too, reproduces these glosses:

> Hyere myn oreyson that my cry may come to þe. In my cry þer stont not þe cloude of synners the whiche were wont to stond by-twene þe and þe wykkyd . . . Y pray you not for erdly ryches but, as ransonyd and asoylyd from þe fyrst captyuyte, y desyre þe kyngdom of heuyn. (pp. 142/84–143/136)

The preceding chapter alerted us to the extent of Hull's preoccupation with the 'lettre' of the psalms. In this, her source anticipates Nicholas of Lyre, and her translation distinguishes itself from its Middle English contemporaries and forebears, with the exception of Wycliffite glosses on the psalms. What also distinguishes her remarkable commentary from its contemporaries and forebears, however, is the way in which it manages to combine close attention to the 'lettre' of David's words with an appreciation of their affective impetus and impact. Not only is Hull interested in what David said, but she is also fascinated by why and how he said it, by the emotions that gave rise to his utterances, and the emotions to which they, in turn, give rise. This is witnessed most powerfully in a series of remarks found at the outset of her commentary. She begins by foregrounding the Psalmist's affective sensibility:

> But Dauid, that languysshyd with loue for desyre of his creator, louyd with hert delycyously . . .

and then goes on to describe the crafting of his pleasing words:

> and [he] made his notis swetewysely and formyd hys word profytably . . .

She concludes by outlining their desired effect on all categories of reader:

> for-to 3eue to the ryghtwys man perseuerance in his goodnes, to the synfulle verrey repentance and to the repentant certeyn hope and to them that ben dede in synne, drede of the peynys of helle. (p. 3/21–6)

By way of contrast, while the prologue to Rolle's *English Psalter* also displays interest in the affective impact of the Psalter's language ('[g]rete haboundance of gastly comfort and ioy in god comes in the hertes of thaim at says or synges deuotly the psalmes' (p. 3)), the hermit makes no reference to David as their human 'auctor', nor, at this point, to his motivation. Rolle's primary interest here is in the 'contemporary' relevance of the psalms for those who read and recite them; what Hull adds to this is a clear awareness of their origin and style.

Nonetheless, in prefacing his English commentary with a simplified version of an academic prologue to an *auctor*, Rolle signals his awareness of twelfth-century applications of literary theory to sacred texts. He gives the book its proper title ('This boke is cald the psautere. the whilk nam it has of an instrument of musyke that in ebru is nablum' (p. 3)) and, like Hull and the Lombard, defines the psalm as sharing formal characteristics with the hymn:

> This scripture is cald boke of ympnes of crist. ympne is louynge of god with sange. Til an ympne falles thre thyngs. louynge of god. ioiynge of hert or thoght. affectuouse

thynkynge of goddis luf. Sange is a gret gladnes of thought of lastand thynge & endles ioy. brestand in voice of louynge. wel than is it sayd boke of ympnes. for it leris vs to loue god with glad chere & myrth & softnes in saule. (p. 4)

As Minnis points out, following the precedent of commentators such as Gilbert of Poitiers and Peter Lombard, Rolle also 'describes the Psalter's 'mater' (= *materia*), 'entent' (= *intentio*), and 'maner of lare' (*modus agendi*)':

The matere of this boke is crist & his spouse, that is, haly kyrke, or ilk ryghtwise man-nys saule. the entent is; to confourme men that ere filyd in adam til crist in newnes of lyf. the maner of lare is swilke. vmstunt he spekis of crist in his godhed. vmstunt in his manhed. vmstunt in that at he oises the voice of his seruauntes. (p. 4)[23]

From the outset it is thus clear that Rolle is grounding his commentary in exegetical tradition. The identity of his primary source as Peter Lombard is well known, but it is likely that he drew also on other authorities (as he says in his prologue, '[i]n expou-nynge. I. fologh haly doctours'). The location of these further sources is, however, problematized by the fact that his *English Psalter* is characterized by a remarkable sparsity of citation.[24] Throughout the entire commentary, the only external authori-ties whom Rolle names are 'saynt Austyne', 'the glose', 'aquila', 'the mayster . . . in the glose', 'Raban and cassiodore', 'Remyge', and 'strab3', several of whom he appears to have borrowed from the Lombard in any case.[25] His failure to mention his pri-mary source by name is explicable by the fact that as a medieval commentator, Peter Lombard does not carry the weight of longer-standing, attested authorities.

Having drawn on Lombardian precedent in his prologue's enumeration of the Psalter's 'mater', 'entent', and 'maner of lare', Rolle's interest in the psalms is of course not primarily that of the literary critic, any more than is the Lombard's. Further, while his exegesis shares features with that of Eleanor Hull (unsurpris-ingly, given the debt owed by both to the Lombard), he does not match her focus on the literal and the historical, and neither, as already pointed out, is he overtly preoccupied by David as *auctor* of the psalms.[26] In fact, David's name, unprompted by its appearance in the text of the psalms, features in his English gloss on only four occasions, two of which are, unsurprisingly, in the commentary on Psalm 50.[27]

---

[23] Minnis, pp. 190–1.

[24] This is a sparsity perpetuated in the Wycliffite RV and is in stark contrast to the practice of the *Glossed Gospels*. On the latter, see Hudson (1988), p. 252.

[25] Rolle's references to Augustine are not surprising, since the Lombard's own commentary draws extensively on his *Enarrationes in Psalmos*. The Lombard also draws on Cassiodorus, cited by Rolle, who also follows the Lombard in citing 'aquila' in justification of the repetitious 'amen. amen' (Ps. 40: 14; cf. *PL* 191, 0414A). The Lombard also cites Remigius on Ps. 72: 4, although Rolle cites him at 146: 9. Rolle's practice does not always map exactly onto that of the Lombard, however: while the hermit claims to draw on 'strab3' (i.e. Strabo) in his interpretation of 148: 4, the Lombard is influ-enced by Cassiodorus, and while Rolle says he is influenced by 'raban and cassiodire' in his reading of 101: 7, the Lombard cites Cassiodorus and Alcuin, the latter of whom is never mentioned by Rolle.

[26] Without actually mentioning him by name, the ever-scholarly Hilton alerts us to his awareness of David as human *auctor* of the psalms at the beginning of *Qui Habitat*: 'þe prophete, at þe inspira-cion of þe holi gost, writeþ a psalme' (Wallner, p. 1/8–9).

[27] David's name appears in the gloss on Psalm 50: 3 and 50: 8. It also features at Psalm 85: 6 (*Auribus percipe domine oracionem meam: & intende voci deprecacionis mee. With eren persayfe till my*

And it is the commentary on this, the most Davidic of psalms, which affords us a particularly revealing insight into Rolle's priorities as exegete. In a gloss which abbreviates vastly the comments of the Lombard, he has very little to say about the psalm's historical circumstances, beginning with a cursory allusion to David's adultery:

> MISERERE mei deus: secundum magnam miserecordiam tuam. Hafe mercy of me god; eftere thi grete mercy. This is the psalme of dauid when he had synned with vris wife. (p. 183)

Although the remarks which follow this insist on David's penitent exemplarity ('Dauid is sett in ensaumpil til men noght to fall. bot if thai be fallen, forto rise, and to shew all maner of meknes, as dauid did his penaunce'), they are most striking for the manner in which they sideline consideration of his sin, replacing it with an injunction instructing the reader to focus on him or herself:

> thou that ere lesse haf na delite that he that was mare fell in till sa gret syn. bot thou may drede and quake *for thi selfe*. (italics mine) (p. 183)

In an exegetical move which appears almost confrontational, Rolle dismisses the Lombard's enumeration of the Psalmist's sins, replacing it with a policing of the self. Do not, he warns, take voyeuristic pleasure in the downfall of a great man of God ('he that was mare'), but look fearfully to the state of your own heart. The Lombard's interest in David as a 'trumpet of the Holy Spirit', whose 'human characteristics were relatively unimportant', is taken to an extreme by Rolle.[28] For Lyre, writing not long before Rolle, David is both *auctor* and *materia* of Psalm 50, but for the hermit, although the Psalmist may be *auctor*, the *materia* is emphatically the sinful self.[29] In his relegation of David to supporting role, Rolle does not, however, go as far as the later Maidstone and Brampton whose commentaries on the Penitential Psalms make no direct reference to the persona of the Psalmist; there is no mention of his name in either text. Yet stripped of their primary status as works authored by (a) human individual(s), for both poetic commentators the psalms take on an identity as articulations of and responses to the suffering love of Christ.

---

prayere lord; and bihald til the voice of my bede. Many dos gret wrange till god: thai pray that he bihald til thaim. and will nouther bihald til god. na till thaim selfe: bot prayand with the lippis. thai suffire thaire hert to rayke in ydel thoghtis. agayns whaim dauid says.i. fand my hert that.i. may pray til the: other men lost thaire hert. forthi ere thai noght herde' (p. 312)) and at 131: 5 (*Et requiem temporibus meis: donec inueniam locum domino, tabernaculum deo iacob. And rest til my tempils: til that.i. fynde stede til lord. tabernakil til god of iacob.* When any erthly thynge bigynnys to delit the til syn; the tempils of thi heued waxis heuy. bot gif the noght til that delite. and than slepe cumys noght til thin eghyn. with this thoght frote thi for heuyd, and shote out slepe and rest of ill delite. and swa thou graithis stede til crist. that is, tabernakil til god. in whilke thou sall serfe him here. this hight dauid and fulfillyd it.' (p. 450)). David's name features in the Psalter and, therefore, the translation and commentary at 17: 51; 77: 70; 88: 4; 88: 21; 88: 36; 88: 50; 121: 5; 131: 1; 131: 10; 131: 11; 131: 17; and 143: 10.

[28] Minnis, p. 47.
[29] For discussion of Lyre's reading of Psalm 50, see Minnis, pp. 108–9.

THE CHRISTOCENTRIC PSALTER

The belief that the true 'mater' of the Psalter is Christ is of course entirely traditional and Christocentric readings of the Psalter are, as we have seen in previous chapters, common in Middle English exegesis. Amongst the complete translations, they are most prevalent in the glossing *Prose Psalter*. A Christological emphasis need not preclude a historical reading: as indicated in the previous chapter, Nicholas of Lyre, the great historicist, insists on reading Psalm 44 as referring to Christ. And we must not forget that as well as the *Postilla Litteralis* on the complete Bible, Lyre was also responsible for the *Postilla Moralis*. Admittedly the latter is significantly shorter than the former, to which it is a supplement, but the fact remains that he was comfortable with the possibility of there being more than one way of reading biblical texts: a text can contain more than one nourishing grain of corn.[30] Eleanor Hull's commentary also manages to reflect the Christological and moral as well as the literal and historical, and the copy of the *Prose Psalter* in BL Add. 17376 includes brief *tituli* delineating the circumstances of each psalm's composition. It is particularly interesting that this should be the case, as the *Prose* translation is resolutely moralizing and often insists on Christian interpretations. The inclusion of historicizing glosses indicates once again that the two modes of reading were not felt to be incompatible: they were not in competition with each other.

More specifically, in Christocentric readings of the Psalter, the Old Testament David is not replaced or usurped by the New Testament Saviour, but is, rather, typologically fulfilled by him. The two were understood to speak together, even by readers of Maidstone and Brampton, who, as already pointed out, make no direct mention of David. However, what a Christian interpretation of the psalms does offer which an Old Testament interpretation cannot, is the reassuring invocation of Christ's redemptive sacrifice. For Maidstone and his audience in particular, the reality of the Passion is a consistent source of comfort. Psalm 31: 11's already optimistic final injunction ('laetamini in Domino et exultate iusti et gloriamini omnes recti corde' [be glad in the Lord, and rejoice, ye just, and glory, all ye right of heart]) is, for the Carmelite friar, only strengthened by recollection of Christ's triumph:

> In 3oure lord God beþ mery & glad,
> 3e þat of ri3tful herte be
> For [he] þat was on rode sprad
> Now sitteþ in his fader se. (p. 59/193–6)[31]

---

[30] See Minnis, pp. 108–9. On p. 109 he provides an illuminating instance of Lyre's moral and literal glosses on Psalm 5.

[31] As in previous chapters, all quotations from Maidstone's Penitential Psalms are taken from V. Edden (ed.), *Richard Maidstone's Penitential Psalms*, Middle English Texts 22 (Heidelberg, 1990). The quotation is taken from the closing stanza of the response to Psalm 31. Of this poem, Edden writes '[The overall scheme leads Maidstone to favour] spiritual interpretations in which the penitent reader may become the speaker of the poem. At no point is there any suggestion of the "literal" (historical) reading in which the speaker is David . . . The speaker in Maidstone's psalms is indeed normally the penitent sinner, i.e the reader' (see V. Edden, 'Richard Maidstone's *Penitential Psalms*' in *Carmel in Britain: Essays on the Medieval English Carmelite Province*, 2 vols (Rome and Faversham, 1992), ed. P. Fitzgerald-Lombard and R. Copsey, vol. 2, pp. 106–24, pp. 108–9).

And for Lydgate, Psalm 42: 5's hard-won expression of hope ('spera in Deum quo-niam adhuc confitebor illi salutare vultus mei et Deus meus' [hope in God, for I will still give praise to him: the salvation of my countenance, and my God]) is solidified by confident trust in the promised redemption:

> Trust in God, and be ryght well certayne,
> Voyde of dyspeyre or ambiguyte,
> For vnto hym I shall shryue agayne,
> My gostly ioy gayne all aduersyte,
> Whyche of my chere ys the felycyte,
> Whyle he ys my socour, allas, whom shall I drede?
> Gayne worldly perylles and infernall powste
> He sparyd nat hys blood for me to blede. (p. 93/137–44)

For Lydgate and his Christian reader, both saved by 'hys [Christ's] blood', there is no need for Davidic 'dyspere or ambiguyte'.

Perhaps unsurprisingly, it is in this same *Judica Me Deus* paraphrase that Lydgate provides us with the most arresting contemporary crystallization of such Passion-based readings of the psalms. Constructing an image in which the cruci-fied Christ is figured as the harp of David, in his commentary on Psalm 42: 4 ('confitebor tibi in cithara Deus Deus meus' [to thee, O God my God, I will give praise upon the harp]) the Saviour becomes the instrument facilitating the performance of the Psalmist's prayers:

> I shall [be] shryue & confesse vnto the,
> In that harpe whyche for owre alther goode
> Was set and wrestyd on Caluary, on a tre,
> When all thy senewys were streynyd on the roode. (p. 92/121–4)

Although the association of the 'cithara' with Christ is traditional, the vivid image of Christ the crucified harp appears to be Lydgate's own. So too, therefore, does the play on the dual meaning of 'wrestyd' as both 'stretched/contorted' (Christ's body) and also 'tuned' (the harp). Christ, David, and the harp are here elided in one extraordinary figure: the instrument which the Psalmist played is, quite literally, the wounded Saviour.[32]

---

[32] Lydgate is responding to Psalm 42: 4–5 ('Confitebor tibi in cithara Deus, Deus meus: quare tristis es anima mea et quare conturbas me' [To thee, O God my God, I will give praise upon the harp: why art thou sad, O my soul? And why dost thou disquiet me?]). Although Lydgate's image of the crucified harp is particularly vivid, the identification of the Psalmist's harp with Christ is tra-ditional. See, for example, the Lombard's comments on Psalm 56: 9 ('exsurge gloria mea, exsurge psalterium et cithara: exsurgam diluculo' [Arise, O my glory, arise psaltery and harp: I will arise early]), inspired by Augustine and Cassiodorus (*PL* 191: 0531D). It is an interpretation alluded to by Rolle in his reading of the same verse: 'That is, ihesu, that is my ioy, make me to rise in ioy of the sange of thi louynge, in myrth of thi lufynge' (p. 203), although he goes on to offer a more precise gloss differing from that of the Lombard: 'rise psautery, that is, gladnes of thought in life of contemplacioun. and the harpe, that is, purgynge of all vices'. As in previous chapters, all quotations from Rolle's uninter-polated *English Psalter* are taken from H. R. Bramley (ed.), *The Psalter or Psalms of David and certain canticles with a translation and exposition in English by Richard Rolle of Hampole* (Oxford, 1884). In his commentary on Psalm 42: 5, the Lombard does not refer to Christ, but reads 'cithara' as inferior to 'psalterium': he who plays on the psaltery fulfils God's commands without suffering (*PL* 191: 0426B).

As indicated by comments from Rolle's prologue quoted earlier in this chapter, the hermit also follows this same broad tradition in stating that the Psalter's 'mater', 'entente', and 'maner of lare' are fully explicable only when understood to be Christ and about Christ. But although this principle informs his exegesis throughout, not all of his readings are as obviously Christocentric as those of Maidstone, Lydgate, and Brampton, nor as those of his immediate source, Peter Lombard. His commentary on Psalm 101 is a case in point: following Augustinian precedent, the Lombard reads the speaking 'pauper' to whom the titulus refers as Christ ('pauper vero de quo agit titulus Christus est' [the true pauper to whom the title refers is Christ'] *PL* 191: 0905C). He also states very specifically that verse 9 ('tota die exprobrabant mihi inimici mei et qui laudabant me adversus me iurabant' [all the day long my enemies reproached me: and they that praised me did swear against me]) is voiced by him ('Loquitur hic Christus' [Christ speaks this] *PL* 191: 0909C). Rolle, however, makes no reference to Christ at the outset or in his commentary on verse 9, but in a departure from the Lombard is resolute in glossing the psalm as voiced by the individual penitent:

> *Tota die exprobrabant michi inimici mei: & qui laudabant me aduersum me iurabant.* All day vpbraydid til me my fas: and tha that louyd me agayns me thai sware. My fas, that was bifore my fleysly frendis, vpbraydid til me, doand penaunce, wrechidnes that.i. had done. swa dos the deuyl to desayfe men. and that louyd me when.i. oysid seculere life with thaim. agayns me sware. that it is ypocrisy that.i. fare with. and that thai did. (p. 353)

It is tempting to read this gloss as intensely personal and to hear in it Rolle's own voice, complaining about the hypocrisy of former friends, but such autobiographical readings are dangerous, particularly when we do not know if comments have been borrowed from a source other than the Lombard.[33] It is, however, worth noting the occasions on which the concerns of the individual self, whether Rolle's or not, feature in the commentary. A particularly haunting instance is found in the hermit's response to Psalm 101: 12–13 ('dies mei sicut umbra declinaverunt et ego sicut faenum arui. Tu autem Domine in aeternum permanes et memoriale tuum in generationem et generationem' [My days have declined like a shadow, and I am withered like grass. But thou, O Lord, endurest for ever: and thy memorial to all generations]). His translation reads:

> My dayes as shadow heldid: and.i. dryed as hay [. . .] Bot thou lord dwellis withouten end: and thi menynge in generacioun & generacioun. (p. 354)

and his commentary:

> My dayes like till me heldid away fra the day lastand. that thai ere bot as shadow: that is, myrk and vayn, passand withouten profit. and.i. dryed as hay. that is,.i. lost the

---

This is the reading adopted by Rolle: 'He shrifis in the harpe that dos godis biddyngis, and is in tribulaciouun, thankand god. he that dos godis biddyngis, and suffirs not anguys, he shrifis til god in the psautery' (p. 158).

[33] Maidstone's reading of this verse as spoken by Christ is entirely traditional: 'Alday þei dryuen me to scorne, / Men þat myne enemyes were, / And þei þat preisiden me biforne / Afturwarde aзeynes me swere; þenne was I tugged and totorne, / Feet, honde, eзen, mouþ and ere, / Til euery lymme hadde lyf lorne, / þe turmenters vpon me tere' (p. 86/609–16).

fayrhede of heuen,.*i. vanyst* [. . .] Thou dwellis lord, that thou delyuer me and *safe me fra vanyssynge*. & thi menynge, that is, hetynge of endles life, and of life that now is: thorgh the whilke thou thynkis on vs, and we on the. that is, in this generacioun, & in a nother vndedly. (Italics mine) (p. 354)

It is his use of the verb 'to vanish' that is fascinating. He is not saying anything dramatically different from the Lombard who, at the same moment, talks of 'dying' and 'being forgotten' (*PL* 191: 0910D–0911A), but his invocation of the notion of vanishing (which can mean 'decay' or 'waste away' but also means 'disappear from view') is powerful, particularly when considered in the context of the hermit's interest in self and reputation. For Rolle, the Christian faith, expressed here in terms of psalm-based devotion, offers the self a chance to escape oblivion, to remain present and visible. By means of a God who eternally 'dwellis', it offers mortal man the opportunity of 'endles', 'vndedly' life.[34] It would be a mistake, however, to suggest that every time Rolle omits to mention Christ or makes reference to the penitent individual, he is doing so out of a misplaced preoccupation with the self. It is often simply the case that his exegetical priorities require him to privilege the personal resonances of the psalms over their other significances. Always working under the assumption (stated in his prologue) that the true 'mater' of the psalms is Christ, he does not need to reiterate this Christ-based typology from psalm to psalm. He is, for example, dismissive of Christocentric readings of Psalm 31, stating firmly in his commentary on verse 1 ('Beati quorum remissae sunt iniquitates et quorum tecta sunt peccata') [Blessed are they whose iniquities are forgiven, and whose sins are covered]) that:

> Here the prophet spekis in his person that does penaunce for his synn, and says. blisfull ere thai, and sall be in heuen, whas synnes ere forgifen in verray contricyon and shrift. (p. 111)

Where Eleanor Hull, inspired by the Lombard, takes the text as an opportunity for a quasi-homiletic excursus on John the Baptist and Christ, Rolle does no such thing. For him, the psalm functions most effectively when viewed as a penitential prayer and a comment on the processes of penance.

However, as already noted, the exegetical practices of the Yorkshire hermit and the St Albans noblewoman do have features in common. In the context of Middle English responses to the psalms, their academic commentaries stand out by virtue of the fact that they do not allow themselves to collapse into stock, Passion-based reflections, but remain engaged in the detail of the text, albeit in rather different ways. After her aforementioned New Testament excursus, Eleanor Hull's return to close textual analysis is seamless. And where Lydgate, for example, swiftly cedes

---

[34] Once again, Maidstone reads this verse as uttered by Christ: 'My dayes passed as shadow of li3t, / I welewede so doþ þe grase; / I wente as man wiþouten my3t, / Whereuer I trad was blody trase; / Whenne I þus deulfuly was di3t/þat neuer dud no trespase, / Centur[io] seyde, 'We done unri3te, / For trewely, Goddes son þis wase' (p. 87/633–41).

translation of Psalm 53: 4 ('Deus exaudi orationem meam auribus percipe verba oris mei' [O God, hear my prayer: give ear to the words of my mouth]):

> God, graciously here thou my prayere,
> The wordes of my mouth with ere perceyue

to meditation on Christ's sacrifice:

> As thou on the rode hast bought me dere,
> So make me able thi mercy to receyue;
> Yf that the fende with frawde wolde me deceyue,
> In thi ryght side ther be my resting place;
> Ther ys my confort, as y clere conceyue,
> Whych may me mende, whill y haue tyme & space. (10/9–16)

Rolle's commentary, germane to the verse in its focus on hearing, is noteworthy:

> Here me, for I aske the noght the floure of this warld that sone dyes, that an ill man knawis noght. bot I aske thi selfe, that is floure of all thynge. forthi thou persayfe my wordis. that ere shewynge of my herte. my enmys, thof thai here thaim, thai vnderstand thaim noght. for thai knaw noght bot vanyte. (p. 192)

Of course, such comparison with Lydgate is of limited value, since the latter's few psalm paraphrases are so different in scale and intent from Rolle's large-scale enterprise. It is, nonetheless, instructive on occasion and can alert us to similarities as well as differences. Despite Lydgate's allusion to the historicizing exegesis of Nicholas of Lyre, his overwhelming focus on the Passion makes impossible any sustained pursuit of this mode of reading. His movement is always towards the typological and the moral, and although his emphasis differs from Rolle's, this at least they have in common.

READING AND (RE)WRITING

Thus far, this chapter has considered readings that engage with the psalms on a particularly literary level, as well as interpretations which foreground their specifically Christian resonances. In different ways and to different extents, both are key characteristics of psalm exegesis in late-medieval England. What this investigation, combined with that of the preceding two chapters, has indicated is the remarkable elasticity of the psalms. It is possible to 'do' a lot of things with the Psalter, although, in a medieval context, it invariably finds its ultimate mooring in Christ.

In a manuscript culture in which every act of scribal copying is also an act of reading, the psalms have the potential to become particularly elastic and capacious texts. In the second half of this chapter, attention turns to scribal activity as a form of psalm reading, looking first at the transmission history of the complete Psalters before returning to consideration of the paraphrased and abbreviated Psalters. It will be suggested that a compelling case can be made for the scribes of the Middle English psalms as inattentive on occasion but imaginative and engaged on others.

Nicholas of Lyre's commitment to the 'letter' of the Bible is such that, unsurprisingly, he is concerned by the possibilities of textual corruption in a scribal culture. In a revealing comment in his *Postilla Litteralis*, he states:

> One should, moreover, bear in mind that the literal sense, which should be our starting-point, as I have said, seems to be greatly obscured in these modern times. This is partly through the fault of scribes who, misled by similarities between letters, have in many places written something which differs from the true reading of the text (*veritas textus*).[35]

Obviously, Lyre is talking here about the transmission of the Latin text of the Bible as a whole, while we are focusing on English texts of the psalms alone. His comments are, however, relevant to our analysis. In a manuscript culture, whether the exemplar is Latin or English, biblical or not, the potential for copying to become or lead to misreading is great. In the late fourteenth century, concerned perhaps by the possibility of damage to his own literary reputation, Chaucer issues his scribe, Adam, an infamous ultimatum to copy more carefully:

> Adam, scriveyn, if ever it thee bifalle
> Boece or Troylus for to wryten newe,
> Under thy long lokkes thou most have the scalle,
> But after my makyng thow wryte more trewe (1–4)

The psalms, lacking a living human *auctor*, were not so fortunate. Although the Wycliffites, acutely aware of the dangers associated with 'incorrect' biblical texts, policed to some extent the copying of their English psalms (most notably in Bodley 959), not all translations and paraphrases of the psalms received such attention. Manuscript versions of the English psalms vary widely.[36] In many circumstances, these variations can be accounted for by error, as Lyre feared, and as we will see. Additionally, however, they are often explicable by other means: LV, for example, alters EV in two different ways and for two distinct reasons. First, because it is an idiomatic reworking of the earlier text and second, because it is written in awareness of dispute over the accuracy of the original, adopting on many occasions the readings of Nicholas of Lyre, as explored in Chapter 3. Manuscripts of the *Prose Psalter* also preserve a variable text: in some cases, differences can be accounted for by a further movement towards idiomatic fluency, but in others it seems that the

---

[35] Quoted in Minnis and Scott, pp. 268–9. The Lombard, too, was concerned by 'textual corruption' and 'the tampering of previous readers in their very act of transmitting [the psalms]' (see M. L. Colish, '*Psalterium Scholasticorum*: Peter Lombard and the Emergence of Scholastic Psalm Exegesis', *Speculum* 67 (1992), 531–48, p. 544).

[36] As indicated in Chapter 3, for the translators of the Wycliffite bible, the text of the Latin Psalter was the subject of some dispute. In Wycliffite theory at least an awareness of the Hebrew original, providing an opportunity for the authoritative resolution of competing readings, is eminently desirable. Once translated into Middle English, however, the text of the psalms becomes rather less stable and, on occasion, radically unstable. For other translators of the psalms in the late Middle Ages, questions regarding the accuracy of the source text did not tend to arise. Although there were obviously differences between the Old Latin and the Gallican, and although Rolle, for example, seems to have worked from the latter with traces of the former, in general whatever Latin text was in use seems to have been regarded as stable and authoritative by those translating it.

approach to the source(s) has differed slightly. In the case of the *Metrical Psalter*, discrepancies between the six copies are of a distinct character and are differently motivated: no manuscript provides evidence that the source has been re-consulted and there is little attempt to move from the verbatim vernacular to a more idiomatic rendering. Neither, given the limited North Yorkshire circulation of the text, is there much evidence that specifically northern terms have been replaced by more widely known alternatives. Instead, the differences are, by and large, those of rhyme. On some occasions, as we saw in the last chapter, the divergences are minimal ('þa/ma' might be replaced by 'swa/þa', for example) and can be accounted for by the vagaries of memory and/or scribal inattention. On others, however, the differences are substantial and deliberate, and while they do not tend to alter the translation significantly, they do create a more complex system of versification.

Rather differently, in the case of Rolle's *English Psalter*, such changes as there are to the translation are often prompted by issues of comprehensibility: as we have seen, more southerly scribes have a tendency to gloss or replace northern dialect terms. In general, however, there is relatively little tampering with the text, even in the Wycliffite *RV*. But the latter's more dramatic, albeit inconsistent, changes to the commentary alert us to a further way in which the English psalms prove to be particularly variable: it was not only the translation which could be changed, but (in the case of those Psalters containing one), the gloss or commentary as well.[37] With the exception of the Wycliffite *RV*, this is particularly significant in the penitential paraphrases of Richard Maidstone and Thomas Brampton: in both of these texts, the theoretically unbiased activity of scribal copying is often supplanted deliberately by a form of re-writing which is itself a re-reading of the (English) original and which, in turn, invites a re-reading of the psalms themselves. However, before considering scribal re-readings of Maidstone and Brampton, it is worth pausing on the textual history of the complete *Metrical* and *Prose* Psalters.[38] For although neither elaborates on the psalms in the same manner as Maidstone and Brampton, variations between different manuscript readings of both translations offer evocative indications of the ways in which scribal activity could often involve deliberate re-calibration of the text.

In the case of the *Metrical Psalter*, it is clear that Vespasian and Egerton are the earliest of the six extant manuscripts containing the text, but there has not as yet

---

[37] As the work of Anne Hudson and before her Dorothy Everett has demonstrated, the textual history of RV is complex: 'Dorothy Everett in 1922 proposed that amongst the manuscripts known to her there was a fairly clear break in the tradition in the course of Psalm 84. Before this point the manuscripts could be divided into two fairly distinct groups, which she called R[evised] V[ersion] 1 and R[evised] V[ersion] 2. After it there were three groups of manuscripts, the first two RV 1 and RV 2, containing short commentaries that diverged in some degree but which differed less than in the opening section, and the third, RV 3, found only in one manuscript (now divided into two parts) and incomplete, which dealt with the material at enormous length and entirely independently' (Hudson (1988), p. 259).

[38] I am not pausing on the textual history of Rolle's Psalter, as analysis of the Wycliffite revisions to the commentary would be a large-scale enterprise and is, in any case, better deferred until after the publication of all three volumes of Anne Hudson's EETS edition. Neither am I pausing on the Wycliffite Psalter, since the content of the glosses found in several LV manuscripts was considered in the previous chapter.

been any full scholarly discussion of which of the six might represent the version closest to the notional 'original'. Editing the Psalter in the nineteenth century, both Stevenson and Horstmann used Vespasian as their base text, and for reasons which the proceeding discussion will at least partially clarify, it seems likely that this manuscript does contain a version of earlier origins than those found in the other five manuscripts. Bodley 921's text, for example, is notable for containing some obvious scribal errors which do not appear in Vespasian or any other manuscript. Psalm 2: 11 ('servite Domino in timore et exultate ei in tremore' [serve ye the Lord with fear: and rejoice unto him with trembling]) provides a good example of this. In Vespasian, the translation reads:

> Serues lauerd in drede at wille,
> And with quakinge glade him tille.

This 'wille/tille' rhyme also appears in the Harley, Egerton, and Corpus Christi manuscripts. In Bodley 921, however, the rhyme has disappeared and instead we read:

> Serues to god in drede
> And with qwaking glades him til.[39]

It would be possible to read this as a deliberate attempt to reproduce the Latin more precisely ('at wille' is padding and has no equivalent in the Gallican), but given that the scribe of Bodley 921 generally maintains rhyme throughout, this seems unlikely. It is simply an inadvertent omission, much more likely to have originated in 921's careless copying than in any anterior version.[40] On other occasions, Bodley 921 shares its erroneous readings with Bodley 425: such, for example, is the case with the copying of Psalm 68: 3–4 ('veni in altitudines maris et tempestas demersit me laboravi clamans raucae factae sunt fauces meae defecerunt oculi mei dum spero in Deum meum' [I am come into the depth of the sea, and a tempest hath overwhelmed me. I have laboured with crying, my jaws are become hoarse, my eyes have failed, whilst I hope in my God]). In Vespasian the translation reads:

> I come in heghnes of þe see,
> And þe storme it sanke me.
> I swanke criand, haase ere made
> Chekes mine for pine I hade;
> Mine eghen waned me of sighte,
> Whil I hope in mi god of mighte.

Three distinct rhymes are in use here ('see/me'; 'made/hade'; 'sighte/mighte') and these pairings also appear in the Egerton, Harley, and Corpus Christi manuscripts.

---

[39] This part of the Psalter is missing from Bodley 425.

[40] There are further signs of scribal carelessness in Bodley 921. See, for example, Psalm 56: 2 ('Miserere mei Deus miserere mei quoniam in te confidit anima mea' [have mercy on me, O God, have mercy on me: for my soul trusteth in thee]). In Vespasian the translation reads: 'Hafe merci of me, god, haf merci of me, / For mi saule traistes in þe.' All manuscripts contain this 'me/þe' rhyme other than Bodley 921, which preserves the obviously erroneous duplication: 'Mils of me god miles of me / for mi saul traistes in me.'

However, in Bodley 425 and 921, while the same rhymes are maintained, the equivalent of 'chekes mine for pine I hade' is omitted, leaving 'made' without a rhyme.[41] This is, again, an obvious error of omission, explicable by scribal inattention. On neither occasion has the translation been deliberately altered or consciously improved; the text has been mis-read rather than re-read.[42]

At other notable moments, however, the translation witnessed in Vespasian does appear, in other manuscripts, to have been the subject of deliberate alteration, not of substance but of style: in all manuscripts other than Vespasian, the insistent couplets rhyming aabb (and, on rare occasions, quatrains rhyming aaaa) are varied by the introduction of quatrains rhyming abab throughout Psalms 26, 44, and 67. Although it is of course theoretically possible that these quatrains were native to the translation in its earliest form, it seems much more likely that they were an innovation, perhaps functioning to alleviate the tedium of copying and/or reading. So, Psalm 26: 1 ('Dominus inluminatio mea et salus mea quem timebo? Dominus protector vitae meae a quo trepidabo?' ['the Lord is my light and my salvation, whom shall I fear? The Lord is the protector of my life, of whom shall I be afraid?') reads thus in Vespasian:

> Lauerd mi lightinge es in lede,
> And mi hele; wham I sal drede?
> Lauerd forhiler of mi life;
> For whate sal I quake, swerde or knife?

but, in all other manuscripts, becomes:

> Louerd mi lihting mi hele so rif
> Whom sal I drede whil þat I wake
> Louerd forhiler of mi lif
> Who is for whom þat I sal quake (reading taken from Corpus Christi)

Similarly, Psalm 44: 2 ('Eructavit cor meum verbum bonum, dico ego opera mea regi. Lingua mea calamus scribae velociter scribentis' [my heart hath uttered

---

[41] There are further indications of a particular association between the Bodley manuscripts, witnessed in part by variations noted in Chapter 3. For a further example of shared miscopying, see Psalm 27: 4 which, in Vespasian, reads: 'After þair werkes gif to þa, / And after nithe ofe þair findings ma; / After þair handwerkes yhelde til am, / Yhelde foryeldeinge of þa to þam.' Two distinct rhymes are in operation here ('þa/ma', 'am/þam') and are maintained in all other manuscripts excepting the Bodley specimens which both repeat the same identical rhyme: 'after þair werk giue to þo / after miht of þar findinges als so / after þair werk yeld to þo / yeld for yelding þo to þam so' (Bodley 921).

[42] On one obvious occasion, however, readings unique to the two Bodley manuscripts are not evidence of a shared error. See Psalm 78: 1 ('Deus venerunt gentes in hereditatem tuam polluerunt templum sanctum tuum' [O God, the heathens are come into thy inheritance, they have defiled thy holy temple]). Vespasian reads 'God, folke come in þin eritage; / sothli þai fortrade þi kirke hali', a reading which is more or less identical to that of Egerton, Harley, and Corpus Christi. But in Bodley 425 and 921 we read 'God genge þine eritage come inne(ine) / Þi heli kyrke(kirke) þai fortrade with sinne.' 'Sinne' is not mentioned at this point in any other manuscripts. Whether this is intentional or not, Bodley's translation is arguably an improvement: 'fortrade with sinne' is a fuller rendition of 'polluerunt' than the bare 'fortrade' (trampled); at the same moment, Rolle has 'fylid'.

a good word, I speak my works to the king. My tongue is the pen of a scrivener that writeth swiftly]) reads thus in Vespasian:

> Mi hert riftet gode worde to bringe;
> I sai mi werkes to þe kinge;
> Mi tunge rede-pipe maister-writer,
> Ofe swiftlike writande be þer.

but all other manuscripts have:

> Mi hert rifted gode word þurgh me
> I telle þe kynge werke of mi hande;
> Mi tunge rede-pipe mot master be
> Writer of swiftli writande. (reading taken from Harley)

And finally, Vespasian's Psalm 67: 3 ('sicut deficit fumus deficiant; sicut fluit cera a facie ignis sic pereant peccatores a facie Dei' [as smoke vanisheth, so let them vanish away: as wax melteth before the fire, so let the wicked perish at the presence of God]) reads:

> Als wanes reke, als wane þa;
> Als meltes wax face of fire fra,
> Swa sinful forworthe þai
> Fra þe likam of god in ai.

But in all other manuscripts we find:

> Als reke wanes, wane to noht
> Swa wax meltes againe fire
> Als sinful to gronde be broht
> Fra godes face is faire and shire (reading taken from Harley)

Beyond varying the tedium of the rhyming couplets, it is difficult to see why these changes are made. The original translations of the Latin are not questioned, although there are some minor variations of vocabulary. Neither is there any sustained attempt to make the vernacularization more comprehensibly idiomatic: both renditions of Psalm 44: 2, for example, are difficult to follow. In fact, the reading preserved in Harley et al. seems to introduce error, separating the 'master' from the 'writer', misrepresenting Vespasian's more accurate translation of the Latin 'scribae' by the compound 'master-writer'.[43] On occasion, the altered rhyme scheme also necessitates more creative padding. While, as is always the case in the *Metrical Psalter*, this does little to alter the meaning of the Latin, it is further evidence that the goal of the revisions is not increased fidelity to the source. The revisions might rid Psalm 26: 1 of its 'swerde or knife', but they add 'to gronde be broht' as a periphrastic rendering of Psalm 67: 3's 'pereant' and the 'faire and shire' of the same verse has no grounding in the Vulgate.

---

[43] Rolle's reading maps more easily onto the Latin: '*My hert riftid goed word: I say my werkis til the kynge. My tonge pen of mayster swiftly writand*' (p. 163).

Of course, it would be pleasing to argue that all three stylistically revised psalms were of particular liturgical significance, as that would provide an obvious reason for their singling out in the textual tradition of the *Metrical Psalter*. This could be suggested of Psalm 26, the first of the Nocturns, all of which are frequently set apart from other psalms in their manuscript presentation, generally by means of substantially enlarged initials. It is not, however, easily applicable to Psalms 44 or 67, neither of which appears to have been of notable liturgical significance; they feature, respectively, in Monday and Wednesday Matins in both the monastic and secular traditions.[44] Why these particular psalms should have been re-written/re-read remains something of a mystery. What such re-writings/readings do suggest, however, is that for scribes of the *Metrical Psalter*, the English translation itself is not sacrosanct. Unlike the Gallican original, the vernacular rendition can be altered and varied. It does not have the same authoritative force as its forebear.

Turning to the later *Prose Psalter*, differences between witnesses to the text are also striking, albeit for very different reasons. As indicated in Chapter 1, the four extant manuscripts of this Psalter are related in evocative ways. BL Add. 17376 and Cambridge, Pepys 2498 share the fact that they are written in Samuels' 'Type II' London English. Pepys and TCD 69 contain a number of the same texts (although the two are 'certainly derived from different exemplars' (Hanna)), and finally, Dublin and Scheide deposit 143 share a scribe. Despite their many connections, it should not surprise us that each preserves a slightly different text of the *Prose Psalter*. What might, however, interest us is the character of these divergences. For while changes to the text of the *Metrical Psalter* are overwhelmingly stylistic, differences between copies of the *Prose Psalter* suggest that the relationship between source and translation was (re)considered more than once. Establishing which, if any, of the four extant manuscripts contains a version of the text closest to the 'original' translation would, however, be a complex undertaking, beyond the scope of this study. We must, therefore, content ourselves with the observation that different versions of the text circulated in the fourteenth century and that while the variations are sufficiently striking to suggest that on occasion the relationship between translation and source might have been reconsidered, they are not substantial enough to indicate that any more than one translation of the entire source text lies behind the versions extant in the four English manuscripts.

In Chapter 3's analysis of the *Prose* translation, the frequency with which Additional's and Pepys' English translation silently erodes the language of the Psalter, replacing it with glosses derived from its Anglo-Norman source (the existence of which is veiled by the appearance of the Latin text in all four manuscripts), was noted. This overwhelmingly consistent silencing of translation by gloss is not, however, a feature of the *Prose Psalter* preserved in TCD 69 nor, to a lesser extent, in Scheide deposit 143. While, for example, Psalm 1: 1 ('beatus vir qui non abiit in consilio impiorum et in via peccatorum non stetit et in cathedra pestilentiae non sedit' [blessed is the man who hath not walked in the counsel of the ungodly,

---

[44] See Harper, Appendix 2, 'The Psalter', pp. 242–65.

nor stood in the way of sinners, nor sat in the chair of pestilence]) reads thus in Additional and Pepys:

> Blesced be þe man, þat ȝede nouȝt in þe counseil of wicked, ne stode nouȝt in þe waie of sinȝeres, ne sat nauȝt in fals iugemen (p. 1)[45]

in the Dublin manuscript we find:

> Blesced be þe man þat haþ noght go in þe counseil of wykkyd men & haþ not stond in þe waie of sinful men, & haþ not syt in þe chayer of pestylence þat ys to seyne of vengeaunce or of fals iuggement.[46]

Unlike the Additional rendition, the Dublin version includes not only the moral gloss on the Vulgate's 'cathedra pestilentiae' (the chair of pestilence), but a translation of the Latin, via Anglo-Norman ('chayer of pestilence') followed by two alternative glosses. To take another instance, while Psalm 41: 11's 'dum confringuntur ossa mea' (whilst my bones are broken) reads 'þer-whiles þat myȝtes ben frusced' (from Old French 'fruissier') in Additional, in the Trinity manuscript and Scheide we have 'þer-whiles my bones or myȝtes beþ broke or proschyd' (p. 51).[47] And to return to a translation which featured in Chapter 3, Additional's Psalm 90: 12 ('in manibus portabunt te ne forte offendas ad lapidem pedem tuum' [in their hands they shall bear thee up lest thou dash thy foot against a stone]) reads 'Hij shul bere þe in hondes, þat tou ne hirt nouȝt perauenture þy gost wyþ vices' (p. 113) and Pepys' reads 'þai schullen beren þe in hondes þat þou ne scalt noȝt hirten, þerauenture, þi gost wiþ vices'.[48] In TCD 69 and Scheide deposit 143, both gloss and translation are provided:

> Hij shul bere þe in hondes perauentur þou hurte noȝt þi goste or [þi] fote with vice or att stone.[49]

Admittedly, the relationship between translation and gloss is not consistently articulated. In the case of Psalm 1: 1, for example, it is clear that 'þe chayer of pestilence' is the translation, glossed ('þat is to seyne') by 'vengeaunce' or 'fals iuggement', but the hierarchy is not similarly clarified in 41: 11 or 90: 12, in which gloss and translation (presented in varying order) are divided by a simple 'or'. However, the fact remains that the *Prose Psalter* version in TCD 69 and, on occasion, in Scheide deposit 143 does not mirror that of Add. 17376 or Pepys 2498, but instead attempts to provide its English reader with a closer rendition of the unglossed Psalter, supplemented by moral glosses.

Such a technique, while it goes some way towards disambiguating text and gloss, inevitably results in a wordy, at times indigestible, English translation. Lacking Additional's sometimes awkward jolting between the literal and the abstract, Trinity's

---

[45] As in previous chapters, unless specificied otherwise, all quotations from the *Prose Psalter* are taken from K. Bülbring (ed.), *The Earliest Complete English Prose Psalter*, EETS OS 97 (London, 1891).

[46] Black and St-Jacques, vol. 1, p. 105.

[47] Pepys has 'my miȝttes ben tobroken' (Black and St-Jacques, vol. 1, p. 27).

[48] Black and St-Jacques, p. 59.

[49] Black and St-Jacques, p. 135.

translation is nonetheless marked by the equally jarring repetition of the explanatory 'or', or 'þat is'. There are other indications, however, that behind the Trinity text in particular there lies a concern to produce an idiomatic, comprehensible version of the psalms in English. In comparison with the Additional copy, the Trinity version is marked by the concessions that it makes to English word-order. So, for example, while Psalm 37: 3 ('quoniam sagittae tuae infixae sunt mihi et confirmasti super me manum tuam' ['for thy arrows are fastened in me: and thy hand hath been strong upon me') in Additional reads '[f]or þyn a-sautes ben ficchid to me, and þou confermed vp me þyn helpe' (p. 45), the Vulgate's 'super me' is idiomatically repositioned in the Trinity version ('For þyn a-sautes ben prikkyd to me, and þou confirmyd þin help vp me'). Additional Psam 50: 9's 'super nivem dealbabor' (I shall be made whiter than snow) is also very literally rendered as 'made why3te vp snowe', but in Trinity the comparative adjective is introduced ('made whytter þan snowe' (p. 61)). And while in Additional Psalm 52: 6's 'ossa eorum qui hominibus placent' (the bones of them that please men) are 'þe bones of hem þat plesen to men' (p. 63), in Trinity they are 'her bones þat plesed'. Whilst obviously preserving a version of the translation also witnessed in Additional, the Dublin manuscript has different priorities. Without necessarily revisiting the Anglo-Norman source, the person(s) responsible for the Trinity text has, in some ways, a greater confidence in the abilities of his audience. Presenting his readers with a 'straight' translation of the Vulgate (via the Anglo-Norman), he goes some way towards allowing them to apply the glosses as they see fit. Unlike the individual(s) behind Additional 17376's version, he does not 'read' the psalms to his audience, but provides it with the tools to 'read' them itself.[50] The *Prose Psalter* was clearly a text with which intelligent scribes were dealing in a thoughtful manner.

The *Prose Psalter* version with which Pepys presents us differs again. In its effacement of gloss by translation it is akin to Additional rather than Trinity, and its syntax and terminology also coincide more frequently with that of the former than the latter. As Ole Reuter suggested some time ago, however, the text in Pepys 'is in some respects closer to the French than [that of] the Additional MS'.[51] He points out, for example, that Psalm 67: 32's 'venient legati' (ambassadors shall come) becomes 'legats shul cumen' (p. 80) in Additional, but in Pepys is rendered 'many folk schullen comen'. Using as comparison the fifteenth-century glossed Anglo-Norman Psalter in Bibliothèque nationale 6260, he indicates that the Pepys translation actually corresponds more closely to 'la multitude viendra' (the multitude will come), although Pepys, like Additional, presents the Latin 'veniant legati' alongside the English translation.[52] And similarly striking instances can be noted

---

[50] It is worth noting that on occasion, the translation in TCD 69 is more accurate than that in BL Add. 17376. For example, Psalm 38: 4 ('concaluit cor meum intra me et in meditatione mea exardescet ignis' [My heart grew hot within me: and in my meditation a fire shall flame out]) reads thus in BL Add. 17376: 'Myn hert wex hote wiþ-inne me, and fur bigan to brenne in my þou3t' (p. 47), but in TCD 69, 'exardescet' is correctly rendered 'schal berne'.

[51] Reuter, p. 9.

[52] TCD 69's reading here is the same as in BL Add. 17376. The Anglo-Norman in BL Add. 44949 reads 'les letat3 uendrount' (f. 140v).

throughout the Pepys text. To borrow one more from Reuter, in Additional, Psalm 83: 6 reads '[b]lisced be þe man of whom þe help is of þe' (p. 103), while in Pepys it reads '[b]lissed be þat man þat is conseiled of þe'.[53] The Gallican text preserved in both manuscripts reads '[b]eatus vir cuius est auxilium abs te' (blessed is the man whose help is from thee), but Pepys' English rendering is again much more akin to that of BN 6260 ('Beneit soit l'omme qui est conseillé de toy' [Blessed is the man who is counselled by you]).[54] Such readings raise intriguing questions. Does Pepys preserve an earlier version of the translation, undertaken with both Anglo-Norman and Latin sources to hand? And do Additional and Trinity contain lightly (albeit differently) revised translations, undertaken without so acute an awareness of the source, or with the specific goal of closer fidelity to the glossed Latin text? Or does the Pepys text itself represent a later revision, undertaken by a reader looking afresh at the Anglo-Norman intermediary? The last possibility is perhaps the least likely, but whatever the sequence of translation and revision, the textual history of the *Prose Psalter* reminds us again that the English psalms, unlike their notionally stable Latin original, are acutely variable texts. To a greater or lesser extent, the act of writing them down is always itself an act of re-reading, inviting further re-reading on the part of their audience.

READING AND DOING

The English psalms not only solicited active engagement on the part of their scribes, who were as much readers as writers of the texts which they copied, but also demanded active engagement on the part of their contemporary audiences. Reading did not only lead to (re-)writing but also to acting and re-acting. The psalms were to have an energizing impact on those who read them. They are texts which ask to be *done* as well as *read*, or, put another way, they seek a reading which is also a doing. As Will suggests in an oft-quoted instance from Langland's C-text, the psalms are tools with which to labour:

> The lomes þat Y labore with and lyflode deserue
> Is pater-noster and my prymer, placebo and dirige,
> And my sauter som tyme and my seuene p[s]almes.[55]

The reading of the psalms is a form of work; deployed correctly, they effect change in the user and his environment. As Zieman has commented on the same passage, '[r]ehearsal of the Psalter does not simply secure one's own salvation but is socially productive.'[56] This sense that any profitable, productive reading of the

---

[53] Again TCD 69's reading is the same as in BL Add. 17376.

[54] The Anglo-Norman in BL Add. 44949 also preserves the same construction (f. 172r). For further striking examples, see Reuter, pp. 9–10. As he points out, there are also many instances in Pepys when it is clear that 'the Latin text has been referred to in the translation as well as the French'.

[55] D. Pearsall, *Piers Plowman—A New Annotated Edition of the C-text*, Exeter Medieval Texts and Studies (Exeter, 2008), Passus V, lines 45–7, p. 112.

[56] Zieman, p. 178.

Psalter is, or should result in, moral activity is commonplace and is prompted by the psalms themselves, which from their very outset are preoccupied with the living of a good life. Psalm 1: 1 is a case in point: the blessed man is he who has lived well:

> Blessed is the man who hath not walked in the counsel of the ungodly, nor stood in the way of sinners, nor sat in the chair of pestilence.

Following from this biblical emphasis, Augustinian exegesis is equally insistent in its foregrounding of authentic psalmody as consisting not only in reading and reciting songs of praise and penitence, but also in an active living out of godly principles. The ideal reader certainly reflects *on* the psalms, but he/she also uses this reflection to lead *out* from the psalms into the enacting of their tenets. In a telling comment on Psalm 118: 104 ('a mandatis tuis intellexi, propterea odivi omnem viam iniquitatis' [by thy commandments I have had understanding: therefore have I hated every way of iniquity]), for example, Augustine remarks:

> Sed quid est quod ait, *A mandatis tuis intellexi?* Aliud enim est, *Mandata tua intellexi*; aliud est, *A mandatis tuis intellexi.* Nescio quid ergo aliud se significat intellexisse a mandatis Dei: hoc est, quantum mihi videtur, *faciendo mandata Dei* pervenisse se dicit ad earum rerum intelligentiam, quas concupiverat scire.

> [But what do these words mean, 'Through thy commandments I get understanding'? The expressions 'I have understood thy commandments' and 'I get understanding through thy commandments' are different. Something else then he signifies that he has understood from the commands of God: that is, as far as I can see, he says that *by doing the commandments of God* he has arrived at the understanding of those things which he had longed to know.][57] (italics mine)

Richard Rolle demonstrates neatly that such an emphasis found its way into conventions of medieval reading. His *English Psalter* is shot through with the aware-ness that 'doing' the psalms is the most meaningful way of reading the psalms, not least in its ultimately Augustinian comment on 118: 104:

> He says noght that he vndirstode the comaundmentis. bot of thaim. for doand thaim. and of exercise in thaim he cumys til the heghnes of wisdome. (p. 426)[58]

Similarly, in his gloss on Psalm 26: 6 ('Circuivi et immolavi in tabernaculo eius hostiam vociferationis. Cantabo et psalmum dicam Domino' [I have gone round, and have offered up in his tabernacle a sacrifice of jubilation: I will sing, and recite a psalm to the Lord]), Rolle very specifically equates the voicing of the psalms in praise with the living of a good life ('thus is sayd in the glose: and I sall say psalme til lorde: that is I sall shew goed dede til his honur' (pp. 96–7)).[59] And in

---

[57] *Enarrationes in Psalmos* (PL 37, 1566).

[58] This interpretation of the psalm is borrowed directly from the Lombard who, in turn, cites Augustine (*PL* 191, 1095D). For further evidence and exploration of this awareness in Richard Rolle's *English Psalter*, see A. Sutherland, 'Biblical Text and Spiritual Experience in the English Epistles of Richard Rolle', *RES* 56 (2005), 695–711.

[59] Immediately prior to this statement, Rolle has presented psalmody as the act of singing 'in dilata-bilte of contemplacyon'. Although his language suggests that this is an intensely private experience, akin

commenting on Psalm 101: 5 ('Percussum est ut foenum et aruit cor meum, quia oblitus sum comedere panem meum' [I am smitten as grass, and my heart is withered, because I forgot to eat my bread]), he equates the eating of 'panem' (bread) not with the reading of God's word but with the doing of his will:

> Smytyn.i. am as hay and my hert dryed: for.i. forgat to ete my brede. That is,.i. am made dedly as hay, that lityl whill haldis the grennes. whils we dwell in kepynge of godis laghe we ere grene. when we syn oure hert dryes. and we forgete to ete oure brede. that is, to delit vs in godis worde doand it. (p. 353)[60]

It would also appear that for the Wycliffites, as much as for Richard Rolle, the correct 'reading' of the Psalter is one which is also a 'living' of it, as suggested by the General Prologue:

> Wel were hym þat coude wel vndurstonde þe Sauter and *kepe it in his lyuyng* and seie it deuoutli and conuycte Iewis þerbi, for many men þat seien it vndeuoutli and lyuen out of charite lien foule of hemsilf to God and blasfemen him whanne þei crie it ful loude to mennus eeris in þe chirche. *Perfor God 3yue grace to vs to lyue wel in charite and seie it deuoutli and vndurstonde it treuli*, and to teche it openly to cristen men and Iewis, and brynge hem þerbi to oure cristen feiþ and brennynge charite.[61] (Italics mine)

However, if spoken by an individual who is not in a state of charity and has no intention of fulfilling in action the godly principles that he is articulating, the Psalter itself becomes blasphemous.

But what was understood by the active reading of the Psalter? What did it mean to 'do' the psalms in a medieval context? At the most basic level, it seems that a person 'does' the psalms by living according to the fundamental tenets of biblical doctrine. A mainstay of patristic exegesis, translated readily into the medieval context, was that the ten-stringed harp on which David played before God was representative of the Ten Commandments, those foundations of contemporary Christian catechesis. Alluded to by Augustine and following him, by the Lombard (*PL* 191: 0326D), Rolle cites this glossing tradition:

> This boke is cald the psautere, the whilk nam it has of an instrument of musyke . . . and it is of ten cordis and gifes the soun fra the ouerere thurgh touchynge of hend. Alswa this boke leres to kepe the ten comaundments and to wyrk noght for erthly thynge. (p. 3)

---

to that of *canor* ('that ioy is & criynge when a haly saule is fild with cristis luf, that makis the thoght to rise in til soun of heuen, or the soun of heuen lightis thar in. and than that man may loue god in heghynge of voice. All the clerkis in erth may noght ymagyn it, ne wit what it is, bot he that has it'), Rolle is careful to position it within an ecclesiastical setting, glossing 'tabernakile' as 'haly kyrke' (p. 96).

[60] Rolle is drawing on the Lombard here (PL 191: 0907D–0908A) but the emphasis on the doing of God's word is his own; the earlier text speaks only of keeping it ('oblitus sum comedere panem meum, id est verbum Dei custodire, quia praeceptum quod Deus dedit, omisit' [I forgot to eat my bread, that is, to keep the word of God, because the commands which God gave, he disregarded]). Eleanor Hull's commentary also has, on occasion, a similarly practical bent; commenting on Psalm 31: 3, for example, she states 'Ye schul know that a man may speke to God in many maners, as in delycyous desire of herte and in profytable true speche of mowthe and in true syht of the yen and in heryng norychyng goodness and in resonable almys-doyng with handys, and in werkyng hele by goyyng of the fete for-to norysche pesse.' Barratt (1995), p. 31.

[61] General Prologue to the Wycliffite Bible, chapter 10. See Dove (2010), pp. 58/2016–59/2023.

It is also referenced in the *Prose Psalter*, where Psalm 32: 2's 'psalterio decem cord-arum' (the psaltery, the instrument of ten strings) becomes 'þe techynges of þe x. comaundement3' (p. 36).[62] This reading of the psalms as delineations of basic doctrine may explain in part the otherwise somewhat puzzling interest that the Wycliffites have in the Psalter. As Hudson suggests, while Wycliffite interest in the gospels is comprehensible, the movement's preoccupation with the Psalter is less so:

> The gospel commentaries [of the Wycliffites] were evidently inspired by a desire to make available in the vernacular a bulk of traditional exegesis of a kind that would facilitate the understanding of the literal sense at the centre of the biblical message. The Psalm com-mentaries [ie., the Wycliffite revisions of Rolle's Psalter] are a little more obscure: even though this book was traditionally the most familiar part of the Old Testament, Wycliffite stress upon the model afforded to contemporary Christian society by the instructions and implications of the epistles make it perhaps surprising that these were not chosen for effort [i.e. for fuller commentary] in preference to the Psalms.[63]

If, however, the 'implications' of basic Christian doctrine are to be located in the Old Testament psalms as well as in the New Testament gospels and epistles, Wycliffite interest in the Psalter becomes more intelligible. We 'do' the psalms, then, by living lives of New Testament obedience to these Old Testament precepts.[64]

In terms of specifically Christian doctrinal readings of the Psalter, the Penitential Psalms play a pivotal role. As a group of seven they could be mapped conveniently onto existing catechetic and doctrinal frameworks. For example, recognizing the Penitential Psalms as a distinct group, the Lombard links them to the sevenfold Spirit who can erase all sins which man commits in the seven ages of his life ('per septiformem Spiritum posse deleri quidquid in septenario hujus vitae committi-tur' [by the sevenfold Spirit who can erase whatever has been committed in these seven ages]), as well as to the seven forms of remission from sin ('scilicet baptismus, eleemosyna, martyrium, conversio fratris errantis, remittere in se peccanti, fletus et satisfactio pro peccatis, communicatio corporis et sanguinis Domini' [namely bap-tism, alms, martyrdom, conversion of erring brothers, remission of sinning against each other, weeping and satisfaction for sins, partaking of the body and blood of the Lord]).[65] Borrowing from the Lombard, Rolle reads their numerological significance identically:

> The seuen psalmes of the whilk this [Psalm 6] is the first. bygynnys all in sorowand gretynge and bitternes of forthynkynge, & thai end in certaynte of pardoun. And thai ere seuen, that we wit that thurgh the seuen giftis of the haly gast all synne may be

---

[62] This is a reading that it shares with Rolle: 'syngis til him in psautery of ten cordis, that is, stire 3ou to serue til charite, in the whilke ten comaundmentis is fulfild' (p. 114). See also *Bonum Est*'s comment on Psalm 91: 3 ('In decacordo psalterio cum cantico in cithara' [upon an instrument of ten strings, upon the psaltery: with a canticle upon the harp]): 'þe rihtwys man makeþ murþe to god, ffor he scheweþ to him his Merci, and his soþfastnes in a ten-stringed sautri, þat is, in folfillyng of his comaundementes' (Wallner, p. 57).

[63] Hudson (1988), p. 248.

[64] The fact that the psalms also ask for more demanding readings will be considered later in the chapter: as the Wycliffites said, they are the most difficult of biblical texts.

[65] *PL* 191: 0104A-B.

doen away, that is wroght in seuen dayes of this lif. And alswa for thare is seuen maners of remyssioun of synn baptem. almus dede. Martirdome. turnynge of neghbure til
god. forgifynge til him that synnes in vs. satisfaccioun and gretynge for synn. comu-
nynge of sacrament of the autere. (pp. 21–2)

and a similar gloss is found in Eleanor Hull's commentary.[66] Hull also goes further
than the Lombard and Rolle in suggesting that the Seven Penitential Psalms have
been specifically 'ordeynyd . . . for-to put awey and efface the vij dedly synnys'.[67]
The commonplace nature of such mapping of psalm to sin in medieval readings
is emphasized by the fact that Maidstone and Brampton both allude to it.[68] In
the light of such glossing, it is easy to see why, as demonstrated in Chapter 1, the
Middle English psalms, particularly but not exclusively the Penitential, were such
comfortable bedfellows with materials of basic catechesis.

It would be unfair, however, to suggest that one can only do profitable work with
the psalms by living according to basic principles extracted from them. Medieval
understandings of 'doing' the psalms were subtler than this, encompassing a more
nuanced notion of what it is to 'do'. Readings were by no means focused exclusively
on practical enactment; they were not anti-contemplative, nor did they dismiss the
value of thoughtful, even intellectual, engagement with the scriptures as a form of
work. One of the most striking Middle English evocations of psalmic labour is that
of Thomas Brampton, who in his paraphrase of the Penitential Psalms, translates
Psalm 142: 10 ('Doce me facere voluntatem tuam, quia Deus meus es tu' [teach
me to do thy will, for thou art my God]) very simply as '[t]eche me to performe
thy wylle'.[69] 'To performe' functions here as a translation of the Vulgate's 'facere';
an alternative rendition would be, of course, 'teach me to do thy will'. The verb 'to
perform', however, was used to denote a range of actions in the Middle Ages: one
does not perform only by 'doing' in the literal, practical sense discussed previously,
but also by voicing the psalms, thereby speaking that which is otherwise silent, or
completing that which is incomplete.[70] Viewed thus, the very act of devotional
reading and recitation is in itself a type of activity before God; actively engaged
upon, it contributes to the reconciliation of the penitential self with the divine and
constitutes part of that devout life towards which ideal psalm reading leads. There
is, as Susan Boynton puts it, a 'redemptive instrumentality' inherent in 'the act of
psalmody' as 'one of its salvific effects'; the very recitation of the psalms has the

---

[66] Barratt (1995), p. 9: 'And for that ther ben ordeynyd vij, that we schold leue surly that al the
synnys þat we done in the vij of thys lyfe mow be effacyd by the vij 3eftys of the holy goost. The holy
goost ys callyd a speryt of vij formys that he enformyth man in quykenes of lyfe for-to do wel and
he sleyht al the synnys of our vij by the vij 3eftys of his grace by whiche euery sinner may come to
remissyon of his synnys.'

[67] Barratt (1995), p. 9.

[68] For Maidstone see, for example, his stanza on Psalm 50: 12: 'God make in me my herte clene, /
þi ri3tful goost in me þou newe, / Fro synnes seuen þou make it shene' (pp. 77/465–7). For Brampton,
see his response to Psalm 50: 19: 'If þou wolt offre to god of heuene / A spyryt of grete repentaunce /
Thogh þou be gylty of synnes seuene / A sorowfull herte ys goddys plesaunce' (p. 389).

[69] Kreuzer, p. 403.

[70] For an exhaustive cataloguing of the resonances of the verb 'to perform' in Middle English, see
the MED.

potential to be a form of productive labour, a type of work.[71] But, as the quoted remark from the Wycliffite prologue suggests, for this to be the case, the psalms must be spoken devoutly and with feeling. In Psalm 37: 9, the Psalmist character-izes his penitent utterance as a roar from the heart ('Afflictus sum et humiliatus sum nimis; rugiebam a gemitu cordis mei' [I am afflicted and humbled exceed-ingly: I roared with the groaning of my heart]) and it is to this quality of agonized feeling and voicing that the true speaker of the psalms must aspire. In his com-mentary on this verse, the Lombard, drawing on Cassiodorus, likens such roaring to that of a wild animal ('a simili leonis et aliarum belluarum' [in the likeness of a lion and other wild animals]).[72]

Although Rolle does not adopt this vivid analogy, his translation of 'rugiebam' by 'romyd' ('I am tourmentid and.i. am mekid ful mykill:.i. romyd fra the sorow of my hert' (p. 139)) is evocative. 'Romien' is a verb used elsewhere in Middle English to denote the cry of wild animals and, sometimes, a howl of insanity. 'Rugiebam' is a verb also remarked on by Eleanor Hull ('[R]yght as þe roryng of a lyon comyth of a gret desyre whan he coueytyth to deuoure hys pray, ryght so ys grete þe wey-lyng of myn hert for-to pursue and folowe pardon od my mysdedys. And þer-for he seythe: Rugiebam a gemitu cordis mei. For þis cause he seythe rugiebam for-to schewe þe strenght of his sorrow'), whose commentary is preoccupied throughout by the tone of the Psalmist's voice.[73] In her investigation of the insistent first verse of Psalm 101 ('Domine exaudi orationem meam et clamor meus ad te veniat' [Hear, O Lord, my prayer: and let my cry come to thee]), for example, she draws attention to the modulating pitch implied by 'oratio' and 'clamor':

> Now see how þis oreyson ys brokyn out in-to a crye and notyht here þe gret dezyr he had that his oreyson schold be herd, when he seyd aftyr that his crye schold come to þe fader.

before pointing out, as quoted earlier in this chapter, that this exemplifies 'a fygure that ys callyd [*epimone*], that is *crebra repeticio sentencie*, that this ofte repetyng. [Ofte repetyng] ys verrey schewyng of þe dezyre'.[74]

The ideal reader of the psalms is, Hull suggests, David himself, who feels as he speaks:

> For ther-of the throte werbyl, the notys and the tonge forge the word, but yf the hert syhe for loue, hit is non hymne, y behyht you. But Dauid, that languysshed with loue

---

[71] Boynton (2007), p. 906. Viewed thus, the speaking of the psalms might be placed within J. L. Austin's category of 'performative utterances' (utterances that 'do' something) as distinct from 'con-stative utterances' (utterances that simply describe something). For as in Austin's description of per-formatives, so in the penitential recitation of the psalms, 'the issuing of the utterance is the performing of an action—it is not normally thought of as just saying something'. See J. L. Austin, *How To Do Things with Words*, William James Lectures 1955 (Oxford, 1975), pp. 6–7. While employing Austin's performative/constative distinction, I am aware of the fact that this is not a rigid categorization which he maintains throughout *How to Do Things with Words*.

[72] *PL* 191: 0384B.   [73] Barratt (1995), p. 80/617–21.

[74] Barratt (1995), p. 141/71–142/73. As Barratt points out, the commentary is here indebted to Peter Lombard (*PL* 191: 0906D-0907A).

for desire of his creator, louyd with hert delycyously and made his notis swetewysely and formyd his word profytably, for-to 3eue to the ryghtwys man perseuerance in his goodness, to the synfulle verrey repentance and to the repentant certeyn hope and to them that ben dede in synne, drede of the peynys of helle.[75]

Hull's use of the term 'profytably' is important. In Middle English literary culture, the devout (as distinct from mindless or blasphemous) voicing of the psalms enjoyed a particular reputation as a worthwhile form of verbal activity, witnessed most powerfully by Ymaginatif's rebuke to Will in Passux XII of *Piers Plowman* B:

And thow medlest thee with makynges—and myghtest go seye thi Sauter
And bidde for hem that yyveth thee breed.[76]

While Will wastes time on the frivolous sport of versification, he could be engaged in the infinitely more productive activity of psalm recitation and prayer. It is, then, fitting that the speaker of Maidstone's penitential paraphrase (itself, ironically, a 'makyng') should take the opportunity to reflect regretfully on his 'wantoun word & ydel ooþ' in responding to Psalm 37: 2 (p. 59/205).[77] While 'ydel' words yield no return, the heartfelt voicing of the psalms, in which the speaker is now engaged, *does* something. This interest in voicing is, to a great degree, prompted by the psalms' own insistent reflection on their status as utterances before the divine. They frequently seem caught between anxiety lest God will not hear:

Hear, O Lord, my prayer: and let my cry come to thee. Turn not away thy face from me: in the day when I am in trouble, incline thy ear to me. In what day soever I shall call upon thee, hear me speedily.[78] (Psalm 101: 2–3)

and certainty that He is able to hear:

For the Lord hath heard the voice of my weeping. The Lord hath heard my supplication: the Lord hath received my prayer.[79] (Psalm 6: 9–10)

---

[75] Barratt (1995), p. 3. Cf. the Lombard on the titulus to Psalm 72: 'Non autem cantat hilariter, qui non amat, sic: Si sit laus et non Dei, non est hymnus, et si sit Dei et non cum cantico, non est hymnus. Oportet ergo, ut sit hymnus, habere haec tria, laudem et Dei, et canticum. In laude confitentis est praedicatio; in cantico amantis affectio' [*He who sings cheerfully, who however does not love, thus:* if it be praise and not of God, it is not a hymn, and if it be of God but not with song, it is not a hymn. It is necessary, therefore, in order that it be a hymn, to have these three: praise and [to be] of God, and song. In praise of confession is preaching; in song of love, affection] (*PL* 191: 0669A).

[76] Schmidt, Passus XII, 16–17, p. 135. In a rather more extreme reading of the psalms, Chaucer's Manciple takes them as sanctioning knowledgeable silence in preference to idle gossip: 'A jangler is to God abhomynable. / Reed Salomon, so wys and honurable; / Reed David in his psalmes; reed Senekke. / My sone, spek nat, but with thyn heed thou bekke' ('The Manciple's Tale', 343–6).

[77] This is not an exegetical emphasis that we find at the same moment in Rolle's *English Psalter*.

[78] For specifically Penitential Psalms exhibiting a similar anxiety, see, for example, Psalm 129: 1–2: 'Out of the depths I have cried to thee, O Lord: Lord, hear my voice. Let thy ears be attentive to the voice of my supplication'; Psalm 142: 1 'Hear, O Lord, my prayer: give ear to my supplication in thy truth: hear me in thy justice'; Psalm 142: 7 'Hear me speedily, O Lord: my spirit hath fainted away.'

[79] For other such declarations, see Psalm 37: 10 'Lord, all my desire is before thee, and my groaning is not hidden from thee'; Psalm 37: 16 'For in thee, O Lord, have I hoped: thou wilt hear me, O Lord my God.' Robert Alter makes a similar point about the psalms' preoccupation with themselves as utterances; see Alter and Kermode, p. 260.

In the context of this latter quotation, what is particularly noteworthy about the psalms is their oft-expressed confidence in the efficacy of speech that is heard by God. When one speaks the psalms in a true penitential spirit, it seems that the act has the potential to effect change in one's relationship with God, to afford one the opportunity of achieving individual reconciliation with the divine:

> *I have acknowledged* my sin to thee, and my injustice I have not concealed. *I said I will confess* against myself my injustice to the Lord: and *thou hast forgiven* the wickedness of my sin. (Psalm 31: 5) Italics mine

Affording the vernacular reader/speaker access to a quasi-liturgical that, crucially, they could understand, the English psalms exploit:

> [T]he power of ritualized language and the ennobling sense of obligation and responsibility that ideally characterized performance of the Office. If the attraction of vernacular theology was the power it gave the *lewid* over their own spiritual fortunes, the ability to wield ritualized language in fulfilment of a commitment made to God would seem similarly to grant a measure of spiritual agency.[80]

READING AND PRAYING

The most productive form of labour with the psalms is, of course, that of prayer. For Rolle, drawing on Cassiodorus, the psalms, as 'chosen sange[s] byfor god', become prayer as one utters them:

> The sange that delites the hertes and lerese the saule is made a voice of syngand, and with aungels whaim we may noght here, we menge wordis of louynge. (p. 3)

For Walter Hilton in the first book of his *Scale of Perfection*, they play an integral role in devotional prayer: their recitation is a feature of the first of his three 'maners' of intercession, suitable for the novice religious:

> For whanne thou seist thi mateyns, thou seist also thi Pater Noster principali; and over more to stire thee to more devocioun was it ordeyned for to seie psalmys and ympnys and siche othere whiche are maad bi the Holi Goost, as the Pater Noster is. And therfore thou schalt not seie hem gredili ne rekileesli, as thou were yvel paid that art bounden with hem, but thou schalt gadre thyn affeccioun and thi thought for to seie hem more sadli and more devouteli than ony other special praier of devocioun, trowande for soothe, that sithen it is the praiere of Holi Chirche there is no praier so profitable to thee whiche is vocale for to use comounli as that is . . . For a man in the biginnynge is rude and boistous and fleiscli . . . And therfore y hope it is most spedful to use this maner of praiere, for to seie his Pater Noster and his Ave Marie and rede upon his sautier and siche othere.[81]

[80] Zieman, p. 116. Here Zieman is actually talking about 'technologies of Latin prayer' but her point is made more forcefully if we recognize these technologies to have been replicated, at least in part, in the form of vernacular psalm translations and paraphrases.

[81] T. Bestul, Walter Hilton, *The Scale of Perfection*, TEAMS (Kalamazoo, 2000). *Scale I*, chapter 27, pp. 59/687–60/705.

This sort of vocal prayer is, he says, a 'siker staaf' for those who cannot yet walk steadily; it is the 'mylk' with which a child is fed and should be used by 'everi man comonli in the bigynnynge of his conversioun'.[82] In recommending the use of the 'sautier' in such elementary contexts, alongside the Pater Noster and Hail Mary, Hilton must have in mind the extraction of basic doctrine and catechesis from the text, discussed earlier. The perceived adaptability of the psalms to the needs and abilities of different audiences is, however, emphasized by the fact that for all their appeal to novice readers, in book two of his *Scale of Perfection*, Hilton specifically recommends their use by those more advanced in the spiritual life.[83] Discussing contemplative prayer, he sets the psalms apart from the rudimentary devotions with which they were coupled in *Scale I*:

> The most special praiere that the soule useth and hath most confort in, I hope, is the Pater Noster, or elles psalmes of the sautier; the Pater Noster for lewid men, and psalmes and ympnes and othere servyce of Holi Chirche for lettred men.[84]

For psalmic prayer to be effective in such circumstances, it must be uttered 'ne in comone manere of othere men by highnesse of vois or bi renable spekynge oute; but in ful greet stilnesse of vois and softenesse of herte'. If undertaken thus, it has the potential to lead to the heights of contemplation:

> There dare no flesch flie delite resten upon the pottis brynke boiland over the fier; right so mai ther no flesch flie resten on a clene soule that is lapped and warmed al in fire of love, boilende and plaiand psalmes and lovynges to Jhesu. This is verray praiere.[85]

This characterization of psalm-based prayer as standing at the threshold of elevated spiritual experience is found also in the writings of Rolle, Hilton's Yorkshire antecedent. As he tells us in the autobiographical *Incendium Amoris*, it was the recitation of psalms that propelled him towards the revelatory experience of *canor*, at the peak of his tripartite model of spiritual progress. Of course, both Rolle in the *Incendium* and Hilton in the *Scale* very probably have in mind the Latin Psalter in the experiences that they narrate and recommendations they make. The former does, however, emphasize that it is not only the Gallican text which has the potential to prompt intense devotion at the very beginning of the prologue to his *English Psalter*. Suggesting that '[g]rete habaundance of gastly comfort and ioy in god comes in the hertes of thaim at says or synges deuotly the psalmes in louynge of ihesu crist', he goes on to claim that for 'thaim that lastes in thaire deuocioun, [the psalmes] rays thaim in til contemplatyf lyf & oft sith in til soun & myrth of

---

[82] It is appropriate that, in the very next chapter of *Scale I*, Hilton should present the psalms themselves as endorsing this sort of vocalized prayer: 'Of this maner of praiere bi speche speketh David in sautier thus: *Voce mea ad dominum clamavi; voce mea ad dominum deprecatus sum* (Psalm 141: 2). David the prophete, for to stire othere men bothe with herte and with mouth seide: With my vois I criede to God, and with my speche y bisoughte oure Lord' (chapter 28, p. 61/729–32).

[83] The appropriateness of the psalms for those more advanced in the devotional life is hinted at briefly in *Scale I* when Hilton details the third 'maner' of prayer (which is 'oonli in herte withoute speche') thus: '. . . this man schal bi hooli psalmes, clene thoughtes, fervent desires, norische the fier of love in his herte, that it goo not out noo tyme' (chapter 32, p. 64/810–12).

[84] *Scale II*, chapter 42, p. 246/3167–9.   [85] *Scale II*, chapter 42, p. 247/3194–6.

heuen.' (p.3) Logically, these remarks must be read as applicable to the vernacular translation which they preface. It is then in keeping with the prologue's emphasis that throughout the *English Psalter* Rolle is careful to link the reading of the psalms to the experience of contemplation. His glosses on Psalm 101 provide us with some striking examples of this. Commenting on verse 22 ('ut annuntient in Sion nomen Domini et laudem eius in Hierusalem' [that they may declare the name of the Lord in Sion: and his praise in Jerusalem]) for example, he interprets 'syon' as 'contemplatife life':

> *That thai shew in syon the name of lord: and his louynge in ierusalem.* Thai that shew wele in syon the name of ihesu. that is, in contemplatife life. in ierusalem. that is, in sight of pes. thai may baldly shew his louynge. for contemplacioun and rest in godis luf ere bath to gidire. (p. 355)

which is a marked departure from the Lombard who glosses Sion (and Jerusalem) very specifically as the church ('Ut jam annuntient [Aug.] (quod non licuit cum interficerentur compediti), nomen Domini, id est laudem de Dei essentia, in Sion, id est in Ecclesia' *PL* 191: 0913B-C).[86] And commenting on verses 27–8 ('Et sicut opertorium mutabis eos & mutabuntur: tu autem idem ipse es & anni tui non deficient' [And as a vesture thou shalt change them, and they shall be changed. But thou art always the selfsame, and thy years shall not fail]), Rolle, again unprompted by the Lombard, makes a specific link with contemplation:

> *And as couerynge thou sall thaim chaunge and thai sall be chaungid: bot thou ert he the same and thi ʒeris sall noght fayle.* That is, as mannys body thai sall be chaungid in new figure, & last tharin. bot thou ert he the same, that is, all hally vnchaungeabil. and thi lastandnes is in the life endles. Gastly, erth is less haly men, that has despendynge of erthly godes. heuens ere mare halymen, that ere gifen til contemplacioun hally. and thai sall dye. and be chaungid fra this warld til the ioy of aungels. (p. 356)

This recurrent coupling of the psalms with contemplative prayer is a defining characteristic of Rolle's commentary, emphasizing the fact that for him 'doing' the psalms involves the labour of intercession as well as the living out of Christian principles.

Such is the connection made in Middle English devotional prose between the psalms and intercession that the aspiring audience is frequently advised to adopt (and imagined as adopting) the words of the Psalmist as the script to his or her own prayers. By this, I refer not to the ordered recitation of liturgical psalms (although, as we have seen, this certainly featured prominently in contemporary devotional routines), but to the apparently more spontaneous expression of the self by recourse to the words of the Psalmist. In their frequent merging of first-person intimacy with non-specific referents, his prayers are adaptable to the circumstances of the individual intercessor, on condition that he or she has reached an appropriate level of spiritual maturity. Rolle's belief that this was the case is emphasized by his commentary on Psalm 12: 1 ('Usquequo Domine

---

[86] [So that they would now announce (which it was not permitted to be interposed when enslaved) the name of God, that is praise of the being of God, in Syon, that is in Church].

obliuisceris me in finem? Usquequo avertis faciem tuam a me' [How long, O
Lord, wilt thou forget me unto the end? How long dost thou turn away thy face
from me?]). Suggesting that the verse is uttered by '[t]he voice of haly men', he
goes on to claim that its words can be adopted as prayer, but by only a select
few ('this wordis may nan say sothly bot a perfit man or womman'). Similarly,
in *Scale I*, Hilton characterizes the second 'maner' of prayer (which is 'bi speche,
but it is not of noon certain special seiynge') by the use of psalm quotation:

> And with that he crieth with desire of herte and with speche of his mouth to oure Lord
> for socour and help, as a man that were in peril amonge his enemyes or as a man in
> sikenesse, schewynge his sooris to God as to a leche, seiynge thus: *Eripe me de inimicis
> meis, Deus meus* (Psalm 58: 2) Lord, delyvere me fro myn enemyes, or ellis thus: *Sana,
> domine, animam meam, quia peccaui tibi* (Psalm 40: 5). A, Lord, heele my soule, for I
> have synned agenys Thee, or sich othere that come to mynde.[87]

Perhaps unsurprisingly, it is in Middle English responses to the intensely introspective Seven Penitential Psalms that we find the most sustained interest in the
voicing of the psalms and their suitability as models for prayer. The commentary
of Eleanor Hull is a case in point. Unlike the expository Augustine, to whom the
commentary is frequently indebted, the affective Hull is keen throughout that we
should try to think ourselves into David's mindset, as indicated by her remarks on
Psalm 50: 6 ('To thee only have I sinned'):

> Now þenke we wel in our reson and þenke we with syhyng hert hou þis word was
> greuos and sorful to þe hert of þe prophete when he seyd: *Tibi soli peccaui.*[88]

Having done so, she suggests, in a manner similar to Rolle, that we are entitled to
speak with the Psalmist:

> He that þis verreyly in al his werkys mekyth hym to God with verrey repentance, he
> may wel sey with good hope with Dauid: *Exultabunt ossa humilitiata.*[89]

As an expansive glosser of the Psalmist's words, she is also eager to explore the ways
in which they are relevant to, and spoken on behalf of, all sinners. A striking example is seen in her treatment of Psalm 6: 2. Beginning with a fairly close translation of
David's words ('Blessyd Lord,' seyth he, 'vndyr-take me nowht so in your furor that
I be conuycte for-to soffre dampnacion. Lord, in your wretthe chastyse me not') she
turns swiftly to a glossing paraphrase of his meaning, still framed as direct speech:

> In this maner seyth Dauid, 'Iuge me not at that dat of iugement that schal seme to
> them þat be loste wretthe and angre for that they haue dysseuyd wretthe,' but as
> ther-of he wold sey, 'Feyre Lord, þou art merciful and I am repentaunt. And þou art
> al-myghty and I feble and wrecchyd. And þou arte [lorde] and I seruaunt. And þou
> art a wyse leche and I a fole seke . . .'[90]

In its repetitive series of straightforward contrasts between saviour and sinner ('þou
art . . . I am'), the glossing paraphrase ('as ther-of he wold sey') clearly offers itself

[87] Chapter 29, pp. 61/740–62/746.   [88] Barratt (1995), p. 109/382–4.
[89] Barratt (1995), p. 119/760–2.   [90] Barratt (1995), p. 10/275–305.

up for the appropriation of readers keen to model their devotions on those of the Psalmist, to adopt his 'entent' as their own.

Such interest in speaking alongside the Psalmist in the articulation of penitential woe is taken to its logical conclusion in the paraphrases of Maidstone and Brampton, where David's identity as originator of the words is not referenced. Although it is unimaginable that contemporary audiences would have forgotten David's role, in these poems his is a part performed by the penitent speaker/reader. I use the term 'performed' (and invoke the notion of 'performance') advisedly, referring not to the straightforward 'doing' of Christian doctrine, nor only to the instrumental act of recitation itself, both discussed earlier. Of course, these interpretations of the term remain valid and active in the proceeding analysis, but here 'performance' is used also to denote specifically the quasi-dramatic way in which the speakers of both poems are required to voice the words of David and to enact the processes of penance outlined by this particular series of seven psalms.[91] In both, the dominance of the first person 'I' (sometimes varied by the plural 'we') insists on the constant presence of this speaking voice, but in Brampton's case, the performative nature of the poem is emphasized particularly by the conclusion of each stanza with the Latin 'ne reminiscaris domine'.[92] Borrowed from the antiphon that in both Sarum and York Breviaries concludes the recitation of the Seven Penitential Psalms and precedes the Litany, his inclusion of the phrase seems designed to key his devotional text into the conventions of the liturgy, and to present it as straddling the divide between private intercession and public observance.[93] This movement between private penitential recitation and a public act of penance is suggested further in both poems by deliberate evocations of the sacramental practices of the church. In Brampton's case, this is achieved by his prologue's introduction of a confessor, a 'brodir ful dere', to whom the narrator tells us he 'schroue' himself prior to his penitential recitation of the psalms.[94] In the case of Maidstone's paraphrase, although sacramental affiliations are less obviously foregrounded, incidental references to 'shrifte' ('confession') suggest that the friar

[91] Both poems create coherent intercessory monologues from the Seven Penitential Psalms. Prefaced with prologues and concluding in 'Amen', they ask for sustained meditative reading and engagement. Of Maidstone's psalms, Edden suggests, they 'move beyond psalm paraphrase, using the psalms as the basis for a single, continuous penitential meditation to be used in private devotion [. . .] the psalms are joined together in one meditation with no breaks between individual psalms. Links are made between them, a single theme unites them and they have a coherent structure.' See Edden (1992), p. 106.
[92] For a fascinating recent discussion of performativity and devotional usage of the psalms, see M. Otter, 'Entrances and Exits: Performing the Psalms in Goscelin's *Liber confortatorius*', *Speculum* 83 (2008), 283–302.
[93] 'Ne reminiscaris, domine, delicta nostra, vel parentum nostrorum, neque vindictam sumas de peccatis nostris.' ('Lord, do not remember our faults, or the faults of our parents, nor exact vengeance for our sins.') Littlehales (1897), p. lx. In her aforementioned *Speculum* article 'Entrances and Exits', Monika Otter makes a similar observation regarding the psalmic intercessions that Goscelin of St Bertin prescribes for Eva of Wilton: 'They are intensely, emotionally private but also keyed to communal worship. They give the individual worshipper a way to make the liturgical prayer his or her own, to fill it with personal content' (p. 292).
[94] Kreuzer, pp. 370–1.

saw his poem as complementing rather than supplanting the formal observances of the church.[95]

READING AND PENANCE

Modulating between an identity as personal devotions and a status as liturgically ordained prayers, often used as preparatory material for confession and penance, the psalms (particularly but not exclusively the Seven Penitential) occupy a curious hinterland.[96] They are, it would seem, texts to be read both privately and publicly, both in solitude and in community, and it is in consideration of this productive tension that we will conclude this chapter. It is in the psalm paraphrases of Lydgate that we find the duality witnessed most dramatically. In the last of the introductory stanzas to his *De Profundis*, for example, he states explicitly that Psalm 129 (alongside the Placebo and Dirige) is recited publicly for souls in purgatory:

> Prestys profite to sowlys with syngyng,
> Thorugh al þe world lasteth ther auctorite,
> Almesse-dede is a notable thyng,
> And lettryd folk loweer of degree
> With De profundis, placebo, and dirige,
> Our ladys sauhter, seid with devocyoun,
> In cherchis yerdis, of what estat they be,
> Whan for sowlys they go in processioun. (p. 80/81–8)[97]

His vivid reading of verse 4 ('Quia apud te propitiatio est; propter legem tuam sustinui te Domine' [For with thee there is merciful forgiveness and by reason of thy law, I have waited for thee, O Lord]) also imagines God's mercy, activated by the 'patent' of the cross, operating in the public, formal arena of the law court:

> Pyte, mercy, haue ther cheef dwellyng place
> Above the hevenly sterryd mansyoun,
> Our advocatys to plete affore thi fface,
> Cleymyng a tytle be thyn hooly passioun,

---

[95] See, for example, Maidstone's comment on Psalm 31: 5: 'þour3e shrifte wol I fro me þrowen / Al my mysdede & mourne among' (Edden (1990), p. 54/123–4). Staley, 'The Penitential Psalms' suggests that Maidstone's poem 'speak[s] directly to a reader whose desire for spiritual enlightenment finds expression in private reading, but a reader who can expect that reading to be guided by a clerical figure'. (p. 231). A similar point is made by Edden in *Carmel in Britain*, in which she states '[t]hrough-out [Maidstone's poem] it is assumed that the penitent sinner will receive the merits of the atonement through the normal channels of the institutional church.' See Edden (1992), p. 117.

[96] Their curious position is also noted by Lynn Staley, p. 244. She comments that '[i]ntended to relocate the penitent within the sacramental life of the church, a sacramental life administered by clergy, the Penitential Psalms were not seen as releasing one from clerical control . . . Nonetheless, when these psalms appear as vernacular meditations, they can take on a life of their own.'

[97] See also the closing stanza to Lydgate's *De Profundis* found in the Harley 2255 version: 'Off this processe to make no delayes / Breeffly compiled of humble true entent, / Late charchyd in myn oold dayes / By William Curteys, which gaf comaundement / That I shulde graunte myn assent / Of that kindred make a memorial, / With *De Profundis* whan so that it be sent / At his chirche to hang it on the wal.'

> Surest patent ffor ther Redempcyoun,
> Other sauffcondit seyn on no party,
> Cros best standard to patyse ther raunsown,
> Right of thy lawe to modyfie with mercy. (p. 81/105–12)

This is no parochial legal establishment, but a setting of grandiose proportions, a 'dwellyng place' above a 'hevenly sterryd mansyoun'. In such an imposing environment, we do not speak for ourselves but have our plea entered by '[o]ur advocatys', Pyte and Mercy, who are richly experienced in such matters. The processes of repentance and salvation are here entirely externalized. Simultaneously, however, Lydgate remains attuned to the resonance that the psalms have in the context of personal devotion. This is particularly true of his *Judica Me* paraphrase, in which the focus throughout is on the applicability of the Psalmist's words to the situation of the individual intercessor. His gloss on verse 2 (For thou art God my strength: why hast thou cast me off? and why do I go sorrowful whilst the enemy afflicteth me?), in its reiteration of first-person singular pronouns, is a case in point:

> For thow lord oonly, bothe in brede and leyngth,
> Of ryght consyderyd, I dar ryght well expresse,
> Thow art my support and my gostly streyngth;
> Why wylt thow, lord, suffyr my sympylnesse
> Forto procede in sorow and in trystesse,
> Whyle my sayde enemyes prowdly me assayle?
> O blyssed Iesu, of mercyfull goodnesse,
> Graunt of thy grace that they may nat preuayle.

The glossing speaker is here entirely preoccupied by the internal realm, by his own feelings and experiences. At this point, that which is external manifests itself only in the hostile threat of 'enemyes' who 'prowdly me assayle', magnified from the Gallican's 'adfligit me inimicus' (the enemy afflicteth me). As indicated by the poem's opening comments recommending reading of the psalm prior to mass, Lydgate is aware that the recitation of *Judica Me* can function as a precursor to public liturgical observance:

> Sey furst thys Psalme, with looke erect to heuyn,
> Iudica me deus, of hole hert entyr,
> Theyr conscience purge from the synnes seuyn
> Or they presume to go to the Awtyer.

but his implicit focus throughout is on the private and personal as the forerunner, or companion, of the public. In fact for Lydgate the two cannot ever be disentangled entirely from each other, as emphasized by his evocation, in *De Profundis*, of 'myn Inward hertyly Orratorye' as the location within which new 'conseits' arise:

> Hauying a conseit in my sympill wyt
> Wich of newe ys come to memorye,
> The prosesse to grounde on hooly wryt,
> Grace of our lord shal be my Dyrectorye
> In myn Inward hertyly Orratorye (pp. 77/1–78/5)

At this moment, the public and the private coalesce evocatively in the imagined architecture of the self. That which is external and performed publicly is also, properly, internal and enacted personally.

This sense that the Psalter can function meaningfully as an aspect of both public and private devotional activity also features at moments in Rolle's *English Psalter*. In sporadic departures from the Lombard, for example, he emphasizes the psalms' relevance to penitential processes. Such is the case in his commentary on Psalm 6: 9 ('discedite a me omnes qui operamini iniquitatem, quoniam exaudivit Dominus vocem fletus mei' [depart from me, all ye workers of iniquity: for the Lord hath heard the voice of my weeping]) in which the focus on penance and compunction is his own:

> Here he shewis that tha that duellis in thaire synn sall be departid fra all that does penance; the voice of his gretynge he kallis compunccioun of his synne.[98]

A similar emphasis can be heard in Rolle's gloss on Psalm 37: 6 ('putruerunt et corruptae sunt cicatrices meae a facie insipientiae meae' [my sores are putrefied and corrupted, because of my foolishness]) in which the Lombard's reference to the cleansing power of baptism is replaced with his own, to the healing power of penance:

> Myn erres, that is, the wondis of my synnes, hale thurgh penaunce, rotid whils.i. eft assentid til syn. and thai ere brokyn when.i. synned eft in dede: and all this is fra the face of myn vnwit: that is, fore my foly, that.i. wild not halde me in the grace that god had gifen me. on this maner myn alde synnes rotis til my self, and ere brokyn and stynkis til other men.[99]

Penitential processes are also alluded to in his commentary on Psalm 31. In response to verse 2 ('beatus vir cui non inputabit Dominus peccatum nec est in spiritu eius dolus' [blessed is the man to whom the Lord hath not imputed sin, and in whose spirit there is no guile]) for example, Rolle states:

> He that has doen plenere satisfaccioun for his synn, god rettis it namare til him, bot he is asoild of synn and pyne.[100]

---

[98] As in previous chapters, all quotations from Rolle's uninterpolated *English Psalter* are taken from H. R. Bramley (ed.), *The Psalter or Psalms of David and certain canticles with a translation and exposition in English by Richard Rolle of Hampole* (Oxford, 1884).

[99] Cf. *PL* 191: 0383A '*Putruerunt*, etc. [Cassiod.] Secunda pars, ubi est narratio, in qua enumerantur miseriae. Quasi dicat: Iniquitates sunt supergressae caput meum, quia *cicatrices meae*, [Gl. int.] id est plagae peccatorum, per baptismum sanatae *computruerunt*, cum jam peccato iterum consentitur *et corruptae sunt*, dum ad actum perducitur' [*They rot*, etc. The second part, where the narrative is, in which miseries are enumerated. As though he says: iniquities surpass my head, for *my sores*—that is, the blow of sins—healed by baptism, putrefy, when now sin is consented to again, and *are rotted*, as long as the deed is prolonged]. Rolle does, however, borrow his emphasis on the difference between consent and action from the Lombard. In his commentary on this verse, the Lombard goes on to demonstrate an interest in alternative readings of the scriptural text ('alia littera'): this is not something on which Rolle dwells.

[100] In these glosses on Psalm 31, Rolle is influenced by the Lombard (*PL* 191: 0318B–0320A), although he again omits the latter's reference to baptism.

and he glosses the 'thorn' of verse 4 ('dum configitur spina' [whilst the thorn is fastened]) as compunction:

> That is. lord, for thi vengaunce touchid me, for to make me meke, and that day and nyght, that is assiduely, turnyd.i. am til the in my wrichidnes, knawand me a wreche, whils the thorn is festid. that is, whils compunccioun for my synn is festid in my hert.

In his 2002 *Viator* article, Kevin Gustafson speaks of Rolle's translation as promoting a kind of interiorized spirituality—a 'potentially destabilizing kind of vernacular theology'—and he is right to do so.[101] None of these references to penance specify it as something which needs to be clerically ordained and supervised. The penitential language which Rolle uses ('satisfaccioun', 'compunccioun', 'penaunce') could refer simply to privately endorsed and enacted procedures. Nonetheless, on at least one, if not two, occasions in his commentary on Psalm 31, Rolle does suggest that the act of confession which penance necessarily entails should be voiced before an audience. Translating and remarking on verse 3 ('quoniam tacui inveteraverunt ossa mea dum clamarem tota die' [because I was silent my bones grew old; whilst I cried out all the day long]) he is specific in his endorsement of oral shrift:

> *ffor.i. stilled eldid my banes; whils.i. cried all the day.* ffor.i. stilled that was noght to still. *that is shrift of mouth*, my banes eldid. that is, the strenght of my saule failed.[102] (italics mine)

and his closing comment on verse 5 ('[d]ixi confitebor adversus me iniustitiam meam Domino et tu remisisti impietatem peccati mei' [I said I will confess against myself my injustice to the Lord: and thou hast forgiven the wickedness of my sin]) to the effect that God 'forgifis syn at a heghtynge of shrifte' also appears to sanction voiced confession, if we read 'heghtynge' to refer specifically to the raising of the voice.[103] That Rolle should endorse oral confession at this point is all the more striking in the light of Peter Lombard's Augustinian gloss on this verse, which suggests that intent to confess ('confitebor') is sufficient to stimulate divine forgiveness ('tu remisisti'):

> [Aug.] Magnum est ergo quod ait, dixi: Confitebor vel pronuntiabo, alia littera. Nondum pronuntiat, promittit se pronuntiaturum. Et Deus jam dimittit, quia hoc ipsum dicere, scilicet pronuntiabo vel confitebor, quodammodo pronuntiare est, non ore, sed corde; nondum est vox in ore, ut homo audiat confessionem, et Deus audit.[104]

It is, however, noteworthy, and in keeping with Gustafson's emphasis, that at no point does Rolle specify that the audience for 'shrift of mouth' should be clerical;

---

[101] Gustafson, p. 296.

[102] The Lombard also reads this verse as referring to confession. Although he does not specify it to be 'confessio oris', the context of his remarks makes clear that he is referring to the voicing of sin (*PL* 191: 0318D–1319C).

[103] See *MED*, heien (*v.*), 1(a).

[104] *PL* 191: 0321A [Therefore he is great who said, I say: I will confess or I will proclaim, according to a different letter. He who does not yet proclaim, promises that he will proclaim. And God now remits, because in itself this act of saying, namely I will proclaim or I will confess, is saying in some way, not with the mouth, but with the heart. The voice is not yet in the mouth for man to hear confession, and God hears].

in the context of his commentary, oral confession could just as easily be intended for the ears of God alone. We are a long way from the more explicit recommendations of Eleanor Hull who, in responding to Psalm 6: 6 ('quoniam non est in morte qui memor sit tui in inferno autem quis confitebitur tibi' [for there is no one in death that is mindful of thee and who shall confess to thee in hell?]) is careful to identify the appropriate audience as involving both the human and the divine:

> [T]her-for eueryche for hym-selfe awht for-to hast hem for-to ȝeld hys account with terys and pure confescyon to God and to hys curate ubi est tempus uenie, tempus curacionis.[105]

Thomas Brampton also draws attention to the importance of confession, and in his response to the above-quoted Psalm 129: 4 ('quia apud te propitiatio est; propter legem tuam sustinui te Domine' [for with thee there is merciful forgiveness and by reason of thy law, I have waited for thee, O Lord]) specifies explicitly that it should be performed publicly:

> A lawe of mercy þou haste ȝeue
> To þem þt wollen no synnes hyde
> But clenly *to a preste* þem schreue
> And leue rebellyoun and pryde. (p. 398/stanza 106) (Italics mine)

As suggested, Richard Maidstone also refers to the necessity of 'shrift' in his paraphrase of the seven psalms, commenting for example on Psalm 31: 5 ('delictum meum cognitum tibi feci, et iniustitiam meam non abscondi' [I have acknowledged my sin to thee, and my injustice I have not concealed]) that:

> þourȝe shrifte wol I fro me þrowen
> Al my mysdede & mourne among.[106]

And although he does not specify an audience for this 'shrifte', there is nothing in his commentary suggesting that he would have any difficulty with recommending oral confession before a priest. But the confessional arena is not the only public space imagined by Maidstone. Like Brampton, albeit on a less grandiose scale, he envisages alternative environments for his speaker, the most obvious being that of the royal court. In his response to Psalm 6: 9, he speaks as the subject of an irate King:

> Now, curteys kyng, to þe I calle,
> Be not vengeable, put vp þi swerd!
>   In heuen, whenne þou holdest halle,
>   Lat me not be þeroute isperde! (p. 51/69–72)

---

[105] Barratt (1995), p. 15/487–9. In her notes (p. 211) she comments that she has been unable to identify the source of the Latin 'ubi est tempus uenie, tempus curacionis' [when the time is come, it is the time of healing]. She does, however, point out that 'tempus curationis' appears in Ier. 14: 19.

[106] Edden (1990), p. 54. Maidstone's familiarity with exegetical trends is emphasized by his commentary on Psalm 31: 4 ('quoniam die ac nocte gravata est super me manus tua conversus sum in aerumna mea; dum configitur mihi spina') in which he links the 'spina' with the pain caused by sin: 'For boþe day & nyȝt also / On me þi honde liþ heuyly, / And I am turned in my woo, / Whil þorn hit prickeþ greuously; / For prickeþ me perelouse þornes two / Of synne & payne, þis fele wel I' (p. 54).

This fear of exile from the noble court is also alluded to in his closing comment on Psalm 37: 3, where his speaker beseeches the lord to:

> [] sende counforte vnto þi kny3t
> þat fer is flemed out of þi lande.[107] (p. 60/215–16)

It is, however, in Brampton's recasting of the Penitential Psalms that we find the most sustained interest in their operation in the public sphere. As noted in the previous chapter, he uses the psalms to critique contemporary injustices and, on one notable occasion, his speaker imagines himself as something of an itinerant preacher, proclaiming vociferously the importance of penitential reformation:

> Myn help myn hele it lieth in the
> For euer I cry in town and felde
> Aftir * * * *Ne reminiscaris et cetera.*[108]

Here, the internally focused penitent has been replaced by his urgently vociferous counterpart, declaiming psalmic precepts in the open spaces of urban and rural England.

More consistently, however, Brampton positions the psalms in the more limited public space of clerically ordained confession and penance, and as noted, keys them throughout into the communally marked liturgy. That he is keen to exploit the dramatic resonances of this space is indicated to us from the very beginning of his poem: in both the A and B versions, the paraphrase begins with a vividly depicted (though differently imagined) tableau, inviting us to view the penitent speaker. In A, we read:

> In wynter whan the wedir was cold
> I ros at mydny3t fro my rest
> And prayed to Jesu that he wold
> Be myn helpe for he my3t best
> In myn herte anon I kest
> How I had synned and what degre
> I cryed knockyng vp on my brest
> Ne reminiscaris Domine.

and in B:

> As I lay in my bed
> And sickenes Revid me of my rest
> What maner life þt I had led
> For to thynke me thoughte it best
> A non my hert began to brest
>   I saide lord haue mercy on me
>   I cryed knockyng on my brest

---

[107] See also his closing comment on Psalm 101: 3: 'Ne putte me not out of þi halle, / But teche me turne a3eyn to þe' (p. 83/567–8).
[108] Kreuzer, p. 373. This forms part of a comment on Psalm 6: 8: 'turbatus est a furore oculus meus inveteravi inter omnes inimicos meos'.

* * * Ne reminiscaris domine.[109]

Although these stanzas clearly introduce a poem of devotional intent, there is no explicit reference, such as we find in Maidstone's prologue, to its nature as psalm paraphrase. Insisting on the particular experience of a first-person singular narrator, Brampton is totally preoccupied with setting the confessional scene.[110] In both versions of his poem we are then introduced to a second figure, to whom the speaker makes his confession:

> Myne hert for sorowe began to blede
> I sent aftir a brodir ful dere
> Of hym me thought I had great nede
> I schroue me to hym or I yede
> Of thought of worde þeis thre
> I cryed to god wt great drede
> Aftir * * * Ne reminiscaris domine.

and who in turn advises him to read and recite the Penitential Psalms as remedy for his sins:

> This brodir was ful wise of lore
> And saide theis synnys forgeuyn are
> If þou purpos to syn no more
> God of his mercy will þe spare
> [. . .]
> Ferthir more for thy trespas
> That þu hast done to god of heuyn
> If god will lend þe life and space
> Thou schalt sey the psalmys sevyn
> The better with god þu maist be evyn.[111]

Although this fictionalizing prologue, making audible a pastoral interaction between penitent and 'brodir', gives way almost immediately to the body of the poem, a paraphrasing response to the seven psalms which never refers back to this prefatory scene, its inclusion is nonetheless evocative. Strictly speaking, it implies that we are reading Brampton's narrator reading the psalms, multiplying the layers of distance from the text. It also reminds us not only of the Psalter's role in devotional praxis, but also, very differently, of the ways in which Middle English translators positioned and invited their audience to position the psalms within literary contexts. For Brampton's poem (particularly in the B version) sounds, initially at least, more like a medieval dream vision than a biblical translation. Often opening with an elaborately imagined scene involving a troubled and sleepless narrator, dream

---

[109] Kreuzer, p. 370.

[110] In fact, Maidstone's unremarkable prologue ('To Goddes worshepe þat [dere vs] bou3te, / To whom we owen to make oure moon / Of oure synnes þat we haue wrou3te / In 3ouþe and elde, wel many oon; / þe seuen salmes are þour3e sou3te / In shame of alle oure goostly foon, / And in Englisshe þei ben brou3te / [For synne in man to be fordon]') appears in only two manuscripts, both of which contain Edden's ß version.

[111] Kreuzer, pp. 370–1. Quotations are taken from the B text.

poetry may well have been a conscious influence on Brampton. The opening lines of Chaucer's earliest dream vision, *The Book of the Duchess*, are particularly illuminating in terms of the generic light that they shed on Brampton's later poem:

> I have grete wonder, be this lyghte,
> How that I lyve, for day ne nyghte
> I may nat slepe wel nygh noght:
> I have so many an ydel thoght,
> [. . .]
> Defaulte of slepe and hevynesse
> Hath [slain] my spirite of quyknesse,
> That I have loste al lustyhede;
> Suche fantasies ben in myn hede,
> So I not what is best too doo.
> But men myght axe me why soo
> I may not slepe and what me is.
> But nathelesse, who aske this
> Leseth his askyng trewly.
> Myselven can not tel why
> The soothe, but trewly as I gesse,
> I holde it be a sicknesse
> That I have suffred this eyght yere.[112]

Chaucer's introduction is obviously more discursive and detailed than that of Brampton; his narrator is overtly preoccupied by the fact that he cannot sleep and he is more expansive on the subject. Further, Chaucer's text lacks the obvious devotional tenor so apparent in Brampton. But there are certain similarities in the situations of the two narrators; both are alone in bed (this becomes apparent slightly later in Chaucer's poem), neither can sleep, and both blame this on sickness. And the similarities persist; Brampton's narrator, troubled by his sleeplessness and blaming it on an acute awareness of his own sin, sends (as quoted above) for a 'brodir ful dere' to whom he can confess his sins and who advises the recitation of the Penitential Psalms. In a related move, Chaucer's narrator also resolves to deal with his sleeplessness in a 'text based' manner, by asking someone to fetch him a book to read:

> So whan I sawe I might not slepe
> Tyl nowe late this other nyght,
> Upon my bedde I sate upright
> And bade one reche me a booke,
> A romaunce, and he it me toke,
> To rede and drive the nyght away.[113]

---

[112] H. Phillips and N. Haveley, *Chaucer's Dream Poetry*, Longman Annotated Texts (London, 1997), pp. 50–2/1–4 and 25–37. For prefatory material to other late-medieval dream visions, see *The House of Fame*, *The Parliament of Fowls* and *The Prologue to the Legend of Good Women* in the same volume. See also, for example, *Pearl* and *Piers Plowman*.

[113] Phillips and Haveley, p. 52.

Again, obviously, there are real differences between the two: Brampton's narrator is clearly operating within a devotional sphere and is set his reading as penance ('[t]he better with god þu maist be evyn'), whereas Chaucer's chooses his own book (a 'romaunce') and reads simply to pass the time (to 'drive the nyght away').[114] And finally, although the similarities between Brampton's preface and the conventions of dream poetry seem incontestable, the friar's poem of course lacks the one defining ingredient of Chaucer's *Book of the Duchess*, and of dream poetry as a genre— namely, the dream itself. While Chaucer's narrator proceeds to fall asleep and to re-emerge into a dream landscape, Brampton's does not sleep and is virtually erased from the poem by the psalm paraphrase that follows the preface.

Given this, what did Brampton have to gain by generically quoting from the dream vision in his introductory lines?[115] What does the allusion lend to his poem that we do not find in that of Maidstone? Put simply, literary dreaming was taken very seriously in the Middle Ages, and certain types of dreams were thought to carry messages of real import and often supernatural significance. So by opening in a manner reminiscent of the conventions of such visionary literature, Brampton's preface leads us very deliberately to expect a poem in which we are granted access to an authoritative voice. And despite the absence of the dream itself, this is indeed exactly what happens; following immediately upon the confessor's injunction to recite the Penitential Psalms ('Be gyn and sey wt mylde stevyn / Oft * * * *Ne reminisc et cetera*') the narrator's voice modulates into the biblically authoritative voice of the Psalmist (or at least a vernacular paraphrase of the same) and the fictionalizing prologue gives way to scripturally based meditation.[116] Yet, although the poem's initial and specific literary pretensions are not maintained throughout the text, the fact remains that we have been invited to consider the psalms in the light of poetic convention. And it is a way of reading which Brampton's (and Maidstone's) use of a simple rhyme scheme encourages us to keep in mind.

Using an image derived from the Old Testament poetry of the Song of Songs, in the Prologue to his *English Psalter*, Rolle describes the book as 'a garthen closed, wel enseled, paradyse ful of all appils'. Eleanor Hull also uses a horticultural

---

[114] I am indebted to Nick Perkins for pointing out that just as Brampton might be drawing on devices associated with dream poetry, so Chaucer may allude to some conventions and commonplaces of devotional poetry at the outset of *The Book of the Duchess*.

[115] Of course, Brampton is by no means the only late-medieval author to draw on the conventions of dream poetry in a poem that does not actually feature a dream. Some devotional lyrics also appear to set themselves within this generic context; see, for example, 'Als i lay vp-on a nith / Alone in my longging, / Me þouthe i sau a wonder sith, / A maiden child rokking' (C. Brown revd. G. V. Smithers, *Religious Lyrics of the Fourteenth Century* (Oxford, 1952), pp. 70–5). See also 'As I lay vp-on a nyth / My þowth was on a berd so brith / That men clepyn marye ful of myth / Redemptoris mater' in C. Brown, *Religious Lyrics of the Fifteenth Century* (Oxford, 1939), pp. 108–9. I am indebted to Nick Perkins for his observation that, at its outset, Thomas Hoccleve's *Regiment of Princes* also positions itself as a 'waking dream' in a manner similar to Brampton's opening: 'Musyng upon the restelesse besynesse [. . .] / As I lay in my bedde apon a nyght, / Thought me byrefte of slepe the force and might.' See B. O'Donoghue, *Thomas Hoccleve—Selected Poems* (Manchester, 1982), p. 73/1, 6–7.

[116] Kreuzer, p. 371.

analogy to describe the 'gloryous sauter' as the book 'wher-þorow al holy wryt borionyht and florysschyt and bryngyth forthe frute'.[117] While Hull's metaphor suggests abundant fecundity, that used by Rolle intimates both fertility ('paradyse full of all appils') and chaste enclosure ('garthen closed, wel enseled'). That his reading should suggest both is remarkably apt since Middle English translations of, and commentaries on, the psalms indicate that they were approached with a dual, though not necessarily contradictory, attitude. On the one hand, the Psalter is indeed a 'hortus conclusus', an inviolate mystery, which should be vernacularized and read in only the most literal manner. The spartan translations of the *Metrical Psalter* and of Rolle provide ample testament to this. On the other hand, however, the Psalter is a book ripe for interpretative adornment or, to borrow Hull's image, a garden which flourishes and grows, engendering multiple readings.[118] The 'growth' of the Psalter can be seen in the moralizing additions to the *Prose Psalter* and, rather differently, in the Wycliffite LV glosses. It is, however, most strikingly witnessed in Rolle's commentary and, further, in the Wycliffite revisions to that commentary. For all its hidden mysteries, the temptation to read the Psalter as a complete compendium of moral theology is great.

[117] Barratt (1995), p. 38/509–11. The common appearance of images of the Bible as a 'fructuous landscape' in the Middle Ages is pointed out by J. A. Alford, 'Richard Rolle's *English Psalter* and Lectio Divina', *BJRL* 77 (1995), 47–59, p. 47.

[118] Another, equally valid, interpretation of Hull's metaphor could be that it suggests those who read the Psalter will themselves bear spiritual fruit in their 'doing' of the text.

6

The English Psalms?

This book began by considering documentary evidence for the circulation of the vernacular psalms in the late Middle Ages, looking first at extant wills and testaments and second at manuscripts containing the primary material. It moved from this introduction through a consideration of theories of translation to an examination of the English psalm versions themselves. In the fifth chapter, trends of vernacular exegesis were explored. This final chapter brings together codicological, theoretical, and interpretative questions to consider the English psalms in their material context. What do extant manuscripts tell us about the ways in which the vernacular psalms were used?

GESTURES OF DEFERENCE AND DISPLACEMENT

In the previous chapter, reference was made to the ways in which the English psalms straddle the divide between private intercession and public observance, and to their duality as texts which have the potential to function effectively in both solitary devotional practice and in communal liturgical celebration. This echoes similar observations on the nature of the Psalter made in Chapter 1 of this book. It is also linked to another of that chapter's key contentions, namely that liturgical and quasi-liturgical activity persisted within an increasingly vernacular devotional climate and that the latter developed and built upon rather than eroded the former. A key aspect of the English psalms' dual functionality lies in the fact that, in their manuscript context, they almost invariably make themselves simultaneously available to audiences wanting to use them in (frequently vernacular) practices of personal piety as well as to audiences eager to tie their own private activity into the more obviously communal (Latin) liturgical observances of the church. They achieve this by including, in different ways and to different extents, some element of the Gallican original alongside the vernacular translation. The psalms are, then, accessible not simply to readers of the English alone but also to those who can read the Latin and/or (the two are not necessarily the same) those who want to key their English devotions into the rhythms of the Latin liturgy. These manuscripts act as constant reminders of ongoing interactions between Latinity and vernacularity throughout the late Middle Ages.

Of course, the presence of Latin and English in codices containing the vernacular psalms, both complete and paraphrased/abbreviated, has been observed on several occasions in this book. Issues of manuscript presentation have been repeatedly touched upon, and it has been noted that while some volumes include the full Latin text, most include only a partial version of the original. In some this takes the form of Latin prompts to individual verses of the Psalter, while others contain initial incipits for the 150 psalms only. Such incipits are often, though not always, distinguished from the vernacular by means of size, colour, underlining, or formality of script—and sometimes by a combination of such features. Full discussion of such matters has, however, been deferred until this final chapter, where we have space to consider the nature, effect, and implications of this linguistic hybridity in proper detail. Underlying this discussion is a basic question fundamental to our understanding of the material under scrutiny in this book and raised first in the Introduction: when viewed in their manuscript context, how English were the English psalms?

With this in mind, it is the task of this chapter to consider the interaction between (as well as, on occasion, the absence of interaction between) the Latin original and the English translation on the pages of manuscripts containing versions of the vernacular psalms, both abbreviated and paraphrased. Such an investigation has important implications for our understanding of the ways in which these psalms functioned in context. More broadly, it also requires us to revisit some of the theoretical issues associated with translation first outlined in Chapter 2 and recurrent throughout the course of this book. In impressing upon us the role played by both source (Latin) and target (English), these manuscripts remind us of the reality of the translation process as a movement between two languages. For all Rolle's partially stated unwillingness to admit the reality of language difference, it is of course an unavoidable fact. In their attempts to articulate a visual relationship between these two languages, some might be said to emphasize a clear hierarchy of descent from authoritative original to deferential vernacularization. In others, however, the Roman model (outlined by Copeland) of translation as 'displacement' and 'substitution' of the original is arguably more applicable. If there is a struggle for supremacy between the two languages, it is perhaps the emerging vernacular which gains the upper hand.[1] Yet one of the questions which this chapter will consider is how appropriate it is to invoke such models of hierarchy and contestation in the context of the English psalm manuscripts. Interpreting the two languages as vying for supremacy on the page, the Latin insisting on its traditional status as 'the firmly installed language of privilege', all the while being subverted by the ascendancy of a precocious vernacular, is tempting but may not always be productive. Might we not, in line with Zieman, query such a narrative in which the vernacular, 'associated with an aspiring laity', is always presented as

---

[1] Copeland (1991), p. 36.

'competing with, and even subverting, Latin as the firmly installed language of privilege'? [2] Is it not, instead, possible to understand the source and target languages as operating in cooperation? What these manuscripts may indicate is that Latin and English worked together to enhance the experience of psalm reading in the late Middle Ages.

A competitive reading which insists on a hierarchy of languages certainly carries some weight: the inclusion of the Vulgate text, whether in full or in part, serves to ground the vernacular, visually and aurally, in the long-standing authority of the Latin scriptures. This is particularly the case when red ink or underlining is used to distinguish the original from its translation, or when an enlarged, if not more formal, script is used for the former. As Malcolm Parkes points out, '[w]hen a particular script [is] preferred for a certain text, or kind of text, that [has] a special significance for readers, the image of the handwriting could itself acquire an emblematic significance by association'.[3] There are, however, limitations to a reading which insists on the inferiority of the vernacular, which can only ever operate as a conduit to the authority of the Vulgate. For although it is beyond doubt that the late-medieval proliferation of vernacular psalm versions is driven, at least in part, by a desire to make traditionally Latin material accessible to a wider audience, the insistent presence of Vulgate material in most manuscripts should caution us against reading the evidence as indicating the wholesale replacement of the old by the new. Rather than surviving as the skeletal remains of a decaying mode of devotion, the Latin reminds us that, on the page at least, the two languages had to coexist. In visually foregrounding the two languages in their manuscript contexts, the English psalms bear compelling witness to the ambiguous and shifting relationship which late-medieval vernacular literature had with the Latin culture on which it drew.

In a statement unwittingly—yet crucially—relevant to the English psalms (quoted once in Chapter 2, but worth reiterating here), Wogan-Browne et al. describe thus the situation in which contemporary 'vernacular literatures' found themselves:

> In annexing Latin's cultural authority, vernacular literatures demonstrate their ability to do anything Latin can do, while marking their difference from Latin; asserting the prestige of Latin texts and *auctores*, they also seek to assimilate that prestige, in an endless shuttling between gestures of deference and gestures of displacement whose most obvious effect is to tie the theory and practice of vernacular writing permanently to the question of its status in relation to Latin.[4]

Most immediately applicable to the emergence of the primarily secular vernacular *auctor* these remarks can nonetheless be mapped productively onto the

[2] Zieman, p. ix. Although the material (vernacular, with Latin prompts) on which I am focussing is distinct from the purely Latin material with which Zieman is concerned, her questioning of a competitive narrative is nonetheless relevant and useful.

[3] M. B. Parkes, *Their Hands Before Our Eyes: A Closer Look at Scribes—The Lyell Lectures Delivered in the University of Oxford, 1999* (Aldershot, 2008), p. 127.

[4] Wogan-Browne et al. (1999), p. 322.

material situation in which the English psalms found themselves in the late Middle Ages: extant manuscripts consistently evoke the authority of their Latin source. The authority of that source, as the divinely inspired word of God is, of course, not questioned. Yet the notion that its authority derives from the simple fact of its Latinity *is*, arguably, queried. The Vulgate text is included not because—or not *simply* because—of its venerable status as Latin original but because it is useful. Questions of hierarchy and prestige aside, whether we are talking of paraphrased or complete Psalters, at the most basic level, manuscripts include Latin incipits for a practical reason: they were the most common means by which the psalms were identified in the Middle Ages. Although there is some use of numbering in copies of the Wycliffite and *Prose Psalters*, and even, on occasion, in manuscripts of Rolle's English commentary, in general Latin incipits seem to have provided the most efficient reference system to the psalms.[5] Persisting in the context of the English translations, they alert the reader to his or her location in the Vulgate text with which they may well have been more aurally familiar.[6] If a reader needs to identify an English psalm, or to use the translation to follow liturgical recitation in Latin, such incipits are the most helpful means of facilitating cross-referencing. In the case of manuscripts which include the full Vulgate text alongside a complete, more or less literal, English translation of the relevant psalms, we can extrapolate further and suggest that they lend themselves to use in educational contexts, in which the vernacular could be used to parse the grammatically unfamiliar Latin.

In different ways and to different extents, English psalm translations present themselves, in their manuscript environment, as of a status comparable to that of their Latin source. As this chapter will demonstrate, it is the word 'comparable' that proves key: time and again, these manuscripts ask us to 'shuttle' back and forth between the Latin and the English. Wogan-Browne's 'gestures of deference and gestures of displacement' are endlessly repeated on their pages.

PARAPHRASED AND ABBREVIATED
PSALTER MANUSCRIPTS

As indicated in Chapter 1, the two anonymous verse paraphrases of Psalm 50, appearing respectively in the Auchinleck and Thornton manuscripts, are both accompanied by at least part of the Vulgate text on which they are based. In the case of Auchinleck's *Dauid þe Kyng*, every two (sometimes three) couplets of English verse are punctuated by relevant quotation from the Latin which, although

---

[5] For evidence of numeration in Rolle manuscripts, see Hanna (2010) where he notes that in the uninterpolated copy of Rolle's Psalter in Cambridge, Sidney Sussex College 89 'the psalms are numbered at the opening by their order in the nocturn in a medieval hand' (p. 14). And in the uninterpolated copy in Eton, Eton College Library 10, the psalms are 'numbered in arabic in the margins, similarly the nocturn numbers at the openings of each section' (p. 63). In London, British Library Royal 18 C.xxvi the psalm numbers have been added as running titles, 's. xv/xvi' (p. 111).

[6] Some complications to this system in the case of the English psalms will be noted in the course of the chapter.

it is written in the same script as the vernacular, is distinguished from it by the use of red ink, introduced on each occasion by a blue initial of the same size.[7] By such means the Latin (which is never quoted in full, always ending in '& c') asserts its difference from the brown-ink English paraphrase and indicates that it is the original to which the latter responds. However, the relationship is not simply one of superior to inferior, as suggested by the fact that after each red-ink quotation from the Latin, the vernacular is introduced by a two-line blue initial decorated with red penwork. Such is the case, for example, with the opening 'L' of the first line, 'Lord God to þe we calle', which dwarfs the Latin and announces its own presence in emphatic terms. While the Vulgate may be the poem's source, the vernacular elaboration is of merit in itself.

Thornton's presentation of the Latin is slightly less systematic: each Middle English stanza is prefaced by quotation from the Vulgate, although only the first six verses are given in full (with standard abbreviations), the remainder being represented by brief cues. On the first folio (102r), every Latin verse is introduced with a red initial (in the case of 'Miserere', the 'M' occupies the space of three lines) while the remainder is in the same brown ink as the English. On the second folio (102v) the red initials are dispensed with. But although Thornton's distinguishing of Latin from English is not as rigorous as Auchinleck's, both scribes (and/or their exemplars) clearly regarded inclusion of the Vulgate as necessary. Since they paraphrase loosely rather than translate literally, and do not include the full text of the psalms, the poems were obviously not used, nor intended to be used, as English–Latin cribs. The Latin does not serve an educational purpose, although the dutiful reader might seek out the full Gallican text on the basis of the cues offered. For most others, however, it seems likely that the Latin serves as a reminder of the status of both poems as responses to biblical material with which they may well have been aurally familiar from liturgical contexts. The fact that its function is primarily decorative does not, however, indicate that the Latin is without purpose. Even if it is not understood, by its very presence and by the simple fact of its difference from the vernacular, it may well alert audiences to the necessity of a reverent mode of reading. It exploits the obvious power of what Zieman would call 'ritualized language'.

In many of the manuscripts containing Maidstone's *Penitential Psalms*, the Latin seems intended to function rather differently. Audiences are more obviously invited to engage thoughtfully with the Vulgate as an aspect of their reading experience. All manuscripts containing Maidstone's poem, complete and partial, reproduce the Vulgate text, in full or in part, and in the great majority, the Latin is distinguished from the vernacular by means of colour. In Oxford, BodlL Laud Misc 174 (one of the relatively few manuscripts to preserve Maidstone's poem in full), for example, each complete Latin verse, with standard abbreviations, is supplied in red, prefaced by a blue initial with red penwork flourishes which become more expansive in the latter part of the text. The verse is then followed by the relevant vernacular stanza, written in brown ink throughout. The poem's relatedness

---

[7] See the high-quality digital reproduction of Auchinleck at <http://auchinleck.nls.uk/>, ff. 280rb–vb.

to biblical material is highlighted further in this manuscript, and in several others, by the introductory 'here begynnyth þe seuen psalmes' (f. 1r) and concluding 'here endun þe vii psalmes / here begynnyþ Benedicite' (f. 24v), both in red.[8] Such incipits and explicits draw attention to the text's status as a reproduction of a liturgically familiar set of psalms rather than to its nature as literary artefact.

The more or less standard scheme of red-ink Latin introduced with a blue initial and followed by brown-ink vernacular also operates in Oxford, BodlL Douce 141, which contains Maidstone's Psalm 50 in the company of more substantial devotional and homiletic material in the vernacular. Following immediately on *The Abbey of the Holy Ghost*, it begins with no introduction at the very bottom of a folio (f. 145r) with the first verse in Latin and the first two lines of the paraphrase (a space is left for a three-line 'M'). Apparently deciding that Maidstone's poem deserved more of an introduction than this, the scribe then begins the paraphrase again at the top of the verso page, with a four-line blue initial 'M' decorated with red penwork, followed by the full Latin verse in red. This is a system which is replicated throughout. The full Latin text is also included in Oxford, BodlL Digby 102, where the poem appears towards the end of the manuscript (on f. 128r a red marginal note introduces it as the 'vij psalmes' and on f. 136r it is concluded with 'Explicit vij ps'). The Vulgate original is in a bigger script than the English throughout and is consistently underlined in red. But other than these fairly standard features of presentation, the poem's *mise-en-page* in Digby is anomalous and interesting: it is set out entirely as prose, although red slashes divide the verse lines throughout. Its omission of linear verse divisions suggests that attention is being focused less on the poem's artistry and more on its status as biblical vernacularization and commentary. Insofar as the prose layout of the English mirrors the prose layout of the Gallican, the manuscript also invites a comparative reading of the two languages in a way that manuscripts which foreground the difference between Latin prose and vernacular verse do not. In fact, in its prose arrangement, combined with its use of size and underlining to distinguish the Latin from the English, the Digby 102 copy of Maidstone has visual affinities with copies of Rolle's English translation and commentary. Clearly, for some scribes and readers, Maidstone's was a paraphrase to consider in relation to its biblical source in an act of earnest and reflective meditation.

In the case of Maidstone manuscripts more generally, the prominent inclusion of the Latin also contributes to a very particular sense that the paraphrase is being deliberately keyed into the devotional rhythms of the liturgy, providing the reader with the opportunity and terminology to meditate on its resonances in the vernacular. Maidstone's affinities, both linguistic and codicological, with primer-based devotion have already been noted in the course of this book, but it is worth adding that in Oxford, BodlL Digby 18, which follows the standard

---

[8] As is generally the case in manuscripts containing Maidstone's poem, in Laud Misc 174 the psalms are not numbered and there is no gap between them. In keeping with the manuscript as a whole, they are very neatly presented, although they distinguish themselves from its further contents by means of their larger script.

system of presentation for the text, his poem is followed immediately by a copy of the 'ne reminiscaris' prayer (which, as we know, often follows the Penitential Psalms in primers) and then, beginning on the same folio (64v), by the litany. The inclusion of a calendar at the opening of the manuscript indicates incontrovertibly that Maidstone's poem was being read as part of a liturgical, or quasi-liturgical, pattern of prayer. In further confirmation of this point, it is also worth reminding ourselves of the fact that Maidstone's poem actually finds its way into a Latin Book of Hours in New York, Pierpont Morgan Library, M.99 (ff. 92r–159r). Given that the poem is being read in such contexts, the foregrounding of the liturgically resonant Latin makes perfect sense.[9]

Of course, there are manuscripts containing Maidstone's poem in which the Latin is not so obviously highlighted. In Oxford, BodlL Ashmole 61, for example, the Latin and English are not differentiated by any means other than the slightly enlarged Latin initial which introduces each of the Seven Psalms. And in Oxford, BodlL Douce 232, although the Latin (in full, with standard abbreviations of individual words) is in a more formal script than the English, it is in the same brown ink. Finally, in the manuscript roll preserved in London, BL Add. 11306, the Vulgate and the vernacular are written in a consistently neat hand using the same brown ink. Although spaces have been left for initial letters at the beginning of each verse, suggesting that the scribe intended to add red or blue detailing at some point, this was never executed.[10] On each of these occasions, however, it seems likely that economic concerns (both financial and spatial) had a part to play, and the fact remains that however undistinguished—and indistinguishable—the presentation of the Latin might be, it is a constant presence in manuscripts containing Maidstone's poem. The vernacular poem is, it would seem, at its most meaningful when considered in conjunction with its Gallican original. For some, the Latin may have been purely ornamental but for others it appears likely to have played its part in a devotional engagement with the resonances of both source and target languages.

The story differs somewhat in the case of Brampton's penitential paraphrase. In some manuscripts, the layout is very similar to that of Maidstone's poem, the full Latin text accompanying the English response. The copy in London, BL Sloane 1853 is a case in point. It is introduced on f. 3r with 'Hic incipiunt septem psalmi penitentiales de latino translati in Anglicum' (here begin the Seven Penitential Psalms translated from Latin into English), an *incipit* which makes no reference to the text's status as expansive verse paraphrase. Brampton's poem is given an identity only in relation to its source ('de latino translati'), to which it advertises its debt throughout: each verse of the Vulgate is written in red ink, introduced with a blue initial, and is followed by the verse paraphrase in brown ink, introduced with alternate red and blue initials. However, the vernacular still makes its presence felt.

---

[9] Digby 18 attributes the poem to Rolle: On f. 38r (in red) we read 'Here bigynneþ þe prologue of þe seuene salmys in englysche by Richard hampole heremyte.'

[10] At the end of the poem (on leaf 40 as the manuscript is now preserved), the scribe has added 'Qui scripsit carmen sit benedictus amen' [may he who wrote the poem be blessed].

As with the presentation of the Auchinleck Psalm 50, Sloane's version of Brampton also insists visually on the importance of the English paraphrase. While each of the Seven Psalms is introduced by a two-line blue Latin initial, decorated with red ('D'(omine)) in the case of Psalm 6, for example), this is matched immediately below by a two-line red vernacular initial, decorated with blue ('L'(ord) in the case of Psalm 6) introducing the verse translation. It is tempting to read this apparent jostling for space on the manuscript page as indicative of an emerging vernacular engaging competitively with the traditional preeminence of the liturgical Latin, claiming that it has the same right to be heard. Here, for the first time in this chapter, we might be said to witness an attempt to displace the linguistic preeminence of the original. However, that the two languages could work in cooperation, and were recognized as capable of doing so, is indicated by the Sloane scribe's treatment of Psalm 50. Beginning '*M*iserere mei' in the Latin and '*M*ercy lord' in the English, the psalm is introduced with a single, four-line 'M' in place of the two initials (the first Latin and the second English) that he uses for the other six psalms.[11] It is of course a fortunate coincidence which allows the two languages to work in tandem on the manuscript page. But that the scribe recognizes and capitalizes, quite literally, on the equivalence of Latin and English at this point is significant, as well as being indicative of his own thoughtful engagement with the work of transcription. As we will see later in this chapter, scribes did not always manage to resolve such coincidences so neatly.

While Sloane 1853, including the full Latin original alongside the poetic paraphrase, invites a reading similar to that invited by manuscripts containing Maidstone's poem, other manuscripts containing Brampton's poem differ markedly, and dispense entirely with the Vulgate. In both CUL Ff.2.38 and Cambridge, Magdalene College, Pepys 1584, for example, the only appearance that Latin makes is in the '*ne reminiscaris*' refrain which concludes each stanza and which is not distinguished from the rest of the text by means of script, colour, or size. Of course, both CUL Ff.2.38 and the closely related Pepys 1584 are obviously devotional compilations and contain nothing to suggest that Brampton's poem should be read as anything other than a devout, meditative text, but the fact that they do not include the Vulgate text is striking. Readers are being invited to engage with the poem without registering explicitly its status as a paraphrase of biblical material or an adaptation of liturgically familiar phraseology. The offering of the title '[t]he seale of mercy' as an alternative to 'the vij salmes' in Pepys 1584 suggests further that an attempt is being made to assert a literary identity for the poem independent of its psalmic indebtedness. Such features of manuscript presentation tally neatly with the suggestion, made already in this book, that Brampton's paraphrase is a particularly accomplished verse elaboration on the psalms which stakes a claim for itself to be considered as a vernacular work of some literary merit in its own right.

---

[11] See the reproduction of Sloane 1853, f. 14v as Figure 1.3. The infilled, four-line 'M' at the bottom of the page functions as the initial for the Latin 'Miserere' as well as the English 'Mercy'.

This being the case, it should not surprise us that manuscripts containing Lydgate's highly wrought psalm paraphrases are also somewhat inconsistent in advertising their indebtedness to the Latin original. Some make perfectly clear Lydgate's reliance on the text of the Bible: the copy of *Judica Me Deus* in Oxford, BodlL Hatton 73, for example, distinguishes Latin from English by means of red ink (with a blue initial) for the former (ff. 5r–6r). And the copy of *De Profundis* in Oxford, BodlL, Laud Misc. 683 (a quarto volume containing only Lydgate) differentiates the two languages even more clearly. Throughout, the full Latin verse is reproduced in red ink (with a blue initial and some marginal red flourishes) and is then followed, after a space, by the English verse elaboration, in brown ink. On other occasions, however, the Latin is dealt with in a perfunctory manner, appearing to have been added as something of an afterthought. Such is the case, for example, with Oxford, BodlL Ashmole 59's presentation of Lydgate's *Deus in Nomine* (ff. 69v–70v). At the very top of f. 69v we are told that the poem is a '[t]ranslacioun of þe salme deus in nomine tuo', which follows a note at the bottom of the previous folio (f. 69r) informing us that we are about to encounter 'þe salme of deus in nomine tuo' translated 'owte of latyne in to englisshe by Lydegate daun Johan'. Yet for all this emphasis on the poem's status as a 'translacioun' from 'latyne in to englisshe', the scribe in fact supplies us with no more than minimal Vulgate incipits which he has scribbled in the margins in the same brown ink as the rest of the text. On two occasions, he puts the incipits in the wrong place and has to cross them out and reposition or replace them. Clearly, in the mind of this scribe at least, Lydgate's accomplished English verse takes precedence over the Latin biblical material to which it responds. As was the case with the two Brampton manuscripts discussed earlier, our focus is guided resolutely to the vernacular. We are not being asked to 'shuttle' between two languages in quite the same way as we are asked when reading Maidstone manuscripts.

Should we, then, read this downgrading (and, on occasion, omission) of the Latin as symptomatic of an aggressive act of territorial expansion on the part of the vernacular? It is certainly tempting to do so, but it does not tell the whole story. In common with so much contemporary vernacular literature, the English psalms rely for their claims to authority and excellence on their annexing of Latin 'prestige', whether that annexing is advertised or not. A translation cannot properly exist without an original.

THE ENGLISH PRIMER MANUSCRIPTS

When we turn to the vernacular psalms preserved in the primers, however, we find that once again the comparative positioning of Latin and English raises pressing questions about the nature of the relationship between the two languages in late-medieval England. Our attention is demanded insistently by both Vulgate and translation, which feature throughout the extant manuscripts in different ways and to different extents. In fact, the layout of the psalms in the English primer manuscripts impresses upon us more forcefully than any other contemporary codices the importance of viewing vernacular literature in the context of its Latin affinities. Reading the psalms in these manuscripts and observing attempts to negotiate space for the two on the page alerts us to the tensions, as well as harmonies, in the out-workings of any relationship between original and translation.

The fact that both languages feature is not surprising: with very few exceptions, everything about these manuscripts suggests that they were intended to function in liturgical and quasi-liturgical contexts. Whether they were being used in church services by devout individuals wanting to follow the recitation of the Latin liturgy, or in the context of private, extra-ecclesiastical but nonetheless ordered devotion, inclusion of the Latin incipits would have served to anchor the reader in the aurally familiar rhythms of public prayer.[12] Although none of the extant manuscripts contains any of the figural illumination so characteristic of Latin Books of Hours produced in England and on the Continent, they are very clearly modelled on such Latin books of private devotion. Several contain elaborate, professionally executed illustration and decoration: they are not volumes designed to be hidden away. Almost all use the formal textura script characteristic of Latin Books of Hours and also preserve the latters' substantial, often illuminated, margins around a neatly contained single column of text, conveying an impression of space and, on occasion, luxury. With the exception of Oxford, University College 179, they also replicate Latin volumes in terms of their shape and size: all are obviously intended for private use, the smallest being that contained in London, BL Add. 17011, which could fit easily into a pocket. Unsurprisingly given its size, this volume contains no marginal decoration, nor any of the gold leaf illumination characteristic of other English primers, but its neat script is far from cramped and its layout far from miserly. Each folio preserves the substantial margins typical of Latin prayer-books, reminding users of the primer's liturgical origin and function.

Among the most impressive of the English primer manuscripts is Oxford, BodlL Rawlinson C. 699. Slightly larger than the 'standard' primer, it contains a significant amount of catechetic data in addition to its liturgical material, but it is the latter which is presented with most care and ornamentation. Gold leaf is used extensively throughout, marking the beginning of each psalm and, often, of individual verses within each psalm. While the initial to each psalm is gold, enclosed in alternately blue and red boxing, the smaller initials to individual verses are, alternately, blue with red decoration and gold with blue decoration. In addition, elaborate border decoration, incorporating intricate vines, sprays, and flowers, marks each Hour as well as other important divisions, including the beginning of the Penitential psalms. Smaller than Rawlinson but nonetheless visually appealing is Oxford, BodlL Douce 246, which survives in its original fifteenth-century binding and is, of all extant primers, the most engaging as a book of private devotion. Part

---

[12] As is well known, in chapter 9 of her *Book*, Margery Kempe refers to herself as kneeling in church, 'heldyng down hir hed, [with] hir boke in hir hand, praying owyr Lord Crist Jhesu for grace and for mercy'. It is possible, though of course unproveable, that a vernacular primer is the sort of book that Margery Kempe might have owned. See B. Windeatt, *The Book of Margery Kempe*, Longman Annotated Texts (Harlow, 2000), p. 83/658–60.

of its appeal of course lies in its evocative inclusion, on fol. 8ᵛ, of the note 'Deyd Agnes Orges my wyff Hausaber in Harflu(r?) in the 3ere of our Lord miiijᶜᶜᶜᶜxlvj', providing us with a tantalizing glimpse into its early provenance.[13] But it is also very sensitively presented and illuminated. Its use of gold leaf is not extravagant but works effectively when combined with finely executed borders decorated with burgundy, green, blue, and black detailing.[14] The copy contained in Oxford, BodlL Ashmole 1288 also insists visually on its liturgical affinities, incorporating extensive gold leaf and a significant amount of marginal decoration at important points. Its incomplete state, however, is suggested by the fact that although several further folios are apparently ruled for marginal decoration, they remain blank. Clearly, it was intended to be more luxurious than it is as it now stands.[15] Another copy whose visual appeal is somewhat dulled (though for reasons rather different from those which pertain in the case of Ashmole 1288) is that found in London, BL Add. 27592. While the surviving text, in its use of gold leaf illumination, suggests that as a whole the manuscript was of a decorative status comparable to that of the two Bodley manuscripts already discussed, miniature hunters have removed a significant proportion of what would have been illustrated initials. Entire folios that, on the evidence of other primers, would have contained elaborately detailed borders, have also been removed. The beginning of Matins itself, for example, is missing, as is the beginning of the Penitential Psalms, meaning that the first complete text is that of Psalm 50.

Not all primers are this finely decorated or executed, however, and in this context, the copy in Oxford, BodlL Douce 275 is particularly noteworthy. While it is in a neat and consistent hand throughout, its illuminations are basic and its margins not those of a luxurious liturgical volume. It has large gold leaf initials on a blue and burgundy background at the beginning of important offices and devotions, but the marginal decoration is simple and there is no use of further colours other than the standard blue and red. It appears to be trying to look like a liturgical volume, but its illustrations are not executed by as sophisticated an individual as those whose work we see in other of the Middle English primers. In other manuscripts, however, no attempt is made to approximate the luxuriant detailing of liturgical volumes: the primer in Glasgow, University Library Hunter 472, for example, uses the textura script and generous margins characteristic of Books of Hours but contains no gold leaf illumination. That in Oxford, University College

---

[13] This indication of provenance was noted in Chapter 1.

[14] See the reproduction of f. 11r on the dust-jacket of this book. Opening with Psalm 50: 17, cited in part in Latin and in full in English ('Domine labia mea aperies. Lorde þou schalt opene my lyppes and my mouþe schal schew þy preysynge'), this folio marks the beginning of Matins.

[15] The fact that Ashmole 1288 was heavily used is indicated by the state of f. 9r, on which Matins begins (see the reproduction, as Figure 4.1). Below the red-ink introduction 'here bigynneþ mateyns of oure lady modir of oure lord ihesu crist' is a seven-line 'L' marking the opening of the vernacular Psalm 50: 17 'Lord þou schalt opene my lippis' (the abbreviated red-ink Latin incipit 'Dne labia' has been forced outside the ruled area and nudges the decorated border). Blue on a gold background infilled with blue and burgundy vines, the initial's ink is very smudged, perhaps suggesting that it has been touched repeatedly.

179 has absolutely no affinities with liturgical texts in terms of size, layout, script, or detailing. Both are manuscripts to which we will return.

As stated earlier, the English psalms in these primers are, without exception, accompanied by quotation from their Vulgate original. In the great majority of cases, this takes the form of red-ink incipits, which tend to be of one or two words only, prefacing individual psalms. In the humbler manuscripts, this is a scheme which works well and creates an impression of clarity; such, for example, is the case in London, BL Add. 17011, which also marks verses using alternating blue and red English initials. One imagines that it would have been fairly easy to use this vernacular manuscript to follow Latin liturgical recitation: its previously noted small size indicates that the user could have done this unobtrusively. A similarly basic scheme is used in Glasgow, Hunter 472. However, in manuscripts whose decorative scheme is more elaborate, negotiating the co-existence of the two languages can become difficult. The copy in Oxford, BodlL Bodley 85 is a case in point. The beginning of Matins, on f. 7r, is enclosed by a full border (blue and gold with decorative detailing extending into the margins) within which the first item is a full, red-ink Latin incipit to Psalm 50: 17 ('Domine labia mea aperies et os meum annuntiabit laudem tuam' [O Lord, thou wilt open my lips: and my mouth shall declare thy praise]) introduced by a two-line gold-leaf 'D'. This is then followed, immediately below, by a much more substantial four-line decorated blue and burgandy 'L'(ord) on a gold background, which introduces the English translation. Somewhat dwarfing the Latin 'D', the English 'L' attracts the eye and insists on the status of the translation as at least equivalent to that of the Latin. On a smaller scale, this pattern is repeated throughout the manuscript: gold Latin initials introduce individual psalms and are matched immediately by slightly larger English initials encased in gold leaf and decorated with blue and burgundy vines. It is a scheme which leads the scribe into an awkward situation on f. 52r where Psalm 31, which begins with a 'B' in both Latin ('Beati quorum . . .') and English ('Blessed ben thei . . .'), is introduced by two 'B's which almost exactly mirror each other, although the English is slightly bigger.[16] Unlike the Sloane 1853 scribe of Brampton's paraphrase, who registers that Psalm 50 begins with an 'M' in both the Latin and the translation, and replaces his customary two initials with one, the Bodley 85 scribe allows the page to be crowded by a duplication of detail. The difference between the two is telling. The Brampton scribe's dual functioning 'M' acts as an effective demonstration of equality between source and translation, between Latin and English as languages of personal devotion. It suggests, momentarily, that in the process of translation no fundamental change take place. One language simply 'becomes' another. In such a context, issues of deference and displacement do not arise. In Bodley 85, however, the duplication of 'B's might be read as suggesting that the two languages are not working in total cooperation. Both are necessary

---

[16] See the reproduction of f. 52r as Figure 6.1. Both 'B's occupy the space of approximately two-and-a-half lines but although they almost exactly mirror each other, the 'B' which begins the English 'Blessed' extends a little further across the page than that which begins the Latin 'Beati'. The marginal foliage extending down from the English 'B' is also longer than that which stretches up from the Latin 'B'.

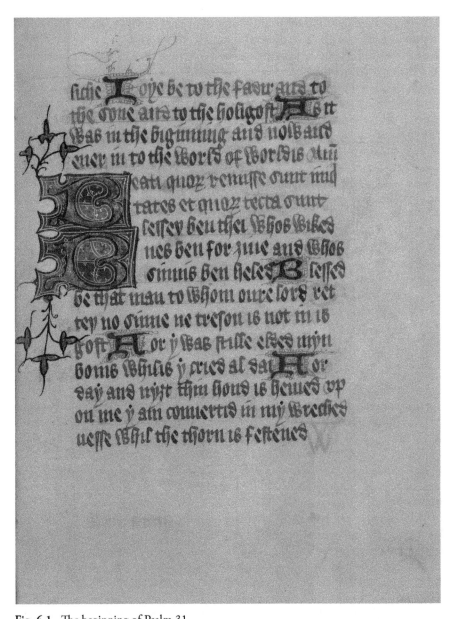

Fig. 6.1. The beginning of Psalm 31

and neither will cede any ground to the other. In this particular situation, intimations of cultural competition are difficult to avoid.

In other primer manuscripts, the size and decorative features of the vernacular script mean that there is little space left for the Latin. In London, BL Add. 27592, for example, the Vulgate cues are so brief and abbreviated as to be virtually invisible, were it not for the red ink in which they are written.[17] They are, in addition, outsized by the two-line gold initials which follow them, and which highlight the beginning of the English translation rather than the Latin original. In the Ashmole 1288 primer, the situation is rather more extreme: as discussed, in this manuscript the opening of Matins (f. 9r) is heralded by an intricately infilled seven-line 'L', marking the beginning of Psalm 50: 17 (in English). It occupies almost half the width of the written area within the intricately decorated border and leaves so little room for the abbreviated red-ink Latin incipit 'Dne labia' [Lord, open thou my lips] that the scribe has to move beyond the rulings, encroaching into the top right-hand area of the border in an attempt to squeeze in the words of the Vulgate.[18] The Latin source is, quite literally, marginalized. At the beginning of the Penitential Psalms (f. 55v), the layout is neater: a line at the top of the bordered area is reserved for the red-ink Latin incipit ('Domine ne in furore tua ar' [O Lord, rebuke me not in thy indignation]). This is then followed, on the line below, by a six-line blue 'L' on a gold leaf background, decorated with blue and burgundy vines and leaves, marking the beginning of the English translation 'Lord repreue þou not me . . .'. Yet although the Latin is here accommodated within the spatial arrangements of the page, the impression remains that it is the vernacular psalm on which we should be focusing our devotional attention.[19] An interesting exception to this apparent trend towards the privileging of the vernacular, however, is to be found at the beginning of Matins in Cambridge, St. John's College G.24. Here, it is emphatically the decorated and infilled Latin 'D'(omine) which dominates the page, taking up over half the width of the bordered area and occupying a ten-line space. Yet for all 'D's apparent mastery of the page, it is worth noting that the Latin incipits in this primer are no fuller than those in any of the manuscripts already discussed.

The delicately illuminated Douce 246 provides us with evidence that other scribes remained undecided on how to present and incorporate both Latin and English on the manuscript page. The primer begins, on f. 11r, with the Latin incipit to Psalm 50: 17 in red ink, underlined in the same. It is introduced by a one-line gold initial 'D'(omine labia mea aperies) infilled with burgundy and encased in blue. This incipit is followed, immediately below, by a bigger (three-line) blue

---

[17] See, for example, 'Dne ex' [Hear, O Lord] for Psalm 101 (f. 22v) and 'ps de profundis cla' [out of the depths I have cried] for 129 (f. 23v).

[18] See the reproduction of f. 9r as Figure 4.1.

[19] The practice of incorporating the red-ink incipit, of the same size as the rest of the text, in the bordered area and following it with a much bigger illuminated vernacular initial is also followed in Rawlinson C. 699's aforementioned primer. At the beginning of Matins (f. 7r), for example, the very brief incipit ('Dne labia') is in the top right-hand corner and is matched, on the left side, by a four-line blue 'L' on a gold leaf background, infilled and decorated with blue and burgundy vines and sprays which extend into the margins and form part of the border.

'L', encased in gold and infilled with a burgundy vine and blue leaves, marking the beginning of the English translation. But after this, the use of gold leaf for the Latin initial ceases. Psalm 94, on the same folio, for example, is prefaced by a red-ink Vulgate incipit ('venite exultem') but the gold is reserved for the three-line 'C' which introduces the English translation ('Come glade we . . .'). And the same scheme is in use at the beginning of the Penitential Psalms (f. 43v): prefaced by a red-ink introduction 'here begynneþ þe seuene psalmes' and incipit 'Domine ne in furore tuo arguas', it is not until the two-line English 'L'(ord in thi wodenesse) that gold leaf is used. In the aforementioned Douce 275, by the time that we reach the Penitential Psalms (f. 30v), Latin incipits have disappeared: a red-ink introduction tells us 'here bigynneþ þe seuen psalmes' and immediately below we find a four-line gold 'L', infilled and surrounded with blue and burgundy, marking the beginning of the translation. It is a scheme contrasting with that used at the beginning of Matins (f. 1r) where a full red-ink incipit 'Domine labia mea aperies & os meu' precedes the five-line 'L' introducing the translated psalm.

Of course, whatever the visual status (in terms of size, colour, underlining, positioning, etc.) of the Vulgate *incipits* in these manuscripts, their function is the same: their brevity surely indicates that their primary purpose must have been to facilitate liturgical cross-referencing, psalm by psalm, for those not literate in Latin. At the most basic level, they function in place of a system of numbering and are, quite simply, necessary. This being the case, further speculation as to the nature of their interactions with the vernacular psalms they accompany might be argued to be pointless. But the very fact that the English psalms rely on them in order to be fully functional is worthy of note, confirming Wogan-Browne's assertion that in the late Middle Ages the 'theory and practice of vernacular writing [is tied] permanently to the question of its status in relation to Latin'. It would be a mistake, however, to regard this as necessarily limiting or stifling. Going some way towards facilitating the matching of English translation with Vulgate original, it is conceivable that the *incipits* could have been intended to serve an educational purpose in tandem with their devotional emphasis. The fact that the two were by no means at odds was emphasized in the very first chapter of this book. In fact, one of the extant Middle English manuscripts (Glasgow, Hunter 472) contains a particular indication that it was intended for educational use. Beginning with a cross-row (an ABC, prefaced by a two-line red-ink cross and concluding in 'est. amen') it then launches directly into catechetic basics (ff. 1–5v) including the Lord's Prayer, the Hail Mary, and the Creed, etc. After this, it contains a calendar and primer (f. 6r–71v), followed by further catechetic essentials (ff. 71v–87r). As discussed, Hunter 472 is among the most decoratively basic of the Middle English primers and it seems eminently possible that this relatively humble volume was intended for use as a school text: in fact, a marginal annotation from a later reader states that it is a good and profitable book 'for a man that can not understond Latyn'.[20]

---

[20] Prior to the opening of the text, the flyleaves have been used by a fifteenth-century reader to copy out further prayers.

But it cannot be the case that the English translations were simply intended to guide readers towards a better grasp of the Latin. The vernacular does not always serve as the humble handmaid to the Vulgate. Rather, it seems more likely that the traffic was two-way. Yes, the English could have been used to parse the Latin, although as I will discuss later in this chapter, the extensive abbreviations of the Vulgate language would have made this problematic for many. Equally, however, one could argue that the Latin was being used as a springboard to launch the pious reader into a world of vernacular prayer and devotion. As we know very well from other contemporary texts and contexts, by no means does Latin function in the manner of a straitjacket stifling vernacular development and creativity. As Bruce Holsinger has commented, in a striking phrase first quoted in the introduction and of particular relevance here:

> [F]ar from exercising a conservative or regressive grip upon vernacular invention, [Latin] liturgical cultures functioned as powerful engines of vernacular making.[21]

Nonetheless, it is difficult to see how, in practice, these vernacular primers could have functioned in educational contexts as English to Latin prompts without a degree of cumbersome manoeuvring on the part of the user. Outside the context of liturgical recitation, a reader wanting to follow the full Latin text simultaneously would have needed to have had two volumes open at any one time.[22]

However, in two of the extant vernacular manuscripts, this dilemma is solved: both Glasgow, Hunter 512 and Oxford, University College 179 contain the full Latin text of the liturgical primer in conjunction with its English translation, with which it alternates verse by verse. In fact, at the beginning of the first office (f. 37r), Hunter 512 uniquely advertises itself as 'Matines of oure ladye in latyn and englisch'.[23] In almost all ways, this manuscript mirrors the layout of the contemporary volumes already discussed: it is of a size appropriate to personal use, preserves the single columns, large margins, and ornamented initials characteristic of Books of Hours (although it lacks figural illustration), and is written in a neat and consistent textura. It differs, however, insofar as our visual attention is drawn insistently towards the Latin. The aforementioned beginning of Matins, for example, is heralded by a six-line blue and burgundy initial 'D'(omine labia me aperies) on a gold leaf background, infilled with burgundy and blue decoration. It is an introduction which, quite literally, dwarfs the subsequent English translation, marked by a one-line red 'L', and contrasts strikingly with the opening of Matins as presented in Bodley 85, Douce 246, Ashmole 1288, and Rawlinson C.699. Further, although the same brown ink is used for both English and Latin throughout, the latter consistently distinguishes itself by means of red underlining which serves not only to highlight the difference in language, but also, perhaps, to suggest a hierarchy of sorts: it is the Latin text to which the English is responding.

[21] Holsinger, p. 300.
[22] Even Hunter 472, which begins with an alphabet, has only the minimal red-ink incipits characteristic of most other extant primers.
[23] See the reproduction of f. 37r as Figure 1.1.

It seems perfectly possible, then, that Hunter 512 was intended to function as a schoolbook of sorts, designed for use in a formal educational environment or in the context of more informal relationships (familial and/or clerical). For the non-Latinate it provides an accessible introduction to the practice of parsing, even translating. Yet once again, to view the English as humble handmaid to the Latin would be to miss the point. A volume such as Hunter 512 could have been used by readers keen to further their knowledge of Latin. But equally, it may have proved useful to those interested in the practice of translation *from* Latin *to* English. It is the target language which is of as much interest as the source in Hunter 512. The manuscript accompanies this literal function with extensive catechetic material promoting the moral health of the reader.[24] It is an educative volume in the fullest sense of the word.

The survival of primers containing complete English and Latin translations of the psalms is not surprising: as discussed in Chapter 1, the Psalter was viewed as a foundational text in facilitating the acquisition of literacy and it makes sense to suppose that it would have been used to support and encourage the practice of translation from Latin to English, promoting understanding of the workings of both. Contemporary evidence in fact confirms that this was the case, the anonymous 'Cambridge Tract 1' commenting that:

[I]n skolis þei construen þe Sauter, gospel and pestil on Englische, and so lernen to make translacion from Latyn into Englische. And þei writen in Englische wiþ þe Latyn, to rede it aȝen ȝif it need to haue it freschly in mynde.[25]

It is of course obvious that the Hunter 512 primer was not produced or used in precisely this way. Its English rendition of the psalms is not an independent effort constructed in a classroom setting but, as discussed in Chapter 4, has close and obvious affinities with the Wycliffite translations. It must have been deployed as a basis for parsing and is unlikely to have originated from a practice exercise in the art of translation.

However, the contents and layout of the only other extant fully bilingual primer, contained in Oxford, University College 179, suggest that it may well derive from such a context. Singled out as anomalous in Chapter 4's discussion of primers, University 179 differs from all other extant contemporary volumes in three key respects, excluding its bilinguality, which it obviously shares with Hunter 512.[26]

[24] Hunter 512's substantial body of catechetic material (in the vernacular with the exception of the last two items) is as follows: the ten comaundments; the seuene deedly synnes; the seuene werkis of mercy bodily; the seuene goostly werkis of mercy; thre principal vertues (feith, hope and charity); the fyue bodily wittis (Seynge, Heerynge, Smellynge, Taistynge, and feelynge); the fyue goostly wittis (Mynde, Undirstondynge, Wille, Resoun, and ymagynacioun); the seuene ghiftis of the hooly gost; the foure cardynal vertues; the seune sacramentis; the sixe maner consentyng to synne; ffour thingis neden to ech man if the word of god schal profite to hym; the articles of bileve; quotations from John 15 and Leviticus 19; Pater noster; Credo; Ympne (Ihesu swete is the loue of thee); Oracio ad sanctam crucem; De sancta Katerina antiphona.
[25] Dove (2010), p. 93/141–4.
[26] In one respect, its bilinguality differs from that of Hunter 512, in which the liturgical material appears in both Latin and English, while the catechetic additions are in the vernacular only (with the exception of the last two items). In University 179, by contrast, both liturgy and catechesis are bilingual.

First, in its size and shape (close to modern A4) as well as layout and presentation, it has nothing in common with Books of Hours. Second, its treatment of the Latin and English differs from that to which we are accustomed. And finally, its translation of the psalms has no obvious or consistent connection with either Wycliffite version. Dealing initially with the first point, University 179 makes no use of gold leaf or illumination and has no borders or marginal decoration. It is written in the same brown ink throughout, punctuated with red initials, and does not use the neat textura characteristic of other primers. It is simply not designed to be of aesthetic appeal; University 179 is a functional volume, a devotional and catechetic notebook.[27] As to the second point, the scribe alternates Latin and English throughout, verse by verse, as is the case in Hunter 512. It is, however, noteworthy that he reverses Hunter's mode of presentation: rather than underlining the Latin original, he (or an early reader) underlines in red (somewhat inconsistently) the English translation, leaving the Vulgate text unadorned other than by the red initial with which each verse begins. It is the vernacular on which our attention is focused, the apparently unique translation from the Latin.

Turning to the third, and perhaps most significant, difference, University 179's translation of the psalms falls comfortably into neither Group A nor B as outlined in Chapter 4, although it inevitably has some similarities with both.[28] Most interesting in this context is Psalm 101: 2–4 ('Domine exaudi orationem meam et clamor meus ad te veniat. Non avertas faciem tuam a me: in quacumque die tribulor inclina ad me aurem tuam. In quacumque die invocavero te velociter exaudi me. Quia defecerunt sicut fumus dies mei et ossa mea sicut gremium aruerunt' [Hear, O Lord, my prayer: and let my cry come to thee. Turn not away thy face from me: in the day when I am in trouble, incline thy ear to me. In what day soever I shall call upon thee, hear me speedily. For my days are vanished like smoke: and my bones are grown dry like fuel for the fire). The verse is translated thus in the Group A primers:

> Lord, here þou my preier; and my cry come to þee. Turne not awey þi face from me. In what euer dai y am trublid, bowe doun þin eere to me! In what euer dai y schal inwardly clepe þee, here þou me swifteli. For my daies han failid as smoke & my bones drieden up as critouns. (Cambridge, CUL Dd.11.82)

---

[27] For a full list of contents, see *IMEP* VIII (Ogilvie-Thomson), pp. 121–4. It does contain many of the catechetic basics (in Latin and English) such as the Lord's Prayer, the Creed, the Absolution, and a Confession. But it also contains several additional prayers (again, in both Latin and English) including intercessions to be made before meals. In it we also find a copy of the Abbreviated Psalter of St Jerome in alternate Latin and English.

[28] Psalm 6 begins (f. 38r) 'Lord yn þi wodenes repreue not me ne yn þi wreþ sle not me. Lord haue mercy on me for y am syke. Hele me lord for my bones be togeder strublid. And my soule ys strubled ful moch but þou lorde forsoþe.' Psalm 31 (f. 38v): 'þey be blessed whace wikkidnesses be for3iffen and whace synnes be hid. þat man ys blissed to wam oure lord put no syn ne in whace spirit ys no trecchry.' Psalm 37 (f. 39r): 'Lord yn þi wodenes repreue not me ne in þy wreþ sle not me. For þyn arwes be fastned on me & þou hast confermed þyn hand on me. þer is no helþe yn my flesch fro þe face of þi wreþ.' Psalm 50 (f. 39r): 'God haue mercy on me after þi grete mercy. And after þe mochnes of þi for3iffynges do awey my wikkidnes.' Psalm 101 (f. 40v): 'lord here myn orison and my cry come yt to þe. Turne þi face fro me in what day þat y am strublid bowe þyn ere to me. In what day þat y clepe þe whitly here me. Ffor my dayes han fayled as smoke and my bones haue dried as a lappe.'

and thus in Group B:

> Lord, here my preiere: and my cri come to the. Torne nou3t a wey thi face fro me. In
> what day y be in tribulation bowe thyn ere to me. In what day I clepe to the swiftly-
> che here me. For my dayes faylede as smoke and my bones ben dreyed as kretones.
> (Cambridge, St. John's College, G 24)

In University 179, however, we read:

> Lord here myn orison and my cry come yt to þe. Turne þi face fro me in what day þat
> y am strublid bowe þyn ere to me. In what day þat y clepe þe whitly here me. Ffor
> my dayes han fayled as smoke and my bones haue dried as a lappe.

Aside from University 179's obvious omission of the Vulgate 'non', turning the
Psalmist's plea for attention into quite the reverse, it is the translation of 'gremium'
[firewood, but also lap or flap of skin] that is of most note here. It is a word
which caused some problems for Middle English translators: the *Metrical Psalter*
has 'krawken', Rolle 'kraghen', the *Prose* 'craukes', and EV 'croote'. LV translates
'gremium' as 'critouns', but in one manuscript this is glossed 'ether leefing of fri-
jng' and in two others 'that is, that that dwellith in the panne of the friyng'.[29]
Maidstone's paraphrase is similarly explanatory ('my boones beþ dryed & al þour3e
soke / Like a þing þat is forfryed' and Brampton's is purely allusive ('My boones
weren strong and myghty made / But now þey clynge and waxen all drye'). It is
only in University 179, however, that 'gremium' is translated as 'lappe'. According
to the Middle English Dictionary, 'lappe' has several possible meanings: it can
denote a lap or bosom but can also indicate a loose flap of clothing or skin. Both
meanings apply to the Latin 'gremium', which can also denote 'firewood'. It seems
that most Middle English translators picked up on the word's association with
charred remains, but University 179's vernacularization indicates that 'gremium' is
probably being understood as a loose flap of skin or clothing (which, in context,
makes more sense than 'lap' or 'bosom'). It is possible that such a departure from
prevailing Middle English tradition indicates that the translation is an independent effort, conceivably originating in the sort of educational environment evoked
by the author of Cambridge Tract 1. The fortunate survival of University 179
reminds us that for all the emphasis that the act of translation places on the target language, the constant activity of psalm vernacularization in the Middle Ages
means that the source language is being consistently engaged and re-engaged with.
The goal of these translations is not the replacement of one language with another
but the encouragement of an active relationship between the two. Nowhere is this
more obviously testified than in the two extant fully bilingual primers.

COMPLETE PSALTERS

We turn now to manuscripts containing Middle English translations of the entire
book of psalms, beginning with the earliest (the *Metrical*) and progressing to the

---

[29] See V. Edden, 'And my boonus han dried vp as critouns: the history of the translations of Psalm
101: 4', *N&Q* 28 (1981), 389–92.

latest (the Wycliffite). Obviously, given the variety of translations and the very different dates of the manuscripts in which they are preserved, it is neither easy nor desirable to trace as consistent a tradition of presentation and decoration as it is in the case of the primers, with the exception of University 179. They range from substantial and ornate to small and relatively humble, and from the carefully designed and executed to the rather more hurried and informal. But despite their differences, they almost all preserve the Gallican original—or, more commonly, some element of the same—alongside the vernacular translation. As was the case with the abbreviated and paraphrased Psalters, it is worth considering what role the Latin plays in such contexts and, in particular, how audiences were expected to negotiate movements between the two languages.

It is also worth prefacing this discussion by registering one further more or less consistent feature of the complete *Middle English Psalters*: almost without exception, they use decoration to mark liturgically important moments in the text. In most cases it is the eight-fold liturgical division which is observed (Psalms 26, 38, 52, 68, 80, 97, and 109 are marked in addition to Psalms 1 and 150), although some preserve the older ten-fold liturgical division, highlighting in addition Psalms 51 and 101.[30] Probably deriving from the thirteenth century, when scribes were inspired by the decorative patterns of French Bibles, the prevalent eight-fold division functions by highlighting the psalms (sometimes referred to as the Nocturns) with which, in secular use, Matins begins throughout the week, as well as the first psalm (109) recited at Sunday Vespers.[31] Quite what function this decorative scheme was meant to perform in English language Psalter manuscripts is not entirely clear. We have no evidence that vernacular translations were intended to supplant the Vulgate psalms for the purposes of public liturgical recitation. The ornamented divisions are not, however, simply relics of the traditional *mis-en-page* of Latin Psalters, incorporated into manuscripts containing English translations in an attempt to replicate the somewhat stately authority of the latter. On the contrary, they retain a degree of functionality insofar as they help readers to map the English translation onto its Vulgate original, should they wish to wish to follow, in the vernacular, the liturgical recitation of the Latin. At the same time, they act as bookmarks, guiding readers as they navigate their way through the dauntingly hefty complete Psalter.

The six manuscripts of the *Metrical Psalter* follow in this tradition of highlighting liturgically significant psalms. But putting the question of decoration aside for a moment, the relative positioning of Latin and English in all the extant *Metrical Psalter* manuscripts offers further intriguing indications of possible use. In terms of the amount of Latin material, none includes anything more than incipits, varying in length between copies. However, the manuscripts differ from those containing the primers in incorporating cues to individual verses as well as to complete psalms.

---

[30] Given the devotional emphasis placed on the Seven Penitential Psalms in the Middle Ages, it is interesting that none of the complete Psalters appears to distinguish them decoratively from the rest of the text. It may well be that they were seen as having a discrete identity, isolable from the Psalter as a whole.

[31] For background, see Harper, especially chapter 5 'The Psalter'.

Surviving in the form of very frequent but brief lemmata, the Vulgate does not appear as a compendious authority to which the English translation pays homage. It is, rather, a necessary source of reference into which the English translation must be 'keyed' in order for it to function appropriately.

In two copies of the *Metrical Psalter*, the Latin incipits and the full English translation form a body of continuous text at the centre of each page. In London, BL Egerton 614, each vernacular psalm begins with a Latin incipit to the first verse, introduced with a red initial. This is followed by very brief cues, sometimes nothing more than 'Et' or 'Sed', to individual verses, the initial letter alternating between red and blue. A similar pattern is adopted in Oxford, BodlL Bodley 921: the first line of each psalm is provided in Latin (with a larger blue initial decorated with flourishes extending into the margin) followed by the English rendition, all at the centre of the page. The first word of subsequent verses is then also supplied in Latin (marked by alternating blue and red initials) prior to the English verse translation. In Cambridge, Corpus Christi College 278, the presentation differs somewhat: each psalm begins with its Latin incipit, incorporated into the main body of the text as in Egerton 614 and Bodley 921, introduced by an enlarged blue initial decorated with red lines. The Latin incipits to individual verses are, however, detached from the main body of text, and appear in the margins (the left hand on verso pages, and the right hand on recto pages). Since the manuscript is carefully ruled throughout, it is very clear which incipit belongs to which couplet or quatrain. The same system is adopted in Oxford, BodlL, Bodley 425: the first full Latin line (with standard abbreviations) appears in the main body of the text, distinguished from the English translation by virtue of its bigger size and by the two- (or more) line blue initial decorated with red flourishes. Cues to individual verses, marked by alternating blue and red initials, are then supplied in the margin of each page. Two features make the matching of the English with the Latin very straightforward; first, careful and consistent ruling means that, as in Corpus Christi 248, the cues are exactly parallel with the English translation. Second, the marginal cues are mirrored by alternating blue and red paraph marks at the head of the English line to which they relate (in some cases, blue initials are matched by blue paraphs and red by red, but the pattern is in general that of alternation).

In the two remaining copies of the *Metrical Psalter*, all of the Vulgate material appears in the margins. London, BL Cotton Vespasian D. vii positions the abbreviated first line of each psalm (in red ink) in the right-hand margin.[32] Incipits to individual verses (using standard abbreviations) are also provided in the same margin, written in black ink with the initial letter infilled with red. Particularly noteworthy is the fact that the scribe (or an early user of the manuscript) has linked together the English rhyming couplets by means of two red lines ('braces') which join each other in pointing towards the marginal Latin incipit that they translate. These lines serve the dual purpose of highlighting the rhyme and clarifying the translation's relation to the Latin. The layout of London, British Library Harley

---

[32] See the full-page reproduction of BL MS Cotton Vespasian D.vii f. 1r as Figure 6.2. The entirety of Psalm 1 and the beginning of Psalm 2 appear on this folio.

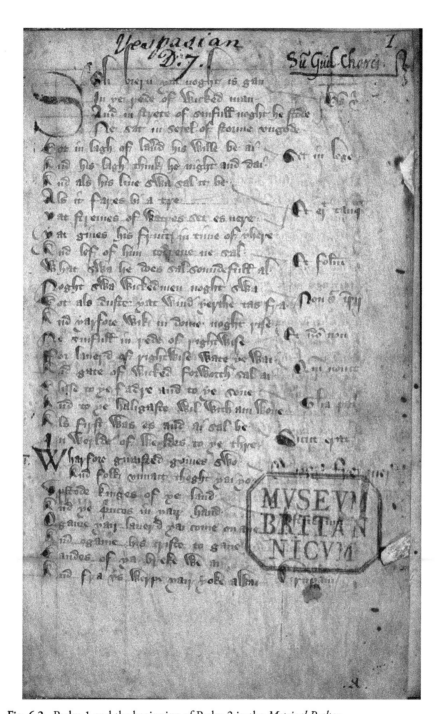

Fig. 6.2. Psalm 1 and the beginning of Psalm 2 in the *Metrical Psalter*

London, British Library MS Cotton Vespasian D.vii, f. 1r. Reproduced by kind permission of the British Library. © The British Library Board

1770's *Metrical Psalter* is similar to that of Cotton Vespasian D. vii; the abbreviated Latin first line of each psalm is given alternately in red and blue in the right-hand margin on recto pages, and in the left on verso. Incipits to individual verses are also provided in the margin, again with alternating red and blue initials. Like Cotton Vespasian D. vii, Harley 1770 also uses red lines to link together rhyming couplets, joining to form an arrow apparently intended to point to the marginal Latin incipit of the verse which they translate. On recto pages, the system functions well: the cues are in the right-hand margin and the arrows point directly towards them. On verso pages, however, the situation is more problematic: while the cues are in the left-hand margin, the arrows are in the right-hand margin, and point to the right. It is an oddity which suggests that the arrows are scribal, added to the text as it was written, and, possibly, that the incipits were added later, forced by lack of space to the left of the page after the quires had been bound together. Other indications, however, suggest that in this manuscript the red lines do not serve only to link English translation to Latin incipit, but also to highlight the occurrence of rhyme. Whoever was responsible for these arrows was as interested in drawing attention to the vernacular versification as he/she was in highlighting the link with the marginal Latin. The treatment of Psalm 2: 1–2 can serve as an example.[33] The Latin incipit of verse 1 ('Quare fremuerunt gentes') is followed by a single line extending towards a reproduction of that incipit ('Quare fremuerunt') in the right-hand margin. The vernacular translation, in the form of a rhyming couplet:

> Wherfore gnaysted genge swa
> And folc ful unnait þoht þai þa

is followed by two lines, meeting in a point, which gesture towards an empty space in the margin. There is no incipit for them to highlight. The translation of verse 2 ('The kings of the earth stood up, and the princes met together, against the Lord and against his Christ') is then spread over two couplets, reading:

> Vpstoden kinges of þe lande,
> And þe princes in þar hande
> Agayn þar God þat come in an
> And agayn þar crist to gan (f. 158r)

Yet while the two lines which extend into the right-hand margin from 'lande' and 'hande' meet in a point at the Latin incipit for the verse ('Astiterunt reges'), the two lines which then extend from 'an' and 'gan', meeting in a point, gesture towards a void; there is, once again, no text for them to highlight. The situation is resolved differently in Cotton Vespasian D. vii, where the concern is more obviously to mark the connection between Latin and English. Here, the two rhymes are indicated by two sets of converging lines, the ends of which are used as the basis for a larger arrow which then points towards the marginal Latin incipit. Although the system of red lines in this pair of manuscripts appears, on the face of it, very similar, there are obviously different priorities informing the two.

---

[33] See the reproduction of f. 158r as Figure 6.3.

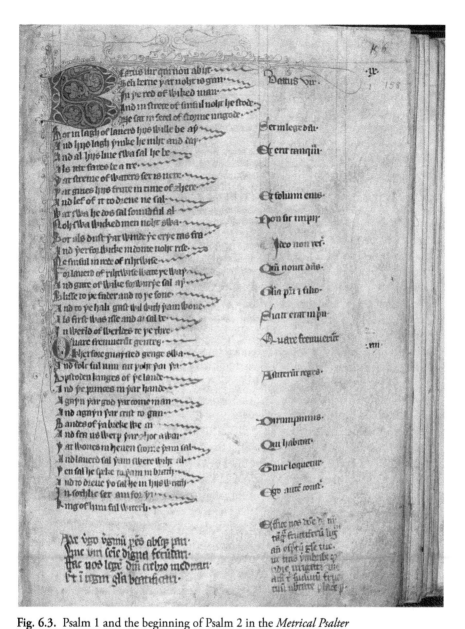

Fig. 6.3. Psalm 1 and the beginning of Psalm 2 in the *Metrical Psalter*

London, British Library MS Harley 1770, f. 158r. Reproduced by kind permission of the British Library. © *The British Library Board*

To varying degrees, then, all extant manuscripts of the *Metrical Psalter* indicate that the matching of English translation to Latin incipit was of real importance for both scribe and reader. But why? As with the primers, at the most basic level, the incipits serve as a system of identification, very probably intended to facilitate some form of liturgical cross-referencing. However, the fact that all copies include cues to individual verses as well as complete psalms might suggest that a rather different mode of comparative reading is being encouraged. These manuscripts are intended for readers wanting or needing to match the entire English translation closely and continuously with the Latin original. It is tempting to speculate that they would have functioned particularly effectively in monastic/religious establishments, in which users might have needed to keep track of antiphonal psalm recitation. In the case of Vespasian D.vii, by far the smallest of the manuscripts containing the *Metrical Psalter*, private reading in tandem with auditory participation in the Latin liturgy seems likely. As noted, the scribe (or an early reader) goes to some lengths to clarify the relationship between the translation and the original. Short of pre- senting the translation in parallel with the full Latin text, he does all that he can to facilitate the sort of comparative reading that paraliturgical use would require. It would have been perfectly possible for an attentive individual to use the Vulgate cues to keep track of liturgical recitation while using the vernacular translation as a basis for prayer. Although Egerton 614 is bigger and slightly more luxurious than Vespasian D.vii, it may have been intended for similar purposes, along with Bodley 921. It is, however, worth pointing out that using either for comparative reading would have been challenging, since neither goes to the same lengths as Vespasian D.vii to link the Latin and the English. More specifically, neither has the ruling which makes such reading unproblematic.

When compared with Bodley 921, with which its text of the Psalter has so much in common (as explored in Chapters 3 and 5), the scribe of Bodley 425 makes a significantly more concerted effort to highlight the interactions between English translation and Vulgate original. Where 921's verse incipits are minimal and some- what sporadic, 425's are both more comprehensive and frequent. Not only this, but its careful use of ruling does much to facilitate the matching of Latin with English, as discussed. If one were trying to refer to the vernacular verse rendition while simultaneously listening to (or, conceivably, reading) the Latin original, Bodley 425, with its more emphatic system of signposting, would have been much easier to use than Bodley 921. That the compiler (who may or may not have also been the scribe) of this manuscript had a particular interest in the translation of biblical, devotional, and catechetic material from Latin to the vernacular is indicated by the manner in which the additional English contents of the manuscript (verse para- phrases of the four Gospel Capitula, the *Veni Creator, The Athanasian Creed*, and the *Ave Maris Stella*) are presented. With the exception of the Gospel Capitula, all have Latin cues accompanying them in the right-hand margin, mirroring precisely those which accompany the *Metrical Psalter*. It is quite possible that the codex was intended for an audience not (yet?) confidently literate in Latin, who stood to benefit from the provision of a basic crib to scriptural and liturgical material. Once again, though, we should not read the traffic as one-way, the English translation simply providing a means of accessing the Latin. A more productive reading of the manuscript would be one which sees its compiler as interested in experimenting with the vernacular as a language of devotion. Additionally, the fact that the manuscript's English contents are exclusively verse suggests a sustained interest in the capacities of English as a literary language on its own terms. Bodley 425 may well have appealed to a reasonably learned, competently Latinate audience not looking for a Latin–English crib, but interested instead in exploring the potentialities of the vernacularized and versified biblical and liturgical material which played such an important role in the literary culture of late-medieval Yorkshire.

The company that the *Metrical Psalter* keeps in Corpus Christi 278 and Harley 1770 emphasizes that its appeal (admittedly limited, if we are to go by the evidence of its curtailed circulation) is related to its identity as a translation, although not one necessarily intended only—or at all—for those whose Latin literacy is wanting. The former also contains an Anglo-Norman prose translation of the psalms and the latter both Anglo-Norman (prose) and Latin Psalters: the Anglo-Norman translations in both have been identified by Dean and Boulton as late versions of the Oxford Psalter, a widely circulated early twelfth-century prose rendition of the Gallican Psalter.[34] In Corpus Christi 278, the translations are consecutive, the full Anglo-Norman following the full English. They are the work of the same scribe, and the movement from one translation to the other takes place within a single quire. They are also presented very similarly: just as was the case with the English, accompanying the Anglo-Norman translation are marginal Latin cues to individual verses, introduced with alternating red and blue paraphs, contrasting with the paraphs in the Anglo-Norman text. Short of including an entire Latin text, every effort is being made to facilitate the matching of translation with original, as was the case with the English translation. However, the occurrence of two vernacular versions, so similarly presented, in the same manuscript, also suggests that readers are being encouraged to compare the Anglo-Norman and the English with each other as well as with the Latin: they are both of inherent interest, as vernacular responses to the Vulgate psalms and neither is privileged, in terms of ornament or decoration, over the other.[35] Of course, it could be objected that a comparative reading would be more revealing if the Anglo-Norman, as well as the English, were verse. But Dean and Boulton list only one such translation, which differs from the English *Metrical* version in using tail-rhyme (aab) and in paraphrasing rather than translating literally. We have no reason to assume that it was known to the compiler of Corpus Christi 278.[36] The reasonably accurate Oxford Psalter, based on the Gallican version, is probably a more reliable comparator.

In the case of Harley 1770, comparative reading is encouraged from the outset: the manuscript identifies itself as containing a 'Psalterium triplicatum, in

[34] Dean and Boulton, pp. 240–1, no. 445.
[35] Positioning the two translations side by side in parallel columns would, of course, have made comparison easier, but in terms of lineation, it would have been difficult to match the English verse with the Anglo-Norman prose without wasting a great deal of parchment.
[36] Dean and Boulton, pp. 243–4, no. 449.

verbis latinis, gallicis, et anglicanis' [a three-fold Psalter, in Latin, French, and English]. In reality, however, it is comparison of the Latin and Anglo-Norman that the manuscript presentation most obviously facilitates: the two Psalters occupy the substantial first half of the codex, appearing in carefully matched parallel columns and written in an identical formal script throughout. The *Metrical Psalter*, presented in a similarly impeccable fashion, occupies the last third of the manuscript, its Vulgate incipits functioning entirely independently of the preceding Latin Psalter: it would be perfectly possible to read the verse text in isolation from the rest of the codex. Nonetheless, the fact that it is presented at all in the company of two further Psalters, in a manuscript which we know to have had a monastic provenance, indicates that it may well have been seen as forming part of a 'database' of comparable psalm versions, of use not only to those of limited Latin literacy but also to a more learned readership interested in the processes of translation for their own sake.

Positioned in manuscript contexts which suggest that it was of interest to the learned as well as those of imperfect Latinity, the *Metrical Psalter* seems, at first glance, to distinguish itself from Rolle's English translation. In the prologue to his text, the hermit identifies one of the goals of his version as the directing of those who 'knawe[] noght latyn' towards a knowledge of the Vulgate original. In Rolle's declared hermeneutics of translation, the vernacular is the handmaid to the Latin and there is no jostling for position. Such deference to the authoritative original is reflected in the layout of most extant manuscripts. As Ralph Hanna suggests in his recent Rolle catalogue, extant codices 'generally make careful efforts to distinguish the component portions of the work. They universally have large coloured capitals to introduce each psalm and make efforts to separate the Latin source (virtually always given in full), the English translation, and the commentary.'[37] He goes on:

> [T]he books essentially imitate the format of Rolle's main source, manuscripts communicating Peter Lombard's Psalter commentary (or such standard, widely dispersed commentaries as ps.-Haymo of Halberstadt on the Pauline epistles). The Vulgate text is taken as primary and sacrosanct, its verses set off by regular initial coloured lombards and quite frequently in a larger (or 'nobler', e.g., textura rather than cursive) script, a presentation that re-enforces Rolle's claim that one purpose of the text is to 'cum tille many Latyn wordes' . . . The translation, while not accorded such august treatment, is frequently set off by a coloured paraph and/or underlined in red.[38]

As Anne Hudson has pointed out, it is not altogether surprising that copies of the interpolated Psalter should be characterized by particularly rigorous and consistent attempts to distinguish text from translation, and both from commentary.[39] As Chapter 3's analyses demonstrated, in their manuscript treatment of the

---

[37] Hanna (2010), p. xxxiii.   [38] Hanna (2010), p. xxxiv.
[39] Hudson (1988), p. 259: 'The Lollard versions retain Rolle's translation of the biblical text, neither substituting the rendering from the Wycliffite Bible, nor providing one of their own; the layout in the manuscripts, distinguishing Latin text, translated biblical material, and commentary, and so creating a visual hierarchy, regularises that of manuscripts containing Rolle's original text.' This recalls scribal practice in manuscripts containing the Wycliffite Glossed Gospels. See also the discussion in the introduction to Hudson (2012).

Psalter, the Wycliffites tend to deal carefully with glosses, often keeping them visually distinct from the direct translation (although in practice the boundaries become blurred). In this context, Oxford, BodlL Bodley 288, containing a copy of the interpolated commentary (Hudson's RV1), offers a representative example. A large, scarcely portable manuscript, written in textura in double columns, it very carefully distinguishes all three component parts from each other throughout. The Latin, in display textura, is introduced by alternating red and blue lombards, and is distinguished from the English translation which follows, prefaced with a lombard of the alternate colour and underlined in red. Both are visually set apart from the commentary, which is neither in red nor underlined in red, but is consistently introduced with a red paraph.[40] Such a layout makes clear that the Vulgate text is the authority to which the translation defers, and that the commentary is distinct from the verbatim vernacularization. Further, the provision of a full Latin text which utilizes relatively few of the standard scribal abbreviations of individual words means that the manuscript could have functioned in the way that Rolle apparently envisaged, leading those of limited or no Latinity to an appreciation of the Vulgate original. Among copies of the uninterpolated commentary, that in San Marino, Huntington 148 is also exemplary in its separation of Latin text (textura), English translation (smaller anglicana, prefaced by a red or blue paraph, though not underlined), and commentary (prefaced by a paraph in the alternating colour).[41] The theoretical—and quite literal—marginalization of the source that we witnessed in the case of other Psalter manuscripts is simply not to be found in these Rolle codices, which leave the reader in no doubt as to the importance of the Latin.

In other manuscripts, however, while efforts are certainly made to reflect the Vulgate original's preeminence by placing it at the top of the visual hierarchy, the extensive use of abbreviations in the reproduction of the Latin text make it difficult to see how the Psalter could have functioned effectively as a means of instructing the non-Latinate, if we imagine the goal to have been a full grammatical understanding of the Latin. Oxford, BodlL Bodley 467, for example, would have been monumentally demanding to use in such a manner.[42] Its use of abbreviated forms, which on occasion omit the very inflexional endings that enable the parsing of the Latin, suggests that the non-Latinate would not have progressed very far in attempting to use it as an aid to grammatical understanding of the original. But if we take Rolle literally (he wants readers to use the translation to 'cum tille many Latyn *wordes*' (italics mine)) and understand his goal to have been the encouragement of basic lexical rather than complex grammatical familiarity with the Vulgate, the intended function of the text is more comprehensible.

---

[40] For a full description, see Hanna (2010), pp. 133–4, no. 72.

[41] For a full description, see Hanna (2010), pp. 196–8, no. 107. He also reproduces fol. 105v as Plate 6 at the beginning of the catalogue.

[42] For a full description, see Hanna (2010), pp. 138–9, no. 75. Bodley 467 is, as Hanna says, unfinished. The Latin is in larger script than the English, although how much larger varies. It is neither in red nor underlined in red, although it is possible that red underlining was to be added later in addition to the four-line initials for which space is left at the beginning of each psalm.

It is a devotional English–Latin dictionary, a guide to lexis rather than syntax. As Zieman points out, such 'extragrammatical literacy' did have a status and function in the Middle Ages.[43] Yet used in such a manner, the translation is still likely to be of most use to readers with an element of pre-existing Latinity: abbreviations of individual words do not make sense unless one knows what they are abbreviating, a knowledge which one could not, of course, expect from a truly non-Latinate readership. Further, it has been observed that there are moments at which Rolle's exceptionally literal translation is so obscure as to require a grasp of the Vulgate text in order to unravel its meaning. On such occasions it is the Latin which must be used to 'cum tille' the English rather than vice versa: in an inversion of expected hierarchies, the source is handmaid to the translation. To be appreciated fully, the vernacular translation paradoxically requires a Latinate reader. And that Rolle's Psalter circulated among learned audiences as well as those of less obvious scholarly repute has been apparent since Chapter 1.[44]

Nonetheless, however many abbreviations of individual words are to be found in manuscripts of Rolle's *English Psalter*, the fact remains that most preserve the outlines at least of the full Vulgate text: it is very clearly the authority on which the vernacular relies. Yet while the relationship between the two languages is patently hierarchical, it is not one of straightforward dependence. The English translation, when being used to parse the Latin (and vice versa), is in constant dialogue with its Vulgate source; in most extant manuscripts neither is silenced by the other. In a small but interesting minority, however, the Latin plays a more marginal role, reduced to the sort of cues and incipits that we saw in the primer manuscripts discussed earlier. In London, BL Add. 74953, an early fifteenth-century copy of Rolle (containing a continuation of the interpolated Psalter found in London, BL Royal 18.D.1), a portion of the text is treated in this way. While the Latin in the Royal manuscript (whose copy of Rolle's interpolated commentary breaks off at Psalm 79: 13) is presented in a larger and more formal hand throughout and is sometimes underlined in red (as is the English translation), in Add. 74953 the treatment is less consistent. The continuation is the work of three scribes, the first of whom provides an abbreviated Latin lemma, which is followed by the English, underlined in red and introduced by a red lombard.[45] The second and third, perhaps feeling the first's work to be inadequate to the fulfilling of the prologue's declared goal, then revert to convention by providing the full Vulgate text prior to the vernacular rendition, underlining both in red.

However, in other manuscripts containing Rolle's Psalter, the role of the Latin is diminished throughout. For example, in the mid fifteenth-century uninterpolated copy in Hatfield, Hatfield House, the Marquess of Salisbury, Cecil Papers 328, neither of the two scribes writes out the Latin in full. Instead, both tend to include

---

[43] Zieman, p. 2.

[44] See also the comments in Gustafson: 'I am not suggesting that the *English Psalter* would have been read only by the Latin-illiterate (indeed, the elaborate system of cross-references in a number of the manuscripts suggests very learned readers as well)' (p. 301, note 23).

[45] For a full description, see Hanna (2010), pp. 106–8, no. 55. As Hanna points out, Royal 18 D.i contains Hudson's R[evised] V[ersion]1 while Add. 74953 contains both RV1 and RV3.

only a single line of text, 'scribe 1 very frequently adding "etc" '. Nor is the Latin consistently distinguished from the translation on the page: as Hanna observes, '[s]cribe 1 begins writing the Latin in a bastard version of his text hand but tends, as he proceeds, merely to use a larger script in his normal style . . . Occasionally, the Latin and its translation are underlined in red'. In scribe 2's portion, while 'the Latin [is] in the normal hand of the text, both it and the translation [are] regularly underlined in red'.[46] Additionally, the uninterpolated copy found in the early fifteenth-century Oxford, Magdalen College lat. 52 contains only minimal Latin text. Until Psalm 41 (fol. 69va), incipits are included, but thereafter the 'Latin verses [are] signalled but reduced to tags'.[47]

There is no obvious explanation for the absence of the full Latin from parts of Add. 74953 nor from Cecil Papers 328. Neither is any later than the majority of witnesses to Rolle's text, nor are they small manuscripts with only limited space on the page—both factors which could conceivably account for the diminished role of the Vulgate source.[48] The inclusion of Rolle's prologue (with its suggestion that the English be used to 'cum tille' the Latin) in both Cecil Papers 328 and London, BL Royal 18.D.1 (the partner volume to Add. 74953) might suggest that the scribes did not foresee the impact that the reduction of the Latin might have. As was the case with the primers, the English translation in these manuscripts cannot have been used in any straightforward way to 'cum tille' a Latin original which is represented only in part. However, in the case of Magdalen lat. 52, which contains Rolle's prologue, translation, and commentary as well as his Canticles, considerations of size must have contributed to the virtual absence of the Vulgate text. Noteworthy among Rolle Psalter manuscripts for its diminutive proportions (Hanna records its dimensions as 208mm x 142mm), it is an obviously portable volume and must have been meant for private use (although this does not in itself account for the reduction of the Latin). It may have functioned in a quasi-liturgical manner similar to the primer psalms or to the *Metrical* text in Vespasian D.vii, although of course it differs in providing the commentary as a stimulus to meditation.

The fact that the Vulgate survives only in the form of incipits and tags in Magdalen lat. 52 (and in Add. 74953 and Cecil Papers 328 RV) need not indicate that these manuscripts were intended for non-Latinate audiences to whom the full Vulgate text would have meant little. On the contrary, it may suggest that these copies were made for learned readers who could be relied upon to recall (or have access to) the full Latin original onto which they could then map Rolle's English translation. So literal is the hermit's rendition of the Latin that such manuscripts, containing little in addition to the vernacular translation, would, in fact, have been

---

[46] For a full description, see Hanna (2010), pp. 64–5, no. 34.

[47] For a full description, see Hanna (2010), pp. 180–1, no. 98.

[48] As a point of comparison, it is worth noting that in a late manuscript witness to Rolle's Psalter (the mid sixteenth-century Worcester, Cathedral Library F.166) an abbreviated copy of the text includes the full Vulgate text in textura but moves the English translation (in italics) to the margins. Worcester F. 166 may be a copy of Worcester, Cathedral Library F. 158. For descriptions of both manuscripts, see Hanna (2010), pp. 215–17, nos. 116 and 117.

exceptionally difficult to use in complete isolation from the Vulgate. In the case of Rolle's Psalter, it is sometimes the original that decodes the translation rather than the translation that decodes the original. The two are mutually reliant in a counter-intuitive way.

In one further early fifteenth-century manuscript of Rolle's Psalter (Oxford, BodlL Douce 258) not only is the Latin reduced to incipits, but no more than selections of the text are preserved, 'arranged for use in a votive or requiem mass' (ff. 1–39).[49] As Hanna's catalogue indicates, Douce 258 presents in order Psalms 118 (beginning 118: 7), 138, 21–2, and 24–30 (Psalm 30 ending at verse 6), which it identifies (correctly) as 'þe psalmes of þe passion'. It accompanies these with material from the Wycliffite LV New Testament (the gospels for Christmas, Easter, Ascension, and St Thomas, as well as the general epistles) and the Wycliffite commentary on the Athanasian Creed. Benedictions appear after Psalm 118 and 138, the latter of which reads (ff. 20r–v): 'Lord 3eue hem endeles rest and perpetual li3t shyne to hem. Fro þe 3atis of helle lord delyuer þe soules of hem. I beleue to se goodes of þe lord in þe lond of lyuers. To þee lord we bitaken þe soules of þi seruauntes bothe men & wymmen . . .'. The subsequent Psalm 21 then opens with '*Tibi domine* To þee lord we betaken þe soules of þi seruauntis' before the translation itself ('God my god loke in me') begins.[50] Spatial considerations may, once again, have played a part in the reduction of the Latin: the manuscript measures only 184mm by 125mm, meaning that it is another easily portable volume. But it also seems that the scribe and/or compiler of this manuscript did not intend his or her selection from Rolle's Psalter to be used primarily as an English–Latin crib. The benedictions appended to the psalms, as well as the manuscript's layout, suggest that its focus is intercessory and its purpose devotional. In place of the double columns in which Rolle's text is usually formatted, Douce 258 uses single columns more characteristic of contemporary primers. The Vulgate cues serve to ground Douce's psalms in the resonances of the liturgy, but beyond this, their function ceases. Despite its self-proclaimed identity as (among other things) a means of 'coming to' Latin via English, the manuscript context of Rolle's *English Psalter* indicates that this was not the only use to which the text was put.

Turning now from Rolle's *English Psalter* to the Wycliffite Bible itself, knowing of Wycliffite misgivings regarding the reliability of Latin Bibles circulating in the Middle Ages ('many biblis in Latyn' are '[ful] false') we might expect manuscripts of their own Psalter to contain little of the Gallican text. This does, in general, prove to be the case: few have anything more than basic incipits. Such incipits were probably intended to function simply as a means of identification, supplementing the

---

[49] Hanna (2010), p. 149. For a full description of the manuscript, see pp. 149–50, no. 82.

[50] In general, the Latin incipits to individual psalms (and to sections of Psalm 118) are in red ink. The English translation is underlined in red with the first initial in blue ink, and the commentary is then introduced with a red paraph. So, at the beginning of Psalm 21 (f. 21v) we have 'Deus deus nisi respice in me' in red ink followed by a two-line gold leaf initial 'G(od)' with burgundy infilling and a blue surround, marking the start of the translation.

tituli which often feature in Wycliffite manuscripts and tend to include numbers for the psalms.[51] As is the case with the overwhelming majority of Psalter manuscripts discussed in this chapter, the Wycliffite incipits very probably serve a liturgical purpose. As several scholars have pointed out, scribes of the Wycliffite Bible often go to some lengths to facilitate the use of their volumes in such contexts.[52] Many manuscripts of the complete translation include liturgical calendars and lectionaries which indicate which epistles and gospels are read at mass throughout the year and individual psalms can also 'readily be located in Wycliffite bibles since . . . the format of the Wycliffite psalms resembles the format of a liturgical Psalter' (although there is no 'rule' for locating the proper psalms).[53] Further, volumes containing the psalms also frequently include headings which draw attention to the Psalter's liturgical function, describing it as 'the sauter, which is red comounli in the chirche'.[54] Unlike Rolle's *English Psalter*, instruction in Latinity is not part of the Wycliffite psalms' primary purpose, so there is no compelling reason for scribes to include the full Vulgate text. Neither do they need to provide the Latin text as a means of decoding the English translation: more flowing and idiomatic than Rolle's literal version, the vernacularized LV psalms make sense independent of their Vulgate source.

As noted on previous occasions in this book, although there are no extant copies of the EV Psalter alone, the LV psalms are found in isolation (or with company limited to the Canticles and, on occasion, a litany and/or lectionary and/or some prefatory material) in seven manuscripts.[55] These volumes tend to be very small and were obviously meant for personal use, setting them apart from many manuscripts of the complete Wycliffite scriptures, the large size of which 'would be appropriate in lectern bibles'.[56] In its treatment of the Vulgate original, the late fifteenth-century London, BL Add. 10047 (which includes LV psalms 1–73 and is of dimensions appropriate for use in private meditation), is characteristic of codices whose principal contents are the Wycliffite psalms. Its inclusion of nothing more than brief Vulgate incipits is unlikely to have been dictated by anxieties regarding spatial economy, as was speculated in the case of Rolle's Magdalen lat. 52. It is, rather, representative of general Wycliffite practice, and is driven by the practical and ideological considerations previously outlined. The text is prefaced (f. 1r) by a red-ink introduction 'here bygynnyth the psalms of dauith þat is clepid þe sauter', after which the first verse of Psalm 1 is provided in full in Latin followed

[51] The complications which arose in the implementation of this system will be discussed later in the chapter.

[52] See for example Dove (2007), p. 58. As Dove indicates, the liturgical nature of Wycliffite Bibles has also been remarked upon by Christopher de Hamel, ch. 7 'English Wycliffite Bibles.'

[53] Dove (2007) also points out (p. 61) that over a third of the extant *c.* 250 manuscripts containing the Wycliffite Bible (in part or in full) include a lectionary. For the quotation, see p. 63.

[54] See, for example, the comment in Worcester, Cathedral Library F. 172 (f. 168v) 'Here bigynneth the psautier the whiche is comunely used to be rad in holichirche service.'

[55] Rather like Rolle's Psalter, the notably literal Wycliffite EV psalms might have been difficult to use in isolation from the complete text of the Vulgate. This may explain in part the more impressive survival rate of the LV Psalter.

[56] Hudson (1988), p. 199.

by the first verse in English, both in the same black ink[57]. The two 'B's introducing the original and the translation are enlarged and decorated, the vernacular 'B' being three times the size and considerably more elaborate than its Latin counterpart. Individual verses are then prefaced by alternating blue (decorated with red) and gold (decorated with blue) initials which refer to the English translation rather than the Vulgate original: after the first verse, there is no further Latin text. This scheme is reproduced throughout the manuscript, which, in common with most Wycliffite Psalters, also contains red-ink tituli for individual psalms. It is a format which leaves us in no doubt as to the overwhelming vernacularity of the text; the red ink which often distinguishes Latin from English in primer and Rolle manuscripts is entirely absent from Add. 10047's Vulgate cues.

In London, BL Add. 35284 (*c.* 1400), an earlier small LV manuscript which contains Psalms 45–150 as well as the Canticles and a Litany, the role of the Latin is further diminished. Add. 35284 is by no means an elaborate manuscript; there is no gold leaf and new verses are marked quite simply by alternating red and blue initials. Each psalm is introduced by the briefest of red-ink incipits but reference to the Vulgate extends no further than this, and the little decorative detail that there is focuses once again on the vernacular. The beginning of each psalm is highlighted by an English two-line blue initial (extending to four lines in the case of the Nocturns) decorated with red penwork reaching into the margins.[58] It is a curious feature of this manuscript that these English initials do not interact visually with the Latin cues: they do not share decorative features and are not positioned in close conjunction. Remaining oddly discrete on the page, the incipits are not long enough to be used meaningfully for comparative Latin–English purposes and would be redundant were it not for their role as psalm identifiers. Dislocated from the central linguistic activity of the Psalter, they appear to refer to a text quite other than that represented by the English translation. We are a long way from the ongoing 'shuttling' between Latin and English that any attentive reading of Rolle's *English Psalter* demands. The redundancy of Latin in the context of the Wycliffite psalms is taken to its logical extreme in the early fifteenth-century London, BL Add. 10046, which contains Rolle's Psalter prologue and excerpts from chapters 11 and 12 of the prologue to the Wycliffite Bible, followed by the LV psalms and Canticles as well as the *Quicunque Vult*, with Rolle's commentary (RV).[59] Although the traditional eight-fold liturgical division of the Psalter is marked by Vulgate running-titles at the head of relevant pages, the English translation otherwise stands alone: the Latin has been all but deleted from Add. 10046's psalms.[60] Gold leaf initials match the running-titles for Psalms 1, 26, 38,

[57] For a full-page reproduction of MS BL Add 10047, f. 1r see Figure 6.4.
[58] Psalm 52, introduced with a four-line initial ' "T"(he unwise man seyde. . .)', does not have a Latin incipit, nor a red-ink titulus.
[59] For brief descriptions of the manuscript, see Dove (2007), p. 289 and Hanna (2010), pp. 75–6, no. 39. Between the prefatory material and the LV psalms, there is a short outline of the four senses of the scriptures.
[60] The running-titles are as follows: 'beat vir'; 'dominus illuminacio'; 'dixi custodiam'; 'dixit insipiens'; 'saluum me fac'; 'exultate domine'; 'cantate domino'; and 'dixit dominus'.

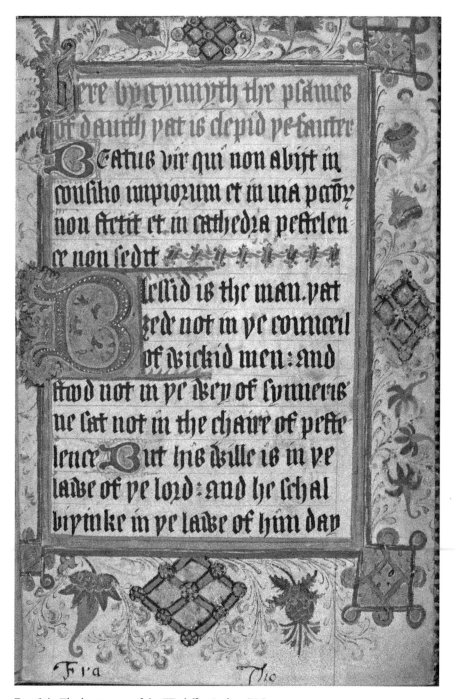

Fig. 6.4. The beginning of the Wycliffite Psalter (LV)

52, 68, 80, 97, and 109 but they are consistent in highlighting the beginning of the English translation. The remaining 142 psalms are also introduced by enlarged initials (two-line blue, decorated with red penwork), but again these refer invariably to the English text.[61] Beyond its function as a key to liturgical recitation, there is little place or role for the Vulgate in Add. 10046's Wycliffite Psalter.

This is not to suggest, however, that the Vulgate is all but displaced in the Wycliffite tradition or that in manuscripts containing the LV psalms we can trace a steady retreat from the authority of the Latin original. On the contrary, the two languages remain involved in active and varied negotiations throughout most extant manuscripts. At the beginning of Add. 10047's individual psalms, for example, when the all but obligatory incipits appear, we often encounter what seems to be a jostling for position between the two languages. In the case of Psalm 1, for example, while the 'B' introducing the Latin 'Beatus' is a one-line blue initial infilled with gold and red and surrounded by a red border, the substantial 'B' introducing the English 'Blessid' occupies three lines and is decorated more elaborately with an increased amount of gold leaf.[62] It is quite likely that the scribe has simply failed to note that the English and Latin begin with the same letter and that the duplication of initials is unplanned; we have seen other instances of this in the course of the chapter. The Latin incipit is helpful in terms of identification and for liturgical purposes, but that is as far as its function extends. The increased decorative ceremony which heralds the English 'Blessid' indicates firmly that this is where our attention should be focused.

Yet, however few and far between, incipits are almost universally preserved, their functionality being irrefutable. The English Wycliffite psalms never appear in total isolation from the Gallican. In fact, on two notable occasions, the Wycliffite version is accompanied by a full reproduction of the Vulgate text. In the mid fifteenth-century Worcester, Cathedral Library F.172, Psalms 1–72: 19 (168v–213v) are presented in alternating Latin and English (the manuscript presumably originally contained the complete Psalter; Hanna suggests that at least seven quires have been lost from the end).[63] A compilation including devotional, catechetic, and moral prose, Worcester F. 172 also contains LV Acts (ff. 48–72), an excerpt from chapter 11 of the General Prologue to the Wycliffite Bible and a copy of the prologue to the interpolated version of Rolle's *English Psalter*, the latter of which immediately prefaces the LV psalms. It is a functional rather than ornate volume in which the psalms are not accompanied by any gold leaf illumination. We know it to have been made for John Vale, servant of Sir Thomas Cook; with the exceptions of the text accompanying the psalms and a brief Latin verse epitaph somewhat earlier, its contents are entirely vernacular. Why the full Vulgate Psalter (up to 72:

---

[61] Some verse divisions are indicated with alternating blue and red capitals. Tituli are underlined in red throughout, as are glosses in the main body of the text. Psalm numbers and some verse numbers have been added in a later hand.

[62] See the reproduction of f. 1r as Figure 8.

[63] For a manuscript description, see Hanna (2010), pp. 118–219, no. 118. The volume is also discussed in R. M. Thomson, *A Descriptive Catalogue of the Medieval Manuscripts in Worcester Cathedral Library* (Cambridge, 2001), pp. 114–16.

19) should have been included in this particular volume is something of a mystery, unless the text was intended to function as a crib for readers unschooled in Latin and/or for an audience who wanted to follow closely the liturgical recitation of the Psalter. It may also be that the scribe was influenced by Rolle's prologue, which he copied immediately prior to copying the psalms, and which refers, as we know, to the use of the English translation as a means of 'coming to' the Latin. Whatever the reasons for its inclusion, however, the presence of the full Vulgate reminds us that even the Wycliffite psalms could be read in meaningful and dynamic conjunction with their problematic Latin source. They do not entirely silence the Vulgate, nor are they intended to do so.

The second manuscript to contain a fully bilingual copy of the LV psalms, London, BL Harley 1896, is of particular interest, as it is the only surviving witness to the complete text in both Latin and English, accompanied by the Canticles. Bigger than the other British Library Psalters already discussed, it is nonetheless of a size which indicates that it may have been a private-use book. Its layout resembles that of manuscripts containing Rolle's translation, although there is no difference between the two languages in terms of script size. Each Vulgate verse (complete although individual words are abbreviated) is presented in red ink, introduced by a two-line blue initial with red flourishes. This is followed by the complete English translation of the relevant verse in faded brown ink, introduced by a slightly enlarged red initial (with blue flourishes). Such a manuscript could well have served an educational purpose, its English translation being used to encourage readers to 'cum tille' the Latin, as Rolle envisaged. In conjunction with this, it is clearly a manuscript intended to function in liturgical contexts, although the scribe becomes slightly muddled in his attempts to indicate devotionally significant psalms. He seems to want to draw attention to the traditional eight-fold liturgical division of the Psalter, as is often the case in manuscripts containing the Rolle and Wycliffite translations, but he fails to decoratively distinguish Psalms 52 and 68, highlighting 51 and 53 instead. Nonetheless, his illustration is quite remarkable in the context of Wycliffite psalm manuscripts, not least because it includes two large historiated initials at the beginning of Psalms 1 and 109, both of which are also surrounded by richly illuminated borders. The 'B' of '*Beatus Vir*' [Blessed is the man] extends to nine lines, and as well as being fully gilded and decorated, encloses a figural representation of an enthroned David playing the harp. And the gilded 'D' of '*Dixit Dominus Domino meo*' [The Lord said to my Lord] stretches to six lines and contains an image of the Father and Son accompanied by the Holy Spirit in the form of a dove.[64] As indicated in Chapter 5, such figural illuminations are very rare in Wycliffite manuscripts, and their inclusion here provides compelling evidence that this volume is consciously modelled on the splendour of

---

[64] Psalm 26 is marked by a seven-line ornamental ' "D"(*ominus illuminatio mea*)' with fully painted and gilded border decoration and Psalm 38 is marked by a six-line ornamental ' "D"(*ixi custodiam vias meas*)'. Psalm 51 (Quid gloriaris) is prefaced by a six-line decorated 'Q' and 53 (*Deus in nomine tuo*) by an eight-line 'D'. An eight-line 'E' marks the beginning of Psalm 80 (*Exultate Deo adiutori nostro*) and a seven-line 'C' the beginning of Psalm 97 (*Cantate Domino canticum novum*).

Latin liturgical Psalters. It is a formatting which serves at once to emphasize the importance of the Vulgate text (it is, after all, the Latin initials which are historiated) whilst at the same time elevating the English translation by suggesting that it is of sufficient stature to feature alongside the Latin original in a manuscript of some pretensions.

These two manuscripts are, however, the exception rather than the rule.[65] In the vast majority of copies of the Wycliffite psalms, it is only the Vulgate incipits which are preserved. But as has been stressed, this should not be read as implying that, in Wycliffite contexts, English translation is intended to slowly erode the dying remains of Latin. For despite the curious dislocation of Latin and English observed in British Library Add. 35284, in several copies of the Wycliffite Psalter which contain nothing more than incipits we witness scribes clearly attempting to negotiate an appropriate relationship between Vulgate and vernacular, indicating that for readers the two languages were intended to operate in some sort of conjunction. We saw something of this suggested in Add. 10047's duplication of 'B's' at the beginning of the Psalter, but encounter it at its most vivid in Oxford, BodlL Bodley 554. Discussed at various points throughout this book, the mid fifteenth-century Bodley 554 is notable for containing a heavily glossed rendition of the Wycliffite LV Psalter, accompanied by the Canticles and other material. It is bigger than the manuscripts discussed previously, though still eminently portable, and contains very little decorative detailing: a functional volume, its predominantly black ink is supplemented only by red and blue penwork. Individual psalms are accompanied by marginal Latin incipits throughout, although there is on occasion some jostling for primacy between these cues and the extensive glosses with which they share marginal space. The Latin opening to Psalm 21 (f. 19v *'Dne Deus meus respice in me'*), for example, is pushed to the bottom of the page by the sheer quantity of commentary. Nonetheless, individual psalms are clearly distinguished from each other: within the main body of the text, each is introduced by a two- (sometimes four-) line blue initial, decorated with red penwork. In the early part of the Psalter, it is the English initial which is afforded such treatment. Psalm 1, for example, is prefaced by a four-line blue initial 'B' with red flourishes which clearly marks the beginning of the English 'Blissed'; the Latin *'Beatus vir'* appears in red in the right-hand margin. At Psalm 41 (f. 21r), however, something rather curious occurs: the scribe begins decorating and enlarging not the initial English letter of the Psalm, as he has done thus far, but the initial Latin. It is, therefore, the 'Q' introducing the Vulgate's *'Quemadmodum desiderat'* (As [the hart] panteth) which is presented in blue ink (two lines) decorated with red penwork, rather than the 'A' introducing the English 'As an hert desirith', which we have come to expect.[66]

---

[65] See, however, San Marino, Huntington Library HM 501 in which the LV psalms (ff. 24v–103v) are accompanied by the full Latin text (Psalms 1–3) and thereafter by the incipit only. That the manuscript also includes the revised version of Rolle's prologue to his *English Psalter* may suggest that the scribe was, initially at least, influenced by Rollean precedent in his bilingual presentation of the psalms, as may have been the case in Worcester, Cathedral Library F.172 (which is also the revised version of Rolle's prologue). For a full description of the manuscript, see Hanna (2010), pp. 202–4, no. 110.

[66] See the reproduction of MS Bodley 554, f. 21r as Figure 2.

On f. 21v, the scribe reverts to enlarging the English initials for Psalms 42 ('God deme þou me') and 43 ('God we herden wiþ oure eeris'), but he then returns to the Vulgate for Psalm 44 (f. 22v) '*Eructavit cor meum*' (My heart hath uttered) and remains with this for the remainder of the Psalter.

The reason for this sudden change seems clear. As has been stressed repeatedly, Vulgate cues operated as a system of psalm identification in the Middle Ages and could function relatively straightforwardly in assisting the reader who wanted to follow liturgical recitation of the Psalter in Latin. To have one's attention drawn to the English initial in such circumstances would have been of little value (although in the case of Psalm 1, it makes no difference). A third of the way through Bodley 554's text, something of this sort must have occurred to the scribe or the individual or institution for whom the manuscript was intended. After some vacillation at psalms 41, 42, and 43, scribal practice is decisively revised and the Latin initial takes visual precedence over that of the English translation. Rather than indicating an abruptly rediscovered respect for the antiquity of the Vulgate, it seems that the Latin's importance lies in its functionality as much as its authority.

The situation is slightly different in the case of the psalms preserved in London, BL Arundel 104, an early fifteenth-century copy of the complete LV Wycliffite Bible, accompanied by a lectionary. Surviving in two volumes, the first of which contains a lectionary and Old Testament (–Proverbs) while the second contains Proverbs–Apocalypse, Dove speculates that Arundel 104 was 'originally conceived as a pandect'.[67] It is an imposing pair of manuscripts, made from good-quality vellum, and survives in fine condition. Although neither volume is remarkably beautiful or ornate, they both include some fine initials (between three and seven lines) in 'orange, pinky-beige and blue on a gold background' with foliate borders in the same colours, and at the beginning of Matthew, the second volume contains an eight-line initial with symbols of the four evangelists.[68] For our purposes, it is Arundel 104's presentation of the Psalter which is of most interest. As Dove points out, the scribe follows general Wycliffite convention in accompanying each psalm with a marginal red-ink titulus and incipit, and in highlighting individual verses with alternating blue and red initials.[69] Fully painted and gilded borders and ornamental initials also mark not only the first and last psalms but also the traditional eight-fold liturgical division of the text. In each case, it is the English translation's initial rather than that of the Vulgate which is decorated (the latter survives in the aforementioned marginal incipit). So, Psalm 26 (*Dominus illuminatio mea*) is marked by a five-line ornamental 'T' ('The Lord is my liȝtnyng'), Psalm 38 (Dixi custodiam vias meas) by a six-line ornamental 'I' ('I seide, Y schal kepe my weies'),

---

[67] Dove (2007), Appendix 4, pp. 244–5.

[68] Dove (2007), Appendix 4, pp. 244–5. She notes that Lindberg describes Arundel 104's text as 'bad' with 'many late and dubious forms and readings'.

[69] As Stella Panayotova points out, these rubrics 'function as a kind of *concordantia* between the English and the Latin text of the Psalms . . . Depending on space and page layout, [they] either begin within the column and spill out into the margin or are written in the margin beside the English *titulus*.' See S. Panayotova, 'Cuttings from an Unknown Copy of the *Magna Glossatura* in a Wycliffite Bible (British Library, Arundel MS 104)', *BLJ* 25 (1999), 85–100, p. 97.

and Psalm 52 (*Dixit insipiens*) by a four-line ornamental 'T' ('The unwise said'). Psalm 68 (*Salvum me fac, Deus*) is prefaced by a four-line ornamental 'G' ('God make þou me saaf'), 80 (*Exultate Deo*) by a four-line ornamental 'M' ('Make ȝe fulli ioye to God'), 97 (*Cantate Domino canticum novum*) by a five-line ornamental 'S' ('Singe ȝe a newe song to the Lord'), and 109 (*Dixit Dominus Domino meo*) by a four-line ornamental 'T' ('The Lord seide to my lord.'). The text on each of the folios featuring these initials is enclosed by elaborately decorated borders and, in common with conventions displayed in the rest of the Psalter, these seven psalms are also accompanied by marginal red-ink Latin cues, although here they are dwarfed by the imposing vernacular initials.

This system of decoration, applied to each of the seven Nocturns, is entirely in keeping with contemporary practice. Theoretically designed to facilitate cross-referencing with the Vulgate Psalter, its highlighting of vernacular initials would, however, have been of limited functionality, not least because in translation no less than three of the seven psalms begin identically with the definite article 'T'(he), a problem which does not afflict the Vulgate text. But where the scribe of Bodley 554 recognizes and redresses this issue a third of the way through his copy, the potential problem does not seem to have occurred to Arundel 104's scribe. It does, though, appear to have struck an early user (probably owner) of the manuscript, who at some point pasted into Arundel 104's Psalter a series of nine historiated initials, of which three now survive. The pasted initials that remain intact mark Psalms 52, 68, and 104, while Psalms 32, 38, 46, 90, 95, and 109 were also at one point highlighted by pastings from the same manuscript, since removed. In an important article published in 1999, Stella Panayotova argues convincingly that the manuscript in question contained an early thirteenth-century copy of Peter Lombard's *Magna Glossatura*.[70] Basing her conclusions on an analysis of the 'short sections of text which survive on the reverse of the three extant images' and the offsets of the six cuttings which are no longer in place, she makes the specific suggestion that the Lombard manuscript was of English origin.[71] Panayotova also points out that Arundel 104 contains two further pastings (both of which remain) at Psalms 66 and 133, both of which appear to derive from a later manuscript.[72]

Considered in the context of this chapter, the most significant aspect of these pasted initials is that, unlike the scheme of decoration native to the layout of this manuscript's page, they relate to the Vulgate text. This is a point noted by Christopher de Hamel, who suggests that the owner of Arundel 104 found the *English Psalter* difficult to use without the standard 'repertoire' of cues to the Vulgate text, the 'traditional liturgical apparatus'.[73] It was for this reason, de Hamel

---

[70] Panayotova, pp. 85–7. The article revises Nigel Morgan's earlier suggestion that Arundel 104's pasted initials derive from an early thirteenth-century *English Psalter* or Bible (see N. Morgan, *Early Gothic Manuscripts*, Survey of Manuscripts Illuminated in the British Isles 4, 2 vols (London and Oxford, 1982–8), vol. 1, pp. 64–5).

[71] Panayotova, p. 97.

[72] Panayotova, p. 97. De Hamel suggests that this later manuscript was a Psalter of *c.* 1370.

[73] De Hamel, pp. 182–3. Making a broader observation which chimes with the preoccupations of this chapter, he also comments that the Latin incipits were so familiar in the fifteenth century that

suggests, that he or she pasted the historiated initials into the manuscript. This argument certainly carries weight in the cases of Psalms 38, 52, 68, and 109. Psalm 52's pasting survives (f. 350r) and is a historiated initial 'D' containing a representation of God casting down arrows on men.[74] The pasting at Psalm 68 also survives (f. 354r) and is an 'S' illustrated with an image of the crucified Christ.[75] Psalm 38's cutting (f. 346v) has been removed but is likely to have been a historiated 'D', as is that which originally marked Psalm 109 (f. 367r). These four psalms are all Nocturns, conventionally highlighted in medieval Psalters, and already marked in Arundel 104 by the scheme of decoration native to the page. Crucially, though, the pastings do not duplicate the existing vernacular initials but provide Latin alternatives which are both more elaborate and more useful, insofar as they work to facilitate the liturgical use of the manuscript. However, De Hamel's suggestion that the pasted initials are intended specifically to supplement Arundel 104 with 'traditional liturgical apparatus' seems more tenuous, though not always unfeasible, when one considers the fact that such pastings do not mark the other three Nocturns (Psalms 26, 80, and 97) whose vernacular initials are all highlighted (as we would expect) by the native decorative scheme. Instead, initials from the *Magna Glossatura* were pasted at the beginning of Psalms 32 (*Exultate justi*), 46 (*Omnes gentes*), 90 (*Qui habitat*), 95 (*Cantate Domino*), and 104 (*Confitemini Domino*), of which only the last now survives.[76] Additionally, as pointed out, pasted initials from a further manuscript survive at Psalms 66 (*Deus misereatur*) and 133 (*Ecce nunc*).

It is possible that the positioning of some of these cuttings could be explicable in liturgical terms. For example, as Panayotova suggests, the pasting accompanying Psalm 95 may have been intended originally to mark Psalm 97 (i.e. the sixth Nocturn); both psalms begin with 'C' and 'the fully painted border on f. 362v, where Psalm 97 is to be found, left no space for additional illustration'.[77] Equally, the pasting at Psalm 90 may be explicable; as Panayotova points out, it 'was part of the five-fold Hebrew division as well as of the fifteen-fold division of the Psalter'.[78] It is conceivable that in highlighting this psalm the owner was simply observing long-standing tradition. It also seems possible that the individual who pasted in the initials to Psalms 66 and 133 was aware that, in their original manuscript context, they belonged to Psalms 26 and 80, two of the Nocturns unmarked by

'individual Psalms were no longer identifiable once their opening words had been translated into English, changing the opening initial'.

[74] 'For lack of space, the initial to Psalm 52 was appended at the lower corner of f. 350r, closer to Psalm 53 and its rubric' (Panayotova, p. 98).

[75] Panayotova includes reproductions of both initials, pp. 85–6. She suggests that the initial marking Psalm 52 probably illustrated the same psalm in the original manuscript (p. 87) and also points out that Psalm 68 was traditionally interpreted 'in the light of Christ's Passion and Resurrection' (p. 91). She also points out (p. 98) that 'the illustration to Psalm 68 was placed at the bottom of f. 354r, completely detached from the rubric in the inner margin'.

[76] The 'C' initial marking Psalm 104 (f. 364v) contains a monk reading from a book on a lectern, with the Holy Spirit descending on him in the form of a dove. Panayotova includes a reproduction, p. 86.

[77] Panayotova, p. 97.

[78] Panayotova, p. 97. Psalm 90 was also recited daily at Compline in both monastic and secular uses.

imported decoration in Arundel 104.[79] In fact, the initials may have been intended for these two psalms in the Wycliffite manuscript before being either inserted in the wrong position or deliberately placed elsewhere due to lack of space; Psalms 26 and 80 begin, respectively, with the same initials as Psalms 66 and 133. Added to this, the fully gilded and painted borders which accompany each of the seven Nocturns in Arundel 104 would have made the correct positioning of all the cuttings something of a challenge. If this series of suppositions is correct, it suggests that the original intention was probably the highlighting of the seven Nocturns (and Psalm 90), in keeping with the decorative scheme native to the manuscript. All of the relevant Latin initials have been pasted in, even if they are not all located correctly.

The pasting of initials at Psalms 32, 46, and 104 is, however, more difficult to explain or justify by liturgical means. According to their position in the Ferial Psalter, Psalm 32 features in Monday Matins in both secular and monastic uses, Psalm 46 in Tuesday Matins for both, and Psalm 104 in Saturday Matins for both.[80] That they featured thus in the liturgy does not, however, help us very much. As we know, psalm recitation was at the heart of liturgical practice in the Middle Ages: 32, 46, and 104 are accorded no more devotional emphasis than many other psalms. It may have been, quite simply, that the owner found him or herself with available 'E', 'O', and 'C' initials and pasted them into Arundel 104 where appropriate space could be found. Equally, though, the highlighting of these particular psalms could be indicative of personal preference.[81] In this context, it is worth noting that the focus of all three is on the offering of praise to God as righteous ruler of his people; thematically at least they are a coherent selection, even if they do not appear to have been of obvious or linked liturgical significance.[82]

Whatever the precise reasons for their selection and positioning, Arundel 104's initials are also of interest for what they suggest about attitudes to the Psalter as an English text. On the one hand, their insertion can be read as an attempt to assert an identity for the vernacular psalms equivalent to that of their Vulgate source: the translated Psalter is of sufficient status to merit the type of elaborate illumination characteristic of its Latin cohorts. The same is also suggested by the

[79] That the initials marking Psalms 66 and 133 'most probably' belonged to Psalms 26 and 80 in their original manuscript context is a suggestion made by Panayotova, p. 97.

[80] See Harper, Appendix 2 'The Psalter'. In secular use, Psalm 32 is the seventh psalm in Monday Matins, and the first in monastic use. Psalm 46 is the second psalm in Tuesday Matins in monastic use and the eighth in secular use.

[81] In her 1999 article, Stella Panayotova suggests that personal preference might account for Arundel 104's highlighting of Psalms 32, 46, 66, 104, and 133.

[82] See, for example, Psalm 32: 10–11 'The Lord distrieth the counsels of folkis, forsothe he repreueth the thouʒtis of puplis; and he repreueth the counsels of prynces. But the counsel of the Lord dwellith with outen ende; the thouʒtis of his herte dwellen in generacioun and into genera|cioun.' See also Psalm 46: 2–3 'Alle ʒe folkis, make ioie with hondis; synge ʒe hertli to God in the vois of ful out ioiyng. [verse 3] For the Lord is hiʒ and ferdful; a greet kyng on al erthe.' And Psalm 104: 1–4 'Knouleche ʒe to the Lord, and inwardli clepe ʒe his name; telle ʒe hise werkis among hethen men. Synge ʒe to hym, and seie ʒe salm to him, and telle ʒe alle hise merueylis; be ʒe preisid in his hooli name. The herte of men sekynge the Lord be glad; seke ʒe the Lord, and be ʒe confermed; seke ʒe euere his face.'

richly decorated codices containing Rolle's *English Psalter* (for example, Bodley 953; Cambridge, Corpus Christi 387 (both unrevised); Lambeth 34; Richardson 36 (both revised)) and by the notable inclusion of historiated initials containing David in Wolfenbüttel, Guelf.A.2 Aug.2, a Wycliffite EV Bible, and in the aforementioned Harley 1896, a Wycliffite Psalter (LV). Even the smaller Wycliffite Psalters and several copies of the Middle English primer, while not opulent or extravagant, are often carefully designed and decorated volumes, suggesting that a degree of reverence is to be accorded to the text which they contain. Such manuscripts enact in visual terms what many of the psalm paraphrases of the late Middle Ages enact in poetic terms: an elevation of the biblical vernacular to a state worthy of literary comparison with its Vulgate predecessor.

On the other hand, the fact that Arundel 104's pastings appear to derive from Latin manuscripts and refer specifically to the Vulgate initials rather than to the vernacular initials already highlighted could be read as suggesting that the English Psalter struggles to assert an identity of its own. It remains perpetually in the shadow of its source, not only for practical reasons relating to liturgical use, but also because it as yet lacks the weight of tradition associated with the Vulgate. This is certainly the view taken by Christopher de Hamel, who suggests that, throughout the Middle Ages, 'in the mind of the devout' the 'true' Bible remained a Latin text. He goes on:

> To a fifteenth-century layman, an English parallel version might seem like no more than a sustained gloss or mirror to the original, to help focus devotion by increasing understanding of the sacred Latin text.[83]

There may well have been readers who, as de Hamel states, regarded the Latin text of the Bible as sacrosanct: as has been frequently observed in this chapter, the English translation often leads the reader directly back to the Latin. Yet the evidence explored in this book suggests that there were other readers for whom the 'true' Bible was the Word of God, irrespective of language. The idea of the English as 'gloss' or 'mirror' to the Latin does not, for example, register those moments when Latin and English remain curiously detached from each other on the manuscript page. The evidence of BL Add. 35284 springs to mind: here, we find no visual interaction between the two languages, the Latin appearing to gesture towards a complete text no longer there.

More importantly, Hamel's statement does not register that when Latin and English *do* interact, the relationship is not inevitably one of superior to inferior. It is of course possible that on occasion the Latin is included as it lends the English an aura of authority or sanctity, but its primary role must be recognized to be functional. Elaborate initials and border decorations do not simply suggest that English Psalters are aping Latin Psalters but that English Psalters are asserting a comparable identity and status for themselves. Far from exerting a stranglehold over the vernacular, interactions with the Vulgate stimulated some of the most remarkable English literary experiments of the late Middle Ages. From the verbatim vernacularizations

---

[83] De Hamel, p. 184.

of the complete book of psalms found in the *Metrical* text and in Rolle's English translation and commentary, to the complex affective paraphrase of Brampton and the aureate renditions of Lydgate, this volume has demonstrated the extent of this variety. In their vacillation between an independent identity as vernacular 'makynges' and an ambiguous status as both indebted to, and expansions upon, their Latin source, they can be situated firmly in the context of wider late-medieval debate on the responsibilities and function of specifically English literature. The vernacular translators of the psalms, dealing in texts so overtly preoccupied with 'voice and persona, both religious and literary', deserve to have their own, often distinctive and powerful, voices heard more widely: 'Lord, opene thou my lippis; and my mouth schal telle thi preysyng'.[84]

---

[84] The quotation is taken from Lawton (2011), pp. 144–6. It has been alluded to previously in the Introduction.

Concluding Thoughts

As anticipated in the Introduction, this book has raised as many questions as it has answered. Clearly, further work is called for in tracing possible connections between Old and Middle English translations of the psalms; analysis of the *Metrical Psalter* has suggested the existence of potentially productive lines of enquiry in this area.[1] More sustained exploration of links between Middle English and Early Modern renditions of the psalms is also a desideratum. The treatment of the Penitential Psalms and their relationship with the development of the literary and devotional self across both periods is an area particularly ripe for future engagement.[2] In mapping the use made of Middle English Psalters, it would also be valuable to consider quotation from and allusion to vernacular psalms in contemporary devotional texts. I have noted elsewhere that scriptural quotation and allusion 'provide the bare bones' around which Middle English devotional narratives are constructed, and the scriptural book most frequently recalled and evoked in these contexts is, unsurprisingly, the Psalter.[3] Investigation of the particular psalms most insistently cited and of the interpretative frameworks applied to them, alongside consideration of their liturgical—and other—resonances, would be likely to provide us with fresh insights into psalm usage in the late Middle Ages. The role that the English psalms play in homiletic literature of the period is another area worthy of exploration.[4] There is also, I am sure, further productive work to be done in situating the practice of psalm vernacularization in the context of contemporary theorizations of the place of the translator and the nature of translation. Additionally, more work is called for on the Wycliffite appropriation and adaptation of Richard

---

[1] The recent publication of Jane Toswell's study of the Anglo-Saxon Psalter (Toswell, M. J., *The Anglo-Saxon Psalter*, Medieval Church Studies 10 (Turnhout, 2014)) will do much to facilitate future work in this area. Among Toswell's areas of interest are the earliest extant vernacular renditions of the psalms and the evidence that we have for the continuing use of Anglo-Saxon Psalters in the later medieval period.

[2] Such work has been commenced by, for example, Lynn Staley (2007) and Claire Costley King'oo (2012).

[3] Sutherland, A., 'The Middle English Mystics', in *The Blackwell Companion to the Bible in English Literature*, Blackwell Companions to Religion, ed. R. Lemon, E. Mason, J. Roberts, and C. Rowland (Chichester, 2009), 85–99, p. 87.

[4] Such work could be facilitated, in the first instance, by use of V. O' Mara and S. Paul, *A Repertorium of Middle English Prose Sermons*, Sermo 1. 4 vols (Turnhout, 2007).

Rolle's *English Psalter*.[5] Most obviously, however, original and substantial research into the extant Middle English primers is required. Who was responsible for compiling these books of vernacular liturgy, and by whom, where, and when were they transcribed and illuminated? Who used these books and how did they use them? Why are some so obviously indebted to the Wycliffite LV while others follow a less clearly defined pattern of translation? And perhaps most enticingly of all, what does the primers' use of the Wycliffite translation(s) tell us about this Bible's early circulation in apparently orthodox contexts?

However, despite these obvious desiderata, what has emerged from this book as it stands is a fresh recognition of the remarkable proliferation of psalm translation, paraphrase, and abbreviation in late-medieval England. Many of the texts explored in the course of these six chapters appear to have been used on a daily basis to bring structure and coherence to lives of devotion expressed in manifold contexts. It is, in fact, no exaggeration to say that the translated psalms formed the backbone of intercessory experience in the late Middle Ages. More reliably than any other biblical book, the Psalter provided the devout with a voice in which to speak to God and an arena in which to hear God speak. Plumbing the depths of misery ('I am poured out like water and all my bones are scattered') and reaching the heights of elation ('. . . my soul shall rejoice in the Lord and shall be delighted in his salvation'), David's words insisted on a particular intensity of personal devotion, of intimacy with the divine.[6] Yet the translated psalms of the late Middle Ages functioned in more ways than this. Not only did they speak of personal preoccupations, but also of corporate affairs and priorities; their voice was simultaneously private and public. And not only were they of catechetic value to the spiritual novice, but they also spoke to and for the devout sophisticate. As characterized by Cassiodorus at the beginning of the preface to his *Expositio Psalmorum* (*c.* 540), the psalms were the most capacious and hermeneutically generous of texts, whose temporal and emotional reach remained unsurpassed:

> Modo enim quidam psalmorum salutari institutione formati, turbidos et tempestuosos animos declinant in limpidam et tranquillissimam uitam; modo promittentes Deum propter salute credentium uisualiter humanandum et ad iudicandum orbem esse uenturum; modo commonent lacrimis peccata diluere, eleemosynis delicta curare; modo sacris orationibus reuerentur attoniti; modo hebraei alphabeti uirtute profundi; modo de passione et de resurrectione Domini salutaria praedicantes; modo lamentantium deploratione piissimi; modo uersum repetitione quaedam nobis sacramenta pandentes; modo canticorum graduum ascencione mirabiles; postremo supernis laudibus feliciter inhaerentes, beata copia, inexplicabile desiderium, stupenda profunditas. Non potest animus fidelis expleri, qui coeperit inde satiari.

> [At one time some psalms endowed with health-giving instruction lead louring and stormy spirits into a bright and most peaceful way of life; at another, they promise that God is to become visibly man for the salvation of believers, and will come to judge the

---

[5] Such work, previously difficult to undertake, is made infinitely more manageable by Hudson (2012–14).

[6] Psalms 21: 15 and 34: 9.

world; at another they warn us to wash away sins with tears, and to atone for faults with alms; at another they express amazed reverence in sacred prayers; at another the power of the Hebrew alphabet gives them profundity; at another they proclaim the saving outcome of the passion and resurrection of the Lord; at another they show deep devotion through the weeping of those who make lamentation; at another their repetition of verses reveals certain mysteries to us; at another they are remarkable for the mounting climax of their song. In short, happily espousing divine praises are rich abundance, indescribable longing, and astonishing depth. The believing mind cannot get too much of it once it has begun to be filled with them.][7]

Taking Cassiodorus as its cue, this book has demonstrated the remarkable extent to which the psalms were—and are—fertile and adaptable texts. To return to Eleanor Hull's metaphor, commented on at the end of Chapter 5, in the 'glory-ous sauter . . . al holy wryt borionyht and florysschyt and bryngyth forthe frute'.[8] The fact that the psalms 'flourished' or produced meaning as they were read by the devout was also pondered by Cassiodorus. Defending the particular eloquence of the Psalter, he claimed that we find meaning in the psalms in the same way in which we find 'uina in uitibus, messem in semine, frondes in racidibus, fructus in ramis, arbores ipsas sensu contemplamur in nucleis' [wine in vines, a harvest in the seed, foliage in roots, fruit in branches, and trees conceptually in nuts]. He went on:

Nam et de profundissima abysso deliciosus piscis attingitur, qui tamen ante captionem suam humanis oculis non uidetur.

[Moreover, succulent fish though invisible to the human eye before being hooked are caught from the deepest pools][9]

For the attentive, patient, and perseverant reader, the Middle English psalms yielded a bountiful crop of meaning. In them, the 'uncertain and hidden things' of God's wisdom were 'made manifest' by means of a language accessible to all (Psalm 50: 8).

As this book has also indicated, however, we cannot speak in terms of a straight-forward 'tradition' of Middle English psalm translation. Since few absolutely clear lines of descent can be discerned in the psalmic literature of the period, it has been found preferable to think in terms of a creative, non-ancestral, nexus of ver-nacularization. While we might have located a predilection for very literal psalm renditions in contemporary practice, we have also noted that for many transla-tors, the activities of translation and interpretation were fundamentally insepa-rable. Translation—even orthodox translation of biblical material—could quite legitimately be an inventive rather than a purely reproductive activity. Further, although this book has demonstrated that there were salient characteristics linking much English psalm exegesis of the late Middle Ages, even here caution must be extended. Different commentators could, legitimately, excavate entirely distinct

---

[7] Adraien (1958), vol. 1, p. 4. Translation from Walsh (1990–1), vol. 1, p. 24.
[8] Barratt (1995), p. 38/509–11.
[9] Chapter 15 of the prologue to the *Expositio Psalmorum*, Adraien, vol. 1 p. 20. Walsh, vol. 1, p. 39.

meanings from one single verse—or word. The apparent simplification of psalmic complexity in some paraphrases of the period was entirely defensible as an interpretation of the Psalter's moral principles and a 'historical' reading of the book was not necessarily at odds with an awareness of its ethical preoccupations. Furthermore, to 'live' the Old Testament psalms in the form of obedience to their prophetic New Testament principles was as justifiable a reading of their 'entente' as an intellectual engagement with their written substance.

One of the most interesting areas into which this book has led us is that concerned with the relative role and status of Latin and the vernacular in contemporary literary culture. It is in keeping with the emphases of current and recent scholarship that my findings have suggested we overstate the repressive role that Latinate culture played in its interactions with emerging vernacularity. Far from stifling devotional exploration and invention, the Latin liturgy provided a template on which English intercessory practice could be modelled and enabled vernacular experimentation in the activity of speaking to—and of—God. The persistent presence of Latin cues in English manuscripts also contributed to the disintegration of any absolute divide between public liturgical prayer and private devotional practice, reminding us that the psalms speak to and for the individual and the community. Without the translated psalms, literal and paraphrasing, complete and abbreviated, prose and verse, the devotional landscape of the late Middle Ages would be unrecognizable.

APPENDICES

APPENDIX 1

English Language Primers

English primers which include psalms (those used in the Little Office of the Virgin and the Office of the Dead as well as the penitential, gradual, etc.):

[1] London, BL Add. 17010

[2] London, BL Add. 17011

[3] London, BL Add. 27592

[4] London, BL Add. 36683

[5] Cambridge, CUL Dd. 11. 82 (printed in Littlehales, H. (ed.), *The Prymer or Lay Folk's Prayer Book* 2 volumes EETS os 105 (1895) and os 109 (1897). *IMEP* xix dates the manuscript to s. xv[1])

[6] Cambridge, Emmanuel College 246 (James, M. R., *The Western Manuscripts in the Library of Emmanuel College—A Descriptive Catalogue* (1904) describes the manuscript and dates it to the late fourteenth century)

[7] Cambridge, St John's College G. 24 (printed in Littlehales, H. (ed.), *The Prymer or Prayer Book of the Lay People in the Middle Ages in English dating about 1400 AD* 2 volumes (London and New York, 1891)

[8] Glasgow, University Library Hunter 472 (v. 6. 22) (late fourteenth century)

[9] Glasgow, University Library Hunter 512 (v. 8. 15)

[10] Oxford, BodlL Ashmole 1288 (1) (dated s. xiv. ex. in *IPMEP*)

[11] Oxford, BodlL Bodley 85

[12] Oxford, BodlL Douce 246 (dated s. xv. ex. in *IMEP* iv)

[13] Oxford, BodlL Douce 275 (dated s. xiv. ex. in *IMEP* iv)

[14] Oxford, BodlL Rawlinson C. 699

[15] Oxford, Queen's College 324 (dated s. xv. in. in *IMEP* viii)

[16] Oxford, University College 179 (dated s. xv. in. in *IMEP* viii)

[17] Yale, University Library Beineke 360 (dated to s. xv. in.)

Reference has also been made to a vernacular primer in Marquis of Bute, HMC 3: 206, but thus far this manuscript has proved unlocatable.

Raymo also alerts us to the survival of parts of a vernacular primer in the fifteenth-century London University Fragment 57 (bound as two flyleaves in John Welles, *The Art of Stenographie* London 1623 (Hartung, A. E. (gen. ed.) *A Manual of the Writings in Middle English* (1967–), volume 7, XX (Raymo) *Works of Religious and Philosophical Instruction*, p. 2569).

Dublin, Trinity College B.3.16 (now 195) has been referred to as a primer but contains only an English translation of the Psalms of the Passion (Psalm 21–30) and of the Athanasian Creed. For a full description of this composite manuscript, see Colker, M. L. with intro by William O'Sullivan, *Trinity College Library Dublin—Descriptive Catalogue of the Medieval and Renaissance Latin Manuscripts* 2 volumes (1991) vol. 2, pp. 386–91, p. 390.

English Language Primers Containing Catechetic Additions

Catechetic additions (generally including basic prayers plus variable amounts of material from the Pecham syllabus) are found in the primers in:

[1] Cambridge, Emmanuel College 246
[2] Glasgow, Hunter 472
[3] Glasgow, Hunter 512
[4] London, BL Add 27592
[5] Oxford, BodlL Ashmole 1288(1)
[6] Oxford, BodlL Bodley 85
[7] Oxford, BodlL Bodley 246
[8] Oxford, BodlL Rawlinson C. 699
[9] Oxford, Queen's College 324
[10] Oxford, University College 179 (also contains the abbreviated Psalter of Jerome in English)
[11] Yale, University Library Beineke 360 (also contains a complete *English Psalter* and the abbreviated Psalter of Jerome in English)

Maidstone and Brampton

Manuscripts containing a complete text of Maidstone's Penitential Psalms

[1] London, BL Add. 36523 (according to Edden (1990) (p. 22), this manuscript contains 'a version of the poem so corrupt (and indeed inventive) that it has little value as a text of the *Psalms*')
[2] Oxford, BodlL Douce 232 (contains only the psalms)
[3] Oxford, BodlL Laud Misc 174
[4] Oxford, BodlL Rawlinson A. 389
[5] New York, Pierpont Morgan Library M.99
[6] Windsor, St. George's Chapel E. 1. 1

A further three manuscripts contain texts which were originally complete, but they now lack leaves or folios:

[1] Aberystwyth, National Library of Wales, Porkington 20
[2] London, BL Harley 3810, Part 1
[3] Philadelphia, Pennsylvania English 1

Manuscripts containing Brampton's Penitential Psalms

[1] Cambridge, Magdalene College Pepys 1584 (so-called variant version B)
[2] Cambridge, Magdalene College Pepys 2030 (so-called 'normal' version A)
[3] Cambridge, Trinity College R.3.20 (so-called variant version B)
[4] Cambridge, CUL Ff.2.38 (so-called variant version B)
[5] London, BL Sloane 1853 (so-called 'normal' version A)
[6] London, BL Harley 1704 (so-called 'normal' version A)

Manuscripts Containing Complete *English Psalters*

The Metrical Psalter

[1] Cambridge, Corpus Christi College 278
[2] London, BL Cotton Vespasian D. vii
[3] London, BL Egerton 614
[4] London, BL Harley 1770
[5] Oxford, BodlL Bodley 425
[6] Oxford, BodlL Bodley 921

The Prose Psalter

[1] Cambridge, Magdalene College Pepys 2498
[2] Dublin, Trinity College 69
[4] London, BL Add. 17376
[3] Princeton, University Library Scheide deposit 143

Rolle's uninterpolated *English Psalter*

[1] Aberdeen, University Library 243
[2] Cambridge, Corpus Christi College 387
[3] Cambridge, Sidney Sussex College 89
[4] Eton, Eton College Library 10
[5] Green Collection (olim Rosebury, olim Phillipps 8884)
[6] Hatfield (Herts.), Hatfield House, the Marquess of Salisbury Cecil Papers 328
[7] London, BL Add. 40769
[8] London, BL Arundel 158
[9] London, BL Harley 1806
[10] Newcastle upon Tyne, Public Library TH. 1678
[11] New Haven, Yale University Library 360 (excerpts)
[12] Oxford, BodlL Bodley 467
[13] Oxford, BodlL Bodley 953
[14] Oxford, BodlL Douce 258 (excerpts)
[15] Oxford, BodlL Hatton 12
[16] Oxford, BodlL Laud Misc 448
[17] Oxford, BodlL Tanner 1
[18] Oxford, BodlL Laud Misc. 286
[19] Oxford, BodlL Laud Misc.321
[20] Oxford, Magdalen College lat. 52
[21] Oxford, University College 56
[22] Oxford, University College 64
[23] Rome, Vatican Library Reg.lat.320
[24] San Marino, Huntington Library HM 148

[25] Worcester Cathedral Library F.158
[26] Worcester Cathedral Library F.166

(Details taken from Hanna (2010).) The manuscripts of the Wycliffite interpolated version of Rolle's Psalter, and their relation to Rolle's text, are described in Hudson (2012–14).

London Manuscripts containing the Psalter in the translation of the Wycliffite Bible (complete in either EV or LV)

[1] Cambridge, Corpus Christi College Parker 147 (Prologue, Lectionary, ONT in LV)
[2] Cambridge, Emmanuel College 21 (Lectionary, ONT in LV)
[3] Cambridge, CUL Add. 6680 (ONT in LV)
[4] Cambridge, CUL Dd. I. 27 (OT, Lectionary, NT in LV)
[5] Cambridge, CUL Mm. 2. 15 (OT, Prol., NT in LV)
[6] Hereford, Cathedral Library O. VII.I (Lectionary, ONT in LV)
[7] London, BL Cotton Claudius E. II (ONT in LV)
[8] London, BL Arundel 104 (2 vols, ONT in LV)
[9] London, Lambeth Palace 25 (Genesis-Deuteronomy in EV; Joshua-Revelation in LV)
[10] London, BL Royal I. C. VIII (Prologue (ch. 1), ONT in LV (rev.)
[11] Longleat House, Longleat 3 (ONT in EV (-NT prologues))
[12] Oxford, BodlL Bodley 277 (Prologue (ch. 1), ONT in LV (rev.))
[13] Oxford, BodlL Douce 369 (Part 1—Num. 20–Bar. 3: 20 in EV. Part 2—Isaiah–Acts in EV (rev. in Luke–John)
[14] Oxford, BodlL Fairfax 2 (ONT, Lectionary in LV)
[15] Oxford, Christ Church College 145 (Lect. in LV, ONT in EV (-prols. Rom–Apoc.))
[16] Oxford, Corpus Christi College 4 (Lectionary, ONT in EV (-prols in NT))
[17] Oxford, Lincoln College, Latin 119 (Prologue, ONT in LV)
[18] Oxford, Queen's College 388 (Lectionary, ONT in LV)
[19] Princeton, William H. Scheide 12 (Lectionary, Prologue, ONT in LV);
[20] Wolfenbuttel, Herzog-August-Bibl., Guelf. Aug. A. 2 (Lect., ONT in EV (-prols. to Mark, Luke))

(All details taken from Dove (2007))

Manuscripts containing the Wycliffite Psalter with the complete or partial Wycliffite Old Testament (EV or LV)

[1] Cambridge, CUL Add. 6681 (OT in EV)
[2] Cambridge, CUL Ee.1.10 (parts of the Old Testament and apocrypha EV (rev.))
[3] Cambridge, St John's College E. 14 (Psalms, Canticles, Quicunque Vult, Prov–Ecclus in LV
[4] London, BL Add. 31044 (Prol. (Ps. –Ecclus.), Ps. –Ecclus. in LV. It also contains the prologue to
[5] London, BL Lansdowne 454 (Genesis–Psalms in LV)
[6] London, BL Harley 2249 (Joshua 19: 19–Ps. 144: 13 in LV) Perhaps vol. II of a four-vol. Bible
[7] London, Lambeth Palace Library 1033 (2 Chron 2: 7 – Baruch in LV)
[8] Manchester, John Rylands University Library, Eng. 88 (Psalms and Song of Songs)
[9] Norwich, Norfolk Heritage Centre I h 20 (Gen–Prov 7: 10 in LV)
[10] Oxford, BodlL Bodley 296 (Gen–Psalms in LV) Presumably vol. I of a two-vol. Bible
[11] Oxford, BodlL Bodley 959 (Gen–Bar 3: 20 in EV)
[12] Oxford, Corpus Christi College 20 (1 Ezra-2 Macc in LV)

[13] Oxford, New College 66 (Gen. –Psalms in LV although the manuscript originally contained more
[14] San Marino, Huntington Library HM 501
[15] Sion College, ARC L 40.2/E. I (Prefatory Epistles, OT in LV)
(All details taken from Dove (2007))

Manuscripts containing the Wycliffite Psalter (LV) with Wycliffite New Testament material only

[1] Cambridge, St John's College E.18 (the psalms of the passion with an LV John and the Articles of the Faith)
[2] Worcester Cathedral Library F. 172 (Psalms 1–83 with LV Acts and a selection of devotional prose)

Manuscripts containing Wycliffite psalms with selections of both Old and New Testament material in the Wycliffite translation

[1] Oxford, BodlL Bodley 771 (a complete EV Old Testament accompanied by extracts from the Epistles and Acts)
[2] Oxford, BodlL Laud Misc 182 (Psalms 1, 2, 4, 5, 6, 36, 50, 70, and 98 are included in a selection of complete LV chapters (Old and New Testaments) and selected verses from the other psalms are quoted again later in the codex)

Manuscripts containing the Wycliffite LV psalms with liturgical and/or catechetic material

[1] Dublin, Trinity College Library 70 (LV Psalms 2: 9–150 accompanied by basic catechetic material)
[2] New Haven, Yale University, Beineke Library 360 (LV Psalms 2: 9–150 accompanied by a primer)

Manuscripts containing the Wycliffite LV psalms alone or with Canticles/litany/lectionary/prefatory material

[1] Dublin, Trinity College Library 72 (lectionary, the LV prologue to the psalms, psalms, and canticles)
[2] London, BL Add. 10046 (part of chapter 12 of the prologue to the Wycliffite bible, psalms and canticles, Quicunque Vult with Rolle's commentary)
[3] London, BL Add. 10047 (Psalms 1–73)
[4] London BL Add. 35284 (Psalms 45–150, canticles, and a litany)
[5] London, BL Harley 1896 (bilingual psalms accompanied by canticles)
[6] Oxford, BodlL Bodley 554 (glossed copy of the psalms, canticles)
[7] Oxford, New College 320 (psalms plus canticles)

Bibliography

REFERENCES

Abbott, T. K., *Catalogue of the Manuscripts in the Library of Trinity College Dublin* (Dublin and London, 1900).

Boffey, J. and Edwards, A. S. G. (eds), *A New Index of Middle English Verse* (London, 2005).

Brown, C. and Robbins, R. H. (eds), *The Index of Middle English Verse* (New York, 1943).

Colker, M. L. (ed.) with an intro. by W. O'Sullivan, *Trinity College Library Dublin—Descriptive Catalogue of the Medieval and Renaissance Latin Manuscripts*, 2 vols (Aldershot, 1991).

Copeland, R. and Sluiter, I. (eds), *Medieval Grammar and Rhetoric: Language Arts and Literary Theory, AD 300–1475* (Oxford, 2009).

Dalton, J. N., *The Manuscripts of St George's Chapel, Windsor Castle* (Windsor, 1957).

Dean, R. and Boulton, M. B. M. (eds), *Anglo-Norman Literature—A Guide to Texts and Manuscripts* (London, 1999).

Edwards, A. S. G., Lewis, R. E., and Blake, N. F. (eds), *The Index of Printed Middle English Prose* (London, 1985) (*IPMEP*).

Hanna, R., *The English Manuscripts of Richard Rolle—A Descriptive Catalogue*, Exeter Medieval Texts and Studies (Exeter, 2010).

Hartung, A. E. (gen. ed.), *A Manual of the Writings in Middle English* 1050–1500 (1967–2005), 11 vols, Vol. 7, ed. R. Raymo, *Works of Religious and Philosophical Instruction* (Hamden, 1986).

James, M. R., *The Western Manuscripts of Emmanuel College: A Descriptive Catalogue* (Cambridge, 1904).

Jolliffe, P. S. (ed.), *A Checklist of Middle English Prose Writings of Spiritual Guidance* (Toronto, 1974).

Lewis, R. E. and McIntosh, A., *A Descriptive Guide to the Manuscripts of the Prick of Conscience* (Oxford, 1982).

Livingstone, E. A. (ed.), *The Concise Oxford Dictionary of the Christian Church*, revd. 3rd edn (Oxford, 2013).

McIntosh, A., Samuels, M. L., and Benskin, M. (eds), *A Linguistic Atlas of Late Mediaeval English*, 4 vols (Aberdeen, 1986).

Mckitterick, R. and Beadle, R., *Catalogue of the Pepys Library at Magdalene College Cambridge*, vol. 5, Manuscripts. Part I: Medieval (Cambridge, 1992).

Morey, J. H. (ed.), *Book and Verse: A Guide to Middle English Biblical Literature* (Urbana, 2000).

Morgan, N. *Early Gothic Manuscripts*, Survey of Manuscripts Illuminated in the British Isles 4, 2 vols (London and Oxford, 1982–8).

Thomson, R. M., *A Descriptive Catalogue of the Medieval Manuscripts in Worcester Cathedral Library* (Cambridge, 2001).

Young, J. (continued and completed by P. Henderson Aitken), *A Catalogue of the Manuscripts in the Library of the Hunterian Museum in the University of Glasgow* (Glasgow, 1908).

THESES AND UNPUBLISHED MATERIALS

Cavanaugh, S., *A Study of Books Privately Owned in England: 1300–1450*, unpublished PhD thesis, University of Pennsylvania, 1980.

Doyle, A. I., *A Study of the Origins and Circulation of Theological Writings in the Fourteenth, Fifteenth and Early Sixteenth Centuries with Special Consideration of the Part of the Clergy therein*, 2 vols, PhD thesis, University of Cambridge, 1953.

Everett, D., *A Study of the Middle English Prose Psalter of Richard Rolle of Hampole*, MA thesis, University of London, 1921.

Harris-Matthews, J. M., *Lay Devotions in Late Medieval English Manuscripts*, MLitt thesis, University of Cambridge, 1980.

Porter, M. L., *Richard Rolle's Latin Commentary on the Psalms to which is Prefaced a Study of Rolle's Life and Works*, PhD thesis, Cornell University, 1929.

Thorn, N., *The Dissemination of the Middle English Psalter*, PhD thesis, University of Birmingham, 1996.

PRIMARY

Adraien, M. (ed.), *Cassiodorus: Expositio Psalmorum*, Corpus Christianorum Series Latina 97 and 98, 2 vols (Turnhout, 1958).

Alter, R. (ed.), *The Book of Psalms: A Translation with Commentary* (New York and London, 2007).

Barr, H. (ed.), *The Digby Poems—A New Edition of the Lyrics*, Exeter Medieval Texts and Studies (Exeter, 2009).

Barratt, A. (ed.), *The Seven Psalms: A Commentary on the Penitential Psalms, translated by Eleanor Hull*, EETS OS 307 (Oxford, 1995).

Bartelink, G. J. M (ed.), *Liber de Optimo Genere Interpretandi (Epistula 57)* (Leiden, 1980).

Benson, L. D. (ed.), *The Riverside Chaucer*, 3rd edn (Oxford, 2008).

Bestul, T. (ed.), Walter Hilton, *The Scale of Perfection*, TEAMS (Kalamazoo, 2000).

Black, R. R. and St-Jacques, R. (eds), *The Middle English Glossed Prose Psalter edited from Cambridge, Magdalene College, MS Pepys 2498*, Middle English Texts 45, 2 vols (Heidelberg, 2012).

Black, W. H., *A Paraphrase of the Seven Penitential Psalms in English Verse*, Percy Society 7 (London, 1842).

Blunt, J. H. (ed.), *The Myroure of Oure Ladye*, EETS ES 19 (London, 1873).

Bramley, H. R. (ed.), *The Psalter or Psalms of David and Certain Canticles, with a Translation and Exposition in English by Richard Rolle of Hampole* (Oxford, 1884).

Brandeis, A. (ed.), *Jacob's Well*, EETS OS 115 (London, 1900).

Brown, C. (ed.), *Religious Lyrics of the Fifteenth Century* (Oxford, 1939).

Brown, C. (ed.), revd. G. V. Smithers, *Religious Lyrics of the Fourteenth Century* (Oxford, 1952).

Bülbring, K. (ed.), *The Earliest Complete English Prose Psalter*, EETS OS 97 (London, 1891).

Burrow, J. A. and Turville-Petre, T. (eds), *A Book of Middle English*, 3rd edn (Oxford, 2005).

Colledge, E. and Bazire, J. (eds), *The Chastising of God's Children and the Treatise of the Perfection of the Sons of God* (Oxford, 1957).

Day, M. (ed.), *The Wheatley Manuscript*, EETS OS 155 (London, 1921).

Dove, M. (ed.), *The Earliest Advocates of the English Bible—The Texts of the Medieval Debate*, Exeter Medieval Texts and Studies (Exeter, 2010).

Edden, V. (ed.), *Richard Maidstone's Penitential Psalms*, Middle English Texts 22 (Heidelberg, 1990).

Edwards, A. S. G (ed.), 'The Battle of the Psalms', *English Language Notes* 8.2 (1970), 91–2.

D'Evelyn, C. (ed.), *Peter Idley's Instructions to his Son* (Boston and London, 1935).

Forshall, J. and Madden, F. (eds), *The Holy Bible, Containing the Old and New Testaments, with the Apocryphal Books, in the Earliest English Versions Made from the Latin Vulgate by John Wycliffe and his Followers*, 4 vols (Oxford, 1850).

Furnivall, F. J. (ed.), *Political, Religious and Love Poems*, EETS OS 15 (London, 1866).

Furnivall, F. J. (ed.), *Fifty Earliest English Wills in the Court of Probate, London AD 1387–1439*, EETS OS 78 (London, 1882).

Furnivall, F. J. and Horstmann, C. (eds), *The Minor Poems of the Vernon MS*, 2 vols, EETS OS 117 (London, 1892–1901).

Greer Fein, S. (ed.), *Moral Love Songs and Laments*, TEAMS (Kalamazoo, 1998).

Hanna, R. and Lawton, D. A. (eds), *The Siege of Jerusalem*, EETS OS 320 (Oxford, 2003).

Horstmann, C. (ed.), with a new preface by A. C. Bartlett, *Yorkshire Writers: Richard Rolle of Hampole, an English Father of the Church and his Followers* (Woodbridge, 1999).

Hoskins, E., *Horae Beatae Mariae Virginis or Sarum and York Primers with Kindred Books and Primers of the Reformed Roman Use, Together with an Introduction* (London, 1901).

Hudson, A. (ed.), *Two Revisions of Rolle's English Psalter Commentary and the Related Canticles*, EETS OS 340, 341, 343 (Oxford, 2012–14).

Hunt, S., *An Edition of Tracts in Favour of Scriptural Translation and of Some Texts Connected with Lollard Vernacular Biblical Scholarship*, unpublished DPhil thesis (Oxford, 1994).

Kail, J. (ed.), *Twenty-Six Political and Other Poems*, EETS OS 124 (London, 1904).

Kreuzer, J. R. (ed.), 'Thomas Brampton's Metrical Paraphrase', *Traditio* 7 (1949–51), 359–403.

Lindberg, C. (ed.), *The Middle English Bible—The Book of Judges* (Oslo, 1989).

Lindberg, C. (ed.), *MS Bodley 959: Genesis to Baruch 3: 20 in the Earlier Version of the Wycliffite Bible*, Stockholm Studies in English 6, 8, 10, 13, 20, 29, 81, 87 (Stockholm, 1959–97).

Lindberg, C. (ed.), *King Henry's Bible. Bodley 277—The Revised Version of the Wyclif Bible*, 4 vols (Stockholm, 1999).

Littlehales, H. (ed.), *Pages in Facsimile from a Layman's Prayer-Book in English about 1400 AD* (London, 1890).

Littlehales, H. (ed.), *The Prymer or Prayer-Book of the Lay People in the Middle Ages in English Dating about 1400 AD*, 2 vols (London, 1891–2).

Littlehales, H. (ed.), *The Prymer or the Lay Folks' Prayer Book*, 2 vols, EETS OS 105 (1895) and OS 109 (1897).

Littlehales, H. (ed.), *English Fragments from Latin Medieval Service Books*, EETS ES 90 (London, 1903).

MacCracken, H. (ed.), *The Minor Poems of John Lydgate*, EETS ES 107, vol. 1 (London, 1911 for 1910).

MacCracken, H. (ed.), *The Minor Poems of John Lydgate*, EETS OS 192, vol. 2 (London, 1934).

Maskell, W. (ed.), *Monumenta Ritualia Ecclesiae Anglicanae*, 3 vols (Oxford, 1846).

McCarthy, A. J. (ed.), *Book to a Mother: An Edition with Commentary*, Salzburg Studies in English Literature; Elizabethan and Renaissance Studies 92; Studies in the English Mystics 1 (Salzburg, 1981).

McSparran, F. and Robinson, P. R. (intro.), *Cambridge University Library MS Ff. 2. 38* (London, 1979).

Millett, B. (ed.), *Ancrene Wisse—A Corrected Edition of the text in Cambridge, Corpus Christi College MS 402 with Variants from other Manuscripts*, 2 vols, EETS OS 325 and 326 (Oxford, 2005).

O'Donoghue, B., *Thomas Hoccleve—Selected Poems* (Manchester, 1982).

O'Mara, V. and Paul, S. (eds), *A Repertorium of Middle English Prose Sermons*, Sermo 1, 4 vols (Turnhout, 2007).

Peacock, E. (ed.), *Instructions for Parish Priests by John Myrc* (London, 1868).

Pearsall, D. and Cunningham, I. C. (intro.), *The Auchinleck MS: National Library of Scotland Advocates' MS 19.2.1* (London, 1977).

Pearsall, D. (ed.), *Piers Plowman—A New Annotated Edition of the C-text*, Exeter Medieval Texts and Studies (Exeter, 2008).

Phillips, H. and Havely, N. (eds), *Chaucer's Dream Poetry*, Longman Annotated Texts (London, 1997).

Pulsiano, P. (ed.), *Old English Glossed Psalters—Psalms 1–50*, Toronto Old English Series 11 (Toronto, 2001).

Hingeston-Randolph, F. C. (ed.), *The Register of John de Grandisson, Bishop of Exeter (AD 1327–1369) with Some Account of the Episcopate of James de Berkeley (AD 1327)*, 3 vols (London and Exeter, 1894–9).

Schmidt, A. V. C. (ed.), *The Vision of Piers Plowman: A Critical Edition of the B-Text Based on Trinity College MS. B. 15. 17*, 2nd edn corrected (London, 2011).

Scott-Stokes, C. (ed. and trans.), *Women's Books of Hours in Medieval England: Selected Texts translated from Latin, Anglo-Norman, French and Middle English with Introduction and Interpretative Essay*, Library of Medieval Women (Woodbridge, 2006).

Simmons, T. F. (ed.), *The Lay Folk's Mass Book or the Manner of Hearing Mass*, EETS OS 71 (London, 1879).

Sisam, C. and Sisam, K. (eds), *The Salisbury Psalter*, EETS OS 242 (London, 1959).

Stevenson, J. (ed.) *Anglo-Saxon and Early English Psalter*, Publications of the Surtees Society, vols 16 and 19 (London, 1843–7).

Wallner, B. (ed.), *An Exposition of Qui Habitat and Bonum Est in English*, Lund Studies in English 23 (Lund, 1954).

Walsh, P. G. (trans. and annot.), *Cassiodorus: Explanation of the Psalms*, Ancient Christian Writers—The Works of the Fathers in Translation 51, 52, 53 (New York, 1990–1).

Wilson, E. (with an account of the music by Iain Fenlon), *The Winchester Anthology: A Facsimile of British Library Additional 60577* (Cambridge, 1981).

Windeatt, B. (ed.), *The Book of Margery Kempe*, Longman Annotated Texts (Harlow, 2000).

SECONDARY

Acker, P., 'A Schoolchild's Primer (Plimpton MS 258)', in *Medieval Literature for Children*, ed. Kline, chapter 9, 143–54.

Alford, J. A., 'Richard Rolle's English Psalter and Lectio Divina', *BJRL* 77 (1995), 47–59.

Allen, H. E. A. (ed.), *English Writings of Richard Rolle, Hermit of Hampole* (Oxford, 1931).

Alter, R., *The Art of Biblical Poetry* (New York, 1985).

Alter, R. and Kermode, F. (eds), *The Literary Guide to the Bible* (London, 1987).

Astell, A., 'Cassiodorus' Commentary on the Psalms as an *Ars rhetorica*', *Rhetorica: A Journal of the History of Rhetoric* 17 (1999), 37–75.

Aston, M., *Lollards and Reformers: Images and Literacy in Late Medieval Religion* (London, 1984).

Austin, J. L., *How to Do Things with Words*, William James Lectures 1955, 2nd edn (Oxford, 1975).

Barr, H. and Hutchison, A. (eds), *Text and Controversy from Wyclif to Bale—Essays in Honour of Anne Hudson, Medieval Church Studies 4* (Turnhout, 2005).

Barratt, A., 'The Prymer and its Influence on 15th Century English Passion Lyrics', *MA* 44 (1975), 264–79.

Barratt, A., 'Dame Eleanor Hull: A 15th Century Translator', in *The Medieval Translator: The Theory and Practice of Translation in the Middle Ages*, ed. Ellis (1989).

Beadle, R., 'Prologomena to a Literary Geography of Later Medieval Norfolk', in *Regionalism in Late Medieval Manuscripts and Texts: Essays Celebrating the Publication* of A Linguistic Atlas of Late Medieval English, ed. Riddy, 89–108.

Bedingfield, M. B., *The Dramatic Liturgy of Anglo-Saxon England* (Woodbridge, 2002).

Bedingfield, M. B. and Gittos, H. (eds), *The Liturgy of the Late Anglo-Saxon Church* (London, 2005).

Bell, D. N., *What Nuns Read: Books and Libraries in Medieval English Nunneries* (Kalamazoo, 1995).

Bell, H. E., 'The Price of Books in Medieval England', *The Library* 17 (1936), 312–32.

Bhattacharji, S., Williams, R., and Mattos, D. (eds), *Prayer and Thought in Monastic Tradition—Essays in Honour of Benedicta Ward SLG* (London and New York, 2014).

Birchenough, E., 'The Prymer in English', *The Library* 18 (1937), 177–94.

Bishop, E., 'On the Origin of the Prymer', in Littlehales, H. (ed.), *The Prymer or the Lay Folks' Prayer Book*, 2 vols, EETS OS 105 (1895) and OS 109 (1897). Repr. in *Liturgica Historica: Papers on the Liturgy and Religious Life of the Western Church*, ed. E. Bishop (Oxford, 1918), 211–37.

Blake, N. F., 'Vernon Manuscript: Contents and Organisation', in *Studies in the Vernon Manuscript*, ed. D. Pearsall (Cambridge, 1990), 45–59, p. 51.

Blamires, A., 'The Limits of Bible Study for Medieval Women', in *Women, the Book and the Godly*, ed. Smith and Taylor, (1995), 1–12.

Boffey, J., '"Many grete myraclys . . . in divers contreys of the eest": The Reading and Circulation of the Middle English Prose Three Kings of Cologne', in *Medieval Women: Texts and Contexts in Late Medieval Britain: Essays for Felicity Riddy*, ed. Jocelyn Wogan-Browne et al. (Turnhout, 2000), 35–47.

Boffey, J., 'The Charter of the Abbey of the Holy Ghost and its Role in Manuscript Anthologies', *YES* 33 (2003), 120–30.

Boynton, S., 'Prayer as Liturgical Performance in Eleventh- and Twelfth-Century Monastic Psalters', *Speculum* 82 (2007), 896–931.

Boynton, S., 'Plainsong', in *The Cambridge Companion to Medieval Music*, Cambridge Companions to Music, ed. M. Everist (Cambridge, 2011), 9–25.

Colish, M. L., '*Psalterium Scholasticorum*: Peter Lombard and the Emergence of Scholastic Psalm Exegesis', *Speculum* 67 (1992), 531–48.

Cooper, H., 'The Four Last Things in Dante and Chaucer: Ugolino in the House of Rumour', in *NML*, vol. 3, ed. D. Lawton, W. Scase, and R. Copeland (Oxford, 1999), 39–66.

Copeland, R., 'The Fortunes of "non verbum pro verbum": Or Why Jerome is Not a Ciceronian', in *The Medieval Translator: The Theory and Practice of Translation in the Middle Ages*, ed. Ellis (Cambridge, 1989), 15–35.

Copeland, R., *Rhetoric, Hermeneutics and Translation in the Middle Ages: Academic Traditions and Vernacular Texts*, Cambridge Studies in Medieval Literature 11 (Cambridge, 1991).

Copeland, R., 'Rhetoric and the Politics of the Literal Sense in Medieval Literary Theory: Aquinas, Wyclif and the Lollards', in *Interpretation: Medieval and Modern*, ed. P. Boitani and A. Torti (Cambridge, 1993), 1–23.

Costley King'oo, C., *Miserere Mei: The Penitential Psalms in Late Medieval and Early Modern England*, Reformations: Medieval and Early Modern (Notre Dame, 2012).

Cré, M., 'We are United with God (and God with Us?): Adapting Ruusbroec in *The Treatise of Perfection of the Sons of God* and *The Chastising of God's Children*', in *The Medieval Mystical Tradition in England—Exeter Symposium* VII, ed. E. A. Jones (Cambridge, 2004).

Deanesly, M., *The Lollard Bible and other Medieval Biblical Versions* (Cambridge, 1920).

Dodson, S., 'The Glosses in the Earliest Complete English Prose Psalter', *TSE* 12 (1932), 5–26.

Dove, M., *The First English Bible: The Text and Context of the Wycliffite Versions*, Cambridge Studies in Medieval Literature 66 (Cambridge, 2007).

Doyle, A. I., 'The Shaping of the Vernon and Simeon Manuscripts', in *Chaucer and Middle English Studies in Honour of Rossell Hope Robbins*, ed. B. Rowland (London, 1974).

Driscoll, M., 'The Seven Penitential Psalms: Their Designation and Usage from the Middle Ages Onwards', *Ecclesia Orans* 17 (2000), 153–201.

Duffy, E., *The Stripping of the Altars: Traditional Religion in England c. 1400–1580* (New Haven and London, 1992).

Duffy, E., *Marking the Hours: English People and their Prayers, 1250–1570: the Riddell Lectures 2002* (New Haven and London, 2006).

Dutton, A. M., 'Passing the Book: Testamentary Transmission of Religious Literature to and by Women in the England 1350–1500', in *Women, the Book and the Godly*, ed. Smith and Taylor, 41–54.

Edden, V., ' "And my boonus han dried vp as critouns": The History of the Translation of Psalm 101, 4', *N&Q* 28 (1981), 389–92.

Edden, V., 'Richard Maidstone's *Penitential Psalms*', in *Carmel in Britain: Essays on the Medieval English Carmelite Province*, ed. P. Fitzgerald-Lombard and R. Copsey (Rome and Faversham, 1992), 106–24.

Ellis, R., 'The Choices of the Translator in the Late Middle English Period', in *The Medieval Mystical Tradition in England—Papers Read at Dartington Hall, July 1982*, ed. M. Glasscoe (Exeter, 1982), 18–46.

Ellis, R. (ed.), *The Medieval Translator: The Theory and Practice of Translation in the Middle Ages* (Cambridge, 1989).

Ellis, R., 'Translation', in *A Companion to Chaucer*, Blackwell Companions to Literature and Culture, ed. P. Brown (Oxford, 2000).

Erler, M. C., *Women, Reading and Piety in Late Medieval England*, Cambridge Studies in Medieval Literature 46 (Cambridge, 2002).

Everett, D., 'The Middle English Prose Psalter of Richard Rolle of Hampole, I', *MLR* 17 (1922), 217–27 (1922a).

Everett, D., 'The Middle English Prose Psalter of Richard Rolle of Hampole, II', *MLR* 17 (1922), 337–50 (1922b).

Everett, D., 'The Middle English Prose Psalter of Richard Rolle of Hampole, III', *MLR* 18 (1923), 381–93 (1922c).

Everist, M. (ed.), *The Cambridge Companion to Medieval Music* (Cambridge, 2011).

Field, S. L., 'Marie of Saint-Pol and her Books', *EHR* 125 (2010), 255–78.

Flanigan, C. C., Ashley, K., and Sheingorn, P., 'Liturgy as Social Performance: Expanding the Definitions', in Heffernan and Matter, *The Liturgy of the Medieval Church*, 695–714.

France, P., Gillespie, S., Hopkins, D., Haynes, K., Braden, G., and Cummings, R. M., (eds) *The Oxford History of Literary Translation in English*, 5 vols (Oxford, 2005), vol. 1 'To 1550', ed. R. Ellis.

Friedman, J. Block, *Northern English Books, Owners and Makers in the Late Middle Ages* (Syracuse, 1995).

Fulton, R., 'Praying with Anselm at Admont: A Meditation on Practice', *Speculum* 81 (2006), 700–33.

Gameson, R. (ed.), *The Early Medieval Bible: Its Production, Decoration and Use*, Cambridge Studies in Palaeography and Codicology 2 (Cambridge, 1994).

Ghosh, K., *The Wycliffite Heresy: Authority and the Interpretation of Texts*, Cambridge Studies in Medieval Literature 45 (Cambridge, 2002).

Gibson, M., Heslop, T. A., and Pfaff, R. W. (eds), *The Eadwine Psalter—Text, Image and Monastic Culture in Twelfth-Century Canterbury* (London and Philadelphia, 1992).

Gillespie, V., 'Vernacular Books of Religion', in *Book Production and Publishing in Britain 1375–1475*, ed. Griffiths and Pearsall, chapter 13, 317–44.

Gillespie, V., 'Anonymous Devotional Writings', in *A Companion to Middle English Prose*, ed. A. S. G. Edwards (Cambridge, 2004), chapter 9, 127–49.

Gillespie, V. and Ghosh, K. (eds), *After Arundel: Religious Writing in Fifteenth-Century England*, Medieval Church Studies 21 (Turnhout, 2011).

Glasscoe, M., 'Time of Passion: Latent Relationships between Liturgy and Meditation in Two Middle English Mystics', in *Langland, The Mystics and the Medieval English Religious Tradition: Essays in Honour of S. S. Hussey*, ed. H. Phillips (Cambridge, 1990).

Goldberg, P. J. P., 'Lay Book Ownership in Late Medieval York: The Evidence of Wills', *The Library* 16 (1994), 181–9.

Greer Fein, S., '*Haue Mercy of Me* (Psalm 51): An Unedited Alliterative Poem from the London Thornton Manuscript', *MP* 86 (1989), 223–41.

Griffiths, J. and Pearsall, D. (eds), *Book Production and Publishing in Britain 1375–1475*, Cambridge Studies in Publishing and Printing History (Cambridge, 1989).

Gross-Diaz, T., *The Psalms Commentary of Gilbert of Poitiers. From Lectio Divina to the Lecture Room*, Brill's Studies in Intellectual History 68 (Leiden, 1996).

Gustafson, K., 'Richard Rolle's English Psalter and the Making of a Lollard Text', *Viator* 33 (2002), 294–309.

de Hamel, C., *The Book: A History of the Bible* (London, 2001).

Hamlin, H., *Psalm Culture and Early Modern English Literature* (Cambridge, 2004).

Hammerling, R. (ed.), *A History of Prayer: The First to the Fifteenth Century*, Brill's Companions to the Christian Tradition 13 (Leiden, 2008).

Hanna, R., 'The Text of *Memoriale Credencium*', *Neophilogus* 67 (1983), 284–92.

Hanna, R., 'Sir Thomas Berkeley and his Patronage', *Speculum* 64 (1989), 878–916.

Hanna, R., 'The Difficulty of Ricardian Prose Translation: the Case of the Lollards', *MLQ* 51 (1990), 319–40.

Hanna, R., *Pursuing History: Middle English Manuscripts and Their Texts* (Stanford, 1996).

Hanna, R., 'Reconsidering the Auchinleck Manuscript', in *New Directions in Later Medieval Manuscript Studies*, ed. Pearsall, 91–102.

Hanna, R., 'Yorkshire Writers', *PBA* 121 (Oxford, 2003), 91–109.

Hanna, R., 'Rolle and Related Works', in *A Companion to Middle English Prose*, ed. A. S. G. Edwards (Cambridge, 2004), 19–31.

Hanna, R., *London Literature, 1300–1380*, Cambridge Studies in Medieval Literature 57 (Cambridge, 2005).

Hardman, P., 'A Mediaeval "Library" In Parvo', *MA* 47 (1978), 262–73.

Hargreaves, H., 'The Vocabulary of the Surtees Psalter', *MLQ* 17 (1956), 326–39.

Hargreaves, H., 'An Intermediate Version of the Wycliffite Old Testament', *SN* 28 (1956), 130–47.

Hargreaves, H., 'The Middle English Primers and the Wycliffite Bible', *MLR* 51 (1956), 215–17.

Hargreaves, H., '*Lessons of Dirige*: A Rolle Text Discovered', *NM* 91 (1990), 511–19.

Hargreaves, H., 'The Latin Text of Purvey's Psalter', *MA* 24 (1995), 73–90.

Harper, J., *The Forms and Orders of Western Liturgy from the Tenth to the Eighteenth Century: A Historical Introduction and Guide for Students and Musicians* (Oxford, 1991).

Heffernan, T. J. and Matter, A. E. (eds), *The Liturgy of the Medieval Church* (Kalamazoo, 2001).

Hirsch, J. C., 'Prayer and Meditation in Late Mediaeval England: MS Bodley 789', *MA* 48 (1979), 55–66.

Hoeppner-Moran, J. A., *The Growth of English Schooling 1340–1548—Learning, Literacy and Laicization in Pre-Reformation York Diocese* (Guildford, 1985).

Holsinger, B., 'Liturgy', in *Middle English*, Oxford Twenty-First Century Approaches to Literature, ed. P. Strohm (Oxford, 2007), 295–314.

Hudson, A., 'The Debate on Bible Translation, Oxford 1401', *EHR* 90 (1975), 1–18.

Hudson, A., *The Premature Reformation—Wycliffite Texts and Lollard History* (Oxford, 1988).

Hudson, A., 'The Carthusians and a Wycliffite Bible', in *Ecclesia-Cultura-Potestas: A Festsch rift for Urszula Borkowska OSU*, ed. P. Kras et al. (Kraków, 2006), 731–42.

Hughes, A., *Medieval Manuscripts for Mass and Office: A Guide to their Organisation and Terminology* (Toronto, 1982).

Kelly, L. G., 'Medieval Psalm Translation and Literality', in *Translation Theory and Practice in the Middle Ages*, Studies in Medieval Culture 38, ed. J. Beer (Kalamazoo, 1997).

Ker, N. R., 'Patrick Young's Catalogue of the Manuscripts of Lichfield Cathedral', *MRS* 2 (1950), 151–68.

Kieckhefer, R. *Magic in the Middle Ages*, Cambridge Medieval Textbooks (Cambridge, 1989).

Kline, D. T. (ed.), *Medieval Literature for Children* (New York and London, 2003).

Kreuzer, J. R., 'Richard Maidstone's Version of the Fifty-First Psalm', *MLN* 66 (1951), 224–31.

Kuczynski, M. P., *Prophetic Song: The Psalms as Moral Discourse in Late Medieval England*, Middle Ages Series (Philadelphia, 1995).

Kuczynski, M. P., 'Rolle Among the Reformers: Orthodoxy and Heterodoxy in Wycliffite Copies of Richard Rolle's *English Psalter*', in *Mysticism and Spirituality in Medieval England*, ed. W. F. Pollard and R. Boenig (Woodbridge, 1997).

Kuczynski, M. P., 'An Unpublished Lollard Psalm *Catena* in Huntington Library MS 501', *JEBS* 13 (2010), 95–138.

Lawton, D. A., '*The Destruction of Troy* as Translation from Latin Prose: Aspects of Form and Style', *SN* 52 (1980), 259–70.

Lawton, D. A., 'Voice after Arundel', in *After Arundel*, ed. Gillespie and Ghosh, 144–6.

Lerer, S., 'British Library MS Harley 78 and the Manuscripts of John Shirley', *N&Q* (1990), 400–3.

Lindberg, C., 'The Manuscripts and Versions of the Wycliffite Bible—A Preliminary Survey', *SN* 42 (1970), 333–47.

Lindberg, C., 'The Alpha and Omega of the Middle English Bible', in *Text and Controversy from Wyclif to Bale—Essays in Honour of Anne Hudson*, 191–200.

Marsden, R., *The Text of the Old Testament in Anglo-Saxon England*, Cambridge Studies in Anglo-Saxon England 15 (Cambridge, 1995).

Martin, C. A., 'Middle English Manuals of Religious Instruction', in *So Meny People Longages and Tonges: Philological Essays in Scots and Medieval English Presented to Angus McIntosh*, ed. M. Benskin and M. L. Samuels (Edinburgh, 1981), 283–98.

Meale, C. M., '"alle the bokes that I haue of latyn, englisch, and frensch": Laywomen and their Books in Late Medieval England', in *Women and Literature in Britain 1150–1500*, Cambridge Studies in Medieval Literature 17, 2nd edn, ed. C. M. Meale, (Cambridge, 1996), 128–58.

Minnis, A. J., *Medieval Theory of Authorship—Scholastic Literary Attitudes in the Late Middle Ages*, 2nd edn (Aldershot, 1988).

Minnis A. J. and Scott A. B. (eds), *Medieval Literary Theory and Criticism, c. 1100—c. 1375: The Commentary Tradition*, rev. edn (Oxford, 1991).

Morey, J. H., *Book and Verse—A Guide to Middle English Biblical Literature*, Illinois Medieval Studies (Urbana, 2000).

Morgan, N. J. and Thomson, R. M. (eds), *The Cambridge History of the Book in Britain*, vol. 2, 1100–400 (Cambridge, 2008).

Morgan, N. J., 'Books for the Liturgy and Private Prayer', in *Cambridge History of the Book in Britain*, vol. 2, ed. Morgan and Thomson, chapter 12, 291–316.

Muir, A. L., 'The Influence of the Rolle and Wycliffite Psalters upon the Psalter of the Authorised Version', *MLR* 30 (1935), 302–10.

Muir, A. L., 'Some Observations on the Early English Psalters and the English Vocabulary', *MLQ* 9 (1948), 273–6.

Nevanlinna, S., 'Glosses in Three Late Middle English Texts: Lexical Variation', in *Historical Linguistics and Philology*, Trends in Linguistics—Studies and Monographs 46, ed. J. Fisiak (Berlin and New York, 1990).

O'Neill, P. P., 'The English Version', in *The Eadwine Psalter*, ed. Gibson, Heslop, and Pfaff (London and Philadelphia, 1992).

Orme, N., *English Schools in the Middle Ages* (London, 1973).

Orme, N., 'Schools and School-Books', in L. Hellinga and J. B. Trapp (eds), *The Cambridge History of the Book in Britain*, vol. 3, 1400–557 (Cambridge, 1999).

Orme, N., *Medieval Children* (New Haven and London, 2001).

Otter, M., 'Entrances and Exits: Performing the Psalms in Goscelin's *Liber confortatorius*', *Speculum* 83 (2008), 283–302.

Panayotova, S., 'Cuttings from an Unknown Copy of the *Magna Glossatura* in a Wycliffite Bible (British Library, Arundel MS 104)', *BLJ* 25 (1999), 85–100.

Pantin, W. A., *The English Church in the Fourteenth Century* (Cambridge, 1955).

Pantin, W. A., 'Instructions for a Devout and Literate Layman', in *Medieval Learning and Literature: Essays presented to Richard William Hunt*, ed. J. J. G. Alexander and M. T. Gibson (Oxford, 1976), 398–422.

Parkes, M. B., 'The Literacy of the Laity', in D. Daiches and A. K. Thorlby (eds), *Literature and Western Civilisation*, 6 vols (London, 1972–6), vol. 2, 'The Medieval World', ed. M. B. Parkes (1973).

Parkes, M. B., *Their Hands Before Our Eyes: A Closer Look at Scribes—The Lyell Lectures Delivered in the University of Oxford, 1999* (Aldershot, 2008).

Paues, A. C., *A Fourteenth-Century English Biblical Version* (Cambridge, 1904).

Pearsall, D. (ed.), *Manuscripts and Readers in Fifteenth-Century England: The Literary Implications of Manuscript Study—Essays from the 1981 Conference at the University of York* (Totowa, 1983).

Pearsall, D. (ed.), *New Directions in Later Medieval Manuscript Studies—Essays from the 1998 Harvard Conference* (Woodbridge, 2000).

Pfaff, R. W., *The Liturgy in Medieval England: A History* (Cambridge, 2009).

Pfander, H. G., 'Some Medieval Manuals of Religious Instruction', *JEGP* 35 (1936), 243–58.

Plimpton, G. A., *The Education of Chaucer: Illustrated from the Schoolbooks in Use in his Time* (London, 1935).

Rector, G., 'An Illustrious Vernacular: The Psalter *en romanz* in Twelfth-Century England', in *Language and Culture in Medieval Britain—The French of England c. 1100–c.1500*, ed. J. Wogan-Browne et al. (Woodbridge, 2009), 198–206.

Reuter, O., 'A Study of the French Words in the *Earliest Complete English Prose Psalter*', *Societas Scientiarum Fennica—Commentationes Humanarum Litterarum* 9 (1938), 1–60.

Riddy, F. (ed.), *Regionalism in Late Medieval Manuscripts and Texts: Essays Celebrating the Publication of* A Linguistic Atlas of Late Medieval English (Cambridge, 1991).

Robbins, R. H., 'The "Arma Christi" Rolls', *MLR* 34 (1939), 415–21.

Robinson, P., 'The Format of Books: Books, Booklets and Rolls', in *Cambridge History of the Book in Britain*, vol. 2, ed. Morgan and Thomson, chapter 3, 41–54, p. 44.

Rothwell, W., 'The Role of French in Thirteenth-Century England', *BJRL* 58 (1976), 445–66.

Russell, G. H., 'Vernacular Instruction of the Laity in the Late Middle Ages in England', *JRH* 2 (1962), 98–119.

Saint-Jacques, R. C., 'The Middle English Glossed Prose Psalter and its French Source', in *Medieval Translators and their Craft*, Studies in Medieval Culture 25, ed. J. Beer (Kalamazoo, 1989), 135–54.

Scase, W., 'Reginald Pecock, John Carpenter and John Colop's "Common-Profit" Books: Aspects of Book Ownership and Circulation in Fifteenth-Century London', *MA* 61 (1992), 261–74.

Shepherd, G. T., 'English Versions of the Scriptures before Wyclif', in *Poets and Prophets: Essays in Medieval Studies*, ed. T. A. Shippey and T. Pickles (Cambridge, 1990), 59–83. Repr. from *The Cambridge History of the Bible*, vol. 2, ed. G. W. H. Lampe (Cambridge, 1969), 362–87.

Simpson, J., *Reform and Cultural Revolution*, The Oxford English Literary History, vol. 2, 1350–547 (Oxford, 2002).

Smalley, B., *The Study of the Bible in the Middle Ages*, 3rd edn (Oxford, 1983).

Smith, L. and Taylor, J. H. M. (eds), *Women, the Book and the Godly: Selected Proceedings of the St. Hilda's Conference, 1993* (Cambridge, 1995).

Somerset, F. and Watson. N. (eds), *The Vulgar Tongue—Medieval and Postmedieval Vernacularity* (Pennsylvania, 2003).

Spencer, H. L., *English Preaching in the Late Middle Ages* (Oxford, 1993).

Staley, L. *Margery Kempe's Dissenting Fictions* (Pennsylvania, 1994).

Staley, L., 'The Penitential Psalms: Conversion and the Limits of Lordship', *JMEMS* 37 (2007), 221–69.

St-Jacques, R. C., 'The *Middle English Glossed Prose Psalter* and its French Source', in *Medieval Translators and their Craft*, Studies in Medieval Culture 25, ed. J. Beer (Kalamazoo, 1989), 135–54.

Strohm, P. (ed.), *Middle English*, Oxford Twenty-First Century Approaches to Literature (Oxford, 2007).

Sutherland, A., 'Biblical Text and Spiritual Experience in the English Epistles of Richard Rolle', *RES* 56 (2005), 695–711.

Sutherland, A., '*The Chastising of God's Children*—A Neglected Text', in *Text and Controversy from Wyclif to Bale—Essays in Honour of Anne Hudson*, Medieval Church Studies 4, ed. Barr and Hutchison (Turnhout, 2005).

Sutherland, A., 'The Middle English Mystics', in *The Blackwell Companion to the Bible in English Literature*, Blackwell Companions to Religion, ed. R. Lemon, E. Mason, J. Roberts, and C. Rowland (Chichester, 2009), 85–99.

Tanabe, H., 'On Some English Readings in the Vocabulary of the Wycliffite Bible', in *Philologia Anglica: Essays Presented to Professor Yoshio Terasawa on the Occasion of his Sixtieth Birthday*, ed. K. Oshitari et al. (Tokyo, 1988).

Tanner, N. P., *The Church in Late Medieval Norwich 1370–1532*, Pontifical Institute of Medieval Studies, Studies, and Texts 66 (Toronto, 1984).

Thomas, K., *Religion and the Decline of Magic* (New York, 1971).

Thompson, J. J., *Robert Thornton and the London Thornton MS: British Library MS Additional 31042*, Manuscript Studies 2 (Cambridge, 1987).

Thompson, J. J., 'Literary Associations of an Anonymous Middle English Paraphrase of Vulgate Psalm 50', *MA* 57 (1988), 38–55.

Toswell, M. J., *The Anglo-Saxon Psalter*, Medieval Church Studies 10 (Turnhout, 2014).

Van Deusen, N. (ed.), *The Place of the Psalms in the Intellectual Culture of the Middle Ages*, Suny Series in Medieval Studies (Albany, 1999).

Watson, N., *Richard Rolle and the Invention of Authority*, Cambridge Studies in Medieval Literature 13 (Cambridge, 1991).

Watson, N., 'Censorship and Cultural Change in Late Medieval England: Vernacular Theology, the Oxford Translation Debate, and Arundel's Constitutions of 1409', *Speculum* 70 (1995), 822–64.

Wieck, R. S. (ed.), *Time Sanctified: The Book of Hours in Medieval Art and Life*, 2nd edn (New York, 2001).

Wogan-Browne, J., Watson, N., Taylor, A., and Evans, R. (eds), *The Idea of the Vernacular: An Anthology of Middle English Literary Theory 1280–1520*, Exeter Medieval Texts and Studies (Exeter, 1999).

Wogan-Browne, J., ' "Reading is Good Prayer": Recent Research on Female Reading Communities', *NML* 5 (2002), 229–97.

Wogan-Browne, J. et al. (eds), *Language and Culture in Medieval Britain—The French of England c. 1100–c. 1500* (Woodbridge, 2009).

Zieman, K., *Singing the New Song: Literacy, Liturgy, and Literature in Late Medieval England*, The Middle Ages Series (Pennsylvania, 2008).

Zim, R., *English Metrical Psalms: Poetry as Praise and Prayer 1535–1601* (Cambridge, 1987).

Psalm Index

General Index

Gillespie, Vincent 6, 27, 41, 78, 83
Gradual Psalms 17–8, 20, 279
Gustafson, Kevin 56, 119, 223, 258

de Hamel, Christopher 155–6, 187, 261, 268–9, 271
Hanna, Ralph 24, 34, 36, 42, 44, 50–60, 62, 95, 98, 104, 106–7, 109, 139, 186, 205, 233, 256– 60, 262, 264, 266, 283
Hargreaves, Henry 86, 97–106, 113–14, 136–9,153–4, 179
Harper, John 1–4, 6, 10, 18, 205, 249, 270
Harris-Matthews, J. M. 30, 138–9, 141, 150, 155
Hebrews, Epistle to the 115 (1: 8–9)
Hilton, Walter
    Of Angels' Song 156
    Qui Habitat and *Bonum Est* 42, 127, 130, 179–82, 193
    The Scale of Perfection 6, 215–16, 218
Hoeppner-Moran, Jo Ann 15, 20, 29
Holsinger, Bruce 4–5, 245
Horstmann, Carl 50, 94, 99, 202
Hudson, Anne 32, 56–7, 61, 76–7, 79–81, 87, 89, 93, 107–8, 112–14, 118, 151–2, 155, 187, 193, 201, 211, 256–8, 261 274, 283
Hull, Eleanor 92–3
    nature of Hull's exegesis 122, 126, 189–93, 195, 198, 210, 212, 213–14, 224, 228–9, 275
    source of her *Commentary on the Penitential Psalms* 91, 92–3
    style of Hull's translation and commentary 92, 93, 179, 182–4, 218–19

Isaiah (biblical book) 79, 283

St-Jacques, Raymond 53–4, 91–2, 121–3, 125–6, 128, 130–1, 133–4, 206
Jerome 60, 67–9, 70, 74, 78–9, 85, 88, 89, 91, 117, 186, 190, 191
    English '*Abbreviated Psalter of St. Jerome*' 62, 138, 155, 156, 247, 280
Job (biblical book) 18, 76, 82, 109, 115
John, Gospel of 246 (15), 283, 284
Joshua (biblical book) 283 (19: 19)
Judges (biblical book) 152

Kermode, Frank 7, 214
Kreuzer, J. R. 40–1, 46, 48, 165, 169, 212, 219, 225–6, 228
Kuczynski, Michael 84, 90, 109, 186, 189

Lamentations (biblical book) 90
Lauds 2, 17–18
Lawton, David 6, 50, 72, 95, 272
Lessons from the Dirige 39, 43, 58, 82
Leviticus 156, 190 (23: 9–14), 246 (19)

Lindberg, Conrad 76, 110–11, 114, 117–19, 151–3, 267
Littlehales, Henry 14, 19, 20–1, 28–9, 138, 142–3, 219, 279
Liturgy 1–5, 10, 14, 34, 39, 43, 78, 270
    and (private) devotion 4–5, 16–17, 43, 219, 225, 230, 235, 239, 254, 260, 276
    and the vernacular 3, 33, 34, 39, 43, 52, 73, 246, 274
Lombard, Peter 117–20, 122, 126–7, 129–34, 173, 182, 186–7, 190–4, 196–8, 200, 209–14, 217, 222–3, 256, 268
    Commentarium in Psalmos 268
    Magna Glossatura 187, 256
London, BLMS Arundel 104 267–71, 283
Luke, Gospel of 138 (20)
Lydgate, John 49, 168
    layout of psalm-based poetry 238
    manuscripts of psalm-based poetry 37
    psalm-based poetry of 162–9, 188–99, 220–2, 272
Lyre, Nicholas of 89, 111, 114–16, 119, 149, 187, 189, 192, 194–5, 199–200
    Lyran glosses in B_554 90, 115–19
    Postillae 114, 187, 195

Maccabees 152 (2), 284 (2)
MacCracken, Henry Noble 163, 188
Maidstone, Richard 39, 170
    link with Rolle 169–70
    links with Wycliffite Psalms 170–2, 179, 182
    Maidstone's *Penitential Psalms* 39–40, 165, 167–79, 194–8, 212, 214, 219–20, 224–6
    manuscripts containing 40–6, 55, 169, 201, 281
    manuscript layout of 42–3, 45, 48, 234–7
Mark, Gospel of 151, 283
Matins
    in English language primers 28–31, 139–40, 240–1, 243–4, 245
    liturgical hour of 2, 6, 17, 18, 205, 240, 249, 268
Matins of Our Lady (also Matins of the Blessed Virgin Mary, Hours of the Virgin) 6, 20, 22, 28, 43, 240
Matthew, Gospel of 138 (1), 151 (3: 4, 4: 20–13: 33), 267
Meale, Carol M. 9, 11
The Metrical Psalter 50–4, 56, 88–9, 93–8, 113, 114, 133, 135, 136, 178, 229, 248, 272, 273
    manuscripts containing 50–4, 92, 135, 201–5, 274
    manuscript layout 248–56, 259
    and Old English glosses 74–87, 98–103
    and Rolle's *English Psalter* 86, 103–10
Minnis, Alistair 70, 185–7, 193–5, 200
Morgan, Nigel 10, 13–17, 22, 27–9, 33, 46, 99, 268
Muir, A. Laurence 87